PROBLEMS IN ECONOMIC DEVELOPMENT

Other International Economic Association symposia

*

THE ECONOMICS OF INTERNATIONAL MIGRATION
Edited by Brinley Thomas

THE BUSINESS CYCLE IN THE POST-WAR WORLD
Edited by Erik Lundberg

INFLATION
Edited by D. C. Hague

STABILITY AND PROGRESS IN THE WORLD ECONOMY
Edited by D. C. Hague

THE THEORY OF CAPITAL
Edited by F. A. Lutz and D. C. Hague

CLASSICS IN THE THEORY OF PUBLIC FINANCE
Edited by R. A. Musgrave and A. T. Peacock

THE ECONOMIC CONSEQUENCES OF THE SIZE OF NATIONS
Edited by E. A. G. Robinson

ECONOMIC DEVELOPMENT FOR LATIN AMERICA
Edited by Howard S. Ellis assisted by Henry C. Wallich

THE ECONOMICS OF TAKE-OFF INTO SUSTAINED GROWTH
Edited by W. W. Rostow

ECONOMIC DEVELOPMENT WITH SPECIAL REFERENCE TO EAST ASIA
Edited by Kenneth Berrill

INTERNATIONAL TRADE THEORY IN A DEVELOPING WORLD
Edited by R. F. Harrod and D. C. Hague

ECONOMIC DEVELOPMENT FOR AFRICA SOUTH OF THE SAHARA
Edited by E. A. G. Robinson

THE THEORY OF INTEREST RATES
Edited by F. H. Hahn and F. P. R. Brechling

PROBLEMS IN ECONOMIC DEVELOPMENT

Proceedings of a Conference
held by the International Economic Association

EDITED BY

E. A. G. ROBINSON

LONDON
MACMILLAN & CO LTD
NEW YORK · ST MARTIN'S PRESS
1965

MACMILLAN AND COMPANY LIMITED
St Martin's Street London WC2
also Bombay Calcutta Madras Melbourne

THE MACMILLAN COMPANY OF CANADA LIMITED
70 Bond Street Toronto 2

ST MARTIN'S PRESS INC
175 Fifth Avenue New York 10 NY

PRINTED IN GREAT BRITAIN

CONTENTS

v

Contents

SECTION 4

THE STABILIZATION OF PRIMARY
PRODUCING ECONOMIES

Contents

Part 4
THE STABILIZATION OF PRIMARY
PRODUCING ECONOMIES

ACKNOWLEDGMENTS

THE congress that is here recorded was held in the University of Vienna during the early days of September 1962. The gratitude of the International Economic Association is due to the authorities of the University itself, and especially to Professor Mahr. It is due also to all those in the Government of Austria and in the City of Vienna who made the occasion immensely enjoyable.

The congress, as will appear from this volume, was organized in four sections. The chairmen of each individual section were responsible, in consultation with the officers of the Association, for the programme of that section. Without their work the congress could not have been the success that it undoubtedly was. There were in all some seven hundred participants. A majority were in Section 1, where the discussions were inevitably more formal. In the three other sections, with less than a hundred participants in each, less formal but perhaps more vigorous discussion was possible. It was, indeed, the purpose of the congress to make opportunity for free and general discussion by as many participants as possible.

The holding of this congress was made possible by grants given to the Association by UNESCO and the Ford Foundation. To both of those bodies the Association wishes to express its great gratitude for their support, without which the work that it has done would have been impossible.

E. A. G. R.

CHAIRMEN AND VICE-CHAIRMEN
OF THE SECTIONS OF THE VIENNA CONGRESS

Section 1 : The Determinants of Economic Progress

Chairman : E. A. G. Robinson
Vice-Chairman : E. Lipinski
Rapporteur : E. K. Hawkins

Section 2 : Industrialization and Methods of Increasing
Labour Productivity

Chairman : Clark Kerr
Vice-Chairman : S. Tsuru
Rapporteur : Marjorie Galenson

Section 3 : Techniques and Problems of Development Planning

Chairman : J. Tinbergen
Vice-Chairman : T. V. Riabushkin
Deputy Chairman : R. Dorfman
Rapporteur : D. C. Hague

Section 4 : The Stabilization of Primary Producing Economies

Chairman : W. A. Lewis
Vice-Chairman : M. Byé
Rapporteur : Helen Thompson

OPENING ADDRESS

E. A. G. ROBINSON
President of the International Economic Association
Cambridge University

I

My task this morning is a twofold one : to thank in the name of
the International Economic Association the authorities of the
Government of Austria, of the City of Vienna and of the University
of Vienna which has generously put at our disposal the buildings
in which this congress is to hold its meetings ; to welcome all of
you who have come here as participants in the congress and to
express the hope of the Council and Officers of the Association
that you will find enjoyment and benefit in the programme of work
and of entertainment that we have attempted to prepare for you.

It is particularly appropriate that this congress of the International Economic Association should be held in Austria and in this
beautiful city of Vienna, for the International Economic Association
has many links with Austria and with Vienna. First we like to
remember that Vienna has been one of the three or four great
sources from which our science has developed. The Austrian
school of economists was prolific in the contributions that it made
to the earlier developments of the nineteenth century. Today the
names of professors trained in the Austrian school spring readily to
our minds in many of the great universities of America and of
Europe. But the International Economic Association has more
personal reasons for gratitude. When in 1950 the Association was
founded, the first President should have been Joseph Schumpeter, a
great economist and a great internationalist. He was closely interested in the creation of the Association and helped to plan its
first beginnings. Alas ! he died a few months before the inaugural
meeting of the Association. But we remember with gratitude the
enthusiasm of that great Austrian for all that we have been trying
to do. When he died, it was to another of Austrian descent, Gottfried
Haberler, that we turned for help. It was he who was in fact our
first President and who did much to shape the first developments
of the Association. When the time came for us to appoint a successor, our choice for the second President was Professor Howard

xiii

Ellis, who had studied in Vienna, had married a Viennese and whose first book was concerned with the monetary problems of Austria. But these three by no means complete the story of our indebtedness to Austria and to Vienna. The onerous task of building up the Association was entrusted to a Viennese, Dr. Helene Berger Lieser, and until her resignation three years ago, it was she who planned our activities, organized our conferences, controlled and stimulated our publications. The debt of the Association to her unflagging energies and to her great gifts for international friendship can never be exaggerated. Thus in coming to Vienna we come to a city that is rich in associations for us.

II

The International Economic Association has come a very long way in a short space of time. Fifteen years ago it was an ambitious dream in the minds of a few persons mostly working at that time in Paris. Between 1948 and 1950 some of us, many of them here today, helped to turn that dream into the outlines of a concrete plan. In 1950 we held the first inaugural meeting of the Council in Monaco at the invitation of Jacques Rueff who had presided over our earliest deliberations. At Monaco, the national associations of some fifteen countries became affiliated to the newly-founded International Economic Association. Today thirty-five national associations, covering a very large proportion of the entire world, are affiliated to it. Many of them have, indeed, been created with this objective partly in view. And we have here in Vienna representatives of almost all these nations, concerned to make their contributions to our work and our deliberations.

The International Economic Association exists to promote the international interchange of ideas in the field of economics. We have tried to achieve this in a variety of ways — directly by the spoken word and indirectly by the written work — by translations and publications of a variety of kinds. But our principal method has been by the holding of conferences and courses. We have held during the twelve years of our existence no fewer than twenty-five conferences and courses. The great majority of these have been small conferences of thirty to forty selected specialists in some important and topical branch of economics who have been invited to meet and discuss twelve or fifteen carefully prepared papers over a period of ten days to a fortnight.

On one previous occasion, in Rome in 1956, we have held a congress open to all members of our affiliated associations. Today we are inaugurating another such congress. It has been our belief that from time to time we have a duty to throw open our doors and use our organization to give opportunity for all who may thus be indirectly our members to meet their colleagues and share their discussions. We welcome you and we hope that Vienna will afford rich opportunities to meet in person colleagues whom you have known only in print and to exchange ideas with them here by word of mouth.

III

We have chosen for this congress the subject of economic development. We have chosen it deliberately. Increasingly in recent years we have found that our specialist conferences have been concerned with some aspect or other of this broad subject. Just as in the 1930s almost all schools of economists were concerned with the problems of economic fluctuations and with the causes and cures of the trade cycle, so today we are almost all concerned with attempting to understand the causes of economic growth. We have seen how in the 1930s the strenuous arguments of that period, the statistical analyses, the studies of past history, the construction, criticism and improvement of economic models collectively led on to a better understanding of the causes and cures of the trade cycle. We hope that by similar methods we may come to understand better and to act better to promote economic development and to diminish the extent to which poverty and the misery that flows from poverty do damage to human happiness. For this is, I think, the faith that is in most of us as economists. We believe that humanity progresses by increasing its control over its environment. In terms of physics and of engineering and in terms of biology and the medical sciences, man is increasing year by year his power to control and to turn to his use the world in which he lives. It is the more important on that account that to an equal extent we shall be able to understand, and when necessary to control, the economic forces that determine our power to make use of these great technical advances.

But above all we wish to seek the answer to the question 'What can we do that will effectively increase the rate of growth of the economically backward nations and to secure that, if possible, the gap between them and the more advanced nations shall be closed rather than expanded further?' To answer that question we must first know what are the factors that determine the levels of the wealth of nations at any moment and what are the factors that determine their growth. And to this I hope I shall not shock you if I say that in my view we do not at present know the true and full answer.

We know something, it is true, about the relations of capital supply to growth. But even here I do not think we know the whole story. Four years ago the Association held a fascinating and illuminating conference on capital theory which brought together most of the leading workers in this field. The chief impression that it left on my mind was of the profound difficulties of either defining or measuring the stock of capital in a world of continually changing prices and of continually changing technologies, in which capital equipment grew old by obsolescence rather than by wear-and-tear, survived in active existence beyond its supposed period of depreciation and was replaced by new equipment different both in design and in cost. Much as we have learned, it is extraordinarily difficult — some would say impossible — to say how the growth of the stock of capital, regarded as the stock of actively co-operant equipment, has compared with that of the flow of annual output produced with its help.

If I had been speaking to you even a few years ago I would have been stressing the importance of high levels of saving and invest-ment and high levels of the international flow of capital funds as means of promoting growth. Even today I would not want to underrate the importance of capital, particularly to a backward country. But evidence is accumulating that capital alone is not a solution of the problem of growth. Firstly, a number of countries, not excluding my own, seem to have demonstrated that in some circumstances a marginal increment of capital is not at all auto-matically associated with a corresponding marginal increment of output. Secondly, if one seeks to explain the growth of the more mature countries, only about one-fourth or one-fifth of the whole is to be explained by higher capital per head and three-quarters or four-fifths by other factors. These include everything that we regard as industrial efficiency, both on the side of management and of workers : better education, better research, better choice and planning of industrial processes, better transport and the economies of scale for which better transport gives opportunity, quicker transfer of knowledge from firm to firm and from country to country, above all a dynamic and progressive outlook and a determination and freedom to achieve progress.

But though the greater part of growth seems to derive from things other than actual capital investment, I think we might be wrong to assume that it can be harvested without the capital invest-ment. Very often it is the construction of a new plant which permits the embodiment of the research into new techniques of production, the better factory layout, the labour-saving equipment, the scale appropriate to new methods of production, and without the capital investment the other four-fifths would have been missing.

Knowing, however, that four-fifths of economic growth comes from these other factors, we do well to pause and ask ourselves whether it is possible to do more to promote growth, possibly at lower cost, by operating on these other unspecified factors. But here, to my mind, is the biggest of many vast gaps in our quantitative knowledge. We can, after a fashion, attempt, despite the difficulties I have mentioned, to define and measure the changes in the stock of a nation's capital. But can we ever hope to define and measure its stock of scientific and engineering knowledge, or its stock of economic freedom and opportunity. We can, it is true — and brave econometricians have attempted it for the United States — measure the national expenditures on education and research and the like and try to see how such expenditures, combined with capital formation, have been related to economic growth. But I feel the gravest doubts whether such relations as one may discover in the case of a nation, such as the United States, which is in the van and is required to make progress by her own research, can be transferred uncritically to a backward nation that can draw on the world's existing stock of knowledge and in some degree on the world's stock of trained technologists.

This is a field, indeed, which lies wide open to those brave econometricians who succeed every day in making economics more of a quantitative science. But until they have made progress, it is a field in which most of us will turn — and I suggest for long to come — to the wisdom and qualitative judgments of the economic historians, with their profound knowledge and understanding of the periods to which they have devoted themselves. Can one generalize the historical experiences of the periods of rapid growth and industrialization of the more mature countries and apply any such generalizations in the form of policies for the backward countries? That, of course, is what Professor Rostow has attempted to do, first in a familiar article that we published in the *Economic Journal* and later in his equally familiar book.

We made these problems the theme of a conference of this Association two years ago, and Professor Habakkuk is to address many of you on the same theme during this congress. My impression was that our discussions and the intensive studies that were prepared as a basis for them threw considerable doubt on any over-simplified statement of the actual process of 'take-off' and suggested that change was continuous rather than abrupt. But I myself was left with the belief that very much more examination was needed by economic historians of what Professor Rostow has christened the preconditions of take-off — the institutional and environmental conditions in which rapid progress may be achieved — and that countries which wish to increase the speed of development would do well to examine their institutions and general economic frameworks as well as their potential supplies of capital. And I believe that this applies to mature countries, including my own, which may be lagging, as well as to backward countries. I look forward to our discussions of these problems during the present congress.

There is a second sphere in which a full understanding of our problems requires, I am convinced, the collaboration of the economic historians and the economic statisticians. Are the time-scales of economic development inevitable and incapable of abbreviation? Are there, as has been suggested by Colin Clark and others, natural rates of growth of particular countries that cannot be speeded up except very temporarily? I am not myself at all convinced by the arguments and evidence so far available to support that view. We have seen the very different tempo of development achieved by Italy in recent years, to take but a single example. We have seen the very rapid rates of growth achieved since the revolution in the U.S.S.R. and other socialist republics. We have seen the rapid development of Japan. I do myself believe that it is not impossible that, during the next twenty years, we shall come to understand these processes so much better, that we shall be able to maintain a better balance between the various factors necessary for growth and speed up the whole process. That is what we are urgently trying to do today in Britain.

Still less am I convinced that we cannot do much to shorten greatly the periods of development of the backward countries. As I have already emphasized, they do not need to increase the world's stock of scientific knowledge and skills in order to make progress. They need to increase the rate of its transfer. I can see no reason why one should assume that the time-scales of such transfer should have a predetermined dimension or be in any sense comparable to those required for the initial creation of knowledge.

And here I would like again to stress the considerable part that education can and must play in economic development. This subject is to be the theme of the International Economic Association's annual conference next year. What is required is not primarily that we shall increase the world's stock of knowledge but rather that we shall increase the receptivity of backward countries and their power to absorb and use knowledge. If one looks back at the history of the economic development of northern Europe, it took something like a millennium for us to absorb much of the scientific knowledge known to Greece and Rome and to China and the East. We must not, I think, be surprised if it takes half a century or more for Africa and parts of Asia to absorb the skills, technologies and tempos of a modern society. For some knowledge, it is sufficient if it is absorbed by a small body of managers and administrators. But for a great deal of the working of a modern society it is necessary that the skills shall permeate a large proportion of all the economically active population. Many of these problems of the transfer of knowledge and skills represent the kernel of the problems that Section 2 of our congress will be deliberating.

IV

I cannot hope to look even as superficially as I have done thus far at all the various groups of problems that this congress will be considering. I scarcely need to stress further than I have already done the need to perfect the methods of quantitative measurement of the many factors affecting the potential trends of economies as a means to the better guidance and planning of their development which Section 3 will be discussing. Nor, I think, need I stress the importance of trying to find satisfactory ways in which the more extreme oscillations or primary product prices are prevented from doing havoc to the development of primary producers, but at the same time the incentives are maintained to expand consumption and use resources efficiently. These and many other problems will be considered by Section 4.

I am glad that Section 4 will also be paying much attention to the part played by foreign trade in economic development. This is in my view an element that has been much too much neglected in most of the model-making by economic theorists, whose models are so often, for purposes of simplicity, models of a single closed economy. But when one studies actual instances of economic development, one of the most interesting features is the relation of the growth of exports and of markets to the growth of the internal economy. Was it wholly a matter of accident that the periods of take-off of the United Kingdom, of Japan, of the United States and of a number of other countries, were periods of rapid increase of export markets, so that the ratios of exports to national income were increasing and constraints from the balance of payments were at a minimum? Is it wholly a matter of accident today that many of the countries whose growth rates seem inadequate are countries, such as India and my own country, where the slow growth of exports imposes continuing constraints. I hope that the model-makers will, during the next few years, attempt to build two-country or three-country models to clarify the repercussions of the growth of one country on another, more particularly where the exports of a less developed country have a low income-elasticity in the more developed country. But such models must, I fear, if they are to be useful be much more complex than most of those that we have been accustomed to use. For they must involve the questions of price-relationships and the processes and time-scales of the achievement of price-relationships which can appropriately be neglected in a single-country closed economy model. But I feel sure myself that it is only by adding to complexity in this sort of way that one can hope to understand the infinite complexities of the real world.

There is one final problem to which I would like briefly to refer. It is very much present in the minds of many of us who come from European countries that a major contribution may be made to economic development by the widening of markets and the freeing of trade between countries. At a conference which the Association held a few years ago we tried to analyse and understand the nature and sources of the advantages that derive from the size of nations. What became apparent to us was that the economies of large markets extend far beyond what economists have called internal economies of the scale of the firm, beyond even the size of market which yields most of the ordinary external economies of scale, and continue into a size of market in which the gains are derived largely from increased specialization, increased competitiveness, increased ease of entering a market and such-like factors. I stress this because so many of the emerging under-developed nations are so small — small in population and small in present purchasing power. We all welcome their new-found independence and respect their desires to use their freedoms to develop their own independent national policies free from any restrictions imposed by artificial connections with the metropolitan countries of the past. But there is I think a real problem of how some of these emerging small nations are to escape the penalties of their smallness. It is extraordinarily important for them that the markets of the world shall be open to them, not only for their primary products but also for their first adventures into industrial production. I believe and hope that there is a common determination that the closer relations of European countries shall not work gravely to the detriment of these small nations, and that where they, in the exercise of their own free wills, wish to associate themselves in trading relations with each other or with wider groups of advanced nations we shall create no artificial obstacles to it.

May I express once again to you all, the gratitude of the International Economic Association that you have found time in your busy lives to come and discuss together here in Vienna these great issues. Above all may I express our gratitude to those who have written the papers that we shall be discussing. For many of us this is, I think, an act of faith. We believe that, by the hard thinking and careful analysis of economists with all sorts of different gifts and qualifications, something very substantial can be done to help the world to solve the human problems of poverty and want, and to enable our own countries and the other less developed countries of the world to progress more rapidly and more steadily. It is, I suspect, with those ideas at the back of our minds that we shall approach the scientific discussion of the next few days.

Section 1
THE DETERMINANTS OF ECONOMIC PROGRESS

Chairman : E. A. G. Robinson
Vice-Chairman : E. Lipinski
Rapporteur : E. K. Hawkins

Chapter 1

THEORIES OF ECONOMIC GROWTH IN CAPITALIST COUNTRIES

BY

GUSTAV RANIS
Yale University, U.S.A.

I. INTRODUCTION

THIS paper will attempt to make some assessment of our continuing effort to understand better the growth process in both the mature and so-called less-developed economy contexts. In view of the massive nature of that effort and the necessarily superficial and hurried nature of these comments it should be remarked at the outset that the task has been approached with considerable trepidation, and that apologies are due both to those who may be misinterpreted and to those who may be neglected, due either to a lack of time or a lack of courage.

As is well known, a concern with growth is time-honoured in our profession; in fact, it is no exaggeration to say that our discipline owes its very existence to this preoccupation with the causes and consequences of economic progress. Admittedly the neo-classicists, with some few notable exceptions (e.g. Schumpeter), strayed from the narrow path and temporarily yielded the field to Marx and the socialists. But then traditional interest in growth reasserted itself with renewed vigour after World War II ; and the 'growthmanship' of practitioners eager to solve our problems and those of the less-developed world has not lagged far behind.

This general resurgence of interest, it should be understood, has not led us towards the attempt to construct any single explanatory schema for application across the board. Instead we have witnessed a series of parallel, if closely related, efforts to understand the dynamics of progress in the institutionally disparate settings of the mature and the so-called less-developed economies. We will endeavour to trace these developments separately while pointing out their common roots and divergent emphases where relevant.

3

II. GROWTH IN THE MATURE ECONOMIES

Post-Keynesian capitalist growth theory for the mature economy generically has insisted on placing capital accumulation at centre stage and focussing on the resultant secular increases in labour productivity. It has consistently emphasized the twin conditions governing such increases : the willingness of a society to refrain from consumption and the fact that the investment into which savings may be channelled will result in increased productive capacity along with increased flows of income. In the language of the Harrod-Domar tradition,[1] it is the propensity to save and the marginal capital-output ratio which determine the growth rate.

One hardly needs to be reminded that the body of contemporary capitalist growth theory consists of a series of extensions and modifications of this basic Harrod-Domar relationship. Such modifications have enabled us to considerably improve our understanding of problems of stability and instability, and of the role of technological change in the context of the long-run growth prospects of the capitalist system.

The role accorded to stability represents the major Keynesian heritage of contemporary growth models. Harrod, for example, was himself motivated largely by a concern for the endemic instability of the capitalist system in the original formulation of his model. According to him, when the actual rate of investment falls short of that level required to absorb full employment savings an underutilization of capital will result with a consequent reduction from the full employment rate of growth. His economy is in fact constantly teetering on a razor's edge, the slightest misstep yielding cumulative departures in either direction.

In this general tradition considerable effort has gone into the construction of modern business cycle theories. This includes the work of Professor Samuelson [2] who, by emphasizing the time lags between the above relationships, produced a theory of interaction between the Keynesian multiplier and the post-Keynesian accelerator. The adoption of alternative reasonable values for the relevant parameters then enabled him to deduce a large number of alternative short-run fluctuation patterns for the economy. Professor Hicks' contribution in the same general area then provided us with a more satisfactory explanation of the turning point by introducing the

[1] R. F. Harrod, *Toward a Dynamic Economics*, London, 1948, and E. D. Domar, *Essays in the Theory of Economic Growth*, New York, 1957.
[2] P. A. Samuelson, 'Interaction Between the Multiplier and the Accelerator', *Review of Economics and Statistics*, May 1939.

concept of floors and ceilings limiting the amplitude of oscillations in the course of the business cycle.[1]

Such direct descendants of the Harrod-Domar formulation suffer from the fact that they formally take into account only one factor of production, capital. Because of this neglect of the possibility of factor substitution not only are undue rigidities assumed for the production process but the all-important problem of income distribution and its implications for growth are skirted. It is small wonder, therefore, that subsequent developments link total output explicitly to multi-factor inputs, principally labour and capital. Only in such a context does distribution theory become non-trivial.

This choice of a particular distribution theory is, indeed, crucial to the choice among the alternative growth-theoretic formulations which have been advanced in recent years. It is inextricably tied up with both the basic ingredients of the Harrod-Domar trend of thought : as a prime determinant of the rate of savings or the consumption function, and as decisive in its relationship to investment decisions by providing a theory of the reward for capitalists.

In this context, two major types of distribution theory have been used as building blocks for a variety of growth-theoretic formulations. One, the so-called neo-classical theory, is based on the marginal productivity calculus. It amounts to an impersonal theory of distribution rendered possible by the acceptance of competitive market forces and the possibility of continuous substitution along the production function. The denial of this functional-based distribution theory, either on the grounds of the non-substitutability of factors, the non-measurability of capital or the non-competitive nature of markets, has led to the adoption of a second type of distribution theory which takes us back to the classical tradition. In this tradition, market forces are replaced by personal forces with emphasis shifting from functional to social distribution based on the interplay of certain, not always clearly specified, institutional forces such as the relative bargaining strength of contending groups.

An example of the use of the neo-classical distribution theory is provided by Professor Tobin's dynamic model.[2] This represents one of the more ambitious attempts to produce an explanation of the instability of the growth process by interpreting features of post-Keynesian growth theory with Keynesian-type notions of monetary equilibrium. His distribution theory is similar to Keynes' in that, in addition to the neo-classical assumptions of perfect competition

[1] J. R. Hicks, *A Contribution to the Theory of the Trade Cycle*, Oxford, 1950.
[2] J. Tobin, 'A Dynamic Aggregative Model', *Journal of Political Economy*, April 1955.

in the input markets, he postulates a rigid supply curve of labour in response to money wages. From the viewpoint of growth theory such a distribution-theoretic formulation plays a dual role : on the one hand it provides a vehicle for the determination of the aggregate savings function required for the determination of the growth potential in a two-factor world. On the other, his acceptance of the 'money illusion' assumption provides a vital link to a monetary theory in the Keynesian tradition.

This monetary theory, to be quite specific, postulates that portfolio decisions of wealth holders (business firms and households combined) are made with reference to the choice between real capital goods and monetary assets. The exercise of such a choice then determines the market rate of exchange which is taken as the absolute price level. (It should be noted that this contrasts somewhat with Keynesian-type notions of liquidity preference in which two types of monetary assets are compared by households in the course of determining — with the help of the monetary authorities — the rate of interest.) For Tobin the general price level is thus determined in the first instance by the requirements of portfolio balance.

Finally, given a capital stock in the short run, a general price level is determined in order to satisfy the requirement of labour market balance compatible with the profit-maximizing behaviour of the entrepreneur. And, as a result of the dual function of this price level in satisfying both the portfolio and labour market balance, an equilibrium position, in which both price and employment are given, is determined for the short run.

Then, in the long run, as capital accumulation takes place these same tools are used to describe the movement of the short-run equilibrium position through time. The difficulty which then arises is that the system cannot continue to function indefinitely in this fashion. Ultimately the strain imposed on the portfolio balance by entrepreneurial insistence on labour market balance in the face of workers' rigid money wage demands causes the system to break down. Tobin's theory strongly implies, however, that the ensuing downturn can be halted by monetary action and/or a more rational wage policy on the part of workers.

The above-described model is remarkably broad and includes most of the facets which have generally been recognized as crucial for an understanding of the problem of cyclical instability and its relation to growth. From the point of view of the purposes of this paper, moreover, two further remarks seem warranted. Firstly, the use of the neo-classical distribution theory in this fashion, i.e. to determine the aggregate savings function with the implied assumption that savings are automatically invested, more or less skirts the problem of capitalists' reward for investment and thus seems to leave the motivation for capital accumulation unexplained. This may be called a shortcoming common to all growth-theoretic formulations utilizing the neo-classical distribution theory. Secondly, the central role assigned to monetary analysis indicates a preoccupation with relatively short-run problems of instability reminiscent of another epoch. The more long-run bias of growth theories of more recent vintage has led to a gradual abandonment of this monetary emphasis.

The work of Mrs. Robinson [1] and Mr. Kaldor exemplifies the use of the classical theory of distribution. In a growth model presented to the 1958 Corfu Conference of the International Economic Association,[2] for example, Kaldor, having generally accepted the Harrod-Domar framework, proceeds to disaggregate income recipients into wage and profit claimants, adding the realistic assumption that the propensity to save out of profits is higher (one in the extreme) than that out of wages (zero in the extreme). A distribution theory based on the classical Iron Law of Wages and stipulating an unlimited supply of labour at the existing real wage is then added. Kaldor's conclusions in tackling the Harrod-Domar instability problem are considered to be less pessimistic ; he feels that equilibrium will be restored through a decline in the aggregate savings propensity via changes in the distribution of income — rather than through the adjustment of entrepreneurial investment decisions in the context of a fixed propensity to save.

His model may be viewed as representative of a family of growth theories which are concerned with what may be termed long-run process analysis. By that we mean highlighting the constellation of factors including profits, technological change and entrepreneurial motivations which are so characteristic of the sources of friction in the course of growth in the capitalist system. Ideally, such process analysis should illuminate the potential for long-run public policy in reducing such frictions. Unfortunately, however, the policy orientation which has been so characteristic of short-run stability analysis (e.g. anticyclical policy) has not yet found its counterpart in long-run process analysis. The latter gives us no clear-cut indication of what policy should be followed : A drastic overhaul of the system, as the Marxists would recommend ? The possibility of revising and

---

[1] J. Robinson, *The Accumulation of Capital*, London, 1956.
[2] N. Kaldor, 'Capital Accumulation and Economic Growth' in *The Theory of Capital*, London, 1961.

modifying the system, e.g. *via* established fiscal and monetary instruments, within the existing socio-political framework ? Or, as Kaldor seems to imply, acceptance of the comforting thought that, in the long run we shall not only all be alive, but automatically prosperous. Many of us naturally believe firmly in the second alternative and submit that there are indications (e.g. the recent work of the U.S. Council of Economic Advisors) that the economist, if not as yet the politician, is successfully turning his attention to this problem.

A further logical development in the direction of long-run analysis is exemplified by the work of Professor Solow. His 'Contribution to the Theory of Economic Growth',[1] for example, utilizes a two factor neo-classical model and the Keynesian assumption of a constant propensity to save to analyze the secular direction of the system. Under his remarkably general formulation Solow is able to show that only in the rarest instances will an economy initially find itself in a position in which all magnitudes are expanding at the same constant rate and the relevant capital-labour and capital-output ratios are consequently invariant. Given a stipulated propensity to save, a population growth rate and a production function exhibiting constant returns to scale, the system will be gravitating toward such a von Neumann state only in the very long run — with the slowest-growing factor ultimately setting the pace for the economy as a whole.

This type of analysis may be more precisely characterized as 'long-run prospect' analysis to distinguish it from the previously referred to long-run process analysis. For although the solution of Solow's differential equation provides us with a growth path nominally representing a process through time, the detailed problems of growth and of the frictions impeding growth along that path are not his main concern.

The major significance of his contribution can be said to lie in the fact that it disputes the inevitability of any particular long-run growth pattern for the capitalist system. Any change in either the aggregate production function, the savings habit or the rate of growth of population can significantly alter the system's long-run growth prospects. These conclusions are quite independent of any particular social system and are presented in a framework of remarkably elegant simplicity ; but precisely due to the very abstract nature of the problem investigated the model is quite remote from the policy implications relevant to any one such system.

Even the relatively ambitious latter-day growth models have

[1] R. M. Solow, 'A Contribution to the Theory of Economic Growth', *Quarterly Journal of Economics*, February 1956.

shown some hesitancy in attempting to recapture the classical magnificent dynamics in all its glory. But while population growth remains exogenous to most contemporary formulations, efforts to come to terms with the *deus ex machina* of technological change have been much intensified. Kaldor, for example, in his 1957 *Economic Journal* article [1] attempts to explain the observed secular constancy of the relative shares and of the capital-output ratio by means of an endogenous theory of innovation. The basic ingredients of his theory are his (previously encountered) disaggregated consumption function, an investment-behaviouristic relationship based on entrepreneurial profit expectations and a technical progress function which summarizes the total impact of capital accumulation (capital deepening) and of innovations on labour productivity in a somewhat catchall fashion. (Though Kaldor does not say so, his technical progress function can be shown to be consistent with a Cobb-Douglas type of production function with neutral innovations, a conclusion which illustrates his low regard for neo-classical distribution theory.) Positing a constant stream of technological change, Kaldor seems to introduce a behaviouristic assumption to the effect that innovations are always embodied in capital accumulation. His model then permits him to explain the historical stability of the relative shares and of the capital-output ratio in the long run via the fact that any deviation between the rates of growth of capital and of output will automatically induce an equilibrating action on the part of entrepreneurs.

Others, including Fellner [2] and Champernowne,[3] have addressed themselves to the same problem of 'explaining' the constancy of these historical ratios. Fellner attempts to do so by reference both to the sufficiency of innovational intensity to keep the bogey of diminishing returns (occasioned by a secularly rising capital-labour ratio) at bay, and the sufficiency of innovational bias in response to changing factor endowments to explain the constancy of the relative shares. Champernowne's model, following Kaldor's lead, achieves an 'explanation' through adjustments of the capital-labour ratio via a classical-based equilibrating mechanism between his natural rate of growth of capital (that rate which, given exogenous neutral innovations and population growth, keeps the profit rate from falling) and his warranted rate of growth (that rate which keeps capital fully employed).

[1] N. Kaldor, 'A Model of Economic Growth', *Economic Journal*, December 1957.
[2] W. Fellner, *Trends and Cycles in Economic Activity* (especially Part III), New York, 1956.
[3] D. G. Champernowne, 'Capital Accumulation and the Maintenance of Full Employment', *Economic Journal*, June 1958.

This interest of alternative models in 'explaining' the constancy of the various operating ratios thrown up by history should occasion no surprise. Quite naturally our model builders are concerned with ultimate predictability and the first test of any model which pretends to more than mathematical completeness must be its ability to explain the past. In this respect the most that can be said for the models under discussion is that they are sufficient to roughly explain history; we are still awaiting specific proof that the behaviouristic relationships assumed in any particular case are statistically significant and that a particular theory can consequently be viewed as necessary as well as sufficient to explain reality.

This is undoubtedly one of the reasons why we have of late seen increasing attention paid to the more precise econometric testing of hypotheses needed to scaffold any growth theory which is really viable in terms of our confidence in its ultimate predictive capacity. Certainly it should occasion no surprise if the contemporary age of econometrics also found its reflection in our growth-theoretic formulations. As was previously the case with Walrasian and Keynesian economics we may now be approaching the stage where it will become increasingly possible to adopt specific rather than general functional behaviouristic relationships and turn the ensuing loss of generality into profit via the achievement of statistical verification. In fact, it is one of the basic strengths of our 'bourgeois' methodology that, no matter how attractive and seemingly close to the jugular a particular theory, we ultimately always insist on its corroboration with hard facts.

A prominent example of what might be called the econometric culmination of our concern with growth is provided by the recent re-examination of capital theory with an eye to improving our inadequate understanding of the interrelationship between investment and technological change in the course of the growth process. Professor Solow, for instance, in his 1957 *R.E.S.* article sets himself the task of estimating the contribution to the rate of growth of output of a constant rate of neutral technological change which is assumed to be independent of the factor endowment.[1] With capital and labour growth rates exogenously given and with the output elasticity of capital derived independently from the relative shares, exogenous innovations are awarded the major credit (up to 90 per cent) for output growth. This *prima facie* implausible result has led to a search for a new view of investment, also championed by Solow,[2]

[1] R. M. Solow, 'Technical Change and the Aggregate Production Function', *Review of Economics and Statistics*, August 1957.
[2] R. M. Solow, 'Investment and Technical Progress' in *Mathematical Methods in the Social Sciences, 1959,* Stanford, California, 1960.

according to which technological change demands embodiment in the latest vintage of capital. Given output and the labour force at time t, the age composition of capital, and the production function, the annual rate of innovation can be estimated (here at 2 per cent). The particular production function chosen is neo-classical with labour at time t allocated over the total capital stock according to equilibrium marginal productivity considerations. Still other so-called putty-to-clay models [1] support the neo-classical assumptions only for the latest vintage of capital but hold the capital-labour ratio constant *à la* Harrod-Domar for all other time periods.

The econometric results of much of this work are as yet quite inconclusive but the controversy engendered has been extremely healthy. On the one hand it has meant that our theoretical formulations increasingly reflect the general recognition that substantive progress must come via a better understanding of the interaction between capital accumulation and innovation. On the other hand it has constrained our theory from wandering too far from historical reality and has pointed theoretical and policy questions in the direction of the hidden inputs along any aggregate production function. Improvement factors for labour as a function of educational investment and for capital as a result of research and development expenditures are becoming increasingly featured in this context.

III. GROWTH IN THE LESS-DEVELOPED ECONOMIES

Thus far we have dealt almost exclusively with growth in the mature economy. The question quite naturally arises as to the extent to which this rather formidable theoretical array has helped us understand growth and, perhaps more importantly, the absence of growth in the so-called less-developed world.

There is quite patently a large measure of transferability in the way growth must be viewed in any context. Everywhere it requires abstention from consumption; and everywhere it is governed by certain technological constraints. In other words, the basic Harrod-Domar formulation can never be rejected; in fact, in an environment which is closer to a one-factor world than our own it may, in some sense, be more relevant. Nevertheless, while useful as a device for highlighting the relevant policy choices before a planning commission it cannot pretend to teach us anything about the *process* of

[1] See, for example, the work of L. Johansen, 'Substitution Versus Fixed Production Coefficients in the Theory of Economic Growth : A Synthesis', *Econometrica*, April 1959 ; and E. S. Phelps, 'Substitution, Fixed Proportions, Growth and Distribution', *Cowles Foundation Discussion Paper No. 133*, February 1962.

development. It is not enough, for example, to rephrase the Harrod problem in terms of a Say's Law world and in terms of an insufficiency of investment to absorb the increments to a growing labour force. The problem has become one of understanding how growth is initiated as well as how it is sustained ; and the resulting inquiry requires at the minimum an imaginative adaptation of our economic tools and, very likely, the fashioning of some new ones. The landscape, in other words, is sufficiently distinctive to render the simple transfer of our familiar theoretical constructs extremely hazardous.

The major problem here is that when we view growth in the mature economy, institutional or non-strictly economic factors are by and large neglected as *de minimis* or, at best, admitted as extra models through the rear door. In the under-developed economy this procedure is inadmissible. The general environment has not become sufficiently stabilized to permit exclusive concentration on the economic calculus of resources. In fact, the selective rejection of traditional *ceteris paribus* assumptions may well lie at the heart of an understanding of the whole phenomenon. Analysis of the dynamics of entrepreneurial behaviour, for example, or of administrative mores may well constitute the *sine qua non* for our understanding of a system's basic capacity to initiate and sustain change. A useful approach to a theory of economic growth is thus likely to require a broadening of the analytical framework to include relevant variables from other disciplines, principally the other social sciences.

Ultimately, even such institutional factors must, of course, be restated in terms of testable hypotheses so that they can be organized and absorbed by economic models — not because we have a great predilection for models but because this is the only way in which knowledge can be transferred and extended. The obvious difficulties attending this task — including those resulting from the case of the 'non-existent colleague' and the case of the 'dabbling economist' — have undoubtedly been responsible for the relative caution with which the profession has tackled the formulation of generalized growth theories for the less-developed world.

In fact, the attack to date has been largely inductive. On the one hand it has taken the form of gleaning the maximum insight and information from the economic history of the now advanced economies ; and on the other, of assembling a rather considerable arsenal of miscellaneous growth-theoretic ideas, mainly of an expressly partial equilibrium character and mostly the by-product of policy skirmishes.

One *obiter dictum* before we pursue these two related strands.

There have also been in evidence a few bold attempts to move directly from an interpretation of the past to a general theory of growth and stagnation for our contemporary world. Such premature attempts to 'explain everything' in the Marxian tradition have, however, usually culminated in Rostow-type stages theories in which conceptual rigour is conspicuously lacking and the field is all too often conceded to intuition and judgment in the grand manner.[1] While this sort of an approach may well render a service by providing insights, focussing attention and stimulating others to a more analytical inquiry, it also does us a disservice by its perennially enticing facility, its failure to discriminate between model and extra model considerations and its consequent inability to isolate the key behaviouristic hypotheses.

On the other hand, when history is viewed not as a hunting licence by means of the big brush but as a laboratory in which significant growth-theoretic relationships may be uncovered and tested, it constitutes, certainly in the present state of our knowledge, one of our major potential assets. The work of men like Goldsmith,[2] Kendrick[3] and Kuznets,[4] for example, has contributed greatly to our forward motion by emphasizing the importance of observed historical relationships for the formulation of viable growth-theoretic hypotheses. The rather remarkable achievement of Kuznets, in particular, in ferreting out intelligence on growth and structural change in a large number of less-developed countries has provided us with the quantitative raw materials essential for further theorizing. Chenery's[5] and Houthakker's[6] interesting attempts to derive long-run behaviouristic relationships for the 'typical' growing economy by means of cross-sectional analysis point the way. The search for regularities goes on, and, thanks to the availability of reliable data, the ranks of intuitively plausible but as yet untested hypotheses (e.g. the internationalized 'Duesenberry effect', the 'take-off', the 'backward-bending' supply curve of effort) are thinned.

[1] W. W. Rostow, *The Stages of Economic Growth*, Cambridge, 1960.

[2] R. Goldsmith, *Financial Structure and Economic Growth in 'Advanced' Countries*, Conference on Capital Formation and Economic Growth, New York, 1953 ; *A Study of Saving in the United States*, Princeton, 1955, among many others.

[3] J. W. Kendrick, *Productivity Trends in the United States*, Princeton, 1959.

[4] See, for example, S. Kuznets, *National Product Since 1869*, New York, 1946 ; and *Quantitative Aspects of Economic Growth of Nations* in various volumes of *Economic Development and Cultural Change*, 1956–62.

[5] H. B. Chenery, 'Patterns of Industrial Growth', *American Economic Review*, September 1960.

[6] H. S. Houthakker, 'An International Comparison of Household Expenditure Patterns, Commemorating the Anniversary of Engels' Law', *Econometrica*, October 1957.

Most of the post World War II additions to our theoretical tool kit may be characterized as partial equilibrium notions derived from the pressing policy needs of the period. This is not to say that planning commissions and national or international agencies concerned with development have been exclusively or even largely responsible for theoretical advances in this period ; but it is undoubtedly true that most of the concepts presently in vogue have been induced by and associated with the search for improved allocation decisions in the less-developed economy.

Nurkse's [1] concept of balanced growth and Hirschman's [2] emphasis on imbalance, for example, stem from this basic concern with developmental strategy. Here the importance of external economies and complementarities is weighed against the husbanding of scarce decision-making resources. Likewise, Rosenstein-Rodan's [3] 'big push' and Leibenstein's [4] 'critical minimum effort' theses concern themselves with the need to overcome the gravitational pull of stagnation by means of a concentrated attempt at breakout over a relatively short period of time.

In general, our recent intensive quest for a satisfactory formulation of the investment allocation criteria problem fits this overall description. This quest has led us from a simple factor intensity criterion (e.g. minimization of the capital-output ratio) through the social marginal productivity calculus towards recent syntheses which accommodate the dynamic distributional considerations of Galenson and Leibenstein.[5] Undoubtedly as a consequence of the insistent pressures of policy such formulations have addressed themselves mainly to the relatively more manageable problem of the choice of technology, given a stipulated output mix.

Other formulations, especially those of more recent vintage, have, however, tended increasingly to face up to the more difficult general equilibrium dimensions of the problem. Noted here must be the various planning models which have been emerging, aided and abetted in no small measure by the revitalization of input-output analysis in the favourable climate of the total-mobilization-conscious less-developed area. These include, of course, the pioneering con-

[1] Ragnar Nurkse, *Problems of Capital Formation in Underdeveloped Areas*, New York, 1953.

[2] Albert O. Hirschman, *The Strategy of Economic Development*, New Haven, 1958.

[3] P. N. Rosenstein-Rodan, 'Notes on the Theory of the "Big Push"' in *Economic Development for Latin America*, Proceedings of an International Economic Association Conference, London, 1961.

[4] Harvey Leibenstein, *Economic Backwardness and Economic Growth*, New York, 1959.

[5] W. Galenson and H. Leibenstein, 'Investment Criteria, Productivity, and Economic Development', *Quarterly Journal of Economics*, August 1955.

tributions of Tinbergen, both in his earlier emphasis on the use of shadow pricing [1] and in his later dynamic growth models : [2] the relatively sophisticated planning models of Sandee [3] and Frisch ; [4] and, on a more down to earth plane, the imaginative modified-linear programming work of Chenery and the UN experts.[5]

It is patently clear that any divorce between planning and growth theory must be highly artificial at best. Presumably we must have some understanding of how a system behaves before we can meaningfully concern ourselves with problems of allocation, targets, instruments and constraints. It should, therefore, be no surprise that the aforementioned relatively cautious two-pronged advance of recent years is currently giving promise of yielding simultaneous progress towards the more generalized type of growth-theoretic formulation.

Any such growth model which endeavours to at least begin to 'tie up' in some orderly fashion the miscellany of insights, ideas and empirical titbits which has been accumulating over the years, must be prepared to withstand attack from those who claim that each less-developed economy is *sui generis* and that the task is consequently impossible. It should once again be emphasized, however, that there is a substantial difference between full recognition of the already referred to difficulties involved in considering a range of non-economic variables — and the denial of the scientific method. It is therefore encouraging to note that our theory is screwing up its courage and attempting to move forward again in these directions.

At least in this author's view, most progress in this connection has been made through models which explicitly recognize the existence, in the labour surplus less-developed areas, of a structural condition commonly, if imprecisely, designated as dualism. Dualism is here defined as the existence of a sector or sectors in which the actual distribution of the capital stock and of complementary factors does not permit the market to be cleared and optimal resource use to be effected. Under such conditions of inequality between the proportions in which factors are available and in which they are used, general equilibrium theory becomes invalid and a distribution theory based on an institutional hypothesis must be applied.

[1] J. Tinbergen, *The Design of Development*, Baltimore, 1958.

[2] J. Tinbergen and H. C. Bos, *Mathematical Models of Economic Growth*, New York, 1962.

[3] J. Sandee, *A Long-Term Planning Model for India*, UN, New York, 1959.

[4] R. Frisch, *Planning for Economic Development in India : A Memorandum on the Broad Macro-Economic Aspects of the Problem*, Indian Statistical Institute, Calcutta, November 1959.

[5] For example, H. B. Chenery and M. Bruno, 'Development Alternatives in an Open Economy : The Case of Israel', *Economic Journal*, March 1962 ; and *Formulating Industrial Development Programmes*, Economic Commission for Asia and the Far East, Bangkok, 1961.

Recognition of this important phenomenon has led us to re-formulate some of our growth-theoretic models in terms of at least two sectors, a commercialized or industrial sector and a non-commercialized or agricultural sector. Simultaneously our emphasis has shifted from the phenomenon of increased labour productivity as the relevant performance index to the rate of reallocation of the labour force between the two sectors.

Arthur Lewis [1] was the first to advance the crucial behaviouristic assumption of an 'unlimited' supply of labour, based on the existence of an institutionally-anchored real wage and stating the conditions under which the transfer of the underemployed agricultural labour force could be effected. Lewis' attention was focussed mainly on the creation of the required employment opportunities in the industrial sector and on the consequences of the ultimate 'turning up' of the industrial labour supply curve; but he paid relatively little attention to the agricultural sector and to the causes of that upturn and its implication for the dynamics of the reallocation process. Jorgenson [2] and Ranis-Fei [3] have sought to follow this up by examining the development problem in terms of the complete interaction between the two sectors in the course of the development effort. This enabled Ranis-Fei, for example, to reinterpret the balanced growth criterion in terms of allocating investment funds by ensuring constancy of the intersectoral terms of trade while 'freeing' only those workers from the agricultural sector which can be productively absorbed by the industrial sector. The immediate aim of development policy then becomes the achievement of a so-called turning point which marks the capture of the entire economy by market forces as all factors become scarce and the familiar economic calculus takes over.

Our halting efforts toward a general theory of under-development thus have their common antecedents in the mature economy but have subsequently been forced to proceed along somewhat divergent paths. Casting a shadow over all else is, of course, the requirement that our analysis for the less-developed world must be deepened to include consideration of all such variables in the total environment which have a significant influence on a system's capacity to initiate as well as sustain growth. The operational significance of this fact is that while for most purposes the developed world can be dealt

[1] Arthur Lewis, 'Development with Unlimited Supplies of Labour', *The Manchester School*, May 1954.
[2] D. W. Jorgenson, 'The Development of a Dual Economy', *Economic Journal*, June 1961.
[3] G. Ranis and J. C. H. Fei, 'A Theory of Economic Development', *American Economic Review*, September 1961.

with in a one-sector model this would be unreasonable violence to reality in most of the less-developed areas. To accommodate the pervasive institution-rooted phenomenon of dualism in our analytical machinery, at a minimum a two-sector model is required. It is then the rate of labour reallocation between the two sectors — and not necessarily the change in overall labour productivity — which must be viewed as the index of successful development.

The rediscovery of the importance of the subsistence or agricultural sector as both deterrent and opportunity has moreover helped to focus our attention once again on the so-called natural resource base. Specifically, the importance of population density and population growth has been considerably up-graded — as it has been for quite different, 'stagnationist', reasons in the advanced economies. But while in general the return to the classical hearth has, as already noted, borne considerable fruit this cannot be said for the specific problem of reintegrating demographic variables into our theory. In fact, we are currently more aware than ever of our ignorance about the determinants of population growth ; recent data has cast doubt even on some of our 'safe facts' concerning urban-rural fertility differentials.

Nevertheless, the specific field of growth-theoretic inquiry with potentially the largest pay-off to a more satisfactory treatment — in both the developed and less-developed economy — is undoubtedly the interrelationship between capital accumulation and innovation. While all economists are agreed on some form of interdependence, both the causal order and the strength of any endogenous relationship which may exist are still largely undetermined. We might, for example, hypothesize in a rough-and-ready fashion that innovations induce capital accumulation in the advanced economy and that the reverse holds for the less-developed world. This is based on the notion that in the mature economy diminishing returns have been historically thwarted by innovations and that major bursts of investment must await the creation of the new investment opportunities yielded by technological change. While in a capital abundant context the bottleneck is thus provided by declining investment opportunities patently in the less-developed area it is a shortage of capital which plays this role. Every increment to the savings fund is more than assured employment. It is, in fact, assiduously wooed and competed for by a plethora of investment opportunities. In such a context innovations can be taken down from the formidable technological shelf (provided mainly from abroad) only as fast as capital accumulation renders the required embodiment possible. It is considerations of this sort which may ultimately help in deriving more meaningful behaviouristic hypotheses in this vital area, especially with respect to the less-developed economy.

Finally, a major comparative disadvantage under which less-developed area growth theorists are forced to labour should be mentioned. When we speak of the less-developed area's 'data problems' we are not simply referring to the well-known difficulties with respect to the quality and quantity of contemporary data but also to the fact that, with the notable exception of Japan, the full applicability of the historical empirical record to today's developmental landscape is at best problematical. Perhaps none of our favourite Western European examples has ever gone through an unlimited supply of labour stage in its process of transition to maturity. This inability to depend on the historical laboratory is further compounded by the fact that the post-war economic experience in the less-developed world is itself heavily marred by the vicissitudes of official policies. The econometric problem of estimating almost any functional relationship is very much complicated by the need to include considerations of policy parameters where the underlying economic market behaviour may be heavily distorted. But clearly the growth theorist has no choice in the matter ; whether he finds himself on the inductive or deductive path he must try to distinguish between what 'will be' and what 'should be' when searching for reliable data and meaningful hypotheses among the maze of five-year plans and statistical appendices.

DISCUSSION OF THE PAPER BY PROFESSOR RANIS

Professor W. Krelle, opening the discussion, commented that the paper had been mainly limited to contributions made in English whereas there had been substantial French, German, Italian and Japanese work in this field. It should be possible to draw conclusions from all the work done and seek out the remaining neglected issues.

The Harrod-Domar theory, using as starting-point a very simple identity, could provide only a first and very rough approximation. It had to be substantially enlarged by introducing — on a base of a suitable social accounting system — different sectors of the economy (at least the government, the entrepreneurs, the wage earners and the foreign countries) together with production, investment, consumption, export and import functions connecting the variables of the system and allowing for the study of the influence of different economic policies on growth and long-run structural change. All contributions to the theory of economic growth since Harrod and Domar lay on that road, but nobody as yet was able to include all the important and relevant sides of the problem mentioned above in one theory ; clearly the course of growth theory pointed in that direction. Such a model could give answers to short-run and to long-run problems as well. In the short run, given the magnitudes of the previous period as constants, solutions could be found for the next period ; in the long run the aim would be to find that rate of growth which, once achieved, maintained itself over time. Models of this type would presumably not give unstable solutions, such as were obtained in the Harrod-Domar analysis ; such instability was the result of over-simplified assumptions.

Some results were available from a model of this kind where only foreign trade and government expenditures were considered as exogenous. Changes in the wage rate had almost no influence on the long-run equilibrium rate of growth or on the distribution of income, although there were repercussions on the price level. The rate of interest had a negligible influence on the growth rate, whilst an increase in the capital coefficient was detrimental to growth. An increase in the degree of monopolization, on the other hand, was a favourable factor. In general the equilibrium growth rates were not much influenced by the usual policy parameters, following from the fact that the short- and long-run effects of alterations in these parameters were often opposed. The model showed that a modern free-market economy was in the long run almost certainly stable, or (very exceptionally) unstable only to a slight degree.

Professor A. Heertje said that an important problem in the von Neumann type of growth model was that, whilst the existence of a rate of growth which would maintain itself could be demonstrated, there may be more than one such possible rate implicit in the model.

Professor E. Schneider said that the explanation of growth in a capitalist economy had to start at the level of the firm, because of the vital role played by the entrepreneur. Hence, micro-economic theories must be combined with macro-economics. The driving force of growth in capitalist economies was often disequilibrium, so that theories based on a search for equilibrium rates of growth were not sufficient.

Professor G. Leduc argued that the tools of analysis used in growth theories were developed for countries already past the industrial revolution. It is questionable how far they can be applied to under-developed countries. What was needed was a theory applicable to both developed and under-developed countries. The concepts of saving, investment, price, demand, etc., were clearly generally applicable. Care was required, however, in applying the idea of 'dualism', since it tended to appear only at a certain stage of development and rapidly became a more complex phenomenon. In fact, sociological and institutional factors may frustrate the use of simple models altogether.

Professor T. Scitovsky said that dualism was an important concept, because it provided a realistic means of departing from the assumption of perfect competition. It implied that, in certain markets, there was no complete mechanism for the equalization of prices.

Problems in Economic Development

Professor H. S. Houthakker commented that, although development involved time, it would still be useful to develop the static theories which would explain the differences between the relative income levels of countries at a given point in time. Such a viewpoint might well reduce the emphasis placed on the role of capital in development policy.

Professor R. Mossé said that the shift in emphasis away from investment towards other factors was welcome. These included non-economic factors. The Soviet Union had placed much stress on certain of these non-economic considerations which were known to be important and this might well account for its high rate of growth.

Professor I. Rachmuth said that Marxists took into consideration not only the technical factors, but also the reciprocal relationships between the men and the production process. The vital factor was the form of social organization — who organizes the production process and who benefits from the output? It was important to know whether the economy was orientated towards growth through appropriate planning.

Professor J. Stanovnik argued that the point of departure should be a distinction between 'development' and 'growth'. The former was a structural change, whereas growth is a quantitative matter. The problem was to make the accumulated experience of developed countries relevant to those starting on the development process.

Structural change affects the institutions of a country so that stimulants used in more developed countries may not work in the same way. The older countries began their development in a state of primitive technology and on a small scale, with technical development proceeding autonomously. Development requires a larger scale of operations today, whilst the development of technology in under-developed countries was hindered by their rapidly changing conditions. Theories of economic development must return to the classical tradition, based on the role of the state as an active factor in the situation.

Professor G. Ranis, replying to the discussion, said that it was necessary to challenge the assertion that investment opportunities were less plentiful in under-developed countries than in the more developed. The Western countries had seen a steady decline in the rate of return on capital, which may now have reached a floor. In under-developed countries, however, there was a scarcity of capital and there was a need to accumulate in order to make use of the technical knowledge already available to more developed economies.

Economic models, although inadequate, were essential as a means of rigorous thinking. The methodology used should rest on an empirical verification of any model used. The present tools of analysis should be applied to under-developed countries, even if imperfect, but the relevance of the historical experience of the developed countries must be carefully assessed ; it was doubtful how far the same pattern fitted all the countries which were now developed. 'Dualism' was a useful concept to employ, but its value depended upon the definitions chosen.

Chapter 2

PROBLEMS IN THE THEORY OF GROWTH UNDER SOCIALISM

W. BRUS
University of Warsaw
and
K. ŁASKI
Central School of Planning and Statistics, Warsaw

FROM the many issues which could form the subject of a paper
bearing the above title, we have chosen especially those which are,
in our opinion, related to the experience of Polish economic development. We think that at least some elements of the theoretical
examination of this experience may be of a more general importance.

I. GENERAL APPROACH TO THE FACTORS OF GROWTH

In an increasing number of contemporary works on the theory
of growth we find a more or less explicit acknowledgment of the fact
that a formal quantitative analysis of the factors determining growth
can give, as a rule, correct results only when it is conducted within a
definite socio-cconomic framework. In our opinion, however, the
only fully consistent general approach which accords with this
principle is presented by the Marxian theory of growth. The study
of the development process as a process of the mutual conditioning
of the material and technical factor (productive forces) and the socio-
economic factor (production-relations) is the fundamental methodological assumption of this theory. Marxists hold that production-
relations determine the essential parameters of every formal model
designed to show the quantitative interdependence of the factors of
growth. Changes in parameters, caused by changes of production-
relations, influence fundamentally the elements contained in a
quantitative model, and thus they influence also the theoretical and
practical conclusions derived from it. For the subject we are considering, distinction between the conditions of economic growth
under capitalism and under socialism is absolutely essential.

The process of growth with socialist social and economic conditions and the resulting national economic planning constitute the basic assumption of all Polish works on the theory of growth. Generally speaking there are two essential forces which specifically determine the conditions of growth in a socialist system :

(1) Socialism creates the possibility and necessity to present and solve economic problems on the scale of the national economy treated as a whole. In the terms used by Oskar Lange,[1] there occurs the integration of particular aims into one general economic aim. In such conditions growth — conceived as the basis of an increasing satisfaction of social needs — can be consciously set up as the aim of co-ordinated planned action on the scale of the entire national economy.

(2) Through the nationalization of the means of production and the consequent putting of the basic resources at the disposal of the community, socialism creates the premises of the realization of a general economic aim. The allocation of the factors of production may be effected according to the plan, with a view to the full utilization of the existing growth potential, and the avoidance of obstacles caused by particular private interests.

Both the points mentioned above explain in the most general way the thesis that socialism creates practical possibilities of utilizing in a high degree the national growth potential, and consequently of minimizing the discrepancy between the real and the potential rate of growth. It should not be surmised that the full utilization of the national growth potential is achieved under socialism automatically and without any difficulties. In this paper we shall try to draw attention to numerous theoretical problems concerning these difficulties. For the moment we wish only to say that socialism creates such socio-economic premises as render possible a close approach of the real rate of growth to the potential one. It is particularly important to note that socialism overcomes those limitations which in capitalism are due to insufficient effective demand consequent on the internal inconsistencies of the capitalist mode of production. Quoting the favourite literary metaphor of some economists, we would say that socialism saves Alice from the Wonderland where over-capacity co-exists with unemployed labour — both factors not being utilized because of a 'supernatural' lack of sufficient aggregate demand.

All this is of essential importance for any examination of the

[1] Cf. O. Lange, *Ekonomia Polityczna* (Political economy), Vol. 1, Warsaw, 1959, p. 134.

analysis of the factors of growth in writings on the socialist economy. For easily understandable reasons the use of growth-models based on the Keynesian tradition and emphasizing the problems of effective demand is not considered very helpful. Realistic models of growth in a socialist economy take as their starting-point the problems of the dimensions of available factors of growth, and not the problems of aggregate effective demand, emphasizing thus, above all, 'supply' as limiting the size and the growth rate of production.

Factors concerning the 'supply-side' can be dealt with in two ways: first from the point of view of current labour (labour reserves and their increase; level of labour productivity and its changes). Viewed thus the gross national income (Y) is determined by the product of employment (Z) and productivity (W) defined as gross value added per employee:

$$Y = Z \times W. \tag{1}$$

Secondly, we can approach the same problems from the point of view of stored-up labour (stocks of means of production and their increase; effectiveness of means of production and its changes). Thus the gross national income can be presented as the product of the real productive fixed capital (M) by the effectiveness of this fixed capital (E) defined as gross value added per unit of capital, or

$$Y = M \times E. \tag{2}$$

This twofold approach to factors determining the national income presents sometimes a temptation to unite the elements of formulae (1) and (2) into one formula. In Poland such attempts are known, based among others on the Cobb-Douglas function.[1] However, the use of a Cobb-Douglas type of function is questioned, first of all because of its problematical theoretical quality and the practical difficulty of dividing the increased income into the 'part due' to employment and the 'part due' to the real productive fixed capital (there is an analogous question as to 'ascribing' the increase of labour productivity to the substitution and to the independent technical progress).[2]

---

[1] E.g. J. Pajestka in his work, *Zatrudnienie inwestycyjne a wzrost gospodarczy* ('Employment and Investment in Connection with Economic Growth'), Warsaw, 1961. Regarding the concept of the factors of growth see W. Lissowski, *Zastosowanie relacji majatek-praca-produkcja w programowaniu rozwoju przemyslu* ('The Application of the Ratio Capital-Labour-Production in Planning the Development of Industry'), Warsaw, 1962, and K. Łaski 'Czynniki wzrostu dochodu narodowego w gospodarce socjalistycznej' ('Factors of Growth of National Income in Socialist Economy'), *Ekonomista*, No. 2, 1960.

[2] Such attempts were made recently in Poland by J. J. Lisikiewicz, 'O metodach analizy wplywu postepu technicznego na wydajnosc pracy w przemysle' ('On

The model of growth formulated by M. Kalecki is most often used in Poland in theoretical studies including those for long-term planning. It will also form a suitable starting-point for our discussions.[1]

On the basis of the methodological assumptions expressed by formula (1), the rate of growth of the national income (r) during the period t is determined in this model as follows :

$$r = \frac{\Delta Y}{Y} = a + \beta \tag{3}$$

where ΔY is the increment of national income during the period t, i.e. the difference between gross national income at the period t and at the period $t - 1$;

Y is gross national income at the period $t - 1$;
a is rate of increase in average productive employment at the period t in relation to period $t - 1$;
β is rate of increase in average labour-productivity at the period t in relation to period $t - 1$;

The product $a.\beta$ is omitted as negligible.

Thus the rate of income growth is the sum of the rate of increase in employment and of the rate of increase in productivity. But both the increase in employment and the increase in productivity assume at the same time a corresponding increase in real productive fixed capital and in its effectiveness. Thus the rate of income growth should at the same time be expressed in terms of the methodological assumptions resulting from formula (2) :

$$r = \frac{\Delta Y}{Y} = i \times \frac{1}{m} - a + u \tag{4}$$

methods of analysing the influence of technical progress on labour productivity in industry '), *Ekonomista*, No. 4, 1961, and by Z. Knyziak, 'Inwestycyjne i pozain-westycyjne czynniki wzrostu produkcji przemyslowej w Polsce w latach 1950–60' (' Investment and Non-Investment Factors of Growth of Industrial Production in Poland in 1950–60 '), *Ekonomista*, No. 5, 1960.

[1] In the first place the following work of M. Kalecki should be mentioned : 'Zagadnienia teorii dynamiki gospodarki socjalistycznej' (' On Problems of the Theory of Socialist Economy Dynamics') in the collective work: *Zagadnienia ekonomii politycznej socjalizmu* (' Problems of the Political Economy of Socialism '), 3rd edition, Warsaw, 1960. In addition, in preparing this paper we availed ourselves of Professor Kalecki's latest work, *Teoria wzrostu w gospodarce socjalistycznej* (' The Theory of Growth in a Socialist Economy ') which is now published. We wish to express our profound gratitude to Professor Kalecki for having kindly allowed us to use this material, as well as for his friendly advice and critical comments. There is no need to stress that the authors are solely responsible for the opinions and formulations contained in this paper.

where I is gross productive investment in fixed capital (the increase in inventories omitted for simplicity) at the period $t-1$, put into operation at the period t ;

$i = \dfrac{I}{Y}$ is the rate of investment or the share of gross productive investment in the gross national income at the period $t-1$;

m is investment outlay necessary to obtain an increase in national income by one unit or the ratio $\dfrac{y}{\Delta Y'}$, where $\Delta Y'$ is the increase in national income due to investment ;

a coefficient of the decrease in national income resulting from the actual loss of means of production or the diminution in their effective functioning due to physical depreciation ;

u coefficient of the increase of national income resulting from all kinds of improvements raising the effectiveness of the existing real productive fixed capital.

Kalecki stresses the fact that formula (4) cannot be applied in a capitalist economy, as there the coefficient 'u' is not an independent variable and fluctuates greatly (even in terms of $+$ or $-$) as a result of the business cycle. On the other hand in a socialist economy in normal conditions this coefficient is always positive, reflecting the tendency of continued improvement of the existing productive apparatus. It results therefrom that the magnitude $i \times \dfrac{1}{m}$ becomes a strategic factor determining the rate of economic growth. This argument can be reinforced by emphasizing that in a capitalist economy the rate of investment also is not independent of the magnitude 'm', which really determines the rentability of investments (assuming a given distribution of income between profits and wages).

In comparing the formulae (3) and (4) we see that

$$a + \beta = i \times \frac{1}{m} - a + u$$

as is obvious, since the rate of growth in the national income does not change according as we look at it from the point of view of labour or of real productive fixed capital.

The confrontation of these two aspects is important as it enables us to realize some of the interrelations needed to define the optimal rate of growth in given conditions. One of these very simple but useful truths, brought to light by this confrontation, is the necessity to co-ordinate precisely the factors shown on both sides (of the comparative formula) in order to assure the optimal course of the process of growth. It is obvious, of course, that first of all the key magnitude $\frac{I}{Y} = i$ — i.e. the rate of investment — must be properly established.

The degree of complexity of the problem of properly defining the rate of investment depends on the degree of variability of the remaining factors to which the rate of investment should correspond. Were the economy to develop at a stabilized rate r, with a rate of increase in employment perfectly adapted to secure a balance of the labour force (there is no possibility of change unless there should occur a deficit in the labour force or unemployment) and with a constant rate of increase in productivity (also without any possibility of change assuming that the coefficients m, a and u are constant) — in such a simplified case there would have been a single and constant rate of investment fulfilling the postulate of a full utilization of the growth potential.

Thus, to obtain the optimal rate of growth, it would be necessary to do two things only: first, to establish satisfactorily the un-equivocally determined rate of investment; secondly, to put into operation a mechanism to ensure the actual attainment of such a rate of investment and its maintenance at the same level. Naturally the word 'only' — especially so far as the second point is concerned — should be written in quotation marks as it is not at all a simple matter. This is shown by the voluminous writings on the problems of the theoretical conditions for bringing an economy on to the trend of stabilized growth that corresponds to the potential possibilities. The importance of the earlier mentioned characteristics of a socialist system — creating, as they do, real premises for the direct establishment of a rate of investment on a national scale that corresponds to the postulated rate of growth — is manifest even with these extremely simplified assumptions.

And yet every step toward reality must mean at the same time a progressive relaxation of the assumptions regarding the invariability of the factors present in the model under consideration. In reality the rate of growth of available labour resources, as well as the rate of productivity, are variable. The coefficients m, a and u have different values at different stages, especially when account is taken of different time-horizons. It follows therefrom that the problem of the optimal course of the process of growth does not, and cannot, consist in putting the economy on to the path of a rate of growth stabilized once and for all — that is in attaining a single postulated rate of investment. A full utilization of the growth potential requires in reality a variable rate of growth, and therefore also a rate of investment that varies at least at certain intervals of time.

This means that the criteria for the evaluation of the conditions, within the given social and economic system, for the optimal process of growth, cannot be limited to the possibility of attaining once and for all a definite rate of investment. These criteria include also the essential factor of flexibility in establishing the rate of investment, a proper relation, that is, of investment to consumption in the national income. And this flexibility must be such that it will not cause a lack of effective aggregate demand in relation to productive capacities and thus will not cause any waste of the real growth potential.

We wish to argue that a socialist planned economy creates — and perhaps it does so especially from this point of view — favourable conditions for a full utilization of the national growth potential. In any case these conditions are more favourable than those created by an economy where the general rate of investments depends on the private 'propensity to invest'.[1]

We will return later to this question in relation to certain particular problems, mostly connected with the variability of the factors of growth. As was said in the introductory paragraph, we will try to base our discussion on the experience of our country and on the reflection of that experience in Polish economic writings.

II. ACCELERATION OF GROWTH WITH EXISTING LABOUR RESERVES

May we begin by rejecting the assumption of stability of a — that is the rate of increase in employment. The rate of growth of the national income (r) existing at the starting period t_o is below the limit set by the labour force (there exists a reserve of population able to work and not yet employed) and therefore it can — or it should, rather, in these conditions — be increased. The assumption of stability in the rate of increase of productivity (β), in as much as β depends on the coefficient m, is meanwhile maintained.

This order in our exposition corresponds to the consecutive order of the conditions that actually prevailed in Poland. At the beginning of industrialization of the country (before 1949) our economy had at its disposal comparatively large reserves of unemployed labour (even taking into consideration the then existing

[1] Cf. W. Brus, K. Łaski, 'Istotna tresc marksowskiego ujecia problematyki rozwoju ekonomicznego' ('The Essential Content of Marxian Approach to the Problems of Economic Development'), *Ekonomista*, No. 4, 1962.

technical and organizational level). They took the form in general of disguised unemployment (agrarian overpopulation) rather than of open unemployment.

(a) *The Variability of the Rate of Growth at the Period of Acceleration*

When a' indicates the rate of growth of the labour-force-supply due to the rate of increase of the population with a given ratio of active to total population and $a' > a$, meaning that the rate of increase in employment has been less than the rate of growth of the labour force, so that the growth potential was not fully taken advantage of, this would necessitate a change from the rate $r = a + \beta$ to the rate of $r' = a' + \beta$ (assuming that β remains constant, which is not precisely true even when the coefficient m remains unvariable). A change, however, from the rate r to the rate r' is a very complicated process which cannot follow a uniform path.[1] Though the gradual increase of r to r' means a formal equalization of the actual and of the potential rate of growth, the absolute increase of employment in this situation is still lower than the absolute increase in labour force. If the above-mentioned conditions were stabilized, then employment would grow by a', but simultaneously unemployment would grow also, at the same rate, a'. Thus to stabilize the rate of growth after n years in the year t_n at the level r' there must be some moment between the period t_o and the period t_n during which the rate of growth $r'' > r'$, in order to bring the economy on to the new course of growth. Only after a period during which the rate of growth is sufficient both to absorb the whole current increase in labour force and in addition the surplus of labour from the preceding periods, can growth be stabilized at the level r'. We have, therefore, the following course of the process of changing the economy from the rate of growth r to the rate of growth r', corresponding to the rate of increase of labour force a': $r \rightarrow r' \rightarrow r'' \rightarrow r'$ while $r < r' < r''$. In Figure 1 this process is shown diagrammatically.

Until the year t_o the economy grows at the rate r with the rate of investment i. In the year t_m (intermediate between the year t_o and the year t_n), the economy attains for the first time the rate of growth r' with a rate of investment i'. The line AB shows the development between the year t_o and t_m. The line BC shows the development from the year t_m to t_n, when the rate of income growth and the rate of investments must temporarily increase above r' and

[1] Cf. Władysław Sadowski, 'Zmiana stopy wzrostu gospodarczego' ('The Change in the Rate of Economic Growth'), *Ekonomista*, No. 6, 1958, and especially 'Przyspieszanie dlugofalowego wzrostu w gospodarce socjalistycznej' ('The Acceleration of Long-Term Growth in Socialist Economy'), *Ekonomista*, No. 4, 1961.

i' to r'' and i'' in order to secure the elimination of unemployment. In the year t_n the economy returns to the rate of growth r' with the rate of investment i'. This is the rate adapted to the equilibrium balance of the labour force. The change to the new stabilized growth goes through the points $A \rightarrow B \rightarrow C \rightarrow B$.

This analysis of the probable course of the process of absorption of the unutilized labour force and of the elimination of this source of difference between the actual and the potential rates of growth confirms the complexity of this process. The rate of investment must

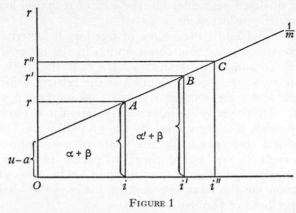

FIGURE 1

On the horizontal axis is measured the rate of investment (i), on the vertical axis the rate of growth of the national income (r). The coefficient of direction of the straight line is $\frac{1}{m}$, the distance from the origin $u - a$, if we assume that $u - a > 0$.

not only increase but even exceed temporarily the long-term optimal level (on given assumption), and decrease again later. It is necessary, therefore, not only to evaluate correctly, organize and finally attain the ultimate ratio aimed at, but also to evaluate correctly, organize and attain the ratios corresponding to the intermediate points. This requires, among other things, even a temporary reversal of the direction of the change in the rate of growth and in the rate of investment.

(b) *Acceleration and the Dynamics of Consumption*

The question arises whether the best solution is an immediate setting of the economy on the new course of growth, taking account of the possibility of flexible planned adjustment of the rate of investment, characteristic of a socialist economy. Such a solution is tempting not only because it shortens the complicated period of adjustment, but because it shortens also the period of losses due to the unutilized growth potential, between the years t_o and t_n.

This would have been in practice the best solution if one could assume that the central planning authorities were completely free in defining the rate of investment. But of course such an assumption is inadmissible. And this is not only due to the numerous technical difficulties connected with the structure of the national product (the necessity to increase violently the share of investment goods), but also to the organizational problems of large investment works, the shortage of qualified personnel and the lack of technical knowledge, as well as other considerations.

The basic problem is the degree of freedom in determining the ratio of investment to current consumption in the national income. The current consumption (defined as $Y - I$) is the more affected, the lower is the starting-point, defined as the relative value r and i, and also the lower the starting level of consumption per head of population. The lower is the figure r in relation to r' (and also r''), so, *ceteris paribus*, the larger must be the growth of i. The growth of i diminishes correspondingly the share of consumption in the national income $(1 - i)$, and during the period of acceleration it restricts the rate of increase in consumption. The consequences of this restriction are the more onerous the lower is the level of consumption per head of population.

From this point of view of course not only is the rate of acceleration of fundamental importance, but also the length of time in which the economy is to take the new course of growth. The shorter is n, the more violent is the growth of i and the fall of $1 - i$, and the slower is the growth of consumption. Thus if we accept even the mildest limiting condition — e.g. that the absolute magnitude of consumption cannot decrease — then it will as a rule be found that the shortest technically possible length of the period n will not be consistent even with this condition. This is still more true if one substitutes the condition that consumption must grow at least at the same rate as the increase of population (so that the consumption per head does not fall), or the alternative condition that average real wages do not decrease.

Let us now consider in detail the problem of acceleration in relation to the dynamics of consumption. It is of great importance to the understanding of certain phenomena that occurred during the first stage of industrialization of Poland. In order to simplify we shall not take into consideration all the intermediary stages of the course between the points $A \rightarrow B \rightarrow C \rightarrow B$.

Before the year t_o the economy grows at the rate r. There is the same rate of growth of consumption, C. This growth is the sum of $\alpha + \beta$, which means that β is not only the rate of growth of labour productivity but also the rate of growth of average real wages. On the other hand population grows by $\alpha' > \alpha$ so that consumption per head grows by $\alpha + \beta - \alpha'$, or slower than labour productivity and average wages β, as $\alpha + \beta - \alpha' < \beta$ when $\alpha' > \alpha$.

By the year t_n the economy will have attained the stabilized rate of growth $r' = \alpha' + \beta$. Total consumption will thenceforth increase at the same rate. Simultaneously the rate of increase in labour productivity and that of average real wages will equal the rate of increase in consumption per head of population, which will amount to $\alpha' + \beta - \alpha' = \beta$.

The final effect is satisfactory. But what happens during the n years between the year t_o and t_n? Let us assume that the decision to increase the rate of growth was taken in the year t_o. This, assuming one year as period of 'maturing' of investment, leads to a change in the rate of investment in the year t_1, and to a change in the rate of growth of the national income in the year t_2.* Essential importance should be attached to the fact, that in the year t_o, when the decision is taken to increase the investment rate in the year t_1, a given rate of investment already exists, resulting from decisions taken in the year t_{-1}. Thus the rate of growth of the national income in the year t_1 and the absolute level of the national income in that year are determined completely independently of the fact whether and to what degree the rate of investment may change. In such conditions, however, any growth of the investment rate does not only mean a reduction of the share of consumption in income — which is always true — but it also means that the level of consumption is absolutely below the level which would have been attained had the acceleration process not been started in the economy concerned.

Let us denote national income, consumption and investments in the year t_o by Y, C and I correspondingly. Were there no acceleration, in the year t_1 these figures would amount respectively to $Y(1+r)$, $C(1+r)$ and $I(1+r)$. If we intend to accelerate growth and establish a share of investment in income amounting to

$$i' = \frac{I(1+r) + \Delta I}{Y(1+r)},$$

then consumption would amount to

$$Y(1+r) - I(1+r) - \Delta I < C(1+r).$$

---

* In practice the gestation period of investment is much longer than one year. This is of the greatest importance to this problem, and especially when the scale of investment expansion is violently changed.

The rate of increase in consumption in the year t_1 will be therefore smaller than $r = a + \beta$, and it must be smaller if acceleration is to be achieved.[1]

The extent of the limitation of consumption depends on several factors, but above all of the magnitude ΔI which in turn depends on the difference $r' - r$ with the given coefficient m. If r' is much larger than r, then ΔI must also be large and it must limit relatively strongly the consumption in the year t_1. It depends further on the magnitude r whether this limitation takes the form of a slower growth, a stabilization or an absolute decline. The lower r, the greater the danger of stabilization or even of absolute decline of consumption in conditions in which it is necessary to increase markedly the rate of income growth.

Independently, however, of different possible quantitative changes, the phenomenon of initial losses of consumption in order to raise the economy to a higher growth path of national income and consumption always occurs in the process of acceleration. It is illustrated by Figure 2 (on a logarithmic scale).

Until the year t_0 the economy (national income $= Y$, real productive fixed capital $= M$, consumption $= C$) has been growing at a stable rate $r = a + \beta$ lower than the potential rate of growth $r' = a' + \beta$. In the year t_0 the decision is taken to increase the rate of investment in order to adapt it to the available labour force. In order to simplify let us assume that there has occurred a single increase in the rate of investment to a magnitude sufficient to ensure the absorption of the whole labour surplus (the increase of population and those unemployed in the preceding period). The rate of investment will increase initially up to i'' (corresponding to the rate of growth of fixed capital r''). Assuming, however, that the maturing period of investment is 1 year, then in the year t_1 national income continues to grow at the rate r. When the rate of investment is increased, this means a decline in the rate of consumption, which in case of drastic changes in proportions may lead even to an absolute fall of consumption. In any case, as it is shown in the diagram, the rate of

[1] Cf. P. Sulmicki, *Proporcje gospodarcze* ('Economic Proportions'), Warsaw, 1962, chapter iii, s. 3.

Bronisław Minc in his *Ekonomia polityczna socjalizmu* ('Political Economy of Socialism'), Warsaw, P.W.N., 1961, pp. 480-1, employs the notion of the year of equalization more or less in an analogous meaning. But by a 'period of equalization' he means a 'period in which the total consumption in different years at a higher rate of investment becomes equal to total consumption at a lower rate'. Regarding the year of equalization see also P. Sulmicki; *op. cit.* p. 138, and S. Polaczek, *Inwestycje w krajach gospodarczo nierozwinietych i ich wpływ na bilans handlowy* ('Investments in Economically Under-Developed Countries and their Influence on the Trade Balance'), Warsaw, 1961. Library of the School of Planning and Statistics in Warsaw.

increase in consumption in the year t_1 is lower than the hypothetical one (that which would occur were there no acceleration, indicated by a broken line). In the year t_2 the rate of growth of national income reaches r'', consumption grows correspondingly at the rate r'', which is higher than the rate r at the initial period. Thus at some moment t_k actual consumption will reach the level of the hypothetical consumption (the point of intersection of the continuous line with the broken one). This moment (year) is described as the moment (year)

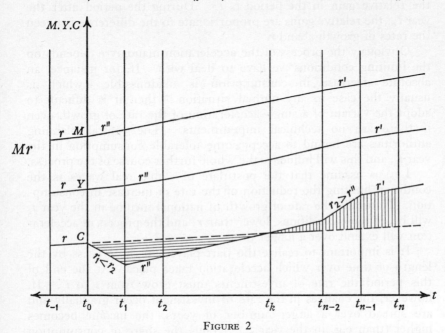

FIGURE 2

of equilization, and the period between this moment and the moment of starting the process of acceleration $(t_k - t_o)$ as the time of equalization.[1] In the following period, if growth continues for a period to be at the rate r'', actual consumption will exceed hypothetical consumption. In the year t_{n-2}, foreseeing the exhaustion of the labour surplus during the year t_n, the planning authorities will decide to decrease the rate of investment for the year t_{n-1} to i', corresponding to the long-term rate of growth r'. Thus between the year t_{n-2} and t_{n-1} there will occur a phenomenon inverse to the one observed during the interval of time from t_o to t_1: income grows still at the

[1] See J. Pajestka, *op. cit.*, who describes the problem of reserves of labour force at the initial stage of industrialization from a somewhat different methodological position.

rate r'', but with a rate of investment $i' < i''$ the increase in consumption is more rapid than r''. From the year t_n, national income, consumption and real productive fixed capital grow at the long-term rate r', which is higher than the initial rate r and corresponds (on the basis of the assumptions we have made) to the potential rate of growth $\alpha' + \beta$. The segment hatched horizontally represents relative losses in consumption (in relation to the hypothetical consumption) during the period t_o-t_k, the segment hatched vertically represents the relative gain in the period t_k-t_n. During the period after the year t_n, the relative gains are proportionate to the difference between the rates of growth r' and r.

Obviously the process of the acceleration manœuvre depends on the limiting conditions we have to deal with. If, for instance, an absolute decrease in consumption is inadmissible — which is usually the case in any normal situation — then it is difficult to adopt the variant of a single acceleration of the rate of growth even if there are no technical impediments. The central planning authorities are bound to accept some tolerable consumption in the year t_1, and this will influence the whole further course of the process.

Let us assume that the postulate of stable real wages is the condition limiting the reduction of the rate of increase in consumption. Naturally the rate of growth of national income in the year t_2 will be, in these conditions, lower than r'' and the process of acceleration will extend over a longer time.

It is important to realize the part played in the process by the length of time over which acceleration takes place. At the end of this period the rate of investments must grow from i to i''. If, however, the changes in the rate of investment occur gradually and are spread over a larger number of years, the income becomes higher (than e.g. in the year t_1). Thus the share of consumption in the income, decreased to $1 - i''$, will represent a larger consumption the higher is the income.

A lengthening of the time over which the process of acceleration occurs is necessary to relieve the conflict between the growth of investment and the level of current consumption, as it makes it possible to have a higher rate of investment i'' when income and consumption have also attained an absolutely higher level. This is the problem facing socialist planning, since — except in special cases of an abnormal character — such planning cannot aim exclusively at a maximum shortening of the period of under-utilization of the labour reserve (though theoretically it would be most advantageous), but it should aim at what is in the given conditions the best compromise between growth with future consumption and the needs of present consumption. Thus even in this relatively simple case of intention to accelerate the rate of growth because it is below the limit set by the labour force, it is impossible to accept the view, still prevalent here and there in Western literature, that the planning authorities are completely free to push up the rate of investment without regard to actual consumption, which is treated as a residuum. The problem of correct choice from this point of view is even more important in conditions in which the labour force is fully utilized, so that the rate of growth of national income is determined almost wholly by the rate of growth of labour productivity (which will be dealt with below).

(c) *The Role of Non-Investment Factors*

In the light of the above discussion it is clear that the strategy of growth during the period concerned must emphasize the taking advantage of all possibilities of shortening the period of under-absorption of the labour force, just so far as that can be done without damaging the actual consumption. In the first place attention should be paid to whatever opportunities are latent in the fields involved by the coefficients a and u. Thus far we have assumed that these two coefficients are constant. This assumption, however, did not correspond to the actual conditions that prevailed in Poland during the initial stage of industrialization, and it does not correspond either to the actual situation in any country which becomes socialist at an intermediate level of economic development.

Countries at an intermediate stage of development have at their disposal a productive equipment which in conditions of capitalism is not fully utilized owing to lack of effective demand. We have, therefore, at the beginning of industrialization not only an under-utilized labour force but also some under-utilized productive capacity, the mobilization of which does not require any investment outlays. With the expansion of investment the violently growing internal demand can be met in some measure by the elimination of shorter working weeks, the increase of the number of shifts, and similar measures. From the point of view of the national economy this is advantageous in general, even though it is not profitable according to a capitalist calculation from the point of view of the particular enterprise because of the comparatively small increase of production. We have here another example of the importance of the power of macro-economic calculation under socialism to take advantage of an existing growth potential.

An analogous part may be played, for a very short period, indeed, by the reduction of repair and period outlay maintenance (provided it does not decrease immediately output capacity in proportion to the reduction of outlay), and especially by refraining from replacing equipment which is out of date from the economic viewpoint. It is true that this equipment gives a very low return, in many cases not even exceeding the wages of the workers employed. It makes it possible, however, to use productively the surplus labour. Thus we can temporarily increase u and decrease a, increasing the difference

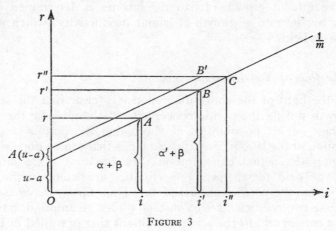

$u - a$, which means an increase in the rate of income growth independently of changes in i. This factor is of special importance since, unlike investment, it produces very quick effects merely by increasing income, in which the share of productive investment may be expected to be greatly augmented.

The increase of the difference $u - a$, achieved mainly by employing gradually a larger labour force on already existing equipment, can be considered as an alternative to applying primitive methods of production in order to take advantage of the so-called saving potential existing in incomplete employment. After the Second World War this alternative was rather commonly used in socialist countries.

The influence of the change in the difference $u - a$ on the process of setting the national economy on a new path of growth can be illustrated in Figure 3.

In comparison with the diagram on page 29 we have here an additional straight line at the same inclination $(\frac{1}{m})$ as the line AC, but at a greater distance from the base of the diagram. This distance is greater by the segment $\Delta(u - a)$, which expresses the average total effect of the increase of u and of the decrease of a during the period (number of years) in which this effect occurs. We assume in this connection, as usually happens in practice, that workers additionally employed as a result of the increase in $\Delta(u - a)$ stay there permanently. In consequence of this effect, the rate of growth r'' is temporarily attained due to the rate of investment i' (point B'). When the temporary effect $\Delta(u - a)$ ceases, at the rate of investment i', we descend to point B on the straight line AC. But if at that moment unemployment is still existing, we must reach point C, that is increase the rate of investment to i'', in order to liquidate unemployment and — according to our previous consideration (page 29) — to come to point B. In view of the fact, however, that some part of unemployed was absorbed by taking advantage of the effect $\Delta(u - a)$, the period of our stay at point C will correspondingly be shorter, which brings, of course, an essential advantage from the point of view of actual consumption. Independently of it, an extremely important advantage consists in the fact too, that the rate of investment grows from i to i' and eventually from i' to i'' when there is an absolutely higher level of income, and thus also at an absolutely higher level of consumption.

It is evident that the problem has been presented here in a schematic way which makes it impossible to consider different possible variants of the course of the process. All this, however, does not alter the fact that taking advantage of the effect $\Delta(u - a)$ facilitates the acceleration of the rate of growth in the most difficult initial phase ; thus it weakens the contradictions appearing in the process as compared with those considered earlier. In Poland this phase played a very essential part especially at the first stage of the Six Year Plan (1950–55).

(d) *Inflationary Pressures*

Our conclusions should not be regarded as implying that owing to the addition of the temporarily acting factor $\Delta(u - a)$ it is possible to avoid completely any sacrifice involved in the increase of the investment rate. The additional increase of income due to non-investment factors will consist in the first place of capital goods and not of consumption goods. Without previous investment no growth in agricultural production is to be expected, and in the countries concerned agriculture produces the main part of consumption goods. On the other hand labour productivity will grow more slowly when non-investment factors are utilized, than if the labour reserve were absorbed by new equipment. There occurs therefore a notable trend towards the increase of employment to the detriment of the factor of the increase of productivity. If it is not possible here to analyse this problem in detail a few remarks seem to be necessary, especially so that this question may be related to the problem of the appearance of inflationary phenomena in the first stage of socialist industrialization.

The growth of labour productivity, amounting in the initial variant to β, plays an important part in the reduction of strains in consumption caused by the acceleration of growth. It is easiest to represent it by denoting the rate of investment as the function of the level of labour productivity (W) and of real wages (w). We have then

$$i = \frac{I}{Y} = \frac{Z(W - w)}{Z \cdot W} - 1 - \frac{w}{W} \tag{5}$$

It follows therefrom that the rate of investment depends on the ratio of wages to labour productivity, assuming that the whole difference $W - w$ is productively invested.

The increase of i calls for a decrease in the ratio $\frac{w}{W}$. When productivity grows by β annually, some increase in real wages is compatible with a decrease of the ratio $\frac{w}{W}$ provided that the rate of increase of real wages is lower than β. If, however, a significant increase of i is required, then the increase of real wages must remain far below β. When β is large enough, real wages can grow, or at least not fall, even if their trend is far below β. But if β decreases, then the possibility of real wage increase, which is far less than β, falls also. When $\beta = 0$ or W is constant, any increase of i requires unconditionally the fall of w to a level determined by the postulated magnitude i. Again when β is positive, but relatively low, in general the required magnitude of the rate of investment will not be attained without a certain decrease in real wages. Thus the danger of decrease of real wages is greater when investment is linked with non-investment than when investment alone is imposed (but within definite limits).

But the level of real wages should not be identified with consumption per head. If, when investment alone is imposed unemployment lasts longer, then employment is lower also at the start. With a given consumption fund, wages will be higher the lower is employment. With an additional utilization of non-investment factors $\Delta(u - a)$ employment is higher in the first stage, while unemployment is lower. With the same consumption fund, wages will be lower if employment is higher. This will be the case also, even when the consumption fund is greater, provided that employment is still correspondingly greater. It would seem that this last case was characteristic of the first stage of rapid industrialization in Poland. At that period real wages increased very little and in the years 1951–53 they even decreased markedly. But the increase in employment was so great in comparison with the growth of population that consumption per head grew during the whole of this period. Even a stabilization, not to speak of a decrease, in real wages is a hard nut to crack for a socialist society. On the other hand, when there is a conflict between increase in wages and increase in consumption per head, it is in the general interest of the economy to solve it to the benefit of consumption.

In these conditions the danger of inflation generally arises. It occurs when real wages cannot rise further, while money wages still must rise by a certain percentage even if only because of payment by piece rates (and also because of some elements in the methods of remuneration leading automatically to increases of money wages from time to time). If efficiency grows by β, then money wages grow by $\dfrac{\beta}{p}$, where $p \geqslant 1/\dfrac{1}{p}$ is the coefficient of increase of money wages in relation to the increase in productivity. But since real wages are to stay fixed, then prices and costs of living must rise also by $\dfrac{\beta}{p}$. Naturally this phenomenon operates more acutely if real wages have to decrease at some time, and much less acutely if real wages are able to rise though to a smaller degree than the 'natural' increase in money-wages.

It should be remembered that during the phase of rapid industrialization of a country the growth of average money wages is strongly influenced by rapid changes in the structure of employment arising from the transformation of the general economic structure. Employment increases most rapidly in heavy industry and in building, where relative wages are high, as is necessary to attract labour in the desired direction. The resulting increase of average money wages becomes an inevitable additional factor increasing the inflationary pressure.[1]

[1] Regarding the relations of real wages, nominal wages and changes of prices see M. Kucharski, *Pieniadz, dochod, proporcje gospodarcze* ('Money, Income, Economic Proportions'), Warsaw, 1961, Library of the School of Planning and Statistics in Warsaw (chapter ii). Regarding the problem of inflation in socialist economy see also Z. Fedorowicz, *Zagadnienia rownowagi monetarnej w gospodarce socjalistycznej* ('Problems of Monetary Equilibrium in Socialist Economy'), Warsaw, 1959, and articles : P. Sulmicki, 'Pojecie inflacji w gospodarce socjalistycznej' ('The Notion of Inflation in a Socialist Economy'), *Mysl Gospodarcza* ('Economic

The problems of inflationary phenomena in the introductory stage of socialist industrialization deserve consideration in more detail and separately, both from the point of view of the character of these phenomena and their differences from those that arise in a planned economy to determine and to control the proportion between purchasing power and the volume of goods and services available. This would, however, go beyond the province of this paper. We must confine ourselves to emphasizing that the problem of inflationary phenomena under socialism can be understood correctly only as an element in a complex total of a planned process of setting the socialist economy on the path of long-term dynamic equilibrium.

We have considered the problems relating to the process of the acceleration of growth by employing for production unemployed and hitherto surplus labour. On the assumptions made, this means that — as far as the element of employment is concerned — the potential rate of growth is determined, after the completion of this process, by the rate of growth of population and the consequent rate of growth of the supply of manpower. In practice this is not exactly true as there remains the possibility of change of the active participation ratio of the population by drawing into production a certain margin of persons who are not technically unemployed, but who are free to take up some form of activity. The increase of the ratio of active participation renders possible growth at a higher rate, but only so long as there exist conditions favourable to the increase of this ratio. We have here a problem in a certain sense analogous to those considered earlier, because the utilization of this factor of growth requires a corresponding adaption of the rate of investment. In the interests of brevity we shall not discuss it here, but we wish to make clear that the ratio of participation of the population depends in a great measure on expenditure on social institutions (e.g. crèches and kindergartens which make possible an increase in the participation ratio of women) and in certain other forms (transportation facilities, hostels for workers, etc.).

Thus we touch here on a vast problem of the socio-economic effectiveness of expenditure outlays for the development of the so-called non-productive sector. Besides those mentioned above, the main elements in this field are the expenditure for education and professional training of skilled personnel and for health measures. Again we must note the problem and do not propose to elaborate

Thought'), No. 5, 1957, B. Oyrzanowski, 'Walka z niebezpieczenstwem inflacji' ('Battle Against the Danger of Inflation'), *Mysl Gospodarcza*, No. 5, 1957, and F. Mlynarski, 'Walka z niebezpieczenstwem inflacji' ('Battle Against the Danger of Inflation'), *ibid.*

it. We must stress, however, that this is an extremely important factor in the achievement of a high rate of growth in a socialist economy. The possibility of allocating funds to these purposes directly by the planning authorities according to the criteria of socio-economic productivity — without having to depend on private 'propensity' to meet these needs adequately — is widely adopted in socialist countries, including Poland. This is shown by many indices reaching, and even exceeding, the levels of highly developed capitalist countries, let alone countries at the same level of general development.

III. ACCELERATION OF GROWTH TAKING INTO ACCOUNT TECHNICAL PROGRESS

In the second part of this paper we assumed stability of the rate of growth of labour productivity. We made only passing comments on possible changes of this rate (showing the consequences of increasing the difference $u - a$). We omitted, among other points, the theoretically very interesting problem, which Mr. Kalecki has called the 'rejuvenation' of capital stock, that is the increase of the proportion of new capital in the total of all capital. If we raise the rate of increase in employment, a corresponding growth in average labour productivity will follow. It will be higher than β, though the incremental labour productivity of the newly employed grows at a stable rate β. The effect of the 'rejuvenation' of capital stock will naturally disappear gradually as the process advances, but this does not diminish its importance.[1]

It is clear, therefore, that changes in the rate of increase in employment, and even more so changes in the structure of employment, are bound to influence the dynamics of labour productivity. In spite of this our initial assumption was justified, inasmuch as we wished to eliminate in the first stage of our analysis the basic factor in the increase of labour productivity — that is technical progress, a factor that is fundamentally different in character.

Change in the rate of increase of labour productivity acquires a special importance in conditions when the possibilities of raising the rate of increase in employment are exhausted.

If the rate of employment growth a' cannot be increased, the only way to raise the rate of growth r' is to raise the rate of increase in labour productivity β. We must therefore now proceed to the analysis of this question.

[1] See M. Kalecki, *Teoria wzrostu w gospodarce socjalistycznej* (' On the Theory of Growth in a Socialist Economy ') (*in the press*).

(a) *Technical Progress and the Choice of the Rate of Growth*

The question immediately arises whether the planning authorities have any freedom of choice at all in this field. If we assume that the rate of β attainable at a moment of time is determined unequivocally by technical progress — then there is no such freedom of choice. It seems, however, that such an assumption is an oversimplification. It would correspond to reality only if at every period there were one single method of possible production, and if technical progress would lead to a new method of production, absolutely better than the previous in the sense that in order to attain a given result it is possible to use a smaller volume of labour with the same or smaller investment expenditure.[1]

In practice various methods of production co-exist in any given period and thus at any given state of technical knowledge. And technical progress achieved in the course of this period may also lead to new methods of production which are not absolutely better than the previous ones (e.g. requiring less human labour but higher investment expenditure to attain the given effect). It cannot be considered, therefore, that β is uniquely determined.

(b) *Variability of the Rate of Growth During the Acceleration Period*

In view of the co-existence of methods of production embodying different degrees of mechanization (including also degrees of automatization), planning authorities aiming to accelerate the existing rate of growth may decide to raise the degree of mechanization of investment goods. Let us assume that, during the period preceding this decision, the process of growth was stabilized at a fixed rate of growth $r' = \alpha' + \beta$ and continued for at least n years, representing the average period of life of the different constituents of the real productive fixed capital. Included in this assumption is not only the rate of growth of average labour productivity, but also the rate of growth of incremental labour productivity, defined as the ratio of labour productivity attained in completed investments put into operation in the year t_n to labour productivity achieved in investments put into operation in the year t_{n-1}.

Any increase in labour productivity greater than β and any rate

[1] By 'method of production' we mean here the combination of labour expenditure and investment expenditure inescapably necessary to increase national income by one unit (assuming an unchanged structure). In addition we abstract from the possibility of changes in the methods of production consisting in diminishing investment outlays while the volume of human labour remains constant since we are interested here only in technical progress leading to the increase of labour productivity, which is the essence of technical progress.

of income growth greater than r' will be the result of the above-mentioned decision. But in these circumstances, the coefficient m will increase too. An increase of the coefficient m is inevitable with increasing mechanization and a given state of technical knowledge. Were it possible to increase the rate of growth of labour productivity without any increase of m, there would be no reason to choose methods of production absolutely worse than others co-existing at that time. The increase of the coefficient m is the price to be paid

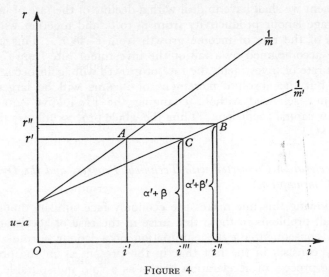

FIGURE 4

for a higher rate of labour productivity resulting from higher mechanization. Let us assume that planning authorities decide on such a single increase of the coefficient m to m'. Let us assume that it will lead to a considerable single growth of incremental labour productivity (in the sense given above) by more than β and in the following years the incremental labour productivity will continue to grow by β. This will in turn lead to the process shown in Figure 4.

This single increase of the capital coefficient from m to m' is expressed by a lower inclination of the straight line having the direction coefficient $\frac{1}{m}$. We assume that the single increase of incremental labour productivity, achieved by this decision, will imply a rate of average labour productivity amounting to β'. And accordingly the increase will grow for once by $r'' = a' + \beta'$, but as point B indicates this will require an increase in the rate of investment from i' to i''.

c   43

It will be impossible, however, to keep up this rate of investment with the given assumptions. We have assumed that the realization of investment at the coefficient m' gives a rate of growth of incremental labour productivity amounting still to β. Accordingly the increase of average labour productivity, which for once was β', will decrease and tend to β. It will reach it after n years, during which the entire productive equipment will 'change' into a new capital coefficient m'. Thus during the period of 'change' of the productive equipment we shall have to deal with a decline of the rate of increase of average labour productivity from β' to β, and together with it, a decline of the rate of income growth from r'' to r'. This process will be accompanied by a fall of the investment rate from i'' to i'''. At this rate of investment, the rate of growth will again become $r' = a' + \beta$, but the absolute increment of income will be larger than were they achieved without changing the productive equipment to a new capital coefficient. Thus the whole process follows the line $A \to B \to C$.[1]

(c) *Acceleration Connected with Technical Progress and the Dynamics of Consumption*

Following this line makes the economy face similar, though not identical, problems to those that arise in the case of acceleration of growth consequent on the elimination of a labour surplus. The analogy consists in the fact that in the present as in the previous case the process of acceleration brings as a rule indisputable gains, the price for which is the increase of the investment rate i, and consequently a decrease of $1 - i$ or of the share of consumption in the income. For a time consumption will grow slower as compared with a hypothetical consumption without acceleration (cf. pp. 27-32 and Figure 1 illustrating the problem of the year and period of equalization). The scale of this reduction in the rate of consumption growth cannot be determined theoretically as it depends on the scale of an inevitable increase in the rate of investment. But at the beginning of the period the consumption must be affected and thus one of the elements of the decision to follow the road $A \to B \to C$ will be the balance of losses and gains in consumption. At the start consumption will grow by less than r', but as income later grows by more than r' (momentarily by r''; thenceforward the difference between r'' and r' grows smaller, but until the complete change of productive capacities — that is during the whole period n — income grows at a rate higher than r'), then, apart from the period of the

[1] See M. Kalecki ; *Ibid.*

single increase of m, consumption grows too at a rate higher than r'. Thus in time consumption as a rule equals and exceeds the hypothetical level of consumption associated with a rate of growth r'.

Despite this fundamental analogy, there are some essential differences between the acceleration connected with the liquidation of labour surplus and the acceleration connected with the increase of labour productivity due to the increase of the coefficient m.

First of all, in the previous case the higher rate of income growth r'' could be maintained for some time, while in the present case the rate of growth rises temporarily to r'' and then falls again. Thus, in the previous case, apart from the starting point when the increase of the rate of investment reaches i''', consumption grows for a time (between the year t_2 and t_{n-2}) at the same rate as the income ; in the present case, on the other hand, during the process of extinction, consumption grows more rapidly than income, as the rate of investment declines continually.[1] It would seem then that acceleration due to changing productive equipment to a higher m will be more advantageous to consumption. This is not so, however. In the present case, that is, due to the increase of m, the effect of a given increment of the investment rate (Δi) in the form of the increase of the rate of growth (Δr) is smaller in comparison with the situation when m remains constant. Furthermore, Δr tends to 0, declining in the process of extinction. Thus, although in the period of 'change' of the productive equipment consumption grows more rapidly than income, this growth of consumption is *ceteris paribus* slower in comparison with the growth of consumption during the period of absorption of the labour-surplus. As a result, the time required to reach equality, k, will be longer in the case of acceleration achieved through changing productive equipment into a higher m, than in the case first analysed.

Decisive for consumption in the long run is, however, the fact that, when the acceleration process is complete, in the first case the economy achieved, at a higher rate of investment, a higher rate of long-term growth than it had at the start $(r' > r)$; now, due to changing the productive equipment to a higher m, the rate of growth r', identical with the initial rate, will need a higher rate of investment. In both cases, after completing the process of acceleration, the actual level of national income will certainly be higher than the hypothetical one. This need not, however, necessarily be true for consumption. In both cases actual consumption in the year t_n can be lower than the hypothetical one, if the impact of increased investment rate will

[1] For simplicity we can assume that r'' and n represent the same magnitudes in both cases.

45

exceed the effect of the increased rate of growth of income during
n years. In other words, in both cases the time of equalization, k,
can — but by no means must — be longer than n.

If this $(k>n)$ should be the case, the single increase of m would
lead to permanent losses in consumption also in the long run.
Indeed, taken from a lower basis the same *relative* increments (at
the rate r') would represent smaller *absolute* increments in consumption, meaning that the hypothetical level of consumption would
never be attained. In eliminating the surplus of labour such a
situation cannot occur. In the period after the year t_n consumption
grows here at a higher rate $(r'>r)$, which means that sooner or later
the actual level of consumption must exceed the hypothetical one.

We do not wish to argue that the process under consideration is
undesirable from the point of view of consumption. The probability
of the time k exceeding n is in general very much smaller than the
reverse situation, in which already during the period of change of
the productive equipment relative gains in respect of consumption
become manifest. And if that is the case, the relative gains will still
continue after the end of time n, since they will be calculated on a
higher basis.

These two cases reflect in a certain sense two stages of development — one extensive and one intensive (this is, of course, a simplification as in reality they cannot be strictly separated one from the
other). Their comparison served the purpose of showing that, from
a certain point of view, the second case may cause difficulty. It is
important to stress this, since the planning authorities are no longer
so bound by compulsions. In considering whether to accelerate
growth by utilizing the labour surplus — that is by eliminating
unemployment — there is no choice for a socialist state whether 'to
accelerate, or not to accelerate'. There is no question regarding
the advantage and necessity of utilizing the possibility created by
socialism of accelerating the rate of growth. The matters of choice
are only the forms and the speed of the process. But in the second
case, the very advantage of the acceleration has to be considered.
Thus all arguments for and against it must be carefully balanced in
order to reduce to a minimum the damaging effects.

In emphasizing the specific difficulties involved in changing the
productive equipment into a higher m, it should be remembered at
the same time that, after the initial reserves have been exhausted,
this is the main means to accelerate the rate of growth, and also
that we have then to deal with an economy that is much more
mature in all respects, and with an absolutely higher level of consumption. It is thus an economy capable of solving much more

complex problems. The experience gained from the second stage of industrialization in Poland fully confirms this view.

(d) *Three Types of Technical Progress*

Finally, attention should be drawn to the fact that, in evaluating the difficulty of accelerating growth in this way, it must be remembered that an essential part is played by an assumption which is by no means inviolable. We assumed that the single increase of the coefficient m indeed increases labour productivity, but the incremental labour productivity (in the above carefully defined sense) at a new capital coefficient amounting to m' continues to grow by β, as it did with the previous coefficient m. Whether this will be so depends on the type of technical progress, and this cannot be predicted theoretically. It is quite possible that the incremental labour productivity with the capital coefficient m' will not grow by β, but by more than β. If this happened after having changed the productive apparatus into a new degree of capital intensity, the rate of income growth would be stabilized at a level higher than r'. The opposite would occur if the single increase of the capital coefficient should yield an increase of incremental labour productivity lower than β. It is clear, therefore, that the gain from changing the productive equipment to a higher m will be different, *ceteris paribus*, with each of these three possibilities, arising from the type of technical progress in the period concerned : if there is a possibility of securing an incremental labour productivity greater than β there will be clear incentives to increase the capital-intensity ; the possibility of increasing the incremental labour productivity is lower than β, the opposite situation will arise (and this not only in regard to increasing the capital-intensity but even maintaining it) ; if there is the possibility of securing an incremental labour productivity equalling β, there will be no incentive whatever in either direction. On the basis of such reasoning, Kalecki deduces his criteria differentiating the types of technical progress, defining the first as encouraging capital-intensity, the second as discouraging capital-intensity and the third as neutral.[1] With given preferences, the planning authorities will be the more disposed to apply additional mechanization designed to increase labour productivity and thus to accelerate the rate of growth, the more capital intensive — in the sense given above — is the type of technical progress.

[1] See M. Kalecki, as above. This definition completes the definition of technical progress contained in M. Kalecki's paper ; 'Z zagadnien teorii dynamiki gospodarki socjalistycznej' ('On Problems of the Theory of Socialist Economy Dynamics') in the collective work, *Zagadnienia ekonomii politycznej socjalizmu* ('Problems of Political Economy of Socialism'), 3rd ed., Warsaw, 1960.

This brief sketch of the problems of adjusting the rate of growth in the light of technical progress seems to confirm the thesis advanced at the beginning of this paper regarding the significance of production-relations in taking advantage of national growth potential and the favourable conditions in this respect created by socialism. The importance is again evident of planned determination of basic macro-economic magnitudes and of possible flexibility in adapting the rate of investment to the varying requirements of the different stages of the development process. Apart from this the problems involved in raising the rate of growth in different conditions of technical progress, bring to light the role of the time-horizon in taking advantage of growth potential. The broad time-horizon of the central planning authorities in a socialist economy renders possible the mobilization of such factors of growth of which otherwise advantage could not be taken. In the light of our discussion above it seems clear, moreover, why it cannot be expected that the premises of strategic decisions concerning development — taken in consideration of long-term and current interests of the society as a whole — will be achieved correctly by the free-working market mechanism. In a socialist economy, decisions of this type are taken outside of the market mechanism, which — as is proved even by the experience of a number of capitalist countries in recent years — is not capable of handling the problems that have been described.

IV. FACTORS LIMITING THE RATE OF GROWTH

The examination of the problem here presented has, by the nature of things, been at a high level of abstraction. This is of advantage in that it enables us to realize better the relevance of some of the problems to the strategy of growth and to visualize the opportunities created by socialism to apply this strategy. But at the same time there is danger in applying the conclusions of this highly abstract analysis directly to an actual situation of much greater complexity.[1] To do this may result in overlooking some of the inevitable difficulties met in the rapid process of growth under socialism.

We are concerned not only with such obvious issues, as frictions and planning mistakes while the rate of growth is being changed and the sectoral proportions involved are changing too. We are concerned with problems of a more general character. Polish

---

[1] Cf. O. Lange's methodologic consideration on this question, among others the importance he attaches to avoiding the error which A. N. Whitehead defined as a 'fallacy of misplaced concreteness' (O. Lange, *Ekonomia Polityczna* (Political Economy), vol. I, Warsaw, 1959, pp. 101-8).

authors have paid a great deal of attention to the study of factors limiting freedom to determine the rate of growth. The theoretical work in this field is undoubtedly a reflection and generalization of practical experience, which showed the complete inadequacy of an approach (in other respects very valuable) to the rate of growth which concentrated exclusively on the general proportions between income, investment and consumption — an approach, that is, from the point of view of the interests of present and future consumption at a very high degree of aggregation. It may seem, for instance, that since there is a certain readiness to suffer some temporary sacrifice in the form of a heavier burden through current investment on current consumption, and since this increased investment makes possible through additional mechanization an acceleration of the rate of increase of labour productivity, there are no obstacles to accepting and achieving a decision to increase the rate of growth of national income. But this is not so. It can be seen that even in this framework the planning authorities are not yet completely sovereign, though there is no question that they dispose of a much wider freedom of choice — the wider the longer is the period of time included into the plan.

Kalecki was the first to study these problems and he proved that the difficulties connected with the acceleration of the rate of growth are related above all to foreign trade, and this both directly and indirectly. In countries strongly dependent on imports of investment goods and, especially, of raw materials (most countries, Poland included, belong to this last group), the acceleration of growth implies directly the necessity to increase imports and — with a well-balanced foreign trade — exports. The acceleration of growth of imports may present, and has presented, difficulties both in respect of supply and of outlet. To overcome these difficulties, it may be necessary to make some less profitable exports or even to take measures against imports. Thus the corresponding investment will have a comparatively high capital coefficient. The price to be paid for the acceleration of growth of national income in the face of difficulties in foreign trade will be acceptance by the planning authorities of the need to increase the coefficient m to the extent required to overcome these difficulties. But this is possible only to some degree. In every situation there exists a certain limit imposed by foreign trade which cannot be exceeded ; it may be nearer or further from the existing rate of growth, but it will not allow the rate to exceed a certain maximum magnitude.

It should also be borne in mind that foreign trade is the universal remedy for a number of difficulties arising during the acceleration of growth, quite apart from any necessity to increase imports. These difficulties are the familiar 'bottlenecks'. The narrowest, if it concerns an important factor, determines the trend of the whole economy. These 'bottlenecks' may take the form of a shortage of natural resources; of a shortage of highly qualified technical personnel and experienced workers; or of a shortage of personnel in some regions while there is satisfactory balance of supply and demand for the labour force as a whole. They may take the form of delays in planning and completing investment projects in some sectors; of limited production capacity in design of office and building enterprises, and so on. Such difficulties may be, and are, overcome by widening these 'bottlenecks' and by adjusting them to the needs of the national economy rather than by adjusting the economy to them. But it often requires additional investment, for example in geological research, housing-construction, personnel training, mechanization of building and construction work and the like. A specific role may be played by difficulties of accelerating the rate of increase of agricultural production, which is of the greatest importance in maintaining the necessary balance of the economy.[1] A rapid acceleration of growth of agricultural production may prove impossible, or on a smaller scale very expensive. Thus, in this respect also, the capital coefficient will increase when the rate of growth is raised.

There is no question that the development of co-operation between socialist countries is diminishing foreign trade difficulties, especially when acceleration takes place simultaneously in all or most of the countries concerned. But since 'bottlenecks' occur, none the less, in all socialist countries and since relations between these countries and the non-socialist countries exist and are expanding, the difficulties described above emerge sooner or later when it is attempted to raise the rate of growth above some level (assuming that it is possible to do so from the viewpoint of the growth of manpower and/or labour productivity).

The increase of the capital coefficient involved in overcoming difficulties in foreign trade and in removing 'bottlenecks' plays an essential part in giving effect to decisions concerning the acceleration of growth. This is illustrated in Figure 5.

The planning authority is prepared to introduce some limitation on current consumption and to raise the rate of growth from r_0 to r_1, or pass from point A to point B by increasing the rate of investment from i_0 to i_1. This implies that the capital coefficient grows from

---

[1] Cf. W. Herer, *Rolnictwo a rozwoj gospodarki narodowej* (Agriculture and the Development of the National Economy), Warsaw, 1962.

m to m'; which increases the average labour productivity from β_0 to β_1. But to attain the rate of growth r_1 difficulties in foreign trade must be overcome and 'bottlenecks' must be removed — the price to be paid for it is the further increase of the capital coefficient to m''. Thus the point B is unattainable and the rate of income growth r_1 is represented by point C with the rate of investment i_2. But though the planning authorities were willing to increase the rate of investment to i_1 as the price of gaining the rate of growth r_1, it is doubtful

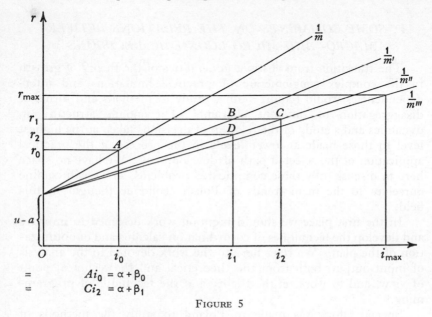

$$Ai_0 = \alpha + \beta_0$$
$$Ci_2 = \alpha + \beta_1$$

FIGURE 5

that they would be willing to make a much greater effort, that is to increase the rate of investment to i_2, to obtain the same result. To simplify the problem we assume that the planning authorities are willing to increase i_0 only up to i_1 — considering for some reason that this is the optimum in given conditions — then they will plan a rate of growth indicated at point D, that is $r_2 < r_1$. This means that in the event of foreign trade difficulties and 'bottlenecks' appearing, the planning authorities choose a lower acceleration of the rate of growth rather than the acceleration to which they would have given priority were there no difficulties or 'bottlenecks'. Finally, on the vertical axis the magnitude r_{max} is shown, corresponding to the share of investment in the income i_{max} at the capital coefficient m''' which results in these conditions and is sufficient to overcome the difficulties mentioned. If the planning authorities were willing to increase the share of investment in the income higher than i_{max} in order to attain a rate of growth higher than r_{max}, then this willingness would be faced by an impassable limit (a deadline) of the maximum magnitude of acceleration of growth. Thus the real range of choice for the planning authorities, when r_o is a rate correlated with the balance of labour force at a given magnitude β_o, is within the magnitudes represented by r_o–r_{max}.

V. SOME COMMENTS ON THE RELATIONS BETWEEN MACRO- AND MICRO-ECONOMIC DECISIONS

The transition from abstract generalities of the theory of growth to the complex conglomerate of practical limitations and inter-dependencies would require both a study of methods and forms of disaggregation of different elements of economic structure in dynamics and a study of the relation of decisions taken at the highest level to those made at lower levels in the process of the practical application of the selected path of development. We have no space here to discuss fully these complicated problems, so we will confine ourselves to the main trends of Polish economic thought in this field.

In the first place we should mention work designed to improve and develop the techniques of co-ordination calculus and of optimization of the plan. We refer here to the work devoted to the analysis of input-output, both from the theoretical and the technical point of view, and to work on the theory and the technique of programming.[1]

Special effort was made in Poland to study the methods of rational choice of investment variants and foreign trade variants. These studies led to a thorough examination in all their aspects of various economic concepts among which the main role has been played by the concepts of 'terminal pay-off period' and of 'maximal rate of exchange'. The specific virtue of these concepts is that, when calculated from a general economic point of view on the basis

[1] First of all the works of O. Lange should be mentioned : 'Model wzrostu gospodarczego' ('The Model of Economic Growth'), 'Kilka uwag o analizie nakladow i wynikow produkcji' ('Some Remarks on Input-Output Analysis'), 'Produkcyjno-techniczne podstawy efektywnosci inwestysji' ('Productive and Technical Foundations of Investment Effectivity') included in *Pisma ekonomiczne i spoleczne 1930–1960* (Economic and social papers of 1930–60), Warsaw, 1961, and *Teoria reprodukcji i akumulacji* ('The Theory of Reproduction and Accumulation'), Warsaw, 1961.
  From the numerous publications on these problems we mention as examples, P. Sulmicki, *Przeplywy miedzygaleziowe* ('Input-Output'), Warsaw, 1959 ; K. Porwitt, 'Wybor ekonomiczny w planie przedsiebiorstwa' ('Economic Choice in the Plan of the Enterprise'), *Ekonomista*, No. 2, 1960; and Wiesław Sadowski, *Teoria podejmowania decyzji* ('The Theory of Decision Making'), Warsaw, 1960.

of macro-economic relations involved in the process of growth, they fulfil the function of parameters in calculation at lower levels which may be concerned with choice of concrete methods of production in new units or with determining the relative advantages of different kinds of exports and imports.[1] These parameters have made it possible to calculate and take decisions at the lower levels while maintaining the necessary degree of co-ordination with basic general trends determined by the central planning authorities.

We have touched on the problem of relations of the highest central level and the lower levels in a socialist economy. This problem is fundamental from the point of view of growth. Known under the somewhat imprecise terms of centralization and decentralization, it became in Poland, especially since 1956, a subject of a great discussion in relation to the so-called model of the functioning of a socialist economy.[2]

The starting-point of this discussion was the thesis that, with the raising of the economy to a higher stage of development, the complexity of economic problems grows also. With it, there is a growing importance of such factors as : the flexibility of adjustment of the structure of supply to the structure of demand (both in production and in consumption) ; economically justifiable substitution of different forms of expenditures ; expansion of different enterprises and sectors related to their economic achievements. It was just from this point of view that excessive centralization was criticized, since this takes the form of concentrating nearly all decisions at the highest level and passing targets and resources to lower echelons only in the form of orders and physical allocations. As a result, the functions of lower echelons (particularly in enterprises) were limited to pure execution of orders only.

The discussion showed that the problem of centralization and decentralization under socialism cannot be considered in terms of centralization or decentralization of *all* economic decisions. It can be considered only in terms of the *division* of centralized and decentralized decisions, with the obvious assumption that the basic

[1] Cf. M. Kalecki, M. Rakowski, 'Uogolnienie wzoru efektywnosci inwestycji' ('Generalization of the Formula of Investment Effectivity'), *Gospodarka planowa* (Planned Economy), No. 11, 1959, and the collective work under M. Rakowski, *Efektywnosc inwestycji* (Investment Effectivity), Warsaw, 1961. And as regards foreign trade W. Trzeciakowski, 'Problemy kompleksowego systemu analizy efektywnosci biezacej handlu zagranicznego' ('Problems of the Complex System of Analysing the Current Effectivity of Foreign Trade'), *Gospodarka planowa*, Nos. IV and V, 1961.

[2] A series of articles *Ekonomisci dyskutuja o prawie wartosci* (Economists discuss the Law of Value), Warsaw, 1957, *Dyskusja o polskim modelu gospodarczym* ('Discussion on the Polish Economic Model'), Warsaw, 1957, and also W. Brus, *Ogolne problemy funkcjonowama gospodarki soyalistycznej* ('General Problems of Functioning of Socialist Economy'), Warsaw, 1961.

macro-economic decisions are centralized. In this connection, the discussion treated broadly the question of the possibility and of the scope for using the market-mechanism within the framework of a planned socialist economy. A lot of space was devoted to the theoretical and practical problems of economic incentives and of prices, as their importance — as macro-economically designed parameters of micro-economic decisions — is growing in proportion to the enlargement of the scope of decentralization.

Beside its direct importance, this 'discussion of the models' was, and still seems to be, of a certain general importance. For it proved, at least in our opinion, that the problem of creating institutional conditions favourable to the full use of potential growth does not disappear once the socialist system is built. Socialism overcomes a number of fundamental contradictions of the capitalist system ; this does not mean, however, that it eliminates all contradictions of every kind, nor that it avoids creating new contradictions arising from the characteristics of the socialist system as such. This implies a necessity for continual search for optimal institutional forms to solve these contradictions, and especially to adapt the functioning system of a socialist economy to the various stages of development, both from a purely economic point of view and a socio-political one. In our opinion this 'discussion of the models' proved also that a socialist socio-economic system provides a possibility of different solutions of the method of functioning of the economy, thus allowing choice of alternatives in this field also, within certain obvious limits.

In mentioning these topics, we have not attempted to deal with them exhaustively (they would require a detailed study in themselves) ; our purpose is to emphasize once again the realism of the Marxian methodological insistence on the necessity of approaching the problem of the development of productive forces in a dialectic unity with problems of the development of production-relations. We are convinced that, unless one takes this aspect into consideration, it is difficult to expect economic theory to make a significant contribution to the study and solution of the complex problems of economic growth.

(The Discussion of the above paper is recorded after Chapter 3.)

Chapter 3

FACTORS INFLUENCING THE ECONOMIC DEVELOPMENT OF SOCIALIST COUNTRIES

BY

K. PLOTNIKOV
The U.S.S.R. Academy of Sciences

I. THE IMPORTANCE OF PRODUCTIVE RELATIONS

THE national economies of the countries of the world socialist system develop with a high rate of growth and continuously on an upward trend. These high growth rates of productive forces under socialism represent a natural phenomenon. They are due to the new and fundamentally different character of the productive relations which have been successfully created in the countries of the world socialist system.

As is well known, productive relations imply specific economic laws which govern the production and distribution of material wealth and determine the dynamics of production. The rates of growth of productive forces are determined also in practice by historic conditions of the development of socialist countries at different stages.

A socialist society, which comes into existence as a result of the revolutionary change of out-moded productive relations, is characterized by a new and higher level of productive forces. Socialism does not merely inherit the productive forces of capitalism. In the process of construction of a socialist society the apparatus of production is transformed to a new basis, new branches of industry are created ; production by machinery acquires a universal character.

The character of the development of the productive forces can be judged from their organization — the dominating method of combining the producer with the means of production. Under conditions of socialism, the development of productive forces finds its expression in a higher organization of production than under capitalism, in a new high degree of social distribution of labour and in the creation of a new material and technical basis of society.

The material and technical bases of socialism take the form of

55

large-machine production, which predominates in the majority of the branches of the national economy. This type of production is based on social ownership of the means of production and is characterized by an advanced and rapidly developing engineering sector, by high concentration of production, by all-round specialization and co-operation within it, by the growth of the cultural and technical level of the working people and by the steady rise of the productivity of labour.

II. THE COMPOSITION OF PRODUCTIVE FORCES

Great importance in any description of the material and technical basis of socialist countries must be attached to the composition of productive forces : their distribution in sectors and branches of material production as determined both by materials and by costs and the distribution of workers between these branches of production. Socialism is impossible without a highly-developed industrial structure in the national economy. Socialist industry plays the leading and essential part in the economy of a country. Alongside this highly developed industry the most important components of the material and technical basis of socialism are an equally developed large-scale mechanized socialist agriculture and a developed transport system.

Experience has shown that after the successful establishment of socialist productive relations some period is required to develop the productive forces for the corresponding level of socialist society. In the Soviet Union the material and technical basis of socialism has been established and the material and technical basis of communism is now being created. In a number of other countries of people's democracy, the creation of the material and technical basis of socialism is approaching completion ; in others the foundations of it are still being laid. Friendly co-operation between socialist countries promotes the equalization of the economic development in all the countries. The tasks of building the material and technical basis of communism in the Soviet Union are closely connected with the development of the economies of the entire world socialist system.

The rapid development of productive forces in the countries of the socialist commonwealth is due to the domination of socialist relations of production in these countries. Social property and socialist productive relations make impossible any anarchic or uncontrolled behaviour of the trend of production. The national economies of socialist countries grow steadily, without any opposing forces. Industrial and agricultural production, socialist accumulation, national income increase rapidly.

III. INTER-STATE ECONOMIC RELATIONS

Inter-state economic relations exert a significant influence on the pace of the development of productive forces. The world socialist system encourages relations of friendly economic co-operation and mutual assistance between the peoples of socialist countries. This technical and economic co-operation between socialist countries in turn considerably affects the volume of the total social product and increases the rate of growth of the national economy. The creation of this new type of international division of labour between countries of the world socialist system, the improvement of planning on the basis of increased co-ordination of the plans of national economies, greater specialization and co-operation of production, foreign trade on a basis of equality and for mutual benefits, scientific and technical co-operation, the use of collective experience in building socialism — all these factors are of a paramount importance. They help to liquidate the backwardness of some countries and to equalize the degrees of economic development of all the countries of the socialist system.

Scientific and technical co-operation, leading to specialization and co-operation in the world socialist system, create favourable conditions for a predominant growth of the production of means of production. This in its turn ensures continuous technical progress and increased labour productivity. In planning the international division of labour, each socialist country develops those branches of heavy industry which best take account of its internal comparative advantages, that is to say, of the availability of raw materials, energy resources, production experience, cadres of skilled workers and the like. Thus socialist productive relations guarantee the rational and planned use of natural wealth.

IV. INDUSTRIALIZATION

The industrialization of a country is the most effective means of creating the material and technical basis of socialism. The process of industrialization has a number of common features in all the countries that have established socialism : the socialist element in industrialization, its planned character, its high tempo of growth, in particular. At the same time there are certain differences between these countries consequent upon their different economic, political, natural and geographic conditions, upon their different levels of development of production, engineering and science and their differences in respect of the availability of skilled labour. The creation of large-machine industry has led to the strengthening of the socialist sector in the national economy. Large agricultural machine-building has also ensured the material means for the technical reconstruction of agriculture on socialist lines.

The predominating growth of industrial production has taken the form of the development, in the first place, of the branches of heavy industry : metallurgy, coal and oil industries, electricity production, machine-building — all those branches, that is to say, which create means of production and which form the foundation of the technical reconstruction of a country.

More advanced engineering has been introduced in all branches of industry, but first of all in those producing the means of production. As a result of high rates of expansion of production of the means of production in each country and of the possibilities of obtaining equipment from other countries of the world socialist system, the proportion of these means of production has increased sharply in relation to the total of all tools and equipment in socialist industry.

The gains derived from the new social system become manifest in total in the rates of economic growth of the Soviet Union and the people's democracies, which much exceed those of capitalist states. The rapid and continuous growth of material production represents an economic law of the new social system that is confirmed by the actual experience of all socialist countries.

Over the years 1951–60, the average annual increase of industrial production amounted to almost 14 per cent in socialist countries as against 5 per cent in capitalist countries. In 1961, industrial production in socialist countries was more than 7 times the level of pre-war 1937 in socialist countries, as against 2·5 times in capitalist countries. The volume of industrial production in 1961 had increased (as compared with the pre-war period) by 5·7 times in the U.S.S.R., by 8·4 times in Poland, by 4·4 times in Czechoslovakia, by 3·4 times in the German Democratic Republic, by 4·2 times in Hungary, by 5·8 times in Rumania and by approximately 14 times in Bulgaria.

The volume of the gross output of industry in the U.S.S.R. for the past three years of the Seven-Year Plan has increased by 33 per cent (instead of 27 per cent envisaged by the plan).

During the period of more than forty-four years since the October

Revolution the Soviet Union has made a leap forward from backwardness to a position in the van of progress and has been transformed into an advanced industrial socialist power. It should be remembered that it has only been during twenty-five of those years that the Soviet people have had the opportunity to build up their economy under conditions of peace.

Remarkable achievements have been made by the Soviet Union in the expansion of industry. Between 1913 and 1961 the gross output of industry increased by 49 times. The production of capital goods increased by 114 times. A versatile engineering industry has been created which is capable of supplying all the sectors of the U.S.S.R. national economy with modern equipment and of satisfying high export requirements. Production of consumer goods has increased 17 times. The main mass of industrial production is produced by types of enterprise which did not exist in pre-revolutionary Russia.

V. AGRICULTURE

Simultaneously with the growth of industry other branches of the U.S.S.R. national economy have been developed continuously on the foundation that it has provided.

Backward and small-scale agriculture has been transformed into a large-scale and mechanized agriculture. The production of grain has reached 8380 million poods, which represents an increase by 66 per cent during the last seven or eight years. The Soviet state plans to achieve an annual grain production of 12,000 million poods by 1965. Production of meat, butter, milk and technical crops has increased considerably. None the less, the growth of agricultural production lags behind the rapidly growing demands of the population and processing industry. The Soviet Government has therefore taken measures to ensure rapid intensification of agricultural production. Capital investment is being considerably increased; the material and technical supplies to collective and state farms are being greatly improved, forms of planning and controlling agricultural enterprises are being perfected. The figures quoted for the Soviet Union and other socialist countries show graphically and convincingly the rapid process of economic development in those countries.

VI. THE CAUSES OF RAPID PROGRESS

It is natural, therefore, to ask what are the causes of the rapid progress of the socialist economies and what are the factors which explain the high rate of growth. To attempt to answer this question does not imply that one accepts the so-called theory of factors of production which has been advanced and is still advocated by some representatives of bourgeois political economy. 'The theory of factors' is erroneous. It treats the economic activity of people at all stages of historic development as a result of the interaction of the three constant factors of production : labour or human activity, capital and land. Moving within the limits of the superficial economic phenomena the advocates of this theory completely ignore profound differences of the social and economic conditions in the life of a nation at different stages of the development of human society, and, in consequence, ignore also the differences due to this or that social form as it affects the combination and interaction of the above factors in different social and economic epochs. At the same time the theory of factors belittles the important fact that the decisive role in the life of the people belongs to labour, i.e. to socially useful and expedient human activity without which no society can exist and develop.

By the factors determining the economic development of a society one must mean first of all those concrete and specific social and economic conditions which exist in this or that country and determine the social form of the expenditure of human labour and cause the growth of the economy. It stands to reason that the available natural resources are of great importance to the development of which human labour is applied, and also the inter-relations between the social and economic and the natural and geographic conditions of production.

The special characteristics of the social and economic conditions in socialist countries, as has been already pointed out, lie in the fact that the economic bases of these countries represent the socialist system of economy and socialist ownership of the tools and means of production. The special factors which explain the more rapid growth of the countries with socialism came into existence and operation precisely on this entirely new economic basis.

VII. NATURAL RESOURCES

Before considering these factors it is necessary to treat briefly the problem of natural resources of socialist countries. The world system of socialism is rich in natural resources. Socialist countries possess now two-thirds of the world's geological deposits of coal, more than half of the deposits of iron ore and bauxites, about 90 per cent of the world's deposits of manganese ore, about 70 per cent of potassium salts and so on.

The Soviet Union can satisfy fully and in growing quantities its needs for the minerals necessary for the expansion of its national economy. At present the Soviet Union takes the first place in the world in the known deposits of iron and manganese ores, of copper, lead, zinc, nickel, bauxite, tungsten, mercury, potassium salts, mica, phosphorus raw material, coal, and one of the first places in the world so far as general deposits of oil are concerned.

Known and expected deposits of mineral raw material in the U.S.S.R. and other socialist countries are sufficient not only for the current requirements of the national economy, but also for the rapid growth of productive forces of these countries during the period covered by perspective forecasts — that is for the forthcoming twenty years. The rational use of natural resources and of the cheapest sources of energy and fuel in the interests both of individual states and of the whole socialist system opens up a vista for the fullest use of the immense advantages of the socialist methods of production.

It need not be said that these immense riches existed in these countries before the revolutions. But they lay untouched. It was only after the revolutions, and especially in the years of the rapid expansion of industry, that these rich deposits of minerals were discovered. Now they are extensively used for the benefit of the peoples of the socialist countries.

Thus, so far as the natural or geographic factor is concerned, the decisive role played by social and economic conditions is clear. This is shown, as the example of the U.S.S.R. and other socialist countries has demonstrated, in the fact that only under the new social and economic conditions have these vast natural resources begun to serve economic construction. In the course of this construction, the geography of these countries has quite literally been changed. Productive forces have been redistributed and backward and absolutely undeveloped areas have been developed.

VIII. LABOUR PRODUCTIVITY

The most important factor in the rapid development of productive forces and of high rates of growth of material production is the steady increase of labour productivity. The superiority of the socialist system over the capitalist one is seen in the fact that socialism creates the solid basis for more rapid growth of labour productivity than under capitalism. Productivity of labour, as V. I. Lenin has stressed, is in the final analysis the most important prerequisite for the victory of a new social system.

May I cite some figures to illustrate the high rates of growth of labour productivity in socialist countries? For the ten-year period 1950–60 productivity of labour in industry increased by 96 per cent in the Soviet Union ; by 128 per cent in Poland ; by 110 per cent in Czechoslovakia ; by 124 per cent in the G.D.R. ; by 119 per cent in Rumania. A single year (1961) witnessed the following increases of labour productivity in industry : by 4 per cent in the U.S.S.R. ; by 7·4 per cent in Poland ; by 5·1 per cent in Czechoslovakia ; by 9 per cent in Rumania ; by 8 per cent in Hungary.

The growth of labour productivity is of special importance in the current stage of development of socialist countries. With the completion of socialist industrialization and the creation of the material and technical basis of socialism in countries of people's democracy, the greater part of any increase of industrial production must come not from an increase in the number of workers employed, but from an increase in labour productivity. The growth of labour productivity is ensured by the development and introduction of new and advanced engineering technology, by more complex mechanization and automatization, by electrification and chemicalization of production, by the zeal of the labour-force and by the increased skill of workers, technicians and engineers.

The law of the increase of productivity requires constant improvement of engineering techniques and the replacement of the existing technology by a new one and the latter by a still newer. This law requires the rapid mastering of new engineering methods, the full use of these in the process of production, the progressive reduction of the time and costs needed to overcome the difficulties of a technique, the improvement of the existing technique, the increase of its productivity, the bettering of technology and organization of production, the effective use of labour resources and the best organization of labour, the constant reduction of expenditures per unit of production and the decrease of the cost of production.

The rates of growth of the economies of socialist countries are to a considerable extent determined by the ratio between the planned scales of production, labour resources and possible demand. In socialist countries there are no 'superfluous' people. At the planned growth of social labour productivity the whole population capable of working is taken into account so that it may be absorbed into actual work and employ most rationally its different abilities, experience, qualifications and the like.

It is necessary to point out that 82 per cent of the total number of the population capable of working were engaged in the U.S.S.R. national economy in 1960. The other 18 per cent were made up of students, the military services and housewives. In the same year the number of the actively employed persons in the U.S.A. constituted only 70 per cent of the population capable of working. Despite such a high percentage of the use of labour resources in comparison with capitalist countries, it still remains possible to attract more of the population available to work into actual labour activities.

The mechanization and automatization of agricultural production, the rapid increase of productivity and the reduction of labour expenditures on collective farmers' subsidiary areas, the development of such public services as canteens, laundries and the like, the further increase of the skills of the labour forces, have all helped to make available additional numbers to work in industry and other branches of the national economy.

Thus, scientific and technical progress and rational use of labour resources will offset the possible shortages of manpower.

IX. TECHNOLOGICAL PROGRESS

The growth of social production under conditions of socialism is based on the planned and continuous development of socialist engineering. Technical progress, automatization and complex mechanization of production represent a uniquely important group of factors which exert a decisive influence on the rate of economic growth. This objective and continuous process is closely correlated with the electrification of the whole national economy, with the industrial use of atomic energy and the development of chemical processes.

Technical progress takes the form, firstly, of the creation, introduction and employment of new and more perfect tools and equipment involving a high degree of mechanization and automatization of production processes ; secondly, of the creation and use of new products and especially of artificial raw materials ; thirdly, of the development and introduction of new productive technology, better use of productive equipment and the perfection of scientific methods of using labour ; fourthly, of the improvement of the organization of labour and the increase of the educational and technical qualifications of the working people.

Automatization is the most effective means of securing a rapid increase of productivity, a decrease of the cost of production and an increase of accumulation. Because of the special features of the socialist social system, such disadvantageous social and economic consequences of the automatization as unemployment, overproduction and the like are impossible in socialist countries. Automatization leads to further reduction of the working day, to the lightening of work, to increase of the material welfare and the cultural level of the nation. In contrast to capitalist countries, there are no limits set to the growth of automatization in the U.S.S.R. and other socialist countries.

In accordance with the development plan of the U.S.S.R. national economy a high degree of mechanization of production will be completed by 1970 throughout industry, agriculture, building, transport and the communal economy. Over a period of twenty years more complete automatization of production will be introduced on a large scale. Cybernetics, electronic computers and control devices are planned to be introduced at increasing rates into the production processes of industry, into scientific and research work, and into planning, calculation, registration and control.

Scientific and technical progress at different rates and on different scales is recorded in all countries. The rapid development of science and engineering has considerably widened the sphere of international relations. The necessity has arisen for scientific and technical co-operation between states in the peaceful uses of atomic energy and in the use of outer space for peaceful purposes. In this connection, the exchange of scientific and technical information, international scientific conferences and the like, have become of urgent necessity. Thus in practice scientific and technical progress is opposed to the arms drive, militarism and the 'cold war' and demands a policy of peaceful co-existence and co-operation between the peoples of different countries.

The present scientific and technical progress of the U.S.S.R. has been made possible by the fact that the Soviet people devoted great efforts and resources to the education of highly qualified specialists, and in particular of scientists capable of mastering modern science and engineering and successfully making further advances.

The planning of specialist education by the state in socialist countries creates the necessary conditions for the most effective use of science and engineering in the interests of the growth of the national economy and the full satisfaction of the needs of a socialist society.

X. THE CONTRIBUTION OF PLANNING

The most important advantage possessed by the economies of socialist countries is their planned character. Their whole economic life is determined and directed by a co-ordinated national economic plan in the interests of the continuous growth of social wealth and the steady rise of the material and cultural level of the national life.

With the establishment of social ownership of the means of production in socialist countries, uncontrolled production, unemployment and economic crises are eliminated. New economic laws have been established and have come into operation. One of the most important is the law of the planned proportional development of the national economy : its planning is based on this law. A planned economy has become a practical necessity.

The experience of socialist countries has shown that without adequate planning and proportionality in the development of different sectors of the economy high rates of growth are impossible.

With the emergence of the world socialist system the scope of the law of planned development has extended considerably and has acquired an international character. This has had a profound effect in accelerating economic growth in all socialist countries.

The law of planned economic development is inseparably connected with the whole system of objective economic laws of socialism. Thus the requirements of these laws are reflected in planning. Planned development necessitates a balanced development of the economy. The most important economic balances are the following : balances between production and consumption of the social product, and especially between production of means of production and production of consumers' goods ; between industry and agriculture ; between individual branches of industry and of agriculture ; between the growth of labour resources and their use in national economy ; between consumption and accumulation in the national income.

It stands to reason that these balances are not all constant and unchanging. They change with the growth of productive forces and the deepening of the social division of labour. In establishing new balances the socialist state starts from previously established balances and from the social needs that arise in each given period.

Changes in the structure of production play a large part in establishing the right balances in the economy. For instance, in the U.S.S.R. fuel industry there is a deliberate policy to give preference in development to the output and processing of oil and gas.

Finally a balanced plan for the economic development of a socialist country requires a planned and regulated socialist policy of industrial location.

Thus the planning of the national economies of socialist countries has a profoundly scientific character, since it results from the requirements of the objective economic laws of socialism and the tasks of technical progress. The experience of the U.S.S.R. and of people's democracies proves convincingly that actual planning is possible only on the basis of social ownership of means of production.

The methods of national economic planning in the U.S.S.R. have developed with the development of the national economy. The wide experience accumulated over several decades has enabled the state and its planning organs to move onwards from quarterly and annual plans to the development of the U.S.S.R. plans for longer periods and finally to the general perspective for a twenty-year period to 1980. Perspective plans for long periods are being produced in a number of other socialist countries.

XI. ACCUMULATION AND CAPITAL INVESTMENT

Large volumes of capital investment have been needed for the industrialization and development of the socialist countries. In the pre-war period investments of state and co-operative organizations (excluding collective farms) in the U.S.S.R. economy amounted to 39 billion roubles (about $43 billion) and for 1941–61 they reached 273 billion roubles ($300 billion). Capital investment in the national economies of other socialist countries has increased enormously.

It may be asked what are the sources of accumulation. At present in socialist countries about three-quarters of the national income goes to the fund of national consumption and approximately one-quarter to accumulation, including stock building. The portion of accumulation in socialist countries is much higher than in capitalist countries.

The problem of accumulation of capital for more rapid industrialization has been solved by the Soviet Union from internal resources. Strict economy in running the economy, the elimination of state financing and the principle of payment related to the quantity and quality of work, has stimulated the growth of labour productivity, the reduction of cost of production and the increase of capital accumulation.

In addition to internal sources of capital accumulation the socialist countries benefit also from mutual assistance and support. The more-developed and richer countries give friendly assistance to less-developed countries. The Soviet Union has helped other socialist countries by building many hundreds of industrial enterprises and smaller units. It has given loans and credits to other countries of the socialist system to the extent of about 8 billion new roubles.

A very great addition to accumulation might be secured through the realization of a policy of peaceful co-existence and disarmament. Enormous resources now cast into the pit of military preparation could be used to meet the pressing needs of mankind. It has been calculated that the resources used throughout the world for military purposes during the last ten years would be sufficient to end the housing shortage in all the countries of the world. Under conditions of universal and total disarmament the total wealth of the world could be more than doubled within twenty to twenty-five years. The Soviet Union and all other socialist countries are sincerely interested in disarmament. As N. S. Khrushchev pointed out in his speech at the World Congress for Universal Disarmament and Peace, the Soviet Union and other socialist countries are forced under the conditions of the arms race to spend great sums for the strengthening of defence. We would be able to use the resources released by disarmament for peaceful constructive purposes for the benefit of humanity.

XII. THE ACHIEVEMENTS IN RECENT YEARS

In any examination of the factors that determine economic growth the objectives of economic development are of great importance. The aim of socialist production is the satisfaction of the material and cultural needs of the members of society ; this aim arouses the vital interest of all workers in achieving the maximum increase of production and implies a material and personal interest on their part in the results of their work, and is thus a powerful factor stimulating economic growth.

This aim of socialist production finds its lively expression in the fact that with the rapid growth of economy there is a steady rise in the national material welfare and cultural level. Since the best general index of the increase of welfare of the nation as a whole is the national income, may I quote a few figures showing the growth of the national incomes of socialist countries and of the shares in them that go to meet the material and cultural needs of the people?

By 1960 the national income had increased as compared with 1950 by more than 2·5 times in the U.S.S.R. ; by twice in Poland and Czechoslovakia ; by 2·4 times in the G.D.R. ; by 2·8 times in Bulgaria ; by 3·8 times in the Korean People's Democratic Republic. Parallel with this, social funds for consumption rose continuously : those parts of the national income, that is, which are available in real or monetary form for the collective (communal) or individual satisfaction of the personal needs of the whole population.

The most powerful integrating factor in the process of the economic development is international trade. The compulsory reduction or even the complete discontinuation of trade with the U.S.S.R. or certain socialist countries is at variance with the working of economic laws, with the principles of the international division of labour and with needs of the time.

Soviet economists consider that wide development of international trade is economically advantageous to all countries and will be conducive to the growth of their economies and welfare.

Widespread international trade, free from discrimination and prohibition, is unquestionably the firmest foundation on which to build up the concept of peaceful co-existence of countries with different social and political systems and a general working co-operation with mutually profitable economic relations between nations. Thus the countries of the world socialist system always stand for the development of mutually beneficial economic relations between all nations and against the closed economic unions that intensify international tension. At the same time that they are developing economic co-operation between themselves and improving the forms of such co-operation, the socialist states stand equally for the development of world trade, because it promotes the consolidation of the cause of peace throughout the whole world. They stand for the convening of an international conference on trade problems to discuss the problem of establishing an International Trade Organisation which will embrace all regions and countries of the world without discrimination.

XIII. PERSPECTIVES FOR THE FUTURE

The economic basis for the participation of the Soviet Union and other socialist countries in widespread international economic interchange is their rapid growth of material production. The main economic objective of the U.S.S.R. during the nearest twenty-year period is the establishment of the material and technical basis of communism. This requires the increase of the volume of industrial production by not less than 6 times and of the volume of agricultural production by 3·5 times. By that date the productive forces of our country will have reached a new level wholly different in character, considerably higher than that of the productive forces of any other country, so that material benefits will have become abundant. Taking them as a whole, in the countries of the world socialist system the total volume of industrial production will have increased by 8-9 times by 1980. As shown by rough estimates, more than two-thirds of the world industrial production will be that of the world socialist system.

In the period covered by the general perspective, the main objectives to be achieved by the countries of the world socialist system are these : the establishment of the material and technical basis of communism and in essentials the creation of a communist society in the Soviet Union ; the completing of the building of the material and technical basis of socialism and to a large extent the creation of the material and technical basis of communism in the other countries of the world socialist system ; the economic over-stripping of the most-developed capitalist countries by the Soviet Union and other socialist countries ; the achievement, in the majority of the countries of the socialist system, of the world's highest standards of life, sufficient to ensure the all-round satisfaction of the material and spiritual needs of the people.

The organic integration of science and production, and high rates of scientific and technical progress represent the most important conditions of the further rapid growth of productive forces in all the countries of socialism.

DISCUSSION OF THE PAPERS BY PROFESSORS BRUS AND ŁASKI AND BY PROFESSOR PLOTNIKOV

Mr. M. H. Dobb, in opening the discussion, said that there was one special analytical point that could be considered first. Professors Brus and Łaski had referred in Section 1 of their paper to the problem of accelerating the rate of investment. They discuss the actual constraints on the speed at which such an acceleration could occur and point out that the conflict between consumption and investment was sharper the *shorter* the period over which this acceleration occurred. In one respect the constraints may be *greater* than they imply, if one considered those imposed by the existing conditions and structure of production. To the extent that the constraints were greater, the conflict between consumption and invest-ment was *less* than they imply. In this context everything depended upon what one considered to be the main limiting factor upon the rate of investment. In a planned economy this had nothing to do with indi-vidual saving propensities, so that growth models that imputed a causal role to savings ratios were inappropriate.

The main (but not exclusive) limiting factor consisted in the existing productive capacity of the capital goods industries. The process of *changing* the rate of investment then became a matter of changing the manner in which the output capacity of this industry was utilized; i.e. changing the proportions in which its output was allocated between this sector and the consumer goods sector. The 'ceiling' on the process of acceleration was when 100 per cent of new investment was devoted to the expansion of the capital goods industry and hence to augmenting the investment potential. In this limiting case consumption during the accelerating period (between t_o and t_n) ceased to increase, but it *did not decline absolutely*. (Of course, its *rate of increase* must decline if there was any rise in the rate of investment, as may also consumption per head if total population was increasing.)

What would probably decline was the *real wage* per worker, because employment was being expanded faster than consumer goods output. This involved, in some degree, that 'redistribution of consumption' between those already employed and those newly employed which was characteristic of an early stage of industrialization. In so far as there was a practicable limit upon such redistribution, for efficiency or incentive reasons, then consumption considerations did place a restriction upon the acceleration process *before* the other limit imposed by productive capacity was reached.

It was in this case, where, for efficiency or incentive (or politico-social) reasons, real wages must be taken as approximately constant, that the problem could be posed a little differently. The conflict could be regarded, within the *short* time-horizon, as being between the rate of growth and the expansion of employment (or the speed of absorbing the labour-reserve). In this situation a premium was placed upon stepping up the growth rate by the transition to more capital-intensive and labour-saving methods of production, a point to which the writers of the paper only come later, in the context of full employment. In the present case the 'interruption' involved was in the growth of employment as well as of consumption. Such a conflict was no more than temporary and vanished in a longer time-horizon, since the higher growth rate would mean *also* a faster increase of employment at future dates. (A higher growth rate by virtue of higher labour productivity under the more capital-intensive technique.) Perhaps this was to be regarded as the economic version of the Biblical paradox to the effect that 'he who seeks to find his life shall lose it' and 'he that loseth his life shall find it'.

The authors' case where consumption falls *absolutely* as a result of accelerating the growth rate seemed to apply to the extent (but only to the extent) that the accelerated investment affected working capital (or turn-over funds) and involved in some form an increase in stocks of goods-in-process at the expense of the flow of final output.

To have made this point may not be quite as trivial as it seemed, because it may serve to underline two more general points. Firstly, what was important in the context of growth was how the surplus or increment which represented the existing growth potential was used to augment that growth potential further. This consideration made for greater flexibility and for more planning possibilities than appeared from a purely static viewpoint. A planned economy, as Professor Plotnikov had emphasized, was, *par excellence*, a growth economy.

Secondly, as the writers of the paper had themselves stressed, what was crucial to any realistic approach to problems in the context of a planned economy was to study first and foremost the constraints on planning decisions which were imposed by the existing production situation. Only when there was a full conceptual picture of these was it possible to appreciate the degrees of freedom that planning permitted — freedom that became greater the further into the future the plans went.

This approach, from the standpoint of production-determinants, contrasted with the British and American approach which began from the opposite end. The habit of seeking the determinants of economic processes primarily from the side of demand, or from the behaviour and attitudes of individual consumers (for 'savers' may be regarded as 'consumers', with a different sign), rested essentially on a view of the economic process as a uni-directional, straight-line affair, a process moving from the input of certain original factors through to the issuance from the production line of certain final consumers' goods. This notion, for example, was implicit in the Austrian process of *Zurechnung*, the imputation of values to 'higher order' goods (in Menger's terminology) from the values of 'first order' goods in terms of marginal productivity. If one considered, by contrast, the well-known von Neumann model of a purely circular growth process, in which all consumption was what the classical economists called 'productive consumption', outputs becoming in turn inputs, then demand determinants in the customary sense of consumers' propensities and behaviour lines no longer came into the picture. Instead the determinants of the growth process were exclusively conditions of production in one form or another. (This was also true, incidentally, of Mr. Sraffa's more static model.) Thus at least, so far (though not only so far) as planning problems consisted of development or growth problems, this type of approach (Western economists might call it essentially classical rather than modern) was the significant and fruitful one. This was one reason why input-output analysis was an ingredient of planning.

One possible objection may be anticipated ; it was no use saying in such circumstances that something called glibly 'planners' preferences' took the place of individual preferences, as some trans-Atlantic writers were wont to do. If this meant simply what planners intend or try to do it had little, if any, explanatory value at all.

Some of the most interesting points in the paper came in Part *III*, in connection with technical change at the stage of 'intensive' development, when full employment of the labour force had been reached. One of these points concerned inflation ; it actually belonged to the end of the previous part, although it was also relevant to Part *III*. The authors state that 'inflationary phenomena in socialism may be understood correctly only as part of a complex of a planned process . . . of long-term dynamic equilibrium'. This was important enough to underline, but in one respect it should go further. Inflationary pressure presumably referred to the retail market for consumers' goods. If this pressure was measured by the relation between the (equilibrium) retail prices level and the wage cost of output (and hence the margin to be bridged, for example, by turnover tax), then *some* degree of enhanced inflationary pressure was inevitable whenever the growth rate was increased, unless this increase marched closely in step with rising productivity in consumer goods production. This relation was, indeed, a simple reflection of the rate of growth. It could be said that it was the price-expression or 'dual' of the structure of production (as regards the relation between the two departments of Marx's scheme). The proposition that, given the level of money wages and of productivity in consumer goods industries, the retail price level was a function of the rate of investment, was one that was recognized by most economists in the socialist countries and by a large number of Western countries. It seemed to be of fundamental importance that all questions of price-level changes, whether up or down, should be viewed firmly within this framework.

One could go further and say that there was little point in speaking of inflationary pressure in a planned economy, except in relation to an unplanned increase in the wage-bill and/or possibly an unplanned shortfall of consumer goods.

There were other points of interest in Part *V* of the paper, where the relationship between micro-economic decisions and macro-economics was mentioned. Obviously any socialist planned economy was, and had to be, a mixture of centralization and decentralization in some degree, involving planned directives with price incentives. Where the line should be drawn between micro- and macro-economic decisions would never be an easy question to answer. Even at its most centralized a line always had been drawn between the strategic framework set by planning directives and operational latitude permitted to lower units within that framework. Such a distinction was of the essence of the Soviet *khozraschot*. Historically speaking, an emphasis on centralization may be appropriate to one period (because the strategic framework was all-important for its main tasks) and an emphasis on de-centralization appropriate to another period.

Dr. R. Regul said that equations (3) and (4) of the Brus/Łaski paper were modifications of the Douglas type of equation. Since these were applicable to closed economies it was important to know whether the GNP concept used included foreign trade or not. It was also important to distinguish between various sector rates of growth. The growth rates for non-agricultural sectors must be different from that of the agricultural sector.

Equation (4) included a residual, 'u', to account for technical improvements, etc. This definition was possibly too narrow; the role of larger markets and the general effects of increased size required an exponential factor, due to time, as a residual.

Professor W. A. Weisskopf commented that high rates of growth were often associated with relatively low levels of income. The richer countries, who had passed through the stage of rapid growth, showed much lower rates of increase by comparison.

Professor R. Bićanić argued that whilst productive relationships had, perhaps, been over-estimated in the paper, productive forces had been neglected. In all economic systems the question as to who manages the productive property was important. The rate of growth was not the same in all socialist countries and this needed more explanation than the 'u' factor. Furthermore, the study of rates of change was not sufficient in itself; this was recognized in the formulae by the introduction of absolute magnitudes. Whilst the investment-income ratio was the central determinant of the paper, consumption still set a limit in a socialist country to the possible size of investment. If consumption was reduced below a certain, critical level consumers put up a resistance which led to the development of an 'underground economy' frustrating the aims of the planners.

The capital coefficient tended to decrease as development proceeded. In the Soviet Union the capital coefficient in the fifth five-year plan had been less than one-half of the coefficient in the first such plan. This economy in the use of capital was applicable in all economic systems; in the early stages of growth the capital coefficient increased, because of the capital requirements of heavy industry, falling at a later stage.

Professor T. Scitovsky said that the wider variety of industries associated with economic growth may increase the unavoidable, minimum absolute level of unemployment. There was also a problem of relative effective demand, concerned with matching the composition of total output with the changing patterns of demand.

Professor I. Rachmuth said that the main principle of socialist production was a continuous expansion of output. The rate of growth was higher than in capitalist countries because the latter depended on the profit motive, which imposed a limit on the possible expansion of production.

Professor E. Heuss commented that whilst investment was central for the achievement of growth it normally meant an improvement in productive methods. Younger countries had more possibilities of doing this than the more developed. This would explain the lower rate of growth of the United States compared with other countries, especially those in the socialist group.

Professor W. Brus, replying to the discussion, said that the authors' approach contrasted with Western theory not in its formal structure of equations, but in the socio-economic conditions assumed. Equation (4), however, was not a modification of the Cobb-Douglas formula; that had a doubtful theoretical validity and, empirically, it was difficult to separate out the contributions made by labour and capital. Hence they had used

73

two separate equations, one to allow for the human factor, the other to allow for productive capital and the effectiveness with which it was used.

The definition of the Gross National Product was the usual Marxist concept of 'material production' excluding services. The model could be applied to an open economy, provided that trade was balanced. Indeed, any discrepancy between demand and aggregate productive capacity would show up as a balance of payment's problem. The authors did not assume that supply would automatically equal demand, but felt that the planning authorities had sufficient powers to bring this about. The authors tried to emphasize that in a conflict between consumption and investment the former could not be regarded simply as a residual. The planning authorities must observe a lower limit to consumption. When discussing inflation much depended on the definitions used; if inflation was defined simply as an increase in the price of consumer goods, they were in agreement with the analysis given by Mr. Dobb.

For the sake of simplicity they had not discussed problems connected with the structure of productive capacity, and even not distinguished between agricultural and non-agricultural sectors. However, the model did allow for further disaggregation as well as for taking into account labour-capital substitution, problems of scale and other factors influencing the capital-output ratio (through the change from m to m').

In replying to specific questions the authors agreed that, whilst it was not difficult to match total demand to total output it was a complicated matter to adapt the 'output mix' to the pattern of demand. Except for the first few years of industrialization there were no problems of unemployment in Poland; there were only occasional difficulties in some regions in finding work for the female labour available.

Professor K. N. Plotnikov, also replying, said that, as author, he was gratified to note that the main thesis of the paper, linking economic development with the productive relationships in socialist societies, had not been widely criticized. The very high rates of growth achieved in socialist countries had the character of inevitability and were conditioned by the new productive relationships.

Whilst there was much factual material in the paper bearing on the reasons for these high rates of growth, there were theoretical factors involved as well. There was a close relation between theory and practice in socialist countries. The high rates of growth achieved demonstrated the close relationships maintained between the different branches of production. The correct balance between sectors was kept by central state planning.

Chapter 4

THE PLACE OF AGRICULTURE
IN BALANCED GROWTH [1]

BY

GIUSEPPE UGO PAPI
University of Rome

I. PRIMARY NEEDS MUST BE SATISFIED FIRST

ONCE basic infrastructures have been created in a developing country, the first thing to encourage in the resulting more favourable economic climate should be an increase in the production of goods to meet the elementary human needs for food, clothes and dwellings. Before anything else, the living conditions of the people must be improved and, barring exceptional cases, economic development should therefore begin with raising the production of foodstuffs, agricultural raw materials, clothing and housing, and should then lead up to producing industrial equipment requiring low capital investment.

This seems the logical sequence — and yet many economists would not agree. Some authors, admittedly basing their argument on highly industrialized economies such as that of the United States, link the prosperity of agriculture to parallel, and often prior, industrial development.[2] Others say that one should raise the purchasing power of farmers by creating more industrial activities and more modern industrial equipment.[3]

I confess I am baffled by these arguments. I can find in them no answer to a very simple question : who is to buy the products of increased industrial activity ? Who is to take them up so as to raise the purchasing power of the workers and producers outside agriculture ?

The problem had best be considered in the setting not of one single country or one single zone, but of the world economy. If we take it for granted that in the initial phase of development first

[1] Translated from the French by Elizabeth Henderson.
[2] See G. U. Papi, 'Agricoltura ed industria sul piano mondiale e nell' opera della FAO', *Rivista di politica economica*, June 1951.
[3] *Report of the FAO Preparatory Commission on World Food Proposals, Washington*, 1947.

priority must belong to the production of goods for the — more or less complete — satisfaction of the population's primary needs, and that the producers of these goods have to produce more of them than they consume if they are to buy other goods and services produced in excess of consumption elsewhere, then it follows that the world's producers of food, raw materials, clothes and simple houses, by producing more of these things than they consume, create effective demand for all the non-primary goods and services others produce in excess of their own consumption. To give an impulse to the economic development of any country it is therefore indispensable to increase productivity, per man and per unit of land, in the production of foodstuffs, agricultural raw materials and essential goods.

Let us take a closer look at the process. First of all, the producers of food, raw materials, clothes and simple houses provide those who have not fully satisfied their primary needs with a larger quantity of goods by which to meet these needs. Secondly, as and when agricultural incomes increase, it becomes possible to produce capital and intermediary goods (machines, fertilizers, textiles, timber, iron and steel) by which to raise the production of primary consumption goods. Thirdly, a certain outlet is created in the primary-producing sector for all other, non-primary, goods and services. Finally, by taking up a certain amount of these latter goods and services, primary producers facilitate the absorption of excess agricultural labour in other sectors of the developing country itself; these labour forces may, for instance, find employment in domestic industry, when the country reaches the point where it can encourage industrial development.

We conclude that a developing country, even if it trades extensively with other nations, has every reason to direct its main efforts at first to raising agricultural incomes beyond the level of demand for essentials, and to postpone to a later date the stimulation of industrial production and of services. The key to development is the growth of agricultural income, and if a country fails to achieve this before all else, the whole development process may be held back; at best, growth rates will vary greatly from one part of the country to another and this is certainly not conducive to balanced growth and adds to the number of problems to be resolved.

II. THE EVOLUTION OF AGRICULTURAL ACTIVITY

Let us recall what Kenneth Boulding has said: 'In our society we are rapidly moving towards the day when one man can produce food for perhaps twenty or even a hundred families, and we may only need to have 5 or even 1 per cent of the people in food-getting and the other 95 or 99 per cent can be released for other things. It is no accident, therefore, but a necessity of economic development, that all industrial expansions have been preceded by, or have gone hand in hand with, a period of agricultural improvement.' [1]

In other words, technical progress in agriculture is translated not into an increase in the consumption of agricultural products, but into the need to shift factors of production to other sectors. This is the reason why in a community where agriculture, too, is in rapid progress, the proportion of factors of production applied to agriculture always declines ; at the same time, the rise in agricultural incomes due to progressively more economical and efficient factor combinations comes to be the very condition of the development of other sectors in any given economy.

In fact, the balanced expansion of the different sectors of any country's economy can be based only on an optimum distribution of factors of production among sectors. The hallmark of optimal factor distribution, as Schultz pointed out,[2] is absence of involuntary unemployment of any factor of production ; this strictly micro-economic concept implies the rule of economic behaviour for individuals, government and public agencies alike. Starting out from optimum factor distribution in this sense, balanced expansion of the economy is conceivable only on condition that the growth of each sector's income is tuned to the elasticity of demand for its own products.

Now, we know from family budgets that the income elasticity of demand is far lower for agricultural products than for industrial products and services. In other words, when a person earns more, he is less inclined to spend more on food than on other things. It follows that the optimum distribution of factors of production can subsist during a development process only on condition that the rate of expansion in the industrial and tertiary sectors becomes a multiple of the rate of agricultural expansion, in the same proportion as the elasticity of rural demand for industrial and tertiary products is a multiple of the elasticity of demand for agricultural products.

Without this proportion in the rise of sectoral incomes balanced growth is impossible. If, for example, industrial income fails to rise to the level appropriate to the income recipients' propensity to spend an additional unit of income on industrial rather than on

[1] K. E. Boulding, 'Economic Analysis and Agricultural Policy', *The Canadian Journal of Economics and Political Science*, 1947, p. 440.

[2] T. W. Schultz, *Agriculture in an Unstable Economy*, New York and London, 1945.

agricultural products, then the terms of trade between industrial products (and services) and farm products would eventually turn against the latter.

This rigorously economic concept of the balanced growth of any country's different sectors of production helps us to understand why it is necessary to develop agricultural income first and to the utmost extent possible.

However, even in strictly economic terms, such a state of affairs is in practice conceivable only in a fully competitive market, such as exists nowhere and least of all in agriculture. Nor is it enough to consider only the elasticity of demand for the various sectors' products ; we must also take into account the elasticity of supply. But, having made these reservations, it still remains an uncontrovertible fact that the tendency towards balanced growth in any country implies the gradual transfer to other sectors of such factors of production as may be in relative excess in agriculture, while only those factors remain which can enter into more productive combinations with land and thereby raise the productivity of all factors.

What has been said about the tendency of factor distribution as among different sectors, applies equally to factor distribution within one and the same sector. Let us again take agriculture. The authorities responsible should deliberately promote the transfer of factors of production from less to more productive employment — for instance, from wheat growing to livestock farming — once the necessary conditions for the latter have been created by adequate investment, say, in rain-deficient areas.[1]

To sum up, it may be said that in the initial phase of economic development all efforts should be concentrated on producing those essential goods which offer the highest returns. This goes for individuals and government alike, and for the latter implies the vigorous pursuit of what we may call a structural policy.

III. THE REASONS FOR LOW INCOMES IN AGRICULTURE

The first essential for an effective structural policy in agriculture is to know, and gradually to eliminate, the causes which tend to keep incomes lower in agriculture than in other sectors of production.

[1] I would quote the example of Italy, where the outflow of rural populations is denuding marginal land. Efforts are being made to increase returns from marginal land, for instance, by improving mountain pastures, increasing orchards (to the extent that domestic and foreign outlets can be found for fruit), and developing timber production to meet the growing demand for wood, paper and pulp.

Very often there is an excess of agricultural population in relation to cultivable land. It is true that every year efforts are made to draw more land into production; but if the rate of population growth tends to rise and the new fields are submerged by families far larger than can enter into effective factor combinations with the land, then a country's economic development gains precious little from new land. The reclamation of uncultivated and the development of new land are not enough to offset excess agricultural population.

Sometimes the excess of agricultural population in relation to land is due to technical progress itself. In the case of traditional crops, especially cereals, technical progress has reduced labour requirements. If technical progress causes agricultural returns to rise and domestic and/or foreign demand for the major food and other agricultural products fails to rise in proportion, commodity surpluses are inevitable and these soon lead to labour surpluses, which keep farm incomes below incomes in other sectors of production.

But there are many reasons other than population pressure why farm incomes are so low throughout the world. One reason is that in wide areas ecological factors make it difficult, not to say impossible, to introduce modern methods of production and farm management; we have only to think of dry climates, deficient water supply, or the prevalence of mountain or marginal hill land, all of which prejudice the results of agricultural activity. The magnitude of the obstacle this can present to development is illustrated, again, by the case of Italy, where 31 per cent of farm-holdings are situated in the mountains and 45 per cent in the hills, so that the amount of land which can be cultivated with success appears severely limited.

Another reason why incomes are lower in agriculture than in other sectors is that very often farm enterprises are numerous, and that most of them may be too small to allow of modern production methods. In large parts of the country agriculture cannot be considered as part of a market economy, and many farmers are unable to produce even what is indispensable for their own consumption; we speak of substandard production. More often, farmers cannot produce quantities which can be sold on the domestic or foreign market and might so raise farm incomes sufficiently to generate a sizeable global demand for other products. In other words, a large part of the rural population cannot insert itself into the circular flow of the economy. Here again, we have proof that in many countries the fundamental reason why agricultural incomes are so low is that too many people are trying to work too little land.

79

Furthermore, agricultural incomes are low because for the most part farm workers are untrained or at any rate insufficiently trained, which makes it difficult for them either to emigrate to other regions or other countries, or to retrain for other activities into which they might move, especially the local processing of agricultural products.

Finally, farm workers of all categories are imperfectly organized and there is not enough credit available to promote the rapid development of intensive production even in areas where it would otherwise be perfectly possible.

If then, agricultural incomes are so often lower than the incomes of other sectors of production, the reasons are not difficult to understand. There are so many of them : a marked disproportion of factors of production ; the large number of enterprises too small to adopt modern production methods ; the exclusion of a large part of the population from the circular flow of production and marketing ; lack of training, ineffective organization of farm workers and deficiency of credit.

But, so long as incomes are lower in agriculture than in other sectors, the disparity of sectoral incomes is likely to be accompanied by disparity in the rate of development of a country's different regions. The backwardness of the productive environment in certain regions is bound to delay their development. This is especially true of regions where the bulk of investment in infrastructures does not, for often considerable periods, generate any incomes additional to those in existence. New incomes can only be expected in the long run, but in the meantime peasant communities are not only slow to assimilate more productive techniques, but also have a steadily growing propensity to consume.

On the other hand, the growth of income is accelerated in the more advanced regions. Public investment in infrastructures for the backward regions itself intensifies demand for industrial products and gives new impulse to the development of the advanced regions. These are better equipped to take advantage of new production opportunities and to put them into effect on the spot, however many special facilities the government may find it expedient to grant to the under-developed parts of the country to attract industries.

IV. THE BETTER UTILIZATION OF THE FACTOR LAND

Structural policy in agriculture should make it its constant concern to improve the efficiency of factor combinations. This implies the better utilization of land on the one hand, and of capital, labour and entrepreneurship on the other.

As regards land, structural policy should endeavour to organize farms of economic size, appropriate to the given conditions of climate, altitude and soil. This means land reform, or the modification of the juridical system of land tenure on the one hand, and on the other hand the combination of uneconomically small holdings into viable units, that is, units capable of producing for sale at home or abroad, at profitable prices. Only in this manner can any region's or any country's agriculture make the transition from a subsistence to a market economy and so create the conditions of lasting growth in agricultural incomes.

(a) *Land Reform*

In many countries the system of land tenure constitutes an obstacle to the improvement in the living conditions of small farmers and farm labour and at the same time to the economic development of the country as a whole.

Several types of land reform have been proposed to remedy this situation. Any reform of the structure of ownership by the redistribution of land depends, among other things, on the relationship between population, land and other resources. In the presence of sufficient domestic resources much may be expected from splitting up the large estates, with their extensive forms of cultivation, among independent and truck farmers and agricultural labourers, with the prospect of more intensive cultivation on smaller holdings.

Similarly, when new land can be taken into cultivation and excess rural population can be absorbed in viable farm-holdings, there is room for an increase in agricultural incomes through the better utilization of land.

The prospect is different in countries where the density of rural population is on the increase and where the large estates are generally not farmed by their owners but, in small units, by tenant farmers; unless the redistribution of land is such as to increase the size of existing units, land reform alone can then not eliminate one of the worst drawbacks of the agrarian structure, namely, that too many holdings are operated at too low an income level.

In either case any advantages to be expected from land reform as such are likely to be wiped out completely unless concurrent steps are taken to provide appropriate services and facilities for the new farm-holders, either individually or jointly through co-operatives to which they may belong. Cases in point are credit facilities to replace the former landowner as a source of finance and to keep step with the smallholders' growing need to borrow capital, sales co-operatives for better marketing, extension work to acquaint the inexperienced farm-holders with their new responsibilities and to teach them what they need to know, tax allowances to ease the fiscal burden on farmers and farm labour, health services and so on ; all these are among the conditions of success of any land reform.

Land reform tending to adapt the size of farm-holdings to ecological conditions and to the market will, moreover, have to be accompanied by a whole set of measures designed to supplement and maintain the results of the new distribution of land ownership. Land reform is not finished with a mere change in ownership, but must be considered as a continuous process with more than just technical and economic aspects. Very largely, it is a matter of education, to improve the use of land by refashioning the outlook of the men who work it. Man has to be lifted from his isolation to a state of mind where he understands the necessity of working his land in active co-operation with others, so that co-operation in agriculture will follow almost naturally. The history of land reform is full of examples of sorry failure, which go to show that the problems of agriculture do not respond to isolated measures.

The end effect of any land reform is measurable by the degree to which it sets free, or enhances, the population's productive energy. Wholly favourable results can be expected only in exceptional cases ; most often, the real effects will be somewhat different from those originally intended and hoped for. In any event, the effects of land reform depend largely on the particular conditions of a given country, and on the cultural level and state of mind of the population.

(b) *Consolidation of Holdings*

If it is one of the purposes of land reform to organize farm holdings of economic size, it is absolutely necessary that the redistribution of ownership should go hand in hand with a process of regrouping and consolidation of fragmented holdings, even if this is a long-term process. Redistribution of ownership through the splitting up of large estates aims at creating a new pattern of land tenure, often without regard to excessive fractionalization ; consolidation of holdings, on the other hand, tends to maintain, or to create, units of a size to permit rational farming.

Consolidation also implies redistribution, of course, but in common usage the term encompasses other measures as well, such as the building of roads, or soil improvement — anything, in short, that structural policy in agriculture can do to adapt the agrarian structure to technical requirements and to the needs of the people who work the land.

The consolidation of land holdings has a direct effect on the productivity of both labour and land. It considerably reduces the expenditure of labour and capital necessary for production and soil conservation, it provides ready access to dispersed fields and creates the means of better and more economic land utilization. The convergent effects of land reform and consolidation find expression in the size of farm enterprises, in so far as these become better adjusted to the ecological and economic conditions in different parts of any given country.

V. THE BETTER UTILIZATION OF CAPITAL, LABOUR AND ENTREPRENEURSHIP

With respect to the factor capital, one of the major ingredients of structural policy should be to increase and improve the use of technical means in agriculture, such as selected seeds, fertilizers, farm machinery, pesticides, animal feed, etc.

Structural policy should, furthermore, deal with animal and plant health protection, with the volume of investment and of indebtedness in agriculture, with the unification of the most effective credit systems and their diversification to meet the different needs of different categories of farmers and finally with co-operation and mutual aid in agriculture.

With respect to the factor labour, structural policy has to concern itself with the rate of demographic growth, the age and sex composition of the population, the proportion of rural to total population, the cost and productivity of agricultural labour, and the gradual and careful shifting of people from the land to other sectors of production, especially to such tertiary activities as transport, trade and the tourist industry.

To make it easier, or indeed possible, for people to move into other occupations, it will be necessary to have vocational training schools and institutes at all levels, not only for farming activities but for a wide range of others. Many problems have to be considered in this connection, including the proper matching of school and occupational grades, the division of training tasks between school and industry, occupational guidance, specific technical training, retraining, refresher courses and so on.

Structural policy with regard to agricultural labour should also watch over the cost of social protection for the population engaged in agriculture, in the sense of not allowing social charges to become an unduly high cost element in farm produce.

As regards farm management, finally, structural policy should make it its business to spread new technical knowledge among farm entrepreneurs and should do everything possible to promote scientific research. Education and the diffusion of knowledge are the key elements in any development process.

The list of structural problems is long, and I have mentioned only a few to illustrate my point that the solution of all these problems is the only means of raising agricultural income and thereby contributing to the country's economic development.

It cannot be stated too often that the way to a lasting increase in real agricultural income is neither tariff protection nor price support, nor yet export subsidies or tax relief. We must break out of the vicious circle and face things as they are. The fact remains that unless a country's agricultural income can be raised, economic development will be held back or, at best, will take place in a patchy fashion, some regions falling behind others.

VI. THE INDUSTRIALIZATION OF AGRICULTURE

In most non-industrialized countries there exists some sort of mystical faith that all evils can be cured by 'land reform', which is not always well defined in its principles and objectives, and by 'industrialization', or the creation of a wide range of industrial activities, in the belief that these will in all cases prove a source of higher income for the country and can draw excess factors of production away from the land. When people speak of the 'industrialization of agriculture', it is by no means always clear what they mean.

Sometimes to industrialize agriculture is understood to mean applying to agricultural production the results of research and technical improvements which keep succeeding each other in the most diverse fields and raise the productivity of all factors of production. This is no doubt a sound interpretation, but it does not exhaust the full meaning of the evolution towards which agricultural activity tends by historical necessity.

Another interpretation is that the industrialization of agriculture implies that agricultural activity is at the base of industrial activities of growing importance for all countries, namely, the production of capital goods for agriculture and the processing of farm products. This, too, stresses a salient aspect, but still misses the essence of the concept of the industrialization of agriculture.

To my mind, to industrialize a country's agriculture signifies making the bulk of agricultural activity profitable. It means making agriculture as profitable as industry must be if it is to survive on the domestic and foreign market ; it means the utmost possible rationalization of agricultural activity to follow upon the transformation of the productive environment by the creation of infrastructures, the elimination or at least mitigation of the factors which depress farm incomes, the better utilization of all factors of production in agriculture, and the widening of the market for farm produce by regional integration. With such progressive industrialization, agricultural produce, produced on the basis of economic calculations in quantities exceeding the farmers' own consumption, can eventually be sold at home or abroad at profitable prices ; farm incomes can then rise and agriculture will be able to pass more easily from the stage of industrialization to that of commercialization in the widest sense of the word.

The commercialization of farm produce in its turn creates demand for specialized labour in transport and trade and stimulates certain processing industries which are best located near the source of their raw materials ; I have in mind the production of butter and cheese, fruit and vegetable preserves, tinned meats, sugar refining, and the transformation of certain forestry and mining products.[1] Thus commercialization provides outlets for higher agricultural output, with the immediate result that the *per caput* income of the rural population goes up. Farmers and farm labour can afford to consume more and so stimulate the development not only of the above-mentioned industries, but of many others.

Commercialization is the first step towards the diversification of employment, in the sense that part of the agricultural labour force can begin to move into industry, trade and the production of services.

Advanced industrialization of agriculture in any given country tends to increase also the commercialization of farm produce, thanks to a progressive reduction of risks and production cost. The effects of industrialization and commercialization in agriculture tend to be

[1] See R. Hartshorne, 'The Role of the State in Economic Growth : Contents of the State Area', in *The State and Economic Growth*, Social Science Research Council, New York, 1959, pp. 289, 292-4, 297.

'Thus, increased commercialization of the primary industries of an area — farming, mining, forestry, etc. — provides opportunity for the development of a variety of manufacturing industries. Such development, if it takes place, increases the level of living by providing manufactured products at lower cost than either subsistence production or imports, and by attracting labor from the farm increases both the commercial market for farm products and the need for labor-saving devices in agriculture.'

I quote this passage because it is in close agreement with a point of view I personally have defended ever since 1945 (p. 290).

cumulative, and agricultural incomes are the combined result of both.

What needs to be done, then, in any under-developed region, is to raise agriculture from the stage of subsistence farming to industrialized farming first, and then to the stage of the widest possible commercialization. But these results can be achieved only by a structural policy applied in depth within each country's ecological limits.

The first phase in any country's or region's economic development is marked by a considerable extension of general public services (public health, police protection, education) and by a judicious programme of public works (roads, ports, aqueducts, means of transport, power stations) to make the environment more receptive for future private investment.

The second phase is that of rationalization, or industrialization and commercialization, of agricultural activity, with the gradual elimination of subsistence — or infra-subsistence — farming.

As the industrialization and commercialization of agriculture proceed, the rural population must be prepared for social mobility by occupational training of the kind which facilitates a move into other sectors of production — industry, trade and services. At the same time an impulse is given to industries producing capital goods for agriculture, to processing industries for food and agricultural raw materials, and to industries with a low capital-output ratio — all of which have a widening market thanks to the increase in agricultural incomes.

This is the way to arrive at that optimum distribution of factors of production among different sectors, which alone can vouchsafe a country's, or a region's, balanced growth.

VII. AGRICULTURE AS A 'GENERAL PUBLIC SERVICE'

It often happens that the government of a country wants to keep up its agricultural production for social reasons ('agriculture is a way of life'), to ensure a certain level of domestic supplies in case of war, or for export, when other sectors of production prove durably unable to earn enough abroad to pay for indispensable imports of other agricultural products. Policies of this kind have a cost, of course, and this cost has to be divided among different categories of income recipients in a manner which it is not always easy to define and which varies from one country to another.

All countries keep a certain amount of agricultural activity going, even if it is uneconomic ; we may rightly speak of a general public service which the state renders the community for one of the reasons mentioned above. As in all cases of government action, the present cost of maintaining the country's agricultural activity has to be compared with the expected useful results. Both are exceedingly difficult to measure precisely, but this does not mean that the comparison becomes impossible.

Taking the concepts of present cost and useful results as a criterion, every attempt to bring agricultural activity more and more within the purview of the economic principle, every effort to limit the extent of unprofitable farming by a judicious structural policy, every progress in rationalizing agriculture with a view to increasing its returns — all these ultimately amount to a real and true process of industrialization in agriculture.

If such a policy is successful, the result will be that a steadily growing part of agriculture becomes profitable, that the government has to incur smaller cost for supporting the uneconomic parts of agriculture, and that the gap between farming and other incomes narrows.

In the balanced economic growth of any given country the place of agriculture tends to diminish with its industrialization and commercialization. Provided diversified and widespread education and labour training has prepared the ground, every factor of production that is, or becomes, redundant on the land is gradually released for use in other sectors of production.

DISCUSSION OF THE PAPER BY PROFESSOR PAPI

Professor D. Delivanis, in opening the discussion, said that agriculture was characterized by a much smaller demand for capital than industry and the growth in output usually began earlier, because of the localization of demand. The predominant opinion that growth must start with industry may be traced to the Soviet example in the pre-war five-year plans, an example that may have been inspired by political motives. One of the main complications in the early stages of growth was the low elasticity of supply of agricultural products ; this could be avoided by increased imports, investment in agricultural improvements, the better utilization of crops and improvements in transport facilities.

The use of measures to protect agriculture would preserve the production of crops grown under unfavourable conditions. Although farmers may gain, these measures might lead to a net loss for the whole community. The use of price supports would have different effects under varying conditions. Where a crop was entirely consumed at home, for example, such supports would merely redistribute the National Income in favour of agriculture, a result which could be offset by fiscal action. Where a crop was exported, or where stocks were large and production was possible in competing countries, price supports could be very dangerous. This was shown by the experience of Brazilian coffee, Greek raisins and United States cotton. Export premiums, on the other hand, were expensive, contrary to international agreements, and could lead to retaliation by other producing countries.

In under-developed countries, the improvement of agriculture was necessary in order to make way for economic growth. In some cases, however, the use of high price supports did nothing to reduce costs and increase output, but merely imposed burdens on the consumer. This was so where peasant proprietors rented their land and often sold their crops in the fields, or on the trees, before harvesting. What was needed was to increase the difference between costs and prices, or to increase output.

The farmer who owned his land and employed only himself and his family was not interested in reductions in cost, since he got both the rent and the wages himself. Thus, amongst farmers who were their own masters there was little interest in cost-saving methods and innovations.

Increased output was useful from the macro-economic viewpoint as long as demand was not saturated, increased exports were still possible without a reduction in the proceeds from total exports and additional labour and land were available. The farmers themselves could contribute by increasing their knowledge, or by small-scale investment in transport equipment, minor irrigation works, etc. The latter may not interest the government but might enormously improve the lot of the farmers individually. Increased output (if possible of improved quality), an increased variety and the abandonment of mono-culture constituted the best paths for the growth of agriculture.

Professor A. Kraal said that Professor Papi had spoken of low agricultural incomes, but this must be understood relatively to other incomes in the economy. It was possible that farmers in all countries earned less per hour than unskilled labour outside agriculture, especially if the value of all kinds of government supports were deducted from their income.

The basic error was to seek to raise incomes and support the industry by steps that increased output. If it was desired to support agriculture for social reasons, the support should be directed to farmers as such, and should not affect output. Similarly, it was wrong to increase investment in agriculture, with a given labour input, in order to increase output. It would be better to try and raise incomes by reducing labour inputs.

Excessive increases in agricultural output not only made it difficult to obtain balanced growth in the economy, but also caused complications for countries overseas as well.

Record of Discussion

Professor F. Perroux argued that agriculture could best be considered within the framework provided by a model, with two sectors, being developed and tested at the Institut de Science Économique Appliquée. It was not sufficient to analyse the influence of industry over agriculture, or vice versa, nor to explain the transfer of labour from agriculture to industry. The fact was that, once the industrial sector had become established historically, innovation began and spreads particularly in this sector. This was because the urban, industrial sector was based on a system of complementary processes and included factors whose speed of reaction and adaptation was greater than that of the agricultural sector.

Inequality in innovation was one of the fundamental reasons for inequalities in productivity and incomes between the two sectors. The model was, therefore, fundamentally, that of an active (or dynamic) sector, linked to a passive sector.

An active, or 'dominant' sector exercised its influence :

(a) Through the effects of scale by increasing (through its demand, or by eliminating a bottleneck) the rate of growth of the passive sector.

(b) Through the pure innovation effect, by acquiring a larger share of total demand ; i.e. by reducing the size of the passive sector, but it also imposed on the latter an increase in the rate of growth of productivity.

These principles were applicable either to developed or under-developed countries.

Developed Countries.—Starting from an initial equality in the supply and demand relationships between the two sectors (assuming a closed system and a situation of reciprocal supply and demand), it was possible to show that an agricultural surplus necessarily appeared as soon as there was an inequality in innovation. This demonstration began with the price and income elasticities of demand of each sector for the products of the other. The remedy was either for the agricultural sector to export its surplus, or to obtain a transfer of incomes from the industrial-urban sector which payed artificially high prices and thus subsidized agriculture.

Movements of labour and capital should be introduced after the movement of goods. The transfer of labour into industry tended to reduce the inequality in productivity and rates of growth between the two sectors. It was population of working age that were transferred, so that the agricultural sector had, in effect, carried the cost of their training, for which it had not been re-imbursed. The question of capital movements was very complex ; the tendency for capital to be invested in the most profitable sector was counteracted by a large number of public investments, or investments subsidised by the state. However, the transfer of capital to agriculture in search of capital gains, or for speculative purposes clearly did not have any relation to the better allocation of capital resources.

Flexible and quantitative planning could introduce order into the process by controlling monopolies, rectifying the spontaneous movements in the terms of trade between agriculture and industry and organizing a concerted export of the surpluses. Planning only achieved these aims in the face of pressure groups, whose viewpoint was never a substitute for the functional analysis of interrelated growth paths.

Under-developed Countries.—These economies were not articulated with respect to prices, flows and information. They were orientated towards the external world by the structure of their capital and the direction of their trade. So much was this so that the established industry was in touch with the rest of the world, but not with traditional agriculture. A policy of balanced growth would consist in linking the outward-looking sectors of the economy with the indigenous economy and organizing in a systematic way the spread of innovation through the country.

The Keynesian models, based on the propensity to save and invest, were not applicable. It was necessary to use models elaborated at the ISEA which started from two fundamental propensities, the propensity to work and the propensity to innovate. These latest models used Cobb-Douglas functions, modified to take account of uncertainty. It was hoped to demonstrate the general case of multi-sectoral models, with two or more active and passive sectors.

Professor A. N. Damaskenides commented that the policies put forward by Professor Papi were not the most suitable for the over-populated agricultural countries of southern Europe. The aim there should be to make the best use of scarce land by creating labour absorbing activities, both agricultural and industrial, such as intensive cultivation and light industries. Priority should be given to sectors using plentiful and cheap labour ; since capital is a scarce factor of production, investments should be carried out in those projects, whether agricultural or industrial, in which the ratio of capital to output was low.

Professor M. Pohorille said that it was difficult to tap the potential savings of the agricultural sector, especially as it was necessary to avoid the adverse effects of forced savings. Farmers must be brought to see the advantages of economic growth and realize that their own incomes would be increased. This required the appropriate changes in social and economic conditions which would promote growth. Industry and agriculture must be integrated, so that the former could meet the needs of the latter and investment could take place in the agricultural sector.

The state may need to encourage this process and the Polish example showed how it could be done. An agricultural development fund had been set up in 1958, financed by compulsory deliveries of products to the state, paid for at lower prices than the farmers could obtain in the free markets, or from the normal state purchases. The fund was used for investment projects for the benefit of the agricultural sector as a whole. The farmers themselves made additional, voluntary contributions to the fund from their total earnings.

Dr. H. Fouquet said that distribution played an important part as an intermediary between the farmer and the consumer. Governments often wanted low food prices for political and social reasons, but the oligopolistic conditions of trade and distribution often meant that the whole burden of the lower prices fell on the farmers. It was possible to have high prices for the consumer and low prices for the farmer at one and the same time.

Professor G. U. Papi, replying to the discussion, said that it was agreed that any price or income stabilization policy must be accompanied by structural changes and that protective policies would damage the interests of other countries. Perhaps it was now possible to look forward to a time when policies could be harmonized between countries so as to permit structural changes to be made, without necessarily damaging other economies. The main problem was how to increase agricultural incomes; industrialization, by itself, was no solution. If the agricultural problem was not solved first, industrialization would cause more social problems as the population increased.

Chapter 5

EDUCATION, RESEARCH AND OTHER UNIDENTIFIED FACTORS IN GROWTH

BY

INGVAR SVENNILSON
Stockholm

I. TRENDS IN THEORY AND THEIR RELATION TO ECONOMIC POLICY

THE assumption: *ceteris paribus* is, indeed, a necessary pre-requisite for any theory that aims at explaining certain specific char-acteristics of an economic system. Without this assumption the theoretical tools cannot be sharpened. Without it, economics deteriorates to a descriptive or institutional science incapable of explaining economic development.

The *ceteris* has, however, to be chosen according to the type of economic phenomenon we want to explain. The main body of economic theory has been designed to explain short-term variations. Interest has, then, been concentrated on variations in quantities such as demand for and supply of factors and products, and their relation to income and prices. In the short term, the social and technological framework within which such variations take place can as a first approximation be assumed to be unchanged; as a con-sequence, the quantity-price-income relations can be assumed to be stable. A next step in the analysis will be to let quantity-price-income relations shift, regarding these shifts as the result of *exogenous* factors which are kept outside the theoretical model.

However, it has often turned out that the *ceteris paribus* cannot be maintained without abstracting from obvious causal relationships between the variables of the theoretical models and shifts in their interrelations. The *ceteris paribus* has, then, to be reduced in scope. A classical example is the development of Keynesian theory. In his *General Theory* Keynes did not take into account the fact that investment, as a result of capital accumulation, leads to a shift of supply functions. This fact was taken as a starting point for the extension of the Keynesian theory along the Harrod-Domar line. A more general expression of such a development of economic theory is that functions expressing economic relationships are found *not to*

92

be reversible. As a result of a movement along such a function, the conditions contained in the *ceteris paribus* assumption change in such a way that we will not turn back to the point from which we started. Once this fact has been recognized, we have evidently embarked on a theory of processes over time, perhaps resulting in 'growth', where a number of 'exogenous' conditions are integrated into the analysis. Even such dynamic theories have, however, their *ceteris paribus*.

There is, on the other hand, also a long tradition of analysis that has broken away from the classical delimitation of economic variables and has taken as a starting point for the analysis processes within the *ceteris paribus* field. This tradition is marked by such names as Adam Smith, Malthus, Marx, Veblen, Max Weber and Schumpeter. They have formulated theories of social and institutional transformation as an integrated part of processes of economic development. Along this line, research has developed based on historical and sociological methods. It has dealt with problems of the social and institutional conditions for invention and innovation, entrepreneurship and market domination, supply of labour, education, consumption and savings, flows of capital, etc. This type of research has been stimulated by the new interest in speeding up the transition from 'under-development' to more developed conditions in the poor parts of the world. It has become evident that in these countries a condition for development has been a policy concerned with broad changes of the social and institutional framework within which economic policy in a narrower sense may be evolved.

This diversity of trends in research and doctrine poses problems both for theory and policy in the field of growth.

For social science there arises a problem of integration versus disintegration of theory. It has to be accepted that various aspects of a process of growth have to be studied with different methodological instruments. Some can be attacked by developing the tools of 'economic' analysis in the traditional sense, leaving a wide field of 'other factors' as a *terra incognita*. Other aspects of a process of growth have to be studied by using sociological, psychological or political science methods. At the same time, the results of these various types of research must be related to each other. The need for integration of the various 'social sciences' is today stronger than ever before. This integration has to be reflected in the organization of social science studies at our universities. The isolation of economics, tending towards econometrics, from other social sciences that often exists has as far as possible to be broken, even if for obvious reasons a certain degree of specialization must remain.

From the point of view of economics, an integration will mean that 'other factors' will have to be given a place as interrelated variables in economic models. The integration may even have to go deeper. The very concepts of economic analysis, which reflect the institutional conditions of a given society at a given time, must be adjusted to changing social conditions. As an example, it may be mentioned that a study of under-developed countries may lead to new conceptual ideas of employment and underemployment. As another example, 'labour input' may have to be broken up into various new elements.

Such an integration and an adjustment of 'economic theory' to new research about 'exogenous' factors is strongly needed from a policy point of view. The formulation of economic theory may be regarded as expressing a bias as regards essentials in a process of growth. In any case, it may intentionally or unintentionally convey false ideas about the relevant parameters of action for development policy. Economists have to confess that their formulation of growth theory has not always been adequate for solving the policy problems of under-developed countries. Methods of national accounting have been uncritically applied. Economists may also be partly responsible for the fact that the shift of emphasis in development policy from the volume of investment towards various types of social and institutional change has come about so late. A growth policy that is well balanced must be supported by economics that are conceptually adjusted to the actual social and institutional conditions, and that have as far as possible integrated factors which have traditionally been regarded as 'exogenous'.

A central notion in any theory of growth must evidently be '*productivity*'. I shall in the following pages concentrate attention on the problem of how various social phenomena might be related to productivity trends. The traditional theory of production relates output to the input of capital and labour, assuming a given supply of 'land' and a given state of — or exogenously determined change in — 'technical knowledge'. It assumes that, at a given input of capital and labour, the most productive methods of production 'known' are applied. On this basis, econometric studies of past historical growth have been made, separating the contribution of labour, capital and technical change. The results of such studies have formed the basis for forecasts and planning.

Modern development of economics is to a large extent oriented towards penetrating behind the façade of this rather simple theory. The efforts are concerned with the forces behind technical change and in this process the highly aggregated concepts of 'capital' and

94

'labour' tend to be dissolved. The field of study is so rich that I shall only try in a very general way to indicate some of the aspects that seem to be of special importance.

II. EDUCATION

One of the trends in modern society is the expansion of formal education as an institution separated from the production process itself. Education in this form may to a varying extent serve several purposes, all of which from a general 'development' point of view may be highly important. Education may be regarded as an *'investment'* in a productive agent. There are, however, also *'consumption'* aspects of education : it makes a direct contribution to the 'standard of living' and creates a lasting 'consumption asset'. The 'consumption effect' and the 'production effect' of education may be regarded as *complementary* from the point of view of the 'social values' that form the basis for our conception of 'growth' in a wide sense. The increased production of goods and services made possible through the productive effects of education may in the future assume a greater value, according to prevalent scales of preferences, to the extent that it will be combined with a better education of the population as 'consumers'. The relative weight attributed to the 'consumption' and the 'production effect' of education may be expected to vary between poorer and richer countries and will be reflected in the 'content' of education. Starving countries would be expected to spend relatively more on education for production, while countries approaching 'affluence', at the same time increasing leisure time, would be expected to spend more on education for 'consumption'.

This character of a *'joint production'* with varying emphasis on 'wool' and 'meat' (to draw a parallel with the classical textbook case) makes it questionable whether any close correlation can be found between the aggregate amount of education — measured by the investment cost or the number of student-years embodied in the labour force — and the growth of production. In studying the productive effects of education we evidently must choose a more differentiated approach. We have to distinguish between systems of education, methods of education, curricula and levels. There are also inventions and innovations in the field of education, which may increase the efficiency of the investment in education, including the cost of spending more years in the classroom.

The economics of education is emerging as a science in its own right, corresponding to the study of other types of production. It

95

is still in an early experimental stage. There are problems of measurement which are unsolved, and knowledge about the 'production function' is still rudimentary. It would therefore be premature to try to integrate the 'education industry' into aggregate economic growth models, even if it is evident how in principle this could be done.

A general outline of the economic problems of education can be indicated in terms well known from the theory of real capital investment. The *gestation period* for the individual finished product of education is long. It can be varied within wide limits, and one main problem from the point of view of growth is how far to prolong education with regard to its marginal effect on production. As in the case of 'land', the 'fertility' of the human raw material is widely scattered. As regards the enrolment rates in higher education, the 'law of declining marginal return' will, therefore, sooner or later appear on the stage. As a result of imperfections in the social selection system, students are, however, not enrolled in an order corresponding to that of 'land' in the textbooks. A democratization of the selection process may postpone the advent of declining marginal return.

The length of education, as well as the choice of the types of education, has to be economically adjusted to the pattern of future production of the country concerned, whether under-developed or highly developed. The choice is complicated by the fact that labour with the different types and levels of education is in a position of *complementarity from a production point of view*. Too many lawyers in an otherwise under-developed environment will yield a low or even negative marginal return. The number of university engineers must be balanced against the number of lower level technicians. The marginal return of increasing the 'engineer density' of the population may decline beyond a certain point, at least if we extend the concept of 'growth' beyond what is included in national accounts as 'production'. We should not presume that, under all circumstances, the marginal return of higher education in art, humanities and social sciences is necessarily lower than that of education in science and technology. (It may be proper to make this observation in a place of old refined culture such as Vienna.)

The difficulty of making an adequate investment decision in the field of education is immensely increased by the fact that this is a very *long-term investment* which affects 'production' several decades ahead. There are not only uncertainties about rates and directions of growth and about technological trends that determine the demand for and the productivity of labour with various types and levels of education. Even if we disregard uncertainty, we cannot take the future economic development for granted and adjust education to it. Education will evidently have an effect on the overall rate of growth. In this respect, there is a parallel with decisions about the rate of real capital investment. Decisions about investment in education must be related to prevailing preferences as regards the time-flow of production and consumption. This relation is complicated by the fact that the possibilities of replacing special types of education by other factors of production are often strictly limited. A condition of perfect or almost perfect complementarity often exists which creates *bottleneck* problems as regards various types of educated skills, specialized workers, teachers, doctors, architects, chemists, mathematicians, etc. In so far as growth must be balanced between sectors of the economy, the balance of education as regards specialization and levels will, therefore, determine the future growth that is made possible. There will be no chemical industry, if chemical engineers are not available. Supply will to a large extent determine future effective demand.

In one important respect, the human character of educational capital as distinct from that of real capital creates a special problem for analysis and policy. By educating students, we may create people better able to invent and innovate in the field of technology, political life, organization and culture. This will affect the trend of technology and production in a way that is unique, when compared with investment in other factors. In econometric studies, various shares of overall growth have been imputed to the volume of capital and labour, leaving an unexplained technological trend as a residual factor. In some studies, the rise in the average level of education of labour has been added as another factor that explains a (comparatively small) share of overall growth. This analysis, however, overlooks the fact that technological trends may largely be explained by qualities in the population that are related to education. This effect will not be brought out by a correlation analysis based on broad aggregates ; it is closely linked to comparatively small groups within the population engaged in the pursuit of research, invention and innovation. Even if the results within this field are largely of a stochastic nature — the view of a great son of Vienna, Joseph Schumpeter — their systematic relation to education in society of today cannot be overlooked.

There are good reasons to stick to the traditional pattern of economic thinking and regard education as *another factor* in economic growth. Policy should be balanced as regards allocation of resources between investment in education and real capital. They can to some extent be substituted for each other and thus compete for available resources. We must also take into account that they are to some degree complementary from a production point of view. Increased education will increase the marginal productivity of real capital, and *vice versa*. The bottleneck position of some types of education, especially of higher education, and its far-reaching effects on the social and technical transformation of society, give it, however, a special place in analysis, policy and planning directed towards growth.

In this connection we have to take into account that economic growth is inseparably dependent on a transformation of society as regards technology, sectoral structure, location of industry and population, social services including education and the general cultural, social and political environment of the population. This complex transformation must be systematically prepared and planned, and plans have to be transferred from drawing boards, offices and committees into operation. The capacity to perform this transformation within a limited period of time and to do it in an effective way depends on the supply of various types of highly educated professionals. The demand for such people is, thus, only partly related to the *level* of development that is reached at any point of time but partly also to the *rate of growth* that is desired. A rate of growth of 6 per cent a year will demand a larger number of administrators, educationalists, scientists, engineers and architects, than a rate of growth of, say, 3 per cent a year. Countries who try to accelerate their growth often find this sector — and not the rate of real capital investment — to be *the* bottleneck. New plans for industry, public services including education, urban and rural development, are too slow to develop. To the economist, this phenomenon can be described in terms of the familiar *acceleration principle*.

From these considerations follows the conclusion — self-evident but often overlooked — that the evolution of education cannot be determined as a demand derived from an independent forecast of production. Educational policy and planning should be regarded as an integral part of development planning, the scope and direction being determined by the rate of growth, the kind of growth and the kind of society in general that we want to see in the future.

These are long-term considerations. In the *medium-long-term* other problems arise, which call for a *strategy* for the more near future. The root of these problems is the length of the gestation period for the formation of educational capital. A prolongation of studies not only delays the entry of students into industry. Higher education is to a large extent the education of teachers, or even of teachers for teachers. An expansion of the educational system

98

makes it necessary to divert an increased number of graduates from research and employment in industry to teaching. This *feedback* may over a number of years seriously reduce the 'output' from the educational system, especially on its narrow peak — the doctoral level. On the other hand, the supply of people to research and industry will grow faster in the long run. A problem, then, arises of the *timing* of economic expansion. The growth in the next decade has to be weighed against more long-term growth. The choice will partly depend on the teacher-student (the 'capital-output') ratio of the educational system at various levels — thus, on its internal efficiency. It would be an important task for economists to explore the logistics of such processes over time as a basis for growth policy.

III. KNOWLEDGE, SKILL AND INNOVATION

Formal *education* should be regarded as one link of an integrated system for *generating and transferring knowledge*. Other links in the system are *research* institutions and the *production system* ('*industry*') itself. As an intermediary functions a many-faced system of *documentation* :

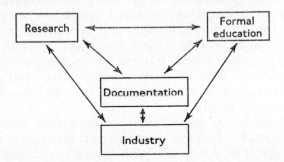

In modern society, this is a highly diversified and complicated system. On its efficiency depends the progress of technical knowledge and its application. One of the main innovations in modern society is that the functioning of this system is not regarded in a *laissez-aller* fashion. It has become an object for policy. We may invest in its various parts in order ultimately to speed up the rate of economic growth.

The efficiency of this system can be formulated in terms of the relation between input of resources and output in the form of production of goods and services. One would not, however, expect easily to arrive at a measurement of the yield of various types of investment in this field. This, for several reasons. First, the process within each sector is of a complicated cumulative nature. Second, there are complicated circular chains of interaction between the various sectors of the system — research, education and industry. Third, it is not only in the sector of formal education that the gestation period may be long ; the effects on production may also be scattered over a long period. Fourth, the relation between input and output is stochastic, especially in the case of research and industrial innovation. Research in this field has in any case to begin with partial studies of the behaviour of the system. A vast literature on such problems has grown up in late years.

I shall here restrict myself to a few observations, which seem to be relevant from a policy point of view.

(a) *The Functional Integration of the System*

In reality, research, education and industry are not entirely organized as separate institutions with different specialized functions : they merge into each other. Higher education is, or should be, integrated with research. Research may be conducted within industrial units. The distinction between basic and applied research is tending to disappear as industrial production becomes more scientific. On the other hand, the 'development' of processes and products cannot be sharply distinguished from 'research'. Formal education is combined with training in 'production'. Education may take place in 'built in' units within industry, and production itself may be regarded as a 'learning process', which may be speeded up by systematic education.

Innovations in the organization of this system may accelerate economic growth. Research may become better integrated with industrial activities, education with research and industry with education.

(b) *Innovations and the 'Learning Process'*

Innovations may be defined as shifts in the production function, resulting in increased productivity. A well-known description of the process of innovation has been the following. The inventor and the scientist create 'inventions' that accumulate into a pool of 'technical knowledge'. The entrepreneur-innovator creates a new combination of such technical elements, profitably adjusted to the current market conditions. In such a process there may be considerable time-lags, perhaps of several decades, between an invention and its application. In the end, the industrial 'innovator' adds to 'technical knowledge', which is usually assumed to be available to anybody. It will sooner or later be imitated by other enterprises.

This description of a process of invention and innovation must be modified in various respects in order to arrive at a more realistic interpretation of its characteristics.

First, it overlooks the tendency towards *integration of research and industry*. Those engaged in research and development work, whether inside or outside industry, may today be regarded as partners in innovating activities. Innovations are often not spontaneous but planned, with the expectation that research will provide the necessary inventions. In this way, the time-lags in the invention-innovation process may be reduced to zero, and as a result technological progress may accelerate.

Second, the earlier treatment of innovations naturally tended to emphasize the role of the big, striking innovations, that historically dominated cycles of growth. The diversification of industrial technology in highly developed industrial systems makes it less likely that any single innovation will dominate an overall process growth. Various studies also have shown that innovations in the form of the gradual improvement of earlier innovations play an important role. It would also be misleading to reserve the term 'innovation' for the activities of top management and research. Labour all along the line may improve methods of operation or the quality of products. On all levels, a '*learning process*' may develop that gradually increases efficiency. In some special cases, it has been possible to study the course of such 'learning processes'. The improvement in efficiency, which takes place in this way, may only partly be described as the result of increased technical 'knowledge'; in part it takes the form of growing 'skill' acquired by repeated experience and training. An important aspect of the efficiency problem is how to speed up this 'learning process'. It can be achieved through systematic organizational studies such as motion studies. It also depends on systems of incentives for all participants in industrial operations, and not only on profit incentives.

It is an open question how much weight in overall growth should be attributed to large discontinuous innovations and how much to the broad and more continuous stream of small innovations. The latter type of innovation may very well carry greater weight.

Third, the linking of research to industrial innovations and the broad stream of innovation poses special problems for the *transfer of technology* between various parts of the economic system. Technical knowledge and skill become to a large extent invested in the individual industrial unit and in its labour-force. It forms what may be labelled its '*know-how*'. The transfer of this 'know-how' to other units may be restricted in various ways. First, only part of this 'know-how' can be documented as 'knowledge'. Some of this knowledge may be freely available, other parts may be subject to patent and licensing, while other parts may, at least transitionally, be kept secret and only slowly 'leak out'. Many details of knowledge as well as the skill acquired can only be transferred by instruction and training; the transfer will, then, depend on such conditions as the willingness of firms to receive apprentices and on the movement of personnel to other firms.

Other types of institutions may serve as intermediaries, transferring 'know-how' from one producing unit to another. Professional societies, independent research institutes or educational institutions may serve this purpose. Firms delivering machinery may advise their customers how to use it, drawing on experiences from various enterprises. A growing importance as a transfer medium may be attributed to independent consulting firms who serve various clients.

The transfer of knowledge and skill is thus a very complicated process. If restrictions to transfer were reduced, innovations would be more easily spread, and the progress of technological standards would be accelerated. The problem is evidently one of economic organization. Restrictions to transfer form an element in the game of a competitive system; a delay in transfer will increase the profit of the progressive firm and will stimulate its efforts to keep abreast of competitors. This stimulus to innovation must, however, be balanced against losses due to slow transfer.

These transfer problems also have an international aspect. Owing to various forms of national integration, technical knowledge and skill may more easily be disseminated within a country than across national frontiers. It is part of the 'external economies' of national industries that they may reach different levels of knowledge and skill in different countries. These conditions form the background of the difficulties encountered in 'technical assistance' from more-developed to less-developed countries. Other difficulties are the lack of education in the receiving countries and the lack of experience in adjusting technology to the conditions of less-developed countries. One conclusion that can be drawn from an analysis of the nature of the transfer problem is that an effective international technical assistance has to take into account the knowledge and skill that has been accumulated within industrial units. The knowledge-skill that exists in the producing units is spread among their employees, who complement each other in team activities. Individual experts are, therefore, much less effective than teams representing an integrated enterprise. The team method is used when industrial firms establish subsidiaries in other markets. The team can transfer the knowledge-skill of the mother firm to the new unit by planning, organization, information, demonstration and training. The success of such operations indicates a method for technical assistance that with advantage could be used also in cases when the technical assistance is divorced from investment and ownership.

It has been said that 'ideas know no frontiers'. To the extent that this applies to technology, the need for organizing an international market would be no greater than in the case of the winds that blow across seas and continents. This picture does, however, only to a limited extent correspond to reality. The process of transfer is complicated and the market structure is far from perfect. One of the main problems in the field of growth is to improve international marketing of knowledge and skill in order to reduce the disadvantages of less-developed countries.

IV. MOBILITY OF RESOURCES

The case of knowledge and skill is just one example of the general rule that growth can be accelerated by increasing the mobility of factors of production.

Capital equipment is to a high degree 'fixed' as regards location and technical design. The mobility of capital is, therefore, mainly dependent on replacement. The durability of capital equipment is mainly responsible for the rigidity of a production system that has once been established, partly so for sound economic reasons. There are, however, imperfections in the replacement process that reduce the rate of growth and that may be overcome by a more adequate economic policy. One may mention the fiscal rules for depreciation allowances which may affect the replacement policy of firms. Probably more important, however, is a public policy that aims at reducing features in the market restricting competition within national and international markets. Actually, the most important effect of a policy aiming at reducing monopolistic elements and government protection of trade or producers may not be that it reduces profits but that it reduces the cost of production by speeding up the transformation process.

The inertia in the transformation process is, however, also linked to the restricted *mobility of labour*, locally and occupationally. Obsolete capital and industries may be kept running for a long period because immobile labour has to accept lower wages than those of other industries. Such obstacles to transformation may partly be overcome by minimum wage laws or by inter-industry solidarity in the wage-bargaining of centralized trade-union systems. But the effect of such policies may only be that low-wage employment is exchanged for unemployment in 'depressed' areas or industries.

One of the main innovations of economic policy after the Keynesian revolution is the initiation of a new labour-market policy aiming towards increasing mobility of labour between occupations and geographical areas. The new policy involves that society is prepared to cover the cost of re-education and retraining, the loss of income during this period and the cost of travel and re-settlement of families. Labour mobility was earlier largely regarded as an 'exogenous factor' outside the influence of economic policy. The new labour-market policy (as it now is formulated for example in Sweden) is based on the estimate that from the point of view of society as a whole it is profitable in terms of growth to invest a considerable part of the GNP in transfer of labour between areas and occupations. The short-term gains corresponding to differentials in productivity may be large; even larger gains may accrue in the long run as a result of a more rapid development of 'growth industries'.

This 'new deal' in labour-market policy links up with the Keynesian full-employment policy in another important respect that is relevant from the point of view of growth. The employment policy may stop short of 'full employment' because bottlenecks are reached in some industries before other industries have become fully employed. Inflationary tendencies, partly emanating from the wage level, may, if the general level of employment is raised further, appear in the bottleneck industries and spread to the entire economic system. The new labour-market policy may help to remove this obstacle to full employment, break the bottlenecks by increasing mobility of labour and, thus, establish a more even front of full employment in all industries. The short-term gain may amount to only a small per cent of the GNP. But, again, forces of growth may be released in industries which, otherwise, would tend towards technological stagnation because of a low level of employment. The out-flow of labour from these industries would force them to modernize their structure, including the capital structure.

V. PLANNING

A common denominator for the factors of growth that have been discussed above is that their growth effects may extend over a long future period and that policy, consequently, must be adjusted to the *long-term development* of the economy. Immediate action in the field of education, research, innovation and allocation of capital and labour must be oriented so as to agree with the long-term transformation and growth of the economy. Mobility of factors is not enough : equally important is in which *direction* they move. A good adjustment in these respects will diminish the risk of mistakes in investment, smooth the path of transformation and, consequently, make a contribution to the rate of growth. A development of the *technique* of long-term forecasting and planning thus forms an important element of growth policy.

In highly centralized economies of the Soviet type, forecasting may be identified with planning by the central government. Even in such cases, however, there is a considerable scope for independent decisions of individual citizens and uncertainties exist about new technology and developments abroad. Long-term plans may, therefore, serve as targets, but the possibility of future revisions of the plans must reasonably be anticipated at the outset.

In decentralized *market economies* the element of uncertainty is for several reasons more predominant. The development of industry and the innovating activities are ultimately dependent on private decisions. As a rule foreign trade has a bigger share, and its development depends on economic trends abroad. In '*mixed*' *economies*, government provides the infrastructure for private activities. These are also influenced — although in a way that is difficult to forecast — by government policy in the field of public finance, central banking, labour market and foreign trade. Any projection of future trends must, therefore, be based on a combination of government plans for action and forecasts of private reactions to this policy. Uncertainties speak for *flexibility* in planning. Plans must be subject to '*rolling adjustment*', as new experience is gained, and plans for the near future may be envisaged as a first step in a more long-term *policy strategy*, including alternative lines for action corresponding to alternatives of development in the 'market'.

At the same time, there is also in a 'mixed' economy a need to indicate some *broad 'targets'* for long-term growth. These may, even if provisional, serve as a guide for the planning by various private and public units within sectors of the economy. There are advantages in a decentralization of planning activities which also have been recognized in the Soviet system. A combination of full-employment policies with national planning and forecasting will, in the first place *induce* firms and sectors, private and public, to take a longer view. A national system of planning and forecasting may also provide information to each unit within an economy about plans and trends in its other parts. It may, finally, become an instrument for co-ordinating sector plans by giving them a direction consistent with overall targets and trends.

One of the main innovations in the field of growth policy after the last world war has been the development of long-term planning activities in the 'market' economies of Western countries (such as France, Japan and Sweden). This innovation is being spread to other countries of a similar type. An expression of this tendency is the recent OECD declaration that member countries should aim, as a 'collective target', at a 50 per cent increase of their production in the 1960 decade. To the extent that this target generally is followed by action, a firmer basis has been created for planning and expansion in each country separately. This development opens fascinating perspectives for a more general co-ordination of planning activities in various parts of the world.

DISCUSSION OF THE PAPER BY PROFESSOR SVENNILSON

Dr. S. P. Pant, in opening the discussion, said that any attempt to increase the rate of growth of the economy must start from the application of known technology to the human and natural resources available. At present educational planning does not always assist in this process ; it needs to be integrated into general economic planning.

Experience in some under-developed countries showed that there tended to be shortages of specific skills, a surplus of unskilled labour and an imbalance of supply and demand in respect of graduates of higher education. The development of education must proceed along with increased capital investment.

The main question was that of deciding how much to increase education and in what form. There were doubts whether the concept of the 'marginal return' was useful for practical purposes ; an alternative approach would be to develop a long-term plan to show estimates of the number of different skills required in each sector. From these requirements an educational programme could be obtained. It was difficult to decide how much detail to include in such a programme ; if too much educational specialization was permitted there might be bottlenecks and training difficulties. Too little specialization may lead to deficiencies in training programmes.

In considering education it was wrong to use a purely economic approach ; co-operation is required with other social sciences, as well as with pure science and technology. The basic process of education is the transfer of knowledge and technology between persons. Formal education was not the only way of doing this, and often not the chief way in which it occurred ; it took place all the time in everyday life. The role of formal education was to provide the capacity to acquire knowledge.

Professor D. Delivanis argued that the many different reasons given for the slow rate of growth of some economies were not sufficient in themselves. It is necessary to use many different techniques to obtain a full explanation of their retardation. There were many obstacles to growth which arose from the poor functioning of administration (both public and commercial), as well as from social and political reactions to change caused by ignorance on the part of people and their leaders. One of the roles of education was to reduce the waste and other consequences that flow from the above factors.

Professor F. Machlup said that much work had been done in the United States in assessing the rate of return obtained from expenditures on elementary, secondary and higher education, as well as on training, learning on the job and research and development. This work was associated with the names of Friedman, Schultz, Blitz, Becker, Mincer, Ewell and Griliches. It was confined, necessarily, to measureable magnitudes, both costs and benefits. However, one of the most important costs — the value of incomes forgone during the period of education — can only be estimated in a speculative and controversial fashion.

The method employed for comparison of benefits and costs was to measure differentials in earnings and correlate them with the length of the learning period. The results obtained showed high average rates of return, especially for elementary education, whilst higher education showed lower returns of 8-10 per cent per annum.

Very high rates of return had been shown to accrue to research and development expenditures. For example, in the case of the development leading up to the production of hybrid corn two alternative calculations had been made : (a) calculating the hypothetical inputs that would be required with old techniques to obtain the actual outputs produced with the new techniques ; (b) calculating the hypothetical outputs to be expected from the old techniques by employing the inputs actually used with the new methods. Using the more favourable of these two approaches, a rate of return of 700 per cent per annum was obtained on the original development expenditure. Such high rates of return on successful, individual projects gave little guide as to the average returns obtainable on research and development expenditures on a national scale. When this is done the social returns are still thought to be as high as 100 per cent per annum.

The main difficulty with these calculations is that the social marginal costs of research and development may be underestimated, since the salaries paid to the scientists and engineers engaged in the work may be much less than their social opportunity costs. There is a strong complementary relationship between present research and educational activities and therefore between research at present and research in the future. The opportunity cost of personnel employed on research and development work was the loss of their services for teaching and training future research workers, and hence a reduction of the flow of research results available in the future. This cost far exceeded the money incomes of scientists, which was the item entered as a cost in the above calculations of rates of return.

Professor H. S. Houthakker argued that one of the major complications of economic analysis was the fact that labour is not homogeneous; this particularly affected any discussion of education. In older, traditional societies there was no rational allocation of labour to various jobs. This can also be true of advanced societies if there were barriers to the acquisition of education.

Education improved both specific and general skills, and the importance of the latter was often underestimated. Education also provided objective criteria of inherent abilities, especially intelligence, and it could be used, therefore, to determine what opportunities are open to people. Probability methods could be used to analyse this aspect, since the role of education could be viewed in terms of raising the probability that each person would find the job for which his abilities were most suited.

Professor G. Leduc argued that it was not satisfactory to talk of 'unspecified factors' in economic development without attempting to identify them. The growth formulae which list only labour and capital must be extended to include other factors. The role of education and research was particularly important. Many examples could be quoted, especially from Africa, where projects had failed because of lack of research. Education was expensive for under-developed countries and must be properly programmed, along with other investments. It was a very suitable subject for aid from richer countries.

Professor V. K. R. V. Rao said that it was questionable whether the methods of economics could be fully applied in the field of education; these doubts were intensified by the suspicions attaching to some of the results already achieved. For example, the 'joint supply' analogy applied to the consumption and investment sides of education was too simple to be useful. There were three different products of education: general training, professional services and technical services. Different investments in educational 'capital goods' are required to produce these different products. For example, technical college teachers were required to produce technical skills, and so on. Education must be viewed, therefore, as a tiered system. In India, for example, the 'capital goods' tier had been neglected.

Record of Discussion

The 'period of production' of education was also important, especially when integrating education into general planning. It takes time to produce teachers. Furthermore, individuals become frustrated when trained for jobs which do not materialize at the time that their training is completed. In the short run adult education is also important in terms of developing literacy, simplifying language problems and improving communications. Perhaps the general aim of education should be to shorten the period of specialized education and lengthen that of general education.

Professor R. Ulavic argued that when discussing education, along with other unidentified factors in growth, it was necessary to take account of the differences between the approaches used by Marxists and Western economists. Factors regarded as exogenous by Western economists would not be treated as such by Marxists. The latter feel, for example, that an extra contribution to increased productivity was obtained in Socialist countries because of the worker's knowledge of the aims of planning and the fact that his wages were known to be proportional to his product.

The production and consumption aspects of education were difficult to separate out, especially their respective effects on labour productivity. The qualitative aspects of consumption were important, as well, and difficult questions were raised as to whether consumers could be allowed free choice in education. The importance of this in planning for development lay in the general problem of finding the correct proportions between physical and non-physical consumption at different levels of development.

Dr. S. Stanley said that the distinction between the consumption and investment aspects of education was not illuminating; instead it would be better to consider the human and political aspects of education apart from the direct and indirect effects upon production. Directly productive education consisted of all forms of practical training, whilst indirectly productive education consisted of that secondary and academic education which created a pool of men and women capable, not only of acquiring further specific skills, but also able to produce leaders in all walks of life.

Professor C. Anderson said that the under-developed countries had placed much emphasis on education as a means of increasing production. However, there was insufficient knowledge about the kinds of education required. It was also necessary to persuade people to take the form of education required, since there was a widespread tendency to seek traditional forms of education. The Soviet Union had wide experience of this problem and had made extensive use of many methods — monetary incentives, the lure of opportunities open to educated persons, coercion and inequality of educational opportunity.

One special problem arose from the hostility often shown by newly independent countries to expatriates, often the only people able to accelerate the educational programme. Economists can contribute significantly to educational planning problems, but most of their work in the field so far can be characterized as 'demographic book-keeping'.

Dr. M. J. Bowman argued that the use of rates of return in analysing education meant employing a type of marginal analysis (even if the rates actually calculated were technically average rates) which was essentially static. This was not sufficient, since it was being applied to a dynamic system. Particular attention had to be paid to the time period of output and the long gestation period involved in educational investments. The rate of return approach could still be helpful, especially if used with appropriate 'shadow prices'; high rates of return, for example, would indicate the existence of bottlenecks in specific fields.

In under-developed countries there was often an acute shortage of sub-professional people due to the rigid structure of opportunities open to graduates. In periods of rapid change and development all production functions were changing, with implications for social productivity stretching right into the future. It was difficult, in these circumstances, to distinguish between the consumption and investment aspects of education, because much depended on the viewpoint of the person concerned and the time period considered. It was possible that the link between education and economic development lay in the way in which a cumulative educational process brought society to a 'threshold point' at which structural change became possible on a large scale.

Professor S. Lombardini said that it had been found in Italy that economic growth had been hampered by lack of labour mobility, which was linked with educational development. It was difficult to assess the marginal productivity of education because of the importance of its indirect effects, which are not measurable. Considerable uncertainty was also introduced by the rigidity of the institutional framework. It was essential to decide educational expenditures along with the investment expenditures of other sectors in one plan. Much more attention should be given to the factors that determine the size and allocation of the resources devoted to education.

Professor C. G. Uhr said that the problem of relating investments in education to changes in productivity required that we first obtain statistically measurable concepts of inputs and outputs in education. Work carried out in Finland showed that there was a high correlation between the growth of productivity and the expansion of educational facilities. It was still necessary, however, to isolate the exact way in which education contributed to raising the growth rate of the economy.

It was possible to place too much emphasis on vocational education, leading to a loss of flexibility in the labour force. When technology was changing rapidly, it was necessary to allow for a high rate of obsolescence in education.

Dr. J. Auerhan said that research had been carried out in Czechoslovakia on the role of science in production in order to try to answer the question whether it was possible to arrive at an optimum development of science for planning purposes. The results, which were still tentative, suggested that this could be done. An index had been calculated to try to measure the 'relative amount of science'; this index showed the number of workers engaged upon scientific research per 100 workers in industry. In the older, industrially-developed economies this index varied between 5 and 8; it had been forecast that, by 1970, it would rise to 10-15 and, by 1980, to between 20 and 30. The number of scientific workers rises as fast as industrial production, but the number of those engaged upon research and development rises faster than the number of engineers and the total labour force as a whole.

Professor I. Svennilson, replying to the discussion, said that whilst there were some doubts as to whether this subject could be integrated into economic science it was clearly necessary to organize thinking about education along economic lines. Already there has been a revision of education policy because of the intervention of economists. It was dangerous to simplify in this field, as had happened in the case of certain econometric models. A more precise, quantitative analysis was required, probably employing marginal analysis of a sophisticated kind. One problem was that discontinuities were very common and would affect the results obtained.

When considering the dualism that existed between consumption and investment in this field it must be recognized that 'joint production' was an important part of education. The clear distinction between investment and consumption aspects was no longer possible, and it was not helpful to talk of a 'capital goods' sector of education. There was no simple relationship between an educated worker, his firm and the output to which he contributed.

Chapter 6

HISTORICAL EXPERIENCE
OF ECONOMIC DEVELOPMENT

H. J. HABAKKUK
Oxford University

HISTORY contains a large number of case studies of successful and
of frustrated economic development. From the detailed study of
these it is possible to gain a general sense of the combinations of
circumstances which in the past have been favourable to development. But it is not feasible to concentrate this experience into
anything which can be dignified with the name of lessons of history.
All I have attempted to do in the present paper is first to consider
an hypothesis about the form which economic development has
taken, and secondly to examine four out of the many relevant
influences on that development.

I. THE FORM OF ECONOMIC DEVELOPMENT

Professor Rostow has argued that a 'take-off' has been an
essential part of economic development.[1] I do not propose to
consider the wider ramifications of this theory but only the assertion
that there is a short and decisive interval in the history of a society
in which changes take place which ensure that henceforth growth is
its normal condition. The core of the hypothesis I take to be the
belief that sustained and gradual growth is, in the nature of things,
impossible.

The strongest reason for supposing that a take-off is necessary
comes from a consideration of the behaviour of population. The
argument which supports Rostow's view is that a period of very
rapidly rising *per capita* income is necessary to break through the
population barrier. Any *gradual* growth of income per head — the
argument runs — will be absorbed or neutralized by the growth of
population so that what emerges will be a growth of the total economy
but not an increase in income per head.[2] An initial rise in income

[1] W. W. Rostow, 'The Take-off into self-sustained Growth', *Economic Journal*,
LXVI, March 1956 ; *The Stages of Economic Growth* (Cambridge, 1960).
[2] H. Leibenstein, *Economic Backwardness and Economic Growth* (New York,
1957).

lowers mortality (because well-fed people are less liable to disease and their governments better able to spend on public health) and may possibly stimulate fertility. The consequent increase of population causes diminishing returns to natural resources ; and furthermore the proportion of active adults is reduced so that they have to share their income with more dependents. In these ways the effect of the forces making for an increase in income per head is exhausted in an increase in the number of heads at the old levels of income. As a result, there will be an increase in total output, but its composition will remain much the same. The market for new types of goods which rising *per capita* incomes would have provided does not emerge. In addition the increase in population prevents an increase in the supply of savings and, on the demand side, diverts saving towards a widening rather than a deepening of consumption. Where the initial increase in incomes was due to an increase in investment it will tend to be halted. But, the argument continues, there is a limit to the rate of population growth which can be induced by an increase in *per capita* income, and therefore what is necessary is a rapid rise in *per capita* income beyond the point at which it stimulates a rise of population. Such a rise will permit both higher savings and a demand for new types of goods and will thus allow higher growth rates in the future.

How far, in fact, the forces making for growth are diverted into the maintenance of more people at the same income per head rather than devoted to an increase of income per head will depend principally on two factors : on the response of population to a rise in *per capita* income, and on the response of natural resources to the increase of population. If the response of population is slow and that of natural resources rapid, then a gradual increase in *per capita* income is less likely to be frustrated.

So far as Western Europe was concerned there was certainly a marked acceleration of population growth in all the industrializing countries, and it is probable, if not certain in all cases, that *per capita* incomes would have risen more rapidly had population grown more slowly. But there were limitations on the responsiveness of population to increases in *per capita* income. In the early stages of European industrialization, mortality was primarily determined by the occurrence of epidemics, and by the character and incidence of endemic diseases, and these were much more influenced by factors such as climate than by income levels ; moreover, in so far as industrialization was accompanied by urbanization, its initial effect was sometimes to raise mortality. So far as fertility is concerned, conventions about marriage and family size set fairly narrow limits to the rapidity with which it could respond to increasing living standards. Indeed the increase of births is generally to be attributed not to rising living standards but to the transformation of social institutions and especially to the growth of the proletariat and the change in the position of the peasantry : and the full force of this transformation was in general felt only after some decades of growth. In England, for example, population increase did not exceed one per cent per annum until the early nineteenth century by which time the economy had experienced several decades of economic expansion. I shall return to the question of population later ; the only point I wish to make now is that in Western Europe population was not so sensitive to an increase in *per capita* incomes as to create a population barrier which could only be surmounted by a very rapid rise in incomes.

Moreover, the initial increase in *per capita* incomes also made possible higher savings, and in most Western European countries this effect was probably significant, especially as the initial increase in incomes usually took the form of a substantial increase enjoyed by relatively restricted groups. Whatever the unfavourable effects of population increase, they cannot have been exerted by inhibiting saving since in this case rising population would have been accompanied by persistent inflation.

The other side of the equation is the responsiveness of the supply of natural resources. In this case too, in the conditions of Western Europe in the nineteenth century, agricultural output seems to have been fairly responsive to the growth of population, in the sense that there was no systematic tendency during the early stages of growth for the terms of trade to move in favour of agriculture.

Thus, though there was some tendency for an initial increase in *per capita* income to be transformed into a larger population at stationary *per capita* incomes, population growth was rarely so responsive or agriculture so unresponsive as entirely to frustrate the forces behind the initial increase. Moreover, the increase in total population which characteristically occurred in the early stages of most nineteenth-century industrializations was not uniformly unfavourable in its effects on growth. It made investment in transport facilities profitable, it allowed certain industries to achieve economies of scale, and it stimulated invention.

My argument is not that a population barrier to sustained growth never exists but only that it was not a barrier in the nineteenth-century industrializations, and that we cannot deduce from the behaviour of population the universal necessity for a take-off.

Nor does it appear in fact that a 'take-off' has been an invariable feature of economic development. Where reasonably long statistical series of total output are available they show a long climb at varying speeds rather than one unique burst.[1] These statistics may not always be a reliable indication of what happened, particularly when they are smoothed by a moving average, but there seems little doubt that many countries' development took the form of a slow increase over a long period rather than a take-off.

This seems to me evidently true of the growth of Great Britain. Here development took the form of the gradual linking together of a smaller number of points of growth which were initially widely dispersed — dynamic regions surrounded by wide areas which remained for a long time poor and stagnant. In this process three influences were of critical importance. First is the process analysed long ago by Adam Smith : the cumulative extention of the market in conditions of political stability and the increased division of labour which resulted. Superimposed upon this long-term movement were two influences exerted over shorter periods. Most accounts of the development of English industry would not attach considerable importance to the low level of agricultural prices from 1720 to 1750, the effects of which were analysed long ago by Malthus. 'This great increase of command over the first necessity of life did not however produce a proportionate increase in population. It found the people of this country living under a good government and enjoying all the advantages of civil and political liberty in an unusual degree. The lower classes of people had been in the habit of being respected both by the laws and the higher orders of their fellow citizens and had learnt in consequence to respect themselves. The result was that their increased corn wages, instead of occasioning an increase of population exclusively, were so expended as to occasion a decided elevation in the standards of their comforts and conveniences.' The consequent increase of demand for industrial goods was a powerful stimulus to growth in the simple manufacturing industries of the period. The low prices of food in these decades were partly the result of a fall in costs, due to improved agricultural techniques, and to this extent they represent an increase in total income. But to some extent they were the result of a fortuitous succession of good harvests and therefore represent a transfer of income from the producers to the consumers of food, i.e. a redistribution in favour of those with a relatively high marginal propensity to consume manufactured goods.

The third element in the process rose from the relation of the

---

[1] See S. Kuznets, 'Quantitative Aspects of the Economic Growth of Nations : VI. Long-Term Trends in Capital Formation Proportions', pp. 22-3, *Economic Development and Cultural Change*, IX, Number 4, Part II, July 1961.

British economy in the eighteenth century to overseas areas of primary production. In the aggregate these areas had a high propensity to import British manufactures and when the terms of trade moved in their favour they imported increased amounts. Since the major part of their exports to Britain were luxuries, particularly sugar, their propensity to buy British manufactures was greater than that of the English consumers of their products ; and therefore the increase in their demand was not offset by a decline in the domestic British demand for manufactured goods. In the 1750s and again in the later 1780s and 1790s, a rapid growth of exports reinforced the effects of the growth of the domestic market.

It is the increase in demand from these causes, enjoyed over a relatively long period of time, which seems the principal explanation of the acceleration of the growth of the British economy. Once innovation had started in one area or sector, it tended to reverberate through the economy ; the inventions in spinning stimulated improvements in weaving ; the construction of railways called forth improvements in machine tools ; the improvements in one form of transport accelerated the adoption of competing innovations.

Much of the growth which took place elsewhere in the nineteenth century can be explained in essentially similar terms, i.e. by an extension of demand from a small number of original centres of growth. In this process the English demand for imports was obviously of considerable importance. Thus English imports of timber stimulated growth in Scandinavia and English imports of grain stimulated growth in several regions of recent settlement. Professor North has recently argued that the English demand for cotton from the southern states of the U.S.A. was a main influence on the growth of the U.S.A. before the civil war.[1] This type of derived growth was of course marked by wide fluctuations, but one cannot plausibly say that it was characterized by one and only one decisive phase.

These cases of derived growth can in principle be distinguished from those where growth was primarily the result of a conscious attempt to borrow the new industrial technology and where the extension of demand from the more advanced areas played a relatively small part. The distinction is not entirely clear-cut in practice but is a useful working classification. The most evident examples of the second category are those European countries whose resources were broadly similar to those of England, in the sense that they had iron and coal and an existing textile industry to which the new techniques

[1] D. North, *The Economic Growth of the United States, 1790–1860* (1961), p. 189.

could clearly be applied — countries which had lagged behind the English in the early stages of industrialization but not decisively behind.

Now of these two types of growth it is the second that exhibited most discontinuity. As Professor Gerschenkron has argued, the later a country started to industrialize, the more likely its development was to take the form of 'great spurts'.[1] The two cases which have been examined in most detail are Russia's development in the 1880s and 1890s and Italy's in the 1890s. Where a substantial back-log of technology had been built up it tended to be absorbed in a relatively short period of time. In some at least of the European late-industrializers the growth was characterized by a period of very rapid development, longer than the boom phase of a single cycle, but short compared with the critical phases of English development — a period of rapidly rising output per head and considerable structural changes.

Even these great spurts, however, seem to have arisen not from the essential nature of development but from the peculiar role of railways in nineteenth-century development. Railways were the piece of advanced technology most obviously worth borrowing by an area which had lagged behind, and in all such areas the first railway boom was a critical event. Railways had generally to be built as systems rather than piecemeal and therefore they made large demands on local resources. Their construction created a demand for the products of other industries, particularly iron and steel, and also created a sense that the economy was going somewhere and a confidence in the future. Moreover, because the capital markets were compartmentalized the heavy demands of the railway for capital were not met by depriving industry of funds ; railways attracted the savings of the passive investors of the more advanced countries. Nor, since they drew mainly on unskilled labour, did they make serious inroads among the European latecomers on the labour available for industry. A railway boom therefore tended to be a general boom. These remarks apply of course to railway building in almost any country. What was peculiar about such building in the countries which were late to industrialize is that phases of development which in the advanced countries were spread over a long period were compressed into a much shorter interval and had therefore more revolutionary effects.

[1] A. Gerschenkron, 'Economic Backwardness in Historical Perspective' in *The Progress of Underdeveloped Countries*, ed. B. Hoselitz (Chicago, 1952) ; 'The Rate of Industrial Growth in Russia since 1885, *Journal of Economic History*, Supplement VII, 1947 ; 'Notes on the Rate of Industrial Growth in Italy, 1881–1913', *Journal of Economic History*, December 1955.

Not only was the first railway boom important, so was the first subsequent trade revival. Railway booms normally ended in a crash and a severe cyclical depression. The crash itself often cleared away a good many of the obstacles to further advance ; moreover, in the next trade revival, the railway system was usually extended — main lines were completed and subsidiary lines started — and the demands of railway construction, though now less 'maniacal' were still sufficient to give a boost to other industries ; finally, it was usually in this trade revival that the external economies created by the existence of a railway system really began to exert their effects. Where the opportunities so created were considerable, investment continued to rise even during the depression phase of the following cycle and the 'great spurt' emerged, indeed the great spurt might be defined as two successive booms and the absence of a cyclical depression following the second of them.

This is to put the matter in too simple and systematic a form since the precise relation of railway building and the great spurt was influenced by the particular characteristics of each area. Thus in Italy there was considerable railway building from the 1860s on but rapid growth did not set in until the 1890s, possibly because of post-Risorgimento exhaustion, possibly because of the lack of an adequate centre of initiative before the German industrial banks set up in the 1880s. But although there were wide variations in individual cases it would not invalidate the general point : that the discontinuity among the 'late industrializers' was essentially due to the characteristics of the railways, to their attraction for governments, the indivisibilities in their building and the external economies they created.

II. CONDITIONS FAVOURABLE TO DEVELOPMENT

So far we have been concerned with the form of development, with particular reference to the question how far it was characterized by a take-off. What can be said about the conditions which were favourable to development ? The attempts often made to distinguish between the 'pre-conditions' or 'pre-requisites' of growth and growth itself have not it seems to me been fruitful. From most of what are classified as pre-conditions — a supply of entrepreneurs, of skilled labour and finance — prove on examination to be essential manifestations of growth. Moreover, there is scarcely one of these pre-conditions which cannot be shown to have been absent in the case of some acknowledged instance of successful growth. Indeed it is not difficult to cite cases where the absence of what is commonly regarded as a pre-condition proved to be a positive stimulus to growth. Thus, for example, the easy availability of finance and an efficiently organized capital market are commonly ranked as prerequisites. But it was precisely because of their lack of these prerequisites that the late European industrializers developed industrial banks. And the initiative of these banks certainly contributed powerfully to development. An analogous argument applies to the case of another prerequisite — abundant labour — for it was the scarcity and dearness of labour available to American industry in its early stages which stimulated the invention and adoption of labour-saving and mass-production methods. Most of the so-called prerequisites are generalizations from the experience of English industrialization, and countries which were later to industrialize were often able to devise effective substitutes whenever their conditions did not correspond to those of England.

The factors favourable to development are so varied and have historically combined in so many different ways that I see no possibility of isolating a small number of crucial variables. All I propose to do is to consider the historical experience on four points where it seems to me to have particular relevance to the problem of development at the present day.

The first point relates to the initiating factor in development. Here if one has to single out one influence, priority must be given to the widening of markets. Under the pressure of demand, old attitudes were modified, social obstacles to growth were removed, new methods were invented and specific bottlenecks — shortages in entrepreneurial skill, in skilled labour and capital — were overcome.[1] There are it is true some cases where the capacity to respond to widening markets was temporarily checked by some particular shortage. But if one confines one's attention to those areas which were successful in developing in the century before 1914, the main dynamic was provided by increases in market possibilities rather than by independent changes in the supply of factors of production. The shortage it proved most difficult to alleviate was that of entrepreneurs. In countries with a long history of previous growth a supply was readily forthcoming from a wide variety of sources, from landowners, merchants and small masters in industry of the pre-factory type. In a country which lacked an adequate class of indigenous entrepreneurs, but where other countries were favourable, entrepreneurs were imported. The foreign entrepreneurs called forth local entrepreneurial ability ; they stimulated competition and imitation and they provided opportunities for local inhabitants to

[1] See A. K. Cairncross, *Factors in Economic Development* (London, 1962), chapter 13.

acquire industrial techniques and administrative experience. In the successful nineteenth-century industrializations even this shortage proved to be very short-lived, once a stimulus had come from the side of demand.

The increase in market possibilities arose in a variety of ways. The orders from government-sponsored railways — directed to local industry by a tariff or by more direct means — provided a market for nascent heavy industry in a number of countries. In some cases steps were taken to secure for the local industries the domestic market in goods which had previously been imported ; and once a wide range of industries had been established, there were possibilities of a cumulative process of balanced growth. But the possibilities were restricted in the early stages of economic growth, which are the stages of most interest in the present context. This is why in several of the most successful of the older industrializations exports played an important role and in a number of them foreign demand was the source of a substantial part of the initial impetus.

Potential export markets were so much greater than the domestic market that an area which had a marked advantage in a particular line of production could expand on the basis of exports in a way which would have been impossible had it been restricted to the domestic market. The expansion of the export sector drew resources away from sectors of low productivity and underemployment ; it afforded some economies of scale ; it stimulated investment in other sectors ; and where it put pressure on domestic resources it stimulated invention and innovation.[1] The export sector was sometimes a manufacturing industry ; thus cotton textile exports played a crucial role in the early industrialization of Britain and Japan. But the most striking instances of growth ignited by expansion of exports were the regions of recent settlement. In these areas the expansion of exports provided the stimulus for the development of their resources — not only the direct stimulus of an increase in income but the galvanizing effects of foreign contacts ; it also enabled these areas to import the capital necessary for the purpose.

A large part of the economic growth of the nineteenth century can be explained in these terms : by a process of transmission from the more advanced areas and their increased demand for imports. This growth did not necessarily take the form of industrialization. The comparative advantage of some areas was so decidedly in primary production that industry was inhibited, except for the processing of raw materials and the manufacture of the simpler con-

[1] C. P. Kindleberger, 'Foreign Trade and Economic Growth', *Economic History Review*, second series, XIV, No. 2, December 1961, pp. 289-91.

sumer goods. But in most of them the increase in incomes sooner or later generated a local market sufficiently large to support a significant industrial base.

It is often argued that the circumstances which made international trade so effective an engine of growth in the nineteenth century were essentially temporary. Clearly, in principle, the rapid growth of one area is capable of inhibiting as well as stimulating growth in less-developed regions. Were the circumstances, which in the nineteenth century ensured that growth in one region exerted a powerful stimulus over a wide area, peculiar to a bygone phase of growth ?

There is one sense in which nineteenth-century developments were unique, the importance of textile exports as a generator of growth. Both Britain and Japan exported textiles to areas which were sufficiently developed to afford such imports but not sufficiently developed to make their own textiles. This stage of development was from its very nature temporary and it is unlikely that textile exports will ever again be a springboard for industrialization.

The nineteenth-century experience was exceptional in a more fundamental sense. The regions of recent settlement — simply because they were areas of abundant land — had a very decisive relative advantage *vis-à-vis* the industrial areas in the production of foodstuffs. Since they were nearly all in the temperate latitudes, these regions produced many of the same foodstuffs as were produced in the industrial countries. As a result, primary production in the overseas regions expanded not only because industrial incomes were growing but because there was a contraction in the agriculture of the industrial areas taken as a whole.[1] The regions of recent settlement were also particularly attractive to European migrants and these migrants were a powerful factor in the diffusion of advanced technology. Moreover, the fact that these areas were peopled from Europe and shared European institutions facilitated a movement of capital. Most of them also were — again because of the abundance of land — areas where incomes were high from the start and where therefore there was a substantial market for manufactured goods, goods moreover of the same general type as those produced in the older industrial areas.

The poorer, more densely populated and long-settled areas of primary production also enjoyed a greatly increased demand for their products in this period : cocoa, palm oil and ground-nuts from West Africa, for example, coffee from Ceylon, tin and rubber from Malaya. The reaction of these areas did not of course fall into a uniform pattern — there was indeed a great diversity of response —

[1] Cairncross, *op. cit.* p. 197.

but there are certain characteristics common to most of them. The increase in exports from such areas was often considerable ; in the last thirty years of the nineteenth century, for example, the value of Burma's exports increased by an average of 5 per cent per annum. But in general the increase was achieved by an increase in the total resources employed in production and did not lead to cumulative improvements in productivity. It is easy to underestimate the changes in these countries produced as a result of the increase in exports, but as a broad generalization it remains true that in their case international trade as an engine of growth did not generate enough power to stimulate a cumulative expansion.

Why did these economies fail to respond more vigorously to the stimulus of foreign demand ? The answer does not seem to be primarily the absence of overhead capital, for at least some of these areas, e.g. India, were provided with railways and port facilities ; and banking systems were also introduced. One reason that has been suggested was that these areas were not capable of replacing the primary production of the more advanced areas. While Australian and North American wheat expanded at the expense of European wheat production, tropical products had to depend for their market exclusively upon such increases of demand as flowed from the rise of income and change of taste in the advanced economies.[1] This was certainly an important difference. But as we have already said the demand for the products of these undeveloped areas was in many cases increasing rapidly. I am inclined to think that a more important difference is in the technological characteristics of the production functions of the commodities which these areas produced for export. These technological characteristics influenced the extent to which an export sector induced subsequent developments because they determined the nature of the inflows of labour and capital and the distribution of income within a particular region.[2] And it has been plausibly argued that the export of a plantation type commodity was less likely to stimulate growth than a grain crop or the production of livestock, commodities better suited to production by family-size farms. One can think of several other explanations of greater or less force according to the particular area in question. But one explanation which seems to be fairly generally relevant is the persistence in these areas of traditional agrarian structures unfavourable to the transmission of the impulses derived from foreign trade.

The implication of the historical experience on this point is not

[1] Cairncross, *op. cit.* p. 197.
[2] R. E. Baldwin, 'Patterns of Development in Newly Settled Regions', *The Manchester School*, XXIV, No. 2, May 1956.

that export sectors did not still have an important role to play in development but only that they are unlikely to promote vigorous growth without extensive changes in agrarian structure.

This leads to the second point at which historical experience bears with particular relevance on the present : the role of agriculture. All the successful nineteenth-century industrializations were accompanied in their early stages by an increase in agricultural output, and in the countries of Europe — which are the most relevant for the purpose — this increase involved in many cases not only the introduction of new techniques but the transformation of the system of land tenure and ownership. This increase in agricultural output is not to be regarded as a pre-condition of growth, if only because it usually accompanied rather than preceded the acceleration of growth. It is rather a part of the growth which requires explanation, but an essential part in the sense that, with the possible exception of Holland in the seventeenth century, there are no cases of successful growth where unresponsiveness of domestic agriculture was made good by imports of agricultural products. Even Britain and Japan did not begin to rely heavily upon such imports until relatively late in their development.

This coincidence of successful development and agrarian improvement does not seem to be accidental. For agrarian improvement performed certain functions which could not have been performed by imports of food, even if these had been available on very favourable terms. Broadly speaking, it performed four functions. (a) It facilitated the supply of labour to industry ; for even where there was surplus labour, in some sense, in agriculture, before the transformation of the agrarian structure, it was often not available to industry, or was available only on terms which gave small dispersed handicraft industry an advantage in relation to factory industry. (b) The increase in agricultural productivity facilitated investment. Where the government taxed agriculture in order to promote industry, the higher the level of productivity in agriculture the easier the burden was to bear. Where the finance for industrial investment was derived mainly from industrial profits, the increase in agricultural productivity prevented the appearance of the curb on accumulation most feared by Ricardo : the rise in the subsistence wage as a growing population pressed on limited supplies of land. (c) In some cases, the agrarian improvements made possible an expansion of exports which helped to pay for imports of machinery and raw materials. (d) Finally, the increase in agricultural productivity provided a domestic market for industrial goods, and thus a basis for the establishment of new industries.

The relative importance of these functions varied from country to country. Agricultural reform was important in releasing labour for the towns in Russia and Germany ; in Russia and Japan agriculture was taxed to support industry ; exports of raw silk in the case of Japan and grain in the case of Russia earned foreign exchange at a critical stage in their industrialization. But the function of agricultural improvement which seems to have been of the most general importance was the creation of a domestic market for local industries in the earliest and most difficult stages of their growth. The importance of this consideration is most clearly seen in the case of India in the later nineteenth and early twentieth centuries — a country which had many of the prerequisites for industrialization (a railway system, indigenous and foreign entrepreneurs, raw materials ; and abundant labour) but where agricultural production between the 1880s and the 1930s seems to have remained virtually constant in face of a population increase of nearly one hundred million.

The responsiveness of agriculture in Europe was partly the result of the fact that techniques were available, particularly the introduction of artificial grasses and root-crops. These were primarily land-saving improvements ; the open-field system, under which a large part of the cultivatable land was left fallow each year — a system which had developed during the centuries in which Europe was sparsely populated — afforded considerable opportunities for raising the productivity of land by the introduction of new crops. But these crops also raised the productivity of labour, because they reduced the seasonalness of agricultural work.

But there is the additional point that, in some areas, the agrarian structure was well suited for the introduction of the new techniques. In England, particularly, well before the Industrial Revolution, there were relatively large farms, worked for the market by tenant farmers who had considerable supplies of capital. The existence of this type of agrarian structure was one of the factors most favourable to England's economic development. It is true, of course, that this structure was itself the result of the earlier growth in the English economy, but it was of critical importance that, in the eighteenth century, when other conditions were favourable for an acceleration of growth, the process was not halted by an inelasticity in the agriculture sector. Where peasant proprietorship was the dominant form of agricultural enterprise, and even more where share-cropping prevailed, the agricultural sector acted as a damper on growth — not so powerful as to preclude growth where other conditions were favourable, but strong enough to impede growth even, for example, in France and Italy. There are a great many reasons why the economic history of southern Europe was so much less successful than that of the north in the nineteenth century, but one reason is that there was less scope for increasing agricultural productivity. It is not merely that the new root-crops and grasses were not suited to the climate of these regions. Because they were, in general, densely populated in relation to resources there was no reserve of capacity in their agriculture such as was represented by the fallows of open-field agriculture.

There is probably some contrast between the effectiveness of the techniques available for raising agricultural productivity in open-field Europe in the eighteenth and nineteenth centuries and those now available in most contemporary under-developed areas. The introduction of root-crops and grasses promised a large increase in productivity for the expenditure of quite a modest amount of capital. But the technical possibilities for agricultural productivity in contemporary under-developed areas are nevertheless very considerable, in some cases greater than those of nineteenth-century Europe. The really striking contrast is not in the technical possibilities but in the power of the social obstacles to their introduction. In England, the main social obstacles to the introduction of new techniques had been decisively weakened well before the Industrial Revolution : agriculture was in the hands of capitalist tenant-farmers. In countries like Germany and Russia, where serfdom, the fragmentation of holdings and communal rights of ownership or cultivation still survived, the reform of the agrarian social structure was undertaken by the state and pushed through rapidly and with relatively small regard for individual interests, which were sacrificed to the aim of increasing the efficiency of agriculture. Thus the existence of state authority, capable of transforming the agrarian structure and anxious to do so, was one condition of the elasticity of food supplies in the earlier phases of European industrialization.

But not only was the agriculture of most Western European countries unusually responsive to an increase of demand. There were also influences working on population which ensured that the forces making for an increase in *per capita* incomes were not entirely neutralized by an increase in numbers. This is the third point on which history is illuminating.

In most parts of pre-industrial Europe (and in those parts of the world which were settled from Europe) there were powerful and long-established mechanisms tending to keep the increase of population in line with resources. The central part of these mechanisms was the age at marriage and the frequency of marriage. From very early in European history, the social unit was the nuclear family —

the husband and wife and their children — as opposed to the extended family or kinship group. In the nuclear family, the individual man was responsible for the support of his wife and their children. Thus marriage was, from early times, associated with the setting up of a separate household, and there was a strong tendency for a man to marry only when he could support a separate household, and support it at a conventional standard of living well above the physiological minimum. It is not my intention to trace the roots of the nuclear family back into European history, but I am sure that this institution (and the attitudes to marriage which it implied) was of immense importance in European economic development. It provided a rough-and-ready mechanism which limited the power of population growth to depress living standards ; and in favourable circumstances it made it possible to retain permanently an increase in *per capita* incomes. For though such an increase had a tendency to stimulate population growth, it also raised men's notions about the standard of living which they expected before they embarked on marriage.

This is one respect in which European experience differed from those areas, e.g. India and China, where some form of kinship group or extended family prevailed — the family which covered several generations or several degrees of relationship. In these extended families, the obligation to support children was much more widely diffused than in the nuclear family, much less firmly fixed on the father ; and the obligation to have children, in order to extend and continue the group was much more powerful. Marriage was not directly linked, as in Western Europe, to the establishment of a new household ; the newly married couple took their place in the existing family household. As a result the age at marriage in such areas was lower and the incidence of marriage higher than in Europe. This seems to have been a difference of long standing and to provide the principal reason why the living standards of India and China were below those of Europe before the Industrial Revolution. Compared with pre-industrial Western Europe, population growth in countries such as India or China was, therefore, determined more by variations in mortality than by variations in fertility, and for this among other reasons it responded more rapidly to any improvement in economic conditions. There was therefore a much more serious population barrier to economic growth.

There is a second feature of European demographic history which is relevant to economic development. The marked and continuous fall in European death rates did not start until the later nineteenth century, and European death rates did not reach very low levels until the end of that century. By this time many parts of Europe had already experienced a long period of economic growth. Moreover, by the time death rates had reached low levels, birth rates were already falling. The fall in birth rates was, at least in part, the result of attitudes towards family size and marriage which were of long standing and which ensured that when an increased number of children survived their early years, fewer would be born.

By contrast, the under-developed regions of the contemporary world have experienced a much more rapid fall in death rates ; this fall has been the result of foreign medical techniques introduced without major changes in economic standards or in social attitudes ; the fall in death rates has taken place before any fall in birth rates, and without demographic mechanisms which in the advanced countries helped to adjust the rate of population increase by a reduction in birth rates.

Nineteenth-century Europe was favoured by a third exceptional circumstance. Where population growth did press heavily on resources, the existence in the temperate zones of great regions of unsettled and fertile land provided opportunities for migration, and emigration mitigated the fall in living standards in some areas and helped to make possible a rise in living standards in others.

Thus if we ask why, in nineteenth-century Europe, the forces making for an increase in *per capita* incomes were not frustrated by pressure of population the explanation lies not only in the strength of these forces but in three circumstances relating to population : the European family structure ; the timing of the fall in death rates ; and unusually favourable opportunities for emigration. The crucial point seems to be that Western European birth rates, on the eve of industrialization, were already lower than those now prevailing in many under-developed regions, and that a sustained and marked fall in European death rates did not start until the economies of Western Europe had already acquired momentum. It was for this reason that the forces making for an increase in *per capita* incomes — forces which were initially of very modest strength — were able to persist. Attention is generally concentrated on the fact that European industrializations were accompanied by a rapid rise in population — a doubling, for example, in the U.K. between 1800 and 1860, and in Germany in the last seventy years or so of the nineteenth century. But it is perhaps more significant that, as a result of restraints on population growth, population was smaller, in relation to resources, in most parts of pre-industrial Europe than in contemporary undeveloped areas.

Problems in Economic Development

It is clear that a great many circumstances were responsible for the economic development of Europe, but, if I had to select the two most important circumstances, I should choose the two I have just dealt with : the responsiveness of the agricultural sector and the restraints on population growth. It was because of these that the widening of market possibilities was not brought to a halt but stimulated a cumulative process of expansion. This is the justification for supposing, as a very rough-and-ready generalization, that what had previously delayed European development was not so much inadequate productive capacity as inadequate demand. The characteristic situation in contemporary under-developed countries is obviously different. There the existence of inflationary pressures suggests not a deficiency of demand but bottlenecks on the supply side.

The historical record suggests a fourth reflection. Economic development in the last hundred and fifty years has been predominantly confined to Europe and the countries settled from Europe — with the important exception of Japan. Even within this region, development has been limited. The U.S.A., Germany, the U.K., France and Russia accounted for approximately 80 per cent of the world's manufacturing production in 1870 ; though the proportions between them changed greatly, they still accounted for about 75 per cent on the eve of the Second World War.[1] Or, to take another indication, Western Europe and the areas settled from it in North America and Australasia accounted for 57 per cent of the world's incomes in 1938 and for not far short of two-thirds in 1949.[2] Moreover most of the countries which were successful in developing enjoyed *per capita* incomes well above those of the contemporary under-developed areas, even before the classic industrial revolution. Many of them, too, had already exhibited a capacity for technical progress. Thus, for example, progress towards manufacture by interchangeable parts was made in Sweden, France and the U.S.A. *before* these countries felt the impact of the new English technology. France had a strong scientific tradition ; and even in Russia, which was the most backward of the major European countries in the nineteenth century, there were centres of scientific research from the time of Lomonosov. Thus the diffusion of technology which has taken place since the later eighteenth century has only been markedly successful in regions which had some similarities even before the Industrial Revolution.

[1] *Industrialisation and World Trade* (League of Nations, 1945).
[2] S. Kuznets, 'Quantitative Aspects of the Economic Growth of Nations : I. Levels and Variability of Rates of Growth', *Economic Development and Cultural Change*, V, No. 1, October 1956, p. 17.

The only striking exception to the generalization is Japan, which, starting from a state of economic life less developed than that of any European country on the eve of industrialization, grew very rapidly from the 1880s onwards. The growth is the more remarkable since, at least until after the First World War, the producer-goods industries — which played a large part in other late industrializations — were not of much importance. Even in the case of Japan, however, there are certain similarities to the European experience.

In the first place agricultural productivity increased rapidly. Mr. Johnston has estimated that between the 1880s and the 1910s output per head in Japanese agriculture more than doubled.[1] It is true that this increase was achieved within an agrarian structure based on small units of cultivation, and by increasing intensity of cultivation often achieved under the threat of starvation. On the other hand, in this case too the increase in agricultural productivity was preceded by agrarian reforms. The content of the agrarian reforms of the Meiji regime was different from that of the European reforms associated with the abolition of serfdom ; but by converting feudal payments in kind into fixed money payments the Meiji reforms gave Japanese cultivators the means as well as the incentive to increase output. Again, though rice cultivation was the predominant form of agriculture, there is this similarity with the European experience — that technical methods of increasing output were available which were relatively inexpensive in capital (in the Japanese case, improved seeds and fertilizers). This increase in agricultural productivity made a direct contribution to raising the level of income per head ; it released population for employment in industrial pursuits ; it contributed to the growth of the Japanese domestic market ; and it made possible a rapid expansion in exports (especially raw silk) which enabled Japan to import machinery and raw materials.

The economic development of Japan took place in the face of a rapid increase in population. The population doubled between 1880 and 1935. This is, it is true, no greater an increase than in the U.K. in a comparable period of her industrialization, but Japan was very much more densely populated in 1880, in relation to natural resources, than the U.K. in 1800. The development of Japan does therefore show that even a country which is densely populated at the start can generate enough momentum to break through the 'population barrier'. The circumstances which made it possible in this particular case warrant much closer examination than is possible

[1] Bruce F. Johnston, 'Agricultural Productivity and Economic Development in Japan', *Journal of Political Economy*, LIX (1951).

in a short paper. But it must be remembered that even after eighty years of rapid industrialization, real output per head in Japan is still far below that of most of the industrialized countries of Europe. Moreover, the disparity would certainly have been greater had not Japan not begun to exhibit some of the demographic traits of the more industrialized countries.

I have concentrated in this paper on the early stages of economic development rather than on the factors which determine variations in the rate of development of advanced economies. My impression is that, in these early stages the influences which may be broadly defined as social were of greater importance than the strictly economic factors. Some of the most important social influences have not been touched on at all, e.g. those which determined the degree of prestige attached to economic achievement in any given society, the sources from which entrepreneurs were drawn and the amount of optimism they showed.

————

DISCUSSION OF THE PAPER BY PROFESSOR HABAKKUK

Dr. J. Marczewski, in opening the discussion, said that Professor Habakkuk's paper on the historical experience of economic growth had two rare qualities — plenty of substance and an exceptionally condensed form. It would be interesting to test the main findings of the author by confronting them with the experience of a country possessing historical statistics going back to the early eighteenth century. The Institut de Science Économique Appliquée had prepared such statistics for France.

The author's fundamental finding was that population growth had not been sufficiently responsive to increases in income in Western European countries to cause economic growth to be hindered by a demographic barrier. This proposition, unlike that of the 'take-off', was entirely verified by French data for the eighteenth and nineteenth centuries. This could be seen by examining the average annual rates of growth (computed for each ten years from 1700 to 1959) of population, agricultural production and industrial production.

(1) Population and agricultural production increased constantly except during the war periods of 1870, 1914–18 and 1939–45.
(2) Agricultural production increased much faster than population.
(3) Of nineteen observed decades, fourteen were characterized by parallel accelerations and decelerations in both series.
(4) There were five decades where these parallel movements did not occur ; three of them exhibited an acceleration in agricultural out-

put, accompanied by a slowing down in the growth of population. For example, the period 1835–44, when there was an increase in industrialization, and the twenty-year period 1885–1904 following the introduction of agricultural protection in France.

(5) The two cases where deceleration of agricultural production accompanied an increase in the growth of population were those of the great depression of 1873, caused by the development of transport and, hence, competition from overseas, and the years 1904–14, where both movements were so weak as to be smaller than the margin of possible error.

The experience of agricultural production and population in France from 1700 to 1959 showed that the increase in population had not been a barrier in the way of increasing agricultural output, since the growth of the latter was always faster than the growth of population. On the contrary, the growth of agricultural output adjusted itself to the demand for agricultural products, an inelastic demand depending more on the numbers in the population, rather than on their incomes. The increase in incomes per head had, nevertheless, an important role to play. It enabled agricultural production to grow faster than population and it also enabled the growth in production to continue even when the increase in population slowed down.

When the rates of increase of population and industrial production were compared, it was found that:

(1) The increase in industrial production was much faster than either that of population or agricultural output.

(2) Increases in the rate of growth of population go together with accelerations in industrial production. The inverse was only true when very deep depressions occurred (1848, 1873, 1929–32) and in war periods (1870, 1914–18 and 1939–45).

It can be said, therefore, that the growth of industrial production depended upon the income, more than on the numbers of the population. Far from stopping the growth of industrial production the increase in population acted as a stimulus.

Both for agriculture and industry the reaction of production to demand (whether due to an increase in numbers or in incomes per head) was much faster than the reaction of population to increases in income. In fact, this last reaction is hardly perceptible, because the rates of growth of population have been small ever since the eighteenth century. Because of this, French experience does not confirm Professor Habakkuk's second finding that there was a marked acceleration of population growth in Western Europe in all the industrializing countries. In France there was some acceleration of population growth in the middle of the eighteenth century, but the natural, incremental rates remained almost always lower than 0·5 per cent. However, between 1750 and 1880 natural growth rates were higher than the overall average of 0·33 per cent which prevailed from 1700 to 1931. The fact that French experience turns out to be an exception to the author's generalization is not entirely surprising. French demographic evolution is a special case and its peculiarities have not yet been fully explained.

Professor Habakkuk had gone on to claim that there had been no systematic tendency for the terms of trade to move in favour of agriculture in the early stages of growth. In France, however, the terms of trade had moved in favour of agriculture from 1700 to 1905–13. The terms of trade of the agricultural sector do not depend only on population ; they depend first of all upon the relation between agricultural and industrial production. Since industrial production increased faster than agricultural production during the nineteenth century, it was not astonishing that the terms of trade had moved in favour of agriculture, despite the great elasticity of agricultural production relatively to population change. It was only since the beginning of the twentieth century that the tendency had been reversed and the terms of trade began to move against agriculture, probably because of the slowing down of population increase and the relative saturation of demand for agricultural products.

French experience did confirm Professor Habakkuk's findings that there was no evidence of a period of 'take-off' as a necessary concomitant of economic development. The series for the French physical product showed that, since 1720 and up to 1960, there had been continuous development with periods of acceleration (1750–80, 1820–47, 1850–73, 1896–1913, 1920–30 and 1949–62) interspersed with periods of deceleration, but not decline. This referred to long-term trends affecting the decennial averages ; annual data showed a more irregular movement. No evidence for a period of 'take-off' could be found.

Basing himself on British experience, the author had mentioned three main factors in industrialization :

(1) The extension of the home market, as discussed by Adam Smith.
(2) The fall in agricultural prices from 1720 to 1750.
(3) The development of exports.

The extension of the market had certainly been important in France, where, after the wars fought by Louis XIV, a long period of relative peace permitted the growth of internal trade and where the speculations of John Law seemed to have stimulated economic activity.

The second factor, the fall in agricultural prices, did not occur in France. They had generally risen since 1720, although there was a fall in prices at the end of the seventeenth and the beginning of the eighteenth centuries. The third factor, the development of exports, had been very important during the whole of the eighteenth century up to the Revolution, especially trade with French territories overseas.

Professor Habakkuk had put forward an hypothesis concerning the role of trade between Great Britain and primary producing countries. The

latter, he had argued, had a high propensity to import British manufactures, which meant that their imports from Great Britain increased
when the terms of trade moved in their favour. He had further suggested
that the propensity to buy British goods was larger in those countries than
that of British consumers for the imported, luxury exports which they
sold to Great Britain.

There were five questions to ask on this thesis :

(1) Was it well established that the terms of trade had moved in
favour of primary producers ?
(2) Was it necessary to establish the fact to explain the increase in
British exports of manufactured products ?
(3) Had it been proved statistically that the propensity to buy British
manufactured goods was higher in primary producing countries
than the propensity to buy luxury imports in Britain ?
(4) Was it necessary to establish that proposition to explain the
increase in British exports ?
(5) Why should British internal demand have diminished, since,
owing to the multiplier effects of growing exports, the income of
the population was rising ?

The trade mechanism existing between Great Britain and primary
producing countries could be analysed differently. British exports were
growing because Great Britain had a practical monopoly in new manufactured goods corresponding to new needs. This increase in exports
increased incomes through the multiplier process. This growth in
incomes stimulated : (a) the demand for agricultural products, (b) the
internal demand for manufactured goods, (c) imports of luxuries and
(after the repeal of the Corn Laws in 1846) other agricultural products.
Value productivity was higher in industry, so that exports of manufactured goods favoured the growth of industrial employment, whilst the
increase in agricultural imports slowed down the rise in farm incomes and
agricultural prices. The exodus of agricultural labour to industry was
stimulated. It was correct, therefore, to say that foreign trade had played
an important part in the acceleration of British industrialization. However, the mechanism seemed to be somewhat different from that put
forward by Professor Habakkuk.

The author had stressed the important role of railway building in the
industrialization of many countries and this factor had contributed to the
industrial and economic development of France. Rostow had argued
that the 'take-off' in France between 1830 and 1860 had been caused by
railway building. It was not possible to agree with this, since construction had developed considerably only after the law of 1842, by which time
the industrialization of the country was already under way.

In general the French experience of the last three centuries seemed
to confirm the fundamental findings of the author, including his insistence
that it was useless to distinguish between 'growth' and the 'pre-conditions'

to growth. The above observations bore on the economic interpretation of the facts, rather than on the facts themselves.

Professor J. Mertens de Wilmars commented that the paper had been concerned with the particular, historical experience of Europe in the nineteenth century. There were lessons to be drawn from this experience, especially if it was not limited to that of the United Kingdom only.

The first point was clearly the fundamental importance of the population factor. Professor Habakkuk had subtly stressed the effects of population growth on the level of development. This had been done within a broad perspective which did not use the simple, quantitative concept of a 'demographic barrier'. When discussing the population balance Professor Habakkuk had brought in the part played by the European concept of the family as a stabilizing factor on the rate of growth of the population. This involved socio-economic relationships which go beyond the usual discussions of economists in quantitative terms.

The second point concerned the role of agriculture; it had played a determining part in eighteenth-century European development and, whilst not the cause of development, it was one of its fundamental features. Professor Habakkuk was right to stress that there were technical possibilities for increasing the agricultural output in the world which had not yet been employed in under-developed countries. Aid to under-developed countries must not neglect agriculture; apart from reducing the malnutrition prevalent in the world an increase in agricultural incomes would broaden the markets for other goods and increase government revenues. Since three-quarters of the world's population were concerned with agriculture, investment in that sector might play the part formerly played by railways as a stimulant for the development process. Agriculture could also play an educational part in this process. It was not possible for under-developed countries to reach European levels of industrial technique very rapidly. Agriculture provided a good training school in which to learn advanced techniques.

The third point concerned the importance of social factors. Family structure had played a big part in nineteenth-century European progress. It was necessary to think in terms of a social balance, taking into account the social conditions, as well as the resources and population available.

Another essential precondition for development in Europe had been land reform, and this remained true at the present time. It was notable that the author's paper did not attribute decisive importance to capital formation. This was another aspect of the view that economic factors had not been as important as the human and social factors. There were two general lessons that could be drawn :

(1) It was essential to educate humans in rational economic activity. This was best done by modernizing agriculture.

(2) The need to make structural adaptations to the economy was more important than capital investment.

Record of Discussion

Professor G. C. Allen said that the task of the economic historian was to confront the economic theorist with the facts, a task brilliantly done by Professor Habakkuk. He had stressed the fact that political and social changes were more important in promoting development than purely economic factors. Economic development could take place under a variety of institutions, although it required good government and a suitable environment in which entrepreneurs and investment could flourish.

Some people responded better to conditions overseas; in the late nineteenth and early twentieth centuries the Chinese had been good entrepreneurs overseas, but there was little development at home, where governments were bad and policies subject to frequent change.

For many countries foreign trade had been the primary factor in development. This was probably linked with the greater specialization that accompanied such trade and which gave the stimulus to local growth. Malaya, for example, was probably the most specialized economy in South East Asia, but it also had the highest income per head. It was true that such specialization led to risks that there would be fluctuations in income, but such risks could hardly be avoided in any rapidly developing economy.

Agricultural improvements were clearly of crucial importance, not only because of the resultant growth in output, but also because of the new economic attitudes fostered amongst the rural population. The rise in agricultural productivity in Japan before the Meiji Restoration, for example, was associated with the commercialization of agriculture, the appearance of an entrepreneurial class and opportunities for industrial wage employment for which the peasants had been prepared in Tokugawa times.

The early stages in the development of advanced economies had been characterized by few capital intensive industries, although those that existed were important. The most important changes had been small, technical improvements, adopted by firms without major structural changes. The same had been true of Japan in Meiji days, including such items as the building of earth roads and the introduction of simple machines.

Another feature of importance was the need for an efficient division of function between government authorities and industrial enterprises. It was clear that more state interference in the United Kingdom might have helped to raise the technical efficiency of certain industries. The success of the Japanese silk industry could be accounted for in these terms, where standardization was achieved by state intervention.

The role of education in the development process was very mixed; in some under-developed countries workers and producers were conservative and resistant to changes in methods of production. At the same time they quickly learnt to want the consumer goods associated with the more developed economies of the West. The spread of education may stimulate consumption, and inhibit capital formation. In cases where local traditions made consumption habits resistant to outside influences the reverse may be true.

Problems in Economic Development

Dr. M. Moalla argued that it was necessary to ask why economic development had taken place first in the United States and Western Europe. The author had highlighted the factors that explained the origins of such development; historical experience was limited to these cases and a point of primary importance concerned the reasons why the poor countries outside those areas remained poor. Have the richer countries enriched themselves at the poorer countries' expense, or not made it possible for the poorer countries to get richer?

The poverty of some areas could be explained in terms of their colonial condition, both in the past and the present. Customs Unions had kept their economies as primary producers, whilst monetary unions meant that profits were not reinvested locally and capital was lost to metropolitan areas. The process of political domination prevented the growth of a national state which could have initiated economic growth and encouraged structural changes.

Under-developed countries were in an unfavourable economic world, where monopolies were powerful and the terms of trade adverse. International trade relationships should be re-organized and world incomes redistributed by the use of foreign aid. The terms of trade should be modified in favour of primary producers, whilst under-developed countries should be permitted to discriminate in their foreign trade. They should also be helped to form regional economic unions. A new world division of labour was required to alter the present pattern of specialization.

The classical process of development described by economists was not appropriate to the development of under-developed countries which must use a shorter time scale than that of older countries. The level of incomes was so low that it was not possible to lower them further in order to raise a surplus of savings for development. Many of them do not have the advantages of an open export market available to the older, developed countries, and it was necessary to widen internal markets to provide a stimulus for economic growth.

For African countries the change in the structure of the economy was towards a more socialist system, but a version unique to Africa. This was the result of delayed development in the past and it was not clear how far such experiments would go.

Dr. J. Z. Wyrozembski said that Professor Habakkuk had put forward the thesis that a period of 'take-off' was not a necessary feature of economic development. This was disputable, especially in view of the fact that the author's evidence was drawn largely from the historical experience of the United Kingdom; there were doubts as to whether the original argument of Professor Rostow fitted this case.

When considering the factors bearing on the accumulation of capital it was the 'net product' that was important; e.g. the Ricardian idea that accumulation depended upon profits plus rent, rather than on the total National Income. In the first period of industrial expansion, for example, it is quite possible that there was no increase in output in some lines, but merely a substitution of handicraft production by factory products.

There had been important social factors at work in the British period of 'take-off' and Professor Habakkuk had not stressed these sufficiently ; the creation of a large working class and the emergence of a small, rich group were associated with the rapid accumulation of capital and revolutionary technical progress. It was possible to disagree with the author's views on the relationship between the low level of agricultural prices in the United Kingdom between 1720 and 1750 and economic growth. Adam Smith had argued that the increase in agricultural production was the main engine of growth and rent was the main source of accumulation ; Ricardo, on the other hand, hoped for low agricultural prices to keep down rents and thus encourage accumulation. These differing theoretical views reflect the different stages of British economic development.

There seemed to be a confusion concerning the role of railway development as a factor in economic growth. It was necessary to distinguish between its effects on growth and its leading role in the business cycle. Another important factor for capitalist countries had been the system of colonization, which had been largely omitted from the paper.

There were three new developments to take into account when considering the present position of under-developed countries ; these would mean that they would not need to pass through all the phases experienced by older economies. First there was the character of modern techniques, which necessitated large-scale operation. The second was the state of modern economics, conscious of the problems of growth and able to help in an objective way in their solution. The third development was the appearance of socialist countries whose experience would also be relevant. Under-developed countries were unlikely to achieve economic growth without planning, a feature absent from the experience of the older, developed countries.

Professor H. J. Habakkuk, replying to the discussion, said that there had been some argument about the role of foreign trade in economic development ; when considering the British experience it was not certain that it could be explained exclusively in terms of a marked comparative advantage as an industrial producer in the eighteenth century. The political connections with primary producers were important as a source of strength for British exports. When the terms of trade were favourable to primary producers British exports to them increased, so that there were periods of twenty to thirty years in the eighteenth century when the terms of trade were against the United Kingdom, yet the volume of exports increased rapidly. This gave an incentive to innovation because of the strain on productive resources. A full analysis of these developments was long and complicated.

The low prices of domestic agricultural products in the 1720s and 1730s which had been noticed by Malthus, meant that there had been a transfer of real income from farmers to consumers. It was possible that the latter had a higher marginal propensity to consume industrial goods. This would help to explain the increased demand for manufactured goods experienced at that time. On top of this domestic demand, overseas sales increased in the 1740s and 1750s.

There was little evidence that a 'capital bottleneck' had been an important factor in Western European development. It was not the inability to save, but the lack of profitable outlets that is likely to have been more important. The availability of capital is suggested by the ease with which London was rebuilt after the fire of 1666, and the way in which financial institutions responded when the demand for funds increased. There were some imperfections at work in the market for capital but they were probably not very important. The case of present-day under-developed countries was generally very different and there was clearly a capital bottleneck to overcome. Europe in 1800 was different from modern under-developed countries both as regards capital supplies and in the diffusion of entrepreneurial ability. The growth of factory industry had been able to draw on men in rural society, with both technical and business skill, which was not true of present-day under-developed countries.

It was difficult to generalize about the part played by political connections and colonial exploitation. It was probable that it had not been a major cause of the retardation of growth in dependent countries ; certainly customs unions could not be described as a form of exploitation and it was doubtful if the colonial connection resulted in the loss of local capital to the metropolitan country. This was certainly not true of India in the nineteenth century, for example ; railway loans had been raised from British capital because of the reluctance of Indians to invest in such enterprises. There were large parts of the world where it was unreasonable to suggest that colonial exploitation was a cause of under-development. In South Africa, for example, the colonial links had been broken more than a century ago. It was also difficult to attribute capital accumulation in Europe to the wealth obtained by colonization. The economic development of Germany had gone through its critical stage at a time when the country had no colonies. Indian wealth had played a part in English history, but it was not connected with economic development ; it was much more a matter of the influence it had wielded on taste, particularly in art and architecture.

Chapter 7

INTERNATIONAL AID AND GROWTH [1]

BY

GASTON LEDUC
University of Paris

BEING an introduction to a general discussion, this paper obviously cannot, and is not meant to, exhaust the problems of which it treats. There exists a considerable body of literature on the subject, even though it did not begin to engage the attention of economists more than fifteen years ago. The author cannot be absolutely certain that he has not missed one or the other of the studies recently published on this question ; in any case, quotations will be limited to just a few which have a direct bearing on the discussion below.[2]

The discussion itself will be divided up as follows :

First we examine the general principles underlying the problem, define what we mean by 'development aid' and briefly review opposing points of view on its usefulness. Then we discuss the different forms development aid may take, distinguishing between those forms which do not involve money and those which do.

---

[1] Translated from the French by Elizabeth Henderson.
[2] For a general discussion of the subject, see F. Benham, *Economic Aid to Underdeveloped Countries*, Oxford University Press, 1961. Benham's conclusions, as always meritoriously objective, are similar to our own. Two other very useful publications are those by the specialist team of the Center for International Studies at the Massachusetts Institute of Technology : M. F. Millikan and W. W. Rostow, *A Proposal : Key for an Effective Foreign Policy*, New York, Harper, 1956, and M. F. Millikan and D. L. M. Blackmer, *The Emerging Nations, their Growth and United States Policy*, Boston, Little and Brown, 1961. See also Eugene Staley, *The Future of Underdeveloped Countries*, revised edition, Council on Foreign Relations, New York, Praeger, 1961 ; and Henry G. Aubrey, *Coexistence, Economic Challenge and Response* (in collaboration with Joel Darmstädter), National Planning Association, Washington, 1961.

For the most recent relevant statistics, see United Nations, *International Economic Assistance to the Less Developed Countries*, Report of the Secretary General to the Economic and Social Council, 30th Session, United Nations, New York, 1961 ; and two reports by the Organization for European Economic Co-operation, *The Flow of Financial Resources to Countries in Course of Economic Development*, of which one, covering the period 1956–59, was published in April 1961, and the other, covering the year 1960, was published by the new OECD in February 1962. The figures of these two reports do not always tally with those of the United Nations.

Special mention should be made of a recent wide-ranging study : P. N. Rosenstein-Rodan, 'International Aid for Underdeveloped Countries', *Review of Economics and Statistics*, May 1961, pp. 107-38. We shall repeatedly have occasion to quote this study and the practical proposals at which it arrives.

Thirdly, we go in some detail into the effects of various forms of financial aid and discuss its effectiveness.

In conclusion, we consider the question of how it would seem desirable and possible to improve the present state of affairs and venture some predictions on the future of international development aid.

I. GENERAL PRINCIPLES

What are we to understand by 'international aid' on the one hand, and by 'development aid' on the other? The answer is not nearly as simple as might appear at first sight. The complex reality underlying these concepts is no doubt responsible for the persisting differences of opinion with regard to the usefulness of aid.

Let us take the three points separately.

A. What is International Aid ?

The word aid seems to us to be susceptible of a wide range of interpretations, beginning at one extreme with everything that serves the purpose at hand, down to the restricted meaning of someone making a free gift, or an unrequited sacrifice (unrequited at least on the strictly economic plane).

If we accept the first interpretation, we would ultimately have to consider as 'aid' every contribution, with whatever object and in whatever form, which somehow ends up by promoting the desired development — or at least which is made with this intention, even if the final result is not exactly as foreseen.

From the point of view of the beneficiary we would have to distinguish between aid involving a liability and free aid, and from the point of view of the donor, between interested and disinterested aid.

But we do not wish to press the point. The best philosophical approach to the question seems to us to make, with François Perroux, a distinction between *gift economy* and *trade economy* — two expressions and concepts which have gained wide currency.[1]

Strictly speaking, the pure gift involves no immediate economic counterpart. It does not rest on any interested calculation. In practice, this means that we can describe as genuine aid only outright grants in money or kind, to some extent such partly commercial transactions as the sale of commodities below market price or their purchase above market price, or yet loans at zero or privileged rates of interest.

[1] We quote, once and for all, the two fundamental works of François Perroux which are relevant to our subject : *Économie et société — Contrainte, échange et don*, Paris, Presses Universitaires, 1960, and *L'Économie du XXᵉ siècle, ibid.* 1961, especially the third part.

It must be admitted, however, that this definition leaves ample room for doubt as to what is or is not 'aid' in any particular case. Let us recall that United Nations experts, for example, consider as genuine aid only official donations and long-term loans of exceptionally long terms, with exceptionally low interest rates and in most cases providing for deferred interest and principal payments. But what are we to make of certain categories of operations, like those of the International Bank for Reconstruction and Development? These are not grants, but their terms are certainly more favourable than could be obtained on the international capital market and at least to this extent they therefore assume the character of aid. An even more positive view would obviously have to be taken of the new International Development Association, which is authorized to lend risk capital at low interest and for very long maturities, with the possibility of repayment in the debtor country's currency and even of conversion into outright grants.[1]

To sum up this first point, we would say that the precise delimitation of the field of aid is often simply a question of convention. It is comparatively easy to say when aid is free, but very much less so to say what part of any transaction involving some counterpart is to be described as aid and what is not.[2]

B. What is Development Aid?

The assistance rendered by economically advanced to less advanced countries need not necessarily have the purpose of promoting (economic and social) development.

---

[1] Other doubtful cases are export credits in various forms and export credit insurance. Advanced countries export at market prices to developing countries and the export credit facilities in question are granted to the exporters. Now, it may be argued that without these facilities the exports would either not take place at all or would be more expensive for the buyers. In this sense export credit falls under the description of international aid. But since it is usually the exporters who ask for help from their own governments, the aid is often purely domestic or, at best, has a double purpose.

Barring exceptions, everything that concerns private transactions (sale and purchase of goods and services, capital investment) evidently does not belong to the field of aid properly speaking. The best-known exception is that of voluntary contributions to the Israeli government's various Funds, and then there are the activities of a number of private missions and foundations, many of which do splendid work in the United States, for example.

[2] In opposition to 'aid' one might speak of 'exploitation' in the Marxist sense. We might add in this connection that the concept of aid seems even more difficult to define in the mutual relations of collectivist economies or in those of communist countries with non-communist under-developed ones. The reason is that in these cases we have no market as a reference base, though admittedly the so-called free world's markets are often also singularly imperfect. See on this point H. G. Aubrey, *op. cit.*, and also François Perroux, *La Coexistence pacifique*, Paris, Presses Universitaires, 1958, vol. 2.

It is conceivable that poor countries may be given purely charitable aid, designed simply to relieve human suffering. This might be described as relief or passive assistance in the elementary form of sharing one's piece of bread, as François Perroux says. We might also, especially in the field of international relations where charitable purposes are of rather recent date, assign to the concept of aid certain purposes which, while not directly of an economic nature, are not altogether disinterested. A case in point is military aid. It is true that it is sometimes hard to draw a strict dividing line between what is economic properly speaking and what belongs to the field of international diplomacy and strategy. Obviously, the military value of an allied country is to some extent a function of the soundness of its economy, and the leader of the alliance will therefore have to help the allies economically, quite apart from any purely military considerations. This is what is known in official United States usage as defence support.

It is also possible that assistance designed to promote development may be given to under-developed countries for the ultimate purpose of preventing such social and international disorders as might follow from the perpetuation of these countries' poverty or a widening of the gap which divides their standard of living from that of the richer countries. In plain words, the purpose might be to prevent the uncommitted nations from swinging right over into one or the other of the two camps which today face each other in what is perhaps no longer the cold war, but does still fall somewhat short of peaceful co-existence.

But here again we do not wish to press the point.[1] What we have to do here is to consider the economic purposes of aid and more specifically those which have a direct or indirect bearing on economic development. The pursuit of these purposes may be linked with motives of self-interest on the part of the donors, but it is equally possible for aid to developing countries to be considered as an end in itself, in a spirit of justice and solidarity among nations.

But here we need to add a few clarifications.

(1) We say as a matter of principle that the purpose of aid is 'development'. Some speak in this context of 'growth'. It would take up too much space to enter into a full terminological analysis here, but we would say that to our way of thinking economic development implies growth, but goes beyond it. As we have explained elsewhere,[2] we consider economic development as an 'overall social

---

[1] See, again, H. G. Aubrey, *op. cit.*, and all the works of François Perroux cited in previous notes.
[2] G. Leduc, *Économie du développement*, Paris, Cours de droit, 1961–62, Chapter II and, for the general questions treated in this report, the whole of Chapter XVII.

phenomenon' with many facets. But there could be no development without economic growth, the essential feature of the latter being an increase of the real domestic product at a pace and in a manner such that national income per head rises continuously even in the presence of rapid demographic growth.[1] With these reservations, we may on occasion use development and growth as interchangeable terms.

(2) We suppose that what we are to discuss here is not simply how to start a regular process of development or growth, which would imply aid towards the 'take-off', to the extent that this concept may be applicable.[2]

The kind of aid we have in mind has rather wider purposes. It is not merely a matter of helping countries to break out of the vicious circle of stationary poverty but, once the growth process has started, to sustain them by making the process as fast and continuous as possible (we deliberately refrain from introducing the notion of acceleration).

Two points need to be made in this connection.

(a) How important is it that the growth process should be fast ? This is a debatable question. It is surely, at least, desirable that the rate of growth of backward countries should quickly come to equal that of the advanced countries (say, an annual compound rate of increase in real *per caput* income of 2 to 3 per cent) and then to exceed it. This would mean that, in relative terms, the gap between the standard of living in 'poor' and in 'rich' countries would cease to widen and that the absolute difference between real *per caput* income would gradually diminish, until one day (in what year ? what century ?) standards of living even out at least approximately.

It is reasonable to assume that the size of foreign aid required is a function of the desired speed of development. The quicker one wants to go, the larger and more prolonged will indispensable foreign aid have to be.[3]

(b) Should a time limit be set to development aid, in so far as it is not solely concerned with the take-off ? This, too, is a question which can be debated — and we hope it will be. The authors

[1] The fact that the improvement is due to an increase in the aggregate domestic product eliminates, to our mind, the effect of a reduction of the population on *per caput* income. The demographic aspects of the problem are numerous and complex, and we do not wish to discuss them here.

[2] See *The Economics of Take-off into Sustained Growth*, edited by W. W. Rostow, 1963. (Proceedings of the International Economic Association's Round Table at Konstanz in 1960.)

[3] This is easy enough to show by means of even quite elementary growth models. These models are so well known that we did not think it necessary to reproduce any of them here, let alone to add another to an already fairly lengthy list.

working at the Center for International Studies at the Massachusetts Institute of Technology, for instance, hold that foreign aid should be continued until the beneficiary countries are able to ensure continued growth by their own means — until, in other words, growth becomes 'self-sustaining'. If we are to believe Paul Rosenstein-Rodan, this may be a matter of fifteen years and the numerical proposals he makes in the study we quoted earlier are based on this assumption. If under-developed countries are to be helped to help themselves, Rosenstein-Rodan proposes a three-stage programme of five-year periods, beginning in 1961 and continuing until 1976. It is interesting to note that the fifteen-year period seems to apply very widely, with the exception of only a few countries like Rhodesia, Mexico, Israel, Trinidad, Jamaica, Hong Kong and Singapore. Quantitatively, aid in the strict sense would be higher in the second than in the first five-year period and would then fall off during the third one. Beyond 1976, private investment flows, which are assumed to increase steadily from one period to the next, would be sufficient to cover the full external needs of a good many countries, including Colombia, Argentina, Mexico, Chile, and even India and Pakistan.[1]

Projections of this kind are, of course, bound to be highly hypothetical. It is much to the credit of their author to have tried to work them out. We shall see later that Rosenstein-Rodan believes that the younger developing countries will need more foreign capital at an advanced stage of their development than at the time of take-off proper. Later on they will again need less and less, in the measure as private and public saving can gradually take over from foreign aid first (public funds) and eventually even from private foreign investment. No doubt, if the latter were to continue, development would be speeded up.

(3) By development we mean development of the backward country as such, within its geographical frontiers, with all the natural and human resources on the spot, but without any implication at all of autarky or isolation. All we assume is that economic progress is possible within the national territory of the country concerned and that progress promises to improve the standard of living by means other than simple emigration. This means that we do not need the somewhat confused and debatable notion of population optimum and that we adopt, as it were, a pseudo-Ricardian approach,

[1] See P. N. Rosenstein-Rodan, *op. cit.*, Table 1, and Appendix Tables 4-A and 4-B. The author adds that it seems likely that none of the Middle East countries will reach the stage of self-sustaining growth within the period 1960–75, except possibly Iraq with its mineral wealth. In southern Europe, Yugoslavia ought to get that far by about 1966 and Greece shortly before 1970.

implying a certain degree of rigidity in the international movement of factors of production — or at any rate of labour, not of capital.[1]

(4) What has to be done, then, is to mobilize the country's own resources and to make the best of its own productive potential — it being understood of course, that any foreign contributions apt to raise that potential are, as a matter of principle, to be regarded as desirable. This is an aspect of the problem to which we shall have occasion to return. For the moment we would merely make the point that these contributions need not necessarily take the form of capital goods, but may, speaking in non-monetary terms, just as well be consumer goods, provided their use ultimately raises the productive potential. A case in point would be aid in the form of subsistence goods permitting the release of a certain quantity of domestic resources from the food production sector and their diversion to the capital goods sector.[2]

C. *Is International Development Aid Necessary ?*

The question whether or not international development aid is necessary is a controversial one, but we do not intend to discuss it here at length.

Authors of liberal complexion, like Brandt, Friedman and Röpke, hold that the best way in which advanced countries can come to the aid of economically under-developed ones is to remove all obstacles to the normal course of business relations in the framework of a competitive free-enterprise economy. This applies both to trade and to capital movements. In this system of thought the advanced countries should play their part actively and loyally, and if they do, their prosperity will progressively spread to the world at large.

This is the theory of transmitted (and induced) growth.

In the view of these same authors, any aid scheme as such implies dangers both on the economic plane (waste, adverse effects on the prosperity of the donor nations) and on the political one. In so far as aid is, on principle, inter-governmental, it is denounced as a means of strengthening, or even of introducing, government intervention in the economy of the recipient countries and so leading, by more or less insidious roads, to collectivist planning.[3]

---

[1] We do not need to take too literally Ragnar Nurkse's well-known saying that 'capital is made at home'. Capital may very well come from outside, and this is precisely one of the essential purposes of aid. Of course, the capital then has to be located and to function 'at home' in the beneficiary countries.

[2] This may be important in populous countries with much disguised unemployment. See the excellent analysis in Ragnar Nurkse, *Problems of Capital Formation in Underdeveloped Countries*, Oxford, 1953, Chapter II.

[3] See especially what Milton Friedman has to say in his article in the *Yale Review* of June 1958, pp. 500-16.

The advocates of aid, including Perroux, Rosenstein-Rodan, Myrdal and others, naturally take a very different view. Without entering into details, we would mention three salient points of their argument.

(1) The ordinary foreign economic relations of a 'trade economy' are held to be insufficient for the creation of the indispensable conditions of a successful take-off and of sustained and durable growth.

(2) It is held to be impossible to count on the 'normal' functioning of frequently imperfect markets for pulling the under-developed countries along in the wake of the advanced ones. We recall in this context Myrdal's theory of cumulative effects.

(3) It is held that the poor countries cannot make the necessary 'big push' or 'minimum critical effort' towards their own take-off without considerable help from outside.

II. THE FORMS OF DEVELOPMENT AID

There are many ways of 'aiding' one's neighbour, even when governments or countries are concerned and especially when it is the intention of the donors to promote the development of the recipients. We shall merely make a brief and by no means exhaustive survey of the different possible forms of such aid. We shall establish two broad categories : aid not involving — or not primarily involving — monetary instruments, and financial aid properly speaking.

This distinction is admittedly rather formal. Non-monetary aid procedures necessarily have some sort of monetary effects, and conversely, what matters to the recipient is not the cash flows of monetary aid but the use to be made of them by transforming them into real flows. Nevertheless the distinction seems useful for purposes of exposition.

A. Non-monetary Forms of Aid

We shall consider three forms of non-monetary aid : technical aid or assistance, commercial aid and what we shall call aid in kind, meaning the unrequited supply of goods and services.

(1) *Technical Aid or Assistance.*[1] Technical assistance is certainly most useful and the time is long past when certain countries, jealous of their technical superiority, rejoiced in the ignorance of others and tried to perpetuate it by restrictive legislation concerning the secrecy

[1] See Maurice Domergue, *Technical Assistance, Definitions and Objectives, Means and Methods, Conditions and Limitations*, OECD, November 1961. (Translator's note : English title not verified.)

of manufacturing processes. The general question of the transmission of knowledge, of the propagation of innovations, of the communication of ideas and procedures in the wider sense, is today recognized as one of the most important problems of development.

It would indeed seem to be a question of absolute priority, in so far as no nation can aspire to progress unless it is in a position to become the principal agent of the changes to be brought about.

To our way of thinking, technical aid or assistance really has three separate fields of application.

(a) Individual education in the widest sense. Aid to this end might be described as 'cultural aid',[1] since its scope is not merely technical but encompasses the mobilization of all the personal resource of the individual as an agent of the desired development. Education is, like health, seen as one of the essential aspects of the formation of 'human capital' and as genuine 'investment'.[2]

(b) The training of specialists in all those branches of activity, including in particular also research, which can make an immediate or remote contribution to development. This is the purpose of technical assistance properly speaking in all the multiple forms which it takes today and which we obviously cannot analyse in detail here.

(c) The transmission of techniques themselves, which is quite indispensable for any improvement in productivity, or in other words, for the more rational use of available resources. The problems involved in this are very delicate,[3] not least because the transmission of techniques has many commercial aspects. It involves questions of royalties and patents, and more generally of organizational procedures which private companies have a perfectly good right to regard as elements of their competitive strength and therefore as a negotiable asset. It might well be worth exploring Svennilson's idea of setting up a private or semi-public company or corporation for the purpose of co-ordinating the transmission of know-how on the part of private firms.

---

[1] As proposed by Maurice Domergue, *op. cit.*

[2] We recall Unesco's numerous publications on the subject, and especially the proceedings of the Conference of African States on the Development of Education in Africa, Addis Ababa, May 15-25, 1961. See also the author's own report to that Conference, entitled 'L'Éducation en tant que facteur fondamental du développement économique et social de l'Afrique', Annex IV of the Final Report.

The concept of 'human investment' is somewhat ambiguous. It is sometimes used — wrongly, to our way of thinking — to describe capital accumulation by means of labour alone.

[3] These problems were analysed by Ingvar Svennilson in his report to the International Economic Association's Round Table at Gamagori, Japan, April 2-9, 1960, on 'The Transfer of Industrial Know-How to Non-Industrialised Countries'. The question obviously assumes different aspects in collectivist countries.

(2) *Commercial Aid*. To speak of commercial aid might seem a contradiction in terms, as implied by the well-known slogan 'trade, not aid'.[1] First heard at the time of the Marshall Plan, this formula is now applied to development aid and is intended to represent trade (including private investment) as the only normal way for advanced countries to be of active, effective and durable assistance to less advanced ones.

This harks back to one of the arguments of the liberal school of thought : provided trade be as free as possible and unhampered by 'artificial' intervention, the developing countries should have no difficulty in getting hold of as much foreign exchange as they need, thanks to the inflow of private capital and above all to the sale of their products (primary products of even manufactures) at 'normal' prices on properly functioning foreign markets.

Trade is, therefore, seen as the most reasonable way of coming to the aid of developing countries.[2]

But this distinction between trade and aid seems to us a bit laboured. Surely, the so-called commercial relations between advanced and less advanced countries can be influenced, and there is no reason why they should not be influenced in the direction of aid to certain categories of trade partners. Generally speaking, it would seem that anything done either to improve the terms of trade for developing countries, or to widen their outlets, or to give them special facilities in the supply of goods needed for development — that all this should be classed as 'aid'. Let us briefly recall the most widespread practices in this category.

(a) Take first the conditions of sale for the commercial exports of advanced to under-developed countries. There are many things a supplier can do to ease the task of his poorer buyers : he can charge lower prices, grant credit facilities, furnish technical assistance alongside with the goods, help in installing plant and equipment and so on and so forth. He may even distribute certain goods free or almost free — a practice on which we shall have more to say under (c) below.

---

[1] Formulating our preferences the other way around, we could also demand *aid, not trade*. Interestingly enough, such a preference is occasionally enounced by certain producers in developed countries who, afraid of competition from developing countries, would rather 'help' them by any means other than opening the domestic market to the importation of the developing countries' products.

[2] In collectivist economies the question appears in a different light. When international economic relations are a government monopoly, it becomes rather difficult to distinguish aid from trade. The aid rendered by the Soviet Union and the People's Democracies to developing countries most often takes the form of supplies in kind or loans repayable in kind, at agreed rates of exchange. Financial loans generally stipulate interest of $2\frac{1}{2}$ per cent a year. These practices are a mixture of trade and aid.

Then there are export credits, with or without insurance and with or without government guarantees. Surely, there is an element of aid in these practices which, according to OECD and United Nations estimates, involved something like half a billion dollars in 1960. Nevertheless, it would be exaggerated to speak simply of charity in this case.[1]

(b) An analogous form of aid consists in the manipulation of the conditions at which advanced countries buy the products of developing ones.

Much could be done, for example, by easing the tax burden [2] on the consumption of certain tropical products, like coffee, cocoa or bananas, which are the main source of foreign exchange earnings for the exporting country. Or one could think of tariff or import quota adjustments on the part of the buyer country — with respect not so much to primary products which generally (though with a few notable exceptions) are free of import duty anyway, but to the manufactures with which a few developing countries are beginning to compete on the markets of advanced nations.

We might even ask whether it would not really be logical for the advanced nations to open their markets to the import of elementary industrial products from developing countries and so to transform their own production structure, while leaving the developing countries free to protect on their domestic markets the nascent industries or those, at any rate, which are not as yet established firmly enough to be freely exposed to international competition. This seems to us to be one of the most difficult problems which the industrialization of developing countries has already introduced into international economic relations.[3]

Along the same line of thought, we might mention anything the advanced countries can do to help stabilize or even raise the prices of primary or base commodities. This subject will be treated separately at the Conference and we shall not trespass upon it here, even though we must refer to it. In some respects and under certain conditions, the mere participation of advanced countries in international stabilization schemes for primary commodities might already be described as development aid. The aid aspect becomes a

---

[1] There exist also proposals to extend insurance to investment proper. See International Bank for Reconstruction and Development, *Multilateral Investment Assurance. A Staff Report*, March 1962.

[2] In Western Germany, the proceeds of consumption taxes on coffee provided the Exchequer for a long time with revenue far in excess of the whole cost of direct aid to developing countries.

[3] See Jean Royer, 'La Structure économique des pays industriels est-elle compatible avec les besoins de développement économique des pays neufs?', *Économie appliquée*, October/December 1959, pp. 483-520.

good deal clearer in the case of stabilization schemes for export receipts and even more so when the declared purpose is a steady and continuous rise of export receipts, that is to say, of the product of export volume times price. However, schemes of this kind are not always harmless and there is nothing to prove that they necessarily contribute to continuous, rapid and balanced growth.[1]

(c) Another way in which advanced countries can come to the aid of developing ones is to give them easier access to trading, or economic, communities within which the handicaps resulting from small (because poor) domestic markets can be eliminated at least in part. The play of complementarity and substitutions, together with the effects of external economies in a 'common market' of a certain size might well call forth new activities capable of assuming the role of development poles. However, the association in one and the same economic community of countries at very different levels of development obviously entails the danger that the weak may be crushed in certain fields by the strong. Caution is therefore indicated if one wants to avoid setbacks or even complete stagnation, the only escape from which would be massive population transfers to the richer zones of the new community. It is a complex problem which we cannot discuss further in the limited space at our disposal. To leave no misunderstanding on the point, we would simply add that any new grouping involves adaptations, and that the conditions of transition are also a field for rational aid.

(3) *Aid in Kind.* Aid in kind takes the form of free supplies, or supplies at a privileged price, furnished by richer to poorer countries to facilitate the latter's economic development.

Very different supplies enter into this description, in particular supplies of goods and services, the latter being akin to technical assistance, which has already been discussed.

They may take the form of technically integrated units, such as whole factories which the donors instal and often initially run in the recipient country.[2] They may, on the other hand, also take the form of a wide range of separate goods, such as machinery, trucks, spare parts, or else, say, books and pharmaceutical products needed for the 'human investment' of which we have spoken.

Are supplies and services of this kind to be considered as 'aid'

---

[1] We shall not here enter into the terminological intricacies of 'balanced' or 'equilibrated' or 'harmonized' growth, on which see the well-known works of Perroux, Scitovsky, Nurkse, Hirschman and others.

On the general problem of commodity stabilization, see the recent United Nations report *International Compensation for Fluctuations in Commodity Trade*, New York, 1961.

[2] There are several examples of this in aid to India since the beginning of her development plans.

only if they quite plainly contribute to capital accumulation? What are we to think of supplies of consumer goods, and especially of food? The question is important, because it involves the use of agricultural surpluses for development purposes.[1] It is also another complex problem.

On the principle of the matter there can surely be no disagreement. Is it not paradoxical, not to say scandalous, that some countries have chronic difficulties in getting rid of their food surpluses, while elsewhere whole peoples suffer hunger?

The case of the United States is significant. It is well known that the famous Public Law No. 480 was voted by Congress in the intention of linking agricultural support policy with the reorganization of American aid in kind to developing countries.

This practice has real advantages both for the suppliers and the recipients. The former have the double benefit of getting rid of their troublesome surpluses and of succouring the hungry. The latter can get for nothing or for a privileged price (which, moreover, can be paid in local currency without any transfer problems) commodities which, if they are food, permit better nutritional balance or, if raw materials (e.g. cotton) provide support for nascent domestic industries.

But there are, admittedly, also certain dangers. For the industrial countries, the question arises whether it is economically rational to encourage chronic surplus production. For the recipient countries, the gift of the surpluses may not always be an unadulterated blessing. Leaving aside the fact that this sort of dumping competition may hurt the interests of other producers of the commodity in question, it is not quite so certain that these practices really are very useful for development. What the countries concerned need most is capital goods and a chance to accumulate capital. Is the supply of agricultural surpluses the best means to this end? Is it not more in the nature of relief than of genuine development aid? The answer has to be qualified, it seems to us. To feed an undernourished population does not necessarily induce it to produce more, but may raise its working potential and enable it to release some resources for investment — in which case the surpluses fulfil the function of a genuine subsistence fund.[2]

[1] See the recent study of the Food and Agriculture Organization of the United Nations, *Development through Food — A Strategy for Surplus Utilization*, Rome, 1961 (revised edition, Rome, 1962), and Professor Jean Valarché's introductory report to the Congress of French-speaking Economists, May 28-29, 1962, 'Le Problème des excédents agricoles', *Revue d'économie politique*, 1962, pp. 131-72.

[2] This is why P. Rosenstein-Rodan, *op. cit.*, proposed that only two-thirds of the proceeds of surplus sales should be considered as investment aid, while the remaining third should be regarded as aid to consumption. The author notes that

To conclude this brief discussion of non-monetary forms of development aid, we would stress again how extremely difficult it is to distinguish in practice between free aid and assistance associated with varying degrees of self-interest. In most cases, it would be better to speak of *aid through trade*, rather than to evoke the contradictory images of *trade, not aid* or *aid, not trade*. The two generally go hand in hand, as Benham astutely observed, with the sole difference that trade generally furnishes the income out of which, via saving, capital can be created, while aid may bring capital directly, either in kind or through monetary channels.

B. Financial Aid

The apparent, if not real, distinction between aid and trade has its place equally in the financial field. If funds are supplied by private capitalists, who lend or invest on their own account, we can hardly speak of aid in the strict sense of the word. The *quid pro quo* is evident. The funds are supplied in view of some direct advantage — interest or profit, not to speak of eventual repayment. May we regard as aid, then, only outright grants and possibly privilege loans on better terms than could be obtained on the international capital market ? In that case the concept of financial aid would be limited to the operations of government and a few exceptional others, such as the International Bank.

(1) *Incentives for the International Movement of Private Capital.* Barring exceptions, private international capital flows are part of trade, not aid. They cannot be moved by anything but self-interest, which does, of course, not prevent the recipient countries from benefiting from them, especially as regards growth requirements.

There was a time, as we all know, when private capital flows represented the normal form of international investment. They still play an important part in the relations between capitalist countries, though today more in the form of direct than of portfolio investment. We know furthermore that since the last war the major part of private international investment was directed to the mineral oil sector and that the bulk of the capital came from the United States.

To give an approximate idea of the order of magnitude involved, we would mention that, according to a recent OECD report, in-

even with this reduction one-fifth of total aid to developing countries could be furnished in the form of surpluses and that in the United States two-thirds of surplus sales may make us as much as 30 per cent of aid to developing countries. The proportion of $\frac{2}{3} : \frac{1}{3}$ seems somewhat arbitrary ; why not $\frac{1}{2} : \frac{1}{2}$, or $\frac{3}{4} : \frac{1}{4}$?

dustrial countries in 1960 placed 2·4 billion dollars of private capital in developing countries under the heading of 'new loans and net investment'. This compares with the 4 billion dollars or so of public funds similarly made available through grants or privilege loans, as we shall see presently.

As regards private capital flows, the aid element can, in our view, have its source only in the originating country, in the form of incentives to invest in backward countries for the purpose of promoting and speeding up their development.[1]

These incentives may be of different kinds. They may consist of unilateral measures, such as tax reduction or exemption for foreign investment income and the profits of the foreign branches of business companies, or guarantees covering certain risks incurred by the investors. The risks covered may, in turn, be of a political or monetary nature, or even of an economic nature to the extent that losses are due to events beyond the control of those responsible for the management of the investment in question. There is an interesting body of legislation on this subject, for instance, in the United States and in Germany.

Guarantees of this kind may also be incorporated in bi- or multi-lateral agreements concerning, for instance, the elimination of double taxation, the creation of a system of joint liability, the exchange of information on investment opportunities, etc.[2]

(2) *Public Funds.* In the past, it was rare for governments to move public funds from one country to another, but today the flow of such funds from advanced to developing countries is the predominant form of international development aid. We shall have more to say later on the difficulties of measuring these flows statistically. For the moment, all that interests us is the relative part played by transfers of this kind in the aggregate flow of capital movements towards the developing countries. According to a recent United Nations study, as much as 63 per cent of the total of these movements during the period 1951–55 were accounted for by inter-governmental transfers of funds, while the percentage dropped to 58 during the

---

[1] These incentives exercise a sort of push on the lender country's capital to go abroad.

Obviously this push will be more effective if it is accompanied by a pull emanating from the borrowing countries. But this is no longer a matter of international aid. More detail on the means employed to encourage international flows of private capital will be found in the reports the United Nations regularly publish on the subject.

[2] Insurance may be possible against some of the risks inherent in foreign investment. See footnote 1, p. 149.

Another way to promote the international flow of private capital is for the creditor country to concede certain monetary facilities to the debtor country to enable it to transfer interest and profits, or even to repatriate capital.

period 1956–59.[1] In the total of public funds during the latter period, the share of grants was

$$\frac{34}{34+23} = \frac{34}{57}$$

that is, roughly 60 per cent ; loans accounted for the remaining 40 per cent.

Apart from the question of their effectiveness, to which we shall devote the whole of the next section of this report, many other problems arise in connection with these inter-governmental capital flows. For the sake of brevity, we shall merely mention a few of those which we believe to be especially important and deserving of careful attention.

(a) Should public funds be given or lent ? We have just seen that on the average of the period 1956–59 the ratio of grants to loans (with respect to public funds) was roughly 6 to 4.[2]

The choice between grant and loan depends on several determinants : the psychological attitude of the owner and the recipient of the capital concerned, the purpose for which it is to be used, the chances or otherwise that a loan can be repaid — quite apart from questions of the rate of interest, conditions of repayment and so on. The Soviet Union, for example, seems to prefer loans to outright grants, but accepts very low interest rates (generally 2·5 per cent).

It may well be that Benham is right and that the course of wisdom lies in a judicious combination of loan and grant. The level of

---

[1] The source of these figures is Table 9 of the United Nations publication *The International Flow of Long-Term Capital and Official Donations, 1951–59*, New York, 1961.

This table gives the percentage distribution of the net international flow of long-term capital and official donations, to all under-developed countries as a whole, as follows :

	1951–55 (Annual Average)	1956–59 (Annual Average)
Total flow	100	100
Net official donations	37	34
Net long-term capital : Total	63	66
Official and banking	26	23
Private	37	42

The figures in the text refer to the respective totals of net official donations and official and banking long-term capital. It may well be that banking capital includes a certain amount of private funds. The term capital seems here to be reserved for public and private loans and direct private investment. Grants are included under official donations — but they are also capital (perhaps destined to turn into income, if they are not invested but used to raise current consumption. We shall return to this point later.)

[2] The grants in question include only monetary ones, not those in kind. Loans may, at least in part, turn into grants, either if a debt is formally pardoned or if the currency of the loan is devalued.

In this latter case the gift is involuntary. It may also happen that the debtor country does nothing to precipitate the devaluation from which it benefits.

development already reached by the beneficiary country will no doubt also influence the choices to be made, in so far as it largely determines the debt-servicing capacity.[1]

(b) Should loans and grants be tied to merchandise movements or not ? Tied loans and grants are sometimes called captive aid, that is to say, aid extended in non-transferable currencies which can be used only for purchases within the originating country.

Beneficiary countries certainly prefer as a rule to be left free to choose their sources of supply. But the alternative may be captive aid or no aid. The most captive aid of all is aid in kind, but this is no reason to condemn it.

(c) Should there be any correlation between the use of foreign funds and their nature and origin ? Is it, for example, reasonable to use grants for investment in infrastructures, especially social overhead capital, which offer no direct and immediate return, and to use loans for what is sometimes called productive investment, especially with respect to the private sector ? All these are open questions. So is the question as to whether foreign capital should preferably be earmarked for specific projects or left free to finance any part of a general development process previously defined as a whole and incorporated in a development programme or plan.

III. THE EFFECTIVENESS OF FINANCIAL AID

To discuss the effectiveness of financial aid towards the development of backward countries exhaustively would require a whole book. We shall here limit our discussion to three major points : the actual size of financial development aid, with reference to a certain number of especially meaningful yardsticks of comparison ; the degree of effectiveness of such aid in relation to the desired end, namely, the development of the assisted economy through the growth of net *per caput* income, and the determination of the optimum volume of aid, from the point of view both of the donor and the recipient country.

A. *The Actual Size of International Financial Aid to Developing Countries*

The size of international development aid is obviously a function of what we conventionally mean by aid. Aid may be twice as high or even more according as we adopt one or the other of the possible

---

[1] See the well-known studies by D. Avramovic on behalf of the International Bank for Reconstruction and Development.

definitions. In the above-mentioned United Nations report we find, for the period 1956–59, a figure of 4·5 billion dollars as the net outflow of public long-term capital and grants (excluding credits through the intermediary of international financial institutions) from the developed countries of the free world (North America, Western Europe, Australia, Japan and New Zealand) to the under-developed countries.

For the same period, the OEEC estimated that its developed member or associated nations put at the disposal of developing countries an amount of 6·8 billion dollars (of which 500 million through the intermediary of international financial institutions).[1]

More recently still, in February 1962, another United Nations document, the report of the Secretary-General to the Committee on a United Nations Capital Development Fund, entitled *The Capital Development Needs of the Less Developed Countries*, gives even more explicit information.

As regards the outflow of capital from developed to under-developed countries, it is shown that for the originating countries long-term capital outflow and official donations represented, during the period 1956–59, a contribution of 8 dollars per year and per inhabitant, and in the aggregate amounted to only about 3 per cent of gross domestic saving in these countries and just a little more than ½ per cent of their gross domestic product. Official donations accounted for about half these flows.[2]

As regards recipient countries, it is stated, with reference to 1958, that foreign capital inflow into under-developed countries on the average represented 4 dollars per inhabitant, ranging from 2·3

---

[1] The chief reasons for the differences in the results of the calculations are analysed in the appendix of the UN report *The International Flow of Long-Term Capital and Official Donations, 1951–1959, op. cit.*
The figure of 4·5 billion dollars mentioned in the text is made up as follows :

	billion
Official donations :	2·2
Long-term capital :	
Official and banking	1·0
Private	1·3
	4·5

Since private loans cannot, strictly speaking, be considered as aid, the latter in fact amounted to 3·2 billion dollars.

[2] The capital flows in question include long-term private loans, but not the funds which under-developed countries get from international organizations and which are for the most part contributed by developed countries ; however, during the period under consideration the amounts involved were not large.
Without private capital, the figures quoted in the text would be reduced as follows : 5·8 dollars per head, 2·09 per cent of gross domestic saving and 0·41 per cent of GNP. See United Nations, *The International Flow of Long-Term Capital and Official Donations, 1951–1959*, New York, 1961, *op. cit.* p. 34.

dollars in South East Asia to 6 dollars in Africa and more than 7 dollars in the Middle East and Latin America. Taking all under-developed countries together, it is estimated that the inflow of long-term foreign capital in 1958 amounted to about 2 per cent of their gross domestic product.[1]

For the period 1956–59, the inflow of (public and private) long-term capital and public grants amounted to 14 per cent of the recipient countries' total foreign exchange resources, that is, export receipts plus net inflow of long-term capital. The corresponding proportion was only 10 per cent during the period 1951–55. From one period to the next, the increase in the amount of these capital flows was more than 60 per cent and more than three times higher than the increase in the receipts from merchandise exports.[2]

One last, and very important, aspect remains to be mentioned. The effective distribution of this aid both among donor and among recipient countries is exceedingly uneven. Without entering into details, we would merely recall that the United States furnish the overwhelming bulk of the funds in absolute terms, whereas France occupies first place (though her lead is diminishing) if we express the amount of aid in *per caput* terms or as a proportion of national income.

That capital inflow per head of the inhabitants of under-developed countries is very uneven has already been mentioned. It is still more uneven in absolute figures or in relation to these countries' national produce (or income), or their domestic saving, either as a whole or per head.[3]

B. *The Measurement of the Effects of Aid*

It would be interesting to examine how the financial flows of international development aid affect the economy of the recipient country — whether they really do take the form of an effective transfer of capital goods from the originating to the recipient country, whether these transfers really do set off or sustain growth as intended, either by their direct effect or by their influence on private capital flows and on domestic private and public saving. Another question

---

[1] See *ibid*. paragraph 74. Without private capital, these figures have to be reduced by a little less than one-third, to something like 2·8 dollars per head and 1·4 per cent of GNP.

[2] See *ibid*. Table 7. The figures do not seem to include invisible exports, which, however, generally do not account for much in the countries concerned. Without private capital the percentage would be not 14, but 10 (p. 100).

[3] Rosenstein-Rodan (*op. cit*. Appendices) gives astonishingly precise figures. We have had neither the time nor the means to check their accuracy, but they certainly do look plausible.

is whether the size of these financial flows properly express the size of the sacrifice they impose upon the originating countries.

We apologize for being, once more, very brief on all these points and for suggesting lines of research rather than attempting to give detailed answers.[1]

(1) *Effects in the Recipient Countries.* If financial development aid is to achieve its end, it should normally lead to a quantitative increase of investment in the recipient country and hence raise the rate of increase of the aggregate national product (and of *per caput* income, to the extent that this rate of increase exceeds the rate of population growth).

The first result should be a net addition to domestic saving. We have seen that capital inflow (including private capital) amounted on the average to 2 per cent of GNP in 1958; this may imply a 25 or even 30 per cent addition to domestic saving, on the assumption that the latter amounts to no more than, say, 6 to 8 per cent of GNP. Obviously, the situation varies greatly from country to country.

Now, this addition can clearly be effective only to the extent that the financial flows lead to the formation of capital goods and not simply to an expansion of consumption, either directly or by the play of substitution.[2] The next question is whether or not higher investment is reflected in a proportionately more or less equal increase in domestic product. Everything depends on the nature of the investment and on the capital-output ratio.

Perhaps we may legitimately set our hopes even higher. These financial flows may set off a sort of multiplier effect, either by drawing more domestic (public and private) saving into financial investment or even real investment in the subsistence sectors, or by attracting private foreign capital, or both.

A French study by Maldant arrives at fairly conclusive and affirmative results on this matter, at least so far as French government aid to the former French territories in Africa is concerned. It remains to be hoped that these results apply also to other countries

---

[1] It would seem as if the effects of these financial flows on the originating and the recipient economy, as well as on the economies of third countries, could be properly analysed only by an investigation both in monetary terms and in terms of the changes which these transfers bring about in the pattern of real flows of goods and services. One would have to use modern input-output techniques, however difficult they may be to apply to primitive and often largely non-monetary economies. Useful indications along these lines may be found in a recent study by Éliane Betout-Mossé, 'Sur quelques problèmes posés par l'aide aux pays sous-développés', published in *Revue économique*, July 1962.

[2] Among others, R. Nurkse has rightly stressed this point; see Chapter IV of his *Problems of Capital Formation, op. cit.*

and that the methods the author used with apparent success may be tried in other contexts than those of his own research.[1]

(2) *Measurement of the Burden on Donor Countries.* In principle, aid is a burden on those who render it ; it implies a sacrifice. But the measurement of that burden is not as easy as might appear at first sight. In the first place, we must distinguish between loans, which in principle have a counterpart, and grants, which have not, even though they may not always be wholly disinterested. The fact remains that the sequence of events following from the monetary transfers connected with aid may modify, and perhaps greatly modify, the real burden involved for the economy of the donor country.[2]

The burden may become larger if financial aid must necessarily be accompanied by technical assistance, if it leads to orders which have to be subsidized in the supplier country, or if it sooner or later calls for further instalments of aid to make good current deficits in the operation of the plant financed by the original aid. Cases of this kind are known from the history of French aid to overseas countries and territories.

It is equally possible that other factors may reduce the effective burden ultimately imposed by aid on the economy of the originating country. Even aid that is given free may have some counterpart : orders to the firms of the donor country through the intermediary of its merchant companies, more freight for domestic shipping companies, higher calls on miscellaneous services — implying experts' and technicians' fees ultimately to be repatriated to the originating country. If we had proper records of all these two-way flows we could no doubt arrive at certain conclusions. Such attempts as have been made in France in this direction suggest that the real sacrifice which aid imposes on the economy of the donor country is generally lower than the original financial flows. But the whole question remains obscure. It is not impossible that when an advanced country is in a state of less than full employment of its productive

---

[1] This study is quoted by P. Moussa in *Les Nations prolétaires*, Paris, Presses Universitaires, 1959. Maldant worked out a multiplier of 3·2 as between public funds made available by metropolitan France and total investment in the beneficiary countries and territories. Having calculated a capital-output ratio of about 4, he arrived at the result that 1 unit of French aid led to an ultimate increase in local annual product of $\frac{3·2}{4} = 0·8$. At first sight, this seems a very optimistic statement. With improved methods of national accounting it should become possible to determine to what extent it is true.

[2] No such complications arise in the case of aid in kind, to the extent, of course, that it is a gift. But there still remains the question of measurement. What 'sacrifice', for instance, is involved for the U.S. economy when it gives away surpluses with which no one knows what to do and which probably have no value at all on the domestic market?

capacity, the aid commitments may help to promote economic recovery or to speed up the rate of increase of national income. In the long run, one would also have to consider the indirect advantages to be derived from the development of backward countries — the seeds of what some authors felicitously call 'reciprocal development' (François Perroux).[1]

(3) *The Question of the Optimum Size of Financial Aid.* While the figures we have quoted are no more than approximate, they do at least show that although international aid (in the strict sense of the word) is growing from year to year, it is still modest both in relation to the resources of the donor countries and to the needs of the recipient ones. How far should it usefully go ? Is it possible to work out some figures for a sort of general and ideal programme of international financial aid to developing countries over a period of, say, ten or fifteen years ? [2] Here again we shall try to be very brief.

(a) Take the donor countries first. Is there a limit to their capacity to give and to lend ? This involves domestic financial policy and budget surpluses, since both the grants and the loans which make up aid usually draw on public funds. But the overall capacity to furnish aid (by grants and loans) is generally also a function of the donor country's ability to forgo some part of the satisfaction of its own needs and to carry the aid disbursements on the debit side of its overall balance of payments.[3] The recent experiences of the United States go to show that it is sometimes very hard to strike a proper balance between a country's willingness to make sacrifices and its ability to keep its balance of payments in equilibrium.

Considerations of this kind might underlie a calculation of the ideal overall amount of aid to be given to 'poor' countries and of the part of this aid each 'rich' country ought to shoulder. Rosenstein-Rodan's numerical proposals might indeed be taken as a basis for a discussion of this kind.[4]

(b) As regards the beneficiary countries, we would have to determine their 'acceptance capacity'.

There is, in the first place, their borrowing capacity, which is a function of the borrower's ability to service the loans, both domestically and as regards the transfer of interest and principal payments in currencies other than the debtor's own.

---

[1] Some indications on how to measure these return flows are given by É. Betout-Mossé in her above-mentioned study.

[2] This is what the CENIS team at M.I.T. has tried to do in the Millikan and Rostow and the Millikan and Blackmer studies quoted ; see also Rosenstein-Rodans' article in *Review of Economics and Statistics*, May 1961.

[3] See C. P. Lucron, *Croissance économique et investissement international*, Paris, Presses Universitaires, 1961, pp. 24-6.

[4] See Rosenstein-Rodan, *op. cit.*, Table 6 of the Appendix.

But there is also a capacity to absorb donations, at least in so far as they are to serve capital formation (the capacity to absorb any amount of gifts in consumption may safely be assumed to be unlimited).

Without entering into the details of this very intricate question,[1] we note that the capacity to use aid effectively for the purposes for which it is intended is, generally speaking, conditioned by the presence or absence of a number of complementary factors needed to make aid effective — such as skilled labour, new resources, appropriate institutions, public utility services, domestic saving, foreign exchange reserves sufficient to cover an increase in imports following upon a rise of domestic incomes generated by investment financed with foreign aid, and so on and so forth.

In these circumstances it would not seem as if calculations based on the combined effect of intersectoral capital-output ratios and of average and marginal savings rates are sufficient to determine the optimum size of foreign aid.

Nor is it good enough to base such calculations simply on foreign exchange deficits, especially on trade account.[2]

On the other hand, it seems legitimate to assume, with Millikan and Rostow and with Rosenstein-Rodan, that absorptive capacity varies according to the current stage of development. This capacity is rather low in the initial phase of the process, concerned mainly with the preconditions of take-off — that is, when the recipient country has to get physically and intellectually ready to break with the habits of the past and somehow or other to make the big spurt. At this stage technical assistance would seem to be of primary importance.

Later, foreign capital will be needed more and more urgently, especially when it comes to creating the whole set of infrastructures necessary for rapid and sustained growth. (The very nature of these infrastructures, the returns from which are widely spaced and long delayed, suggests that their cost will primarily have to be covered by grants or privilege loans.) Once the growth process is well under way, it may be hoped that the part of external aid will gradually be taken over by domestic saving at a higher marginal rate and by direct and portfolio investment of foreign private capital.[3]

[1] See Millikan and Rostow, *op. cit.*, and B. Higgins, 'Assistance étrangère et capacité d'absorption', *Développement et civilisations*, No. 5. pp. 28-43.

[2] J. Royer, *op. cit.*, estimates that under this heading alone the under-developed countries will need 11 to 12 billion dollars of foreign aid annually between 1962 and 1975. These figures are very far from Rosenstein-Rodan's.

[3] It is on these assumptions that Rosenstein-Rodan, *op. cit.*, bases his proposals for aid to some 80 under-developed countries for each of the five-year periods

IV. CONCLUSIONS : THE FUTURE OF AID

To conclude this overlong and yet sadly incomplete report, we should like to make a few observations on the following three points :

(1) Should international development aid be continued ?

(2) Should it be made more universal ?

(3) When, and at what rate, may it be expected to fall off gradually?

(1) On the first point, there seems hardly much room for disagreement. International aid is useful and should be continued. It is true that development may not always be the sole purpose of aid and that ulterior motives of self-interest may to some extent influence the decisions of the donors. It is equally true that recipient countries do not always make the best conceivable use of the aid they are given. Nurkse is no doubt right when he says, in the last chapter of the book we have quoted more than once, that development action must begin on the home front. But all this does not seem to us to invalidate the statement that not many nations can pull themselves up by their own bootstraps. Whether we speak with Rostow of the take-off, or with Rosenstein-Rodan of the big initial spurt, or with Leibenstein of the minimum critical effort, or yet of the precise role of the capital-output ratio in the growth process, there can be no doubt that any country will reach the stage of self-sustained growth more quickly if it is helped from outside and that indeed thereafter its rate of growth is likely to be faster if aid continues to be forthcoming. It is certainly not for us, as economists, to find it surprising that the highest spokesmen of the world's great countries should so often have proclaimed the need for aid and to have proposed that, internationally speaking, our present decade should become the decade of development.[1]

(2) Necessary as it is, it does seem as if development aid, as

1961–66, 1966–71 and 1971–76 (see Tables 4-A and 4-B in the Appendix). He calculates that aid, properly speaking (excluding private investment), should amount to 4290 million dollars annually during the first period, to 3775 million during the second and to 1870 million during the third. These amounts include a constant 500 million dollars from the International Bank. An alternative solution is presented on the basis of the somewhat different conditions of India. To our mind these figures, even though they exclude aid towards social development as well as the value of agricultural surpluses ear-marked for consumption, are too small to be realistic.

The United Nations report *The Capital Development Needs*, etc. *op. cit.* shows, in Table 3, annual foreign capital requirements beyond 1960 and in some cases until 1976, in the amount of 4·8 to 7 billion dollars, to achieve an annual rate of growth in national income per head between 1·8 and 2·5 per cent. The underdeveloped countries concerned would no doubt consider these limits rather low. There remains, in any event, the question how much private capital might contribute, in so far as aid properly speaking would have to cover only the difference.

[1] *An Act for International Development — A Program for the Decade of Development : Summary Presentation*, Department of State Publication 7,205, Washington, D.C., 1961.

practised today, were susceptible of great improvements. This is why we deliberately refrained in this paper from dwelling too much on purely institutional aspects.[1] We all know that the bulk of aid is today provided on a bilateral basis, each donor nation treating separately with the recipient nations of its choice. There are, it is true, some forms of multilateral aid, both on the world plane and on the regional plane (the Inter-American region, for example, or the Eurafrican region through the association of certain overseas territories with the European Economic Community, or yet the Colombo Plan in which South East Asia is associated with certain developed nations in other continents). Then we have to mention the International Bank for Reconstruction and Development and its recent offshoot, the International Development Association, as well as United Nations' action along the twin lines of technical assistance and financial aid through the Special Fund. Discussions are, furthermore, under way on a proposal for the United Nations to set up a Capital Development Fund, which is to promote the economic diversification and the rapid industrial development of the less developed countries.[2]

In the presence of this complex structure, one might well ask whether it would not be simplest to unify all action at the highest level, and to create, for instance within the United Nations, a sort of general co-ordination and management agency for international aid.[3] Along this line of thought we come close to certain other proposals, for instance, that of P. Moussa for a world tax to be introduced by international agreement, its proceeds being devoted to development aid according to an agreed distribution code. But it is no use indulging in flights of fancy. Decisions of this kind, as Nurkse rightly said,[4] are essentially political. They presuppose the

---

[1] See G. Leduc, *Économie du développement, op. cit.* p. 483 *et seq.*

[2] The United Nations Special Committee drew up a list of 13 principles to govern the creation and working of the Fund. But there was so much opposition that they were adopted only by simple majority.

[3] B. Higgins, *op. cit.* p. 41, proposes that the existing International Development Association should be transformed into such an agency. It might retain its name, but its scope would be considerably widened, so that it might become a worldwide research and management centre for development aid, both technical and financial. Instead of being, as at present, subordinated to the International Bank, it would then come to rank above it. Sir Robert Jackson, *The Case for an International Development Authority*, Syracuse University Press, 1959, proposed the creation of a world development authority, and his proposal was taken up by E. Staley, *op. cit.* p. 458 *et seq.*

[4] P. Moussa, *Les Nations prolétaires, op. cit.* last chapter, and R. Nurkse, *Problems of Capital Formation, op. cit.* Chapter IV.

The argument that international aid is essentially a political matter constitutes a serious limitation upon Rosenstein-Rodan's proposals. These could be carried out only on the basis of a prior international agreement — and where are the 'wise men' who could then be asked to follow and check its application?

existence of some sort of world government or at least a great re-inforcement of the United Nations' present powers, such as even their warmest supporters (including myself) must admit to be fraught with difficulties. It would already be progress merely to co-ordinate as best one may the present forms of aid, to avoid overlapping, to integrate outside aid with some sort of overall programming of the development potential of the beneficiary countries, and to put an end to the current competitive bidding, inspired more by demagogic motives than by any real desire to reduce the gap which divides the standards of living of the world's peoples.

(3) And so to the last point : is it possible at this stage to look forward to the termination of an aid which probably has not even reached its peak yet ? If we are to believe certain authors, aid will have to go on as long as some countries are still in a stage of insufficient development. No time limit is set. In this view, the redistribution of the richer countries' income to the benefit of the poorer ones would have to continue as long as the inequalities which the income redistribution is supposed to even out.

Not everybody is so pessimistic. There are some who think of the termination of aid properly speaking within a reassuringly short period — for what are fifteen years in the life of a nation ? Development aid then appears merely as a transitory phenomenon in the economic history of the modern world. Its effectiveness would be proved by the successive arrival of the eighty or so nations concerned at the stage of self-sustained growth. Thereafter, aid could again give way to trade, and we may place our faith once more in the virtues of the international exchange of goods and services and international private capital movements (at least outside the communist world). For ourselves, we should certainly wish this to happen and indeed for some movement in this direction to begin right now. To quote an astute observer, at this very moment the problem of commercial relations between industrial nations and developing countries is becoming one of the major problems of the 'sixties.[1] The same author finds himself in full agreement with G. Myrdal, whom he quotes [2] as saying, on his return from India, that the economic aspect is a minor one in the problem of development, that the financial aspect is a minor one in economic development, and that the aspect of outside finance is a minor one in finance generally.

More than ten years ago, we said something on much the same

[1] See René Servoise, 'De l'assistance au commerce international — Perspectives décennales', *Revue de politique étrangère*, 1960, No. 4, pp. 316-31.
[2] G. Myrdal, *op. cit.* p. 329.

lines.[1] Nevertheless, we would not now hazard any prediction as to when aid, or at least financial aid, may become redundant. To be realistic, we are inclined to think that on the level of nations just as among individuals, there will always be some of us that are poor. But if we all become more conscious of the interdependence and the common destiny of all human beings, then one-way aid may some day be replaced by mutual co-operation and by such action as is appropriate to a joint enterprise carried forward in a common spirit of lasting victory over ignorance and poverty.

DISCUSSION OF THE PAPER BY PROFESSOR LEDUC

Dr. J. H. Adler, in opening the discussion, said that the subject of aid affected all aspects of economic development and it could not be placed in a subdivision by itself. There was a close connection between aid, foreign trade and financial and technical assistance. There were always political implications to be taken into account and there was no possibility in consequence, of an 'optimum distribution of aid', or of an 'optimum distribution of the burden'. The question was often asked as to whether it was not possible to channel more aid through international institutions, so as to minimize the political problems. Professor Leduc had suggested an agency charged with general co-ordination and management, for example. The need for this was much less than it seemed, because there were already institutional arrangements for this purpose, such as the various consortia set up by groups of countries.

Professor Leduc had mentioned the possible multiplier effect of foreign aid ; it was doubtful whether there was such an effect in the usual sense of the term. It was the form of the investment expenditure that was important ; investment in social overhead capital, for example, might result in higher incomes only after further induced investment had taken place. One possibility was that foreign aid might bring about induced investment financed from 'frustrated savings', a phenomena that had been pointed out by Professor Hirschman. Another function of aid was to extend the absorptive capacity of the economy by widening the scope for further investment : it was likely to alter the social returns obtainable on all investment expenditures.

The capacity of an economy to absorb aid depended upon the supply of co-operating factors available and the internal economic policies followed. The role of economists was to help make the flows of aid more

[1] G. Leduc, 'Le Sous-développement et ses problèmes', Report to the Congress of French-speaking economists, *Revue d'économie politique*, 1952.

effective by programming and the preparation of projects. It was essential to obtain an improvement in the performance of investment projects.

Finally, it should be noted that foreign aid did impose a burden on the donor, so that there was bound to be a limit to the total amount of aid available.

Professor J. Stanovnik argued that it was best to classify any international arrangement as 'foreign aid' if there was no commercial basis for it, or if the latter was purely subsidiary. If that were done it was unlikely that aid could be regarded as a transitory phenomena. The only possible substitute was private capital and it was most unlikely that the flow of capital could once again depend mainly on private funds. One reason for this was that foreign trade could not support the servicing of such flows. The servicing of foreign debts now absorbed 12 per cent of the foreign trade receipts of the under-developed countries. Professor Leduc had estimated that these payments were equal to 14 per cent of the import capacity of those countries. It might well be the case that foreign capital flows were already less in total than debt servicing payments.

As far as foreign trade was concerned the prospect was not encouraging. Exports of foodstuffs were hampered by the operation of Engels' law and the effects of support prices ; for raw materials it was the competition of substitutes that mattered, whilst exports of manufactures were likely to be met by protective measures. Only minerals and heavy manufactures offered any prospects, and both these were highly capital-intensive sectors.

The dualistic nature of under-developed countries was largely due to the flow of private capital and the subsequent need to repay debts. The diversification of the economy meant finding an optimum use for its natural resources. This should be a major policy objective, but it may clash with the aims of private capital. Historically speaking, it was the movement of 'imponderables', rather than the real transfer of goods and services, which had been important. It was necessary to study how these 'imponderables', or unidentified factors in growth, worked under different flows of aid and investment.

Professor L. Baudin emphasized that the basic question was whether the population was ready to use aid properly. The mentality of the beneficiary was important here ; in some cases it was clear that economic progress was not always the main aim of the society. An example of these difficulties was that of hoarding by people with limited needs who had no desire to put savings to productive use. It was clear that the problem of education was basic to most of these difficulties.

Dr. A. Nussbaumer said that it would be a mistake to consider aid solely in terms of capital transfers and investment goods. The importance of the trading policies adopted by the developed and under-developed countries themselves could scarcely be over-estimated. These would determine how far the under-developed countries would benefit from an extended division of labour and the economic growth that followed, as well as the distribution of the multiplier effects of new investment between the donors and recipients of aid. Trade concessions by the developed countries would stimulate foreign investment on a commercial basis and also increase the benefits that under-developed countries gain from aid. The kind of aid given did not have to be considered exclusively by the standards and needs of the recipients ; aid may also assist the donors in policies of income stabilization, etc.

More precise welfare considerations would have to be founded upon the measurement of sacrifices and the results obtained. Increments to and losses from disposable national income in both countries might be used although there would be problems relating to secondary effects, and the measurement of gains and losses to donors and recipients. Should they be measured, for example, in absolute or relative terms ? Can the same weight be attached to an absolute amount transferred from a rich country to one with a low income per head ? It is unlikely that value judgments could be excluded from such comparisons and the amount and type of aid could not be judged purely by economic criteria. The development and use of economic measures is necessary, if only to be able to specify the moral and political content of the decisions taken.

Professor J. L. Cecena Gamez said that some under-developed countries could be described as still under colonial or semi-colonial status and were not free to make their own international arrangements. Certain international monopolies operating in world markets had considerable power over their economies.

Generally speaking, countries free to choose preferred aid 'without strings' on a bilateral basis. A typical example of aid with strings attached was the 'Alliance for Progress', which favoured private foreign investment. Another criticism which could be levelled at aid given by international agencies was that it was accompanied by excessive bureaucracy.

Professor I. Rachmuth said that economic aid between the socialist countries took many forms, but the basis of it was the Council for Mutual Economic Assistance, formed in 1949, amongst the countries of Eastern Europe, and which now included the Mongolian Peoples Republic. Through this body national plans were co-ordinated, although it was important to note that there was no supra-national plan imposed on individual countries.

The second kind of collaboration took place through foreign trade. The Soviet Union had performed a special role in this connection, through exports of capital goods needed for industrial development. Trade credit also had a part to play in these flows of trade.

Another kind of aid took the form of joint enterprises between countries. For example, Rumania, Czechoslovakia, Poland and the German Democratic Republic had combined to build a cellulose plant in the Danube delta. The completed factory would belong to the Rumanian State, but repayment for the machinery, etc., supplied by the other countries would be made out of the current output of the plant.

Finally, much mutual assistance was given in the form of technical aid, provision of information about techniques, research and development. This was exchanged between countries on a gratuitous basis.

Dr. A. W. Doroth Duesterwald said that the period of the 'take off', as put forward by Rostow, was the point at which 'development' becomes 'growth'. Development involved a more than normal increase in the stock of capital, where normal is defined as that rate of investment required to keep pace with the rate of natural increase of the population and the process of technological advance. Development must be defined with reference to the nature of the process, and not by its success in raising the gross national product per head. It was the uncertainty of success attaching to the process that explained why no definite time period can be attributed to it. By definition, an under-developed country would not be able to finance such an increase in the capital stock from its own savings.

Apart from the gap between resources and needs there are also unavoidable tensions in a development process. There was a tendency to anticipate the fruits of development in the form of higher money incomes ; as a manifestation of human weakness this was undesirable, but, at the same time, development needed qualified manpower with appropriate standards of living, education, etc. The state may also be an inhibiting factor, especially if a large part of public budgets, resources, energy and intelligence is preoccupied with such subjects as defence and national security.

No purely economic solution for the problems of agricultural development was likely to be found as long as there was no international division of labour and free world trade. Regional mobility of labour was also an important condition for the rational development and allocation of economic resources. Such mobility required a reserve of housing such as was not likely to be available to under-developed countries.

Israel had accumulated wide experience both as a recipient of foreign technical assistance and, more recently, as a supplier of such expertise. It had been found that it was necessary for such experts to learn before they began to teach in a foreign country.

Professor T. Scitovsky argued that aid should be seen as a means of reducing the inequality of incomes between nations. These were now greater than inequalities between individuals, and economic history had failed to show the existence of any automatic mechanism tending to reduce such inequalities of income and wealth.

There were two ways in which aid might be designed to work towards this end. The first would be to keep the terms of trade favourable to the poorer countries. The second way would be to reform the international payments mechanism. At the moment those countries which had a surplus in the balance of payments acquired additional liquidity, but the surplus was not used in the best way to place resources at the disposal of under-developed countries. Any plan for reform should be designed to accomplish this end.

Professor G. C. Allen said that it was not true, as had been alleged, that private foreign capital had, in the past, gone solely into productive enterprises. In order to be able to operate at all it had been found necessary to invest in the provision of infrastructure, as well as in the more commercial investments. This was true of Western enterprise in China and South-East Asia in the colonial period. It was also not correct to say that capital invested had to be repaid at the expense of the balance of payments; capital had not been repaid in the past; where conditions were favourable to the emergence of a local, entrepreneurial class, it was more usual for local investors to become associated with foreign firms as time passed. Profits were transferred, but it was only in recent years that there had been a repatriation of capital and then usually from areas of political instability. The distinction between economic aid and direct private investment was not as sharp as had been suggested, especially in countries where conditions were favourable to development.

Professor E. James argued that the topic of economic aid raised problems of economic policy or 'economic morality'. Aid was now offered in a different way from that it had taken in the past. After the first world war aid had been transferred between countries through assistance given to different currencies.

In order to avoid waste and the possibility of intervention by monopolies, planning would be necessary and, possibly, supra-national planning as well. Even if such plans were produced, however, they may still include a 'dominating effect' (as analysed by Professor Perroux). In the end it might be necessary to have an international plan for aid to get over these difficulties.

Professor G. Leduc, replying to the discussion, said that Dr. Adler had raised the question of the multiplier effects of inflows of foreign capital. The difficulty was that there was no fundamental study of this aspect of the multiplier which was fully substantiated. The same applied to the idea of the 'capacity to absorb' aid, which had not yet been fully investigated either.

It was agreed that aid was most beneficial when used in a planned framework. The 'dominating effects' experienced by some economies had also been mentioned and it was true that this did occur, especially where monopolies were concerned. The solution probably lay with the more developed countries, who should exercise more control over monopolies, both national and international.

The paper had been written with specific reference to capitalist countries, and the problem of international planning was basically political. In favourable political circumstances it might be possible to envisage the kind of 'world tax' suggested by Professor Moussa to finance an international fund for the provision of aid.

Chapter 8

THE ROLE OF TAXATION IN ECONOMIC DEVELOPMENT

BY

N. KALDOR
Cambridge University

I. FISCAL ASPECTS OF DEVELOPMENT POLICY

1. PROBLEMS of taxation, in connection with economic development, are generally discussed from two different points of view, which involve very different, and often conflicting, considerations : the point of view of *incentives* and the point of view of *resources*. Those who believe that it is the lack of adequate incentives which is mainly responsible for insufficient growth and investment are mainly concerned with improving the tax system from an incentive point of view through the granting of additional concessions of various kinds, with less regard to the unfavourable effects on the public revenue. Those who believe that insufficient growth and investment is mainly a consequence of a lack of resources, are chiefly concerned with increasing the resources available for investment through additional taxation even at the cost of worsening its disincentive effects.

2. In my opinion a great deal of the prevailing concern with incentives is misplaced — except in particular cases, such as in the matter of tax concessions granted to foreigners which *may* increase the inflow of capital from abroad [1] — it is limitation of resources, and not inadequate incentives, which limits the pace of economic development. Indeed the importance of public revenue from the point of view of accelerated economic development could hardly be exaggerated. Irrespective of the prevailing ideology or the political colour of particular governments, the economic and cultural development of a country requires the efficient and steadily expanding provision of a whole host of non-revenue-yielding services — education, health, communications systems, etc., commonly known as 'infrastructure' — which require to be financed out of government revenue. In addition, taxation (or other compulsory levies) provides

[1] But see below, para. 13.

170

the most appropriate instrument for increasing savings for capital formation out of domestic sources.[1]

3. The only feature that is common to most 'under-developed' countries is the shortage of revenue which makes it impossible for them to provide essential public services on the required scale. The common assumption is that these countries are unable to lift themselves out of their predicament because of their very poverty. No doubt the 'taxation potential' of a poor country — the proportion of its gross national product that can be diverted to public purposes without setting up intolerable political and social pressures — is generally lower, and in many cases appreciably lower, than that of a rich country. But more important, in my view, is the low 'coefficient of utilization' of that potential — due to bad tax laws, bad tax administration, or both — which in turn is only partly to be explained by lack of knowledge, understanding or of administrative competence — it is also the result of resistance by powerful pressure groups who block the way to effective tax reform. Accelerated development in all such cases is predominantly a political issue : expert advice can point the way, but overcoming resistance to more effective policies for mobilizing resources must depend on the collective will, operating through political institutions.

4. The inadequacy of public revenue has two important consequences. It forces undue economies precisely in those fields of public expenditure (like health and education) which are more easily sacrificed in the short run, but are the most important from the point of view of long-run development. It also yields persistent budgetary deficits which force the monetary authorities to follow highly restrictive credit policies (to protect the balance of payments and to limit the pace of inflation) which in turn has highly undesirable effects on the pace of economic growth, without fully compensating for the effects of the weakness in the state of public finances on the stability of the currency.

5. Many under-developed countries suffer, not only from lack of revenue, but also from an irrational scale of priorities in the allocation of public funds. Too much may be spent on the (real or fancied) needs of defence, or for ostentatious purposes of various kinds — such as public buildings and ornaments, lavish diplomatic

---

[1] The only alternative is inflation, which by comparison is a clumsy and ineffective instrument for mobilizing resources, since a large part of the 'enforced' reduction in the consumption of the mass of the population, brought about by the rise in prices in relation to incomes, is wasted in the increased luxury consumption of the profit-earning classes. Also, it is difficult to conceive of inflation as more than a temporary instrument for mobilizing resources : once wages rise in consequence of the rise in prices, the rate of price-inflation is accelerated, without securing any further savings.

missions, etc. There is nothing much to be said about all this, beyond noting the fact; and for the rest of this paper we shall consider the problem entirely from the revenue side : what determines a country's 'taxation potential', and how can that potential be more fully exploited ?

6. The 'taxation potential' of a country, as above defined, is obviously greatly dependent on (i) real income per head ; (ii) the degree of inequality in the distribution of income ; (iii) the sectoral distribution of the national income, and the social and institutional setting in which the output of particular sectors is procured ; (iv) the administrative competence etc. of the tax-gathering organs of the government.

7. It is a commonplace to say that taxes can only be paid out of the 'economic surplus' — the excess of production over the minimum subsistence needs of the population. Moreover, in so far as such surplus is not consumed by the people to whom it accrues, but is saved and invested, it can only be made available for the purposes of public expenditure at the cost of reducing the rate of capital accumulation of the community. This is bound to react adversely on the country's economic development except in so far as investment is diverted from inessential or 'luxury' purposes (such as luxury housing) to purposes important for development. It would be more correct to say, therefore, that the taxation potential of a country depends on the *excess of its actual consumption over the minimum essential consumption of the population.*

8. In practice, however, the 'minimum essential consumption' of a community cannot be defined or measured ; it is not just a matter of the strict biological requirements of subsistence (which themselves vary greatly with climate and location) but of social conventions and habits, and the actual standard of living to which the bulk of the population of any particular community has become accustomed. Since governments ultimately depend on the consent of the people whom they govern, it is impossible as a matter of policy to compress, by means of taxation, the actual standard of living *of the mass of the population* outside fairly narrow limits. (If this were not so, the taxation potential would vary enormously with the actual level of real income per head. Supposing this potential were 10 per cent in a country with an income per head of $60 a year, it would be no less than 82 per cent in a country whose income per head is $300 a year. Yet even the richest countries with incomes per head of over $1000 a year find it very difficult to raise more than 30-35 per cent of their GNP in taxation.)

9. It can happen, on the other hand, that the amount of food or

other necessities produced in a country is limited not by the availability of natural resources (land), or by knowledge or ability, but by the customary way of life of the agricultural population, who prefer a maximum of leisure and a minimum of material income, and therefore work just hard enough to cover their immediate and traditional needs. In such circumstances additional taxes levied on them would tend to make them work harder and produce more — i.e. to reduce their leisure, rather than their standards of material consumption. Taxation would then act as an incentive to produce more (as opposed to forcing the people concerned to consume less) and this may not encounter the same kind of resistance, particularly if the increase on taxation is a gradual one. From this point of view, the countries of Africa — where, in general, shortage of land is not a critical factor in agricultural production — are more favourably placed than the under-developed countries of Asia.

10. Excluding, however, the case where taxation may itself serve as an instrument for increasing real income per head, the taxation potential of a country will be strongly dependent on the prevailing inequality in the distribution of the national income, which in turn is closely linked to the relative importance of incomes derived from property, as against income derived from work, and to the degree of concentration in the ownership of property. As between two countries with the same real income per head, the accustomed standard of living of the bulk of the population will evidently be the lower, and the share of unnecessary or luxury consumption larger, in the country in which a larger share of total incomes accrues to a minority of wealthy individuals.[1]

11. From this point of view the under-developed countries of different regions of the globe (or even individual countries within the same region) show the widest differences. At one end of the scale a country such as India, with one of the lowest incomes per head of population, has a high ratio of property income in total income (a ratio that is comparable to that of the country with the highest income per head, the United States) and in consequence has a relatively

---

[1] This is not to suggest that either the inequality of incomes, or the inequality in standards of consumption could be eliminated by taxation. It is not possible or expedient to prevent the owner of the successful business from enjoying the fruits of his success during his lifetime — any more than it is possible to prevent scarce talent from earning its high reward in a socialist state. But clearly not all forms of economic privilege fulfil any positive social function — absentee landlords, for example — and the experience of Western Europe and North America has shown that the consumption of the entrepreneurial class can be reduced within wide limits by means of progressive taxation without interfering either with incentives or the means of continued growth and accumulation. (It is consumption, rather than savings out of profits, which shows a wide difference between countries, according to the nature of their tax systems.)

high taxation potential in relation to real income per head.[1] At the other end of the scale there are some under-developed countries (particularly in Africa) in which incomes derived from property owner-ship are relatively insignificant and in which a wealthy property-owning class can hardly be said to exist.

12. The share of the national income of under-developed countries accruing to property is largely dependent on the pressure of population on the land, and the prevailing system of land owner-ship. In the relatively over-populated countries of the Middle East and Asia, a considerable share of income accrues (or has accrued, until recently) to a wealthy land-owning class who not only pre-empt an undue share of the national resources for their personal ends, but whose very existence bars the way to the development of a more efficient agriculture. Even in countries where the ratio of population to natural resources is relatively favourable (as in many of the countries of Latin America), where the fertile or accessible land is firmly held by feudal absentee owners, incomes derived from the ownership (as distinct from cultivation) of land account for a considerable share of incomes produced. This results in a high ratio of resources being devoted to unnecessary consumption. The same is true of countries in the earlier stages of industrialization, where fortunes made in the course of industrial development virtually escape taxation, and where in consequence a much higher share of the profits earned in industry and commerce are devoted to personal consumption.[2] In view of this, expressed as a proportion of GNP,

[1] Although the 'coefficient of utilization' of that potential appears to be rather low.
[2] In a study of Chile some years ago I found the following percentage alloca-tion of the gross national product between various categories of expenditure :

Chile: Allocation of Gross National Product in 1953
by Categories of Expenditure, in Percentages

Gross domestic investment (public and private)		12
Of which—		
Gross fixed capital formation	9	
Increase in stocks	3	
Government current expenditure		11
Personal consumption		77
Of which—		
Wage and salary earners (69 per cent of active population)	37	
Self-employed (31 per cent of active population)	18	
Recipients of profits, interest and rent	22	
	Total	100

The total share of property in GNP was 34 per cent of which direct and indirect taxation took up little over 12 per cent (i.e. 4·5 per cent of GNP) and about one-fifth (or 7·5 per cent of GNP) was saved. If an effective system of taxation had existed which compressed property owners' consumption by one-half, this would

the 'taxation-potential' of the semi-developed countries of Latin America (with incomes per head of $200-$300 a year) must be fully as large as that of the highly developed countries, although their actual tax revenue is typically only one-half as large.[1]

13. There are some under-developed countries which, while they lack a domestic property-owning class, have important foreign enterprises in their territory (for the exploitation of valuable minerals or the product of plantations), so that a considerable share of their gross *domestic* product accrues to non-residents. Since the right of a country to tax all income arising within its jurisdiction is now firmly established, this provides a source of taxation that is essentially similar to that of a wealthy domestic property-owning class. There is a danger, however, that owing to the comparative ease with which this source can be tapped (by means of export duties, or taxes on income and profits) such taxation may be carried to the point where it inhibits the development of export industries which may be vital to the development of the economy.[2] On the other hand, many under-developed countries have recently been competing with one another in according all kinds of tax privileges and immunities to newly established foreign enterprises in an attempt to attract foreign capital to their own territory, with adverse consequences on their ability to collect revenue. Whilst it can plausibly be argued that an under-developed country gains from the inflow of foreign capital even if the income acquiring from the investments is left untaxed — owing to the wage and salary incomes generated as a result, and the increased export earnings — it is an uncertain matter how far the total flow of capital investment from the developed to the under-developed areas is enhanced in consequence of such policies, and if it is not, such 'beggar-my-neighbour' policies of stimulating development deprive the under-developed countries of revenue without any compensating benefit.[3]

14. Under-developed countries differ also as regards the relative magnitude of the 'non-monetized' or subsistence sector, and the 'monetized' or market-exchange sector, as well as the nature of the

have released resources sufficient to double government current expenditure, or alternatively to increase gross fixed capital formation by 125 per cent.

In the highly industrialized countries of the U.S. and the U.K. the share of the GNP accruing in the form of gross profits, interest and rent is much smaller (less than 25 per cent in 1953) and the proportion paid in taxation much greater. Property-owners' consumption accounted for only about 7·5 per cent of GNP in the U.K. in 1953 as against Chile's 22 per cent.

[1] Tax revenue accounts for 9 per cent of GNP of Mexico, 14 per cent of Chile, 10 per cent of Brazil, 16 per cent of Venezuela (excluding oil royalties).

[2] It is said, for example, that the excessive taxation of the foreign-owned copper mines of Chile was largely responsible for the decline in the share of Chile in the world copper market.

[3] This point will be further discussed in paras. 36-8 below.

prevailing type of enterprise in each. The most appropriate forms of taxation will differ as between an economy where commercial and manufacturing activities are carried on by small traders and one where they are concentrated in the hands of large-scale business enterprises. Similarly, the prevailing forms of land tenure, the nature of social and family relationships, the extent of economic inequality, etc. call for differing methods of taxation of the subsistence sector. The general tendency in most under-developed countries is to throw a disproportionate share of the burden of taxation on the 'monetized' or market sector, and an insufficient amount on subsistence agriculture. The reasons for this are partly administrative and partly political — taxes levied on the agricultural community are far more difficult to assess and collect, and are socially and politically unpopular because they appear unjust — the people in the 'subsistence sector' are, individually, always so much poorer than the people in the market sector. Yet for reasons set out in paras. 17-18 below, it is the taxation of the agricultural sector that has a vital role to play in accelerating economic development; the disproportionate taxation of the 'monetized' or market sector tends to retard economic progress by reducing both the sources and the incentives to accumulation.

15. The general conclusion is that the efficient utilization of the taxation potential of an under-developed country raises problems which vary with the circumstances of each country, though certain features may be common to all of them. The extent and importance of a domestic landowning class; the nature of enterprise in the secondary and tertiary sectors; the role and importance of foreign enterprise; and finally the competence and integrity of tax administration are the main issues in this connection.

16. In the remaining sections of this paper we shall consider separately the issues raised by (i) the taxation of the agricultural sector; (ii) the role of indirect (commodity) taxation; (iii) direct taxation on income and capital; (iv) the taxation of foreign enterprises; (v) compulsory savings; and (vi) problems of tax administration.

II. THE TAXATION OF THE AGRICULTURAL SECTOR

17. The most important common feature of under-developed countries is that a high proportion of the total population is occupied in the so-called 'primary' or subsistence agricultural sector; indeed the proportion of the population engaged in the provision of food

supplies for domestic use is the best available index of the stage of economic development of a country. In the poorest and most backward economies it reaches 80-90 per cent ; in the relatively poor but semi-developed economies it is around 40-60 per cent ; in the highly developed areas it is 10 per cent or less. This means that as development proceeds, the proportion of the working population engaged in producing food for domestic consumption is steadily reduced, and the proportion engaged in manufacturing, commerce and services is steadily increased. In order to make this possible the proportion of food produced on the land which is *not* consumed by the food producers must steadily increase ; this in turn inevitably involves that each family engaged in food production should sell a steadily larger part of its output for consumption outside the agricultural sector. Unless this happens it is impossible for the non-agricultural sector to expand so as to occupy an increasing proportion of the community's man-power. Such an expansion of the 'agricultural surplus' cannot be relied upon to arise automatically as part of the over-all process of growth in the economy. Economic incentives do not operate in the same way in the 'subsistence sector' as in the case of industry and commerce. A shortage of food is not likely to call forth increased production ; a rise in the price of locally produced food may even lead to a *decrease* of the amounts which are offered for sale since it may cause the agricultural families to reduce their amount of work (or increase their own consumption) if their own needs for things which can only be procured with money can now be satisfied in exchange for a smaller quantity of foodstuffs. But since, on account of the nature of food as a primary necessity, a very large part (and if necessary, an increasing part) of the urban worker's income is spent on food, it is the supply of foodstuffs to the non-agricultural sectors which limits the effective demand for the products of the non-agricultural sectors. Hence it is the growth of the demand for labour outside agriculture which is limited by the proportion of food production which goes to the market (as against the food consumed by the food producers themselves), and not the other way round.

18. It follows that the taxation of agriculture, by one means or another, has a critical role to play in the acceleration of economic development since it is only *the imposition of compulsory levies on the agricultural sector itself* which enlarges the supply of 'savings' for economic development in the required sense. Countries as different in their social institutions or economic circumstances as Japan and Soviet Russia have been similar in their dependence on heavy agricultural taxation (in the case of Japan, through a land tax, in the

case of Soviet Russia, through a system of compulsory deliveries at low prices) for financing their economic development.

19. An annual tax on land, expressed as a percentage of the value of the produce per acre, is the most ancient form of taxation both in Europe and in Asia. Up to the beginning of this century the land tax still provided the principal source of revenue in the countries of the Middle East, in India and many other areas (in Europe its relative importance had been declining for a century or so as a result of the diminished relative importance of agriculture in the total national income). Since that time, however, political pressures, combined with monetary changes, have succeeded almost everywhere in 'eroding' the weight of this tax almost completely, and its rehabilitation now faces heavy political and administrative obstacles. Yet there can be little doubt that with heavier agricultural taxation the rate of development of all these countries could be much accelerated.

20. The main political objection to this tax is that it is socially unjust in its incidence since (taking into account needs) it hits the poor far more heavily than the rich farmer. However, it would be possible to avoid the anti-social features of the tax by making it a *progressive tax* varying with the total size of family holdings. Since in most countries that are relatively over-populated, and in which land is scarce, the distribution of the ownership of land is very uneven (with something like one-half of the available land being owned by 10 per cent or less of the agricultural families in typical cases) it is quite possible to exempt the very small farmer from this tax altogether and yet collect adequate revenue by making its incidence progressive on the owners of the larger holdings. A progressive land tax naturally raises the most fierce resentment in all countries where a land-owning class exists, and, to my knowledge, it has not yet been put into practice anywhere.

21. Another objection frequently made against a land tax is that it requires relatively frequent periodic reassessment of each individual holding — a task which is extremely costly and difficult to perform. It would be possible, however, to assess the potential fertility of individual pieces of land *in relation to the national or regional average* on the basis of more of less permanent criteria (such as average annual rainfall, irrigation, slope and inclination of the land, porousness or other qualities of the soil, etc.), and once this work of evaluation of 'potential relative fertility' is accomplished, it need not be repeated at frequent intervals. On the other hand, the actual tax liability could be changed year by year by estimating the average value of output per acre for the country or region as a

whole,[1] and multiplying this by the coefficient which relates the fertility of any particular acre to the national average.

22. It would be technically feasible, therefore, to revive the ancient land tax in a way that would make it both more effective and more in keeping with present-day conceptions of equity by (i) a system which assesses the potential yield of any particular piece of land not in terms of the actual value of output, but in relation to the yield of the *average* land in any particular region ; (ii) by making the tax a progressive one, the effective rates of taxation of which vary with the total value of land-holdings of the family unit. Such a tax would preserve the merit of the ancient land taxes in that it would be a tax on the 'potential output' rather than on the actual output of any piece of land, meaning by 'potential output' the *output which the land would yield if it were managed with average efficiency*. Thus the inefficient farmer whose production is less than the average for the region and for the type of land concerned would be penalized, whereas the efficient farmer would be correspondingly encouraged. Such a tax on potential output is far superior in its economic consequences to any tax based on actual income or profit ; and it is technically feasible to impose it in the case of agriculture (where the nature and quality of land provides a measurable yardstick) in a way which is not feasible for other types of economic activity. It would thus give the maximum incentive for efficient farmers to improve their land and expand their output ; it should also greatly encourage the transfer of land ownership from inefficient to efficient hands, and thereby raise the average productivity of land nearer to that obtained by the best managed farms.[2]

23. Another important advantage of a tax on these lines is that it would operate as a potent instrument of land reform, and its efficiency in this respect could be enhanced to any desired extent by increasing the rate of progression of the tax. It could be made to operate so as to induce the owners of large estates — particularly when the tax schedule is expressed in terms of *effective* rates, rather than *marginal* rates — to sell part of their holding in order to bring themselves into a lower tax bracket, thereby making the distribution of land ownership more equal and at the same time creating a freer

[1] One way of doing this is by making an estimate of the total output of food-stuffs for the country or region and then dividing it by the estimate of the number of cultivable acres in that region. Once statistical estimates had been made for a sufficient number of years, the average value of the produce per acre could be calculated as a moving average of, say, the past five years. In years of drought the tax could be remitted altogether either on a local or a national scale, as the case may be.

[2] A tax reform on these lines would of course be the more efficacious in raising agricultural productivity if it were combined with other measures for improving agricultural productivity — e.g. the provision of cheap credit facilities, the institution of agricultural extension services, etc.

market in land. In many countries agricultural stagnation is largely the result of absentee ownership, and of the unwillingness of existing owners to part with any of their possessions, even if they are incapable of putting their land to good use. By making the land market more fluid, a progressive land tax would enhance the chances of able and energetic cultivators to get hold of the land.

24. In some under-developed regions — as e.g. in most areas of Africa — the traditional social customs and the prevailing system of land tenure etc. have made the establishment of a system of an annual land tax hitherto impossible. Instead, resort was generally had to an inferior substitute — the poll tax — which is levied simply on the basis of the number of adult males in each region. The great advantage of the poll tax is the ease of assessment ; and in countries where there is not much economic inequality in the rural areas this tax is not so obnoxious as it would be in older, over-populated countries where a high degree of economic inequality prevails. Nevertheless, a poll tax can never fulfil the same functions as a land tax based on the *potential* fertility of land. A poll tax, unlike a land tax, does not give the same incentives to improve cultivation ; it does not make for greater fluidity in the ownership and/or occupation of the land. And because it can take into account economic inequality, a land tax is capable of yielding a much larger revenue than a poll tax.

25. The importance for economic development of an efficient system of taxation of the agricultural or subsistence sector of the community cannot be over-estimated. In the absence of a direct tax on the subsistence sector — whether in the form of a land tax or a poll tax — this sector can only be taxed indirectly through taxes on commodities which are bought by the agricultural sector. Such methods of indirect taxation can never, however, fulfil the same function : they do not provide the same incentives for increased production or an increase in marketable supplies, and may even tend to retard the development of the rural regions. Since, moreover, it is impossible to differentiate in indirect taxation between various classes of consumers, and since only a small part of the real income of the subsistence sector may be absorbed by the consumption of products bought for money, the scope for such indirect methods of taxing the subsistence sector are strictly limited.

III. TAXES ON COMMODITIES

26. Whilst commodity taxes are not an adequate method for taxing the agricultural sector, they are bound to be one of the

principal methods of taxing the economy at large and one of the principal sources of government revenue. As a method of taxing the 'monetized' or exchange sector they are superior to direct taxes wherever the economy largely consists of small enterprises, with few employees in each ; in these circumstances income tax is not a convenient or efficient instrument for taxing either the profits of the employer, or (through the PAYE, or deduction-at-source method) the wages and salaries of employees. To assess and collect taxes on commodities which pass through the frontier is relatively simple, particularly where imports and exports pass through a port. And, to an extent not always realized, such taxes may fall partly on the profits of *producers* or *suppliers* (domestic or foreign) and not only on the *consumers* of the taxed commodities.

27. Thus, in the case of commodities imported for domestic consumption, where particular imports are under the control of a single company, or a limited number of companies (either because the bulk of the local market is controlled by a single great merchanting house, or because the imports are controlled by world-wide concerns, as with oil and petrol) the price to the domestic consumers tends to be fixed at the 'optimum monopoly' price ; so that it may not pay the importer to pass on the full incidence of the tax to the local buyer. In this case the import duty is partly a method of taxing the profits of the importer (which is often a foreign company) and only in part a method of taxing the domestic consumer.

28. Similarly in the case of exports of minerals or plantation products, an export duty may be a more effective method of taxing the profits of producing companies than an income tax, particularly where the local operating company is a subsidiary of a foreign company which is also its trading partner, so that the profits shown by the local company may be arbitrary. The danger is, however, that once export duties are imposed, the exigencies of revenue lead them to be fixed at excessive levels with the result that the development of export industries is inhibited.[1]

29. Though it is possible to vary the rate of commodity taxes according to the degree of luxuriousness of the commodity, thereby introducing a certain progression into the tax system, the revenue potentialities of taxes on luxurious goods are limited, since total imports may be small and consumption may be substantially reduced by heavy taxation. To get maximum revenue it is necessary to tax articles of mass consumption — cotton cloth, sugar, flour, beer, tobacco, kerosene, etc. — and this raises all the political difficulties

[1] The expansion of the Ceylon tea industry is said to have been severely hampered through excessive taxation by means of export duties.

associated with a reduction in accustomed standards of living of the mass of the population. But this is not a peculiar feature of such taxes, but of taxation in general. It is impossible to increase the amounts raised in taxation suddenly or substantially without public resistance — whatever form the taxation takes.

30. There is finally the possibility of a *general sales tax*, collected from retailers on a very wide range of articles. Such taxes are a common feature of many developed countries ; the experience of India shows that they can be successfully imposed also in under-developed areas at least where a relatively high standard of public administration exists.

IV. DIRECT TAXES ON INCOME AND CAPITAL

31. The importance which progressive direct taxes on income and capital should play in the tax system necessarily varies with the stage of economic and social development. The experience of a wide variety of countries shows that taxes on income or profits can only be successfully imposed on large-scale enterprises or on the employees of such enterprises. In many under-developed areas the bulk of income tax revenue comes from a few large business firms and from government employees. The extension of the tax to small traders, artisans or professional persons meets with serious administrative difficulties — as there is no way of ascertaining incomes where no proper books are kept, no regular accounts are prepared or audited. It has often been suggested that a more promising form of bringing small and medium traders within the scope of direct taxation would be by means of a tax assessed on the value of their property — by means of a net wealth tax — since property (whether in the form of land and buildings, plant and equipment, or stock-in-trade) is more difficult to conceal than income. However in the few under-developed countries where graduated taxes on net wealth have been introduced (such as India and Ceylon) they operate with a large exemption limit, and they are intended as an additional form of taxation on wealthy individuals and not as a tax on small and medium business, so that there is no actual experience to show how successful such a tax would be in practice.

32. In 'semi-developed' countries which possess large-scale enterprises engaged in industry and commerce, and where a wealthy domestic capitalized class exists, progressive taxes on income and wealth are potentially very important both for mitigating the growing economic inequalities between different classes (and the political and social tensions which are attendant on this) and for reducing

the share of national resources devoted to socially unnecessary luxury consumption.[1]

33. There is hardly any 'semi-developed' country, however, where an efficient system of personal taxation can be said to exist (with the exception of taxes on salaries and wages). In most countries of Latin America, for example, though nominal tax rates mount to fairly high levels — to levels comparable to those in the U.S. or the U.K. — the proportion of large incomes effectively paid in taxation (according to all available evidence), is considerably lower than that falling on small or medium incomes. This is partly due to defective tax legislation — e.g. many countries follow the so-called 'cedular' system of income taxation which imposes a separate tax on different sources of income (and which leaves important sources entirely untaxed) instead of a single comprehensive tax on all income, as in the U.S. or Western Europe. In part it is due to prevailing legal institutions which permit anonymity in the ownership of wealth (mostly on account of the prevailing system of 'bearer shares' in the case of companies or the system of 'benami' in India), and which prevents any effective taxation on incomes derived from capital or on wealth (either in the form of inheritance taxes or of annual taxes on capital). It is also due to sheer inefficiency (and to an unknown extent perhaps also of corruption) in administration, which prevents the existing provisions from being effectively referred even to the limited extent to which existing systems of tax laws would permit.

34. It would go far beyond the scope of this paper to set out the essential requirements for creating an effective system of direct taxation — the more so since these requirements vary considerably with the circumstances of each particular country. I am convinced, however, as a result of studying the problem in a number of countries [2]

---

[1] This objective cannot be attained by a graduated system of commodity taxation alone. Since the same commodities are bought by people of very different wealth — the richer people buying more *kinds* of goods and services, and not just more 'luxurious' goods — and since many of the things on which the rich spend money cannot be effectively taxed — domestic service, foreign travel, antiques, etc. — the spending power of the wealthy classes can never be tapped by means of commodity taxes to anywhere near the same extent as by means of progressive taxes on income or wealth.

It is sometimes argued that in under-developed countries the 'luxury consumption' of the rich is largely spent on services (i.e. domestic servants, etc.) which increases the volume of employment, and thereby performs an important social function. This view overlooks, however, that it is the supply of wage-goods (particularly food) which sets a limit to the total volume of employment that can be offered outside the agricultural sector without creating inflation ; if more people are taken into unproductive employment, there is less room for productive employment. The mere existence of surplus labour in a community does not imply therefore that such luxury consumption is harmless or that it does not involve the use of scarce resources.

[2] Two of these studies have been published. Cf. *Indian Tax Reform*, Report of a Survey (Ministry of Finance, New Delhi, 1956), and *Suggestions for a*

that in all countries which have attained the stage of development at which the need for an effective system of direct personal taxation arises, there are no unsuperable technical or administrative obstacles to its introduction, provided the need is adequately recognized, and the opposition from vested interests can be overcome.

V. TAXATION OF FOREIGN ENTERPRISES

35. The tax treatment of foreign enterprises and of foreign investment raises two distinct problems to under-developed countries. The first concerns the question of how far under-developed countries should go in the offer of special concessions — in the form of immunity from taxation, etc. — in order to attract foreign capital and enterprise to their country? The second relates to the most appropriate method of taxing the profits of foreign enterprises when they are not exempt. Both questions raise difficult problems as a result of developments which have occurred since the Second World War.

36. Foreign investment in its various forms holds out the best hope of accelerated development to many under-developed countries ; it may be indispensable at critical stages of development when industrialization gives rise to greatly enlarged imports of equipment and materials but before there is any corresponding increase in export availabilities to pay for these. Foreign enterprise may be indispensable also in imparting the know-how necessary for the efficient development of local industries. Moreover, in the case of many countries, the production and export of valuable minerals found in their area holds out the only hope of generating the 'economic surplus' which is a necessary pre-condition for their internal development. For many countries, the production of minerals for export forms a considerable share of their gross national product and is the principal source of their public revenue. It is evidently in the interest of under-developed countries that the production of such minerals be developed, and that this should be followed up by the development of processing facilities which gives rise to industrial development ; it is better to export aluminium than crude bauxite, or refined copper than copper ore ; it is better for oil-producing areas to have their own oil refineries so as to export their oil in refined form. Most under-developed countries have neither the money nor the know-how to undertake such developments on their

Comprehensive Reform of Direct Taxation, Sessional Paper IV, 1960 (Government Publication Bureau, Colombo, Ceylon).

own ; moreover, the marketing of many of these commodities is closely controlled by large international concerns.

37. On the other hand it is broadly true that the amount of investment which the large international concerns are ready to undertake both in mining and in processing depends on their over-all view of the requirements of the world market, and their estimate of the annual growth of world consumption. It is therefore *a priori* unlikely that any special concessions (in the form of tax holidays etc.) granted by the producing countries are likely to have any appreciable effect on the *total* flow of international investment. They can have important effects, however, on its allocation : since most basic minerals are to be found in many different regions, it is naturally in the interests of international capital to develop them in those countries which offer the most favourable prospects, both from the point of view of production cost and also from the point of view of the tax treatment of the resulting gains. But this in turn tends to bring about an unhealthy competition in the offer of special concessions to foreign capital. Whilst any *particular* country will normally stand to gain by the offer of such tax concessions, if the concessions offered are relative to the existing tax treatment of foreign enterprises in competing countries, the very fact that the various countries are in competition with one another for getting a larger slice of such investments will cause any new concession offered by one country to be copied by the others, so that in the end they are all deprived of the prospect of obtaining their due share from these developments without benefiting any one of them — the competing concessions will largely cancel out each other.

38. The situation is basically different when the concessions offered to foreign enterprise serve the purpose of developing domestic industries largely catering for the internal market. In such cases tax concessions may well have the effect of increasing the *total* flow of international investment — some particular project of developing a local textile mill, a cement factory or an assembly plant may appear sufficiently attractive when tax concessions are offered when it would not be attractive without.

39. This question of how far under-developed countries *as a group* should go in offering privileged tax treatment to foreign investment (or for that matter, to domestic enterprise) is therefore a complex one which cannot in general be answered one way or another. In cases where the concessions serve the purpose of increasing the aggregate flow of investment it is clearly to their interest to forgo additional tax revenue, even for a considerable number of years, since their rate of economic development may be

greatly enhanced as a result. But in other cases it is not; and in view of the haphazard multiplication of tax privileges of various kinds in recent years there is a clear case for international discussions possibly leading to conventions or agreements, that would eliminate the element of unhealthy competition which undoubtedly exists at present. It is to the interest of under-developed countries as a group that the tax treatment — both the scope and the rates of taxation of enterprises and of the nature and extent of tax holidays etc. granted — should as far as possible, be uniform, and that individual countries should not offer additional concessions except in agreement with the others.

40. The second important issue concerns the manner in which the profits of foreign enterprises engaged in production for exports (or in the import trade) are to be taxed. The most satisfactory method is a tax on the profits arising from local operations. An export duty, as we have noted, can be a potent form of taxation, but it is not a satisfactory substitute for taxation on the basis of profits : if the export duty is heavy, it may have an inhibiting effect on development ; if it is light, it cannot secure adequate revenue. Taxes based on profits are less discouraging to the foreign investor, precisely because their burden depends on the gains actually made ; if the operations turn out to be unsuccessful (either because there were unexpected costs in local operations, or because the market conditions are unfavourable) the entrepreneurs are relieved of them.[1]

41. The problem with profit taxation, on the other hand, is to ascertain the true profit in all those cases where the resident operating companies are merely branches or subsidiaries of international concerns whose trading operations are not at 'arm's length' — since they sell to (or buy from) non-resident companies belonging to the same group. The prices in such transactions are in fact internal accounting prices of the concerns ; it is well known that an international concern operating through a chain of subsidiaries can easily 'shift' its profit from one place to another by changing the price which the subsidiaries (or associated companies) charge to one another. So long as profits are everywhere subject to tax and so long as the rates of taxation are not too different, the incentive for such 'profit shifting' will not be strong, particularly when the rates of taxation are heavier in the countries where the parent companies are situated than in the under-developed countries where the branches and subsidiaries operate. But since the Second World War inter-

---

[1] It is for this reason that export duties, in many cases, are fixed in terms of some sliding scale, the incidence of which varies with the prices actually realized in relation to some average.

national companies have made increasing use of the so-called 'tax-havens' — they established holding companies or subsidiaries in territories where the profits are not subject to tax (or only at nominal rates) or in countries which do not bring into charge the profits earned in the overseas operations of their resident companies.[1] The result has been that an increasing proportion of the profits made by such concerns has been syphoned into such tax-havens, thus depriving both the producing and the consuming countries of revenue.[2]

42. Thus the profits made in the extraction and processing of minerals may be under-stated by invoicing exports at unduly low prices. The profits made in the importation and local distribution of foreign commodities or services may be under-stated by invoicing imports at unduly high prices.[3]

43. Sooner or later the arbitrary allocation of profits in the production or distribution of commodities which enter into international trade will make it necessary for countries to look beyond the accounts of the local companies, and, if necessary, to impute profits to them based on an appropriate share of the total world profits of the companies which operate local branches or subsidiaries. Here again there is a fruitful field for international co-operation. If it were possible to get agreements between the various countries of how they should deal with such problems they could be dealt with far more effectively than if each country tried to act in isolation.

VI. COMPULSORY SAVINGS

44. A relatively new form of raising internal resources for development purposes which has recently been introduced in a number of

---

[1] For a description of the facilities offered by such 'tax-haven' countries cf. Gibbons, *Tax Factors in Basing International Business Abroad*, Harvard Law School, International Program in Taxation, Cambridge (Mass.), 1957.

[2] That this problem is not peculiar to under-developed countries but affects the countries of the parent companies as well is shown by the current efforts of the U.S. administration to get U.S. tax legislation amended so as to bring the profits of foreign subsidiaries and associated companies within the scope of the U.S. Corporation tax.

[3] In the case of the international oil industry the tendency has been to fix the price-structure in such a way that the profits arising from the whole complex of international operations are concentrated on the production of crude oil, and not in refining and distribution of oil products. The reasons for this are partly to be sought in tax considerations (since the royalties paid to the governments of the oil-producing countries qualify as a tax offset in the 'parent' countries) and partly political and strategic. But the result has been that the oil-producing areas obtained more revenue than could have been obtained if a free competitive market had existed ; whereas the oil-consuming countries (both developed and under-developed) have been deprived of revenue (other than in the form of import duties or excise taxes).

countries (e.g. Turkey, Ghana, British Guiana, Brazil and some others) is compulsory savings. This obliges individuals and businesses to apply a certain percentage of their incomes to the purchase of interest-bearing but non-negotiable bonds which are repayable (together with accrued interest) after five, seven or ten years. The scheme is usually administered in connection with income tax or (as in the case of Ghana) in connection with the purchase of cash crops by a marketing board. The advantage of the scheme, as against straightforward taxation, is that as people are merely asked to postpone their consumption and not forgo it altogether, considerations of equity do not require the same kind of differentiation or graduation as is the case with income tax, and in consequence, more substantial amounts can be raised at relatively modest rates. Thus the compulsory levy is generally imposed on wage and salary earners at a flat rate of 3 or 5 per cent on the *whole* of income, though the obligation only extends to people whose incomes are above certain minimum levels. There may be a similar obligation on businesses and professional persons, generally with a higher rate of contribution.

45. It is possible to combine such a scheme with a lottery scheme (like the 'premium bonds' in the U.K.) which might make it more attractive to the majority who are given a chance to win large cash prizes even before the bonds are due for redemption. But the lottery element makes the administration of this scheme far more complicated ; also, it was found in some cases that there was a great deal of moral opposition (by the churches, trade unions and farmers' organizations) to compulsory lottery.

46. It is possible also (though this requires far more administrative preparation) to make the scheme into a universal contributory pensions scheme, drawn up on an actuarial basis, whereby the repayment of the compulsory loan takes the form of a pension upon retirement, graduated according to the amount of the contributions made during working life. A compulsory savings scheme which results in a universal old age pensions scheme is likely to be far more popular than a scheme where the contributors are supplied with non-negotiable bonds repayable after a fixed number of years.

47. A scheme of this kind is only appropriate to under-developed countries which have already attained a stage of development which makes it possible to bring a considerable section of the population within the scope of direct taxation ; or where there is a major cash crop (such as cocoa in Ghana) which is purchased by a central marketing board at fixed prices.[1]

[1] In Ghana, 10 per cent of the price of cocoa is now paid in the form of such bonds.

VII. THE PROBLEM OF TAX ADMINISTRATION

48. It cannot be emphasized too strongly that the efficacy of the tax system is not just a matter of appropriate tax laws but of the efficiency and integrity of tax administration. In many under-developed countries the low revenue yield of taxation can only be attributed to the fact that the tax provisions are not properly enforced, either on account of the inability of the administration to cope with them, or on account of straightforward corruption in the administration. No system of tax laws, however carefully conceived, is proof against collusion between the tax administrators and the taxpayers ; an efficient administration consisting of persons of high integrity is the most important requirement for exploiting the 'taxation potential' of a country.[1]

49. One important condition for this is that the government departments concerned with the administration of taxes should not be over-burdened and this in turn requires that complicated taxes should be avoided unless there is an administration able to cope with them. Yet in many countries there are hundreds of different taxes with a negligible yield — the cumulative result of the gradual accretion of imposts which have long since lost their justification, but which have never been formally withdrawn — the administration of which is a great deal more costly than the amounts collected. Indeed, there is no other field where bureaucracy can be so cumbrous and absurd as in the administration of taxes ; and in many countries there needs to be an infusion of a new spirit, which makes it possible to apply modern techniques of business administration, before any major reform can be accomplished.

50. Many under-developed countries suffer both from an insufficiency of staff and from the relatively low grading of the staff of the tax administration departments. Persons of ability and integrity can only be found for these jobs if sufficient recognition is given to the importance of the tasks which they are asked to perform, and this should be fully reflected in their status, pay, prospects of promotion, etc. Any additional outlay incurred in improving the status and pay of the officials of the revenue department is likely to yield a very high return in terms of increased revenue.

[1] There is a glaring discrepancy, in most under-developed countries, between the amount of incomes of various types as computed by the method of national output statistics, and the incomes declared in tax returns or computed on the basis of tax receipts. In the 'developed' countries the national income estimates based on the 'income' and the 'output' method of computation are more easily reconciled, and do not reveal such glaring differences. It is probably not exaggerated to say that the typical under-developed country collects in direct taxation no more than one-fifth, possibly only one-tenth, of what is due.

DISCUSSION OF THE PAPER BY MR. KALDOR

Professor V. K. R. V. Rao, in opening the discussion, said that it was generally agreed that there was a need to increase tax revenues in all under-developed countries and that the tax potential of such countries was not yet fully utilized. Mr. Kaldor had put forward the proposition that this potential depends on the excess of actual consumption over the minimum essential consumption of the population. It was necessary to amend this to include 'minimum essential private investment' as well, since it was also desirable to reduce unessential private investment in under-developed countries.

The paper had argued that there was a high ratio of property incomes to total national income in under-developed countries. This was based on a misunderstanding of the distribution of property incomes in such countries; they consisted of a large number of relatively small incomes, which were difficult to tax. It was the ownership of industrial property that mattered; an increasing maldistribution of the ownership of such property was almost an index of economic development. Indian experience suggested that the distribution of all property might be less unequal than the distribution of income.

The paper had discussed the role of the subsistence sector as a source of tax revenue and proposed that a progressive land tax be used as a means of obtaining resources from this sector. However, the subsistence sector meant, by definition, under-consumption of food, not a surplus available over and above minimum needs. The bulk of consumption in the subsistence sector was foodstuffs; in India it had been found that the surplus offered for sale by the subsistence sector before the last war was the result of the farmers' need for money to pay taxes, interest to money lenders, etc. In a democratic country rising farmers' incomes led to an increase in the consumption of foodstuffs by farmers. The first aim of any policy should be to raise agricultural productivity.

To tax the potential output of agricultural holdings, as proposed by Mr. Kaldor, was logical but not practical, because of the possible effects upon land holdings. It would be difficult to tax these holdings according to their size, because of the problems of defining 'size' in any meaningful way. However defined, there were very few large holdings in India and the average size of holding was probably too small already for efficiency. A progressive land tax might reduce the size of holdings still further. The experience of high industrial taxation in India had shown that it led to the breaking up of firms into smaller units in order to reduce the total tax burden.

It was unduly pessimistic to say that an agricultural income tax could not be successful. India had such a tax, although it could be criticized on various grounds. There was also no reason why commodity taxes should not work as well in the subsistence sector as in the urban sector.

Record of Discussion

Professor F. Neumark said Mr. Kaldor had stated that an annual land tax in the form of a percentage of the produce per acre had been the most ancient form of land tax. This was not so ; land taxes had usually been levied on the physical volume of production. When the change had eventually been made to a value basis this had been regarded as an improvement.

There were strong doubts, however, as to the feasibility of a progressive land tax as proposed by the author of the paper. There had been some discussion in the non-English literature of the effects of such a tax on incentives, but these arguments might not hold in the case of under-developed countries. Graduation of the tax by size of holding was clearly unjust, because of the differences in potential profits from different crops. Such a tax would also lead to the fragmentation of holdings. Mr. Kaldor's proposed procedure for assessing the tax (paragraph 21) was rational and similar to that in use by the French authorities, but it would probably be too complicated for under-developed countries.

The heterogeneity of under-developed countries was an important factor when tax systems were under discussion. An income tax, for example, had proved workable in Turkey, but had not been useful in Thailand, except in a simple form and in limited sectors. Particular care was needed when using international comparisons of tax burdens ; such comparisons could not show the fact that tax potentials were fairly well exploited in developed countries, but were not yet fully utilized in under-developed countries.

Professor Sir Dennis Robertson said that there was much in the paper to agree with, especially the inefficiency of inflation as a means of stimulating economic growth, and the dangerous addiction of some governments to expenditures on expensive status symbols, such as public buildings and diplomatic missions. There was also the important point concerning the need to avoid complicated taxes that were expensive to administer.

Mr. Kaldor's picture of the peasant as indolent and incapable of response to economic, or any other sort of incentives, was not so acceptable. Other observers with detailed knowledge of such societies did not support this viewpoint. It was doubtful if the growth process required the actual reduction of food consumption in the agricultural sector, but it was clear that agricultural improvements should have a high place in any planning scheme, together with such supporting investments as roads and the provision of credit, etc. Professor D. Walker, in his paper to Section 4 of the Congress ('Marketing Boards'), had underlined the importance of small independent enterprises as sources of economic growth in countries such as Uganda. Fiscal arrangements, as well as other policies, should be designed so as not to hamper the emergence of such indigenous enterprises.

Professor E. P. Reubens said that Mr. Kaldor had mentioned export taxes, but not as counter-cyclical devices. It was in this role, however, that they had been extensively used in the 1950s as a means of capturing the gains accruing to primary producers in the Korean War boom. Such taxes were unlikely to be important at a time when prices were falling, especially when they were levied on a sliding scale that caused the yield to decline as prices fell.

A question of wider importance concerned the relevance of the Kaldor model to different types of societies. It seemed to fit the case of nineteenth-century Japan well ; it was a homogeneous patriotic society, with a docile people dominated by a small, aggressive elite which, in turn, was devoted to abstemious living and resolute saving and investment. There was a strong demand for Japan's export products on the world market (silk and coal) ; at home the land taxes were mitigated in their effects by rising prices, since they had been fixed in money terms in the early 1870s. Rising farm productivity also sustained the payment of these taxes.

At the other extreme was the case of present-day British Guiana. It was divided as a society, both racially and ideologically. The main exports were produced by large, expatriate concerns and faced heavy competition on world markets.

These contrasts suggested that tax systems must be carefully adapted to circumstances. In particular, tax programmes must not exacerbate any divergent tendencies, both social and economic, which might exist in a country.

Dr. A. Loutfy commented that the need for fiscal reform in under-developed countries was widely recognized, as was the injustice of many of the taxes on income and wealth which are now in operation. Keynes had put forward the view that any increase in the progressiveness of taxes would decrease savings and Mr. Kaldor had pointed out in his book *An Expenditure Tax* how people might give up saving in the face of very high taxation.

This reduction in the supply of savings forced firms to rely on self-financing, which raised prices and led to the weakening of competition as firms grew in size. Entrepreneurs were opposed to the simplification of tax systems, however, because of the way in which such reforms would reduce the scope for evasion.

Injustice arose from the way in which the taxes fell on different types of tax payers. Some, such as civil servants, cannot evade taxes, because of the nature of their work, whilst other occupations find it easy to do so. Similarly, some types of firms could not evade taxes because they were forced to keep accounts, whilst others need not do so. It was widely accepted that the yields from taxation were reduced by evasion and fraud, apart from the injustice involved.

Since taxes on income and wealth could be shown to be unjust, low in yield and obstacles to growth (because of the way in which they inhibited savings) it would be better to replace them with a graduated expenditure tax along the lines previously proposed by Mr. Kaldor.

Professor R. Dorfman said that the discussion had turned on the merits of the tax systems in under-developed countries as a means of stimulating development ; in the more developed economies this role also fell on the banking system. Was the tax system being expected to provide a substitute for a developed banking system in under-developed countries ?

It was not true that 'subsistence' farmers did not save, since they did spend a small amount per head on such purposes as the acquisition of land, hoards of gold, etc. These expenditures would release resources for development purposes by locking up purchasing power. It would be interesting to know what use was made of the resources freed in this way.

Professor D. Walker argued that, when considering the African economies, it was necessary to distinguish between the agricultural and subsistence sectors, because there was no true subsistence sector to be found in Africa. Within the agricultural sector there did exist taxable capacity which could be mobilized, if required. Since incomes arose in several forms a variety of taxes were required. There was a good deal of trade in local foodstuffs, for example, which, if exempt whilst export crops were taxed, would result in too large a burden falling on the export sector.

The idea of a land tax was quite impracticable in African conditions. Mr. Kaldor's arguments for this tax on the grounds of incentives were not convincing, although they might work at low levels of output. The Irish land tax was an example similar to the author's idea, but it had had no effects upon output. The farmers often did not understand it, but those who did evaded it.

There had been no mention in the paper of the role of local government. It had been shown possible in Africa to raise a simple income tax at the local government level. This had been based on indicators of wealth — the level of consumption, etc. — known to the local people.

Finally, it was important to ask whether it was necessary to raise the revenue in the first place. There were several examples of countries which already raised quite high revenues in relation to their national income. It was possible to have taxes that were too high and damaged productive enterprises in consequence.

Dr. W. Thweatt said that the proposition had already been put forward that the propensity to save of the recipients of profits was higher than that of those people who received incomes from property. Those receiving profits were more likely to behave like 'economic men'. Landlords, on the other hand, sought more wealth through larger holdings, which was not investment from the point of view of the economy as a whole. It made sense, therefore, to impose higher taxes on rent than on profits.

Professor E. Gannagé argued that a property tax might be a way of reducing the amount of evasion experienced if only income taxes are employed. In the Middle East, for example, oil royalties had risen in importance as a source of revenue, but they had replaced other taxes as their yield increased. It was necessary to ask whether the countries concerned could absorb such large revenues from this source. As far as taxes on land were concerned, the differences of opinion expressed in the discussion as to the practical possibility of such taxes may be due to the likelihood that such a tax is more likely to be successful at certain stages of development, but not at others.

Professor M. L. Dantwala said that Mr. Kaldor had maintained (paragraph 11) that the high ratio of property incomes to total national income in India meant that there was 'a relatively high taxation potential in relation to real income per head'. Whilst it was true that total property incomes were important, individual incomes from this source were not high, and it was on the individual size of incomes that taxation potential depended.

Similarly, the uneven distribution of land ownership to which Mr. Kaldor had also drawn attention did not necessarily imply a high tax potential. In India, the 10 per cent of the farmers who owned 50 per cent of the land often included those with relatively small incomes, often below the exemption limit for taxation.

The difficulties associated with land tenure could be dealt with by reforms in the systems of land ownership ; it was important to ask whether these should come before or after fiscal changes. It was probably better if land reform came first.

Mr. N. Kaldor, in replying to the discussion, said that the paper had covered a wide range of countries with different characteristics and many of the points raised had already been mentioned in it. The question of 'unnecessary private investment', for example, had been included.

Any proposal for a progressive land tax should not consider a rate which exceeds 15 per cent of the value of the produce of the land. It should be remembered that only a small proportion of the total value of the produce (usually not more than $\frac{1}{2}$) acrued to the cultivator in India. The Ricardian theory of rent was relevant to such a situation and it suggested that the surplus could be tapped by taxation. There had actually been a fall in the rate of the land tax in India since the days of British control.

The concentration of land ownership in the hands of a minority was often a stumbling block in the way of improvements which increased agricultural productivity. It might be necessary to encourage some fragmentation at the right level of size of holding. A tax on the value of land was effectively a tax on potential output and this was its great advantage. Poland had a progressive land tax and it seemed to work very well. In contrast, the income tax in Turkey, which had been referred to, worked well for those earning wages and salaries in urban employment, but not for other incomes. In African countries subsistence agriculture was often hindered from developing by a lack of incentives. In general, the essence of the fiscal problem was to get all sections of the population to pay their due share of taxation.

The possible effects upon saving of property taxation had probably been exaggerated. In Western countries with progressive taxation it had been the level of consumption out of property incomes that had diminished, not savings. In under-developed countries, it was generally safe to assume that most property incomes were based on land ownership. In these circumstances a betterment tax on land was suitable.

Chapter 9

THE CONTROL OF INFLATION IN CONDITIONS OF RAPID ECONOMIC GROWTH

BY

D. HOROWITZ
Bank of Israel

In their search for new capital, the developing countries frequently turn to inflationary methods. The temptation to finance development by inflationary means is greatest in developing countries, which strive to achieve forced savings by deficit financing of government budgets and thus to acquire resources needed for investment. The conception that resources for development can be appropriated by governments through inflationary savings is frequently promoted by the consideration that if a country refrains from ambitious development ventures it chooses *ipso facto* stagnation, dependence on foreign assistance for its balance of payments and substandards of living.

If monetary expansion takes place in a country with under-utilized resources, expansion of the physical volume of production following upon monetary expansion through governmental deficit financing may galvanize dormant factors of production which help to balance and set off the effects of monetary expansion. Here, the problem will be, to a great extent, one of the pattern of economic expansion and selectivity of investments. Bottlenecks in skilled labour, raw materials or equipment may frequently limit and retard the expansion of the gross national product, although on the whole there are ample under-utilized resources.

The selectivity of investment and the deliberate change in its pattern may release unutilized resources and factors of production, and help to overcome bottlenecks. Frequently, reorientation of investments, which would increase the supply of one of the scarce resources through training of unskilled labour or import of some specific equipment, or elimination of projects requiring excessive quantities of a certain resource which is in scarce supply, may help to overcome bottlenecks which, with monetary expansion proceeding, would cause inflationary pressures and disparities with all the distortions in the pattern of the economy as their result and concomitant.

The optimum relation between investment in the infrastructure and in branches of the economy, which, after fruition of investment, influence directly the balance of payments, either through replacement of imports or expansion of exports, presents one of the important dilemmas of selectivity of investment. Thus from the point of view of controlling inflation the pattern of utilization of capital imports is, in the last resort, not less important than their availability.

The inclination to give preference to large-scale projects and spectacular ventures frequently reduces the value of the capital imported into a developing country. Another dilemma is the relation of fixed capital to labour. This and many other decisions are involved in establishing the scale of priorities, which — if inflation is to be controlled — must be based on qualitative as well as quantitative controls. Replacement of labour by expensive machinery in countries with surplus of labour and scarcity of capital, the addition to large-scale spectacular projects, are the most frequent and striking shortcomings in the qualitative control of investment.

If resources are scarce, there is one decisive criterion for investment — the alternative use of resources. Too frequently, development projects in developing nations are judged and evaluated without proper regard for the order of priorities. Mostly, the question is posed whether a certain project is desirable on its merits, seldom whether an alternative use of the same resources for another purpose does not rank higher in the scale of priorities. Selectivity as a guiding principle applies, of course, not only to capital, but to total resources, including managerial and technical skills, which in many cases may be the main bottlenecks.

However, selectivity must be seen not only in the context of the order of priorities, but sometimes in connection with the need of a much more painful decision to refrain altogether from carrying out marginal projects, the need for which is less immediate, if the sum total of projects exceeds available resources, as otherwise their implementation would subject the economy to stresses and strains resulting in inflation. In the long run, inflation would slow up development, both because of balance of payments difficulties and physical shortages resulting therefrom, and prices rising faster than resources which can be allocated to development through an increased supply of money.

Nevertheless, in a country with dormant factors of production or under-utilized resources, the policy of monetary expansion may under certain conditions be successful in the short run and up to a limit, by galvanizing and utilizing idle capacity of production.

However, in countries in which, owing to already rapid pace of growth or scarcities, there are no dormant factors of production, or the bottlenecks are of such rigid character that they cannot be overcome by the change in the pattern of investment, the situation is incomparably more difficult. If, in such countries, the monetary authorities validate, through an increased supply of money, claims exceeding in volume the sum total of resources, the fat is in the fire and inflation takes its course. The supply of money is being augmented either by government budget deficits and borrowing from the central bank or by excessive expansion of credit through the banking system. In the long run, inflation takes its toll from nearly all social groups, but in the short run, pressure to initiate an inflationary policy by such validation of claims, through excessive monetary expansion, is of frequent occurrence, as almost every social and economic group is aware of the fact that in the short run it can gain by acquisition of assets through inflation, if it succeeds in maintaining its monopoly or supremacy in the appropriation of resources. This situation results in both rising price levels and increased pressure on the balance of payments, as the surplus purchasing power spills over into excessive demand for foreign currency to buy imported goods which would satisfy the new demand which cannot be met by increased production, and must lead to a deterioration of the balance of payments. Depletion of reserves of foreign currency, physical shortages and unemployment caused by lack of raw materials and other components of production dependent on imports, are the raw inevitable results of such developments.

Development through inflation, or economic growth within the framework of stability as alternatives of economic policy, must, however, first and foremost, be subjected to the test of economic efficacy. Economic stability is not a value superior to all other values and is an imperative desideratum only by virtue of its being a prerequisite for a long-term sustained growth free of economic distortions and extending over a period of years.

Monetary expansion may be the result either of direct government deficit financing or over-expansion of banking credit to private enterprises and less frequently of persistent surpluses in the balance of payments. In the latter case the surplus of foreign currency is being accumulated by the 'monetization' of this surplus in the form of local currency which it creates and which exerts an inflationary pressure. This latter form of inflation is of rather rare occurrence in developing countries, particularly so as with the continuous decline in the prices of primary products and limited import of capital from abroad. Those countries usually encounter balance of payments difficulties and thus inflation generated by a surplus in the balance of payments is a very rare exception.

Inflation develops on the following pattern : primary stage — deficit financing of government budgets and/or rise in wages exceeding increases in productivity ; second stage — expanding credit to government and/or business and increase in the supply of money ; third stage — rise in prices and/or deficit in the balance of payments. This is, of course, a schematic description of a process which leads to two discrepancies : (a) between the external and internal price levels ; and (b) between the volume of purchasing power and the quantity of goods and services available at prevailing prices.

The effects of this development can be traced in various ramifications of economic life. The disequilibrium, of which the price rise is only a symptom, leads to several distortions in the economic structure of the countries afflicted by such a process : as the rate of exchange cannot be too frequently adjusted, the gap between external and internal price levels leads to undue preference for imported goods and a higher propensity to consume these goods, as long as foreign currency is allocated by government at an unrealistic and cheap rate. Local production is penalized and imports are at a premium as the relative price levels of locally produced and imported goods are changed, creating price differentials in favour of imported goods.

In countries with a plentiful labour supply and a shortage of capital, a replacement of labour by labour-saving devices takes place, as capital equipment is being imported at an artificially low rate of exchange.

Simultaneously with the pressure for larger imports, because of the gap between the artificial and the real rate of exchange, exports are being adversely affected by the disparity between a high level of internal costs dominated and determined by inflationary pressures, and prices in the international markets. This disparity is reflected in distortions inherent in unrealistic exchange rates which actually diminish the returns of exporters. The high level of the cost of production cannot be reflected in prices on the foreign markets because of international competition, while the equivalent of the foreign currency earned is converted into local currency for the exporter at an artificially low rate of exchange. At the same time, the internal market is ready, because of the discrepancy between the inflated purchasing power and limited quantity of goods and services available, to absorb the additional quantity of goods at high prices and with greater ease than foreign markets.

Productivity is reduced by the fact that the marginal utility of additional amounts of depreciating cash is rather low and consequently leisure rises in the scale of values of the individual.

A shift from essential to non-essential production is taking place because the imposition of price controls which usually takes place in such situations mainly affects essential goods and keeps their prices rather low, while floating purchasing power and income are diverted to purchase of luxury goods which are uncontrolled and practically form the only free outlet for inflated incomes.

Import of capital in the form of transfer of currency dwindles into insignificance, as the artificial rate of exchange over-valuing local currency is tantamount to an expropriation of a part of the capital imported.

Distortions in the price structure resulting in a distorted pattern of production lead to a distortion in the structure of investments causing further disequilibrium in the future.

The first reaction to inflationary trends in modern political bodies is the introduction of physical controls. By keeping prices artificially low, through administrative controls, without arresting monetary expansion, the floating purchasing power is accentuating the shift to unessential production, and in the last resort consumption rises because of the artificially low price level as confronted with effective demand and rising incomes. Given a scarcity of foreign currency to pay for increased imports, physical shortages develop.

The introduction of physical controls frequently involves rationing, the elimination of consumers' choice and the creation of a black market for controlled commodities. The relative magnitude of the official and the black market is changing in favour of the black market, and the latter makes increasing inroads into the official market. All the time, internal prices rise, while the official rate of exchange remains unmodified. Political bodies are reluctant to change the rate of exchange and to adjust it to new realities. They are inclined to consider the rate of exchange as a matter of prestige and its modification as evidence of the failure of the government in power. Anyhow, usually the progress of this form of inflation, i.e. suppressed inflation, is too rapid to allow for its treatment by a change in the rate of exchange alone, as such changes would have to be of too frequent occurrence. The discrepancy between the internal price level and the artificial rate of exchange has its effect not only on the balance of payments but also on the utilization of existing resources. The criteria for an alternative use of resources are eliminated by the distortions in the price structure and the production pattern. Furthermore, the demand and pressure for credits becomes irresistible, as any credit under conditions of the declining value of money means a substantial profit to the debtor. Thus, such conditions bear in themselves the seeds of perpetuation by permanent credit extension, until the structure collapses both politically and economically and a clean sweep is made by devaluation and fiscal and monetary reform, frequently under a political regime fundamentally different from its predecessor, which was made unpopular by the results of inflation.

Physical controls are effective for short periods of emergency or war, under the impact of a great emotional stress. In such times of trial and tribulation and of far-reaching distortions of the pattern of economic activity, the usual means of financial policies are inadequate to cope with the situation and to dam the rising tide of effective demand. Moreover, in times of physical shortages, the exclusive reliance on monetary policy would lead to widespread distress of broad sections of the population and endanger the social and political stability of the state in a period of emergency. The effectiveness of physical controls is, however, limited in time and conditioned by a state of emergency. In the long run, suppressed inflation, artificially restraining price rises and administrative controls, causes greater distortions and greater difficulties of readjustment when the artificial dikes break down, as they finally must. When stabilization is carried into effect, the floating purchasing power must be absorbed by a more drastic rise of prices.

The alternative course of action is a policy of saturation by using up rapidly reserves of foreign currency to saturate the inflated purchasing power on the home market by increased import. The following step is an increase of indebtedness in foreign currency. In the first phase, a policy of saturation seems less devastating but it has its obvious limitations in the amount of foreign currency available. Moreover, it has the psychological disadvantage that as long as it continues, a kind of morbid prosperity removes all economic and political incentives to rectify the disequilibria as a state of general satisfaction and complacency can hardly serve as a basis for far-reaching and painful but imperative adjustments.

Another instrument of what is considered as an anti-inflationary policy are subsidies. The point of departure is social, but it is soon recognized that this form of social aid is wasteful, as it assists indiscriminately all sectors of the population, even those well able to afford buying at the realistic market prices. A concentration of the same, or even of a lower, amount of money on narrower sections of the under-privileged classes, in the form of direct financial assistance, would have a much more beneficial welfare effect. In the course of time, the system of subsidies degenerates into an instrument for maintaining an artificially low price level of some commodities. In many countries subsidization of commodities in short supply in the immediate post-war period increased the demand for these commodities till it became excessive, aggravating through increased consumption the already existing physical shortages. It is seldom recognized that the underlying causes of disequilibrium, rather than symptoms of price rises, have to be dealt with.

In some cases this policy is adopted with a clear objective to circumvent the wage escalator clause, mainly in order to slow up the price-wage spiral. The shortcomings of the official cost-of-living index are used to subsidize commodities which weigh heavily in the cost-of-living index, thus slowing up the price-wage spiral.

Governments also utilize the differential between the external and internal price level by the creation of the so-called 'grey market'. The government imports directly, or through a subsidiary company, luxury goods and resells them at whatever price the market can carry, thus earning in local currency the multiple of the foreign currency equivalent at the official rate of exchange. That is another device to absorb purchasing power in order to reduce the pressure on the declining reserves of foreign currency.

Another remedy by which the government tries to check inflationary developments is the introduction of multiple rates of exchange, which is only another more extensive form of indirect taxation and of the 'gray market'.

Developing countries face the strongest temptation to finance development by inflationary methods. They try to overcome, by monetary expansion, the handicap of a low rate of saving and of capital formation and of inadequate capital imports from mature economies. For a short time, monetary expansion creates a kind of artificial inflationary saving and the government is able by depreciation of money to appropriate a large part of the national income and in this way to increase investment. Thus, the attempt is being made to force the pace of development by inflationary savings. The attempt to supplement the capital equipment bought through supplier credit, by creation of new money, leads inevitably either to deficit financing of government budgets or over-expansion of commercial banking credits which are both self-defeating expedients.

Anti-inflationary policies encounter in developing countries greatest difficulties, as the success of monetary policy applied by central banks is to a great extent dependent on co-ordination with fiscal policy. However, large budgetary deficits cannot be neutralized by the monetary policy of the central bank alone. Usually, the central bank has to execute its monetary policy under the pressure of monetary expansion caused by budgetary deficits ; while central banks in developing countries are almost invariably subject to governmental interference, even if endowed with a certain autonomy. If budgetary deficits cause the money supply to expand, the only remedy is to compensate for the resultant expansion by a tight money policy and credit restrictions. The orthodox means of influencing money markets, such as open market operations or the manipulation of interest rates, are not very effective in developing countries. An open market policy presupposes the existence of a money market, which in developing countries is either limited or non-existent.

Resale of credits becomes a frequent phenomenon under these conditions. The crude form of obtaining money at nominal rates from banks and reselling it at exorbitant rates in the private money market is one possible variation. The use of bank credit at preferential rates in enterprises for production of goods is more frequent, the inflationary gain being obtained through the sale of these products on the free market, when the very high rate of interest prevailing on the free money market is calculated in the price of goods.

Under these conditions, credit policy is of greatest importance. Moreover, in developing countries the sensitivity of monetary expansion and contraction to the impact of changes in the cost of credit is comparatively low. The orthodox means of rediscount rates and interest rates in general are of little effect as : (a) interest rates to meet the exigencies of the situation would have to be so high as to become politically and socially untenable ; (b) the availability of credit is more important than its cost ; (c) the deduction of interest for tax purposes tends to blunt the effectiveness of this weapon. Central banks, therefore, have to resort to quantitative and qualitative credit controls and to liquidity ratios and similar devices to keep the quantity of money in check. High liquidity ratios imposed on commercial banks may prevent further inflationary increases of bank credit. However, the degree of effectiveness of such a policy will depend on the measure of quantitative expansion of central bank credit to government. The central bank can apply its policy of monetary contraction and credit restriction only within certain limits. If these limits are exceeded, large-scale unemployment may be caused, compelling the central bank to reverse it.

These discrepancies constitute the crucial monetary problem of developing countries.

Thus, attempts made in such countries to accelerate economic development and to counteract the tendencies deepening the gulf between the developed and developing countries without sufficient resources for such acceleration, lead to balance of payments difficulties and to inflation with all its implications.

The limitations of quantitative controls, due to political and other external pressures, do not warrant the conclusion that monetary policy is certainly ineffective in curbing inflationary pressure and neutralizing the detrimental effects of monetary expansion. It is probably the most effective means available for the partial sterilization of excessive quantities of money generated by an attempt to overcome the difficulties of a shortage of real resources such as internal savings and influx of capital. The full effectiveness of monetary policy will depend on its co-ordination with budgetary and fiscal policies and the elimination of the fundamental factors generating inflationary pressures.

For developing countries which do not possess dormant factors of production or unutilized resources which can be galvanized by monetary expansion, an inflationary solution is self-frustrating. Dormant factors of production must comprise not only manpower or equipment, but an optimum combination of labour, raw materials and equipment if they are to be effective in a development plan. Monetary expansion exceeding the capacity of production, based on the optimum combination of all the available factors — skill, labour, capital and raw materials — will not increase the gross national product, even if only one of the factors is deficient and in the last resort it will cause distortions and bottlenecks.

Thus monetary expansion is of no avail in countries which are in need of development and not of activation of unutilized capacity of production. Monetary expansion without concurrent and concrete expansion of capacity of production will, in such countries, lead to depletion of foreign currency reserves and afterwards to physical shortages. As the opportunities to obtain additional means of production mainly from abroad are diminishing, the artificial prosperity will be damped and the volume of money chasing scarce goods will have an impact on prices, availability of goods and the balance of payments.

Thus, inflation can hardly serve as a substitute for formation of capital or for capital imports. Monetary expansion will not do in countries with adverse trade balances, bottlenecks, scarce resources and no dormant factors of production.

The control of inflation in conditions of rapid growth encounters the greatest difficulties. In such conditions the overheated economic activity, over-full-employment and pressure on limited resources become, as a rule, contagious and create a chain reaction of new ventures, with the concomitant pressure on resources. Moreover, the psychological effect of such a situation leads normally to over-estimation of resources and the competition for limited resources and consequently to steep increases in the price of various factors of production. In such a situation, the emergence of bottlenecks becomes inevitable and is greatly aggravated by an inclination towards spectacular investment projects. As far as young and developing countries are concerned, shortage of capital is mitigated only to a very small extent by capital imports.

The flow of private capital from developed to developing countries does not reflect any spectacular capital inflow into the latter. Under conditions of world shortage of capital and investment demand in industrialized countries, the natural flow of private capital is not propelled by force of economic gravitation to developing countries, but rather in the opposite direction. The process of accumulation is further retarded by the fact that institutional saving is in these countries in its embryonic stage and the use of money as a medium of exchange is limited. The margin above bare existence in these populations is so small as to defy any attempt to squeeze out of them savings for capital formation and subsequent investment. These countries cannot lift themselves by the straps of their own boots.

In these nations political and social factors would militate against a policy of forced savings with a view to diversion of resources from consumption to investment, as long as consumption levels are distressingly low.

Although theoretically such policies could be carried into effect by heavy taxation, extremely low wages, introduction of what would practically amount to forced labour in the village communities, the resistance to such measures in any but totalitarian regimes would be so formidable as to defeat their ends. Moreover, in an economy run on the basis of a multiplicity of private decisions of employers, factory owners, landlords, there is no certainty and hardly any probability that resources created by depressing standards of life and consumption would be diverted to investment. In some of the developing countries, a small but wealthy minority at the top of the socio-economic ladder disposes of considerable resources and squanders most of them in conspicuous consumption.

Accumulation of capital alone does not safeguard its use for investment and promotion of economic growth. The will to apply resources for this particular purpose, knowledge, skill and entrepreneurial initiative are the indispensable prerequisites of economic growth. Accumulation of capital frequently assumes, in these countries, the form of hoarding of gold, real estate investment and other non-productive use of capital and even export of capital in the form of foreign currency balances held in the highly-developed countries.

Under these circumstances of a limited import of capital, slow capital formation and reluctance of owners of such capital as is being accumulated to invest it, the temptation to appropriate resources by budget deficits becomes almost irresistible and monetary and fiscal discipline breaks down completely.

However, even under such conditions of great pressure on limited resources, instruments to control inflation to some extent are available.

Savings, and even forced savings through taxation, could serve as an important source of non-inflationary financing. The resources at the disposal of some sections of the population can be diverted to investment by a system of incentives and disincentives, as well as by taxation, while conspicuous consumption could be discouraged.

The importance of savings would grow after the initial push and take-off in economic growth. A policy of providing for some lag in the rise of standards of living behind the rapid growth of the gross national product, incentives of voluntary savings and taxation, could accelerate the process of capital formation to be used for large-scale investment.

A study made by the World Bank in October 1960 quotes the average rates of saving of 19 developing countries in the years 1952–57. The gross and net rate of saving in 19 developing countries were as follows : gross annual savings exceed in all these countries, with the exception of three, 10 per cent, and the net savings reach in 6 of the 19 — 10 per cent or more ; in 4 — it is nearly that rate and in 9 other countries below this level. These data bear witness to the fact that with a certain effort a rate of saving of some 10 per cent on the average could be reached in all those countries, particularly as with increasing incomes the rate of saving could increase more than proportionally.

As to taxation, heavy duties on non-essential to semi-essential commodities can serve as an important instrument for diverting resources from consumption, particularly conspicuous consumption, to investment, and thus make inflationary financing of development superfluous.

All these measures are directed to prevention of inflationary financing of development, and promotion of investment of real resources. The next step could be the development of a capital market which would gradually absorb some of the surpluses accumulated in such countries by entrepreneurs, landlords, etc.

The lag of incomes behind the rise of production and productivity could be provided for by a wage policy slowing up the rise of wages and directing these resources to the development of investment.

All these methods of promoting capital accumulation and saving and diverting surpluses to investment can only be successful if, on the one hand, a too rapid rise of consumption is prevented in the transitional period and if monetary discipline is maintained by the authorities and monetary expansion kept within the limits of the growth of production in real terms. Of course, this policy presupposes the existence of a machinery of research, statistics and information, which would make it possible to prevent any overestimation of resources.

As to the institutional set-up of the machinery for the control of inflation, the most important part of such an institutional set-up is a central bank with broad powers and a far-reaching autonomy. This is essential first and foremost as an instrument of credit control, as inflationary developments are likely to originate from the commercial banking system just as frequently as from government budget deficits. However, the central bank can also serve as a watch-dog *vis-à-vis* the government in not only preventing the resort to the printing press for financing and accelerating development, but also in influencing the general attitude towards problems of inflation and combatting any tendency to create an inflationary gap. This is particularly important as the psychological effect of an overheated economic activity and boom is conducive to attempts to do too many things simultaneously.

But even if all these brakes are applied, they may prove ineffective in the long run. They may slow up the inflation to the pace of a creeping inflation, but still undermine the ability of the economy to compete on world markets. In such cases, an early readjustment of the rate of exchange will serve as an indispensable and formidable means to restore the equilibrium and any delay of such an operation must become very costly in terms of resources and of their utilization. This surgical method of controlling inflation is, of course, the last resort.

The process of inflation itself will be greatly influenced by the size and pace of the import of capital. On the one hand, import of capital — if it exceeds the excess of imports over exports and leads to the accumulation of foreign currency reserves which are monetized — can become in itself a vehicle for the promotion of inflation. On the other hand, ample import of capital from abroad counteracts the temptation to finance development by internal monetary expansion.

The importance of political and social forces in applying the brakes of an anti-inflationary policy cannot be over-emphasized. The temptation to accelerate development even in conditions of rapid growth is intensified by the very fact of a rapid rise of production and of boom conditions. In the short run, all pressure groups are interested in inflationary developments and the policies of pressure groups are determined by short-run prospects.

Overestimation of resources is nearly always a concomitant of conditions of rapid growth. Limitation of monetary expansion by the government within the limits of the growth of production in real terms, credit control, forced and voluntary savings, are all unpalatable remedies from the point of view of the public. So is the lag of incomes behind the growth of production.

Selectivity of investment in order to assure its economically rational pattern encounters great difficulties. Devaluation as the last resort of anti-inflationary policy in a later and more pronounced stage of inflation is politically inexpedient and always encounters opposition for prestige reasons. The central bank is usually exposed to both pressure from the government and criticism by the public in its attempt to put on the brakes in conditions of economic growth. Any action to control inflation under these conditions must therefore combine economic measures with an educational effort to rally political forces behind the policy of sound growth within the framework of stability.

DISCUSSION OF THE PAPER BY DR. HOROWITZ

Professor Howard Ellis, opening the discussion, said that he found himself in complete agreement with the analysis presented by Dr. Horowitz. He then referred to the theory that inflation might bring idle factors of production into use ; he maintained that in so far as this might temporarily occur, it was a measure not of the success of inflation but of the extent to which a policy of monetary expansion had failed to produce inflation. He went on to stress that conditions in under-developed countries were particularly unfavourable for utilizing idle factors of production. Idle plant capacity was virtually non-existent, while unemployment was more structural than cyclical. In these conditions monetary expansion was usually pure inflation.

Discussing the theory that inflation produced forced saving, Professor Ellis said that while it might reduce some consumption it did not necessarily impose saving upon society as a whole. Even if it did, and additional investment took place, the transfer was wasteful and extra consumption by the windfall receivers of forced savings meant that more was transferred than was invested. Moreover, in market economies an increase in aggregate saving did not necessarily result in productive investment, since the savings, in inflationary conditions, might well be 'invested' in such things as gold, foreign exchange and luxurious apartment buildings. Finally Professor Ellis stressed that even if forced savings did result in productive investment, this result was likely to be transient. On the other hand the adverse effects of inflation on the price system, the direction of investment and economic motivation were apt to be lasting and cumulative.

Some comments by *Dr. Kafka*, who was unable to be present, were read by Professor Haberler. Dr. Kafka stated that he was encouraged by Dr. Horowitz' belief, which he shared, that growth could be combined with stability. He took issue with Dr. Horowitz, however, on the usefulness of qualitative control of investment in removing bottlenecks and mobilizing under-utilized resources. He felt that it was usually not the activities of the private investor but those of the state itself which led to misinvestment. What was needed was not an order of priorities (particularly not for the private sector) but a general financial programme to match investment to available resources.

With regard to Dr. Horowitz' point about inflation and foreign indebtedness, Dr. Kafka observed that it was sometimes easier for a country in difficulties through inflation to acquire 'bail-out' loans than finance for development or stabilization programmes.

An important distortion caused by inflation, not mentioned by Dr. Horowitz, was the disintegration of the private sector. This came about through price controls and the extension of government influence over large sections of the economy.

Mentioning the differences between the so-called 'monetarist' and 'structuralist' viewpoints on inflation, Dr. Kafka said that even the 'monetarists', who believed in the essential role of monetary policy in promoting inflation, would not deny that inflation occurred because the monetary authorities multiplied the means of payment only in response to certain stimuli. Where the 'structuralists' seemed to go wrong was in drawing the conclusion that under-developed economies, because of their inflexibility, could not have development without inflation. Monetary policy, specifically the credit restrictions advocated by Dr. Horowitz, could not control inflation except of a very moderate order, or provoked by investment demand of the private sector. Fiscal measures were also inappropriate if inflation was in the public sector.

In conditions of today, stabilization would in bad cases ideally require heavy foreign aid to cover external deficits, step up investment and cushion adjustment for the sectors which had benefited from inflation. Private capital assistance would also be needed (perhaps in the form of stand-by loans) and had in fact often been forthcoming.

Dr. Kafka believed that it was impracticable to 'taper-off' inflation slowly, as it was too easy for 'inflationists' to mobilize resistance to this policy. If foreign aid was not available, the economic objectives of 'tapering off' could sometimes be achieved by fiscal measures.

Professor Haberler said that he was in agreement both with Dr. Horowitz and Dr. Kafka. He gave some further explanation of the 'monetarist' and 'structuralist' viewpoints on inflation in Latin America.

Professor Leduc, who had recently returned from Latin America, also spoke of the 'monetarist' and 'structuralist' controversy there and believed that there was really much in common between the two views.

He declared himself opposed to the idea that development must be associated with monetary ease. He thought that Latin American experience was conclusive on this point. At the same time, monetary authorities in these countries had a difficult and essential task to perform in furthering development without sacrificing external stability. Their policies needed to be co-ordinated with fiscal and social policy, and to be supported by public opinion.

Professor Damaskenides described the case of Greece, as an underdeveloped country with unemployment but no unused resources of machinery and equipment, which had had experience of hyper-inflation during the war and afterwards. In such a country an injection of new money caused a great increase in the velocity of circulation and finally the complete destruction of the value of the currency. After the stabilization of the drachma Greece had been able to increase her gross national product at a satisfactory rate, proving that stability was the best policy for a developing country in these circumstances.

Dr. Regul said that experience since 1945 showed that nowhere had rapid expansion been associated with price stability. He was particularly concerned with cost inflation which had a push effect and always involved price increases, especially where resources were fully employed. What remedies were there ? He agreed with all that Dr. Horowitz had said on the distorting effects of price controls and subsidies. Exchange rate adjustments, such as those of France and Germany, appeared to be effective only for a short time. He agreed with Dr. Horowitz that exchange rate adjustments could not be repeated too often ; would fluctuating rates solve the problem of creeping inflation ?

Professor Scitovsky said that although all economists condemned inflation it was still popular and perhaps economists were too sweeping in their condemnation. For instance it seemed wrong to group together inflations of very different intensities and then to generalize about them. He felt that a more dispassionate and careful analysis was called for.

Mr. Salin shared many of Dr. Scitovsky's views. He pointed out that though economists must necessarily be against inflation, the historical picture was one of centuries of inflation and very short periods of stability. It was probable that at certain times some degree of inflation was necessary, but it was important that in under-developed countries the profits arising from inflation should accrue to the state and not to the private sector.

Dr. Fouquet said that the situation in Latin America was not as catastrophic as had been suggested, and it was difficult to see how inflation could have been avoided. With a very rapid increase in population, as in Brazil, it was impossible to provide the necessary services on a balanced budget.

Dr. Horowitz, replying to the discussion, said that there had been misunderstanding of his treatment of the theory that inflation could in some circumstances call forth savings and utilize idle resources. His thesis was that up to a certain point monetary expansion could put into use idle resources. Beyond that point, workers and entrepreneurs anticipated a further depreciation of money and the rise of prices went faster than the utilization of idle resources. He had also made the point that idle resources were rare in under-developed countries.

He felt that Dr. Kafka was an advocate of extreme *laissez-faire*. For instance, the export of private capital to under-developed countries was negligible. In order to develop, these countries must have access to public capital and because this had to be lent to and used by governments there was a need for selective investment.

He agreed with the view that inflation should not be tapered off, but should be brought at once to a stop after a suitable adjustment of exchange rate. He did not approve of a floating rate because then the investment criterion provided by external prices was lost. He saw no reason to tolerate creeping inflation. If it could be kept down to this point it could be abolished altogether.

He agreed that monetary policy alone could not control inflation. Restriction of credit, heavy taxation and a balanced budget should be combined with the elimination of bottlenecks, selective investment and the increase of production. Dr. Horowitz emphasized that many groups each trying to appropriate more resources and having a vested interest in inflation formed a built-in resistance to stabilization.

Chapter 10

ON SOME DETERMINANTS OF SAVING IN DEVELOPED AND UNDER-DEVELOPED COUNTRIES

BY

H. S. HOUTHAKKER [1]

Harvard University

INTRODUCTION

FOR the analysis of economic development, the principal question concerning savings is whether or not savings increase more than proportionately to income. In virtually all theories of growth, capital formation plays some part, and it is therefore important to know how it can be financed. The question is crucial for those theories — now somewhat discredited — which regard capital formation as the primary means of raising income levels, because suitable variations in the savings-income ratio are then needed to explain why some countries stay poor in the absence of foreign investment. Theories of the latter variety would be left hanging in mid-air if the savings-income ratio did not vary significantly among countries or in the long run.

The savings-income ratio is also of evident importance for development policy. Proponents of a 'big push' policy often count on an increase in this ratio to make the 'take-off' self-sustaining.

The present paper approaches the savings problem by an investigation of data for a number of countries with different income levels. It follows earlier work by Kuznets (1960) and Houthakker (1961). Although these two papers, written independently, were based on essentially the same data, they did not come to quite the same conclusion. Both found that the ratio of personal saving to personal income varied considerably among countries, but they disagreed on the relationship behind this scatter. Kuznets showed that if the countries were grouped by *per capita* income level, savings

[1] The research on which this paper is based was done at Stanford University under the auspices of the Research Center in Economic Growth with the support of the Ford Foundation. The author is indebted to Tsunehiko Watanabe, Neil Singer, Hiromitsu Kaneda and other members of the Center for their help and suggestions.

were relatively higher in the richer countries, whereas Houthakker found that in a linear regression of savings on income the intercept was not significantly different from zero. There were other differences between the two studies, especially in conceptual coverage and in technique of analysis, and these were further reasons for reconsidering the subject. In particular it was desirable to consider more comprehensive categories than personal income and personal savings (this had been done to some extent by Kuznets).

1. *Personal Saving*

Let us first discuss the central point of apparent disagreement in the light of newer data and improved techniques. As regards data, the use of the 1959 and 1960 editions of the *U.N. Yearbook of National Accounts Statistics* permitted the inclusion of 28 countries, as compared to 24 in Kuznets (1960) and 28 in Houthakker (1961), which were both based on the 1958 *Yearbook*. The use of these more recent figures is preferable because the data presumably become more reliable as statistical techniques are improved and because the earlier figures in some cases reflected the disturbing influence of the Korean War. For all these countries together there were 187 annual observations, compared to 202 in Houthakker (1961). As a result of the presentation of the last-mentioned paper at the Tokyo meeting of the International Statistical Institute, a defect of the data for Australia (which appeared to have inexplicably high savings) was uncovered : in that country consumers' expenditures on private automobiles were included in household savings (and also in investment) ; an appropriate adjustment, suggested by the Commonwealth Bureau of Statistics, was subsequently applied to the published data. The period covered was usually 1953–59, supplemented by earlier years if the 1953 data had not been revised between the 1959 and 1960 *Yearbooks*. For the rest the treatment of the basic data was the same as explained in Houthakker (1961). The principal figures on personal saving are set out in Table 1.

For convenience the countries are arranged in four brackets of seven in descending order of personal disposable income and unweighted and weighted bracket means of the savings-income ratios are calculated. The weights, where applicable, are the product of population and the number of years covered, on the theory that the variance of a mean is proportional to the size of the sample on which it is based.[1]

---

[1] That weighting is necessary can also be seen by supposing we had separate figures for each of the 50 states of the U.S. ; these would swamp any unweighted mean, but have no particular effect on a weighted mean.

It is worth noting once more that the savings-income ratios vary greatly between countries. The fact that the extreme ratios appear in very small countries such as Luxemburg, Malta and Panama

TABLE 1

PERSONAL SAVINGS

(Money figures are *per capita* in U.S. dollars of 1955 at official exchange rates)

Bracket and Country	Years Covered	Weight	Disposable Personal Income	Personal Saving	Saving Income Ratio (%)	Group Mean Un-Weighted	Weighted
I						9.1	7.4
U.S.A.	1952–59	1340	1659.1	123.2	7.4		
Canada	1952–59	127	1208.1	84.0	7.0		
New Zealand	1953–59	15	928.0	81.2	8.8		
Australia	1952–58	65	905.0	96.6	10.7		
Belgium	1953–59	63	877.6	95.9	10.9		
France	1953–59	306	835.7	47.7	5.7		
Luxemburg	1952–58	2	801.2	107.3	13.4		
II						9.7	6.2
Sweden	1953–59	58	765.0	58.5	7.7		
U.K.	1953–59	360	737.6	30.7	4.2		
Denmark	1952–58	31	723.2	65.7	9.1		
Netherlands	1952–59	87	476.4	45.7	9.6		
Ireland	1953–59	20	416.5	29.5	7.1		
Austria	1952–59	56	411.9	41.2	10.0		
Malta	1954–59	2	316.8	64.8	20.5		
III						4.6	11.5
Panama	1952–58	6	286.8	-12.6	-4.4		
Costa Rica	1953–59	7	257.8	13.7	5.3		
Jamaica	1953–59	11	235.8	8.0	3.4		
Spain	1954–57	116	234.8	10.7	4.6		
Japan	1952–59	629	199.2	28.8	14.4		
Colombia	1953–59	91	198.7	8.6	4.3		
Ghana	1955–59	24	197.7	9.6	4.9		
IV						4.6	3.7
Mauritius	1952–58	3	197.0	18.0	9.1		
Honduras	1952–57	10	164.0	11.4	7.0		
Ecuador	1952–57	30	134.5	5.2	3.8		
Brazil	1952–58	355	127.7	5.6	4.4		
Rhodesia	1954–59	45	115.5	8.8	7.6		
Peru	1952–58	66	98.0	-3.8	-3.9		
Belgian Congo	1952–59	102	58.3	2.4	4.2		

provides empirical justification for the use of weights. Not much significance should therefore be attached to the unweighted bracket means ; they are given only because Kuznets relied rather heavily on them. In any case they do not present a very clear pattern, though it is true that in the two lower income brackets the ratio appears to be distinctly lower than in the two upper brackets. The rank correlation (as measured by Kendall's tau) between income and the savings-income ratio is only 0·29, which is barely significant at the 5 per cent level.

When weighted means are taken, however, the pattern suggested by the unweighted means disappears completely. This is due in large measure to the preponderance of one large country in each of the brackets (the U.S., the U.K., Japan and Brazil respectively). The fact that Japan, well towards the lower end of the income scale, had a personal savings-income ratio nearly twice as high as that of the United States is enough to cast serious doubt on any simple theory of the savings function. In respect of statistical quality the U.S. and Japanese data are probably as reliable as any in the sample, though it is also true that savings data are usually among the weakest in any national accounts system.

As far as the personal sector is concerned, the basic data therefore do not suggest that over periods of several years the marginal propensity to save is higher than the average propensity. The question is important enough, however, to warrant some further calculations.

In the first place, some linear regressions were computed, corresponding to the 'between countries' regression of Houthakker (1961), but with an improved weighting system, namely with weights inversely proportional to the square of personal income *per capita*.[1] The most immediately relevant of these are the following:

$$S_{pers} = -1·09 + 0·081 \, Y_{pd} \tag{1}$$
$$(2·35) \ (0·011)$$
$$S_{pers} = 0·080 \, Y_{pd} \tag{2}$$
$$(0·011)$$

where S_{pers} is personal saving *per capita* per year and Y_{pd} is disposable personal income *per capita* per year, both in U.S. dollars at 1955 prices and official exchange rates. The figures in brackets are standard errors. As noted previously, the intercept in (1) is much smaller than its standard error and therefore contributes nothing to the explanation; it is omitted in (2). The average and marginal propensity to save of 0·080 in (2) agrees closely with the weighted overall mean of the savings ratio in Table 1, which is 0·0754.

As a further check a non-linear formulation was investigated.

---

[1] This is the weighting proposed but not applied in Houthakker (1961), p. 62, end of second full paragraph. Earlier in this paragraph there is a confusing mistake : the word 'inversely' in line 6 should be omitted.

For this purpose it was necessary to use consumption rather than saving as the dependent variable, because saving may be negative and consequently does not fit into a double-log equation. (A semi-log formulation could be rejected out of hand from the scatter diagram.) The weighting in the double-log case has to be different from the linear case ; in fact it is the same as in Table 1 (population times number of observations). The results are

$$\log C_{pers} = -0.0346 + 1.0004 \log Y_{pd} \qquad (3)$$
$$(0.0209)\ (0.0076)$$

where C_{pers} is personal consumption *per capita*, expressed in the same units as Y_{pd}. The elasticity of C_{pers} with respect to Y_{pd} is evidently not significantly different from one, and again we conclude that for personal savings, proportionality represents the data best. The intercept in equation (3), which of course does not mean the same as the intercept in (2), corresponds to a savings ratio of 0.077, in agreement with (2).

The above does not mean that no better explanation of personal savings can be found ; some attempts in this direction will now be reported. No useful results have so far been obtained by introducing extraneous variables such as the rate of interest (with and without adjustment for inflation), the rate of change of prices, or the money supply *per capita*. Various refinements of the income variable itself proved to be of greater assistance. A breakdown of personal income by type, in particular between income from employment and other income, had already been analysed in the earlier paper. Applied to the data used in this paper we find, as the end result of a number of trials, that

$$S_{pers} = 0.043\,L + 0.120\,P \qquad (4)$$
$$(0.022)\quad (0.041)$$

where L is *per capita* income from employment and transfers and P is other personal income *per capita* ; the units are again the same as for Y_{pd}. In this equation there is no intercept, because it was not significant when introduced. L and P are before tax, since there seems to be no good way of allocating direct taxes by type of income. If *per capita* direct taxes are introduced as a separate variable, they appear with a positive regression coefficient, which does not make sense (though it can be rationalized), so it appeared wiser not to introduce this variable.

The important implication of (4) is that the marginal propensity to save out of income from employment is much lower than that for income from property and entrepreneurship. This had earlier been observed by a number of authors, but never for as wide a range of income as is represented in the present study. While (4) gives a significantly better fit than (2) [1] it does not completely explain the high savings level of Japan, Luxemburg and Malta, nor the low level of France and Panama. For most countries, however, the predicted figure comes within a few dollars of the observed figure for S_{pers}.

There are a number of reasons why the MPS should be higher for P than for L. This is not the place to discuss them all, but one may be mentioned here. It is likely that this difference has something to do with the return on investment available to different classes of people. Employees usually can invest only through intermediaries such as banks, while entrepreneurs in particular can invest directly, and shareholders in equities. The latter two types of investment typically have higher rates of return.

This hypothesis, if true, may also help in explaining international differences in the savings-income ratio. It is true that, as mentioned earlier, the rate of interest was not found effective as an explanatory variable. This may be, however, because the rate of interest used in the analysis was an inadequate measure of the return to investment, since it did not refer to risk capital. Unfortunately more meaningful measures of the return to capital are not easily obtained. The only source available so far is Minhas (1960), who calculated the rate of return (after depreciation) on the non-financial assets of manufacturing industries in the U.S., the U.K., Canada and Japan (also India, which is not included in the savings analysis). His results may be summarized as follows:

TABLE 2

PERCENTAGE RATE OF RETURN IN MANUFACTURING
AFTER CORPORATE TAKES

Country	Period	Rate
U.S.	1949–58	9·17
U.K.	1948–58	9·54
Canada	1948–57	9·91
Japan	1951–57	17·39

Source : Minhas (1960)

Note the striking difference in rates of return between Japan (a high saver relative to its income) and the other three countries (all of them low savers). Of course this evidence, while encouraging, is too fragmentary to establish the validity of the hypothesis.

[1] The percentage of the weighted squares of S_{pers} explained by (2) is 0·67 and by (4) 0·81 ; for (5), mentioned below, it is 0·91.

Other equations of interest are obtained by using the rate of change of income as an explanatory variable, in accordance with a theory of saving put forward by Modigliani and Brumberg (1953 ; see also Farrell, 1959). Before adopting this theory in its strict form it seemed advisable to test one of its principal hypotheses, viz. that in a stationary economy savings are proportional to income. For this purpose the following equation was estimated

$$S_{pers} = -1·04 + 0·040 \ Y_{pd} + 1·591 \ \Delta Y_{pd} \qquad (5)$$
$$(1·60) \ (0·010) \qquad (0·282)$$

where ΔY_{pd} is the mean annual increase in Y_{pd} during the period considered. The intercept is not significant, so the hypothesis under consideration cannot be rejected and (5) can be simplified to

$$S_{pers} = 0·036 \ Y_{pd} + 1·592 \ \Delta Y_{pd} \qquad (6)$$
$$(0·009) \qquad (0·279)$$

A disturbing aspect of this equation is the large coefficient of ΔY_{pd}, which would imply that for each dollar of annual increase in income there is a \$1·60 increase in annual saving. Moreover the pattern of residuals in (6) leaves something to be desired since it under-predicts savings in most of the high-income countries. This may be due to a departure from the Modigliani–Brumberg theory in its original form. The variable ΔY_{pd}, in particular, is not defined in accordance with that theory, which is primarily concerned with the savings-income ratio in an economy with growing aggregate income, rather than with *per capita* figures. A more correct formulation is therefore

$$\frac{S_{pers}}{Y_{pd}} = 0·0200 + 1·36 \ \Delta^* Y_{pd} \qquad (7)$$
$$(0·0124) \ (0·28)$$

where $\Delta^* Y_{pd}$ is the *rate* of growth of aggregate real disposable personal income, and the estimates have already been inserted. The co-efficient of $\Delta^* Y_{pd}$ is still very high. This may be due to simultaneous-equations bias: strictly speaking the savings equation cannot be estimated without specifying a whole system of equations, in which income itself would be endogenous. Unfortunately there is as yet no quantifiable theory of the determination of income levels in different countries, so the single-equation methods used here are probably the best that are available at present.

The theories of saving expressed in equations (4) and (7) are complementary rather than competitive ; they emphasize different determinants of savings, each of them with considerable theoretical appeal and empirical justification. Combining them might give even better results.

Before leaving the subject of personal saving we conclude that nothing in the above calculations casts doubt on the proportionality of personal savings to disposable personal income in the long run. Some results on short-term savings behaviour are given in Section 4 below.

2. *Private Saving and Government Saving*

Although in nearly all countries the personal sector (including households and private non-profit institutions) is the largest source of savings, the picture is seriously incomplete unless other sources are considered as well. One reason for this is the relatively greater role of corporations in the more developed countries. It is conceivable — and indeed true, as we shall see — that corporations take over part of the savings function from individuals by not distributing all of their earnings as dividends. This type of saving is inherent in the legal form of the corporation, and frequently is also encouraged by tax rules. The government, on the other hand, may supplement the savings of individuals by appropriate fiscal policies, usually with a view to stimulating development in low-income countries.

Lack of uniformity in the data made it impractical to analyse corporate savings separately. Instead, the concept of 'private saving' was introduced, this being the sum of personal and corporate saving. Similarly, 'private income' is defined as national income less government income from property and entrepreneurship. Note that transfer incomes are included in personal income but not in private income. To arrive at disposable private income direct taxes on households and corporations were deducted. Data problems, especially in the treatment of government-owned enterprises (which we exclude from the private sector), made it necessary to use a somewhat different set of countries than in Table 1.[1]

The main result is as follows:

$$S_{priv} = -3.08 + 0.117 \, Y_{dpriv} \qquad (8)$$
$$(1.05) \ (0.011)$$

where S_{priv} is *per capita* private saving and Y_{dpriv} *per capita* disposable private income, both in U.S. dollars of 1955 at official exchange rates. The intercept is now definitely significant, indicating that corporate saving is proportionately more important in the richer countries. The saving-income rate implied by the above equation is

---

[1] Countries excluded from the private savings analysis were Australia, Ecuador, Ghana, Japan, Sweden and the United States. The following countries, not present in Table 1, were Korea (South) and Trinidad and Tobago, making 25 countries in all. For a few countries present in both analyses the time periods covered were slightly different.

10·2 per cent at $Y_{dpriv}=200$ and 11·4 per cent at $Y_{dpriv}=1000$, so the disproportionality is quite small. Attempts to refine the private savings equation have not been rewarding so far.

In the case of government saving the main difficulty is to find a suitable explanatory variable. Current government revenue appeared to be as good as anything ; it leads to

$$S_{govs} = 0·60 + 0·100\ G \qquad (9)$$
$$(0·59)\ (0·016)$$
$$S_{gov} = 0·107\ G \qquad (10)$$
$$(0·014)$$

where S_{gov} is *per capita* government saving (as defined in the *U.N. Yearbook of National Accounts Statistics*) and G is *per capita* government revenue, all in the usual units. The intercept in (9) is positive and on the borderline of significance, which suggests that there may be some tendency for governments with low revenues to save relatively more (see also the next section). Equations (9) and (10) are based on data for 27 countries ; neither fits the data particularly well.

3. *Domestic Saving*

Putting private saving and government saving together we arrive at domestic saving, which differs from total saving only by the balance of payment on current account (an item that is not investigated here). Domestic saving is equal to national income less consumption by households and government. It can be calculated for 34 countries, listed in Table 3.

Since the government is now included, it would be no longer appropriate to work with disposable income. The basic relation now is between domestic saving S_{dom} and national income Y, both *per capita* and in the usual units. We find

$$S_{dom} = 0·88 + 0·134\ Y \qquad (11)$$
$$(3·13)\ (0·015)$$
$$S_{dom} = 0·135\ Y \qquad (12)$$
$$(0·014)$$

and proportionality once more seems to be the outcome. But this time that conclusion is not upheld by further analysis. Although the pattern of the weighted means in Table 3 is not much more distinct than it was in Table 1, it does suggest some curvilinearity in the savings-income relationship. Accordingly a double logarithmic regression of consumption on income was attempted, with the following result :

$$\log C_{dom} = -0.003 + 0.948 \log Y \qquad (13)$$
$$(0.047)\ (0.017)$$

where C_{dom} is personal consumption and government expenditure *per capita*. The elasticity is significantly less than one, so Kuznets (1960) is right in declaring the domestic savings-income ratio to be an increasing function of *per capita* national income. Equation (13)

TABLE 3

DOMESTIC SAVING

(Money figures are *per capita* in U.S. dollars of 1955 at official exchange rates)

Bracket and Country	Years Covered	Weight	National Income	Domestic Saving	Saving Income Ratio (%)	Group Mean Un-Weighted	Group Mean Weighted
I							
U.S.	1952–59	1340	1962·7	202·4	10·3		
Canada	1952–59	127	1337·1	156·5	11·7		
New Zealand	1953–59	15	1078·7	183·8	17·0		
Australia	1952–58	65	1019·5	187·8	18·4	14·2	10·9
Luxemburg	1952–58	2	942·7	187·0	19·8		
France	1953–59	306	890·7	109·4	12·3		
U.K.	1953–59	360	855·5	85·0	9·9		
II							
Belgium	1952–59	63	831·4	91·6	11·0		
Denmark	1952–58	31	787·7	119·3	15·2		
Netherlands	1952–59	87	582·8	122·9	21·1		
Austria	1952–59	56	450·9	83·7	18·6	14·2	16·9
Ireland	1953–59	20	416·7	45·2	10·8		
Trinidad	1952–59	6	356·4	29·8	8·4		
South Africa	1952–59	97	308·4	57·0	18·4		
III							
Malta	1954–59	2	307·3	59·4	19·3		
Panama	1952–58	6	303·2	−1·0	−0·3		
Costa Rica	1953–59	7	269·0	35·2	13·1		
Spain	1954–57	116	255·8	28·7	11·2	12·2	21·2
Jamaica	1953–59	11	247·6	23·4	9·5		
Greece	1952–59	56	233·4	18·2	7·8		
Japan	1952–59	629	228·2	56·4	24·7		
IV							
Mauritius	1952–58	3	225·3	40·9	8·1		
Colombia	1953–59	91	212·8	23·5	11·1		
Chile	1952–59	49	209·2	1·7	0·8		
Portugal	1953–59	62	182·3	15·7	8·6	10·2	11·0
Honduras	1952–57	10	168·4	15·9	9·5		
Brazil	1952–58	355	144·6	18·4	12·8		
Ecuador	1952–59	30	143·1	15·4	10·8		
V							
Philippines	1952–59	64	134·9	3·4	2·5		
Rhodesia	1954–49	45	126·9	24·7	19·5		
Peru	1952–58	66	109·8	1·3	1·1		
China (Taiwan)	1953–59	65	94·5	9·9	10·5	9·5	9·1
South Korea	1953–59	154	83·7	5·6	6·6		
Belgian Congo	1952–59	102	72·1	12·0	16·7		

fails to explain the low savings of the United States, Canada and the United Kingdom and the high savings of Japan and some smaller countries, but that is clearly too much of a challenge to any explanation of saving in terms of income levels only.

Finally the principle of equation (7) was applied to domestic saving (ignoring the apparent non-proportionality) with the following result

$$\frac{S_{dom}}{Y} = 0 \cdot 046 + 2 \cdot 07 \, \Delta^* Y \qquad (14)$$
$$\phantom{\frac{S_{dom}}{Y} = 0} (0 \cdot 019) \, (0 \cdot 42)$$

where $\Delta^* Y$ is the growth rate of real national income. Since the coefficient of $\Delta^* Y$ is highly significant, the Modigliani-Brumberg effect is clearly present, but again there is a question whether the coefficient of $\Delta^* Y$ is not unreasonably large. It also appears that both (7) and (14) overstate savings in low-income countries. The positive intercept in (7) and (14) is hard to reconcile with the original Modigliani-Brumberg theory, which considers only savings for old age.

Summing up Sections 1-3 we see that personal savings appear to be proportional to disposable personal income, but that corporate savings seem to be responsible for a higher overall rate of saving in high-income countries, though this may be partly offset by a tendency for governments to save more in poor countries, due to curvilinearity in the long-run savings functions. Income change (as distinct from income level) is a significant determinant of saving, and so is the breakdown of personal income by types (income from employment and other).

4. *Short-term Savings Functions*

The emphasis in this paper has been on comparisons between country means, each mean covering seven or eight years in most cases. The savings functions thus exhibited are clearly of a long-term nature. In addition analyses were made of the annual observations themselves, for which purpose the data for different countries (which are expressed in the same units) were pooled. This amounts to assuming that the marginal (but not necessarily the average) propensities to save are the same for all countries. The techniques used are explained in Houthakker (1961), including a proposal for appropriate weighting of the observations which was first carried out in the present paper.

In order to separate long-run and short-run effects, the annual observations for each country in this analysis are always expressed as deviations from the country's mean for the whole period covered. This transformation has been indicated by a prime attached to each symbol. Thus Y' is the difference between *per capita* national income in a particular country and year and that country's mean *per capita* national income during the period covered. The short-run equations that follow are not always the exact counterpart of the long-run equations given in Sections 1-3 because different variables may be significant in the short run.

The most important results are given below, in much the same order as the long-run results. For personal saving we find corresponding to (2), that

$$S'_{pers} = 0.274\ Y'_{pd} \quad (R^2 = 0.68,\ 159\ \text{degrees of freedom}) \quad (15)$$
$$(0.015)$$

indicating that the marginal propensity to save is much higher in the short run than in the long run. The absence of an intercept in (15) and in all following equations does not indicate proportionality of savings to income because the intercepts (which vary among countries) have been absorbed in the transformation mentioned in the preceding paragraph. The short-run equivalent of (4) is

$$S'_{pers} = 0.184L' + 0.402P' \quad (R^2 = 0.66,\ 158\ \text{degrees of} \quad (16)$$
$$(0.020) \quad (0.048) \qquad \text{freedom})$$

where the division of income into L and P is again shown to be helpful.

In the case of private saving it appears that depreciation D is also significant in the short run :

$$S'_{priv} = 0.360\ Y'_{dpriv} - 0.643D' \quad (R^2 = 0.40,\ 140\ \text{degrees of} \quad (17)$$
$$(0.038) \qquad (0.174) \qquad \text{freedom})$$

The sign of the depreciation variable is correct, and the closeness of its coefficient to one suggests that in the short run depreciation and savings are substitutes.[1] For government saving there are also additional variables in the short-run equations :

$$S'_{gov} = 0.348G' + 0.078(\Delta Y)' - 0.169(Y - G)' \quad (18)$$
$$(0.032) \quad (0.019) \qquad (0.019)$$

The negative sign of disposable income in (18) is somewhat puzzling ; it would imply that, for constant government revenue and income change, the government saves more as national income is lower. This

[1] In the UN system of national accounting, savings are always defined net of depreciation. An alternative explanation of the phenomenon just observed is that in the basic data the breakdown of gross savings into net savings and depreciation is subject to considerable error. If so, gross saving might be a better dependent variable than net saving.

may be related to the possible tendency, mentioned in Section 3, for governments to save more in low-income countries, though (18), of course, is a short-run equation. Actually (18) does not give a good fit, despite the low standard errors, so perhaps it would be unwise to read too much into it.

For domestic saving, finally, the following two equations are obtained :

$$S'_{dom} = 0.402Y' \quad (R^2 = 0.65, \text{ 196 degrees of freedom}) \qquad (19)$$
$$(0.033)$$
$$S'_{dom} = 0.443Y' - 0.245D' \quad (R^2 = 0.65, \text{ 195 degrees of} \qquad (20)$$
$$(0.033) \quad (0.160) \qquad \text{freedom})$$

The inclusion of D' is barely justified and does not change the rest of the equation much.

It is interesting to note that in all the equations of this section the short-run MPS is some three or four times as large as the long-run MPS. This fact may be useful in the development of an integrated theory of savings, valid for both the long and the short run. Further research is needed on this point, and also on the application of the Modigliani–Brumberg approach (equations (7) and (14)) to short-run savings behaviour.

REFERENCES

Farrell, M. J. (1959), 'The New Theories of Saving', *Economic Journal*, **69**, pp. 678-96.

Houthakker, H. S. (1961), 'An International Comparison of Personal Savings', *Bull. Intern. Statist. Inst.*, **38**, pp. 56-69.

Kuznets, S. (1960), 'Quantitative Aspects of the Economic Growth of Nations ; V. Capital Formation Proportions : International Comparisons for Recent Years', *Economic Development and Cultural Change*, **8**, No. 4, Part II.

Minhas, B. S. (1960), 'An International Comparison of Factor Costs and Factor Use', Memorandum No. C-17 of the Stanford Project for Quantitative Research in Economic Development. (Published by North-Holland Publishing Company.)

Modigliani, F., and Brumberg, R. E. (1953), *Utility Analysis and Aggregate Consumption Functions, An Attempt at Integration* (mimeographed).

———

DISCUSSION OF THE PAPER BY PROFESSOR HOUTHAKKER

Dr. E. Szczepanik, in opening the discussion, said that Professor Houthakker's findings concerning the rate of saving were based on the experience of some 25-28 countries. It was impossible to know whether the conclusions would have been the same if more, or fewer countries had been used. The data employed was in the form of the standardized national income accounting framework devised by the United Nations; the very consistency of this framework, when applied to diverse economies, may hide wide variations in the coverage of the statistics and the methods used to collect them.

In the paper, countries had been grouped by income brackets, so that widely divergent countries were found in the same classification. Certain rich countries had low rates for personal savings, whilst Japan, for example, had a high rate; such differences might well be due to different attitudes to thriftiness. The results suggested that comparisons of growth paths would have been more instructive than the static comparison used. Institutional factors were also important, especially the role of savings banks and other monetary institutions.

The paper had discussed the possible relationships between the rate of return on capital and a high rate of saving out of income. It is possible, however, that the high rate of saving may precede the high rate of return in time; the rate of return may be more closely linked to the intensity of utilization of capital.

A similar problem related to the question as to whether changes in personal savings always preceded increases in corporate savings over time. This was not always the case and, indeed, no clear distinction could be drawn between business savings and personal savings. Many influences were at work on these two categories and they would depend upon the stage of growth reached, psychological factors, etc.

In primary producing countries the annual fluctuations in such aggregates as income and savings depended upon external factors, such as the weather, or changes in world markets. Since these changes were relatively large from year to year any short-term analysis was almost meaningless.

Finally, there were statistical difficulties of some magnitude. It was well known, for example, that figures for depreciation were the result of arbitrary calculations in many national income series. Savings were themselves one of the most difficult concepts to measure; they were often calculated as residuals, or were produced from direct estimates of investment expenditures. It was questionable whether it was worthwhile using sophisticated methods on data obtained in this way.

Mr. N. Kaldor said that the analysis had been based on the use of figures net of depreciation. This was misleading, since such figures were often based on tax allowances, which did not correspond with what was actually written off by businessmen.

There was another hypothesis which was possibly more significant than those examined by Professor Houthakker. This was that the observed differences between saving-income ratios could be accounted for by differences between the distribution of incomes between sectors and the role of business incomes in the total. The latter was probably especially important. The classical economists, including Marx, had stressed that savings were not a matter of choice for the business sector, but a necessity for survival in the competitive struggle.

The failure to distinguish between business savings and other savings had led to an apparent error in the paper where the high rate of return on capital in Japan was attributed to the high savings-income ratio. In fact business savings ratios in Japan were not significantly different from those in the United States, but the share of profits in the national income was much higher.

The differences in personal savings could be accounted for in terms of the differing roles played by unincorporated enterprises. The savings ratio for the latter group (excluding agriculture) was as high as that for incorporated business (say, 70 per cent). The important difference appeared to be between property owners, who were low savers, and entre-preneurs who were high savers. It was important to consider savings over a person's lifetime; early savings were offset later by dis-saving after retirement. Growth in both population and incomes, however, served to ensure that the positive saving exceeded the dis-saving. In the United States, however, it had been noted that aggregate personal savings were equal to the total personal investment in residential property.

Professor A. Kraal said that the national incomes of many countries included estimated items which were quantitatively important; in some cases, they may well account for some of the relationships found. Could it be that some of these relationships had been introduced by statisticians?

Professor F. Neumark argued that the problem of hoarding could not be separated from any discussion of savings statistics. The true incomes received may be hidden and the amount saved underestimated. This type of evasion would vary in importance from country to country.

Professor B. P. Pesek said that Professor Houthakker employed a statistical device which implied a peculiar hypothesis about the transfer of cultural-economic values. In his analysis the *per capita* income and savings figures were weighted by the size of population of each country. If the results were used to try and predict the behaviour of a member of a poor nation after economic development had raised his income, the weighting system implied that, for example, the chances are 180 million to 50 million that an average Indian would behave like an average American, rather than like an average Englishman, once his income reached the Anglo-American range. Other evidence, however, would seem to indicate that the reverse would be more likely to happen.

The weights used could be regarded as indices of the attractiveness of the behaviour of an average member of one nation for an average member of another, an index that depended on the population size of various nations. This was not a tenable hypothesis. Professor Kuznets had used no weighting system in his similar calculations, so that his conclusions were not affected by those now produced by Professor Houthakker.

Professor H. S. Houthakker, replying to the discussion, said that it was important that theories should be tested against the facts, but the accuracy of the data available for this purpose was often a matter of degree ; if estimates were available they should be used. The explanation of savings behaviour could not be left in terms of such ideas as 'thriftiness'. The pattern of savings must be related to other magnitudes.

The question had been raised as to whether the large, random variations in income experienced in the short period by primary producing countries did not invalidate any short-term analysis. This was not so, since correlation analysis could deal with this type of variation if there were a sufficient number of cases to study.

When discussing the role of savings by businesses it was not helpful to talk in terms of their decisions being made out of 'necessity'. This was a vague concept for use in economics, especially as there was always some choice open to businessmen in their decisions.

It was unlikely that the statistical results obtained were affected by any bias introduced by the statisticians when the original data was collected. The system of weighting used was justified on the grounds that samples of different sizes were being used ; if these were not weighted the error terms in the regression analysis would not be homostochastic.

INDUSTRIALIZATION AND METHODS OF INCREASING LABOUR PRODUCTIVITY

Chairman : CLARK KERR
Vice-Chairman : S. TSURU
Rapporteur : MARJORIE GALENSON

Chapter 11

FACTS AND OBSERVATIONS ON LABOUR PRODUCTIVITY IN WESTERN EUROPE, NORTH AMERICA AND JAPAN

BY

ANGUS MADDISON
O.E.C.D.

1. POST-WAR rates of productivity growth in Western Europe and Japan have everywhere been above their long-term trend. In several countries growth has been faster than nearly all recorded historical experience. This is true of Japan, Germany, Austria, Italy, France and the Netherlands, where output per man increased at 6·7 per cent, 5·2 per cent, 5 per cent, 4·3 per cent, 3·9 per cent and 3·7 per cent respectively in the 1950s. Even in the U.K., Denmark and Belgium, where growth was much slower, the growth rates of 2 to 2·5 per cent were much better than they had achieved over any sustained period in the past. Amongst the industrial countries, it is only the U.S. and Canada which have shown no acceleration in growth.

2. It is not possible in this paper to elaborate on measurement problems. However, a great deal of research has been done in recent years on the real product statistics used here, and it seems clear that further research will not invalidate our basic observation on the acceleration of growth. If we wish to compare our figures with those for Communist countries, we should, of course, change our concept to that used in those countries where total output usually refers to commodity production only. Available evidence indicates that the adoption of a Soviet definition of GNP would not affect our estimate of Western output to any great extent, but it would increase both the rate of productivity growth for the post-war period and its growth relative to earlier periods, because productivity is increasing relatively slowly in the service industries, which have increased their share of total economic activity. In the case of Germany, the figure for productivity growth would be 6·8 per cent on Soviet concepts instead of 5·2 per cent, in the U.K. 2·9 per cent instead of 2 per cent and in the U.S. 2·5 per cent instead of 2 per cent.

3. What has caused this acceleration of productivity growth in the post-war period? It seems reasonable to suppose that some recovery processes have been involved, particularly in view of the retardation of growth which was caused by two world wars and the great depression. This is all the more plausible in view of the fact that there has been no acceleration in the U.S. and Canada. However, growth continued to be fast long after old levels were regained, and it looks more and more as if some process of rejuvenation has occurred whose effects are lasting or, at least, that 'recovery' must be interpreted in some sense wider than mere reversion to trend. We must therefore see what changes there have been in the post-war economy which might explain the acceleration of growth.

4. One general feature of the post-war scene is the buoyancy of demand. In practically all countries, except the U.S. and Canada, unemployment has been at lower levels than ever before and there has been a continuous pressure on prices. The sustained expansion of demand has had its most direct impact on output through fuller utilization of resources but it has fostered productivity growth as well.

5. One way in which prosperity has an apparent effect on productivity is by eliminating disguised unemployment. In most European countries long decades of stagnation and instability had given people a preference for sectors of the economy where they maintained a modicum of independence and security, even though their living standards were low. The typical case is agriculture, but there are other sectors of the economy which provided a refuge, particularly retail trade and some services.

6. It is difficult to measure the degree of disguised unemployment but it is remarkable that in practically every country agricultural productivity has risen much faster than total productivity in the 1950s and agriculture has released manpower on a massive scale. If we assume that the 1·4 million who left German agriculture in the 1950s were really in disguised unemployment, then the increase in overall productivity would have been 4·5 per cent instead of 5·2 per cent per annum. However, this is an extreme case, and in most countries this factor is not a significant explanation of growth rates. In any case, the assumption that all the people leaving agriculture were really unemployed is an extreme one. This once-for-all bonus is therefore only a small part of the reason for accelerated growth.

7. It is sometimes argued that the structure of output in the 1950s has been particularly favourable to growth in Europe and Japan because of the structure of demand. It has, in fact, been a period of intensive activity in the consumer durable industries where

there are particularly good returns to scale. There is something in this argument, but not a great deal when we subject it to quantitative tests. In most European countries growth of output is only fractionally lower in the 1950s if consumer durables are eliminated. The extreme case is Denmark where annual GNP growth would have been 0·5 per cent lower without durables. The effects on productivity were probably at maximum about a quarter of a per cent a year. It is therefore doubtful whether the structure of demand has affected productivity growth to any significant degree.

8. A factor which has exercised a favourable influence on resource allocation has been the reopening of the economies to international trade. The removal of trade and payments restrictions and the impact of the recovery in world trade from the stagnation, war and autarky of the 1913–45 period was analogous in its effects to the elimination of disguised unemployment we have already analysed, except that it affected all production factors and all sectors of the economy to some degree. This factor has probably had its greatest impact in Germany where commodity exports rose from 8·6 per cent of GNP in 1950 to 16·6 per cent in 1960, but it has also been of notable significance in many other continental countries and Japan. It is noteworthy that the share of exports in GNP has not risen in the 1950s in the slowest growing countries—the U.K., the U.S. and Canada. It is not possible to quantify the influence of the more enlightened post-war trade policies but the rate of productivity growth is, in fact, closely related to the degree to which exports have risen as a fraction of GNP. This factor has been operative continuously since 1948 when quotas and payments restrictions began to be lifted, and it seems likely to continue for another decade as tariffs are removed in an enlarged Common Market.

9. Apart from the direct effects on productivity of commercial policy, we should also note the indirect impact of the creation of a workable system of international payments which, for all its defects, has permitted governments to follow expansionary demand policies without fear of deflationary shocks from abroad. Payments problems have, of course, been frequent, but with the exception of the U.K. they have not been deflationary in their effect, and there has been no attempt at the vicious beggar-your-neighbour policy of the inter-war years.

10. The main way in which high demand has affected productivity is via investment. In almost all the countries under consideration, except the U.S., the rate of investment in the 1950s was half as high again as it had ever been before. In Germany and the Netherlands investment averaged a quarter of GNP in the 1950s, in Japan

and Norway it was higher, and in several other countries it was over a fifth of GNP.

11. The reason for the higher rate of investment is that entrepreneurs have had high profits and expectations of profit because of the rapid expansion of demand. It is difficult to show how profits in the 1950s compare with the past, but it is at least possible to get some idea of the extent to which they have differed between the slow- and fast-growing countries. We have done this by adding together the yield and the capital appreciation of equity capital as shown by stock market quotations. In order to convert the returns into real values we have divided by the cost of living index. Capital appreciation is, of course, affected by expectations as well as by actual returns, and the degree to which the future is discounted will vary between countries. This is, however, exactly the mixture of considerations which entrepreneurs have in mind when they take investment decisions. It can be seen that the rate of return is highly correlated with investment rates and productivity growth. In Japan the annual return on capital has been about 33 per cent, in Germany about 24 per cent as compared with 10 per cent in the U.S. and 4 per cent in Belgium.

12. In most countries governments have played a substantial role both by providing incentives to entrepreneurs and by their own activity. A large range of anti-cyclical fiscal and monetary action has ensured full employment and steady growth of demand. Most governments wield a good deal of control over investment, either directly or indirectly, but not all of them have used their powers to stimulate growth. In several cases governments have been important suppliers of savings and have provided funds over and above their own investment requirements. The countries where government has saved most are those with the highest investment rates. In Austria and Norway government saved 8 per cent of GNP, in Germany 7 per cent, and in the Netherlands and Sweden about 5 per cent in the 1950s. In the U.K. and the U.S. where growth and investment lagged, government saving has been about 2 to 2·5 per cent of GNP. In fact, the publicly controlled sector in the U.K. has been in deficit. In Belgium government saving has been negative.

13. It has become somewhat fashionable to decry the influence of investment on economic growth and there has been a considerable revival of production functions which show that the big factor in growth is a residual trend. I think that a good deal more work is necessary on the role of investment, but I am convinced that it is the key factor in growth. It is, of course, true that there have been

substantial differences in the return from investment in different countries. I do not think that these have been due to differences in the structure of investment, though this may be true in some extreme cases, nor is it due to differences in the relative price of investment goods. In fact, a revaluation of investment at U.S. relative prices in the fastest growing European countries — Germany and Italy — would reduce their already low ICORs.

14. In my view there are four main factors which help explain intra-country differences in the incremental capital-output ratio. One of these is the degree of capacity use. In many production functions these variations in capacity use are not taken properly into account. If the degree to which the existing capital stock is used increased gradually, then the incremental capital-output ratio will tend to be lower than otherwise. It seems likely that this was the case in Germany and Japan where there was not only overt spare capacity in the early 1950s but also opportunities, not present elsewhere, of reactivating war damaged capital stock by small complementary investment or repairs. In the U.S. and Canada the reverse situation occurred with some decrease in capacity use in the 1950s. This is a once-for-all effect and its termination should lead to an increase in the ICOR in Germany and Japan, and a temporary lowering of the ICOR in the U.S. and Canada.

15. Another reason for differing ICORs is the fact that some countries have had faster increases in labour inputs than others. It seems obvious that, other things being equal, the capital requirements per unit of output will be smaller in a case where labour is increasing than where it is stable. The evidence seems to bear this out. The smallest ICORs have been in countries where the labour supply has increased most, and this is even more true if we take into account the disguised unemployment we have mentioned above. Capital widening has been cheaper than capital deepening.

16. It could also be argued that the burden of replacement has weighed more heavily on slow-growing countries than on fast-growing countries. However, if we allow for the fact that the quality of capital is constantly tending to improve, there will always be some productivity bonus from replacement, and countries which do less replacement will not get the bonus. Nevertheless, countries which have done proportionately more scrapping will tend to get slower growth from a given amount of gross investment.

17. Even if we allow for all these factors, there has still been a substantial difference in the rate of return from capital deepening in different countries. The reasons for this are various, but I think the following are important. One is the improvements brought

I 235

about through better specialization in international trade. Perhaps the most important variable is the starting level of productivity. Most industrialized European countries have a productivity level just over half of that in the U.S., in Austria and Italy it is somewhat under half, and in Japan it is about a quarter of the U.S. level. If we assume that the U.S. is operating at the fringe of known technology (naturally, there is quite a range within the U.S.) whereas the other countries are proportionately below, then it seems reasonable to assume that given favourable demand conditions they will be able to push their rate of capital deepening further than the U.S. without running into diminishing returns. It is certainly significant that the fastest productivity growth and lowest ICORs have been in countries where the absolute productivity level was lowest. Here we have another recovery element which fosters productivity growth and keeps down ICORs which is not a matter of catching up to your own trend but of catching up to the leader, and making good investment opportunities missed in the past because of wars. There are, of course, other factors which affect the returns to capital deepening, particularly the attitudes and skills of entrepreneurs and workers.

18. It is obvious from the above analysis that the high rates of productivity growth and the profitability of investment in the 1950s were due to some extent to exceptional factors. Improvements in economic policy have also played a role and should lead to a continuance of better growth. The problem is to decide what we should regard as normal performance. First of all it should be clear that the productivity growth potential is not the same for all countries but depends on the starting-point. All the countries we are considering have social institutions and attitudes to growth which should permit them to catch up to American productivity levels if they can push their investment high enough for a sustained period. I would therefore expect most West European countries to have a faster growth than the U.S. for quite some time, Italy should grow faster than most of Europe, and Japan faster still. The integration of European trade should help this catching up process. The ultimate slowdown in growth rates will probably take place before American levels are reached because the U.S. productivity differential is partly due to some natural resource advantages, but these are, however, not too great in view of modern technology and possibilities for trade. As between countries, the impact of earlier temporary factors may have an influence for some time to come, for some of the momentum of high growth and investment can be sustained if it is properly nurtured. A good deal of economic growth depends on

expectations, and up to certain limits a better psychology will generate better growth.

19. The implications of this argument for future policy depend to a large extent on the type of experience of the country concerned, in the past, although there are some obvious morals which apply to all countries — avoid wars, maintain high levels of demand and co-operate with your neighbours. Countries with a very fast rate of growth like Germany and Japan have benefited from once-for-all gains which are too good to last, and they must try to ensure that the adjustment to slower growth rates is made smoothly and that the rate remains high. In both of these essentially private enterprise economies I would expect the declining marginal efficiency of capital to manifest itself in falling profit rates and I would expect the rate of investment to fall somewhat. Apart from the physical returns, they will be squeezed by a tighter labour market situation which will have a direct effect on wages, and the ability to raise prices in compensation will be affected by their international competitive position. As I see it, this adjustment is inevitable ; the main thing is to avoid too sharp a movement. Nevertheless, there will still be factors operating in Germany to keep productivity above normal for the next decade.

20. Countries with a slow rate of growth would do well to see if they cannot achieve a take-off to faster growth. It is, of course, difficult to postulate what rate of growth they should aim at, and the rate will depend to some extent on the absolute starting level. My own hunch is that any European country with a productivity growth below 3 per cent ought to be seeking to do better.

21. As far as the U.S. is concerned, I have argued that its productivity growth potential is slower than that in other industrial countries, given an equal degree of success in policy. This does not imply that it could not do better than in the 1950s when demand was not adequate to ensure full use of recourses, and policies were generally less successful than in Europe.

(The discussion of this paper is recorded after Chapter 12)

TABLE 1

VARIOUS MEASURES OF LABOUR PRODUCTIVITY, 1950–60

	GNP per Man	Material Product per Man	GNP per Man adjusted for Disguised Unemployment	Annual Average Compound Rates		
				Output per Man in Agriculture	Output per Man in Industry	Output per Man in Services
Austria	5·0					
Belgium	2·5	3·9	2·3	5·3	3·5	1·1
Denmark	2·5					
France	3·9		3·6	2·9		
Germany	5·2	6·8	4·5	6·5	5·7	2·7
Italy	4·3		3·8	4·1		
Netherlands	3·7	4·7	3·6	5·8	4·4	2·5
Norway	3·2	3·6	2·6	3·4	2·9	2·6
Sweden	2·9					
U.K.	2·0	2·9	1·9	3·9	2·8	1·0
U.S.	2·0	2·5	1·8	3·2	1·8	1·5
Canada	1·9	3·0	1·0	4·8	1·7	0·4
Japan	6·7					

TABLE 2

RATES OF GROWTH OF GNP PER MAN

	1870–1913	1913–50	1950–60
Austria			5·0
Belgium			2·5
Denmark	2·1	1·0	2·5
France		1·1	3·9
Germany	1·6	0·6	5·2
Italy	0·8	1·0	4·3
Netherlands	0·7	0·7	3·7
Norway	1·4	1·6	3·2
Sweden	2·5	1·5	2·9
U.K.	1·1	1·2	2·0
Canada	2·3	1·2	1·9
U.S.	2·5	1·6	2·0
Japan	3·9	1·3	6·7

TABLE 3

ABSOLUTE LEVELS OF OUTPUT, EMPLOYMENT AND
OUTPUT PER MAN, 1960

	GNP at U.S. 1955 relative Prices $ billion	Employment millions	Output per Person employed $	Output per Person as % of U.S.
Austria	9·7	3,574	2714	44·1
Belgium	13·4	3,495	3834	62·3
Denmark	7·1	2,236	3175	51·6
France	68·5	19,775	3464	56·3
Germany (F.R.)	90·7	25,295	3586	58·2
Ireland	2·3	1,099	2093	34·0
Italy	51·5	20,209	2548	41·4
Luxembourg	0·6	148	4054	65·8
Netherlands	16·1	4,324	3723	60·5
Norway	5·7	1,478	3857	62·6
Sweden	11·9	3,071	3875	62·9
Switzerland	8·5	2,420	3512	57·0
U.K.	84·3	24,632	3422	55·6
Canada	31·2	6,074	5137	83·4
U.S.	426·0	69,195	6157	100·0
Japan	71·1	44,720	1590	25·8
Rest of World	505·0	954,160	529	8·6

TABLE 4

GROSS DOMESTIC INVESTMENT AS A PROPORTION OF GNP

	1870–1913	1920–38	1950–60
Austria			22·2
Belgium			16·5
Denmark	13·6	12·0	18·1
France			19·0
Germany		13·6	24·0
Italy	11·2	16·3	20·8
Netherlands			24·3
Norway	12·7	15·1	29·8
Sweden	8·1	13·3	21·4
U.K.	9·2	10·2	15·8
Canada	17·6	15·5	24·8
U.S.	20·7	15·6	18·0
Japan		15·4	28·2

TABLE 5

GROSS INCREMENTAL CAPITAL-OUTPUT RATIO

	1870–1913	1920–38	1950–60
Austria			3·8
Belgium			5·7
Denmark	5·6	6·4	5·1
France			4·4
Germany		4·9	3·2
Italy	6·9	7·3	3·5
Netherlands			4·8
Norway	5·2	5·2	8·8
Sweden		3·9	6·4
U.K.	6·0	4·5	6·2
Canada			6·6
U.S.	5·6	6·6	5·4
Japan		3·1	3·1

TABLE 6

THE RETURN ON EQUITIES IN SELECTED COUNTRIES

	Belgium	France	U.S.	U.K.	Netherlands	Italy	Germany	Japan
Average yield on shares (October 1961)	3·3	1·7	3·0	5·7	3·4	2·5	2·5	4·1
Average annual increase in share prices, 1955–61	2·7	13·3	8·6	8·9	15·8	19·4	23·0	30·5
Average annual increase in cost of living, 1955–61	1·6	5·2	1·8	2·7	2·5	1·9	1·9	2·5
Real annual return on capital	4·4	9·6	9·8	12·1	16·8	20·1	23·7	32·6

Chapter 12

INDUSTRIAL LABOUR PRODUCTIVITY IN
NON-WESTERN COUNTRIES SINCE 1945 [1]

BY

WALTER GALENSON AND JOHN R. ERIKSSON
University of California

I. PURPOSE OF THE PAPER

THE purpose of this paper is a limited one : to present the available data on trends in labour productivity for all countries except the United States, Japan and the nations of Western Europe (the latter are covered in a separate paper by Angus Maddison). In the course of our research, we discovered quickly that pre-World War II data are to be found for only a handful of the countries with which we are concerned, so that we were obliged to take the year 1945 as the inception of the period with which we deal — and even then, we have not always been able to go back that far. We have generally eschewed attempts at analysis of the underlying factors which produced the observed trends. Presumably, that is the function of the rest of the papers submitted to this section.

We have also confined ourselves to the non-agricultural sectors of the economy. This is not to say that agricultural productivity is not relevant to economic development. On the contrary, it may be a key variable, particularly where there are severe population pressures. But the data problem is insurmountable at present ; indices of agricultural output and employment which even approximate reality, simply do not exist for most of the countries in our sample. Of course, since industrialization is usually regarded as one of the main bench-marks of economic development, productivity figures for the industrial sector, even though they do not tell the whole story, are of great theoretical and practical significance.

II. PROCEDURE

It proved possible to secure useable statistics on output and employment, from which productivity indices could be calculated,

[1] The authors are grateful to Professor Dale Jorgenson for his advice at various stages in the preparation of this paper.

241

for 41 countries. Included in the sample are such relatively developed countries as Australia and Canada, and many of the newly emerging nations of the world that are still on the threshold of industrialization.

Our chief reliance was on publications of the United Nations Statistical Office and of the International Labour Office. These were supplemented by publications, both official and unofficial, of the several countries. The data are not all of equal reliability, even though the UN and ILO try to set minimum standards for the publication of figures submitted to them by member nations. Such standards are often lacking in the case of the numerous sources other than the publications of the international agencies to which we have had to resort.

Ideally, we should have liked to compute the productivity indices from (a) indices of value added in the manufacturing sector, and (b) employment in manufacturing. Although this is a limited sector, it is less ambiguous than the 'non-agricultural' or 'industrial' sectors, and it usually has the advantage of better statistical coverage. If we had hewn strictly to this line, however, our final sample would have been very small. On the output side, it was necessary to employ a variety of indicators, measured in gross as well as net value, and covering on occasion extractive and service industries. In some cases, the indices covered only 'census', or modern industry, limited to enterprises meeting specified minimum standards with respect to enterprise size and the use of machinery. Similarly, on the employment side our data include, in addition to manufacturing employment, indices of non-agricultural employment, employment in the socialist sector (for some communist countries) and various combinations of these. Because of limited space, the sources and specifications of the data selected for final use are not included in this paper, but they may be secured in mimeographed form on application to the authors.

These preliminary remarks are essential lest the reader be misled by the apparent precision of the final results. Many heroic assumptions had to be made to fill gaps in the data, which in any event, because of their highly aggregative nature, should be looked upon as general orders of magnitude at best. One of the more difficult problems involved the deflation of production data which were available only in current prices, and where that was necessary, the results are particularly speculative. Moreover, many of the nations in which we were interested have been collecting data for a very limited period, and their statistical services are not yet well developed. Despite all of these limitations, we are convinced from our study of the data that they tell a significant story, one that will be borne out by the more detailed inquiries that are just now getting under way.

After assembling the productivity data, it appeared from inspection that their trend over time was best described by an exponential function of the type $y = ae^{rt}$, where r represented the compounded rate of productivity growth. Accordingly, a function of this type was fitted to the data for each country by the method of least squares. As a partial check on the appropriateness of the particular function chosen, linear functions were also fitted to the data. Confidence intervals for the regression coefficient were determined for both functions at a 95 per cent level of confidence. Correlation coefficients and the number of 'runs' in the residuals from the fitted curves were calculated for each function.[1]

The Data

The results of these calculations are shown in Table 1. For six of the 41 countries, in the population — the Dominican Republic, El Salvador, Honduras, Indonesia, Peru and South Africa — there was no discernible trend. In the case of Peru, if three of fourteen years (one high, two low) are eliminated, an exponential rate of productivity increase of about 2 per cent is obtained, but for the remaining five countries, no clear pattern emerges even with the exclusion of an atypical year.

For four additional countries — Costa Rica, Malta, South Korea and Tanganyika — the width of the confidence limits renders dubious the significance of the trend rates. This result springs from a combination of a small number of observations and one or two extreme values.

In the remaining 31 countries, however, industrial labour productivity has tended to increase fairly consistently since 1945. Measured by the correlation ratios and the distribution of the runs, the exponential function gives a clearly superior fit in nine cases and a slightly better one in nine, while the linear function was superior in five cases and slightly better in four. For the four remaining cases, the two functions were about equally descriptive of the data. The most general conclusion which can be drawn from the statistics is that labour productivity in the 31 countries for which there are significant trends has tended to grow at an

[1] For a description of the so-called runs test of goodness of fit, see Wilfrid J. Dixon and Frank J. Massey, *Introduction to Statistical Analysis*, New York, 1957, pp. 287-9. The runs statistic provides a test for linearity and supplements the correlation coefficient as a measure of goodness of fit. For truly random residuals, the mean value of the statistic employed is 0·500.

exponential rate. Averaging the data for all 31 countries, the exponential rate of increase is seen to be 5·3 per cent, with a 95 per cent confidence interval of ±0·31 per cent.

There is considerable variation among the countries in the specific rates at which productivity increased. Using the exponential rates, the distribution of the 31 countries by 2·5 per cent class intervals is shown in Table 2. Three countries were below 2·5 per cent, and 3 above 10 per cent.

An additional word of warning should be inserted at this point. Some of the high rates have been called into question, particularly those for nations in the communist bloc. For example a U.S.-calculated production index for East Germany,[1] if employed, would have the effect of reducing the rate of productivity for that country from 7·83 per cent to 6·23 per cent. The Soviet rate would be reduced sharply on the basis of any one of the numerous Western indices of Soviet industrial output.[2] The nature and paucity of Mainland Chinese statistics render it difficult to draw any meaningful conclusions about the extremely high rate shown for that country.

III. SIGNIFICANCE OF THE DATA

A priori, there is no reason to assume any necessary relationship between industrial growth and increasing productivity of labour. Conceivably, where factor proportions favour labour intensive technologies, labour productivity might remain static, or even decline, as industrial output grew. South Africa appears to have been a case in point : since 1945, industrial output more than doubled, but since the labour force increased at almost the same rate, output per man rose very little. In Western economic thinking on development, the labour productivity ratio is not generally regarded as a critical variable. The rule is maximization of output through the use of that combination of capital and labour which yields the highest marginal return on cost, and this of course is not necessarily inconsistent with declining labour productivity. If in a given situation additional output could be secured more cheaply through the employment of more labour than through the purchase of more machinery, the additional labour would be hired, and with capital remaining constant, the productivity of labour would probably fall. In this situation, recourse to capital intensive methods for the purpose

---

[1] See Wolfgang F. Stolper, *The Structure of the East German Economy*, Cambridge, 1960, p. 272.
[2] The most recent index, that of Raymond Powell (then unpublished), yields a rate of 6·84 per cent for Soviet productivity growth since 1945.

of insuring rising labour productivity would normally be considered irrational.

It is interesting to find, therefore, that with very few exceptions, where there is an increase in industrial output, labour productivity does increase. This occurs both where labour is scarce and where it is abundant relative to capital. Moreover, the rate of increase tends to take a particular form, that of an exponential function of time.

This phenomenon can result from numerous combinations of the underlying production and employment series. Thus, if we represent the growth function by the expression $\frac{P}{L} = ae^{rt}$, where P is an index of production and L is an index of employment, it can be seen that if employment remains unchanged, an exponential growth in the rate of output would produce the same rate of labour productivity increase. If employment is increasing, the specified rate of productivity increase could be obtained only through a higher rate of output increase. To cite an example, productivity increased at almost precisely the same rate in Brazil and Taiwan, but in Brazil this was achieved by a combination of a 184 per cent increase (over a twelve-year period) in production together with a 17 per cent increase in employment, whereas in Taiwan, for a similar period, production rose by 488 per cent and employment by 133 per cent.

Thus, identical rates of productivity growth can have radically different implications for development, not only economically, but from a political and sociological viewpoint as well. If there is unemployment or underemployment, a productivity increase combined with an increase in employment is obviously preferable to an identical rate of productivity increase with stable employment. Thus, in the case of Egypt, productivity rose by 6 per cent from 1950 to 1960 but employment remained unchanged, with no resultant improvement in the employment situation. In Puerto Rico, on the other hand, an 8·6 per cent annual increase in productivity was achieved despite the fact that industrial employment increased by more than 35 per cent from 1950 to 1960.

While the data do indicate the likelihood of a persistent increase in labour productivity once industrialization gets under way, they tell us very little, without a good deal of further analysis, about the specific rate of increase that may be anticipated. From a cursory inspection, however, it appears that the communist model of industrial development, in which emphasis is given to concentration of investment in manufacturing and mining, and where modern technologies in heavy industry are regarded as desirable almost regardless of factor proportions, yields high rates of increase in industrial

TABLE 1—LABOUR PRODUCTIVITY TRENDS

(1)	(2)	(3) Exponential Rate of Productivity Increase	(4) Confidence Interval at 5 per cent Level	(5) Correlation Coefficient-Exponential Function
Country	Period	(%)	(% ±)	
Argentina	1945–60	2·39	0·410	0·9578
Australia	1945–60	3·47	0·596	0·9580
Brazil	1946–58	6·85	1·176	0·9716
Bulgaria	1948–61	6·31	0·763	0·9821
anada	1945–60	2·61	0·214	0·9899
Chile	1945–60	4·20	0·935	0·9320
China (Taiwan)	1948–60	6·82	0·971	0·9778
China (Mainland)	1949–59	11·88	3·058	0·9464
Colombia	1953–59	2·19	0·633	0·9790
Costa Rica	1953–57	4·57	6·803	0·7769
Czechoslovakia	1948–59	7·80	0·936	0·9858
Dominican Republic	1950–58	1·65	3·432	0·3942
East Germany	1950–59	7·83	0·535	0·9965
El Salvador	1955–59	1·10	5·336	0·3542
Finland	1945–60	6·00	0·455	0·9914
Greece	1950–60	7·61	0·955	0·9864
Guatemala	1948–60	3·82	0·414	0·9868
Honduras	1953–58	− 1·69	6·946	− 0·3205
Hungary	1949–60	3·72	1·390	0·8833
India	1947–59	3·32	0·526	0·9728
Indonesia	1954–59	− 8·07	12·803	− 0·6583
Israel	1952–61	5·69	0·607	0·9944
Kenya	1954–59	2·85	0·877	0·9763
Malta	1955–59	7·80	9·492	0·8337
Mexico	1945–60	4·62	0·427	0·9872
New Zealand	1945–60	2·43	0·206	0·9892
Pakistan	1950–57	11·36	2·542	0·9758
Peru	1945–58	0·31	1·726	0·1116
Philippines	1949–60	7·68	1·259	0·9740
Poland	1949–60	7·71	0·566	0·9946
Puerto Rico	1950–60	8·64	1·395	0·9810
Rhodesia	1954–59	5·35	2·562	0·9452
Rumania	1950–60	7·98	0·611	0·9949
South Africa	1945–58	0·85	1·098	0·4564
South Korea	1955–59	8·66	4·216	0·9666
Tanganyika	1953–59	9·47	3·142	0·9608
Turkey	1950–58	5·71	2·748	0·9225
U.S.S.R.	1946–59	9·63	1·251	0·9793
U.A.R. (Egypt)	1952–59	6·06	1·199	0·9900
Venezuela	1950–59	10·82	0·862	0·9952
Yugoslavia	1950–61	4·41	0·664	0·9779
Average for 31 countries	1945–61	5·30	0·310	0·8699

* E indicates a clear advantage for the exponential function, L a clear advantage for the are inconclusive as between the two functions. N.S. indicates the absence of a significant

(6) Randomness of Residuals (expected value at 0·500)	(7) Annual Linear Rate of Productivity increase (%)	(8) Confidence Interval at 5 per cent Level (% ±)	(9) Correlation Coefficient- Linear Function	(10) Randomness of Residuals (expected value at 0·500)	(11) Summary of Goodness of fit *
0·427	2·47	0·446	0·9538	0·427	(E)
0·001	3·61	0·733	0·9424	0·001	(E)
0·197	7·13	1·685	0·9480	0·197	E
0·078	6·31	0·523	0·9914	0·617	L
0·497	2·64	0·255	0·9860	0·231	E
0·108	3·56	0·755	0·9379	0·108	(L)
0·733	7·60	1·513	0·9578	0·010	E
0·262	11·83	3·145	0·9431	0·262	(E)
0·400	2·33	0·711	0·9767	0·400	(E)
0·500	4·85	7·013	0·7858	0·500	N.S.
0·013	7·46	0·512	0·9953	0·424	L
0·500	1·50	3·231	0·3821	0·500	N.S.
0·643	8·65	0·968	0·9907	0·040	E
0·500	1·12	5·705	0·3393	0·500	N.S.
0·622	5·75	0·389	0·9931	0·035	(E)
0·533	8·90	0·977	0·9896	0·262	(E)
0·471	4·04	0·483	0·9841	0·296	E
0·400	− 1·67	7·295	− 0·3035	0·400	N.S.
0·392	3·76	1·409	0·8829	0·076	(E)
0·236	3·29	0·480	0·9767	0·576	L
0·300	− 7·05	12·591	− 0·6140	1·000	N.S.
0·143	6·13	0·969	0·9877	0·143	(E)
1·000	3·09	0·906	0·9784	1·000	(L)
0·500	9·45	12·265	0·8167	0·500	N.S.
0·214	5·01	0·678	0·9732	0·035	E
0·032	2·40	0·225	0·9868	0·035	N
0·629	12·69	3·195	0·9697	0·371	E
0·821	0·27	1·788	0·0953	0·510	N.S.
0·279	8·45	0·979	0·9867	0·197	N
0·076	8·29	0·646	0·9939	0·175	N
0·405	0·60	1·738	0·9762	0·405	(E)
0·300	6·22	2·740	0·9532	0·300	(L)
0·606	9·25	0·939	0·9910	0·024	E
0·085	0·88	1·045	0·4863	0·085	N.S.
1·000	10·36	5·229	0·9643	1·000	N.S.
1·000	12·29	4·355	0·9556	0·200	N.S.
0·200	5·61	2·453	0·9345	0·200	(L)
0·005	8·50	0·324	0·9982	0·287	L
1·000	6·69	1·401	0·9888	1·000	N
0·048	12·41	0·894	0·9961	0·405	L
0·175	5·08	0·913	0·9689	0·015	E
0·069	5·51	0·167	0·8660	0·001	(E)

linear function. (E) and (L) indicate a less decided advantage. N indicates that the tests relationship in both cases.

labour productivity. The other side of the coin may be low productivity in agriculture and in the service industries, and lagging productivity in light manufacturing. In our 31-countries sample, all of the communist bloc countries had rates of productivity increase in excess of 7·5 per cent, except for Hungary, where the revolution of 1956 had obvious repercussions on production, and Bulgaria, which had an extremely high rate of increase in employment.

TABLE 2

EXPONENTIAL RATES OF PRODUCTIVITY INCREASE
FOR THIRTY-ONE COUNTRIES

A. *Less than 2·5 per cent*
   Argentina
   Colombia
   New Zealand
   Egypt
   Finland
   Israel
   Rhodesia
   Turkey

B. *Between 2·5 and 4·9 per cent*
   Australia
   Canada
   Chile
   Guatemala
   Hungary
   India
   Kenya
   Mexico
   Yugoslavia

D. *Between 7·5 and 9·9 per cent*
   Czechoslovakia
   East Germany
   Greece
   Philippines
   Poland
   Puerto Rico
   Rumania
   U.S.S.R.

C. *Between 5·0 and 7·4 per cent*
   Brazil
   Bulgaria
   China (Taiwan)

E. *Over 10 per cent*
   China (Mainland)
   Pakistan
   Venezuela

Leaving aside the communist bloc, the more developed nations in our sample — New Zealand, Australia, Canada — were at the lower end of the productivity growth spectrum, suggesting that the rate of productivity increase is in part a function of economic maturity. The only countries which might be placed in the developed category in which productivity rose by more than 5 per cent since 1945, Finland and Israel, were subject to very special circumstances which might explain their deviation from an expected pattern.

It is worth noting that the Latin American nations fared relatively poorly in terms of productivity advance. There was no consistent productivity increase at all in the Dominican Republic, El Salvador and Honduras. Argentina, Colombia, Chile, Guatemala, Mexico and Peru were at the lower end of the scale, and only in Brazil and Venezuela were substantial rates of increase achieved.

One final note of caution is necessary in interpreting the data. Other things being equal, an increase in manufacturing, or industrial, productivity is generally desirable in a developing economy. But it does not necessarily imply a proportional, or for that matter, any increase in the welfare of the population concerned. A very rapid rate of manufacturing productivity advance might be achieved by the adoption of capital-intensive techniques. One of the results might be an increase in unemployment, but since the unemployed are not usually included in the denominator of the productivity fraction, this would have no effect on the productivity data, though its impact on welfare might be severe. Similarly, rapidly increasing manufacturing productivity might be offset by stagnation in service industry and agricultural productivity. All of these factors would have to be taken into account in any assessment of developmental progress.

DISCUSSION OF THE PAPERS BY MR. MADDISON AND BY PROFESSOR GALENSON AND MR. ERIKSSON

Chairman : PROFESSOR CLARK KERR

Professor Erik Lundberg (Sweden) opened the discussion on Mr. Maddison's paper, nominating him for the title of the 'European Kuznets', in recognition of his brave attempt to derive long-time series. His courage in drawing conclusions from data for policy pronouncements was also praiseworthy. On a few points, however, Professor Lundberg had some doubts. He was not convinced that post-war rates of productivity growth in Western Europe were above their long-term trend ; he believed on the contrary that the post-war rates were a reversion to trend, and that the slower growth rate in Sweden, for example, could be attributed to the fact that it had moved off the old trend line shortly after the war. Nor could he agree that forces with lasting effects, beyond mere recovery, had emerged in the post-war years. He considered that the 1950s were an exceptional decade, with special features not likely to continue into the next decade. In Western Europe, demand pressures had been evenly distributed over the entire economy during the 1950s. This had begun to change, and the uneven development of demand and production would seriously strain the mobility of resources and the flexibility of the European economies.

Mr. Maddison's method of measuring profits or annual return on investment, in order to explain investment rates, involved some circular reasoning : high investment, stimulating demand and creating inflationary prospects, causes rapid capital appreciation as well as high yields.

Professor Lundberg voiced an objection to the highly aggregative approach, which was especially dangerous when policy issues were considered. Differences in investment ratios among countries should not be compared without reference to the varying composition of total gross investment, e.g. private and public sectors ; housing, which is partly determined by the rate of population increase, etc.

Finally, it was important to note that the big differences in productivity levels among countries which Mr. Maddison noted are the result of gaps within the countries between the average or marginal firms and the best practice. In Western Europe, the best practice is quite up to the American level, but the disparity between the best practice plants and the average is much wider than in the United States. The closing of this gap requires mobility of capital and labour, from the declining to the growing industries, and the faster transmission of new techniques within the country. 'Disguised unemployment', a slippery concept as Mr. Maddison used it, can appropriately be applied to this productivity gap within a country. In conjunction with the shifting demand conditions which are producing excess capacity in some sectors, the internal productivity gap calls for flexibility and mobility ; this, and not high investment *per se*, is the major policy issue for the 1960s.

Professor Melvin Reder (United States) expressed his confidence, based on extensive acquaintance with Professor Galenson's work, in the care and judgment with which the very detailed statistical tables in his paper had been compiled. Although many of the figures must be unreliable, they are as good a collection as is presently obtainable, and it was a great service to have presented them in one source. He wanted to comment on only one point : on the question whether the trend in labour productivity is exponential or arithmetic. The growth rate for the more advanced countries, as Professor Galenson pointed out, seems slower than for the others ; if this is true, and if these countries are not 'slow growers' for other reasons, then it follows that they were growing faster at some earlier stage of their development, i.e. before 1945. This suggests that the exponential trend may not be applicable to the whole range of historical experience. This question must be explored by combining essentially inter-country studies, such as Professor Galenson's, with the analysis of the long-time series available for advanced countries, especially the United States.

On Mr. Maddison's paper, Professor Reder had two comments. First, the composition of output was a very important determinant of productivity growth, which the remarks in Section 7 tended to minimize. (Mr. Maddison had stated in his oral summary that he had changed his mind, and now believed that the structure of demand was a significant factor to be taken into account in productivity comparisons, particularly in the United States-European comparisons. In the United States, the proportion of national output accounted for by services was twice as high as in Europe, and productivity increases have been slower in this sector.) One reason why the rate of growth of man-hour productivity has tended to slacken is the tendency for demand to shift to items in which individual differentiation is important. Product improvement, which is not adequately recognized in price and output series, also uses resources, and hence acts as a brake upon what is measured as man-hour productivity. In comparing growth rates of socialist countries, which can more effectively concentrate consumer demand upon standard items, with those of capitalist nations, this factor may be an important source of bias.

Section 11 in Mr. Maddison's paper was open to criticism in two respects: (1) The measure of return on capital is inappropriate because rates of capital appreciation as measured by stock prices reflect not only present and expected profits but also the rate at which they are paid out as dividends, which is quite another matter. Furthermore, since payout rates are negatively correlated with investment, *ceteris paribus*, the relation between return on capital and investment tends to be understated. (2) An opposite bias arises from neglect of the *ceteris paribus* effect of investment in increasing profits. This effect plays an important role in most contemporary models of the growth process. Indeed, it is possible, although not very likely, that the observed association between investment and profits could be entirely due to this link without any reflection of an incentive effect.

Professor John W. Kendrick (United States) noted that both authors dealt with output per person engaged in productive activity. Often, employment or persons engaged series are the only input estimates available, and their ratio to output is of interest in indicating changes in manpower requirements per unit of output as a result of changes in organization and technology, and factor substitutions. But he hoped that work would continue towards implementing more refined productivity concepts for an increasing number of countries in the future. Most economists preferred man-hours as a measure of labour input. The relationship of net output to non-human factor inputs was also of interest. As Professor Galenson pointed out, output per worker is not the 'critical variable' in management calculations, since a net saving per unit of output in *total* input of scarce resources is sought.

If 'total factor productivity' estimates were available for the various countries, their ranks with respect to rates of productivity change might well differ from those shown for output per worker estimates. It is also probable that the dispersion among countries in levels of total factor productivity would be less as of a given date than the dispersion in levels of output per worker.

Regarding the quality of the estimates, both authors were careful to point out the substantial margins of error, and Professor Kendrick wanted to add only two observations. For a number of countries, Professor Galenson was forced to deflate value added in manufacturing by an overall price index, either the wholesale or the consumer price index or variants thereof. It is preferable to deflate value added by the double-deflation method. But even if the gross value of production were being deflated, the overall price indexes cited are unlikely to be appropriate with respect to commodity coverage, weights, and, in the case of consumer prices, the distribution of income. Mr. Maddison's estimates are probably better with respect to the real commodity content; but the gross national product deflators are notoriously weak in the service area, especially the gross product originating in government, where wage- or salary-rates are often used. This results in downward bias, the more so, the greater the relative importance of service.

Secondly, if there is a positive correlation, as there probably is, between levels of output per worker and rates of improvement in quality of commodities, international productivity comparisons will tend to be distorted. In the United States, almost half of research and development outlays are for product improvement; if real product estimates could adequately reflect this qualitative factor, the relative growth and productivity performance of the United States and other advanced countries would look better.

With respect to Professor Galenson's figures, one must be careful to note the sector coverage (as well as the time spans), since those countries in which the estimates cover handicraft industry might be expected to show higher productivity advance, other things equal, due to the effect of the relative shift of labour to modern manufacturing establishments.

Both sets of estimates are nevertheless useful for analysis as long as close precision is not required. They both suggest the phenomenon of convergence, which is a reasonable result. As more under-developed countries complete the pre-conditions for effective adoption and adaptation of advanced technology, their growth rates should accelerate. Certainly the foreign aid and investment policies of the United States have sought to speed reconstruction and growth. It would be cause for surprise and concern if convergence were not occurring. Of course, at some future date, as more countries approach the frontiers of knowledge in an increasing number of industries, growth rates may be expected to slow down somewhat.

The reasons Mr. Maddison adduces for the higher post-war rates of productivity advance are provocative. Emphasis should also be placed on the heavy value accorded to productivity advance as a means of reconstruction and development after World War II. The will to accelerate productivity advance gave rise to institutions such as the European Productivity Agency and the various national 'productivity centres', which played an important role in speeding the diffusion of technology both among nations and among the firms of various industries within the countries.

Record of Discussion

Finally, Mr. Maddison was correct in stating that productivity growth could have been greater in the United States in recent years. (Incidentally, Mr. Maddison's figures for the United States show a rate of productivity increase higher before World War I than after it; this is contrary to the results of Professor Kendrick's research, and due to a defect in the census data.) Since 1955 or so, it could be argued that we are in the downward phase of the Kuznetsian 'long-swing', aggravated by monetary and fiscal policies which have squeezed the rate of return on investment so that the level of new investment has been inadequate to ensure full employment — and maximum productivity advance. With improvement of these policies now under way, and with the sharp acceleration in growth of the labour force and in family formation beginning in 1964–65, the likelihood is that American economic growth in the decade ahead will look better than in the decade past.

Professor V. K. R. V. Rao (India) commented that the inclusion of international trade in Mr. Maddison's list of favourable influences on productivity could just as appropriately read the other way : increased productivity stimulates exports. He was not satisfied with Mr. Maddison's calculation of profit ; for entrepreneurs, other factors were more important than the appreciation of shares, which is of greater concern to the investor. Professor Galenson's figure for India was wrong; there was very little increase in productivity in the last ten years. And that Pakistan actually has the highest rate of increase is extremely doubtful. In general, the quality of the data was so poor, and the sector coverage so limited — figures on manufacturing alone, for example, are of no interest — that he had to register an objection to the whole of Professor Galenson's paper ; it was not worth doing.

Professor Giovanni Lasorsa (Italy) pointed out the difficulty of comparing periods of time because of the influence of special events which might have effected changes in the structure of the economy. Legal and political events could not be neglected. In Italy, for example, agrarian reform had a profound influence on productivity in agriculture, particularly in the south, because it produced a shift away from monoculture to a plural crop cultivation. Mr. Maddison might also have mentioned the importance of mobility as a factor increasing productivity — for example the population movements of persons in the economically active age groups from southern to northern Italy, which resulted in an increase in productivity in both areas.

Professor D. J. Delivanis (Greece) registered his disagreement with some of Mr. Maddison's conclusions : that increased productivity in Western Europe is in part the consequence of two world wars (in which Sweden and Switzerland were not involved) ; that people stayed in agriculture for security (they stayed only until more profitable opportunities became available elsewhere) ; and that productivity in Europe would not reach the American level (there is no theoretical reason why it cannot exceed that level). Mr. Maddison had neglected to mention the influence of expected price rises on demand, and the fear of inflation as a more important factor in the purchase of shares than expected yields.

Dr. W. E. G. Salter (Australia) criticized the methodology of both papers, which used imperfect statistics to draw conclusions. Professor Galenson's figure for Australia, for example, was way off. Deductions from figures should take account of confidence limits — the margin of error in the data probably exceeds 25 per cent — and hunches should be distinguished from facts.

Miss Audrey Donnithorne (United Kingdom) pointed out that Professor Galenson's figures included the period of post-war rehabilitation for some countries and excluded it for others, thus vitiating comparison. In China, for example, rehabilitation did not begin until 1949. A factor which may well affect labour productivity, but which is rarely mentioned, is the age structure of the working population. Changes in the age composition of the working force should be taken into consideration, as well as demographic trends affecting the total population or the total working force.

Mr. Felix Trappaniers (Belgium) asserted that the increase in intra-European trade after the war was an important stimulus to increased productivity through the reallocation of resources. In the United States, this factor had operated before the war. A levelling off might be expected in the increase from this source in the future.

Dr. Desmond C. Corner (United Kingdom) also stressed the importance of trade ; if exports as a proportion of national product had risen in the United Kingdom as much as they did in Germany in the last decade, the productivity increase would have been much greater. Another point to consider is that, for both the United States and the United Kingdom, the use of output per man figures, rather than output per man-hour, understated the actual increase in productivity because of the fluctuations in economic activity.

Dr. Kurt W. Rothschild (Austria) noted that the crucial question was the weight to be given to each of Mr. Maddison's factors influencing the growth of productivity. The 'catching-up' effect had perhaps been over-estimated ; we have now had a history of some two hundred years of considerable technical progress, yet very wide differences in productivity persist. International trade, which has been mentioned as a stimulus to productivity growth, may have hampered the development of modern industries, in which the fastest gains can be made, in the less advanced countries, at the same time that it stimulated productivity in the traditional industries. Thus trade may have proved a brake on the 'catching-up' process by acting as a barrier to the growth of new sectors.

Dr. Rothschild warned against the assumption of the continuation of present trends, which may lead to forecasts very wide of the mark. Mr. Maddison's view that the rate of productivity growth will decline in advanced countries because demand will shift increasingly to services, where productivity increases more slowly than in manufacturing, may be mistaken. The belief has long been that agricultural productivity increased relatively slowly, and this belief has been contradicted by the post-war experience. Present trends in distribution and new office machines indicate that considerable productivity gains are possible to services too.

Two observations were relevant to Dr. Reder's argument that productivity gains would be lower in wealthier countries because incremental income tends to be spent on a wider variety of products, thus sacrificing some opportunities for economies of scale. The nature of demand will not be completely independent of the advantages of technological progress and economies of scale. In the nineteenth century, consumers had dresses made to order, and there was consequently more variation than today; but technological progress has led to the advance of the clothing industry despite rising incomes. Secondly, the satisfaction of a fickle and shifting demand is not necessarily a postulate of welfare economics. A large part of the present demand for varied products is artificially stimulated by advertising and sales pressure; if that is true, it is not so much the rise in real income, and the consequent change in the structure of demand, but present-day selling methods which have a dampening effect on productivity increases.

Dr. Gyorgy Cukor (Hungary) thought that Professor Galenson's figure for Hungary was unrealistic. He explained the great importance of productivity in socialist countries, but in the macro-economic sense and for the long run. Other factors were taken into consideration too, such as employment. Mr. Maddison's statement that total production in socialist economies included only commodities was not so; electricity was included, and other similar types of production. Services were omitted in part because they are difficult to measure; e.g. is productivity in the laundry industry to be measured by the price of cleaning or the increase in output of washing machines?

In answer to the points raised in the discussion on his paper, *Mr. Maddison* characterized some of the criticisms of the measurement of productivity as irrelevant. The point that quality improvement was not included would be a good one if the United States alone were being considered — here it might raise the rate of productivity increase 2 or 2·5 per cent; but the same quality factor applied to all countries so that it did not affect international comparisons. Nor were quality changes all in the same direction; each successive visit to the United States, for example, indicated that the food was getting worse. He contended that the OECD data were reasonably reliable, better certainly than the data Dr. Galenson used, and that the margin of error was not 25 per cent; the figure for one country for one year might be that far off, but not the figure for the decade. The table on profits, he agreed, was very shaky; he had included it to stimulate work in the field. Profits were the weakest part of the national accounts. In answer to Professor Lundberg, there were no data on the long-term rate of productivity increase for Europe, and he did not know what it was. The emphasis on intersectoral shifts was, furthermore, a statistician's approach and not an economist's. Mr. Maddison took issue with Professor Galenson's view of the significance of the labour productivity ratio. For the economy as a whole, in the macro sense, labour productivity is the crucial variable ; it is labour which is the factor to be economized.

Professor Galenson, in his summing up, pointed out that many speakers had objected to his data for their own countries. He objected too. But the objections should be directed to the source : the national account and employment statistics submitted to the United Nations. There was no 'on-site' inspection of statistics ; if some of the figures submitted were dubious, all he would say is that, sooner or later, the truth will out, as the Chinese discovered in the year of the great leap forward. In the meantime, the official data were all that were available. In answer to Professor Rao's criticism of the limited coverage of the data, manufacturing is important *per se*. It is a key sector in development, the most rapidly growing sector, and the exponential growth of productivity there has disquieting implications for employment in the developing countries. Finally, he would agree with Mr. Maddison on the global importance of labour productivity.

Chapter 13

STAGES OF INDUSTRIALIZATION
AND LABOUR PRODUCTIVITY

BY

J. PAJESTKA
Warsaw

THE purpose of this paper is to analyse the factors determining
labour productivity in the various stages of economic development,
and particularly during the initial phases of accelerated industrialization in the developing countries.

1. I presume it useful to consider the growth of labour productivity as a constituent of the general process of economic development. Therefore, it seems very useful to examine labour productivity
in its long-run changes and in aggregated effects — as presented by
the notion of the general, social labour productivity. This approach
pays attention above all to the macro-economic conditions of a
steady growth of labour productivity. On the other hand, the conventional understanding of the factors determining the behaviour
of labour productivity can be characterized as a micro-economic
approach.

A proposition I would like to present is that, at the initial stages
of an accelerated industrialization, the principal importance should
be attributed to the macro-economic, structural conditions of the
long-run growth of labour productivity. In further stages of economic development the factors appropriate for the conventional,
micro-economic approach grow in importance.

2. A substantial difference between the highly developed and the
under-developed economies can be found in the fact that while the
first are in the possession of structural conditions of a self-sustaining
growth, the others do not possess such conditions. Particularly, the
developed economies possess well-developed productive capacities
with a structure and economic characteristics allowing for enlarging
continuously, improving and better utilizing the capital stock and
for employing productively a high percentage of the labour force.
Such conditions do not prevail in the under-developed countries.
Therefore, for the developed economies, there exists a very large
scope for productivity improvements. For the under-developed
economies those possibilities are very limited. It is not so much

productivity improvements, but creation of new economic conditions which is most decisive for economic progress in those economies.

Problems of growth of labour productivity should be considered in a different way for the under-developed economies than for the developed ones — in accordance with their economic conditions, with the stage of their economic development. This means, above all, that they should be considered in the context of the general process of economic development.

3. At the early stages of industrial development, the material factors creating conditions for an accelerated growth play the most important role in the increase of labour productivity in the long run. Other factors, particularly those influencing the human behaviour in production, although also very important, have relatively less significance. That is why, when analysing the social conditions, the institutional arrangements, etc., favourable for increase of labour productivity, attention should be paid not only to how they influence the human behaviour in production, but also — and this is very important — to how they favour creation of material conditions of an accelerated development.

The above proposition can be supported by indicating certain features pertaining to the industrialization process carried on in the developing countries nowadays.

It can be stated, on the basis of historical experience, that the sociological factors do not create, as a rule, any paramount obstacle for economic development. All nations are able to acquire the contemporary industrial civilization, and the process of social adaptations to the new technical, economic, and social conditions of industrial civilization proceeds together with and on the basis of the changing material conditions in production and consumption, although it certainly takes time.

During the first stages of the historical development of industrial civilization, the social and economic factors had to produce the new production techniques and the new social organization of production. Nowadays, for the developing countries, they have only to take the techniques available and the organization of economic activities already experienced. This should be much easier, and actually one can state that the process of social adaptation to the already existing, introduced techniques is relatively easy and can be accomplished in an accelerated way. There is sufficient historical demonstration for that.

It can be observed that, in general, it is much easier to borrow the new techniques, where — assuming they can be introduced because of economic reasons — the human beings can adapt themselves to them, than to achieve a gradual and steady progress in production techniques which must originate and grow out of the existing socio-economic conditions. Thus, it is easier to introduce into any country the modern system of transportation and communication, the industrial techniques, than to achieve a steady progress by way of improving the technical methods, implements and institutions, e.g. in agriculture, where they very often have to develop out of the existing, traditional socio-economic conditions.

The great ability of human beings to adapt themselves to the conditions created by new production techniques, and the fact that techniques available nowadays have favourable economic characteristics, mean that this path of economic development brings about fast growth in labour productivity for countries still retarded in economic development. This particular path can be defined as accelerated industrialization. Industrialization consists, in fact, in applying the new production techniques on a large scale, in imposing them upon the society. 'Imposing' does not, of course, mean that the new production techniques are introduced against the will or interests of the society, but only that they are an exogenous factor and bring about changes in internal relations, conditions, attitudes, etc.

Since, then, industrialization is the most important method of raising labour productivity, conditions favourable for fast industrialization and factors determining it are, at the same time, of significance for increase of labour productivity.

4. Increased capital formation is a paramount factor of an accelerated economic development. Capital investment is, indeed, an indispensable way of introducing new production techniques and benefiting from the high levels of labour productivity they bring.

Accordingly, as macro-economic factors determining the growth of labour productivity one should consider the factors determining the volume of capital investment.

There are two principal factors determining investment volume in the developing countries :
(1) social savings,
(2) the capacities to transform savings into real investment.

For the developed economies, capital investment is analysed mainly or solely as a function of savings and demand for capital goods. In many of the growth models, the investment ratio is given as equal to the savings ratio without qualifications. This approach may be right for those economies, as they possess the abilities to produce capital goods in a wide range. Therefore, the problem of transforming the savings into real investment is rather disregarded in theories. This problem is much more difficult for the under-developed economies, however. They lack the necessary capacities to produce the capital goods and, therefore, the transformation of savings into investment has to be achieved, to a large extent, via foreign trade. This way, however, is only possible whenever they can sell their surplus on the foreign markets, to finance the purchase of capital goods. It is our opinion that, for many of the under-developed countries, the capabilities to transform savings into investment constitute a most important factor limiting the growth of capital formation, often more important and insurmountable than the generation of savings.

The factors determining the investment volume and therefore also the long-run growth of labour productivity can, then, be formulated in the following way : (1) factors bringing about increase in social savings, (2) factors increasing capabilities for capital investment, in which capacities to import capital goods have a great importance at the earlier development stages. The first group of factors can be found in the field of income distribution ; the second, in production structures, conditions of world markets, foreign trade policies, etc.

It is only a corollary of the above that the social and institutional framework most favourable for the steady and high growth of labour productivity is the one which can solve the problems of income distribution and development patterns allowing for a fast progress in industrialization.

The above interpretation of the factors determining the growth of labour productivity seems rather different from the conventional understanding. It seems useful, however, and even indispensable for a correct understanding of the real factors which can bring a high level of labour productivity for the developing countries. All the methods influencing human behaviour in production, such as economic stimuli, administrative measures, improving human relations, etc., though undoubtedly relevant for productivity, amount to very little unless accompanied by a sound and fast development of the productive apparatus.

The macro-economic approach to the labour productivity has, moreover, a particular significance for the cases where the long-run growth of labour productivity comes into conflict with its behaviour in the short-run and considered from a narrow angle.

5. In providing arguments for the above propositions, it seems worth while to discuss certain relevant problems :

(i) Labour productivity can be measured per unit of man-power and per unit of labour actually employed.

The first of these concepts of labour productivity is broader than the second one and, indeed, quite useful in macro-analysis. Gainful employment in comparison with unemployment means, in the light of this concept, a rise in labour productivity. In the micro-economic analysis it is only the second concept which can be meaningfully applied, and this concept is actually used for measuring labour productivity in the various sectors, firms, etc.

Employment creation is one of the most important ways of increasing the social labour productivity. This statement may sound strange to the micro-analyst, accustomed to considering employment and productivity as two opposed means of increasing output. It is not a fallacy, however, and a similar operation is made when applying labour productivity measured per man-hour and per man-year.

Employment creation should be rightly considered as a very important means of increasing labour productivity, from all conceivable points of view. First, it means a real jump in the labour productivity of a man, from zero value to a positive value. Second, when employment creation takes place in the modern sector, it effects high labour productivity in comparison to the average productivity. Third, wherever it takes place, it creates, as a rule, a certain scope for further productivity improvements.

(ii) It is not an abstract situation for the developing countries in which increase in output per man-power is achieved simultaneously with or even by way of, a decrease of output per person employed in a certain sector. This may come about in many of the developing countries utilizing the surplus labour in agriculture and other traditional sectors as well as in the modern sectors (e.g. by increasing employment in the existing plants up to the full utilization of the technical productive capacities).

Though it may be controversial, I would not hesitate to call the described development as meaning growth of the social labour productivity.

A particular case with regard to the above is that which occurs in connection with the choice of techniques. More labour intensive techniques mean lower labour productivity in a certain activity, but may contribute to the higher social labour productivity measured in output per unit of man-power.

It needs to be emphasized, however, that the social labour productivity should be necessarily considered in the longer run. Therefore, it is not in all cases certain that, for example, relatively labour intensive techniques are more favourable for the long-run growth of labour productivity.

There is one very important point which comes up in the

discussed context. Employment creation provides a certain scope and favourable conditions for productivity improvements. Particularly employment increase in the modern sector is a necessary prerequisite of the development of skills, spreading of the technological knowledge and imposing upon people the industrial discipline. That is also why the employment creation should be considered as an important means assuring the long-run growth of labour productivity.

(iii) Utilization of the surplus labour in agriculture can be of particular significance when it is utilized for capital works in agriculture itself and when it produces an additional food surplus, thus permitting an increase in the total volume of capital works in the country. The same is true, *mutatis mutandis*, for utilization of the surplus labour in other sectors.

Then, what may actually happen is that, by way of a temporary decline of labour productivity in a given sector, favourable conditions are created for a long-run growth of labour productivity.

(iv) Let as assume a situation in which balance of payments difficulties hamper the expansion of capital investment. In such a situation, which is quite common in the developing countries, promoting exportable production and substitutes for imports is a way of increasing a country's capacities to import capital goods and thereby to increase capital investment.

It would seem shortsighted to consider the sectors producing the exportable surplus or import substitutes from the narrow point of view of their sectoral labour productivity. The most important result they produce is to expand the capital investment capacities, which causes the growth of labour productivity in the longer run.

The above are but examples showing that the macro-economic approach to labour productivity problems is quite fruitful for the developing countries. It is so because the real roots of labour productivity growth lie, at the early development stages, in macroeconomics — in the general conditions and ways of economic development.

6. When a country achieves the structural conditions favourable for economic development, that means with regard to industry — for a fast and steady expansion of industrial capacities—other factors affecting labour productivity grow in importance. They are similar to those envisaged by the more developed countries, and known as the 'human factor'.

The 'human factor' has always had great importance for progress in production and productivity. Man is shaping the economy, although he is also being shaped by it. The state of economic underdevelopment indicates, however, that there is something deficient in this interaction. It is our thesis that a favourable change in the inter-relations and interactions between man and economy can be facilitated by imposing industrial techniques upon the society. That is why we consider that the social and political conditions creating the necessary economic basis for this change (as discussed above) are, at the same time, most favourable for economic progress, reflected in labour productivity. When, however, the new industrial techniques are established, influencing directly the human factor becomes more and more important.

The desired changes in the 'human factor' can be defined as :
developing of skills — technical, managerial, etc. ;
developing of human attitudes favourable for economic progress.

In other words, there is the problem of the capabilities and of the will, which should go hand in hand in order to produce a steady progress in productivity.

Many problems are faced by the developing countries striving to develop the 'human factor' together with the solution of other development tasks. Very instructive lessons can be drawn out of these experiences. Is there, however, any regularity which can be observed with regard to the ways and methods applied on the various stages of industrial growth ? It seems doubtful, and it is particularly doubtful whether the historical experience of the developed countries could be relevant for the new developing countries.

DISCUSSION OF THE PAPER BY PROFESSOR PAJESTKA

Chairman : PROFESSOR V. K. R. V. RAO

Professor Subbiah Kannappan (United States) opened the discussion on Professor Pajestka's paper. He took issue with the thesis that in developing countries a macro-economic approach with emphasis on long-run factors and social productivity was more fruitful than conventional micro-economics. Conventional economics had a greater role to play than Professor Pajestka assigned to it. Although it is true that sociological factors are not insurmountable obstacles to industrialization, one cannot there-fore conclude that productivity increases are mainly dependent on the accumulation of physical capital. There are at least three other sources of productivity increases : superior organization and management of enter-prises ; more effective borrowing and adaptation of the technical know-ledge of the advanced countries ; and improvement in labour commitment, mobility and discipline. Professor Pajestka's vista is in one sense too sweeping and in another too narrow. His long run is far too long, and virtually ignores most of the short-run and pressing problems of utilizing human resources in economic growth, or of providing for labour supply in the requisite quality and in the appropriate locations. Even assuming that the long run elasticity of the supply of labour is infinite, or at least positive, there are lags in the responses of the labour market. The requirements for trained man-power are not always anticipated in advance. Even where there is public investment in education and training, to the extent that valuable skills are acquired only on the job, it appears likely that for a considerable period of time, there will exist relative shortages of skilled, especially high-talent, man-power. This will be particularly critical in the area of research and innovation, which the under-developed countries will have to undertake themselves if methods and techniques are to be realistically adapted to the local cultural environment as well as relative factor endowments.

Professor Pajestka's approach is narrow, however, because of its exclusive focus on the 'industrial' sector. Relatively high labour productivity may be attained in the industrial sector while the non-industrial sectors are stagnant. The employment potential, and consequently the creation of external economies through trained man-power and the building up of entrepreneurial experience, may be limited. Furthermore, high figures for labour productivity do not necessarily indicate a satisfactory yield on capital invested. Since capital is a scarce good, it must be wisely allocated. The record does not support Professor Pajestka's optimism in respect to raising agricultural productivity solely through the utilization of surplus man-power. Both agriculture and marketing and distribution have their own claims to capital.

Professor Pajestka's stage concept is arbitrary and unrealistic. One set of problems cannot be postponed, certainly not for so long, while awaiting the achievements of structural conditions favourable for economic development. He is unrealistic in projecting teleologically an ultimate stage of development as if the problems arising at intermediate phases are irrelevant to the final outcome. Agreed that industrialization is the desired goal ; some guide-lines would be needed to select the industries which are worth developing, the extent to which complementary investments would be required in education, agriculture or distribution, the phasing of the programme of industrialization, etc. More understanding is needed of the functioning of the labour market and of the phenomenon, even in India with its vast reservoir of human resources, of the relatively high cost of industrial labour and the acute shortages of skilled and professional man-power. Finally, the most advanced techniques recommended by Professor Pajestka would accentuate technological dualism in the under-developed economies. None of these problems can be solved without the aid of micro-economics, nor can they be deemed of secondary importance for the under-developed countries.

Mr. Pavel Turcan (Czechoslovakia) supported Professor Pajestka's thesis with the example of the development of Slovakia, a traditionally agricultural region which was industrialized in fifteen years. With 29 per cent of the population of the country, and a contribution to the national product of well under 20 per cent, Slovakia was allocated about 30 per cent of total investment during the fifteen-year period. The fact that the under-developed region received support from an advanced industrialized economy, and was not compelled to construct its own industrial base, made accelerated development possible. In the first phase, the creation of industrial employment for the surplus agricultural population was emphasized, on the basis of the exploitation of local resources of primary products. This permitted the rationalization of agriculture. At the same time, transportation and public services were enlarged and improved. In 1948 agricultural workers were four times as numerous as industrial workers in Slovakia, but today they are about equal. Now the task in Slovakia is the same as for the country as a whole : the most rational utilization of labour through the construction of large-scale enterprises, mainly metallurgical and chemical, with a very high level of labour productivity.

M. Bertrand de Jouvenel des Ursins (France) suggested that production rather than productivity should be stressed in development. Higher productivity alone might create unemployment which could not be absorbed elsewhere in the economy.

Professor Delivanis pointed out, in connection with Professor Pajestka's suggestion that industries producing exports or import substitutes furthered long-run social productivity because they produced foreign exchange, regardless of the short-run productivity of these sectors, that in Greece, when self-sufficiency in wheat was achieved, total imports nevertheless increased, because of the preference of wheat growers for foreign commodities.

Professor Pajestka asserted, in answer to the points raised from the floor, that he had not meant to rule out other factors in development in his emphasis on capital formation. Education and skill were certainly of fundamental importance. Nor indeed was capital the only significant external factor. As for employment creation, he had already noted in his paper — and Mr. Turcan had understood this — that it was one of the most important ways of increasing social labour productivity in the long run, even though, in the short run, output per man did not rise in the enterprise or sector, or perhaps even fell.

Chapter 14

PRODUCTIVITY GROWTH AND ACCUMU-
LATION AS HISTORICAL PROCESSES[1]

BY

W. E. G. SALTER

Department of the Prime Minister, Canberra

THIS paper belongs as much to the field of growth-model theory as productivity analysis. My first excuse is that the objectives are similar: Productivity analysis seeks to understand the reasons for divergent rates of growth between inputs and outputs; and growth-model theory seeks to define the relationships between the rates of growth of output, labour, capital and technical knowledge. My second excuse is that the particular problem in growth-model theory that I propose to examine is how the capital stock an economy inherits from the past influences its present rate of growth. This is a question that has some relevance to the effect of different stages of industrialization on productivity — although in this paper I am concerned only with theory and have resolved to eschew all practical implications.

In examining the role of an economy's capital stock, I am not concerned with equilibrium rates of growth that may eventually be established ('Golden Ages'), but rather with the process by which an economy moves from one point on its growth path to another. Most of what I have to say centres on the role of an economy's inherited capital stock as the repository of its recent history. Thus the argument develops at aggregate level ideas that originally had their rationale in the field of industry productivity analysis.[2]

I. GROWTH AS A PROCESS IN TIME

An economy in the process of growth is, so to speak, sandwiched between its past history and its expected future. From the past it has inherited a capital stock, the physical form of which reflects

---

[1] To our great regret we have to record the death in November 1963 of Dr. Salter, one of the most brilliant of the younger generation of Australian economists, in Lahore, where he was acting as adviser to the government of West Pakistan. We print the paper as he wrote it.

[2] Especially chapters iv and v of my *Productivity and Technical Change*, Cambridge University Press, 1960. I am grateful for the help given to me by T. W. Swan in refining the analysis of this paper.

past investment and technique decisions. From the future expectations are thrown back about new techniques, variations in factor prices, and new demand conditions. And, in the present itself, new technical knowledge, new savings and perhaps new labour, are available to be incorporated into the economy.

How do these links between the past, present and expected future interact ? Hicks' *Value and Capital*, and the theory of expectations, throw some light on how the expected future influences decisions taken today ; and Marshall's analysis of long- and short-period equilibrium provides some clues on the role of fixed capital carried over from the past. But these are only fragments of an answer. Once we venture outside the notion of a self-contained present — with, say, technical knowledge, demand conditions and factor supplies, as the sole determinants of what happens today — theory becomes very much more complicated, since for each variable, past and expected values, as well as present values, become relevant in determining what happens today ; and this, in turn, is the raw material for tomorrow's history.

The whole question of the way these links in time bind together past, present and future events is an extremely difficult one, as yet largely unexplored in economic theory. But, there is one simple and direct relationship binding the present to the past that is perhaps capable of analysis with our present tools. Durable capital equipment links the present and the past, so providing a medium by which past events may extend their influence into the present.

This aspect of capital is usually side-stepped in growth-model theory by the assumption — made explicitly in Swan's 'Meccano set' model [1] and implicitly in most others — that capital is a fluid factor of production free to change its physical form. The assumption is perhaps not very restrictive if the objective is to take a very long view and ask, for example, under what conditions an economy will settle down to a 'Golden Age' equilibrium rate of growth. But it is restrictive when we are concerned with the actual time-path of an economy. Consider, for instance, the analysis of capital accumulation involved when we regard 'capital' (however measured) as a fluid factor of production.[2] Total supplies of capital in each period consist of current net investment plus capital accumulated in the past. Successive periods therefore imply total supplies of capital

[1] T. W. Swan, 'Economic Growth and Capital Accumulation', *Economic Record*, No. 63, 1956.
[2] Mrs. Robinson in *The Accumulation of Capital* (London, 1956) treats capital as a 'treaclely' factor in that it is recognized that different techniques co-exist, and that entrepreneurs 'leap-frog' from one to the other. But this is regarded as an adjustment problem that does not impart any special characteristics to the model.

K_1, K_2, K_3 .... These together with available supplies of labour lead to a sequence of techniques, A, B, C ..., implying values of total output Y_1, Y_2, Y_3 .... Strictly speaking, these values refer only to notional equilibria that would be reached if the whole economy were adjusted to these techniques. Only if the capital stock were wholly transformed in each period into the physical forms appropriate to A, B, C ..., would the values Y_1, Y_2, Y_3 ... be achieved. In fact, however, the rate at which the capital stock may be so transformed is limited by the rate of gross investment. This year technique A^* is appropriate and is reflected in the physical form of current investment ; but, before a fraction of industry is equipped with A^* equipment, either technical progress or capital accumulation have made technique B^* appropriate ; and so on with new techniques appearing before their predecessors have worked their way through the capital stock.

Output, and output per head never reach their notional values, Y_1, Y_2, Y_3 ..., and $\frac{Y_1}{N_1}$, $\frac{Y_2}{N_2}$, $\frac{Y_3}{N_3}$ ... but fall short by an amount reflecting inability to transform the physical form of the capital stock.

It is clear, then, that one consequence of the assumptions of fluid capital and instantaneous adjustment is that they prevent analysis of the actual time-path of an economy. Moreover, realized output is always less than notional output ; and, in so far as this affects saving, it means that the whole character of an economy's growth is different, as well as its time sequence. But, more important than either of these difficulties, the assumption of fluid capital effectively cuts off an economy from its own past history. At each point of time, the economy is assumed to start off, as it were, with a clean slate independent of its past history and techniques. One of the points that I wish to establish is that there are mechanisms by which an economy's past history — booms and slumps, wars, past variations in technical progress and savings, and population growth — has an influence on current investment and techniques — an influence that is perhaps as important as even current technical knowledge. But, obviously, to do this requires dropping the idea of capital as something that adjusts its physical form instantaneously, and seeking instead for a schema in which capital is the accumulated sum of acts of physical investment, undertaken at various times, and reflecting the conditions of the past.

II. A NEO-RICARDIAN MODEL

Consider at a point of time, t, an economy that has been experiencing technical progress and capital accumulation. Total output,

Y_t, is the sum of the output produced by the various age-groups of capital equipment (or for simplicity, 'plants'), making up the existing capital stock.

$$Y_t = \int_{t-e}^{t} y_{(z)} \, dz \qquad (1)$$

where y is the present output (conveniently measured as 'net output' gross of amortization) of plants constructed between the present, t, and $t - e$ where e is the age of the oldest plant in operation.

Similarly, total employment, N_t, may be regarded as the sum of the labour force of the various age-groups of plants.

$$N_t = \int_{t-e}^{t} n_{(z)} \, dz. \qquad (2)$$

These two relationships reflect characteristics of the capital stock, and as such contain a good deal of information about the past history of the economy. For example, the distribution of output and employment between different age-groups of plants depends to a considerable degree on past rates of gross investment, reflecting in turn past booms and slumps, wars and variations in saving. Moreover, comparison of the distribution of employment with that of output reflects the techniques embodied in the capital stock. Thus (1) may be rewritten as :

$$Y_t = \int_{t-e}^{t} n_{(z)} \frac{y_{(z)}}{n_{(z)}} \, dz \qquad (3)$$

i.e. each age-group's output is its employment times its output per head reflecting the technique embodied in that year's crop of capital equipment.

This technique, in turn, is a reflection of the technical knowledge and factor prices ruling at the various plants construction dates, ranging from the present to perhaps fifty years with the past. In this sense, the capital stock and hence our age-group distributions of output and employment, reflect the history of the economy, including its technical history, over some decades.

In developing a model based on these premises, the first step is to determine the equilibrium conditions which define a self-consistent position at each point of time. This involves three sets of conditions involving respectively :

(i) the output, y_t, and the technique, $\frac{y_t}{n_t}$, of plants currently being added to the capital stock :

(ii) by analogy, the technique and output of plants built in earlier periods, together with any variations since their construction date ; and

(iii) the conditions defining the oldest plant still in operation, and hence *e*, so as to determine from how far back into the past the existing capital stock derives.

In order to focus attention on the main issues, assume an economy operating according to competitive principles in which full employment and full utilization of capacity is maintained by variations of the interest/profit rate (or by a central planning bureau). Assume that technical knowledge falls into two categories : that which requires investment to be utilized (a new machine) ; and that which can be incorporated into existing plants without investment (time and motion study). For simplicity, assume a zero 'Wicksell Effect', i.e. the price of capital goods remains constant in terms of consumption goods ; and that entrepreneurs (or planning cells) are myopic and expect the future to be the same as the present. An appendix sketches the way in which these assumptions may be relaxed, and some of the consequences of doing so.

In terms of these assumptions, consider new plants. We may write :

$$y_t = F_t(n_t, G_t) \tag{4}$$

as the best-practice production function. y_t is the output of plants built at t, n_t their labour, and G_t gross investment at t. This function is similar in concept to an ordinary production function except that its relevance is restricted to new plants, including replacements. This is appropriate for only when building new plants do entrepreneurs have a full choice of techniques. By the same token, it is obviously nonsense to talk of a grand production function involving all output and all employment since the bulk of output and employment at any one time is produced by existing plants using fixed capital equipment embodying techniques chosen in the past.

The form of the best-practice production function reflects, of course, technical knowledge at t (of both varieties, that requiring and that not requiring investment) ; so that with improving technical knowledge there is a different production function for each year.

The choice of techniques then follows the well-worn lines of production theory. Take G_t as given and as a function of total output, i.e.

$$G_t = sY_t \tag{5}$$

where s is the gross savings ratio, assumed fixed for simplicity (although it would be possible to build in any other savings behaviour considered relevant).

n_t and y_t are then defined by the usual maximizing condition that the marginal product of labour, $\dfrac{\delta y_t}{\delta n_t}$, equals the real wage, w_t.[1]

Turning next to plants built in earlier periods, similar conditions define their output and technique. The production function is the one relevant at the construction date, j, while gross investment at j, G_j, and the wage rate, w_j, determine their technique. Hence y_j and $\dfrac{y_j}{n_j}$, defined in terms of the values when the plant was first constructed, are given by :

$$y_j = F_j(n_j, G_j) \tag{6}$$
$$G_j = s Y_j \tag{7}$$

and
$$\frac{\delta y_j}{\delta n_j} = w_j. \tag{8}$$

At time, t, however, we are more interested in the actual values, including any changes since the plants were built. The more important of such changes are variations from the original designed capacity, physical deterioration of plant involving either more labour for maintenance or a smaller output, and technical improvement that can be introduced with the original capital equipment (improved methods of management, for example).

The first, variation in capacity working, has been assumed out of existence since, in this analysis, we are not very interested in such short-term factors.

The second, physical deterioration, could be treated in a number of ways. It is perhaps sufficient to regard employment in each plant as fixed and output as falling with age — in effect labour is diverted from production to maintenance. Thus, if physical deterioration reduces output at a steady rate u, the actual output at time t of plants built at time j with an original output of y_j may be written as

$$(y_j')_t = y_j e^{-u(t-j)}. \tag{9}$$

(If one wishes to build in a more complicated ageing function this can be done at the cost of more complicated mathematics.)

---

[1] Since the analysis is gross of amortization, the analogous condition for investment needs to be expressed as $\dfrac{\delta y_j}{\delta G_j} = R_j$ the gross rate of return on investment including amortization. This subsumes of course an anticipated life of investment involving in turn questions of durability and expected obsolescence. Hence, the choice of technique is really very much more complicated than set out here. A more detailed analysis covering these points is set out in 'The Production Function and the Durability of Capital' (*Economic Record*, No. 70, 1959, p. 47).

The third factor, technical progress incorporated without investment after the plant has been built, may be treated in a similar way. Assume such improvements come forward at a rate v and are immediately adopted. The effect on output is similar to physical ageing (but positive) since both are simple functions of time. Thus a positive term, v, may be added to (9) to give

$$(y'_j)_t = y_j e^{-(u-v)(t-j)}. \tag{10}$$

(If desired, one may interpret v to include other influences on productivity, such as greater labour effort.)

Turning back to our original expression $Y_t = \int_{t-e}^{t} y_{(z)} \, dz$, each

value of y in this expression refers to its current value. It is now possible, and rather more convenient, to recast the expression in terms of the output of each age-group of plants when first constructed, plus any subsequent variation due to physical deterioration and technical progress, etc., not involving investment, i.e.

$$Y_t = \int_{t-e}^{t} y_{(x)} \, e^{-(u-v)(t-x)} \, dx \tag{11}$$

where x is the construction date of each age-group ranging between the present, t, and $t - e$. Similarly

$$N_t = \int_{t-e}^{t} n_{(x)} \, dx \tag{12}$$

since, on our assumptions, the labour force of each age-group does not vary over its life.

It remains to define how far back into the past the capital stock stretches, i.e. the value of e. This may be done quite simply by utilizing the condition that capital equipment disappears from service when quasi-rents are zero — or, in other words, when receipts equal prime or operating costs.[1] Remembering that output is measured as net output and that labour costs are accordingly the only prime costs, this condition may be written as :

$$y_{t-e} \, e^{-(u-v)e} = n_{t-e} \, w_t$$

[1] Scrap value is assumed zero. The same condition applies for replacement decisions — as may be seen by breaking a replacement decision into its two parts : a decision to build a new plant when profitable, and a decision to scrap an old plant when no longer profitable to operate. For a general discussion of this condition see 'Productivity and Technical Change', chapters v and vii ; and for a proof that it is implicit in replacement decisions, see pp. 57-86.

or

$$\frac{y_{t-e}}{n_{t-e}} e^{-(u-v)e} = w_t. \tag{13}$$

Thus e, the age of the oldest plant (or plants) still in operation, is defined by the condition that the actual output per head at t of such plants equals the current real wage w_t — which is the same as saying that wages exhaust the product and that quasi-rents are zero.

This is a key relationship. It defines how far back into the past the capital stock stretches. Further, it indicates that this time-span is a function of the level of real wages, which, in effect determine how much of the fossilized history embedded in the capital stock influences present total output and productivity.

This part of the analysis may be formalized by the concept of a 'capital stock function' — a function that describes certain characteristics of an economy's inherited capital stock. The rationale is as follows : Each year's gross investment produces physical capital equipment, which, provided sufficient labour is devoted to its maintenance, is capable of producing output virtually indefinitely. Thus, at any one time the total output of the economy may be increased or decreased by not scrapping or by scrapping existing capital equipment. But to do so involves using more or less labour. In this sense, the output that can be extracted from an inherited physical capital stock is a function of the amount of labour employed in conjunction with it. Thus, in this particular sense of varying the age of equipment in use,

$$Y_t = \psi_t (N_t) \tag{14}$$

or

$$\int_{t-e}^{t} y_{(x)} e^{-(u-v)(t-x)} dx = \psi_t\left(\int_{t-e}^{t} n_{(x)}dx\right). \tag{15}$$

It is possible to say something about the shape and determinants of this function. In an economy experiencing technical progress and/or capital accumulation, each year's 'crop' of capital equipment is normally more technically advanced than its predecessors in the sense that it yields a higher output per head.[1] Hence, while Y_t is a rising function of N_t, it will rise at a declining rate since, as one moves back through the capital stock, the output per head of each age-group progressively falls — by how much depends on the past history of the economy. In other words, the shape of the capital

[1] There can be perverse cases : for example, if technical change has been highly biassed towards capital-saving methods ; or if the past history of factor prices has led to progressively less mechanized techniques.

stock function depends on the distribution of output between plants of various age-groups compared to the distribution of employment.

Differentiating both sides of (15) with respect to e so as to find the effect of varying the age of equipment yields :

$$\frac{\delta Y_t}{\delta e} = y_{t-e}\, e^{-(u-v)e} \text{ and } \frac{\delta N_t}{\delta e} = n_{t-e}$$

and since e is the only form of variation,

$$\frac{\delta Y_t}{\delta N_t} = \frac{y_{t-e}}{n_{t-e}}\, e^{-(u-v)e} \tag{16}$$

or, the ratio of output lost to employments lost through scrapping additional plants (or vice versa) is the output per head they yield. Hence, the marginal product of labour derived from the capital stock function is the output per head of the oldest (or marginal) plant or plants still in use, which, in turn, equals the current real wage.

What is involved in this mechanism is an additional form of variation by which the marginal product of labour and the real wage may be equated.[1] This derives simply from the fact that one way of obtaining more or less output with more or less labour is to vary the operating life of equipment already in existence.

The elasticity of this capital stock function, written as

$$A_t = \frac{\delta Y_t}{\delta N_t} \cdot \frac{N_t}{Y_t}$$

has some interesting properties. One may be conveniently noted now. So far as variations in e are concerned :

$$\frac{\delta Y_t}{\delta N_t} = \frac{y_{t-e}}{n_{t-e}}\, e^{-(u-v)e}$$

so that

$$A_t = \frac{y_{t-e}}{n_{t-e}}\, e^{-(u-v)e}\, \frac{N_t}{Y_t} \tag{17}$$

indicating that A_t equals the ratio of the output per head of the oldest age-group of plants compared to the average output per head for the economy as a whole.

The value of A_t depends, of course, on the past history of the economy. For example, an economy with a history of rapid technical change will, other things equal, have a lower elasticity than an economy with a history of slow change. Output per head of the

[1] But note that it is not a wholly reversible mechanism. If, for example, a sudden influx of labour takes place, it may not be possible to extend the life of existing equipment beyond a certain limit because that previously scrapped cannot be brought back into service.

economy as a whole will be high compared to that of older plants because of the rapid progress since their construction date. Again, an economy with a history of a high rate of replacement (and scrapping) will tend to have a low elasticity compared to an economy with little replacement since output per head of older plants will be higher if replacement is rapid. Further, to the extent that past booms and slumps are embedded in the relevant part of the capital stock, these will affect the value of A_t — and perhaps change its value quite markedly from year to year. In all these ways, this elasticity, A_t, is a convenient short-hand way of summarizing something of the past history of the economy.

To sum up progress to date: We have a system consisting of two basic functions. One, a production function,

$$y_t = F_t (n_t, G_t)$$

relates to current technical knowledge and is relevant to new plants currently being added to the capital stock. The other, a capital stock function

$$\int_{t-e}^{t} y_{(x)}\, e^{-(u-v)(t-x)}\, dx = \psi_t \left(\int_{t-e}^{t} n_{(x)}\, dx \right)$$

describes characteristics of the existing capital stock and thus the past history of the economy.

Given total labour, N_t, and gross investment G_t as a function of Y_t, we have a determinate system. As shown, the equilibrium conditions follow conventional lines except that the marginal product of labour equals the wage rate in two senses, one for new plants, and one for plants just about to be scrapped, i.e.

$$w_t = \frac{\delta y_t}{\delta n_t} = \frac{y_{t-e}}{n_{t-e}}\, e^{-(u-v)e}. \tag{18}$$

III. SOME CHARACTERISTICS OF THE MODEL

This is a model of an economy caught, as it were, in mid-flight, and ready to be set in motion. But before taking this step consider some of its characteristics.

First, note that viewed even in a static sense, the model does not involve the measurement of capital. This is important, not so much in itself, but because it offers a means of escape from the tyranny of the aggregate production function, $Y_t = F_t(N_t, K_t)$ and the restrictive form of comparative statics imposed by the need to regard capital as free to change its physical form with each variation in technique.

The trick by which these problems have been avoided is to work in terms of investment. The justification for doing so is that at any one time accumulated capital is not a factor of production with alternative uses ; only gross investment is free in the sense that, like labour, it can be used to produce alternative products by alternative techniques. In the model, accumulated capital is treated as what it really is : a 'who's who' of individual items of plant and equipment. Instead of information about its amount, the model relies upon information about the distribution of output and employment between the various age-groups of this 'who's who' of physical capital. It is not so much the amount of such capital we are interested in, but rather what it can do : produce so much output involving so much employment. This treatment more or less parallels that of land in the Ricardian model, in which it is not necessary to measure the amount of land since this underlies the function relating output and employment. In fact, the capital stock function in this model parallels the output-employment function in the Ricardian model except that age-groups of capital equipment are the determinants rather than degrees of fertility — and, of course, the Ricardian function is fixed whereas the capital stock function changes with time as the economy generates new history.[1]

A second consequence of breaking away from the notion of a self-contained present is to introduce into the analysis a new class of restraints — historical restraints that depend on the past history of the economy. In the model, the output produced by given factor supplies depends on both technical and historical considerations. The technical considerations, depending on current technical knowledge, influence the character of new plants currently being added to the capital stock. But, in addition, historical considerations reflected in the economy's inherited capital stock, also play an important role in determining the level of output, wages, profits and productivity. They do so in two ways : One is the rather mechanical sense in which total output is the sum of output of plant built in the past. The other is the more positive sense in which past events affect the present through their influence on the shape of the capital stock function. This is explored in greater

---

[1] This is not to deny that there is some flexibility : Some capital equipment can produce different products and some can be combined with varying amounts of labour. But, in such cases, the restraints are not technical knowledge but rather arise out of the characteristics of capital equipment in existence — 'historical' facts. The parallel with Ricardo is the case of land that is capable of producing alternative crops.

detail in the following section. But already it is apparent that the level of real wages, for example, is determined by both technical and historical considerations. This is clear since the equilibrium condition for wages may be expressed in terms of the elasticity of both the current (technical) production function (α) and the (historical) capital stock function (A), i.e.

$$w_t = \alpha_t \frac{y_t}{n_t} = A_t \frac{Y_t}{N_t}. \tag{19}$$

The parallel with Ricardo is again clear : technical restraints correspond to 'the state of the arts' ; historical restraints to the character and distribution of available land.

Parallel with these two forms of restraint there are two forms of substitution between labour and investment. A given amount of gross investment may be employed to raise output per head in two ways : the first is by increasing the degree of mechanization in new plants — the standard neo-classical form of substitution ; the second is by additional replacement investment, which, by bringing the existing capital stock more up-to-date, also raises output per head. In the model the level of real wages provides the link between these two forms of substitution through the equilibrium condition that real wages equal the marginal product of labour in new plants and the average product of labour in plants about to be scrapped. Hence a rise in real wages has two effects : a higher degree of mechanization in new plants : and higher standards of obsolescence leading to shorter lives for existing physical capital.

Finally, the way in which factor shares are determined in the model is of some interest. For new plants, the share of wages under competition is given by the elasticity, a_t of the production function (4). However, the share of wages for the economy as a whole is given by the elasticity, A_t, of the capital stock function (15). This is apparent when using (17) A_t is written as :

$$A_t = \frac{y_{t-e}}{n_{t-e}} e^{-(u-v)e} \frac{N_t}{Y_t}$$

and since

$$\frac{y_{t-e}}{n_{t-e}} e^{-(u-v)e} = w_t$$

$$A_t = \frac{N_t w_t}{Y_t}. \tag{20}$$

It is easy to see why it is the capital stock function that is relevant to the share of wages at any one time. When we speak of the share of wages in output produced from an existing capital stock, we are really making a comparison between wages and quasi-rents yielded by existing capital equipment. This is in contrast to new plants where the rate of interest or profit is relevant. But it is relevant only as an ex-ante concept before the investment is made. Once it has been made the returns become quasi-rents ; and whether they exceed or fall short of the anticipated rate of return is not of much significance. Certainly, the capital equipment is there and will go on producing so long as it can yield positive quasi-rents. Hence it is the realized division between wages and quasi-rents (for which the capital stock function is relevant) that is actually of significance in determining factor shares at any one time.

Factor shares for the economy and new plants are, of course, related. Writing the two elasticities, or shares, as a ratio, we obtain

$$\frac{\alpha_t}{A_t} = \frac{w_t \dfrac{n_t}{y_t}}{w_t \dfrac{N_t}{Y_t}} = \frac{\dfrac{Y_t}{N_t}}{\dfrac{y_t}{n_t}}. \tag{21}$$

Thus, the ratio of shares equals the inverse ratio of output per head for the economy as a whole compared to that of new plants. Hence the share of wages in new plants is lower than for the economy as a whole — a proposition that is consistent with the gradual erosion of quasi-rents over the life of plants as technical progress and accumulation raise real wages and render them progressively more obsolescent.

IV. MOVEMENT

The next step is to examine how this model moves through time. Complex issues involved for a system such as this, which generates its own history, quickly become very involved. Hence, I have little to say about its growth path, or whether it reaches an equilibrium rate of growth. Instead I propose to concentrate on the mechanisms involved in its movement — how rather than where to. This, incidentally, is needed to round out the previous sections which are incomplete to the extent that they define equilibrium conditions without indicating the mechanisms by which equilibrium is achieved.

The following elements, all functions of time, disturb each equilibrium position as fast as it is created :

(i) New technical knowledge becomes available leading to a superior production function compared to that hitherto available for the choice of technique of new plants.

(ii) Gross saving takes place, and the labour force may increase. Both need to be absorbed into the economy.

(iii) Existing plant and equipment physically deteriorate.

(iv) Technical improvements, etc., capable of being utilized without investment become available and are incorporated into existing plants.

The problem is to trace through the reactions to these new elements. As a first step, consider the following rough sketch :

The new techniques induce entrepreneurs to build (or, at least, plan) new plants. This creates a demand for labour and investment : the demand for labour depends upon both output of the new plants and their unit labour requirements (reflecting the embodied technique) ; similarly, the demand for investment depends on the output of new plants and their unit investment requirements.

The labour force for new plants may be drawn from three sources : (i) the increase in the labour force ; (ii) labour released from plants which are scrapped because of physical deterioration ; and (iii) labour employed on other plants. The first two sources of labour are available at the existing level of real wages. Other plants, however, are earning surpluses over operating costs at the current level of real wages, and therefore will not release labour unless forced to do so by a rise in real wages.

This may be achieved in either one of two ways. The owners of new plants may bid up the money wage. With a constant price level real wages rise and some of the older existing plants are forced to close down as real wages rise above their output per head. Their quasi-rents disappear, and their labour force is freed. (The assumption of a constant price level is not necessarily inappropriate, for although money incomes increase, output also increases by virtue of the transfer of workers from old plants with low output per head, to modern plants with a relatively high output per head.) The alternative is for prices to fall. As some of the new plants enter production (employing, say, the labour released from plants which have physically deteriorated) output increases. Against a constant money income, prices fall, so raising real wages and releasing labour for the remaining new plants. Whatever the means, the important feature of this mechanism is that the new plants increase the demand for labour, and, by raising its real price, induce a transfer of labour from one of the least productive avenues of employment — older plants just on the margin of obsolescence.

The rise in real wages not only frees labour, but also reduces the labour demanded by new plants in two distinct ways : higher real wages induce more mechanized techniques in the new plants ; and the costs of labour-intensive industries rise relative to capital-intensive industries, with the result that the proportionate expansion of labour-intensive industries is less than that of capital-intensive industries. By these means the demand for labour by new plants is reduced.

If the economy is to remain fully employed, gross investment in new plants must match full employment gross savings. This may require adjustments to the interest/profit rate. The effects on the demand for gross investment are analogous to those for labour noted above.

This rough sketch indicates that the problem is basically one of a transfer of resources from existing to new plants, a process in which increases in real wages are a key equilibrating factor. The process may be given more precision as follows :

Differentiating the expression

$$Y_t = \int_{t-e}^{t} y_{(x)} \, e^{-(u-v)(t-x)} \, dx$$

with respect to time indicates the element making up the change in total output, i.e.

$$\frac{dY_t}{dt} = y_t - y_{t-e} \, e^{-(u-v)e} \left(1 - \frac{de}{dt}\right) - Y_t \, (u-v). \tag{22}$$

The first term is the output of plant currently added to the capital stock. The second is the output of plant scrapped. It falls into two parts : the output of plant with an age $t - e$; and the output of plant scrapped (or retained) because of any change in e. The last term reflects the change in the output of all existing plants, consisting of a negative term (u) reflecting physical deterioration and a positive term (v) reflecting technical improvement, etc., capable of being incorporated without investment.

The corresponding labour flows are given by differentiating

$$N_t = \int_{t-e}^{t} n_{(x)} \, dx$$

with respect to time, yielding :

$$\frac{dN_t}{d_t} = n_t - n_{t-e} \left(1 - \frac{de}{dt}\right). \tag{23}$$

The interpretation is similar to that of (22) except that there is no third term because of the convention of regarding physical

deterioration and technical improvements, etc., not involving investment as leaving unaffected the labour force of existing plants.

These relationships structure the problem. To give precision to
the mechanisms involved we need to examine the demand and supply
of factors involved. From the current production function for new
plants, $y_t = F_t(n_t, G_t)$ we can derive the functions for the demand
for labour and gross investment generated by such plants, i.e.

$$n_t = \alpha_t \frac{y_t}{w_t} \tag{24}$$

and

$$G_t = \beta_t \frac{y_t}{R_t} \tag{25}$$

where α_t and β_t are the elasticities with respect to labour and gross
investment of the production function.

These are the familiar derived demand functions for factors of
production theory (although restricted here to the demand of new
plants). They are highly interrelated, reflecting the nature of current
technical possibilities, their labour and investment-saving biasses, the
elasticity of substitution (and, in a multi-product system, the relative
opportunities for expansion of labour-intensive and investment-
intensive industries). In fact, they are analogous to those of a
static system, for at the forward margin of the capital stock, where
all factors are mobile, this system operates according to the principles
of the static general equilibrium model.

Turning to the supply of factors available to new plants, available
gross investment is given by (5), i.e.

$$G_t = s Y_t.$$

The supply of labour for new plants involves rather more com-
plication. (23) may be written as :

$$n_t = \frac{dN_t}{dt} + n_{t-e}\left(1 - \frac{de}{dt}\right) \tag{26}$$

indicating that one component is the increase in the labour force,
$\frac{dN_t}{dt}$, taken as given, and the other the labour released from plants
scrapped, including those involved in any change in e. This, however, is related to the level of real wages and defined by the condition
(13), i.e.

$$w_t = \frac{y_{t-e}}{n_{t-e}} e^{-(u-v)e}.$$

We need therefore to know how the rearward margin of the capital stock defined by this condition moves with time. Differentiating (13) with respect to t yields : [1]

$$\frac{dw_t}{dt} = e^{-(u-v)e} \left(1 - \frac{de}{dt}\right) \frac{\delta\left(\frac{y_{t-e}}{n_{t-e}}\right)}{\delta n_{t-e}} - (u-v) \frac{de}{dt} \cdot \frac{y_{t-e}}{n_{t-e}} e^{-(u-v)e}$$

from which

$$-\frac{de}{dt} = \frac{\dfrac{dw_t}{dt} - \dfrac{\delta\left(\frac{y_{t-e}}{n_{t-e}}\right)}{\delta_{t-e}} e^{-(u-v)e}}{\dfrac{\delta\left(\frac{y_{t-e}}{n_{t-e}}\right)}{\delta_{t-e}} e^{-(u-v)e} + (u-v)\dfrac{y_{t-e}}{n_{t-e}} e^{-(u-v)e}}$$

Multiplying by

$$w_t = \left(\frac{y_{t-e}}{n_{t-e}} e^{-(u-v)e}\right)$$

and writing

$$h = \frac{\delta\left(\frac{y_{t-e}}{n_{t-e}}\right)}{\delta_{t-e}} \frac{1}{\dfrac{y_{t-e}}{n_{t-e}}}$$

we obtain

$$-\frac{de}{dt} = \frac{\dfrac{dw_t}{dt} \dfrac{1}{w_t} - h}{h + (u-v)} \tag{27}$$

which substituted into (26) yields the following supply function for labour available to new plants :

[1] In this differentiation $\frac{y_{t-e}}{n_{t-e}} e^{-(u-v)e}$ is broken up into two parts $\frac{y_{t-e}}{n_{t-e}}$ and $e^{-(u-v)e}$. Differentiation of the latter part is straightforward. Differentiation of the former part involves going back to the basic functions $y = y(x)$ and $n = n(x)$ which are integrated over the range t to $t-e$ to give (11) and (12). These basic functions imply the existence of a function $\frac{y}{n} = \frac{y}{n}(x)$ which, differentiated by t, yields

$$\frac{d\left(\frac{y}{n}\right)}{dt} = \frac{dx}{dt} \frac{\delta\frac{y}{n}}{\delta x}.$$

Hence, when $x = t - e$,
$$\frac{d\left(\frac{y_{t-e}}{n_{t-e}}\right)}{dt} = \left(1 - \frac{de}{dt}\right) \frac{\delta\left(\frac{y_{t-e}}{n_{t-e}}\right)}{\delta_{t-e}}$$

In effect, differentiation involves changing the age-group under consideration, first by fractionally changing the point from which we are standing looking back (t) ; and then changing how far we are looking back (e).

$$n_t = \frac{dN_t}{dt} + n_{t-e} \left(1 + \frac{\frac{dw_t}{dt} \frac{1}{w_t} - h}{h + (u - v)} \right) \tag{28}$$

This may be interpreted as follows : $\frac{dN_t}{dt}$ is the given increase in the total labour force ; n_{t-e} is the labour employed by plants built $t - e$ years ago. As such it reflects one aspect of the recent history of the economy. If the economy experienced a boom e years ago n_{t-e} will be high ; and low if it experienced a slump. Generally the value of n_{t-e} reflects all the factors — demographic, technical and economic — that determined how much labour was engaged by new plants e years ago.

Whether the amount of labour released exceeds or falls short of n_{t-e} depends in the first place on the proportional rate of increase of real wages, which, as noted, influences the life of existing equipment through its effect on the ability to earn quasi-rents. But the extent to which it influences the life of equipment depends on three parameters, h, u and v.

The parameter, h, reflects a second aspect of past history. Written as :

$$h = \frac{\delta \frac{y_{t-e}}{n_{t-e}}}{\delta_{t-e}} \frac{1}{\frac{y_{t-e}}{n_{t-e}}}$$

it is clearly the proportional rate at which the output per head of new plant was increasing e years ago. This is relevant because if, for example, past history were such that $\frac{y}{n}$ of new plants increased considerably e years ago (i.e. rapid technical progress) then a given increase in real wages will render fewer age-groups of plants obsolete — $\frac{y}{n}$ rises quickly from one age-group to the next. But, if the rate of increase of $\frac{y}{n}$ was low e years ago (slow technical progress) a given increase in real wages renders more age-groups obsolete and releases more labour — $\frac{y}{n}$ rises slowly from one age-group to the next.

The remaining elements reflect the rate of physical deterioration (u) and technical progress, etc., independent of investment (v). As might be expected, when there is no increase in real wages, the greater u the more labour is released by scrapping, and the greater

v the less labour is released. But, in their relation to an increase in wages, these factors operate in an opposite way because then the effect on the gradient of $\frac{y}{n}$ between successive age-groups becomes relevant.

In summary, then, the amount of labour released from old plants depends on : (i) the rate of increase of real wages ; (ii) on two historical factors reflecting the amount of labour employed by plants built e years ago, and the rate at which $\frac{y}{n}$ was then increasing ; (iii) the rate of physical deterioration ; and (iv) the rate of technical progress etc., not involving investment.

This system of demand and supply function of factors for new plants :

$$n_t = \alpha_t \frac{y_t}{w_t} \qquad\qquad G_t = \beta_t \frac{y_t}{R_t}$$

$$n_t = \frac{dN_t}{dt} + n_{t-e}\left(1 + \frac{\dfrac{dw_t}{dt}\dfrac{1}{w_t} - h}{h + (u - v)}\right) \qquad G_t = sY_t$$

illustrates the mechanisms by which the economy moves forward a step in time, adding new capacity, and discarding existing capacity.

One thing that emerges clearly is the role of variations in real wages as the equilibrating factor relating labour usage in new and old plants. The basic reason why wages should have this role is that the price of continuing to use outmoded techniques is the extra labour costs involved, so that variations in real wages influence the balance between these extra labour costs and the investment costs involved in utilizing new and up-to-date techniques.

Also, the nature of the interaction between the technical and historical restraints mentioned earlier is now somewhat clearer. Technical restraints are relevant in determining the shape of the demand function for labour to man new plants. Historical restraints play the major role in determining the share of the supply function for such labour. To return to the analogy with the Ricardian system $y_{t-e}\, e^{-(u-v)e}$ is the output of land at the margin of cultivation $\frac{y_{t-e}}{n_{t-e}}\, e^{-(u-v)e}$ is its 'fertility', and h is the rate at which 'fertility' increases as the margin of cultivation is withdrawn to better land. (Again the caveat is relevant that in the model these restraints are continually changing as it generates new history.)

Both types of restraint are, of course, relevant in determining the extent of the increase in real wages, the technique chosen for new plants, and their output. But, it is interesting to see that to the extent these historical restraints influence current events, there is a kind of historical 'echo effect'. Today's events are influenced by events e years ago ; and these in turn will influence events e' years in the future ; and so on. As the economy moves forward each past event leaves a diminishing mark on subsequent events at intervals equal to the life of capital equipment.

The system of demand and supply functions also illustrates the mechanisms by which each momentary equilibrium is reached. The nature of this equilibrium, however, deserves some comment. It is not short-term in the Marshallian sense since investment is involved ; nor is it long-term since the physical form of 'capital' is not adjusted to the technical and economic currently prevailing ; rather it is an amalgam of both in which short- and long-term elements are combined. The economy has adjusted itself as far as is profitable to current technical conditions given the capital stock that it has inherited, given that gross investment is limited and implies a current cost, and given that equipment in existence has no current cost and is there to be used or not.

In fact, classical long-run equilibrium is a special case of the momentary equilibrium concept of this model. To see this clearly, consider successive momentary equilibria with unchanging technical knowledge, zero 'net saving', a 'balanced' age-composition of the capital stock, and a constant labour force. In such circumstances, the only new element that occurs with time is physical deterioration. The owners of these plants, having foreseen the exact date when such deterioration will have eliminated their quasi-rents (with the perfect foresight that is also an attribute of long-run equilibrium) will have made depreciation allowances just sufficient to create a demand for labour in new plants equal to that released from plants scrapped. Real wages, techniques, the rate of interest and total output are unchanged ; and the present value of the quasi-rents of the capital stock equals its initial cost less depreciation.

In such a situation, each momentary equilibrium is exactly the same as its predecessors. Thus long-run equilibrium (or the stationary state) is the special case of the present model where conditions are such that a series of unvarying momentary equilibria results — the processes and mechanisms are exactly the same. In fact, the term stationary state is really a misnomer. For, while the values of each variable are constant, the stationary state is not without movement since labour is continuously being transferred from old to new plants. What the present model does is to seize on this movement, generalize the mechanisms involved and apply them to other situations where the exacting conditions for a series unvarying momentary equilibria (or long-run equilibrium) are not realized. It enables us to take a stationary state, disturb it by, say, an act of saving, and then trace out the resulting series of momentary equilibria as it sets off on its long and tortuous path in search of a new long-run equilibrium.

Given this concept of momentary equilibrium, successive equilibria trace out in a kind of way the growth path of the economy. Of course, at the highly simplified level of this model, many abstractions are involved : no gestation periods, constant expectations, no problems of effective demand, perfect competition and so on. These are very great abstractions. Nevertheless, this schema does suggest some kind of framework for analysis of growth paths. But how one derives such a growth path is at this stage frankly beyond me. I have no more positive suggestion than putting the whole model (including a given set of past history) on a computing machine and then exploring its behaviour.

It is possible, however, to take a little further analysis of the factors that determine the rate of growth of output at any one time.

We have already :

$$\frac{dY_t}{dt} = y_t - y_{t-e}\, e^{-(u-v)e}\left(1 - \frac{de}{dt}\right) - (u - v)Y_t \qquad (22)$$

and

$$\frac{dN_t}{dt} = n_t - n_{t-e}\left(1 - \frac{e}{dt}\right). \qquad (23)$$

Substituting (23) into (24) and making use of (13), i.e.

$$w_t = \frac{y_{t-e}}{n_{t-e}}\, e^{-(u-v)e}$$

yields

$$\frac{dY_t}{dt} = y_t - n_t w_t + \frac{dN_t}{dt}\, w_t - (u - v)Y_t. \qquad (29)$$

This expression implies that the increase in total output consists of (i) the gross profits (including amortization) of new plants $(y_t - n_t w_t)$; (ii) the earnings of the increase in the labour force $\frac{dN_t}{dt}\, w_t$; and (iii) the subtraction or addition to output from the net effect of physical deterioration on existing plants and technical progress, etc., not involving investment. In the special case where the labour force is constant, and there is no physical deterioration or technical progress, etc., not involving investment, the increase in output equals the gross profits of new plants.

286

The reason why the model throws up what might seem to be an unusual proposition is as follows : The output lost as a result of scrapping always equals the wages of the labour engaged in producing such output. Thus, provided the amount of labour transferred to new plants is small, the net increase in output is equal to the gross profits of new plants. In effect, labour is transferred from marginal existing plants where its marginal product equals its average product, to new plants where its average product exceeds its marginal product by an amount sufficient to meet the necessary level of gross profits in such plants. Thus, in this case :

$$\frac{dY_t}{dt} = y_t - n_t w_t$$

$$= n_t \left(\frac{y_t}{n_t} - w_t \right)$$

$$= n_t \left(\frac{y_t}{n_t} - \frac{y_{t-e}}{n_{t-e}} \right) \tag{30}$$

i.e. the net increase in output is the amount of labour transferred (n_t) times the difference between its average product in each use. Looked at from the viewpoint of profits, it is gross investment which makes this transfer possible, and, as might be expected under marginal productivity conditions, the extra output resulting equals the earnings of such gross investment.

Reverting to the expression :

$$\frac{dY_t}{dt} = y_t - n_t w_t + \frac{dN_t}{dt} w_t - (u - v) Y_t$$

writing from (25)

$$y_t - n_t w_t = G_t R_t = \beta y_t$$

and from (19)

$$w_t = A_t \frac{Y_t}{N_t} = \alpha_t \frac{y_t}{n_t}$$

and using $G_t = s Y_t$ the following alternative expressions may be obtained for the logarithmic rate of growth of output :

$$\frac{dY_t}{dt} \frac{1}{Y_t} = \beta_t \underbrace{\frac{s}{G_t}}_{y_t} + \frac{dN_t}{dt} \frac{1}{N_t} A_t - (u - v) Y_t \tag{31a}$$

or

$$\frac{dY_t}{dt} \frac{1}{Y_t} = \beta_t \underbrace{\frac{s}{G_t}}_{y_t} + \frac{dN_t}{dt} \frac{1}{N_t} \alpha_t \frac{y_t}{n_t} \Big/ \frac{Y_t}{N_t} - (u - v) Y_t. \tag{31b}$$

The first term $\beta_t \dfrac{\dfrac{s}{G_t}}{y_t}$ is the contribution gross investment makes

to the rate of growth of output. The second term is similarly the contribution made by the rate of growth of the labour force. The alternative forms appear because the model involves two ways in which additional labour may be used : either in new plants or by not scrapping old ones. The marginal product of labour is equal in each use so that the contribution made by the rate of growth of labour is also equal whatever use is involved (so long as only small changes are involved).[1]

It is of interest that these expressions for the rate of growth of output bear a family resemblance to the equivalent expressions derived from an aggregate production function $Y_t = F_t(N_t, K_t)$, i.e.

$$\frac{dY_t}{dt}\frac{1}{Y_t} = \beta' \frac{s}{\dfrac{Y_t}{K_t}} + \alpha'_t \frac{dN_t}{dt}\frac{1}{N_t} \tag{32}$$

where α'_t and β'_t are the elasticities of labour (N_t) and 'capital' (K_t).

The resemblance, however, is something of a fraud. In the first place, all such expressions for the rate of growth of output, if based on marginal productivity assumptions, are simply fancy ways of saying that the increase in output is the addition of each factor times its marginal product.[2] In the second place, the similarity between the two expressions is more apparent than real. For the rate of growth of output derived from the aggregate function depends on technical restraints ; while that derived from the present model involves, in addition, historical restraints. In the latter case the economy, having two forms of restraint will, in a sense, take the line of least resistance. For example, suppose the production function for new plants is such that there is a low elasticity of substitution between labour and investment. The demand for labour generated by new plant will then tend to be inelastic, leading to a greater than otherwise transfer of labour from old plants, and reduction in the life of existing capital. In effect, the economy devotes more of its gross investment to bringing its existing capital stock up to date

---

[1] Note that in the second form, the ratio $\dfrac{y_t}{n_t} \Big/ \dfrac{Y_t}{N_t}$ is added to indicate the proportional effect on total output Y_t.

[2] We have seen that (31a) and (31b) derive from an expression of this kind, i.e. (29). Similarly (32) derives from

$$dY_t = dK_t \frac{\delta Y_t}{\delta K_t} + dN_t \frac{\delta Y_t}{\delta N_t}$$

obtained by differentiating $Y_t = F_t(N_t, K_t)$. (See Swan, *op. cit.*)

than to increasing the degree of mechanization of new plant. Alternatively, if historical conditions are such that a very large rise in real wages is needed to free a given amount of labour from old plants (n_{t-e} is small, and h large) then this encourages an increase in the degree of mechanization in new plants so as to reduce their labour requirements.

Clearly, there is much to be done in exploring how different kinds of technical and historical restraints affect the growth path of an economy. But all I wish to establish at this point is that the historical restraints are relevant and that they have an important bearing on the growth path.

V. CONCLUSIONS

Leaving aside the false precision implied by model-building, the main points that seem to emerge from this paper are :

(1) In growth-model theory, the assumptions of homogeneous capital and instantaneous adjustment imply growth paths that are, in effect, only adjacent long-run equilibrium positions.

(2) One line of escape from this difficulty is to treat explicitly 'capital' as a 'who's who' of inherited capital goods. This dispenses with the need to measure it, avoids the assumptions of homogeneity and instantaneous adjustment, and provides a means of introducing something of the economy's history into the analysis.

(3) Using Ricardian principles, and regarding 'the production function' as only relevant to investment decisions, most of existing analysis can be fitted into this framework. However, both 'technical' and 'historical' restraints become relevant to substitution between labour and investment, to productivity and to factor shares.

(4) As part of the mechanisms involved, variations in real wages relate labour requirements of new investment to physical capital already in existence. Through these mechanisms the past history of the economy, such as past booms and slumps and past rates of productivity increase, influence the techniques embodied in equipment currently being added to the capital stock.

(5) The equilibrium concept is relevant to analysis of growth paths, and is a generalization of classical long-run equilibrium.

(6) While the interaction between 'historical' and 'technical' restraints requires a great deal of further investigation, both clearly influence the rate of growth of output and productivity.

APPENDIX

The purpose of this appendix is not to attempt a generalization of the model, but rather to indicate briefly that the main assumptions are not highly restrictive.

Expectations

Expectations of the future (however derived) clearly are an additional element to be taken into account in the technique and investment decisions involved in new plants. One aspect is the question of when to 'break in' on a series of expected (but imperfectly known) new techniques. This involves complicated exercises in probabilities and discounting. Another aspect is the influence of expected changes in factor prices on the choice of techniques. This requires that a distinction be made between the current wage rate, w_t, and an expected future wage rate that is the average of the wage rates expected to apply over the future period that the plant or equipment will operate. Thus the basic condition for wages needs to be re-written as:

$$w_t = \pi \, \alpha_t \frac{y_t}{n_t} = A_t \frac{Y_t}{N_t} \tag{i}$$

where π is some factor relating current and expected average wages over the expected life of new plants.

Since expectations have an important effect on current technique decisions and hence the behaviour of the model, it may well be the 'future facts' (or their present images) have as significant a role as the 'past facts' highlighted in this paper.

A Multi-Product Economy

One consequence of extending the analysis to a multi-product economy is that the mechanisms need to be thought of in a general equilibrium context, i.e. equations (4) and (15) need to be interpreted as applying to individual industries and related by the condition that marginal value products are equal. In particular (18) becomes for the ith good:

$$w_t = p_{it} \frac{\delta y_{it}}{\delta n_{it}} = p_{it} \frac{y_{it-e}}{n_{it-e}} e^{-(u-v)e} \tag{ii}$$

where p_{it} is the price of the ith good at t.

A corollary is that since there are now many different values of e, the influence of past events (such as a boom) on the present will be spread over a period of years, and thus be much less direct than implied by the model.

A second consequence of a multi-product economy is that the 'Wicksell Effect' becomes relevant once capital goods are treated as a special class of goods. There are no difficulties in introducing this into the model and the only point of substance is that historical as well as technical factors become relevant in determining the relative price of capital goods and consumption goods.

Imperfect Competition

In principle, imperfect competition can be introduced into this model in the same way as it is treated in a general equilibrium model, i.e. by recasting (ii) above in terms of marginal revenue rather than prices. This, however, is only a formal solution. It seems probable that once entrepreneurs have some freedom from competitive discipline in relation to replacement and scrapping decisions, the mechanisms of the model are very much less precise.[1]

'Machines' and 'Plants'

Since gross investment involves individual 'machines' as well as complete plants, it needs to be recognized that scrapping and replacement conditions for individual machines are more complicated than for complete plants. The main problem is that 'machines' generally do not produce a recognizable product so there can be no question of rises in real wages forcing them to be scrapped; rather rises in real wages render their replacement profitable.[2] The mechanisms involving transfer of labour need to be interpreted in this sense in so far as they relate to old and new machines rather than to plants.

DISCUSSION OF THE PAPER BY DR. SALTER

Chairman : PROFESSOR V. K. R. V. RAO

Mr. Nicholas Kaldor (United Kingdom), opening the discussion on Dr. Salter's paper, pointed out that he operated under a handicap — or an

-----

[1] *Productivity and Technical Change*, p. 90.
[2] For a discussion of this question see *Productivity and Technical Change*, p. 83.

advantage — because he had received the paper some weeks earlier and had been able to study it as it deserved. It was a most interesting and subtle paper, but the kind of comments it called for would not be readily understood by the audience which, because of delayed distribution, had just received it.

Dr. Salter was quite correct in recognizing that technological progress was almost entirely embodied in material instruments, and was not a function of the mere passage of time. Superior instruments had to be constructed; this depended on the infusion of new capital, which in turn depended on the share of gross investment in the national product. Dr. Salter was also right in presenting capital stock as the product of different stages of human knowledge, comparing it to a museum exhibition of machines from the past through to the present. There is no such thing as an aggregate production function.

However, Dr. Salter assumes implicitly that labour distributes itself rationally, like Ricardo's use of land, according to its fertility; this is not true today in the United States or in the United Kingdom, where employment changes less over the cycle than production and where there is excess capacity in all vintages of plants. Mr. Kaldor's main disagreement with the Salter model could be put generally as the difference between the neo-classical and Keynesian systems. Dr. Salter is still a child of neo-classicism. On the crucial definition of savings, Dr. Salter makes them a simple linear function of total income, whereas they are a function of the distribution of income, or the share of profits. The statistics on the proportion of business investment financed out of undistributed profits prove this. Real wages are the equilibrating factor in the transfer of resources from old to new plants in the Salter model, because new equipment causes profits from the old machines to disappear (in the marginal plant, the marginal product of labour equals the real wage). But in the real world entrepreneurs 'satisfize' rather than maximize, Mr. Kaldor thought, and the adoption of a technological innovation depends on whether the expected discounted stream of profits for a certain number of years will cover the cost of the equipment. The period depends on expected obsolescence, and this is decided according to a rule of thumb — in the United States it is three years. Hence it is entrepreneurial expectations on profits which determine the rate of investment and technological progress.

Professor Melvin Reder stated that a United Nations study of the textile industry provided empirical support for Dr. Salter's notions of obsolescence; the results were firmly neo-classical. However, he would add to the age of a machine, as a determinant of its productivity, what has been done to it since it was originally installed, and also the factor of relative prices at present and not only in the past.

Professor John T. Dunlop (United States) agreed with Dr. Reder that the nature of technological change today made the textile industry atypical. Expenditures in the current year change productivity; for example, the introduction of centralized traffic control in railroad systems increases the productivity of old stock. In other industries, new automatic regulators have become important. The introduction of oxygen processes in the steel industry is another example of this kind of innovation.

Dr. Desmond Corner suggested that perhaps technological change was faster today than it was in the nineteenth century, when the textile industry was developing. Certainly the situation in the transport industry differed from the textile industry experience.

Mr. Odd Aukrust (Norway) pointed out that the importance of technology and 'know how' had been recognized only in the last five years, although the pioneering article by Tinbergen had appeared ten years ago. Already there was a trend away from the aggregate Cobb-Douglas function; Leif Johansen and Robert Solow had made attempts to disaggregate.

After paying tribute to Dr. Salter for his outstanding paper, which presented a powerful model based on simple postulates, Mr. Aukrust put three questions to him : Did he agree with an estimate attributing 90 per cent of the increase in productivity to 'know-how'? Dr. Salter linked the present with the past; how would he explain the high post-war investment demands? Professor Simon Kuznets has attempted to estimate long-run changes in growth rates; could Dr. Salter link empirical facts with his theory, and explain differential growth rates?

Professor Harvey Leibenstein (United States) wondered whether we should not be more concerned with what goes on in men's minds than with the unique relation between the building of capital stock in the past and investment in the present.

Mr. Kjell Eide (Norway) suggested that the Salter approach to the question of the age structure and productivity of the capital stock should be qualified by the recognition of a significant tendency for the employment of relatively highly-skilled labour to work on the latest capital equipment. Skills have been increasing rapidly in the advanced countries, and new and rapidly developing industries employ a large proportion of highly qualified man-power. Observed differences in productivity between old and new capital equipment may therefore to a considerable extent reflect differences in the quality of labour and only partially measure improvements in technology in the usual sense. He thought that the average skill level of labour could be included in Dr. Salter's model without too much difficulty, adding an extra dimension and increasing its theoretical and empirical usefulness.

Professor Leslie Fishman (United States) asked whether raising real wages would, in Dr. Salter's model, increase the **rate** of technological change.

Dr. Salter asserted, in his response to the questions raised during the discussion, that many of the factors suggested as additions to his model could in fact quite easily be incorporated into it. The point made by Professors Reder and Dunlop, and Dr. Corner, on the effect on the productivity of old capital stock of current expenditures could be handled. Mr. Eide's suggestion could also be incorporated : skills could be treated in the same way as capital investment ; they become obsolescent in the same way — the quasi-rent of skilled workers is gradually whittled away until the level of unskilled wages is reached. He also thought that Mr. Kaldor's savings function could be fitted into the system.

In answer to Mr. Aukrust, Dr. Salter asserted that it was impossible to identify the separate contributions of investment, schools, technology and 'know-how' to economic growth. Nor was it yet possible to explain differences in growth rates with his model. The model could, however, be made cyclical, and the role of demand taken into account. In the 1930s, for example, because of inadequate demand, technology may have got ahead of investment. But in general, he would say that his theory had a long way to go before it could be applied to the real world.

To Professor Leibenstein, he stated that he certainly agreed on the prime importance of human beings in economic development. To the question whether raising real wages would stimulate technological change, the answer was : no ; it would create unemployment or inflation.

Chapter 15

THE EFFECTS OF TECHNOLOGY
ON PRODUCTIVITY

BY

SHIGETO TSURU
Hitotsubashi University

1. THE central theme of this paper is a renewed plea for careful distinction between the real aspect and the value aspect in economic theorizing; and for this purpose it might be better to start the discussion with an example which appears to reflect insufficient awareness of the need for such a distinction.

We are treated with an increasing number of studies which purport to quantify the effects of technology on productivity by separating them from those of capital accumulation.[1] The point I intend to make can be illustrated by any one of them, but here I shall use a modified version of the Johansen's model as a starting point. Seeing that how to measure capital is a knotty problem, he proposed a model which did not require statistical figures for the stocks of capital in the empirical analysis. His model is in terms of industry production function; but I modify it into the aggregate production function.

2. Let the production function be the Cobb-Douglas type

$$Y = AK^\alpha L^{1-\alpha} \tag{1}$$

with usual assumptions of constant returns to scale and neutral technological progress. The factor A subsumes shifts in the production function and may be expressed as Ae^{rt}. Dividing both sides of (1) by L and defining $m \equiv \dfrac{Y}{L}$ and $k \equiv \dfrac{K}{L}$, we obtain

$$m = Ae^{rt}k^\alpha. \tag{2}$$

[1] Not intended to be exhaustive, the list of such literature may include: R. Solow, 'Technical Change and the Aggregate Production Function', *The Review of Economics and Statistics*, August 1957; R. Solow, 'Investment and Technical Progress', in *Mathematical Methods in the Social Sciences 1959*, edited by K. J. Arrow, S. Karlin and P. Suppes, 1960; B. F. Massell, 'Capital Formation and Technological Change in United States Manufacturing', *The Review of Economics and Statistics*, May 1960; E. D. Domar, 'On the Measurement of Technological Change', *The Economic Journal*, December 1961; and L. Johansen, 'A Method for Separating the Effects of Capital Accumulation and Shifts in Production Functions upon Growth in Labour Productivity', *The Economic Journal*, December 1961.

From this, we derive a relation

$$g(m) = r + \alpha \cdot g(k) \tag{3}$$

where $g(\ )$ expresses the rate of growth, telling us that the growth rate of labour productivity can be decomposed into the rate of 'technological change' and the growth rate of capital-labour ratio multiplied by the elasticity α. The ratio for which statistical measures have been calculated by Solow, Massell, etc., is $r/g(m)$ which we shall designate as a. Then (3) can be rewritten as

$$a = 1 - \alpha \cdot \frac{g(k)}{g(m)}. \tag{4}$$

Assuming that the cost minimization principle is carried through with no monopoly power, we obtain the condition

$$\frac{cK}{\alpha} = \frac{wL}{1 - \alpha} \tag{5}$$

where c and w are the costs which are associated with the use of one unit of capital and labour, respectively. We may call them the real profit per unit of capital and the wage rate per unit of labour. From (5), we obtain

$$\frac{K}{L}(\equiv k) = \frac{\alpha}{1 - \alpha} \cdot \frac{w}{c} \tag{6}$$

hence, we derive a relation

$$g(k) = g(w) - g(c) \tag{7}$$

inasmuch as we assume the elasticity α to be constant. Inserting (7) into (4), we obtain

$$a = 1 - \alpha \frac{g(w) - g(c)}{g(m)}. \tag{8}$$

Now, since $w = (1 - \alpha)\frac{Y}{L}$ or $\frac{w}{m} = 1 - \alpha$, and α is assumed to be constant, $g(w)$ has to be equal to $g(m)$. Further, if we write $g(c)/g(w) = h$, we can simplify (8) into

$$a = 1 - \alpha + \alpha h. \tag{9}$$

Here the expression h is something similar to the reciprocal of Johansen's 'w', or the 'relative increase in wages'. If capital grows at the same rate as output, obviously c has to be constant inasmuch as $\frac{K}{Y} = \frac{\alpha}{c}$ from the cost-minimization condition. And in this case $g(c) = 0$, simplifying (8) into

$$a = 1 - \alpha. \tag{10}$$

3. Let us look at the equation (9) again. α is the relative share of capital which has been known to be fairly stable, in mature countries like the United States, in the vicinity of 0·25. Given this stable parameter α, all that we have to know is the value of h in order to estimate the effects of technology on labour productivity. And it is Johansen's claim that h can be estimated without concerning us with the precise definition of the capital concept since it is the ratio between the rate of change in the cost per unit of capital and the rate of change in the cost per unit of labour. *A priori*, this ratio can be

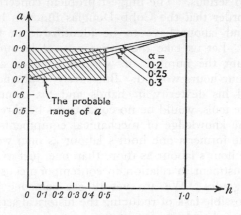

FIGURE 1

inferred to be rather small. Not only in theory, but in the real world also, $g(w)$ tends to be equal to $g(m)$, whereas $g(c)$ or the rate of change of the profit rate is likely to be nearer to zero than to $g(w)$. Thus we may guess that h in most instances has the value less than 0·5. On the basis of such empirical guesswork we can plot the equation (9) as in Figure 1. And there it can easily be seen that the range within which a can move is fairly restricted, possibly between 0·7 and 0·9.

4. What is the significance of the value of a as measured by the use of the equation (9)?

Firstly, apart from theory or substance, the arithmetical fact that the range within which a can move is very narrow, lessens, it appears to me, the significance of the result we obtain. Suppose that someone undertakes a laborious task of measuring a for a number of countries like the U.K., Germany, France, Italy and Japan using the Solow method for the U.S.A., carefully compiling the statistics to make them comparable and consistent, and obtain the results showing that a is equal, let us say, to 80 per cent for the U.K., 78 per cent for Germany, 82 per cent for France, 75 per cent for Italy and 84 per cent for Japan. Can we draw from such an array of figures any significant conclusion as regards the degree of contribution which technological progress has made, in these countries, to raising the productivity of labour?

Secondly, the restrictive assumptions underlying the equation (9) should be examined more closely. The usual assumptions implied in the aggregate Cobb-Douglas function, as well as the assumption of profit maximization under the competitive condition, are, I believe, not too serious. The biggest problem concerns the matter of units. In order that the Cobb-Douglas function be applicable, both capital and labour have to be identifiable in homogeneous physical units. Let us take the easier case of labour. It is easy enough to count the number of workers engaged and even the number of labour-hours worked. But surely, a Japanese worker of 1870s, with all his dexterity in hands and his common-sense in handling simple tools, would be no equal to his brethren of 1960s in literacy and the knowledge of mechanical equipments of all sorts. If we count the former's one hour's labour as one, we must count the latter's one hour's labour as more than one, just as we would do the similar adjustment in relation to contemporaneous labourers of two different grades. We are yet to see someone perform this seemingly impossible task of reducing the historical series of labour-hours worked to a homogeneous unit.

The case of capital is far more complicated, as has been pointed out by Joan Robinson and others. Johansen's claim that his method can skirt around this difficulty is tenuous, for the rate of profit, or 'the cost associated with the use of capital', is a ratio which, no matter how unambiguous it may be, still presupposes a particular way of measuring the denominator, capital. Between the restrictive concept of capital as a factor consistent with the aggregate Cobb-Douglas function and the concept of capital conventionally used in the calculation of the rate of profit, there is a long series of bridges that have to be crossed ; and few of them are easy to cross. Let us postulate, for example, a world in which there is only one kind of machine. 'Ideally what one would like to measure is the annual flow of capital services' (Solow). Now, a machine, like a labourer, has a finite life of its own. So long as it is in active use, it can be assumed to render more or less the same 'quantity' of service every year. But the *value* of a machine, which is relevant to the profit rate calculation, depreciates as it nears the end of its life. One might try to get around this difficulty by taking the gross stock instead of the net stock. But then, a change in the durability of the machine could affect the gross stock magnitude without changing the 'quantity' of current services rendered.[1]   Secondly, a machine, like a labourer, can be improved in its performance capacity through technological progress without any change in durability or in a number of labour-hours required to produce it.   Should not such a machine be counted, in the Cobb-Douglas function, as a multiple of the simple machine? Here is a problem quite similar to the case of the labour factor mentioned earlier.   Thirdly, compare two machines exactly alike in all respects (including their durability and age) except that one is drawn from an economy with a higher product-wage rate.   As Joan Robinson pointed out, 'the value of the two machines is different, and the investment required to create them is different.   A difference in value remains if we deflate them by the wage rate, for in two economies with different product-wage rates the rate of profit and therefore the rate of interest are different.'[2]   Furthermore, the real world makes use of a thousand and one different types of machines, both substitutive and complementary.   A formidable index number problem arises here.   In addition, the concept of capital that is relevant to the profit calculation subsumes not only fixed capital but also working capital.   Some economists would, even now as in the classical era, prefer to include what Marx called 'variable capital' (wages payment in advance of the sale of products) as a part of capital.

In other words, capital is essentially a value concept; and one cannot escape from its value implication as affected by the rate of interest, the time pattern of wage rate changes, etc., unless we assume a radically simplified economy of one-type machine with no technological change.

Now, suppose we close our eyes to all the knotty problems in crossing a series of bridges which extend across the aggregate Cobb-Douglas function and the real world and look at the equation (9) without specifying the significance of a.   Call it, for example, simply the 'a-ratio'.   Both α and h, i.e., the capital's share and the relative growth rate of the profit rate with respect to the wage rate, are empirically observable magnitudes.   The a-ratio can be derived for any economy in which α is measured to be fairly stable over a span of years and the reasonably accurate statistics of the profit rate and the wage rate are available.   We refrain from identifying the a-ratio with the degree of contribution which technological progress makes to raising the productivity of labour; but could we not at least

[1] On this point, Solow simply says that 'there is nothing to be done about this'. (*Op. cit., The Review of Economics and Statistics*, p. 314.)
[2] Joan Robinson, 'The Production Function and the Theory of Capital — A Reply', *The Review of Economic Studies*, No. 62, p. 247.

say that it measures some kind of *real* (as contrasted to *value*) contribution of a certain occurrence to some kind of *real* (as contrasted to *value*) increase in products ? *A priori*, we are not prevented from answering this question in the affirmative. The *a*-ratio is in the world of *real* magnitudes and α and *h* are in the world of *value* magnitudes ; and the equation (9) tells us that the former is determined by the latter. Such a relation or its inverse is not at all unusual in the neo-classical theorizing as is exemplified by the equating of the marginal physical product of labour with the wage rate under the competitive condition. We have been quite accustomed to the theorizing of this type that most of us do not even suspect that here lurks a methodological problem which becomes peculiarly relevant in connection with certain types of problems. Before going any further, we can at least say that the *a*-ratio as determined by the equation (9) is, though intended to be *real* in its content, highly dependent on the workings of the type of economic system to which α and *h* are inseparably related. In other words, it is conceivable that with the same technological progress a socialist economy will be characterized by the *a*-ratio different in magnitude from that in a capitalist economy. It is for this reason that I propose to trace, in what follows, somewhat elementary steps in the discussion of technological progress with a view to distinguishing the real aspect and the value aspect.

5. The economist who showed the keenest awareness of the need for distinguishing the value aspect from the real (or physical) aspect was, I believe, Marx.[1] But it is not necessary to dwell upon his systematic discussion of this problem in order to realize what is involved here. Economists like Keynes and Harrod, who performed a pioneering role in the development of modern macro-economic theory, were, in their own way, aware of the peculiar difficulty which presented itself in the matter of the choice of units — the difficulty

---

[1] See, in particular, chapter 7 of volume I of *Capital*, entitled : 'The Labor-Process, and the Process of Producing Surplus-Value'. (In the German edition, currently available, this is chapter 5.) It was natural for Marx to insist upon such a distinction since he was concerned especially with the analysis of the *peculiarly capitalistic character* of the social relations of production. Cf., for example, 'The labor-process . . . is human action with a view to the production of use-values, appropriation of natural substances to human requirements ; it is the necessary condition for effecting exchange of matter between man and Nature ; it is the everlasting Nature-imposed condition of human existence, and therefore is independent of every social phase of that existence, or rather, is common to every such phase. . . . As the taste of the porridge does not tell you who grew the oats, no more does this simple process tell you of itself what are the social conditions under which it is taking place, whether under the slave-owner's brutal lash, or the anxious eye of the capitalist, whether Cincinnatus carries it on in tilling his modest farm or a savage in killing wild animals with stones.' (*Capital*, vol. I, Foreign Languages Publishing House, Moscow, pp. 183-4.)

which stemmed from the double character (the value and the physical) of the production process, especially of the economic system as a whole. In criticizing Pigou's method of arriving at the net national dividend by deducting 'normal' obsolescence, Keynes made a revealing comment : 'Since this deduction is not a deduction in terms of money, he is involved in assuming that there can be a change in physical quantity, although there has been no physical change ; i.e. he is covertly introducing changes in *value*'.[1] Keynes' solution was, as is well known, to adopt the labour-unit and/or the wage-unit 'by taking an hour's employment of ordinary labour as our unit and weighing an hour's employment of special labour in proportion to its remuneration'.[2] This is an approach remarkably close to that of Marx, except that in the latter's case 'ordinary labour' as the unit is visualized to change its quality historically.

Harrod, too, wrestled with a similar problem when he posed the problem of whether neutral technical progress required new investment and answered that it was a question of definition — that the answer depended on whether a labour standard of value is chosen or a goods standard of value. His preference was for the latter for a number of reasons which we shall not go into here.[3]

The distinction between a labour standard and a goods standard corresponds to that of the value aspect and the physical aspect. Whereas micro-economics for a capitalist society can navigate almost entirely in the world of values, macro-economics, especially of the dynamic type, finds it difficult to dissociate itself from the real or physical aspect of its subject matter. In this sense, the fact that Keynes, who was interested more in the short-run problem with no technological change, chose a labour standard and Harrod, who was concerned with a dynamic economics, chose a goods standard is easily understandable.

Having said this, I must add immediately that problems in dynamic macro-economics, so long as it is intended to be economics, cannot avoid navigating in the world of values also, and that our task is a peculiarly difficult one of combining the two aspects in an appropriate manner.

6. The real or physical aspect of production can only be described and does not easily render itself to abstract analysis. Whatever the type of economic system a society may have, the process of production in the society as a whole involves the exertion of efforts by all kinds of men, with differing qualifications, who operate upon nature with

---

[1] Italics in original. J. M. Keynes, *The General Theory of Employment, Interest and Money*, pp. 38-9.　　　　[2] *Ibid.* p. 41.
[3] See R. Harrod, *Towards a Dynamic Economics*, pp. 28-34.

objects fashioned out of nature in the circumstance of natural endowment and social environment not necessarily uniform everywhere. Operating workers, at any point of time, may be endowed with heritage, both technical and cultural, which is the accumulation passed on from their forefathers. Those selected few who are in the position of making decisions for a producing unit may have an aggressive outlook conditioned by the social milieu or by their innate propensity, and again they may not have it. Language is no less a factor in the situation, as can easily be surmised from the comparison of the three countries : Japan with the phoneticized media, China with innumerable characters requiring years to master, and India with multi-lingual heritage not adapted yet to modern science and technology. It should be mentioned, moreover, that the problem of material balance in terms of use-values is quite relevant to the real or physical aspect of production.

Once we turn to the value aspect of production we cannot escape, in our discussion, from the framework of a particular economic system in which production is carried on. In general terms we could say that the value aspect of production would have the following components, all expressed in the same unit so that the addition is feasible :

$$\boxed{\text{Cost of raw materials and fuel}} + \boxed{\text{Replacement cost}} + \boxed{\text{Value added}}$$

But how this unit comes about is dependent on the mode of production (as, for example, the competitive pricing in a private enterprise economy or the accounting pricing in a centrally planned economy) and how the value-added component is distributed among various categories is certainly not independent of the class relations of that society. In a feudal society, for example, the ruling class could claim a sizable portion of the value added on the basis of their *status* without in any way participating in the production process. In a capitalist society, at least in theory, knowledge as such does not receive its own marginal product, although few will doubt the substantial contribution it makes in the real or physical aspect of production. In a centrally planned economy it is perfectly possible deliberately to calculate the *value* reward for 'knowledge' in approximate accord with its obvious contribution in the real aspect. Again, the rentier income, as Keynes observed, may well be a historically transient category even within the framework of capitalism. Capitalism may well be a most efficient economic system ; but to admit this does not absolve us from recognizing the efficacy of specific value relations which characterize different modes of production.

7. Technological progress, too, has its real and value aspects. Whether it takes place in the Soviet Union or in the United States, its real aspect can be described in almost exactly the same way. How to describe it, probably, would be the task of an engineer who would have to focus upon multiple causal relations in which the development of basic science, quality of labour, specific resources endowment, etc., would all have to be brought in. Essentially, the nature of this task is a description which ends up with a demonstration that the ratio between the physical output and the labour (both direct and indirect) input has risen — the ratio which we usually call 'the productivity of labour'. In such discussion of the real aspect it is not necessary that the unit of labour shall be in terms of the abstract concept of historically unchanging simple labour. In fact, it is generally understood that here labour is in terms of the biological unit which commonly changes its quality over time. Focussing our attention to this ratio, we can pose an inquiry as to relative contributions of various *real* factors to the rise of the ratio. A number of factors which are relevant may be enumerated :

(A) Education and training which enhance the quality of labour.

(B) Public health and medical services in general which contribute towards maintaining the continual effective performance of operating workers.

(C) Cultural amenities which have the function of raising the morale of workers.

(D) Industrial harmony which can elicit a greater degree of co-operation from the working class than the lack of it.

(E) The improvement in the media of communications, including the modernization of language.

(F) Social and political tensions of constructive character, including what Rostow called 'reactive nationalism'.

(G) Social innovations in the sense of 'new methods of inducing human beings to compete and cooperate in the social progress' (Kuznets).

(H) Technological innovations of both 'proper' and 'derived' types.[1]

(I) The mere increase in the scale of production entirely apart from any technological change.

[1] Cf. Charles Kennedy, 'Technical Progress and Investment', *The Economic Journal*, June 1961, p. 294.

It is hard to deny that each one of these factors, in varying degrees in different historical circumstances, has been relevant to the raising of labour productivity ; and it is probably harder to assign quantitative weights to them in a given situation.

In the Japan of the last quarter of the nineteenth century, when she is said to have accomplished the Rostovian 'take off' with a remarkable speed, the factors like (A), (E) and (F) above were undoubtedly of major importance, making it possible to achieve the 4 to 5 per cent annual growth rate with the net investment ratio of less than 10 per cent. A value relation like the capital-output ratio is bound to reflect such specific circumstances of the country in the real aspect. And so long as we confine our attention to the real aspect, it is not very meaningful to ask what percentage in the rise of labour productivity was due to technological innovations and the remainder due to the increase in the 'quantity of capital' per worker.

8. If we limit ourselves to quantifiable magnitudes, it is, of course, not impossible to set up a model through which we might indicate certain logical relations implied in technological progress as viewed from the real aspect.

Assume an economy which produces corn only with the aid of tractors which, however, can be improved upon. Let us assume that the total quantity of corn (Q) to be produced remains constant, as well as the total number of tractors (K) in operation at any time. Tractors are replaced as they wear out, and the number of them replaced each year (D) is, of course, determined by the durability (n), or

$$\overline{K} = nD.$$

The number of workers engaged in the production of tractors (L_i) is determined by their physical productivity (m_i), or

$$D = m_i L_i.$$

The number of workers in the sector of corn production (L_c) is, we assume, uniquely determined by the number (a) needed to operate each one of the tractors, or,

$$L_c = a\overline{K}$$

and their productivity (m_c) can be related to Q as follows :

$$\overline{Q} = m_c L_c.$$

It is clear that m_c cannot be independent of a, nor is it independent of m_i if the latter fails to make the tractor bigger and better. Defining

$$L \equiv L_i + L_c$$

304

we can express, on the basis of the above relations, the social productivity $Q/L(\equiv m)$ as

$$m = \frac{anm_im_c}{1 + anm_i}.$$

In such an economy, the nature of technological progress in the broad sense can be of the following types :

(1) a declines, or the number of workers in the corn sector needed to operate the given tractor can be economized due to, say, an improvement in the technical qualification of the corn sector workers. In this case, it might be assumed that m_c rises exactly to offset the decline in a. Then, obviously, the numerator remains constant while the denominator falls, thus raising the value of m.

(2) n rises, or the durability of tractors is lengthened without any change in other variable. In this case, too, m rises as a result.

(3) m_i rises, or an innovation takes place in the tractor producing sector without any change in the type of tractors made. Again, m rises as a result.

(4) m_i falls but m_c rises more, so that the product m_im_c is bigger than before, or a new and bigger type of tractor is introduced with no change in a or n. Upshot will be the rise in m as in other cases.

The model of this type is essentially physical and makes no mention of the wage level or of the 'quantity of capital'. However, it is possible, within the limitation of the real aspect, to refine the model further by introducing both. If we write w for the real wage rate in terms of corn and v for the wage-value of a tractor, we can say

$$v = \frac{w}{m_i}$$

since the number of workers required to produce one tractor is $1/m_i$. Further, the total number of tractors in existence, K, can be expressed as

$$K = \frac{1}{a}L_c.$$

Thus the wage cost of the *gross* stock of tractors is

$$vK = \frac{w}{am_i}L_c.$$

Dividing this by output or $Q(=m_cL_c)$, we obtain a ratio which we might call the 'capital-output ratio', written as

$$\frac{w}{am_im_c}.$$

This, incidentally, is an expression for the 'capital-output ratio' which could be derived from a model different from ours here.[1] It

[1] Cf. S. Tsuru, 'A Note on Capital-Output Ratio', *Keizai Kenkyu*, April 1956.

implies that the ratio can remain constant even if productivities change so long as the real wage rate rises *pari passu* with $am_i m_c$. Various other abstract relations could be derived with the aid of a model like this. But it is essential to remember that its applicability is limited to a type of situation where value relations in the Marxian sense of the term can be entirely abstracted.

9. Once we move to the value aspect of technological progress, we enter the world which, no matter how abstract, cannot escape from the efficacy of a particular mode of production. The concept 'capital', for example, now acquires an institutional dimension. Under capitalism, 'capital' is the basic unit of economic activities guided by the principle of maximizing the return to itself. Thus the return to 'capital' is an institutional category and as such it constitutes an essential component in the process of price formation. Technological progress, as viewed in this world of value relations, is inevitably related to this process of price formation ; and it is characteristic under capitalism that innovations are introduced by a private entrepreneur, a category of men who are in the driver's seat, so to speak, who receive special reward for their successful introduction during a limited duration of time before they are generally imitated. Once a specific innovation becomes prevalent, the special reward disappears and competition forces the relevant price to go down. It is possible to discuss in detail, by the method of comparative statics, how prices may change as a result of this or that type of technological progress which we enumerated in the previous section.

What is especially important in the dynamic value aspect of technological progress, however, is the special reward which accrues to pioneering entrepreneurs ; and it is perfectly conceivable that under another mode of production such a reward takes a non-economic form for the manager of a firm while monetary rewards are given more directly to scientists and engineers.[1] In other words, the question like 'How are the fruits of technological progress distributed between capital and labour ?' cannot be answered independently of a particular mode of production in which it takes place. This is the reason why we cast serious doubt, in Part I, on the method of estimating the effect of technological progress, as distinguished from that of capital accumulation, on raising the productivity of labour — the method which essentially depended on the relative share of a factor in the value aspect of production.

---

[1] A 'social innovation', as defined by Kuznets in our earlier section, makes this possible.

Record of Discussion

DISCUSSION OF THE PAPER BY PROFESSOR SHIGETO TSURU

Chairman : Mr. ODD AUKRUST

Dr. Gyorgy Cukor (Hungary) opened the discussion on Professor Tsuru's paper with the declaration that he agreed with the criticisms made there of the attempts to separate the effects of technology and capital on labour productivity through the use of the Cobb-Douglas production function, or some other production function, and that he would merely expatiate on Professor Tsuru's argument, stressing the practical aspects which were of the greatest interest in socialist countries.

Three methods of measuring productivity increases were available : the traditional quotient of index numbers ; a production function ; and input-output analysis. Contrary to some recent criticism of it, the traditional method is the principal one used in the socialist countries, and the preferred method of John W. Kendrick in his important study. The factor of technological progress is well expressed by the labour productivity and the capital-output ratios, or by the combination of the two, 'total factor productivity'. On the other hand, the production function in its original form, the Cobb-Douglas, included only two factors of production so that productivity could increase only through the rise of the capital-output ratio. Actual experience has contradicted this assumption ; Solow has shown that capital per working hour declined in the United States about 20 per cent from 1930 to 1949, while at the same time labour productivity rose considerably.

To the question whether an increase in productivity can be explained by the use of a production function, whether the increase can be traced back to its source, the answer is that although the production function yields an explanation it is an ambiguous one. The study of Olavi Niitamo on productivity in Finnish industry from 1925–52 employed seven different production functions, which included cyclical factors, a measure of the general level of education and a trend expression which was a function of time only, in addition to changes in the amount of capital and labour. The various equations fitted the actual values equally well. Furthermore, in each case the rise in productivity was attributable to one factor, all the others remaining unchanged. When the attempt was made on the basis of Niitamo's functions to find the productivity increase in ten years from an assumed increase of 25 per cent in the quantity of labour, a 100 per cent rise in the quantity of capital, and a 35 per cent rise in the 'level of education', the answer was a range from 20 to 35 per cent. This is hardly a precise answer for planning purposes. Nor would it be a simple matter to derive the production functions for individual branches of industry, which planning also demands.

The third method of productivity analysis, input-output analysis, is a logical extension of Professor Tsuru's model. It permits the computation of live and embodied labour, in the Marxian sense, employed both directly and indirectly in the production process. The two other methods over-estimate the quantity of capital, because the rise in productivity itself reduces the amount of labour required to produce capital goods, and both omit, in order to avoid double counting, the energy and materials consumed in production. For individual branches of industry, however, raw materials and energy consumption must be included as inputs. Technological progress usually involves a saving in the use of materials and energy ; this 'productivity' increase, as well as the increase of the productivity of capital and labour, can be distinguished and traced back to the sectors in which they originated by input-output analysis. This method has obvious advantages for planning. So far the widespread use of input-output analysis has been restricted by the scarcity of input-output tables. In Hungary, where the first one was computed for 1957 and the second for 1959, it is intended to make them an organic part of statistical work for every other, or at most, every third year.

Professor Harvey Leibenstein, commenting on Professor Tsuru's diagnosis that the confusion of real and value aspects had led to errors in the measurement of the effects of technological progress on productivity, wondered whether this was really the essence of the difficulty. According to Professor Tsuru, the real aspect of technological change cannot be measured. The actual changes in the production process which occur when an innovation is introduced can only be described, by an engineer or scientist. This real aspect exists irrespective of the economic system involved.

It is because economists cannot measure technological change directly, but instead attempt to measure the extent to which increases in income are due to increases in labour and capital, with the residual presumed to accrue because of technological progress, that we may be misled. For, Professor Tsuru argues, the distribution of the product depends on the nature of the system, by which he has in mind such broad categories as capitalism versus socialism, and hence the same real phenomena may yield different effects in different systems. A basic question which enters into consideration here is who gains from technological progress. Professor Tsuru argues that under capitalism it is the entrepreneur ; unfortunately, he does not define the word entrepreneur, nor does he consider patents, copyrights and other institutional arrangements under which the producers of ideas reap some of the benefits flowing from them. They may not get all the fruits. But this is true of all factors of production in any economy ; there must be consumer surpluses, for without them there would be no trade. It is precisely here that the Marxist labour theory of value fails as a tool of analysis.

One cannot say offhand in which type of economy the producer of ideas gets a more adequate share of the fruits of such ideas. For example, it is not clear to what extent socialist countries pay for ideas discovered elsewhere. Professor Tsuru seems to imply that the distribution of the national product can be completely determined by the economic system, but is this really true? Distributive shares probably depend on more than 'socialism' or 'capitalism'. For example, the degree of competition, and the incentive and reward system, are two of many factors that may determine distributive shares in any broad type of economic system.

Professor Tsuru's main point, that institutional arrangements may affect distributive shares, is acceptable in principle. But do such institutional changes really affect shares significantly? This is an empirical question which as yet has not been answered. Professor Tsuru has discovered a possible methodological criticism of some of the current methods of measuring the effects of technological change on productivity. But the essence of the matter is not the pitfall involved in ignoring the distinction between the real as against the value aspects of economic phenomena. The essence of the matter is factual. How do economies work? Can those who 'run economies', if such an expression can be used, change factor returns to a significant degree without changing productivity? To answer such questions, we would have to know how different systems of incentives and motivations affect technological progress, and the relation between different incentive systems and distributive shares. Unfortunately, we do not have such information today.

Mr. Nicholas Kaldor registered his agreement with Professor Tsuru's conclusions, but not with his emphasis. The attempts made by Solow and others to isolate the contributions of capital and technology to productivity increases are futile and based on circular reasoning. That the profit share indicates the net contribution of capital at the margin of production is not based on empirical evidence, and this has nothing to do with the nature of the system. The Cobb-Douglas and all other production functions are not based on empirical research; the notion that there is a production function in the aggregate sense is a myth. The assumptions that the function is homogeneous and linear, that there is unit elasticity of substitution between capital and labour, and constant returns to scale, are based on nothing except the requirement that marginal productivity explain distributive shares. These exercises are without any value. In practice, it is impossible to distinguish the contribution to productivity increases of capital or technology or labour.

Professor Melvin Reder defended marginal productivity in general, and Professor Solow's work in particular. He pointed out that the attempt was not primarily to measure technological progress; the residual measured the difference in time static equilibria in two periods and it included economies of scale and other factors in addition to what we commonly mean by technological progress. To reject all the hypotheses behind the production function would also involve the rejection of current statistical practice in the measurement of national income.

Dr. Edward Denison (United States) observed that Professor Tsuru's paper was a frontal attack on the marginal productivity theory. The marginal product was what we were really after in productivity analysis, and not distributive shares, which required the heroic assumption of perfect competition. Professor Tsuru stated that distributive shares did not differ radically between countries and over time. The growth of capital stock and output, on the other hand, does differ very much over time — consider the pre-1929 and the post-1929 figures, for example — and between countries. Some Israeli data, for example, indicated that capital accounted for 75 per cent of the increase in output; the figure is not always 10 per cent or 25 per cent.

Mr. Odd Aukrust conceded that Mr. Kaldor might be correct in characterizing as idle research the attempt to measure contributions to increased productivity by production functions — a field in which he had been involved too — but he could not accept Mr. Kaldor's reasoning. In defence of the Cobb-Douglas function — and some of the variations used had less restrictive assumptions on returns to scale, etc. — it was consistent with sound production theory; furthermore, the test of a theory was in its ability to conform to facts, and on this criterion, reasonable success had been attained with it. He agreed with Dr. Reder that if the whole theory were thrown out, the national accounting system would have to go too.

Professor V. K. R. V. Rao inquired why Professor Tsuru had written that it was meaningless to ask what weight could be assigned to his list of real factors in productivity growth. It was important for countries where capital was scarce to identify the other causes of growth.

Professor Tsuru expressed gratitude to Dr. Cukor for developing the constructive implications of his paper, which he himself had felt to be largely negative. He suggested that Professor Leibenstein had misunderstood his use of the term 'values', by which he meant the social relations of production in particular economic systems; but at any rate, Dr Leibenstein had stated that the assessment of technological progress was essentially a value problem, and in this they agreed. To Dr. Rao, he would answer that technological progress was essentially embodied in gross capital investment, and that it was difficult to separate out the role of technology versus capital in the real sense. Dr. Denison was correct; his paper could be taken as an attack on the marginal productivity theory. This he had learned from Mr. Kaldor and Joan Robinson. The point made by Dr. Reder and Mr. Aukrust about the necessity of throwing out the whole system of national accounts, he did not grasp. Dr. Reder's defence of marginal productivity was understandable in terms of chess: one had to follow the rules if one wanted to play the game. But he envisioned the role of economics as somewhat different from that of a game.

Chapter 16

WAGES, PRODUCTIVITY AND INDUSTRIALIZATION

BY

LLOYD G. REYNOLDS
Yale University

I. INTRODUCTORY

THIS discussion is oriented toward an economy in which economic growth is accelerating significantly. In particular, there is a rapid growth of manufacturing, power, transportation and other modern industries. The agricultural sector, still dominant, is beginning to shrink in relative terms. The economy is creeping over the threshold of economic development.

In this context, I ask what difference the behaviour of wages makes to the rise of labour productivity. There is obviously a circular relation between these variables. The advance of productivity, determined mainly by factors examined in other papers at this conference, provides a basis for real wage increases and determines their maximum amount. But there is also a feedback effect from wage behaviour to productivity itself. My paper is concerned with several aspects of the feedback.

It seems best to attack the problem at three levels, ranging from the most aggregative to the most micro-economic. We begin with the general level of real wages, proceed to consider major types of wage differential and conclude with the responsiveness of the individual worker to wage incentives.

II. THE GENERAL LEVEL OF REAL WAGES

There is a famous model of economic growth which is frequently, though perhaps unfairly, placed on the shoulders of Professor Arthur Lewis.[1] Its lineage goes back to Marx and Ricardo, and perhaps even further. It is a model under which growth proceeds at a

[1] W. Arthur Lewis, 'Economic Development with Unlimited Supplies of Labour', *The Manchester School*, May 1954, pp. 139-92 ; and 'Unlimited Labour : Further Notes', *The Manchester School*, January 1958, pp. 1-32.

constant level of real wages. Labour being in excess supply, there is no reason for wages to rise. The constant real wage level provides maximum opportunity for capital accumulation through reinvestment of profits, and this leads to a maximum rate of expansion for the modern sector of the economy.

The implication of the model is that intervention to raise real wages in the early stages of the growth process reduces the funds available for reinvestment. This will retard the upward shift of demand curves for labour, the rate of increase in employment opportunities and the rate of growth of national product. If one is obliged to raise real wages for political reasons, this must be regarded as a regrettable necessity.

This apparent clash of economic and humanitarian considerations is undoubtedly genuine in part. From one standpoint it is the familiar clash between the interest of the present generation and future generations. But I suggest that the starkness of the clash is mitigated by several considerations which are not always taken into account.

(1) The familiar model takes the schedule of marginal productivity of labour as independent of the level of real wages. But in practice, raising real wages is likely also to raise the productivity schedule. The first effect of a real wage increase is to permit a more ample and diversified diet. The increase in food intake raises the worker's physical strength and energy, increases his mental alertness, renders him less susceptible to illness and disease and prolongs his working life. The favourable effect of all this on productive capacity is scarcely debatable.

A less obvious point is that a higher level of nutrition makes the worker a better subject for other types of 'investment in human beings'. Children who are always hungry cannot take full advantage of educational opportunities. Public health measures cannot be fully effective if food availability is too low. Thus better nutrition increases the size of the coefficients relating inputs of medical, educational and training services to outputs of productive energy.

Labour productivity is likely to rise also because of the shock effect of higher wages on management methods. There is much evidence that, where labour is very cheap, it is used carelessly and inefficiently. Production standards are low, supervision is lax, and little attention is paid to selection, training and retention of qualified workers. A substantial rise in wages may lead management to set higher production standards, supervise more carefully and give greater attention to selection and training. This possibility is usually assumed away in economic theory by supposing that firms are already operating on their production functions. This assumption is debatable even for industrial nations ; and it is quite unrealistic for the less developed countries, where there is often a wide gap between potentiality and performance.

(2) The capitalist profits which appear in the Lewis model are not necessarily reinvested. One must remember that classical economics was written for classical Englishmen, who apparently got little enjoyment from life. They put their money back into more factories instead of leading a gay life in tropical resorts. This was no doubt commendable. But it is unsafe to assume that all capitalists in the presently developing countries will behave in the same way. To the extent that profits are consumed rather than reinvested, the argument for wage restraint is weakened.

(3) The usual models take the agricultural sector as passive, as simply a reservoir of surplus labour. But if the economy is developing rapidly, one must expect that productivity and living standards in agriculture will be rising. For reasons which cannot be detailed here, but which are widely accepted, sustained industrial progress is not feasible unless there is also substantial progress in the agricultural sector. But if rural incomes are rising, and if one accepts a substantially higher wage in industry as necessary for recruitment purposes, then industrial wages must also be rising at somewhat the same rate.

(4) Finally, one cannot overlook demand considerations. Classical growth theory, written for a Say's law world, was entirely supply-oriented. But in private economies, at least, aggregate demand has to be considered even at an early stage of economic development. Some rate of increase in real consumer expenditure is needed to induce a continued high level of investment in industrial capacity.

I do not draw the conclusion that governments and trade unions in the developing countries should be encouraged to undertake indiscriminate wage-raising. How far this is wise must be a matter for separate judgment in each country. I suggest only that the economic disadvantage of real wage increases is typically less than appears on the surface. It is even conceivable, though perhaps not likely, that in the early stages of development real wage increases may be costless in the sense that they are more than offset by consequent increases in productivity.

III. THE STRUCTURE OF RELATIVE WAGES

We turn next to the kinds of wage differential needed to draw people into areas of expanding labour demand. We shall consider differentials between rural and urban labour, between unskilled workers and skilled craftsmen and between the manual occupations and the professional and managerial occupations.

A preliminary question : in a situation of labour surplus, why does one need earnings differentials to induce labour mobility ? Will not the mere opening up of new jobs be sufficient to attract workers from stagnant sectors of the economy ? There are two answers to this question. First, it is necessary to have differentials wide enough to offset differences in training costs, risks, inherent attractiveness and other features of particular occupations. These are the famous 'equalizing differences' pointed out long ago by Adam Smith. Second, it will usually be desirable to have differentials somewhat wider than this to speed the redistribution of labour. Labour mobility is notoriously sluggish and imperfect. It may take substantial differentials to bring quick results. If the objective is rapid redeployment of labour, it is wise to err in the direction of differentials which are too wide rather than too narrow.

(1) This is true, first, as regards the earnings gap between the countryside and the towns. Food, rent and other basic necessities cost more in the city. Moreover, urban life is more expensive because the style of life is more elaborate and the list of conventional necessities is longer. But it is this urban way of life which is attractive, particularly to the young and vigorous who preponderate in the migration from village to city. To keep the flow going requires an urban wage level which permits workers to enjoy city-style housing, clothing and recreation, and which enables them to compare their new situation favourably with the old.

(2) Within the urban sector, the growth of construction, public utilities and manufacturing stretches the occupational structure in an upward direction. There is a substantial increase in demand even for unskilled labour, but the demand for the higher skills rises disproportionately. Economic development means among other things a sustained boom in construction. There is need for many more carpenters, electricians, bricklayers, plumbers and so on. In manufacturing, one needs a great increase in skilled production workers and maintenance mechanics.

Large wage differentials help to direct labour into these rapidly expanding occupations. Conversely, a niggardly wage policy can be a serious barrier to recruitment. The experience of the U.S.S.R. in this respect is well known. During the 1920s there was an effort to level down occupational differentials and to achieve greater equality of personal incomes. But this provided little incentive for workers to enter the skilled and technical occupations in which demand was rising rapidly. As these difficulties became apparent, the Soviet government in 1931 announced a change of policy in the direction of wider differentials.

During the last few years there has been renewed discussion of wage policy in the U.S.S.R. and some effort to narrow occupational differences once more. This suggests that training and redistribution of labour has now caught up with demand to the point where the wide differentials needed in the 1930s are no longer required. A narrowing of the skilled-unskilled differential is also observable in most of the Western industrial countries over the past half-century.

The extent to which occupational differentials must be widened for recruitment purposes depends partly on whether potential manpower bottlenecks are foreseen and attacked systematically through training programmes. If future needs are visualized and adequate supplies of labour are provided in due season, one can get along with smaller differentials than are necessary if labour must be attracted belatedly through market incentives. Fortunately, the training time for most manual occupations is so short that workers for a new plant can be trained faster than the plant can be built. But though the problem is inherently quite manageable, somebody has to manage it. Either the industry in question, or some organ of government, must see that training facilities are available and that workers are recruited and trained by the time at which they are needed. Systematic effort in this direction can reduce the pressure on the wage structure.

(3) Industrialization brings a great expansion in the demand for administrators and professional people — agronomists, chemists, accountants, engineers, even economists. Since these occupations involve trouble and responsibility, a long period of training and sometimes scarce natural talents, one must expect their market rate of pay to be high relative to the earnings of manual workers. This was true for generations in the Western industrial countries. In the U.S.S.R., one of the most rapidly industrializing economies of our time, industrial managers, engineers and other professional people also enjoy a marked income advantage.

At this point the requirements of efficient resource allocation appear to collide head-on with considerations of social justice. How can one justify a situation in which the top occupational groups earn ten times as much as the bottom ones? This is a major socioeconomic problem confronting the countries now embarking on industrialization.

The most basic line of attack on this type of inequality consists of massive investment in facilities for vocational education. The salary advantage of the professional-executive occupations at an early stage of development rests partly on supply restrictions arising from inadequate educational facilities. These educational bottlenecks can be broken by building more agricultural colleges, engineering schools, medical schools, teacher training colleges and other technical training institutes. It is debatable how one can best train civil servants and industrial managers, but they also need to be trained in large numbers. As an increased flow of graduates from institutions reaches the labour market, the earnings of the higher groups will tend naturally to fall. Thus inequality is reduced in a way which does not conflict with effective staffing of the economy.

Long-term projections of demand for technical and professional skills are a useful tool in this connection. In the professional occupations training periods are long, training is basically pre-employment and expensive training institutions are required. If a larger flow of doctors is to become available in 1975, preparatory steps must be taken in 1965. It is in this critical 5 to 10 per cent of the labour force that demand projections and systematic efforts to increase supply really come into their own.

IV. WAGE ADMINISTRATION AND PERSONAL INCENTIVES

One cannot conclude a discussion of wages and productivity without saying something about the reaction of the individual worker to monetary incentives. This is all the more necessary because a good deal of mythology has developed on this subject. The new industrial worker in an under-developed country, it is said, brings from his agricultural past habits and attitudes which make it difficult for him to fit into industrial employment. He is resistant to discipline and routine, inattentive to prescribed duties, prone to absenteeism and turnover. He values leisure highly and his income aspirations reach a ceiling at a low level. Thus his individual supply-curve of labour bends back to the left after a short distance. It is often implied that he finds factory employment basically unpleasant and that he looks back nostalgically to his life in agriculture.

This stereotype rests largely on casual opinions volunteered by management people in the less developed countries. It is true that industrial establishments in these countries often experience low man-hour output, high absenteeism and high turnover. But it is unsafe to conclude that this is due to inherent and unalterable characteristics of the workers, or to accept management's judgment of workers' abilities and motivation.

The readiness of employers to cast all responsibility for low output on the workers may stem partly from secret doubts about management's own competence, and from feelings of guilt at the prevailing level of wages. When employers face the challenge, 'How can you pay such scandalously low wages?' it is convenient to be able to reply, 'These people aren't worth any more'.

There has been little research into these matters, but there are already bits of evidence which run counter to the view described above, and which tend to establish the industrial worker in Asia, Africa or Latin America as not basically different from his counterpart in Europe or North America. The ease with which the worker adjusts to industrial life seems to depend largely on how he is handled by the employer. If the employer treats him as non-rational, if he is given no systematic instruction in his duties, if his earnings bear no visible relation to output, his response will be what one might expect. But if the employer does a good job of selection, wage-setting, training and supervision, a worker fresh from agriculture can quickly attain a level of effort and output comparable to that in the older industrial countries.

I may perhaps be permitted to relate some as yet unpublished results of a study which I directed several years ago in the island of Puerto Rico.[1] The study involved detailed interviews with about a thousand workers, most of whom had transferred from agriculture to industry within the preceding five years. It also involved investigation of about seventy new industrial establishments, in which we secured information on management procedures as well as quantitative data on employment, earnings, output, labour turnover, absenteeism and related matters. The problems examined are sufficiently typical of those found in other industrializing countries that the findings may have some general interest.

We found, first, a surprisingly high level of satisfaction with industrial life. Few workers expressed any desire to return to the strenuous physical effort, low incomes and primitive living conditions which they had experienced in agriculture.

As regards absenteeism and labour turnover, the most striking fact was the wide divergence of experience among establishments in the same type of industry. Some had turnover of only 5 to 10 per cent a year, while others had turnover in excess of 100 per cent. The fact that these establishments were drawing on the same pool of labour suggested that the explanation lay with management rather

---

[1] Professor Peter Gregory, of the University of Minnesota, collaborated with me in this study. A joint volume reporting the findings in detail will be published in the near future.

then with the workers. And this turned out to be true. Some plants, for example, had no pre-employment selection procedure. Anyone appearing at the gate was put to work, and those who did not perform proficiently were later discharged. This naturally produces a high turnover rate. Plants which screened workers carefully before employment showed much lower rates.

There were also surprisingly wide differences in man-hour output. In some industries the most efficient firms had attained output levels more than double those of the least efficient firms (and output levels comparable with those of similar plants in the United States, thus refuting any 'inherent inferiority' of the Puerto Rican worker). The difference lay partly in equipment and production layout, but to a considerable degree in personnel management. The efficient plants invariably used systematic, progressive management techniques, while the inefficient plants were usually managed along traditional paternalistic lines. On this front, as on many others, our findings confirmed the cliché that 'most labour problems turn out to be management problems'.

Because of the theoretical interest attaching to income aspirations, we questioned workers on this point at length and from several directions to permit cross-checks of consistency. The results were broadly similar to those of similar investigations in the United States. Few workers thought that their wages were high enough, or that they were living as well as they deserved. How much more income did they need to live properly? Ten, fifteen, twenty per cent — that 'little bit more' which has turned up in so many other surveys. When asked what they would do with this extra income, they were usually able to specify household furnishings or other items which they already had in mind, and whose purchase waited only on the necessary financing. Their responses did not suggest a low ceiling of aspirations. They were the kinds of response which an economist reared on the doctrine of insatiable human wants would naturally expect.

Why, then, have some writers concluded that workers in pre-industrial countries have low income aspirations and will respond to higher wage rates by working less? This is a complex question, but one clue may be suggested. Workers value money, not as an end in itself, but for what it will buy. If the circumstances are such that transformation of money into goods is blocked, or if the worker is somehow unable to use more goods effectively, then monetary incentives will naturally fail. Such circumstances are not uncommon in the countries we are considering. Transfer of money into goods may be blocked because domestic output of manufactured goods is small, while imports of consumer goods are restricted to conserve foreign exchange. The African migratory worker, who leaves his family behind in the tribal village, does not find effective avenues of enlarged consumption open to him in the city. But if the family moves with him, and his wife becomes an effective consumer, his income aspirations will rise rapidly.

Thus full investigation may reveal that the worker's behaviour is a rational response to his situation, and that strengthening his interest in money income requires changes in the situation rather than any transformation of the worker himself.

If one accepts the proposition that workers normally are responsive to monetary incentives, certain conclusions follow for wage administration. These are sufficiently obvious that they can be suggested rather than described in detail : job rates rather than personal rates ; some scope for advancement in earnings on the same job ; adequate wage differences between successively higher occupational levels, combined with promotion procedures which permit able workers to move up the occupational ladder ; and effective use of payment on an output basis.

More fundamental than specific practices is the general outlook of management. Too many employers in the less developed countries still cling to a traditional, near-subsistence level of wages and excuse this level by explaining that workers do not really want more. Would it not be more constructive to say, 'Of course they want more — let's help them to earn it' ? This attitude is relatively new even in the United States, going back only some forty years. The output results have been sufficiently impressive that our philosophers can now afford to speculate about the harmful effects of an over-supply of material goods. This is a problem about which most of the newly industrializing nations need not worry for a long time to come.

(*The discussion of this paper is recorded after Chapter 17.*)

Chapter 17

WAGES AND PRODUCTIVITY
IN GREAT BRITAIN

BY

K. G. J. C. KNOWLES
Oxford University

DESPITE the early proliferation of industrial institutions, *laissez-faire* has — paradoxically — been dying harder in Great Britain than in many other places and, while the gearing of wages to productivity is evidently of central importance, it is hard to find any appreciable 'effects of wage policies on productivity' or statistical relationship between the two. Thus the OEEC concluded that 'given the antiquated nature of the institutional arrangements in a number of [British] industries, the weakness of the central bodies on both sides, and the lack of any clearly defined norm for arbitrators to take as a guide when making awards, there can be no assurance that wage increases will in future be kept in line with the growth potential of the economy'.[1]

Wage-fixing arrangements have always been slow developers and therefore 'antiquated'; employers and trade unions are too jealous of their autonomy to tolerate anything but 'weakness' in their central organizations; and arbitrators have never been assured of success by relying on 'clearly defined norms'. The hand of history lies heavy on wage differences between industries : wage settlement in Britain is almost (in the words of a financial journal) 'as rigidly stylized as the classical ballet' and, when the stock arguments based on profitability, productivity and the cost of living have been exhausted, the appeal to 'comparability' tends to perpetuate historical relativities. The short-term similarity of increases during 'wage rounds' has been exaggerated; but there is, over the longer term, a perceptible tendency towards uniformity — possibly an institutional rather than an economic effect. Within industries, too, wage rate differences tend to be perpetuated : rigid wage 'structures' determine the form of the changes that can be made.

To this picture, productivity is *de facto* largely irrelevant. Several

[1] OEEC, *The Problem of Rising Prices*, May 1961, p. 447.

recent studies have found, for large numbers of industries, little or no correspondence between increasing productivity and advancing earnings [1] — although in some cases a nominal gearing of wages to productivity is strong or even predominant. Payment by results, despite the uncritical post-war enthusiasm for its extension, is probably obsolescent in the longer term, as mechanization limits the scope for increasing workers' efforts. Moreover, the complexity of such systems of payment is not amenable to national control; and the tendency of pieceworkers' earnings to pull away from time-workers', and then to drag them up in their wake, has probably been one (though only one) of the forces causing earnings to diverge from nationally negotiated wage rates.

In any case, granted the expectation that most workers' wages should rise by more or less similar amounts at more or less regular intervals, a rigid gearing of wages to productivity in particular industries is a dubious ideal; for workers in other industries (notably the public services) have less opportunity of increasing their productivity but no less expectation of advancing their wages. In such a situation, from the national standpoint it should be ensured that the current rise in wages is not greater than that in overall productivity [2] — so that industries where productivity is not rising may enjoy a like wage increase without contributing to further inflation.

Policy makers have concentrated on wage rates (since these alone are subject to some degree of national control), while earnings have received only secondary attention. Thus the 'pay pause' attempted, with questionable success, over most of the past year was aimed at checking the rise of wage rates; and the White Paper on Incomes Policy [3] has deprecated all the stock arguments of national wage negotiation in favour of 'general economic considerations' (the overall rise in productivity). It proposes that wage increases (including sliding-scale increases and the effects of reductions in hours) should be held for the present within the — since the war — unprecedentedly low figure of 2 to $2\frac{1}{2}$ per cent (the 'guiding light').

---

[1] Cf. R. J. Nicholson and S. Gupta, 'Output and Productivity Changes in British Manufacturing Industry, 1948–54', *Journal of the Royal Statistical Society* (Series A), IV, 1960; also C. H. Feinstein in *London and Cambridge Economic Service* (*Times Review of Industry*, December 1960); and W. E. G. Salter, *Productivity and Technical Change*, 1960, pp. 129, 167.

[2] Strictly, the rate of increase in wages should not exceed that in the productivity of consumption goods. (More strictly still, it is the rate of increase in the demand for consumption goods resulting from increases in wages that should not exceed the rate of increase in the productivity of consumption goods.) For even if wages were geared to overall productivity, if the rise in overall productivity reflected a big increase in the productivity of capital goods while that of consumption goods remained static, inflationary pressure would still tend to build up — at any rate in the short run. [3] *Cmd. 1626* (February 1962).

While the importance of earnings is now recognized, there are no specific proposals for controlling the earnings gap.

The reasons for the gap (the amount of overtime called for, the extent of above-standard payments made by individual firms, and the generosity of piecework pricing as well, of course, as higher earnings from improved productivity) lie essentially outside the province of national agreements. Some 'inflators' of earnings — in particular, above-standard payments (although they can hardly all be explained in these terms) — are due to labour-market pressures ; others are probably due to pressures inherent in the piecework system. Piecework, moreover, complicates the gearing of wage increases to the overall productivity increase. For since workers paid by results are continuously receiving wage advances in response to their own productivity, any 'permissible' wage rise should, strictly, discount for these advances. But this would mean a dimming of the 'guiding light' either (a) for all industries or (b) for piecework industries only, possibly to the point of invisibility. (a) alone would be likely to ensure rejection, while the apparent anomaly of (b) might, in addition, induce workers paid by results to limit their output — and hence, frustratingly, their future productivity.

Payment by results will not, however, disappear overnight. There is one possible alleviant which, since it amounts to settling wage rates with reference to actual earnings, deserves consideration : the '*pro tanto*' type of agreement. Normally, any negotiated increase in wage rates results in an increase in the earnings of everyone in the industry ; but a *pro tanto* agreement awards the full increase only to those workers whose earnings are near the minimum rate, while those earning more receive progressively smaller increases. The pros and cons of this have been argued elsewhere ;[1] but if it can help to reduce the variability of earnings within industries it should surely not be neglected as a method of relieving one of the pressures tending to widen the earnings gap and eventually to pull wage rates up in the wake of the highest earnings.

I have been assuming that no political *deus ex machina* — the National Economic Development Council or anything else — will revolutionize, miraculously, the character of 'free collective bargaining' in Britain. Miracles may happen ; but there may also be other possibilities in the interim.

[1] Cf. K. G. J. C. Knowles and T. P. Hill, 'The Variability of Engineering Earnings', *Bulletin of the Oxford University Institute of Statistics*, May 1956.

Record of Discussion

DISCUSSION OF THE PAPERS BY PROFESSOR REYNOLDS AND MR. KNOWLES

Chairman : DR. K. ROTHSCHILD

Mr. E. I. Kapustin (U.S.S.R.) opened the discussion with an account of the relationship between productivity and wages in the Soviet Union. The growth of labour productivity is of decisive importance for raising living standards in the U.S.S.R. : during 1957–61, over 60 per cent of the increase in industrial output was achieved through higher labour productivity, and the figure is expected to rise appreciably higher in the future. Technical progress is the fundamental condition for accomplishing this task — it will account for 80 per cent of the increase in productivity in the next twenty years — but incentives for the workers, both moral (e.g. socialist emulation) and material, are necessary.

While piece rates are still predominant, time rates are being increasingly applied ; the proportion of time-rate workers is 50 per cent in coal, 55 per cent in the chemical industry, etc. This trend is associated with the increase in automated and chemical processes, and in the greater importance of quality in performance. A group bonus system supplements the basic wage in most industries, based on quality as well as quantity of work. Collective bonuses for pieceworkers encourage the learning of several trades to cut losses of working time and for mutual assistance. The wage system increasingly reflects the skill of the worker, the working conditions and the economic importance of the work.

A uniform wage and skill rating handbook now covers about 65 per cent of all jobs in industry.

Since 1952, real incomes of factory and office workers have risen 55 per cent. Productivity has increased more. But living standards have also risen more than wages : working hours have been shortened ; public utilities and services of all kinds have increased, including medical care, education, libraries, pensions. A significant role in the rise of living standards was played by the extension of collective farming.

Dr. Desmond C. Corner, commenting on Professor Reynolds' paper, suggested that he was probably thinking of the United States model of development in his assessment of the relationships among wages, productivity and industrialization. He had envisaged the reallocation of labour during development as occurring only via wage increases in the expanding industries. The British experience, with industrialization starting in the textile industry, is probably more relevant for most of the under-developed countries. Here a cottage industry was transformed into a factory industry, with no intersectoral movement ; and the shift from handloom weaving to power looms was effected by falling prices rather than by rising wages. The United States is an example of economic

323

development with limited supplies of labour and unlimited supplies of land. Urban wages had to be raised initially in order to keep labour from the high productivity land at the frontier. This put a floor under wages, and also encouraged technical improvements.

In most of the under-developed countries today, the situation is exactly the reverse, and a mechanism suitable for American development in the nineteenth century may not be the most appropriate. On the other hand, it is not clear that real wages must remain unchanged even in countries with unlimited supplies of labour. The upshot of the long debate on what happened to real wages in England from the 1820s to the 1840s seems to be that on the whole they rose. Furthermore, in countries with a high proportion in agriculture, as surplus labour is drawn away from land into industry, the productivity of the land may well increase, especially in those places where the amalgamation of small plots into workable farms is not hindered by the existing system of land tenure. As a result, the real wages of workers remaining on the land would tend to rise just as agricultural wages did in England in the 1850s and 1860s. Finally, he agreed with Professor Reynolds that an earlier rise in real wages might well be worth a slightly lower rate of growth in developing countries, especially if this is the price that has to be paid for social and political stability.

Professor Giovanni Lasorsa (Italy) described the Italian 'miracle' of post-war economic development as an example of the 'Reynolds model', with rising real wages facilitating the movement of workers from south to north.

Professor D. J. Delivanis agreed that raising wages stimulated productivity by inducing employers to rationalize.

Mr. Eduard März (Austria) asserted that the feedback effect of wages on productivity was probably more important in the developing countries today than it was in either the United Kingdom or the United States; There are several new elements : the prevalence of some degree of central planning ; the emphasis on heavy industry ; the demonstration effect ; and the presence of trade unions at an early stage of development. The effect of these conditions is pressure for rising real wages, and also for a differentiated wage structure to encourage the acquiring of needed skills.

Professor Carl Uhr (United States) asked for some elaboration of Professor Reynolds' paragraph on 'shadow' wage rates : what differentials would be applicable as against the market rates, and who would make the decisions on them ?

Professor Elliot Berg (United States) noted that Professor Reynolds was trying to get us out of the 'low wage box' in which many economies find themselves — and many economists — via higher productivity. In general, he too thought that higher wages lead to higher productivity, but that the effect is not quantitatively significant. In Africa, most people were not underfed but badly fed, and higher wages would not cure this. The main problem there was the enervating effect of the environment :

climate and disease. Public health measures would be more appropriate than higher wages.

On the other hand, there were associated effects which were both negative and significant : on employment growth, on the balance of payments (through increased imports), on development and redistribution of income. The large role of the state in these economies must be kept in mind ; usually it employs from a quarter to more than half of all wage earners. The total number of wage earners is, however, a relatively small proportion of the total population — less than 10 per cent in many of them. Where the state is a large, or the largest, employer of labour, wage increases have dramatic and immediate effect on public resources available for capital formation. The dilemma is higher wages, or more roads, schools, hospitals.

There are also equity effects. In most under-developed countries indirect taxes, mainly import and export duties, provide most public revenues. But the peasant majorities do most of the importing and exporting, and hence pay most of the taxes, which are used to pay the wages of those employed by government. Already wage earners tend to be a relatively privileged group in many poor countries.

In short, the low wage box that Professor Reynolds is trying to extricate us from is more troublesome than he seems to admit. There is surely room for some movement of wage levels ; in some countries, perhaps even large opportunities exist. But the conditions common in the under-developed world put severe restraints on the wage policy area, and there are no easy ways around them.

Professor Subbiah Kannappan agreed with Professor Reynolds' comments on the Lewis model ; it had led to unwarranted optimism in regard to labour supply at a constant real wage during the course of development. Workers in under-developed countries are consumption and income oriented. However, the gap he mentioned between the market rate and the opportunity cost of labour seems to underestimate the difficulty of transferring labour, which does exist despite an aggregate surplus. The real costs of moving from agriculture are high from the point of view of security, which agriculture affords and industry does not. On the other hand, while one can concur with Professor Reynolds' judgment that the conflict between raising wages and capital accumulation is not rigid and inflexible, it does exist.

Professor V. K. R. V. Rao also believed that a conflict existed between capital accumulation and higher wages. But he preferred the Reynolds to the Lewis model. India had allowed for a large increase in consumption right from the start ; it was more democratic, and it also stimulated production. Constancy of wages is a better prescription for developed countries, where it would indeed increase capital accumulation, than for under-developed. But he was not sure that wage differentials should be the principal method for encouraging labour mobility ; in a planned economy like India it leads to inflation. Monetary incentives should be utilized within an industry to raise productivity, but inter-industrial wage relationships should reflect social policy.

Professor H. A. Turner (United Kingdom) did not think that Professor Reynolds had adhered to his first statement, that he would make no attempt at empirical generalization. For the under-developed countries, Professor Reynolds advocated a decentralized, flexible wage system, with the maximum play given to market forces. This was challengeable. Market forces do not work in many of these countries. Real wages often rise faster than productivity because of the political power of working-class movements. Even an appropriate wage structure does not arise from market forces; witness the high differentials for clerical workers in many under-developed countries, and the existence of many rates for the same job. What is needed is centralized guidance, not flexibility.

The apparent contradiction between the Reynolds and Knowles papers on the question of payment by results is due to the fact that the situation differs in developed and under-developed countries. Rich economies need equality to avoid inflation, but only the rich can afford equality. The problem for developing countries is how to avoid creating wage structures which will be embarrassing later on. He would agree with Professor Reynolds that some large part of real wage increases should take the form of social benefits. In the Congo, real wage increases had led mainly to the expansion of the brewing industry.

Mr. Felix Trappaniers pointed out that the elaborate attempt to create a rational incentive wage system in the Netherlands, tying wages to productivity, had not succeeded.

Professor John T. Dunlop (United States) asked Professor Reynolds to sharpen his advice to under-developed countries : should they follow Arthur Lewis or be more generous ? Real wage increases in the United Kingdom in the early nineteenth century were quite small, and the same was true of the U.S.S.R., and of the United States in the 1860–80 period. But perhaps the rate of productivity increase is higher in the under-developed countries today than in those countries during the early stages of industrialization, as Professor Galenson's paper seemed to indicate. What would Mr. Kapustin advise ?

Professor Carl Knoellinger (Finland) had heard the wage structure at the start of development described as anarchic; Professor Reynolds said it was compressed. Were both true ?

Professor Leslie Fishman emphasized that Professor Reynolds, as was true of most of the participants in the section, ignored the relationship between demand and productivity. This relationship was complex but was crucial to an understanding of the rate of productivity advance in a developing economy. The transition to a machine civilization required an expanding market demand which would justify the investment in new plant and equipment. Higher wages help provide the larger market and act as a 'workers' cruse', much as the 'widow's cruse' of employment theory. The 'widow's cruse' postulates that as investment increases, the increased demand created by the multiplier effect of the investment, validates the additional investment. A 'workers' cruse' postulates that higher wages can, through creating a larger market, call forth enough new investment and technical progress to justify the higher wages. A difficult balance is required between capital accumulation and expanding market demand to justify that accumulation. Decreasing costs, internal and external economies, and technical progress — the categories we economists have used to analyse productivity advance — all require an ever-increasing market demand if they are to be realized.

Professor Walter Galenson questioned Professor Reynolds' description of wage structure in the early stages of industrialization as one of widening differentials, which later narrowed. This was the traditional view, but there was actually very little empirical information on it. A forthcoming study of Pakistan which he had read indicated that wage differentials were very narrow there, and the same situation apparently prevailed in Israel, where of course strong ideological factors were also at work. Secondly, he too would like to ask Mr. Kapustin what sort of wage policy he would advocate in the early stages of development. There was a fall in real wages in the U.S.S.R. under the first Five-Year Plans.

Mr. Gösta Rehn (Sweden) wanted to know what method Professor Reynolds would prescribe for preventing inflation if real wages were tied to productivity increases, as Mr. Knowles had described the system. Or did he recommend inflation as a method of promoting growth ? And would he advise under-developed countries to let the trade unions push for increases in money wages (and if so, what about agricultural wages) ?

Mr. Kapustin answered Professors Dunlop and Galenson by suggesting the following principles, which would be useful in a developing country : (1) Considerable differentiation according to degree of skill to stimulate the acquiring of skills and productivity. (2) Inter-industry differentials to attract labour to expanding industries. (3) The employment of piece rates and bonuses to stimulate production in the first stage, before complex mechanization prevails. On Dr. Galenson's point : real incomes did increase during the industrialization of the U.S.S.R. because of the liquidation of unemployment, the shift of low-wage agricultural workers to industry and the extension of education and the introduction of medical care. The rise in real income was, however, lower than in later periods because no foreign aid was given the U.S.S.R., and they had had to industrialize themselves.

Professor Reynolds, in a general summary answer to the questions raised during the discussion, asserted that payment by results was still suitable for many types of work despite the spread of automation ; he disagreed with Mr. Knowles that it was tending to become obsolete. The effect of such a system on inflation, and the wage drift, were different issues ; he was concerned in his paper only with the effect of incentive pay on output. On wage structure : he would agree that people did not move only because of differentials ; but they did help to lubricate the process of labour mobility. The disadvantages of wide differentials had, however, been adumbrated in the discussion : they tend to stick, and they are difficult to reverse. Forecasting, training and labour market organization should be utilized as much as possible to produce flexibility of labour resources. Large wage differentials might then be considered evidence of failure on these other fronts. Expenditures on housing, social security systems and other government services should be included in the real wage level ; these are a method of reducing differentials in fact.

He had been misunderstood on some points. He had not meant that under-developed countries should follow the United States model, or the British. Or that wages should be left to market forces. He had talked about the criteria for wage policy, implying some degree of government control. But many of the same forces must be dealt with, whatever the system. Had he advocated a soft policy, was he in favour of rising real wages during the period of development ? No ; he had suggested only that there were some arguments in favour, to be weighed against the arguments on the other side. Wage restraint and capital accumulation were generally recognized as a desirable policy ; he wanted to point out that there was another side to it, including the favourable productivity effects of a higher real wage level, and its significance as a stimulus to demand.

Mr. Rehn had propounded some unanswerable questions on how to prevent inflation of the money wage level. As to whether he favoured inflation : his threshold of tolerance was rather high, and he was much more alarmed about unemployment. On the question of trade unions pressing for wage increases in developing countries, he would say only that it was lucky for some of the western countries that unions had developed late in the course of industrialization.

Chapter 18

CONTRIBUTIONS OF MANAGEMENT TO PRODUCTIVITY

BY

S. CARLSON
Uppsala University

I. THE PROBLEM

WHAT contribution can the management of the individual industrial firms make to the industrialization process, what particular managerial skills need to be developed and what policies should be pursued? These are our problems. The setting is the following:

1. We shall limit our analysis to the under-developed countries, i.e. to the management problems of the pre-industrialized milieu.

2. We shall examine these problems from the point of view of management itself, and by management we here mean top management. That is, we shall mainly be concerned with the growth problems of the individual firm, and with the management policies related to these growth problems.

3. Furthermore, we shall mainly consider the indigenous industrial firms. Subsidiaries of foreign companies and joint foreign and local ventures will only be brought into the picture with reference to their general influence on management practices. In spite of the fact that they may be of considerable importance for the industrialization process, under certain circumstances, we shall not be able to go into their special problems.

Thus, there are severe limitations to the scope of our discussion. Still, the subject is immense and we shall only be able to touch on some of its most important aspects.

II. THE POLICY-MAKER AND HIS ENVIRONMENT

The policy-making tasks of management are twofold: it has to establish the policies regarding the representation of the firm towards the outside world, and the policies relating to the organization and administration of the internal operations. We may illustrate this setting by the following picture:

THE FIRM

Internal operations

THE OUTSIDE WORLD

The Commodity Market	The Capital Market	The Labour Market	Non-market institutions

The outside world we are here concerned with is the particular milieu of the under-developed country. Let us first have a look at this milieu and see how it affects the policy-making tasks of the management. In doing so we are fully aware of the fact that the conditions vary very much from country to country, and that on practically every point one should add some reservations. But life is too short for all that.

(a) *The Commodity Market*. Most of the under-developed countries are not only poor, they are also small. Their internal markets are therefore often quite limited. Furthermore, since the main source of income generally is agriculture, the effective demand for consumption goods and equipment is often concentrated in relatively short seasons. This means that in many cases the marketing uncertainties for new products are considerable, and that there is a special need for market research. Generally the management of the local industrial firms does not dare to develop new products and new channels of distribution, but prefers to concentrate an expansion on goods which hitherto either have been imported or produced by handicraft methods, and for which marketing channels already exist. It will have to fight against a consumer preference for imported products — the strong nationalistic sentiment which expresses itself in so many other ways seldom affects the consumers' product preferences. But if it succeeds, it will soon establish a monopoly position. This position is safeguarded by the limitation of the market, the high transport costs and the general lack of competitive tradition.

If we look at the market for the goods the firm needs to buy, it is to a large extent an overseas market, which means high transport costs and long delivery times. In an under-developed country there is a lack of dependable local suppliers for equipment, for spare parts or for semi-finished products. The raw materials available locally are often different from those used in the industrialized countries, and it is generally up to the buying firm to establish the necessary grading and standards. For all these reasons the choice between 'to buy or to make' becomes much more difficult than in an industrialized milieu.

330

(b) *The Capital Market.* In most under-developed countries the traditional financial institutions are mainly interested in the primary commodity trade and the import business. The banks are often subsidiaries of European or American banks which, as Nevin has pointed out,[1] do not operate as their mother companies did, when Europe and America were in their early stages of industrial development, but as they do today in a highly industrialized setting. They have meant much as introducers of bank management skills to the under-developed countries but they are not equipped to handle the risks which a financing of an early industrial development involves. Because of the uncertainty regarding the ownership of land and regarding the values of industrial assets in the case of a liquidation, the young industrial firms represent pretty poor risks, and the only thing the banks generally can do is to supply short-term credit. There is seldom any market for shares and bonds, and as a result people with money are not interested in buying minority interests in, or in giving long-term loans directly to, industrial firms. In some countries special development banks have been established for medium- and long-term industrial financing but their resources are generally insufficient. In addition there are, of course, the money lenders, but the rates they have to charge are by necessity much higher than the rates of the established financial institutions. One of the characteristics of the under-developed countries is, in fact, the existence of two quite separate financial markets, one high rate and another low rate, and one of the problems for the management of the industrial firms is how to get over from the former to the latter.

With the organized capital market closed or non-existent for everything but short-term trade credit, the industrial firms try to finance their investments in machinery and equipment by long- or medium-term commercial credit. Otherwise the accumulation of profit becomes the main source of finance. Summing up, the problem of finance is much more of a preoccupation for management in the under-developed countries than in the industrialized parts of the world.

(c) *The Labour Market.* One of the main characteristics of the pre-industrialized milieu is, of course, that while generally there is a vast supply of unskilled labour, there is a shortage of skilled or professional people. And of all skills, what Harbison calls the 'organization-building ability'[2] is often the rarest, while it at the same time is the most needed. Temporarily, at least, the industrial firm may

[1] Edward Nevin, *Capital Funds in Underdeveloped Countries*, London, 1961, ch. 3.

[2] F. Harbison, 'Entrepreneurial Organization as a Factor in Economic Development', *Quarterly Journal of Economics*, LXX (1956), p. 367.

import some skilled staff, but this is no happy solution. It is also excessively expensive.

As regards the unskilled labour force there exists sometimes a similar division into one high-price and one low-price market as we found with reference to capital. But here the price relates to the buyer and not to the supplier. The little fellow can generally get his labour cheap. When the industrial firm increases in size, the unions will be more influential, and the government authorities will find it both more important and easier to enforce existing wage laws. The raising of the productivity of unskilled workers through proper organization, training, nutrition and wage incentives becomes one of management's most important problems.

(d) *Non-Market Institutions.* In general I believe one will find that the more dominant an industrial firm is in its branch or in the local community, the more important are its contacts with government institutions, local authorities, trade associations, etc. The importance of these relations increases, of course, with the degree of governmental control of the economy. Being often both a dominant supplier and employer in the local community, and generally operating under all kinds of governmental restrictions, the industrial firm in an under-developed country will be very dependent on its official relations. Sometimes it may be even more important to be on good terms with various planning and licensing authorities than with suppliers or customers. But these relations require special managerial skills and cunning and they must generally be handled by the top manager himself.

III. MANAGEMENT POLICIES AND SKILLS

The environmental factors here described influence the management policies in several ways. These policies are of course also influenced by tradition : the family enclave, paternalism, the status system, etc. In some ways, the tasks of the management of an industrial firm in an under-developed country may be simpler than in an industrialized country. The top manager is less of an innovator in the Schumpeter sense than an imitator and adapter. His market position is generally more protected. But on the whole he has a more difficult job, at least if he wants his firm to grow, and it is with the growth problem that we are concerned here.

Of all the environmental circumstances, the absence of a properly functioning capital market is probably the factor which has the most detrimental effect on management policies. For financing one has mainly to resort to the family and to friends, which leads to a constant preoccupation with the question of financial control. An operation which would influence the present balance of control is often avoided even if it might be highly profitable. If some members of the financing group are unwilling to plough back profits into the firm, they will get the others to follow suit. This system of finance leads easily to nepotism. Representatives and friends of the various interests have to be offered management posts irrespective of their competence. The more uncertain such a member of the management team feels in his job, the more reluctant he will be generally to employ competent subordinates and to delegate authority to them.

The problems of finance become even more complicated under inflationary conditions. As Hirschman has underlined, it is difficult to learn that capital equipment needs to be continuously maintained, and not only repaired after it has broken down.[1] But to understand that more and more money must be invested in plants, machinery and inventories, if the physical production capacity is to remain the same, is even more difficult. Proper management policies in this respect are often hampered by lack of understanding both by accountants and by tax officials.

As regards market and product policies, we have noticed above that the management generally prefers to concentrate an expansion on goods that have hitherto either been imported or produced by local handicraft. While in the latter case we may find a conscious drive towards cost reduction, quantity expansion and development of new markets, the import substitution seldom leads to any particular dynamism. When the protected market has been skimmed, there is little incentive for any further expansion, and as a result of the monopoly position rarely is anything done regarding qualitative improvements. An industrial firm which has succeeded in breaking into the export market has much more inducement for cost reduction and expansion, and one can see the effect of this on its management policies. The management of these firms talk about their foreign sales with great pride, and one can sometimes observe the stimulating effects of these sales all through the organization.

There is much to be said regarding management policies with reference to choice of technology, to work force organization, to training of staff and to work incentives, but these topics have been treated in other papers and should not be repeated here. Let us instead try to see what can be done in order to induce more growth-promoting management policies in general.

[1] A. O. Hirschman, *The Strategy of Economic Development*, New Haven, 1958, ch. 8.

If I could make a list for Santa Claus of what I would like most, it would definitely include the establishment of proper financial institutions : an improved market for industrial stocks and bonds, an adaptation of the policies and operative practices of the commercial banks to the needs of the local industry, and the establishment of special industrial development banks. If the management of the industrial firms were financially less dependent on family groups, it would have more freedom to run its investment and personnel policies without consideration to the balance of control. Progressive management policies would also be helped by taxation rules permitting liberal depreciation allowances and favouring the establishment of capital reserves. Company laws requiring a fairly large amount of publicity regarding the firm's economic status would help to loosen up the present urge for secrecy. As regards product development and marketing, the stimulating effect of competition through imports should not be entirely forgotten, and the attempts of the industrial firms to develop export sales should be aided in every way. The policies favouring a more even distribution of income will also have an influence on management policies. As long as management expects a market for its products only among a small upper class while the masses have no possibilities to increase their consumption, one cannot expect any growth promoting policies.

But a change in the environment is not enough. The management's own skills in policy-making and policy-implementing need also to be improved. This is a question both of formal education and of practical training. But it is only when an organization reaches a certain size and complexity that the importance of the particular managerial tasks becomes obvious, and it is mainly in such organizations that the need for special education and training for such tasks is felt. In the under-developed country, this means the army, perhaps the civil service, but rarely industry. Some of the best top managers have come from the army or the civil service. If, however, somebody in industry should want to get professional management training, he has not much of a chance. The higher educational institutions may, at best, be geared to produce technicians, accountants, etc., for industry, but they are seldom equipped to give their students a basic training in the analysis of cost, finance, marketing and administrative problems. Still, for the development of managerial skills formal education is not enough. In addition the professional student must have a chance to observe and to practise under proper supervision, and this becomes very difficult in an industrial society composed of relatively small family firms. It is here that the subsidiaries and the joint ventures with foreign industrial firms can make one of their most important and lasting contributions to the industrialization process. Another problem is that even if there exist people with the proper management training, the family traditions and the paternalistic system may prevent them from getting a chance to apply their skills, before they have forgotten what they have learned.

The need for a change in the present system is felt among the younger groups both in industry, in the central planning organizations and in the governments. By the establishment of professional societies, junior chambers of commerce, management training centres, etc., where an interchange of ideas and experience could take place, and management problems could be discussed more and more openly, much could be done to professionalize management and to break the present isolation of individual firms. Something can also be learned from abroad from, e.g. the German or French middle-sized family firms which recently have gone through the kind of managerial changes that the under-developed countries will have to face, and from firms in other under-developed countries which are more advanced than the average. The trouble is that the experiences and practices of these firms are much more difficult to study than the super-administrations of the American or European industrial giants, which now are the object of so much attention.

(The discussion of this paper is recorded after Chapter 19.)

Chapter 19

THE CONTRIBUTION OF WORKERS TO PRODUCTIVITY GROWTH

BY

H. A. TURNER
Leeds University

THIS topic can be discussed at at least three levels. The individual's attitude to the factors on which productivity growth depends — his response to material incentives, his willingness and ability to adapt, innovate and co-operate — is largely determined by a complex of social and cultural pressures and conditions, some of which may be specific to employed people, or even to particular sections or communities of employees. It is secondly well recognized that any continuing workplace group tends to establish its own internal structure of relationships (which may little coincide with that designed by the management concerned) and, particularly, that such 'informal' groups often evolve and enforce their own standards and methodology of productive performance.

This paper examines the 'workers' contribution' at a third level, that of workers' formal organization. It especially discusses (if only as the most tangible subject for terse analysis) trade unionism's bearing on and attitude to the technological, methodological and structural changes involved in productivity growth. But it should not be forgotten that the other two levels are also operative ones, which interact with that of formal organizations.

Trade unions *should*, of course, be interested in increasing productivity because the level of real wages is largely governed, if not absolutely determined, by the relevant economy's *per capita* product. This is true of economies of all types — communist, capitalist, or simply 'under-developed' — though with varying expressions. Recent experience, however, provides further reasons for unions to concern themselves with productivity. In several industrial countries, the major obstacle to the continuing maintenance of full employment has been the incapacity of production to match demands for income (including those of the unions themselves) at high employment levels ; here, a faster productivity growth would facilitate the accommodation of those demands, rather than their containment by unemployment or underemployment. While in certain 'under-developed' economies — particularly where independent govern-ments are new and major private employers foreign — employees, though very much in the minority, are the only substantially organized popular force, and have been able to extract concessions so en-dangering the prospects of development that the unions invite the risk, if not of suppression, then of government control. Here, an increased concern with productivity may help unions to retain their independence.

However, general and long-run interests of this kind are not necessarily obvious at the operative point — in relation to the in-numerable specific changes in techniques, working arrangements and employments that advancing productivity implies. To start with, such changes are generally initiated from above and may appear to workers as demands (or impositions) upon them, made in their employers' interests. That they also raise those employers' general capacity for concession is not always immediately self-evident : the whole issue, in effect, is often obscured by distributive complications. Secondly, some large part of the rise in average real wages associated with productivity growth takes the form, not of improvement in the standards of particular classes of employees, but of a change in the labour force's composition — a gradual increase in the proportion of skilled and salaried workers, an increase in better-paid industries' share of employment, and the like. Where productivity rises slowly, again, this may mainly benefit new entrants to employment, and up-gradings among existing workers be effectively limited to occasional promotions that are resented by the workplace group as undermining its solidarity.

But in any case, trade unions are not usually the embodiment of a 'general will' but of organized group and sectional interests, separate and diverse. And to all particular interests, innovation is certainly not automatically beneficial. Technological advance may historically have contributed only marginally to unemployment : but if unemployment is already widespread its marginal effect is often peculiarly striking, and may be disproportionately blamed for the general circumstance in which it merges. But even where pro-ductive change involves no significant or enduring labour redund-ancy, it may still threaten the *relative* status of particular groups. This explains, for instance, the obstinate retention of their job-demarcation rules by several British craft unions in face of a genera-tion's near-full employment. One might perhaps theorize that technical change produces in succession specialized groups of workers, which benefit disproportionately to the average productivity growth when the innovation round which they crystallized is recent, but which in turn fall behind — or even suffer absolutely — as their speciality itself obsolesces. If this were valid, then near half the workers would at any one time be relatively disadvantaged by technical change ! At least, it is worth noting that some types of workers' association (including unions and 'professional' bodies) are very much concerned with relative status.

Most of these problems would, of course, be minimized where the rate of productivity growth was *already* so high that everyone palpably benefited to some extent. But a faster rate of advance would also involve greater individual displacement, and greater disturbance of working methods and arrangements that workplace groups and even trade unions may have adapted to a protective routine. If, as Perlmann suggested, organized workers tend to be preoccupied with 'job-control', managerially-initiated innovation is likely to appear as a major hazard to that ambition.

How important is all this ? About the factors that determine whether growth rates are high under the current conditions of advanced economies '. . . the only important point that can be established is that a necessary, and almost sufficient, condition . . . is (a general expectation) that the demand for products will continue to grow rapidly'.[1] If this is true, the major contemporary determinant of economic growth would appear to be government policy. Though trade unions can complicate the task of maintaining high demand and employment intolerably, by their wage policy or by restrictions on the general mobility of labour.

But the direct responsibility for innovation lies with particular managements : and at this level unions or their members may at least delay and limit advance significantly — if not by direct resistance or obstruction, then by the imposition of conditions on particular innovations that substantially reduce their advantages to managers, or even by an implicit sabotage. The key to a willing acceptance of productivity growth's detailed implications thus appears to be, not merely that no significant section should suffer absolutely or enduringly in consequence of innovation, but an effective practical translation of the general interest in such growth into specific sectional benefits.

An acceptance of innovation, however, is by no means the same thing as an active promotion of it. Excluding the unions in communist countries, which during the Stalin era, at least, appeared primarily as agencies to foster production, the average attitude of

---

[1] *National Institute Economic Review*, London, February 1962, 'Policies for Faster Growth'.

trade unionism still appears effectively neutral to technical innovation. Historically, this is itself something of a change. 'No Trade Union ever encouraged invention', said a then-prominent British critic a century ago.[1] But already by the 1890s a Royal Commission, examining the rules and regulations of hundreds of British unions, found no surviving trace of hostility to invention or improvement.[2] And the Webbs, in what is still the most far-reaching survey ever made of union practice, then commented[3] that '. . . the old attempt of the handicraftsman to exclude the machine has been definitely abandoned. Far from refusing to work the new processes, the Trade Unionists of today claim a preferential right . . . to perform the new service. In asserting this preferential claim to continuity of employment, they insist that the arrangements for introducing the new process . . . are matters to be settled, not merely by one of the parties to the wage-contract but . . . on the principle of Collective Bargaining (when) the Trade Union always proceeds on the fundamental assumption that under no circumstances must the "improvement" be allowed to put the operative in any worse position . . . (with) sometimes the further claim . . . that the wage-earner should receive some of the advantages to be derived from the improvement. . . .' In essence, Slichter's conclusion, more than forty years later, that American unions were predominantly concerned to control productive change, not obstruct it, is identical,[4] and the Selekmans in 1950 still only confirmed that in the U.S.A. '. . . majority union policy . . . *accepts* technological advance, provided there are proper safeguards for workers'.[5] There remain, of course, in both countries, sectors — shipbuilding in Britain and construction in the U.S.A. — where union practice constitutes a fairly clear handicap to productivity : and these cases are offset by others in which unions have deliberately pressed employers to improve it. Certain modern American instances of the latter kind particularly caught the imagination of European labour leaders a few years ago :[6] but even in the 1890s, again, the Webbs were able '. . . to observe that, with the acceptance of this new policy by the employers, and its complete comprehension by the workmen, it is not the individual capitalist, but the Trade Union, which most strenuously insists on

---

[1] *Trade Unions and their Tendencies*, Edmund Potter, F.R.S., Social Science Association, 1860.
[2] Royal Commission on Labour, Majority Report, 1894.
[3] *Industrial Democracy*, 1897, chapter on 'New Processes and Machinery'.
[4] In *Union Policies and Industrial Management*, 1941.
[5] 'Productivity and Collective Bargaining', *Harvard Business Review*, March 1950.
[6] For instance, Report of TUC Productivity Mission to the U.S.A., 'Trade Unions and Productivity', 1950.

having the latest improvements . . .' and to quote several instances to that effect.[1] But this extreme of union practice remains, apparently, as generally exceptional as its opposite.

Since the war, however, union leaders of every tendency have repeatedly declared themselves for higher productivity. And a consciousness of some need on this front is reflected in the establishment of specialized 'productivity services' by union organizations. Of twenty-one national union centres (federations, i.e.) in twelve countries that replied to an EPA questionnaire in 1958, ten had Productivity Departments, distinct from their economic research services. But this development is much less marked at the actual industrial level — it is extraordinary, for instance, that only two European metal- and machine-workers' unions were then reported as thinking fit to have such an organ. And the actual work of these union productivity services seems little concerned with productivity promotion as such, but rather with the analysis of innovation's consequences for workers and with assistance to unions in negotiating conditions — new wage-systems, employment guarantees, etc. — for managerially-initiated developments with which the unions' other officers are unfamiliar : in effect, these services reinforce the established function of 'control'. A survey of American unions' technical services by two of their Research Directors similarly noted of their industrial engineering services' functioning that . . . 'At times (unions) co-operate in this area . . . of automation and other technological progress'.[2] But after citing certain notable instances they add : 'Such extreme co-operation is rare, however, and unions are more concerned with assuring wage earners their just share of the results of increased productivity than they are with methods of increasing it'. The President of the Belgian Christian Union Confederation similarly explained its appointment of several production experts after the 'productivity protocol' agreed with the national employers' organs in 1954 : 'It is our duty to see that the employers and their technicians are matched with worthy opponents — union specialists who can advance and defend the interests of the workers'.[3] It seems significant that services of this kind have been most elaborated in countries where unions largely developed after Taylorist techniques of labour utilization had already been widely applied by employers, and had to be accepted as a fact rather than (as occurred

[1] *Industrial Democracy*, again ; the 'new policy' being that outlined in the preceding Webbsian quotation.
[2] E. M. Kassalow and A. Weinlein, *Union Research and Technical Services in the United States*, EPA, 1958.
[3] M. Auguste Cool, to an inter-European union conference in Vienna, December 1958.

in Britain during the inter-war period) resisted. This partly explains why the German unions should now be relatively well-equipped in such services.

Nevertheless, in elaborating their techniques to control innovation and share its benefits, unions are in fact performing a considerable service to productive advance itself. There are social costs to innovation which expert union 'control' tends probably to minimize. Particularly, union bargaining of innovation reduces its threats and bogeys at least to manageable disturbances, and often converts them to opportunities of gain to workers. It thus forestalls individual and group resistance to change : by making innovation negotiable it also makes it acceptable — or even, in demonstrable cases, welcome. Employers and managements who insist, as some still do, that innovation's consequential arrangements are a 'managerial function' (the British Engineering Employer Association's term) are thus obstructing its routes as effectively as the most obstinate of restrictive unions. Such things as rigid job-demarcations, arbitrary output limitations, deterrent or prohibitive impositions on the use of improved tools, etc. — whether applied by unions proper or by 'unofficial' or informal groups — generally represent defensive distortions of a proper and desirable function of workers' organization, which are likely to diminish further as unions improve their equipment to negotiate such things as job-classifications and evaluations, 'workloads' and wage-structures in the light of moving technical fact. The risk is not in the attempted control, but in an inadequate equipment for the task.

It may be argued, of course, that the general demands of trade unions — for more pay, more leisure, greater job-security and so on — are themselves an incentive or pressure to productivity growth. And certainly, exacting unions may serve as stimuli to managements. But these effects of union pressure are incidental to the 'consumptionist' function of unions, just as those described above are incidental to their 'protective' function. How much further should unions go towards becoming 'productionist' agencies for labour mobilization ; towards the Soviet model ? In a newly industrializing country there is, at least, something to be said (though not unconditionally) for that approach — for the reason already given and for others. But as industrialism consolidates, and the working-class becomes 'structured' and sectionally stabilized, the danger of a 'productionist' approach is that if the unions fail to meet the protective needs of employees, they will evolve alternative 'informal' techniques to serve that purpose, which may amount to a subterranean but continuous resistance to managerial innovation.

Unless the unions retain the confidence of the workers, they will thus fail to fulfil even their major incidental function of facilitating innovation and change : it seems notable, in fact, that if Western unions have become more 'productivity-minded' since the war, those in certain communist economies are apparently reassuming protective and representational functions.

One frequent contemporary argument is that 'direct workers' participation in management' — a demand pressed by several labour movements — would apply a largely-untapped reserve of experience and initiative among workers themselves to productivity advance. 'Workers' self-management' in Yugoslavia certainly seems to be associated with a high rate of growth, but (other considerations apart) implies also a unique form of economic organization. In other countries, devices like employee representation on management boards, elected Works' Councils and formal 'joint consultation' have sometimes apparently been helpful as a communicative channel in implementing change, but mainly where the unions' own bargaining activities do not embrace direct negotiation at the workplace over the exercise of managerial functions. There is little evidence that these devices release a flood of employee initiative : an official Italian survey of 147 elected plant committees in 1958 showed that only 15 concerned themselves with production questions, and then in a very limited way — the promotion of suggestion schemes and the like. The Israel example of union assumption of managerial responsibility, though glamorous, does not seem so encouraging on closer inspection. And other experiences suggest that for unions themselves to become involved in 'participational' procedures may again compromise their essential protective functions.

A good deal, again, might be said about the effects of alternative forms of union organization on productivity growth — for instance, that 'industrial' unions are better than 'craft' or 'general' unions. But the main way in which unions can encourage productivity growth remains via wage policy. At the risk of trespassing on another discussion at this Congress, the writer will assert (he regrets, dogmatically) that, in an advanced economy at least, the need is for a national wage structure that equalizes net advantages for comparable skill and responsibility throughout its effective area, in which wage payments approximate in their security and stability to salaries, and which is under continuing pressure both to level-up lower wages and to raise wages in general just ahead (but not too far ahead) of average current productivity growth. In so far as union pressure tends towards such a pattern, it is helpful.

This pattern would be *directly* effective as an incentive to managerial efficiency and initiative, however, and two selective incentives to workers would be desirable. First, to performance — that is to accept objectively assessed and agreed 'work-loads'. But second, to accept and welcome innovation : which involves a wage structure carefully graded — and repeatedly revised — in relation to equipments and methodologies. In actual wage practice, these two incentives are often confused. But particularly, they often involve an almost arbitrarily distributed 'wage drift' that not merely destroys uniformity (and even rationality) in the national structure of wage relationships, but incites a general wage pressure so far ahead of productivity possibilities as to be irrelevant to them. These difficulties are not insuperable — some very careful Dutch studies are relevant [1] — but their control demands very close and persistent study and attention by negotiators.

Under sectional and dispersed collective bargaining, the problem is that union leaders tend to become so preoccupied with the periodic general wage round that not merely are these exacting and intricate details of wage structure and wage systems often neglected, but so too are the many other issues which ought to be negotiated in connection with productive performance and innovation. For instance, the British annual average of reported industrial disputes has risen from a few hundred in the 1930s to some 2500 in the 1950s : this rise is largely due to a sharp increase in the number of small 'unofficial' or 'wildcat' stoppages over redundancy, over wage systems and wage anomalies, and especially over detailed working arrangements, work rules and discipline ; these things cause some two-thirds of contemporary strikes. How can the limited resources of professional leadership in unions be released to their key function in relation to productivity growth — that of providing a socially-acceptable route for innovation ?

Some national agreement or 'consensus' on future general wage advances appears to provide at least the framework of an answer. Such central bargains or understandings should, however, be based on reasonably-attainable rates of productivity advance, not on inferior past performance. Otherwise they will not, in some cases, provide enough to make them acceptable to union members or a sufficient pressure on managements : and the risks of mild inflation are preferable to those of stagnation, anyway. But secondly, they should be keyed to a medium period of years — say three or four — so that they can be expressed in relation to substantial and realizable

[1] See, for instance, 'Problems raised by incentive systems in the Dutch Metal Industry', by A. I. Bruggink, reproduced in *Trade Union Research Departments*, EPA, 1959, and other Dutch studies there referred to.

targets of improvement in popular living standards. However, central 'wage-policy' agreements have usually been concerned mainly with a general, all-round wage increase. And finally, such agreements should embody three distinct elements : the minimum all-round increase itself ; an allocation for the controlled negotiation of 'incentives' to specific groups of workers to accept innovation ; and another selective allocation (applicable not merely on grounds of justice but as a penalty on backward managements) to groups that had fallen behind in the past. While if in any one year the actual average rate of wage advance has to be reduced below the target, it should be its general, not its selective, components that suffered. It is, in effect, these elements in wage movements that provide the mechanism of positive labour participation in productivity growth.

DISCUSSION OF THE PAPERS BY PROFESSORS SUNE CARLSON AND H. A. TURNER

Chairman : M. Pierre Gonod

Professor Adolf Sturmthal (United States) opened the discussion with the observation that although the plan had probably been for the two papers to be symmetrical, they did not conform : the contributions of management were discussed in the context of under-developed countries and the contributions of workers, in industrialized countries. He also pointed out that economic growth and the growth of productivity were not the same thing, and that Dr. Carlson's paper referred to growth problems of the firm. He wondered about the level of development Dr. Carlson had in mind ; the reference to taxation rules, liberal depreciation allowances and capital reserves sounded more like Argentina or Italy, or even the United States, than a country just starting on the road of economic development. The Carlson paper concentrated almost exclusively on the conditions under which management operates rather than on what management itself can do to raise productivity. Even if the level of productivity is primarily a function of what Dr. Pajestka referred to as the 'material factors' in countries with meagre capital resources, the role of management is nevertheless not negligible. The results of management performance in one enterprise — prompt delivery, repair services, etc. — become the 'material factors' determining the degree of success of management in another firm.

In one of Professor Turner's passing references to unionism in under-developed areas, he wrote that a concern with productivity might help unions to retain their independence. The verb should have been 'obtain'. It was doubtful that independent unions could exist, except in special circumstances, in countries in which independent modern social groups have not yet developed.

A number of variables determine the nature of unionism, which differs in different circumstances more than Professor Turner suggests. Nevertheless, basically, unions are protective organizations concerned with the relatively short run.

Dr. Turner's highly sophisticated proposal for a wage policy raises the question whether, if wage increases are sectional and differentiated to stimulate productivity, they can also be made compatible with the function of allocating labour which wage differentials must also perform.

Professor Kenneth F. Walker (Australia) asserted that, if it is possible to study economic organization scientifically, there must be broad principles common to the situation of the manager in both developed and under-developed countries. These principles must also articulate with our knowledge of the role of workers in economic development, since these are reciprocal roles. One such principle is surely that managers everywhere respond to pressures of competition and cost; as Clark Kerr has noted, 'the central point in managing the managers is placing them under the proper pressures to perform for society'. In this principle we find common ground between Dr. Carlson and Dr. Turner, for union pressure to raise wages above the rate of productivity growth can be an effective stimulus to raise productivity. So long as union pressure to raise wages cannot be passed on in higher prices, and so long as this wage pressure is not accompanied by enforcement of customary practices restricting efficiency, a strong labour movement may be a positive factor in the process of industrialization. The training and development of educated union leaders, skilled in negotiation and leadership, need attention as well as the development of managers.

A second broad principle is that productivity depends partly upon managerial leadership, and the extent to which it is effectively distributed throughout the various levels of the enterprise. This principle has been observed in operation in developed economies in a number of ways. Comparisons of absence and labour turnover rates in the same industry, for example, show very wide variations, much of which is attributable to differences in management. Studies by Likert and others have demonstrated a positive relation between certain styles of supervisory leadership and efficiency. Fleishman's investigations of the permanence of changes induced in supervisors' styles of leadership by training programmes showed that the leadership style of the supervisor's boss was a more powerful influence. This reveals, in a setting different from that described by Dr. Carlson, how a manager may be influenced by his environment; in particular, how an innovator may fare under conservative pressures. Productivity groups, which have mushroomed in Australia in the last five years, might provide a useful supporting environment in under-developed countries to encourage the manager and technician to innovate and to maintain his drive for productivity. Such groups are also a possible source for comparative study of smaller firms which, as Professor Carlson says, is more important than the study of the industrial giant. Linked with managerial development programmes such groups could form a valuable basis for continuing on-the-job education and for the systematic collection of case material and data on management problems as they occur in the actual working situation of the manager. They could thus help with two of the main problems of managerial development programmes, which are to inject realism and relevance into the programme and to maintain its effect after the initial impact.

A third broad principle which can be seen operating in economies of widely varying degrees of industrialization is that the logic of efficiency may be incongruent with prevailing social norms. After the smoke had risen from the warring interpretations of the Hawthorne studies, it became clear that economic organization never completely embodies the logic of efficiency and that no formal organization ever completely accommodates the personalities of its members. The proposition has been illustrated more dramatically in the process of industrialization of underdeveloped countries where the logic of efficiency has often clashed with social norms expressing non-western values.

Industrialization involves technological, sociological and psychological factors which must be integrated in new socio-technical systems. There is a great deal of evidence that each technology sets characteristic industrial and human relations problems. Studies have shown how the behaviour of industrial work groups varies according to their technological function, and also how managerial organization and practices have been shaped by differing technologies. While the effects of technology may be offset or altered by other factors, the human dimensions are always there, and if they are foreseen, some of the social costs of technological progress may be avoided. If the implications of technological change for industrial relations are ignored, unions may be driven into policies which put a brake on economic growth by enshrining out-dated customary working practices in an effort to prevent the social costs of progress from falling on the workers.

While we cannot expect that the interests of managers, workers and government will ever completely coincide, it does seem that the objective study of industrial enterprise as a socio-technical system in an economic and political environment offers the prospect of a common focus of concern with, and concerted efforts to reduce, the social costs of economic progress and to share them equitably.

Dr. Zofia Morecka (Poland) noted that Professor Carlson had limited himself to the problems of a free exchange economy. Whatever the scope of government intervention, it is not the liberal economy but the regulated one which has been chosen by many developing countries as the way to industrialization, regardless of their political system. That means the existence of a government plan of economic and social development, so that the individual firm operates in the external conditions created by economic planning. The main directions of economic activity are established in the plan — investment, structure of production, financing, etc. — and in that way the plan creates the framework within which management and workers can contribute to the increase of productivity.

One of the most difficult problems in the functioning of a planned economy is the erecting of a mechanism which ties the central plan with enterprises in a way which (a) enables the proper elaboration of the plan from the social and enterprise point of view and (b) encourages the proper realization of the plan. It seems impossible to attain the full identification of preferences of particular groups of workers, enterprises and society as a whole even in a socialist economy, particularly in the early stage of its development. Therefore, ways have to be sought to overcome short-run contradictions between individual and social interests. Various methods have been tried by socialist countries, of which the experiments of recent years in decentralization, which have been going on in all socialist countries, are an interesting example. There has been a variety of solutions, adjusted to specific national conditions, but they have all had the same goal : the achievement of active participation by employees in the management process.

Many interesting changes have been introduced into wage systems, strengthening the incentives to raise productivity. Apart from wage policy, strong non-material incentives may be created in a socialist economy, such as production democracy, the genuine participation of workers in management and the genuine influence of an enterprise on general economic planning.

Professor Turner discusses the role of trade unions in technical progress. In a socialist country, this problem is attacked first of all by giving the unions the right to participate in decision-making on all levels of the social organization. But this does not of course automatically ensure the workers' active co-operation. Other forms have been sought. One of these is a formal organization, separate from the trade unions, of workers' self-management in industry. It has been successful in some fields, particularly in the encouragement of innovations and in training, but some difficulties have arisen in the adjustment of this new form to the customary patterns of management.

The conclusion, based on the experience of socialist countries, is that there is a great variety of paths, methods and forms for the channelling of contributions of workers and management to increasing productivity. Social ownership of the means of production presents the greatest opportunity for industrialization and raising productivity, but it also involves some specific difficulties which must be solved.

Professor Bruno Stein (United States) suggested that 'productionist' unions were likely to be found in authoritarian countries. While from one point of view, the dues levied by them could be regarded as a useful form of taxation to support an auxiliary managerial class, it should be remembered that managerial skills are scarce in under-developed countries. The ingenuity of workers in under-developed countries is probably under-estimated — as t is in the advanced countries — and the attempt to tap this source, as distinct from the trade unions proper, is worth pursuing because the potential contribution is a significant one.

Dr. Philipp Rieger (Austria) asserted that another level existed on which workers' contributions to productivity growth could be made : the strong Austrian labour movement, aware of the close correlation between the growth of real national income and real wages, and of the importance of government policy on economic growth, is therefore aiming at '*Mitbestimmung*' (co-determination) at the national level. Professor Sturmthal's contention that the basic aim of unions is to protect the interests of the workers in the short run no longer describes the Austrian situation. Under modern conditions, even the short-run interests of the workers can be safe-guarded only if macro-economic policy decisions can be influenced. The Austrian labour movement has created special institutions, such as the Chambers of Labour, for making its influence on government economic policy felt. Similarly, a tripartite Price-Wage Commission was set up on the initiative of the Trade Union Federation as a novel experiment to contain cost-inflationary pressures. This was done with considerable opposition from the employers. A cut in tariffs was also forced by the unions. The rate of growth of real national income, which averaged 7 per cent a year in the last decade, will be closer to 4 per cent in the 1960s. This will create a difficult situation for the unions, and they are concerned with reaching the highest possible growth rate that the circumstances will allow.

Professor John P. Carter (United States) stated that Dr. Carlson need not fear that his remarks apply only to small countries ; they also apply to Indonesia, a country of 100 millions. It is a country with a very low level of skills, both managerial and technical. As Dr. Morecka pointed out, governmental restrictions need to be included in the list of factors with which the entrepreneur in a developing country must content. Government policies in Indonesia are both restrictive and volatile, and the prevalence of the 'return commission' (kickback) is not confined to the private sector.

Professor Melvin Reder asserted that it was asking too much of unions to give them a major responsibility for economic growth ; that would impose a severe internal strain on them. It is up to the monetary and fiscal authorities to police the system, and exert discipline on employers, so that they in turn will press the unions into line.

Mr. Gösta Rehn agreed that unions could not be expected to hold down their members' demands for wage increases. But the development of the restrictive, monopolistic type of trade unionism that started early in the United States and in Europe could be prevented by government action. A tradition of free entry could at least be established.

348

Record of Discussion

M. Pierre Gonod (France) suggested that, in the light of the many international differences among trade unions and union policies, the influence of trade unions on economic growth was a subject for research and not, in the present state of knowledge, for generalization.

In summing up, *Professor Carlson* expressed his gratitude to Dr. Morecka for her survey of management problems in a planned society. With the external conditions set for them by the government, they had only to concentrate on techniques and organization of production. As some of the comments had pointed out, his paper did indeed emphasize the external environment of the firm, because it presented more serious problems in under-developed countries than any of the internal issues. He was also grateful to Professor Walker for reporting on the management groups in Australia ; they would be a good source of information on the middle-sized firm. Professor Sturmthal wanted to know which countries he was writing about : he had in mind Latin America, Southern Italy, Turkey — countries where a merchant class exists and where, if they are not worrying about problems of taxation, they should be.

Professor Turner stated that he would accept many of the comments which had been made on his paper. He was particularly interested in M. Gonod's suggestion that the relationship between trade unionism and economic development called for extensive inter-disciplinary investigation. Too much of the thinking on the subject has run in terms of artificial concepts, too-rigid characteristics. Witness all the references in the last day or two to 'unions in advanced capitalist' or in 'socialist' societies or the characterizing of trade unions in under-developed countries as possible 'nuisances'. These sharp dichotomies and distinctions blur the interesting fact that certain convergences have been taking place. In the non-communist countries, pressure has been developing in the unions for economic growth and planning. In the communist countries, pressure has been exerted by the unions towards the democratization of existing planning processes. Professor Sturmthal's conception of trade unions as essentially protectionist is very conservative ; trade unions all over are interested in economic development.

Are trade unions in developing countries a 'nuisance'? They can be. But they can also be useful, not only in the political sphere, but in contributing to economic development. They may help in the adaptation of employees to a new pattern of society, and the system of responses which industrialization demands — particularly to the idea of the labour market. They can provide personal service and social support which were formerly provided by the traditional society. They can be helpful in administration : for example, in developing a wage structure, through consultation and collective negotiation. Despite their fundamentally protectionist role, they can be productionist as well.

349

Chapter 20

EVALUATION OF FACTORS
AFFECTING PRODUCTIVITY

BY

JOHN T. DUNLOP
Harvard University

I. SOME PRELIMINARY POINTS

PRODUCTIVITY is the end result of a complex social process
including : science, research and development, education, technology, management, production facilities, workers and labour
organizations. These factors may be under private or public direction, or they may reflect varying combinations of private and public
activity. Productivity cannot be increased in any country or under
any social system by simple decree. An increase in output per man-
hour or output *per capita* for a country reflects the energy and ingenuity of its whole people. A century of increasing productivity
involves contributions from all industrializing mankind.

Any list of the factors affecting productivity will vary according
as the centre of interest is the productivity of a particular operation,
plant, industry, or an economy as a whole. As with so many other
problems in economics, it is essential to specify what is fixed and
what is variable for the task at hand. In treating the productivity of
a particular plant or industry, the technology of other sectors which
supply materials and equipment and the level of education in the
community, for instance, are appropriately treated as given. These
sessions of the International Economic Association are rather
concerned with the productivity of an economy as a whole
and quite appropriately with factors affecting productivity in the
long run.

A listing of the factors affecting productivity will also vary
depending upon whether the central purpose is general analysis,
policy prescription or quantitative measurement. Such specialized
purposes will dictate particular definitions or groupings of factors.
For some purposes it may be significant to measure the effect of
the changing composition of output or changing industrial structure
upon productivity. The shift of labour from farm to non-farm
industries in the United States, for example, in the period 1909 to

350

1941 is estimated to have raised the annual rate of productivity increase from 1·84 per cent to 2·11 per cent a year.[1] Kuznets estimates more generally that inter-industry shifts account for four-tenths of the total rise in net national product per worker in the United States in the period 1869–1948.[2] But such statistically oriented classifications of the factors affecting productivity, important as they are for many purposes, are not the central interest of these sessions.

The role of the separate factors affecting productivity varies with the given endowments and resources of a country. In one country natural resources may be scarce while human resources may be highly developed ; in another country the reverse situation may prevail. Egypt and Iraq have been contrasted in these terms.[3] The resource situation of a country at any stage of development serves to constrain or to stimulate productivity.

This discussion is concerned with countries already embarked on industrialization. The problems initiating industrialization are presumed to have been overcome. '. . . On even the most preliminary view of the problem, effective government, education and social justice emerge as critically important. In many countries, in diagnosing the barriers to advance, it is lack of these that is of critical importance.' [4] Moreover, our programme invites attention to the factors now operating to increase productivity rather than to those that may have been operative in the early instances of industrialization. The task is to identify the factors — in policy terms, the levers — that tend to increase or even accelerate productivity today in countries at various stages on the road to the industrial society. This discussion is first concerned with the common or the universal factors increasing productivity.

II. THE UNIVERSAL FACTORS

1. *Science and Discovery.* 'The growing capacity of the economy to make technological discoveries has within the last several decades

[1] John W. Kendrick, 'National Productivity and Its Long-Term Projection', in *Long-Range Economic Projection*, Studies in Income and Wealth, XVI, Conference on Income and Wealth, National Bureau of Economic Research, Princeton, Princeton University Press, 1954, p. 95.

[2] Simon Kuznets, Ed., *Income and Wealth of the United States, Trends and Structure*, Series II, International Association for Research in Income and Wealth, Baltimore, The Johns Hopkins Press, 1954, p. 126.

[3] Frederick Harbison, 'Two Centers of Arab Power', *Foreign Affairs*, July 1959, pp. 1-12.

[4] John Kenneth Galbraith, *Economic Development in Perspective*, Cambridge, Harvard University Press, 1962, pp. 9-10.

given rise to the industry of discovery. The rise of this new industry has been far more important than any one of the great inventions that collectively make up the industrial revolution.' [1] The isolated inventor has become relatively less significant compared to the research and development organization. 'There is now an increasing scientific base for technology ; the steam engine antedated thermo-dynamics, but the applications of atomic energy were developed from a discovery in physics.' [2]

The new industry of discovery holds out the prospect not only of increasing productivity but even of an acceleration in productivity. Modern science and research and development are inherently dynamic. New ideas, products, materials and methods are its output. If scientific advance were to be turned off, productivity levels in many developing countries could no doubt continue to increase and to catch up to the economically advanced countries for many years. But further increases in productivity in the most advanced countries would be severely constricted. It now appears that in the advanced countries productivity is now increasing at a faster rate than earlier. Solomon Fabricant reports for the United States : 'A distinct change in trend appeared some time after World War I. By each of our measures, productivity rose on the average more rapidly after World War I than before.' [3] This greater rate of increase has often been attributed to the new role of science.

The new industry of discovery is world wide in its impact. Science and technology know no national boundaries ; they speak in a universal language. 'Science is non-national, singularly independent of the form of government, the immediate tradition, or the affective life of a people.' [4] While pioneering research and development may yield temporarily a significant economic advantage to a country, and continuing innovation may be a significant export industry, modern science and technology assure that any given significant innovation is likely to be emulated.

2. *Educational System.* Education is the 'handmaiden of industrialism',[5] and the educational system is one of the major policy levers of a country seeking to influence productivity over the long

[1] Sumner H. Slichter, *Economic Growth in the United States, Its History, Problems, and Perspective*, Louisiana State University Press, 1961, p. 102.
[2] American Assembly, *Automation and Technological Change*, Prentice-Hall, Inc., 1962.
[3] *Basic Facts on Productivity Change*, Occasional Paper 63, National Bureau of Economic Research, New York, 1959, p. 10.
[4] J. Robert Oppenheimer, *The Open Mind* (New York : Simon and Schuster, 1955), p. 121.
[5] Clark Kerr, John T. Dunlop, Frederick Harbison and Charles A. Myers, *Industrialism and Industrial Man*, Cambridge, Harvard University Press, 1960, p. 36.

period. The primary, secondary and vocational schools and the universities largely shape the versatility and capacity of a work force to be trained and retrained to accord to the occupational and skill demands of industrializing societies. / Moreover, the higher educational system and professional schools supply the critical high talent man-power — scientists, engineers, doctors, executives and administrators. While education is in part a consumer good, desired for its own sake, the educational system has a direct impact on the capacity of a country to increase productivity. Investment in man is not an entirely new idea, since Adam Smith recognized the significance to a nation of 'the skill, dexterity and judgment with which its labour is generally applied'.[1] 'The improvement in the productive powers of labour' today must be attributed more to the educational system than to the effects of the division of labour as Smith did.

3. *Management.* Productivity depends significantly upon the way resources are combined and directed at the enterprise or industry level. This is the task of management, private or public, and the term here is used to include activities of the entrepreneur, innovator and organizer, to use language from a particular social system. But all industrializing countries require managers, and while their functions vary and while societies place them under different constraints and provide different rewards, they have a central operational role everywhere in affecting productivity.[2]

4. *Capital.* The capital to secure plant and equipment and the social overheads is everywhere recognized as decisive to productivity.[3] A high rate of capital formation and a high rate of savings from incremental income were at one stage of the discussion of developing countries regarded almost as the sole requisite for economic growth. But the more recent emphasis on the role of human resources and institutional change does not preclude a central role for capital formation in rising productivity. The capital may come from abroad or from within ; it may be secured from agriculture or natural resources of industrial profits or surplus.

But capital is not an unchanged quantum. In the last half of the nineteenth century in the United States, it appears that capital per unit of output tended to increase. Since World War I, capital-output ratios have declined slightly or remained constant. This recent development has been associated with an increase in the

[1] Adam Smith, *The Wealth of Nations*, Introduction.
[2] Frederick Harbison and Charles A. Myers, *Management in the Industrial World*, New York, McGraw-Hill Book Company, Inc., 1959.
[3] Simon Kuznets, *Six Lectures on Economic Growth*, Glencoe, Illinois, The Free Press, 1959.

amount of energy per unit of industrial capital and marked improvements in managerial organizations.

5. *Labour Force.* The labour force in a number of ways is a determinant of productivity. The size of the labour force, the hours of work and the skill and other qualities of the labour force are among the policy levers. Every industrializing society is concerned to build a labour force [1] — to see that it is recruited, trained and disciplined, committed to industrial life, upgraded to changing requirements and protected from the hazards of industrial life. While the educational system, as has been noted, is significant to the quality of a labour force, the reference here is to those qualities largely developed at the work place.

6. *Motivations.* The productivity of a country, with given natural resource endowments, also depends upon the energy, effort and imagination which the labour force applies to its tasks. Although industrializing countries differ with respect to the ideals and drives which motivate a devotion to duty and responsibility for performance of the work force, they all are concerned to develop an ideology, an ethic, and organizations at the work place to attain high standards. 'Strict supervision and exacting management imposed on a lethargic work force will not suffice ; the personal responsibility for performance and the achievement of norms of quantity and quality of output must be implanted within workers, front-line supervisors and top-managers to be truly effective.' [2]

The concern to increase productivity has resulted in widespread interest among workers and managers alike in incentive methods of pay, bonuses, communication programmes and work level committees. The activities of trade unions, workers councils, joint consultative committees and the like are in varying degree related to the quest for higher efficiency and productivity.[3] There appears to be abundant evidence that workers and managers do not consistently perform at par, and various organizational forms and incentives are sought in different industrializing societies to stimulate, to entice or to compel greater productivity.

The universal factors decisive to productivity listed above are arbitrary in the sense that the list of six could have been compressed to a few or expanded many-fold in order to highlight particular factors in particular countries. There is no need for controversy over such a listing since these factors may be readily subdivided or combined for particular purposes.

[1] Clark Kerr, John T. Dunlop, Frederick Harbison, and Charles A. Myers, *op. cit.*, pp. 165-92.   [2] *Ibid.* p. 43.
[3] H. A. Clegg, *A New Approach to Industrial Democracy*, Oxford, Basil Blackwell, 1960, pp. 81-128.

III. THE PARTICULAR COMBINATION OF FACTORS

The universal factors affecting productivity operate within the limits of the size and natural resource endowments of a country. But the relative significance of these factors on productivity also depends upon the general policies of the elite directing the course and pace of industrialization and upon the stage of industrialization.

1. At the earlier stages of industrialization countries appear to be relatively more concerned with capital accumulation, elementary education and training the labour force, and motivating their people for higher productivity. The population is likely to be close to the traditional society, and the immediate and most oppressive limitations on economic growth require these factors. The traditional society, its family pattern, educational system, culture and values are likely to be resistant in some respects to industrialization and high productivity. The habits of saving, mobility, industrial discipline and urban life often have yet to be established. '. . . The requirements for growth call for a high degree of adaptability to new things and new ways on the part of both consumers and workers.'[1]

The more advanced the stage of economic development, the greater the relative emphasis upon science and technology, the university and professional educational system and managerial development as factors to increase productivity. These factors cannot so readily be imported or borrowed when the country tends to be pushing the limits of knowledge and techniques. While all the factors are operative in advanced countries, the first three are relatively more significant.

2. The first three factors — science, high-level education and management — also tend to be the more decisive factors affecting productivity in the long run. It would be interesting to speculate upon what would have been the increase in productivity in the past hundred years if science, the educational system and management organizations had remained unchanged even though all other factors operative to increase productivity had been fully exploited. While the question is non-operational, there would no doubt be a consensus that the increase in productivity would have been only a very small fraction of the actual record in the advanced countries. It would be in error to derogate the role of capital formation, training the labour force and motivation, but their significance is more short run and more limited in ultimate impact.

3. The factors which are most important as long-run determinants

[1] E. S. Mason, *Promoting Economic Development, The United States and Southern Asia*, Claremont, California, 1955, p. 37.

of productivity are also the factors which are most readily transferable among countries and tend to be most uniform among countries in advanced industrialization. Technology, high-level education and professional management are likely to become more similar among advanced countries to conform to the necessities of modern science and industry. The limitations of resource endowments and the culture of a traditional society are likely over the long run to be less decisive on productivity as industrialization advances. Regardless of their traditions, origins or social system, advanced industrial societies are tending gradually to become more similar by virtue of the impact of these universal factors.

4. There are very considerable differences among industrializing countries in the way in which the universal factors are utilized or organized to affect productivity. Thus these factors may be well adapted or poorly co-ordinated to contribute to increased productivity. There may or may not be any close relation between science and production technology. The aggregate amount and the relative expenditures on primary, secondary and high-level education may be inappropriate to the emerging needs and opportunities of a country. The educational system may not place sufficient emphasis upon the new professions required in industrial society and may be oriented too long to traditional subjects and values. The enterprise managers may lack professional training and may be too oriented to family or party to perform most efficiently. National leaders vary in their sense of urgency and determination to industrialize, and countries vary in their rates of capital formation, even recognizing that natural endowments and stage of development affect the capacity to generate capital. Countries vary in the proportion of the population in the labour force, the use of women in industry and the methods used to train, to shift and to adapt the work force. There are likewise wide differences in methods of wage payments, institutions at the work place and ideologies, ethics and methods used to motivate the work force.

Thus, there are great differences in the way in which different countries — apart from natural resources and stages of development — use the universal factors to influence productivity. In part these diversities arise from fundamental strategies of the elite leading industrialization and in part from the variations in the effectiveness of the policies adopted.

A steady or accelerating increase in productivity is the end product of a complex social process in any country. The major factors or policy levers — apart from natural endowment of a country — tend to be universal. These major factors are science and technology, education, management, capital formation, the labour force and the motivation of workers and managers. The first three of this list tend to be more long run and more fundamental; the last three, more short run and more significant to countries at the earlier stages of economic development. But different elites directing the industrialization process of a country use these factors in different ways. As a consequence, apart from natural resources and stages of development, there are quite different rates of economic growth and increases in productivity.

DISCUSSION OF THE PAPER BY PROFESSOR DUNLOP

Chairman : DR. BURKART LUTZ

Professor G. A. Prudensky (U.S.S.R.) opened the discussion by noting that Professor Dunlop's paper, and indeed the deliberations of the congress, analysed the question of labour productivity much more broadly and thoroughly than the conference on labour productivity at Cadenabbia in 1961. Increasing significance is being attributed to the human factor, and this is undoubtedly a progressive step. The labour force is in fact the main productive force, and Professor Dunlop should have put it in the first group (in his oral presentation) rather than the second.

In the proceedings here, the whole complex of factors affecting productivity has been fully explored : the role of science and technology, the human factor, various regional features, foreign trade, etc. While some of the speakers thought it was possible to abstract from specific regional features affecting productivity, he did not think that this aspect could be neglected, and if he was not mistaken, Professor Dunlop agreed with him on this point.

A methodological note : in economics, reliability of measurement plays a significant role. It is necessary to bear in mind that the traditional method of measuring productivity is only a rough approximation ; and it certainly does not permit the isolation of the contribution of individual factors. Therefore the task now is to develop new methods of analysing productivity growth, particularly through the adaptation of input-output analysis.

Professor Prudensky had been asked by the chairman of the section to give a brief description of the Soviet system of analysing 'reserves of productivity growth', a subject on which much research has been done and which is, at the same time, a practical planning technique in actual use. 'Reserves' include both planned stocks (raw materials, finished goods, etc.), which are an important aspect of planning, and untapped potentialities for productivity growth. The latter covers a wide range, from the improvement of wasteful and uneconomic resource use, including labour time, to the development of new technological methods. Reserves are estimated for the shortest planning period, a month, up to the long-range plans, in which case they include new capital investment. The indexes used in the analysis of reserves are labour productivity, cost of production, continuity of production, utilization of capacity and quality of output. Since the measurement of separate factor influences upon the economic indexes cannot be complete, because of the interrelationships of the factors, the goal of the thorough study of reserves is to help reveal the possibilities for increases in production.

Professor Denison expatiated on some of the points made by Professor Dunlop. 'Productivity', he had stated, 'cannot be increased in any country or under any social system by simple decree.' What is required is some action which would not have occurred otherwise. And in almost every important case these steps to increase productivity impose real costs. Since maximum output is obviously not the only goal of society, policy can be sensibly formulated only by quantitative comparison of costs and benefits, and this holds whether decisions are made by private individuals or by governments. Economics can contribute little unless it can provide quantitative measures of benefits and costs.

Professor Dunlop also stated that a listing of the factors affecting productivity will vary depending on the purposes of the investigation. This is true in another sense than his illustration suggests. There is an important distinction between the factors that may have produced growth in the past, and the factors that might be influenced to alter the future growth rate of a country. For example trade barriers that have remained unchanged over a period, and could not be considered a cause of growth, might, by their elimination, raise productivity and contribute to future growth. In the United States, Professor Dunlop's sixth category, motivations, may be such a case : assuming that they have not changed much in recent decades, they would not be listed as an important source of past growth ; yet there may be important possibilities of improving motivation and raising productivity — for example, by greater use of certain types of incentive pay systems.

The time perspective is also crucial. Most improvements are one-shot actions, which move the growth rate to a higher level without changing its subsequent slope. If eliminating trade barriers raised national income by 2 per cent overnight, 2 per cent would be added to the growth rate computed over a one-year period, but only one-tenth of a point in a growth rate computed over twenty years. Lags are another aspect of the time perspective. An additional year of schooling for each student would add an estimated 0·1 per cent to the growth rate for the United States for the next fifty years, but would add nothing in the first decade when the improvement in the quality of the small proportion of the work force affected would be cancelled by the loss of work of those who remained in school.

Professor Dunlop had indicated what he considered the most important elements of productivity increase. A study of the sources of growth in the United States in 1929–57, which required, admittedly, some strong assumptions, yielded the following results :

The improved quality of labour accounted for 36 per cent of the total increase of real national income per person employed (which amounted to 1·6 per cent per annum). This was the net result of favourable and unfavourable changes. The most significant favourable change was that the average member of the working force in 1957 had spent 4 or 5 more years in school than the average member in 1929, an enormous increase in a 28-year period, accounting for an estimated 42 per cent of the total. There was also a change in the average experience of women workers as many became permanent members of the labour force — plus 7 per cent. Shortening of working hours from 2530 to 2060 a year was the main negative factor, with allowance for the fact that work performed did not decline in the same proportion — minus 12 per cent. An additional minus 1 per cent was charged to a small unfavourable shift in the age and sex composition of the labour force.

The quantity of land per person employed declined, accounting for minus 3 per cent of the growth rate. Capital per man increased, but not greatly ; 9 per cent was ascribed to this factor. Thus 42 per cent of the increase in output per man was due to increased input of resources per person employed, including the improved quality of labour itself. The remaining 58 per cent was due to the increased output per unit of input : 21 per cent to economies of scale associated with the growth of the national economy and regional and local markets, and 37 per cent to the contribution of managerial and technical knowledge (the residual in the calculation). This last factor did not include the improvement of products and the introduction of new products, to which the bulk of research and development expenditures are devoted, since the measurement of net product per man does not include them ; i.e. new or improved products result in no greater national product than if the resources used for their production were devoted to previously existing products.

These results apply only to the period 1929–57. A very different breakdown was arrived at for 1909–29, when, for example, the contribution of capital was much greater and that of education much less. On the whole, these results, tentative as they are, support Professor Dunlop's judgment that science and technology, education and management are the more fundamental long-run factors of growth in advanced countries. His emphasis on the importance of human as against material resources is supported by the experience of the United States.

Mr. Edgar Salin (Switzerland) suggested that the modern belief in factors which are capable of quantitative measurement, combined with the assumption that all nations, religions and races have a common goal, industrialization, have led to the underestimating of the countervailing forces. Max Weber showed the close relationship between the ethics of Puritanism and the capitalistic 'Geist'. An example of the strong anti-industrial force, religious or traditional, which exists outside the European and American continents, can be found in the case of Tibet. He thought that perhaps the special problems of under-developed countries had also been underestimated. Not only savings and investment are important in development, but also natural resources (particularly sources of energy) and export opportunities, which played such an important role in the development of the western countries. Nor should the fundamental importance of the political climate be overlooked.

Professor John Kendrick commented, with respect both to Professor Dunlop's list of factors and to Dr. Denison's sources of growth in the United States, that the various causal factors were in practice interrelated. For example the improvement in the educational level in the United States would not have been so fruitful if technology had remained constant; the contribution of education and technology was in reality a joint product. Furthermore, the continued acceleration of productivity growth from research and development expenditures is doubtful. For under-developed countries too, this source of growth will slow down as they approach the frontiers of knowledge.

M. Pierre Gonod agreed with Professor Dunlop's conclusions. He gave an account of the situation in France, where post-war productivity increases were largely attributable to the growth of the labour force. Research on growth factors was being carried on in conjunction with development planning, because insufficient data on productivity gave rise to one of the principal uncertainties in forecasting. Diffusion of best practice techniques was known to be an important source of future growth; the gap in the building industry, for example, between average and best practice productivity was 40 per cent.

Mr. Felix Trappaniers reported that comparative research had indicated that the structure of labour productivity was similar in many countries despite different levels of productivity; average productivity depended to a large extent on the structure of production, on the types of products resources were concentrated on. He would add to Professor Dunlop's list demand, both internal and external.

Professor Carl Knoellinger characterized Professor Dunlop's list of factors as incomplete unless he was describing a closed economy. He suggested the specific recognition of the gains from foreign trade and the international division of labour.

Mr. Juan Alemann (Argentina) would add another fundamental factor to Professor Dunlop's list: political stability. Argentina had an unusual productivity problem: that of a decrease. Political instability created economic instability. There was extensive government interference in the economic sphere, but it could not be termed planning.

Mr. Kjell Eide requested clarification of Professor Dunlop's statements on the relative importance of the factors affecting productivity at different stages of development. He obviously did not mean that the absolute amount of resources allocated to these important factors should be larger, that resources devoted to research, for example, should ever exceed those allocated to new physical capital. Bearing in mind the high degree of complementarity among the factors, and the wide differences in national policies concerning them, the identification of 'bottleneck' factors at each stage of development probably requires detailed studies in each individual country. Would Professor Dunlop say that it was a mistake for Yugoslavia to devote a relatively greater proportion of her resources to education, even to higher education, than do more advanced countries such as Germany, Belgium and the Netherlands? Considerable caution should be exercised at this stage of knowledge in drawing general conclusions.

Mr. R. Ulavic (Yugoslavia) spoke briefly on the functioning of the worker-management system in Yugoslavia. The organization of work has been much improved, and workers try to educate themselves on the problems of the firm, the technical problems of industry, etc. But there have been some negative effects on productivity : small firms here as elsewhere resist new techniques that may render some of the work force redundant ; a conflict arises between the welfare of the firm and the welfare of the society, with some enterprises retaining too much of their earnings ; and there is a conflict between the remuneration policy needed to overcome the shortage of engineers and efficient managers and the requirements of an egalitarian philosophy.

Dr. Jan Auerhan (Czechoslovakia) asked Professor Dunlop if he could give a rough estimate of the time lag between the development of an innovation and its application in production, a point which is important for planning estimates. He wondered why capital had not been classified among the easily transferable factors.

M. Hubert Sainmont (France) also stressed the interrelationship of all the factors affecting productivity.

Professor Dunlop made a general reply to the questions raised in the discussion under the following points :

1. In the general framework presented in his paper, as in any situation, certain dimensions must be taken as given. Marshall had noted that much confusion in economics resulted from failure to distinguish between what is fixed and what is variable. Revolution and political disturbances preclude an interest in productivity ; economists have to take political stability as given. Certain ideas and motivations must be present in a country before development can occur : in some countries these were embodied in the Protestant Ethic ; in others, in a form of nationalism or ideology. Again, economists must take this as given.

2. It is important to distinguish between the pursuit of economic knowledge and advice on policy questions. The under-developed countries are not going to wait until we decide on the determinants of productivity.

The world is impatient. Scientific work should of course continue at the same time.

3. It is true that all factors interract, but that does not get us very far. Policy levers were what he had sought to identify ; focal points for the policy makers.

4. The role of science and discoveries is increasing. We have not yet begun to see their impact ; we are still on the threshold of the scientific age. He did not agree with Professor Kendrick that constantly increasing expenditures were required for the application of science to technology.

5. The time lag between invention and application is a fascinating question. In the practical world, a rule of thumb is used which puts the period at 5 to 10 years.

6. Productivity growth was not merely a national but an international problem. Capital was certainly mobile, and he had erred in not listing it as such. Foreign trade was definitely important.

7. Too little is known about the factors affecting productivity and their interrelations in different types of societies. He would enter a plea for two types of studies : comparative research on an international basis, an enormous field for work ; and studies within countries on the separate impact of the various factors affecting productivity.

Chapter 21

ROUND TABLE DISCUSSION OF
PROBLEMS OF INDIVIDUAL COUNTRIES

BY SECTION 2 CHAIRMAN

PROFESSOR S. TSURU

Hitotsubashi University

Professor Elliot Berg opened the discussion with a general summary of the situation in Africa. On the aggregate level, the importance of structural changes in early industrialization mentioned by several speakers is particularly great. Until recently, concern with the efficient use of labour resources was secondary ; the major problem was to find the man-power required by the expanding money economy. To induce men to enter wage employment, it was often necessary to permit partial commitment : e.g. the 'task work' system in agriculture and construction, under which men could quit after fixed daily tasks were completed, and the 'ticket system', under which a worker received a month's pay when he had had his ticket punched thirty times. Both methods were in a sense wasteful and chaotic, but they did encourage men to enter wage employment.

On the level of the firm, scarcity of indigenous managerial talent is a severe obstacle to expansion. In all of sub-Sahara Africa, there is probably not a single modern firm with more than one hundred employees which is owned and managed by Africans. Some recent studies by Peter Kilby have indicated the very large differences in productivity between firms in the same industry, apparently due to management factors. The shortage of lower-level supervisors is also acute.

Productivity on the individual worker level has received little attention here, probably because of the implicit assumption that there are no inherent human differences. But the environment may be a problem. The heat and the humidity in much of Africa seem *prima facie* to slow down the tempo of work. Furthermore, the climate is associated with the prevalence of a host of chronic diseases and parasites, which have a general debilitating effect. A puzzling fact, however, is that the most obvious inefficiencies of African labourers appear not in the unskilled categories requiring intense physical effort, nor in the semi-skilled jobs requiring repetitive

363

operations or adjustment to machine rhythms, but in the more complex operations. This would suggest that physical environmental factors are probably not of overriding significance in the productivity picture.

Perhaps more than half the working force in Africa is not yet wholly committed to industrial life. The mythology that Africans do not respond positively to monetary incentives has fortunately been dispelled. It is certainly untrue for the fully committed worker, and although there are still 'target workers' among migrant work forces of some countries, their number is declining.

In short, it appears that while the physical and cultural environment in Africa is less favourable to high productivity than in gentler climates and less traditional societies, the low productivity levels in Africa are due in greater part to factors of skill and organization.

In the past decade in most of Africa, there have been significant increases in output per man in the industrial sector. The first reason is the high rate of capital formation : gross investment was over 40 per cent of GNP in the Rhodesias in some years, and in the Congo around 30 per cent in the early part of the decade. In the French African countries, it was about 20 per cent. In few countries was it less than 15 per cent. The second reason was the rise in wage levels which occurred in many countries and which led to more economical use of labour. Future possibilities for increases are associated with the general economic growth, which cannot be gone into here. It should be noted that increases in man-hour output are probably less important than increases in employment levels in the near future.

Among other factors affecting productivity, the major obstacle to the expansion of productivity in the decade ahead is the secondary-school bottleneck, in relation to the need for lower-level supervisors. Nowhere except in Ghana and Nigeria is the anticipated flow anywhere in sight of expected needs.

Another factor is a political one, the goal of Africanization of posts of responsibility. It is understandable, but the forced updraft of people is bound to exact a price in terms of efficiency. Another heritage of colonialism is the absence of an individual sense of responsibility, and care-free job performance, reflected in the neglect of maintenance of equipment, which has carried over into independence.

A peculiar fact is the widespread alienation of intellectuals ; university-trained Africans tend to regard governing parties with at best a lack of enthusiasm. In some instances, they refrain from serving the government or even leave the country. Not many of the

African doctors and engineers in London or Paris or elsewhere are actually political exiles, but the existence of an international market for high-level man-power, and the real attractions of employment in advanced countries, require some countervailing force, some ideological impetus, if highly-trained Africans are to be kept at home. And this pull rarely exists.

Industrial relations are unsatisfactory. After independence the party tends to take over the control of the trade unions. One result has been increasing difficulty in handling ordinary disputes and grievances of an industrial character. With channels of communication clogged between the workers and the political leadership at the top, grievances tend to fester and to erupt in what appears to the government to be near-revolt.

There are also compensating factors on the political side, most important of which are probably the unleashing of energy, the will to modernize, which come with independence. This is the most important positive force. Except for the development of the will to grow, the prospect for Africa is, on balance, not cheerful.

Professor Kannappan sketched the situation in India. With a population of 440 million (and 14 major languages), employment in the modern sector, including industry, commerce, railroads, post and telegraph, totalled 7-8 million, to which should be added the 5 million in public administration. The bulk of the population and nearly half the GNP are accounted for by agriculture. Labour productivity has increased for two main reasons : the growth of employment in the new, more capital-intensive industries, and the reduction of the labour surplus in the traditional industries (jute, cotton textiles). Emphasis in planning has been on the development of heavy industry and particularly the production of import substitutes. Perhaps inevitably, costs of these products have risen above the world market. Professional managerial and skilled personnel are in short supply. The educational level of the labour force is low.

The trade unions are headed by lawyers and politicians who have more interest in inter-union rivalry than in industry. The system of industrial relations is dominated by government machinery, including compulsory conciliation. Joint employer-union consultation and negotiation are limited, and grievances accumulate.

Until recently, education was oriented strongly toward the liberal arts, with government service the goal. In both industry and government, the administrator dominated the technician. But this is changing. Management training is growing, and with it a tendency to professionalize management. The need for the technical training of the labour force is being felt increasingly. But the most critical area is middle-level management, which at present does not provide efficient supervision.

Mr. Juan Alemann described the non-Europeans in Latin America as 'having no interest in progress or a higher standard of living'. In South Africa, there is a high correlation between *per capita* income and the proportions of Europeans in the total population.

Professor Drewnowski (Ghana) supported Professor Berg on many aspects of productivity in Africa. Although there was a lack of data, productivity was undoubtedly rising with the shift from less to more productive employment. There was some dispute over whether agriculture should be modernized or whether in some branches traditional methods were not in fact better suited to conditions. The tightest manpower bottleneck was the secondary schools, from which middle-level management comes.

Mr. Labhras O'Nuallain (Ireland) suggested that the experience of the Republic of Ireland in the last three to four decades might be of particular relevance to under-developed countries, because its intermediate stage of development was one in which they might find themselves in ten years. Ireland too had secured its independence in fairly recent times.

Of a static population of 2·8 million, of whom 1·1 million are in the labour force, 37 per cent are in agriculture, a very high proportion for Europe, and only 18 per cent in industry. Nevertheless, industry contributes 28 per cent of the national income. *Per capita* national income is $600.

Since 1931 the Republic has followed a policy of high protection and the fostering of domestic manufacturing, with a consequent expansion of the consumer goods industries. Yet up to 1956 the rate of increase in GNP was 1 per cent per annum — virtual stagnation.

Like a number of developing countries, Ireland is very much a one-commodity producer : e.g. of total agricultural exports (constituting over half of all exports), live cattle and livestock products amounted to 75 per cent. Three-quarters of her exports were to Britain, and half of her imports were from Britain.

A recent census revealed an actual fall in population in 1956–61 because of an annual net emigration. This was a salutary shock to the country's pride. A change in pace had already begun to occur after a change in government in 1957, followed by the preparation of an expansion programme. The formation of the European Economic Community, with which Ireland hopes to be associated, also fostered a growth psychology. There has been a decided quickening of interest in economic development.

For that reason among others, production and employment have begun to expand. The rate of growth rose from 1 to 4·5 per cent in each of the three years 1959–61, and emigration has been reduced.

There are many similarities between Ireland and the developing countries elsewhere. Tradition is strong, and innovation and change (in ideas and in production) meet with resistance. Education is classical, and geared to turn out lawyers, doctors, priests and politicians. Industry and commerce carried little prestige until recently. The problem of developing Irish entrepreneurship was acute, and management has begun to provide training courses itself.

For some time wage increases have outpaced productivity increases in manufacturing. In part because of negotiations for entry into the Common Market, there has been increasing concern with costs. Trade unions and employers are trying to arrive at a general policy on wages and prices, and to increase productivity.

Although Ireland cannot yet be said to have reached the take-off point into self-sustained economic development, it has gone beyond the creeping stage and is now approaching the starting gate.

There are serious obstacles to the continued increase of productivity in Greece, *Professor D. J. Delivanis* reported, despite the 6·5 per cent rate of growth of GNP in the last two years. There is a lack of continuity in the economic policies of the government, with a large gap between plans and achievements, and the public services — post, fuel, transportation — are both expensive and inferior. In government and business, decision making is over-centralized, waste is widespread and, as a concomitant of the dislike for manual work, know-how is limited. Entry to some of the professions — e.g. law — is closed to all but the sons of the current practitioners. In general, vested interests are very strong. Greece's association with the Common Market will have a healthy influence on these monopolies, although it has been given a long period, 22 years, to adjust fully. As in Ireland, there is substantial emigration, and of the best young people. Perhaps the effect of this will in time oblige Greek firms and the public services to rationalize. Only remittances from the emigrants and a large capital inflow have made it possible to maintain equilibrium in the balance of payments.

Mr. Karol Krotki (Pakistan) reported that there had been remarkable development in Pakistan after 1947. But he believed that the African situation was more hopeful than the Asian, although Dr. Berg and Dr. Kannappan had given the opposite impression. A principal reason was demographic; and population should not be included in Dr. Dunlop's 'given' factors — it may be the most important variable. There was elbow room in Africa, none in Asia. In Asia, also, societies seem much more set in their ways, much more resistant to change. He could not agree with other points made by Dr. Berg : the lack of maintenance of capital was a habit in Africa, and not an expression of anti-colonialism ; and the 'alienation' of intellectuals was not an intellectual or a political phenomenon but the simple and understandable desire to live, when possible, in the more comfortable West. Professor Carlson's account of the external problems faced by management was realistic but not complete : tariff walls, overvalued currencies accompanied by export bonuses, the Moslem attitude toward the rate of interest, non-productive hoarding and the tradition of wasteful expenditure — all these hampered development. He thought education was one remedy, but education directed towards the practical needs of developing countries. The African and Asian professional men who had had the educational opportunities were highly skilled, but there were no alphabetical telephone books in circulation.

Professor Carl Anderson (United States) stated, of the secondary-school bottleneck cited by several earlier speakers, that it was temporary ; the number of secondary schools was increasing. On the other hand, it should be noted that there were many unemployed among the educated minority. The shortage of trained man-power was worse, he thought, at the highest levels. The *kind* of education was not the cause but the result of development ; he disagreed with Mr. Krotki on this point. At any rate, technical education should be given on the job and not in the schools.

Among the problems faced by educators in under-developed countries were the language problem in some places — a western language had to be taught — and the absence of a supporting culture outside the schools. For example, children enter school with no manual dexterity ; in the West, children have acquired this from playing with toys. A society cannot be built by the schools ; they are a reflection rather than a prime cause.

Dr. Pitamber Pant (India) questioned whether the ideals of people anywhere were an obstacle to development. In most countries there was no manifest disapproval of good living and enjoyment of material goods. On India : its aim was to achieve the maximum balanced rate of growth and to reduce the disparities between sectors to a minimum. It could not hope to achieve the *per capita* United States level — which would, in any case, require for India a total GNP equal to that of the United States, the Soviet Union and Europe, combined. The conflict between productivity and employment was acute in India ; to raise productivity in agriculture, surplus labour must be drawn off. But modern industries have limited demands for labour.

Professor J. H. Davis (Sierra Leone) outlined the problem of increasing productivity in Sierra Leone, which is among the poorest of the under-developed countries. Nearly 80 per cent of the estimated 2·8 million population derives a living from subsistence agriculture. The main crop is rice. The few cash crops include palm oil, coffee, cassava and palm kernels. Only about 80,000 workers are wage earners, 25,000 each in mining and the public sector, and 30,000 in services. Infrastructure is poorly developed and transport facilities are inadequate.

Productivity in agriculture is low, with much underemployment on small holdings. The ten-year Development Plan emphasizes the establishment of a plantation system, by the expansion of co-operatives. That the Sierra Leonan prefers leisure to more pay and is not responsive to the price stimulus is contradicted by the increase in output of coffee in recent years, and by the high productivity, under good conditions, of workers in the diamond and iron ore industries. However, the chronic ill-health of the people, due to the wide incidence of debilitating diseases, is a real barrier to increased productivity. Medical services are at present woefully inadequate. But if this obstacle can be eliminated, there is little doubt that productivity in all sectors of the economy would increase greatly.

Professor John P. Carter (United States) reported his impression, in the absence of statistics, that the productivity of labour in Indonesia, in shipping and on the waterfront, compared fairly well with western standards, with the general level about two-thirds as high. Capital in ships and aircraft is poorly utilized and poorly maintained, because of bad management. An unrealistic official foreign exchange rate, overvaluing the local currency, encourages the carrying on of repair and maintenance work abroad, and discourages the development of a native labour force of skilled mechanics.

SECTION 3

TECHNIQUES AND PROBLEMS OF DEVELOPMENT PLANNING

Chairman : J. TINBERGEN
Vice-Chairman : T. V. RIABUSHKIN
Deputy Chairman : R. DORFMAN
Rapporteur : D. C. HAGUE

Chapter 22

SIMPLE DEVICES FOR DEVELOPMENT PLANNING

BY

J. TINBERGEN
Netherlands School of Economics

I. INTRODUCTORY

IN this paper we propose to list a number of devices for the construction of a development plan. Together they are a complete set of activities to arrive at such a plan. They do not represent the most sophisticated methods known to the author but rather the most practical ones. Their selection necessarily remains somewhat arbitrary and depends on the author's taste. The resulting method of planning is one of successive approximations and not a simultaneous solution of the complete set of interrelated problems which a plan must solve. Each of the following sections may be considered a phase or a stage of the process. It is in the nature of successive approximations that some of the phases must be repeated if the assumptions used are disqualified by later findings. Some of the data to be used may themselves be the outcome of pieces of 'partial research' which can be undertaken independently from the succession of phases.

As a rule, development plans will be based on the assumption that prices do not change. In some cases this may not be a permissible simplification; something will be said about it in Section VI.

II. MACRO-ECONOMIC ESTIMATES

To begin with, estimates are made on the most desirable time path of total national product or income y_t, total savings s_t and total investment j_t. We assume that these figures are known for a base year $t = 0$. The difference between j_t and s_t represents net foreign aid f_t; we assume that it is known for the planning period. The essence of our problem consists of finding the optimum level of s_t

373

or the optimum level of the savings ratio $\alpha_t = \dfrac{s_t}{y_t}$. Both may vary over time. The optimum path must be such that at no moment is it desirable to save more or to save less. In order to judge this we must (i) know its consequences and (ii) have a yardstick to evaluate these consequences.

The consequences of increased savings are a large volume of capital K_t, resulting in a larger volume of production, both for all future. It is doubtful by how much future production will be raised if 1 per cent more of national income is saved in any given year. The simplest theory so far proposed is the one of the constant capital-output ratio. This theory maintains that each addition to the capital stock leads to a proportional addition to national product. The proportionality factor is about 3 or 4 (if a time unit of a year is used) for most countries. For countries using considerable amounts of foreign capital the capital-output ratio may be considerably higher than otherwise would have been the case : the net product added to their national product will be lower than the product obtained from an investment by the amount of interest to be paid to foreign investors.

More refined theories are those using production functions. A well-known example is the Cobb-Douglas function. It shows less than proportional increases in production ; a 1 per cent increase in capital works out into a $\frac{1}{4}$ per cent increase in production only. The wide divergence between these two figures may be interpreted as follows. In the theory mentioned first, the tacit assumption is made that technical and organization progress as well as education develop in proportion to the rise in capital. If this assumption is kept in mind during the further elaboration of the plan, the use of constant capital-output ratios can be accepted. This means that education and technical progress etc. are planned in appropriate proportions.

A simple example may show the practical use of the assumptions just discussed. Let the capital-output ratio be 3 years and the savings and investment ratios in the base year 8 and 12 per cent of national income, implying foreign aid to the extent of 4 per cent. Let it be expected that foreign aid remains at this level. The rate of increase in income, according to our assumptions, will be 4 per cent $\left(\dfrac{12}{3}\right)$ in the beginning. If the savings ratio were raised to 11 per cent, income would rise by 5 per cent annually ; but in the first year consumption would have to fall by 3 per cent (11 minus 8). Similarly, more alternatives can be calculated, as indicated in the following table (expressed in per cent of national income) :

TABLE 1

CHARACTERISTICS OF ALTERNATIVE PATHS OF GROWTH

Rate of Savings	Annual Rise in Income	Initial Fall in Consumption
8	4	0
11	5	3
14	6	6

In order to make a choice the government must evaluate the consequences indicated above. It is the author's contention that at the moment economic science is not able to guide governments in this choice. Insufficient knowledge is available about the preferences of the population ; moreover, the government as well as parliament may wish to deviate deliberately from these preferences if they consider the average citizen less farsighted than seems to be his own long-term interest.

We therefore assume that a choice is made by the government and that, as a consequence, the future development of investment, consumption and income is given.

Our example is over-simplified, in that it suggests a constant savings ratio and a constant rate of increase in income over time. The planning agency may make estimates with varying rates. In all probability the rate of increase in income will not be forthcoming immediately, since investments require time. If the gestation period is three years, the increases in income corresponding with higher savings in year 1 will only show up from year 4 onwards. This feature can be introduced fairly easily into our estimates.

III. SECTOR PLANNING

The next set of problems to be considered refers to the prospective development of demand in a number of sectors. First of all the sectors must be defined. Their number should not be too large ; about twenty may be a good figure. The sectors should be as homogeneous as possible and it is clear that their choice depends on the structure of the country. Some sectors may be chosen because of their possible future importance. One sector may be non-competing imports. Once the sectors have been chosen, all data should be subdivided accordingly.

We start by estimating future demand for *finished* goods ; these may be consumer, investment or export goods.

Consumer demand is estimated from the planned development of income and from expected population figures. Average income per head can be estimated and knowledge on Engel curves will enable us to estimate average demand per head for individual commodities or groups of them. By means of multiplication by population total demand for these groups of commodities can be obtained. A more refined approach consists of using the income distribution. In this case we must not only know the income distribution in the base year, but also the changes to be expected in it. One possibility is to assume that all income intervals will expand proportionately to average income. The method of estimating average demand for a given group of commodities can now be used for each income bracket. Thus a more precise estimate of total demand is possible. For commodities showing a non-linear Engel curve this estimate is better. For commodities with a linear Engel curve the previous method is just as good.

If no family budget statistics are available for the country concerned, figures for comparable countries may be used. Alongside income other factors will sometimes influence demand. In some cases trends may have to be added representing changes in tastes or technological improvements.

Demand for *investment* goods was estimated as one figure (for each year) in the macro-economic approach already. It can be subdivided into demand for, say, buildings, for equipment and for increases in stocks, if we have some initial figures and assume proportional increases. We will discuss a second (better) approximation below.

Export demand may be estimated with the aid of the principles used for estimating consumer demand. Incomes must now be incomes of countries absorbing exports. Since export commodities will not as a rule be finished consumer goods, the relationship between income and demand must be found from other sources than family budget figures.

Having estimated the demand for finished goods we can now estimate the necessary development of production of *intermediate goods and raw materials*, as far as specified by our sector definitions : they are supposed to be outputs of some sector. Their production is estimated with the aid of input-output coefficients. Demand for finished goods is considered the 'final bill of goods' and the result of the operation will be the production programme needed, with the existing structure, to provide for this final bill of goods. It is not certain that the existing structure should be maintained. It may be desirable to develop more rapidly some industries showing comparative advantages ; and to develop less rapidly some industries showing comparative disadvantages. For the time being it is assumed that the existing pattern was chosen in line with comparative advantages. In the project appraisal phase the pattern will be checked and a change may be suggested by it.

The sector-wise production programme just derived may now be used to estimate a *second approximation of the investment programme*, based on sectoral investment programmes. In order to carry this out we must know, for each sector, the capital-output ratio and the gestation period characteristic for it. The desired increase in production in all sectors can then be translated into an investment programme. This will not, as a general rule, coincide with the one calculated before. In order for it to coincide the average capital-output ratio and the average gestation period used in the first approximation would just have to be equal to the properly weighted averages of the sectoral capital-output ratios and gestation periods. Proper weights are those corresponding with the relative increases in production of the various sectors.

Among the sectors considered we may also include some *educational and other social activities*. This enables us to integrate into the plan a plan for training the necessary man-power of all levels. The necessary inputs are buildings and further equipment as well as teachers, themselves an output of some educational institutions. One of the important characteristics of the educational sectors is the long duration of the process. It may well be, therefore, that education becomes a bottleneck to the development process, unless imports of trained man-power are considered possible. The necessary imports can then be estimated.

As a rule the outcome of the sector estimates will constitute a *check* on the figures estimated in the macro-phase. It will be necessary to repeat the calculations of both the macro- and the sector-phase whenever considerable discrepancies occur. This may be an inefficient procedure but it is my belief that it is not. In some simplified cases I think it can be proved that this 'planning in stages' is an efficient approach.[1]

Among the sectors a number will be producing '*national goods*', that is, goods which cannot be exported or imported. Important examples are energy, inland transportation, building, retail and wholesale trade, and a number of services. The production estimates obtained for these sectors can be considered final. Whatever changes in structure will be considered later must be changes in 'international sectors', producing goods which can be imported or exported. Such switches are not possible in national sectors.

[1] J. Tinbergen, 'Planning in Stages', *Statsøkonomisk Tidsskrift* (1962), p. 1.

There may even be scope in introducing the concept of 'regional sectors', producing goods which cannot be imported into or exported from the regions where they are needed. As soon as a plan has to be specified for regions — meant here to be parts of a nation — this concept becomes relevant. It depends on the aims of economic development policies what use can be made of the concept. If these aims imply the fixation, beforehand, of income aims for the various regions, the necessary production of regional goods can be estimated directly, before even the distribution of interregional sectors over the regions is fixed. It is true that this is an approximation only ; strictly speaking the need for regional products may depend on the industry mix of the region. As a first approximation, however, this need may be assumed to depend on total income (or production) only.

IV. PROJECT APPRAISAL

The heart of development programming consists of the appraisal of individual projects and the selection of those to be included in the programme or plan. The bulk of the work involved is of a technological character : the preparation of figures describing the inputs and outputs of each project, both during the investment period and during the operation period. In principle these figures must describe all the 'relevant' features, that is the *contributions made to the aims* of development policy and the *use made of the country's scarce resources*. Since the main aims usually are economic ones the economic aspects of the projects usually rank high ; but several extra-economic aspects are also important, such as the project's contribution to employment, to income distribution among groups of the population and among regions, to education, to health and to the cultural level of the country. Some of these aspects cannot be measured or estimated and may be judged intuitively only. The methods of appraisal to be used have been developed mostly by economists, but their applicability is much more general and it is an error to think that they are imposing economic criteria on extra-economic aspects. They are the only logical way of solving a problem of choice, wherever it comes up. Of course they may be subject to improvement. A prerequisite of making a development plan is the existence of a sufficient *stock of projects*, in the public as well as in the private sector, sufficiently detailed to be carried out when necessary. The preparation of such a stock is an integral part of the total task of planning.

The first question to be dealt with is the one of the most appropriate *'unit'* or *'building block'* to be used in the exercise. Although we suggested, in what preceded, that it is the single project in the practical sense of that word, we think it is better to consider as the unit of appraisal something more complex, expressing the necessary complementarities involved. Our building blocks of the programme to be selected consist, each of them, of one project in an international sector plus a set of complementary investments in the national sectors. An example will clarify matters.

Let the project in an international sector be a weaving factory. For its operation this factory will need energy transportation, building and some services which must be available and which cannot be imported. Productive capacity in these national sectors must be expanded simultaneously with the creation of the weaving unit. We will call these additions to capacity the complementary set of investments in national sectors. Its estimation will be discussed below. Before doing so we must emphasize that the complementarity just discussed does not exist with regard to any inputs from international sectors needed : these inputs can always be imported. It is not true, for example, that the establishment of a weaving unit also requires the establishment of a spinning factory : the necessary yarn may be imported. The possible international-sector investments should therefore all be considered separately in order to find out which of them shows comparative advantages and which does not show them. But each of them should be combined with the complementary set of investments in national sectors.

The next question is the *criterion* to be used. Many criteria have been proposed by the many writers on the subject. Practically all of them can be brought under the general formula of a fraction. The numerator of this fraction expresses the value of the contributions to the aims of national development policy. The denominator expresses the value of the scarce factors used. It is customary to include in the denominator only the value of the factors used during the investment period and not those during the operation period. The latter will then be brought in as negative contributions in the numerator. It would be possible to put them into the denominator. We will stick to the customary method here. The simplest case conceivable shows only one term in both the numerator and the denominator, for instance the contribution to national income in the former and the capital invested in the latter. This is correct if the only aim of development policy is raising the national income and the only scarce factor is capital. If there is another aim, for instance, to increase employment, the numerator should be the 'value' sum of the two aims. This presupposes that we can attribute relative prices to the aims. These prices may be obtained from interviews with

379

policy-makers. In principle they can also be considered as marginal (social) utilities of the aim variables. From the economist's point of view they are autonomous or exogenous ; this illustrates the acceptance, by the economist, of extra-economic elements in policy aims.

If there are more than one scarce factor, a similar problem turns up. Alongside capital, such factors as foreign exchange or trained labour may also be scarce. Their total value in the denominator can only be calculated if we have prices. These prices cannot be considered autonomous, however. They must be so as to equilibrate demand and supply. If the markets considered are in equilibrium the observed prices (market prices) may be used. If the markets are not in equilibrium, fictitious prices must be used, known as *accounting prices* or *shadow prices*. Under some circumstances these prices can be estimated fairly accurately. The price of an imported input which is protected by an import duty should be taken equal to the world market price. If all the investment projects and the factors needed for them are known, the shadow prices can be found by trial-and-error methods aiming at (a) using all of the available scarce factors, and (b) maximizing the contribution to the aims.[1]

In other cases crude estimates of shadow prices can only be made. There are strong arguments to apply a low shadow price for unskilled labour.

Shadow prices for factors may also have to be used in the estimation of the contribution to national income of a project. If among the aims balance of payments equilibrium is chosen, the price to be used for a given improvement in the balance of payments may be taken equal to the shadow price for foreign exchange. Here the price would, then, not be autonomous — unless this aim were considered to have an extra-economic value apart from its economic significance.

Both the contributions to the aims and the scarce factors used should be estimated for a *future* period, in principle the period of the project's lifetime. This implies that the quantities and the prices used need not be equal to those prevailing at the moment of appraisal. The quantities of inputs may diminish as a consequence of a learning process. The prices may change as a consequence of changed scarcity conditions.

On the list of projects to choose from we may not only have alternative projects, but also alternative versions of what is essentially the same project. These alternative versions may differ in the

[1] The problems to be solved are related to but not identical with linear programming problems. For applications of linear programming to this field see H. B. Chenery and P. G. Clark, *Interindustry Economics*, New York, 1959, especially p. 123 ff. and p. 283 ff.

technologies used either for the operation phase or for the investment phase. The different techniques may be characterized by their capital intensities, that is, quantities of capital used per man employed. In some production processes considerable ranges of variation for capital intensity exist and a proper choice may be important especially if heavy weight is given to employment as an objective. The choice just indicated may sometimes be made as a separate 'partial' study, if it is likely to depend only slightly on the precise outcome of the appraisal of other projects.

The use to be made of the criterion described is to select the projects yielding the highest values of it, except for some forms of regional policy to be discussed in the next section. This raises the question where to stop. As a rule the volume of investment will be the figure determining the frontier between projects included in the programme and projects not included. A problem arises, however, when the marginal project chosen in this way makes a negative contribution to the aims. A simple example is presented by the case in which a negative contribution to national income would be made. Such a situation indicates that there is something wrong with the general economic situation of the country considered ; in a general way it indicates that incomes paid are higher than 'the country can afford'. Such a conclusion can only be drawn after a sufficiently large number of projects has been traced and appraised. The conclusion is of considerable importance to the development policy of the country.

V. REGIONAL PROGRAMMES

Sometimes not only a programme for the country at large is required, but also programmes for the geographical subdivisions of the country, to be named 'regions'. This introduces a new dimension into the problems : that of distance and location. In its full consequences this new dimension will make the problems so much more complicated that we cannot hope to solve them in a precise way. The necessary data as well as the necessary theories are lacking. In this essay only the simplest devices will be discussed which must be introduced in order to arrive at regional programmes consistent with regard to some main criteria. Similarly to what is needed for a national plan, we must also now know the *aims of the regional development policy*. Usually, if we speak of a regional policy, some extra-economic aims will be on the minds of the policy-makers. Well-known examples of such aims are the reduction in the differences in income per head or unemployment between the regions. This implies that more investments will have to be made in regions showing low incomes or high unemployment, even if the most attractive projects from the national point of view are not to be found in those regions. The simplest way in which we can now proceed is the following. We make a distinction between 'shiftable' and 'non-shiftable' projects. The former can be carried out in several, if not all, regions, without changing their contribution to national aims. The latter can only be carried out in one region (or a few regions). Each project in an international industry (with the complementary sets of investments in national industries) must now be given a set of 'numbers' indicating the regions in which this project or parts of it can be carried out. The selection of projects for inclusion in the development programme will now be different from what it was in Section IV. Instead of taking first what from a national point of view was the 'best' project, then the second best, and so on, we select now from the projects carrying the number of the region most in need of development only. The first project to be picked now will be the best among those carrying the number of the particular region. The second project will be the second best again among the projects carrying that same number, and so on. When, as a consequence of the projects selected, the region considered has been brought to the level of the next poorest region picking will be from projects situated in both regions. When both have been lifted to the level of the next poorest (third) region, we go on taking in projects of the three regions — in proportions keeping them at the same level. In this way we go on until we have fully used the investible funds available. It will be understood that a large number of variations are conceivable with regard to the criteria used for the needs of the regions, and the degree to which these needs have to be taken into account.

The project selection described in the preceding and the present section must be considered as a correction of the sector estimates discussed in Section III. Sectors showing comparative advantages in production cost in the sense of the theory of international trade will appear to have been expanded more than sectors showing comparative disadvantages. Some of the calculations based on the sector approach, as, for instance, the needs for education, will have to be revised accordingly. The same applies to the refined calculation of investments, including their timing. This again illustrates the trial-and-error character of our method. Strictly speaking, trial-and-error methods are only correct when they lead to a converging series of estimates. This is not necessarily always true. Additional theoretical research will be needed to show the character of the series of estimates. Sometimes a choice exists between different methods of adaptation, some of which are rapidly converging.[1] These may be useful if the total amount of work has to be kept within reasonable limits, but they are not always the best methods from the economy's point of view.

VI. ASSUMPTION ABOUT PRICES

It was already observed in Section I that prices are as a rule supposed to remain constant. It may be said to be the very aim of planning to maintain equilibrium and hence to avoid the necessity of changing prices. There are cases where this assumption is not permitted. Plans may then have to be based on changes in prices. This applies, first of all, to external changes, that is, changes in world market prices as a consequence of external developments. These must be estimated as accurately as possible from pure forecasts, as distinct from plans. Changes in prices may also be necessary as a consequence of some features of the plan. This may be so if exports are increased of a product in which the country has comparative advantages and serves a considerable portion of the world market. The price change must then be functionally related to the rise in exports with the aid of a world demand function. As a consequence of these price changes national income will also be affected and all demand functions depending on it. It is not too difficult to introduce such changes into the formulae of our procedures.[2]

DISCUSSION OF THE PAPER BY PROFESSOR TINBERGEN

Professor Tinbergen defended the idea that it was useful to carry out a development plan in several stages. He thought that, in principle, this was correct though it might not be easy in practice because of interdependences. He was confident that such a procedure was possible as a first approximation and that by a process of successive approximations one could reach a successful result.

It was his practice to distinguish between several phases in development — including the macro-phase, the sector phase and the project phase. He thought one should also add the regional phase, but was not

[1] Cf. Herbert S. Levine, *The Centralized Planning of Supply in Soviet Industry*, Joint Economic Committee, Congress of the United States, Comparisons of the United States and Soviet Economics, Part I, Washington, 1959.

[2] Cf. H. C. Bos and J. Tinbergen, *Mathematical Models of Economic Growth*, chapter 6, New York, 1962.

sure whether this was the ultimate or penultimate one. However, he was sure that the first problem was the macro-economic one, e.g. agreeing on the optimum speed of development. The government should choose a rate of growth as, for example, Turkey had chosen 7 per cent.

So far as planning by sector was concerned, this could be carried out by input-output procedures or, as the Russians would say, by the balance method. The task in this second phase was to estimate the division of total output between sectors and to derive production targets. In his paper, he had suggested that at this stage one should retain the existing structure of the economy. With his recent experience in Turkey, he would now say that one ought here to bring in some of the knowledge from the third phase, and begin to change the structure of the economy. Development meant adding new products which would either increase exports or decrease imports. In Turkey, for example, there had been the question of which industries should be added. In principle this question could be answered by using a dynamic input-output table with investment coefficients. The technique for making a choice was the same as in the third phase. The two main problems were, first, the objective question of what the results of each investment programme had been. Second, there was the much more subjective business of evaluating success. When one wanted to know what was good for a particular country one inevitably had to develop satisfactory criteria. So far as the results of an investment programme were concerned, perhaps one needed a new approach to the secondary consequences of investment projects. It was no longer correct to assume, as Keynes had done, that there was idle capacity. Professor Tinbergen said he had suggested the distinction between national and international industries and had explained in his paper what each of these was. He felt that this was a useful distinction because it led to much simpler operations than the more conventional type of input-output analysis ; the matrix to be inverted was much simpler.

So far as regional planning was concerned there were great difficulties because of regional diversity. Consistent solutions required extreme simplification. However, he thought it possible to simplify the analysis so that the characteristics one was considering became purely qualitative. For example, instead of using transport costs or differences in production costs between areas, one might in the extreme case have industries which could, or could not, go to other regions. This helped one to derive simple rules whereby one could select from a set of projects a programme which would achieve the original aims. However, regional planning presupposed that the government had a regional policy, if only the traditional and passive one of allowing production to take place wherever costs were lowest. Nowadays we were much more inclined to think of some kind of justice being done as between regions.

Professor Riabushkin explained that in the U.S.S.R. planning began from the data on the output of the most important products, the rate of growth of each branch of industry and the rate of growth of the national income. Drawing up natural balances was particularly important. Resources were compared with requirements and allotted to principal consumers. Only a few balances of this kind could be used in long-term planning and these referred to the most important products. However, in operational plans the balances covered thousands of products.

Recently, inter-industrial balances — what Western economists called input-output tables — had attracted the attention of statisticians and planners and interesting work had been done on them in several socialist countries. The balances drawn up for the U.S.S.R. covered a wide range of industries and products and a large proportion of the gross national product. It was not true, as some Western experts alleged, that input-output methods were replacing traditional Russian planning. This was carried out by millions of people through a detailed examination of the economic resources and potentialities of the largest units in the economy.

Professor Riabushkin suggested that planning might be improved by using the inter-industrial balance method. This would make possible a deeper study of the structure of the economy and of the inter-relationships between its different elements. It would also make possible calculations of requirements of material and labour which would otherwise be impossible. Whereas American input-output tables gave outlay on goods and services, the Soviet tables distinguished sharply between goods and services.

At present, the U.S.S.R. produced a cost balance for 83 branches of production and a balance in physical terms for 157 products. Moreover, the product balance always covered the whole volume of any product circulating in the economy. The inter-industrial balance therefore gave a more complete picture of the movement of production from branch to branch, in both physical and money terms.

In planning, there were more than two thousand norms for the use of material and fuel, but these related to very special types of goods and equipment. The inter-industrial balance, on the other hand, gave summary indices for broad product groups. Planning needed both kinds of norms, which were complementary and not contradictory. Data from the input-output tables made it possible for planners to study relationships between different industries. For example, it had become possible to see the relationship between the direct and total consumption of power in various industries. However, too many demands should not be put on inter-industrial balances, nor should unjustified hopes be aroused. These could easily discredit a method which was far from perfect and which needed considerable improvement. It was hoped to develop the balance method in the fullest sense of the word and experimental work had already been done on an estimate of the planned balance for 1962. It was hoped to proceed to an expanded system. This would compare inter-industrial balances in all the years of each planning period, the volume of production in any year bearing a linear relationship to capital expenditure in the preceding years.

Problems in Economic Development

Professor Drewnowski said that while Professor Tinbergen's work had given us what one might call the 'model' model, he was never happy that we distinguished sufficiently carefully between socialist and capitalist planning. The two differed very greatly. An important question in all planning was how to allow for the preferences of the State. These were allowed in by the back door in Professor Tinbergen's model. The old idea that one wanted to maximize national income represented a satisfactory enough simplification for the old, liberal days, but not for contemporary American capitalism. State preferences should be given the same important place in economic models that they had in reality. Otherwise the models would assume away a most important element which was now an established fact of life.

Unless one explicitly introduced the state's preferences, many policy problems simply could not be analysed. For example, the serious question whether one was interested in a higher rate of growth or a particular product mix could not be resolved. Only if state preferences were part of the model could the model users be certain when they were concerned with calculus proper and when with value judgements.

Professor Chenery suggested that state preferences could also serve as a criterion for distinguishing capitalism from socialism. In both, there were state and consumer preferences, but the 'shape' and 'sphere of influence' of the state's preferences differed considerably. These differences could be said to constitute the distinction between the two systems.

So far as regional planning was concerned the great problem was how to fit the region into the whole nation. One might decide to favour a particular region, but how far should this go? In a programming model one could introduce a restriction when one wanted a certain amount of economic activity in each region. He was not sure how far Professor Tinbergen's procedure would give the right selection of projects, but felt that even if successive revisions would not lead one to the same solution as a more complete model, there would not be very big differences.

Professor Boudeville commented that, with regional models, Professor Tinbergen was concerned with those industries which could be more or less easily shifted from one region to another. Did he look at the growth and shape of new industries? For the growth of an industry in a region would itself lead to a shift in the balance of industry between regions.

Dr. Desai thought that Professor Tinbergen's model, and other models used in the analysis of development policy, were open to a fundamental criticism. This was that they relied entirely on a statical vision of economic development. The statical approach no doubt had its merits, but economic development, being essentially a series of dynamical processes, required at dynamical approach. (He was using the words static and dynamic as defined by Professor Frisch.) There was no doubt, first, that the response of the variables of the model to development policies would have a time-form. These responses may be damped or explosive, oscillatory or non-oscillatory. Also, the correction policies undertaken by the development authorities would themselves have a time-form, such as proportional, integral or derivative. In addition, a number of time-lags would have to be taken into account, each lag with its own location, length and distribution. To neglect all dynamical considerations when planning for development would be to court avoidable and unnecessary difficulties. Of such avoidable difficulties one example would suffice. When faced with an unexpected downward movement in output the authorities may suppose, quite erroneously, that it was a permanent one, and they may therefore proceed to change their policies; whereas closer analysis might have revealed that the down-swing in question was in fact a self-correcting and transient one. It is clear that such errors would create additional pressures on the economy and add to the complexities and the real costs of the process of economic development.

Development planning, he thought, could be considered with advantage in terms of closed-loop control systems. Professor A. W. H. Phillips of the London School of Economics had done path-breaking work, in terms of such models, in the context of the dynamical analysis of stabilization policy. And this work had a direct bearing on investigations relating to development policy. Clearly, the dynamical dependence of output (O) on development expenditure (E) would be a crucial relationship in a closed-loop control model. In general, this dependence can be expressed by the following hypothesis:

$$O(t) = \int_0^1 f(m)E(t-m)dm + k + e(t).$$

That is, at any point of time t output depends linearly on the magnitudes of development expenditure at earlier points of time in the interval between t and $(t-1)$. In the above relationship, $f(m)$ is the time-form of the dependence of output at any point of time t on development expenditure at any point of time $(t-m)$. Further, $e(t)$ represents all changes in output other than the direct changes in response to variations in development expenditure. And finally, k is the constant term. A closed-loop control model can be built around the nucleus of such dynamical relationships. Such a model would also incorporate the relevant feed-backs and feed-back loops, and take into account not only the speeds of response in various lags, but also the appropriate structural constants and the policy parameters. For development planning such a model would appear to be an essential desideratum.

Dr. Eastman wondered whether the suggestion that the price of an imported input protected by an import duty should be taken as equal to the world market price implied a policy conflict if the plan was acted upon. Goods valued at world prices would presumably be imported rather than produced at home, whereas the tariff was intended to cause a rise in home output.

Problems in Economic Development

Professor Bićanić suggested that planning required one to consider at least eight dimensions, including institutions, space, time, methods and techniques. Since complete centralization of planning was impossible, one also had to agree on which decisions were of strategic importance. He disapproved of central planning and was currently working on the idea of poly-centric planning.

Professor Bićanić argued that the capital coefficient must now be regarded as more important in economic development than the investment quota. Unlike Rostow, he regarded the first period of development planning as one of creeping over the threshold rather than taking off. The capital-output ratio was likely to rise initially from two to six or eight and then fall to about three. Would Professor Tinbergen agree that such a change would occur regularly and predictably in various countries? Technical progress was clearly more important for the capital coefficient in most countries than had been thought.

Since macro-economic planning was not merely a simple sum of all micro-economic activities, he wondered how the planners would reconcile the two.

Professor Leonard stressed the importance of raising national income per head and not simply in the aggregate. The economist had tended to ignore his responsibility to point to the problems caused by rapidly-rising population. However, the latter had an impact on consumption and on the need for such things as health services and schools. It was the duty of economists to bring the population problem to the attention of governments and to ensure that it was allowed for in development plans.

Professor Meissner wondered how Professor Tinbergen's four steps tied in with planning at the level of the individual firm. If private enterprise was to have a future, could one give 'simple advice' for micro-economic planning? How similar was the methodology to that of macro-economic planning and how much did it differ? This was particularly relevant in developed economies like the U.S.A. where 'what was good for General Motors was good for the country'.

Dr. Szczepanik said that the macro-economic objectives discussed by Professor Tinbergen often represented a kind of *ex-post* econometric frill. In such cases it would be misleading to attach operational significance to them. In under-developed countries, not only the capital-output ratio but even income per head was not calculable in a meaningful way. Why should one attempt to produce figures where the margin of error exceeded the annual rate of change? One might see the validity of Professor Tinbergen's approach for long-run or perspective planning but a four- or five-year plan was not long enough to take account of most of the objectives he mentioned. Accordingly, emphasis should be laid on physical production targets and not on financial investment targets.

Dr. Szczepanik further suggested that there was a need for a new approach to growth methodology. In the planning process, development expenditure replaced capital formation as the basis of a dynamic calculus,

388

but there was still no satisfactory theoretical framework into which the concept of development expenditure could be fitted.

He also wondered whether, in formulating plans, a major difficulty was not the shortage, rather than the abundance, of projects. For the supply of technical personnel was a limiting factor. Even the World Bank appeared to suffer from it. The problem was not the choice of techniques but the choice of technicians.

Professor Tinbergen, replying to the debate, said that when he spoke of planning he meant Government activity, whether there was much or little of it. The public sector always existed and the aims of planning depended on the institutional structure. It was not realistic to assume that a country had only one aim. In the West, one needed to work towards four or five main aims.

Professor Tinbergen would not comment on movements in the capital-output ratio, but agreed with Professor Bićanić that a country had to go through a difficult process of crossing the threshold. This had happened very obviously in Sweden and Japan. He stressed that education was important and that it played a big part in development in the U.S.A.

As for whether the macro-economic phase should be first or last in very small countries, he agreed with Dr. Szczepanik. In the larger countries he preferred the Western, macro-economic approach. It was better to think and talk in terms of the rate of growth of income rather than the rate of growth of the output of steel, coal, etc. The outputs of these commodities were not independent but related, and the central aim had to be settled first. He agreed that sometimes technicians were more scarce than capital, but an important example of a country where the situation was exactly the opposite was India. The real problem in India was the balance of payments deficit and the difficulty of acquiring capital which that implied. He also agreed that a macro-economic plan was not simply the aggregate of several micro-economic plans. For the last word on this, one had to turn to a detailed model with sectors, projects, etc.

Professor Tinbergen differed from Dr. Desai on the practical issue. Dynamic input-output models were unrealistic in the short-run. He was therefore inclined to think that they were of little use in short-run analysis but extremely valuable for long-run analysis.

He agreed that he had ignored qualitative aspects and knew that incidental arrangements like land reform were important. He thought that a mixed economy was best and the real question was where the optimum division between state and private industry lay. However, while he agreed that qualitative factors were important, he thought they were less so than, for example, Professor Rostow suggested. Professor Chenery has asked for a more sophisticated approach when experience increased, and he agreed with that. This had always happened in the U.S.S.R. Trial-and-error rather than simultaneous equations had been used so far, but now there was a change. Perhaps there was also an optimum to the degree of formalization of the model ; a lower degree was probably better in the U.S.S.R. So far as the form of planning was concerned, the project was often concerned with the enterprise and it depended on the kind of economy one was dealing with whether or not one left decisions at the level of the firm to the individual or not. Nevertheless, with all important products, such as steel, the last word must certainly lie with the public authority.

Professor Tinbergen agreed with those speakers who had stressed the importance of the population problem and of income distribution. Savings did not necessarily have to come merely from those with high incomes and the equalization of incomes should be an aim to be pursued simultaneously with increasing growth.

Replying to Dr. Eastman, Professor Tinbergen thought it was correct to take the world price as the accounting price. It was self-deception to say that an industry's level of costs was satisfactory if one could import more cheaply than one could produce at home. One needed to take world prices in order to discover one's position relatively to the rest of the world. Professor Tinbergen could see cases where one might put regional planning before project planning. If one wanted to equalize incomes one could then see the consequence for regional industries. Regional policy was so complex that no regional model was possible; there were too many variables.

On the basic question of aims, Professor Tinbergen agreed that he had been concerned mainly with the simpler aspects of the problem. Nevertheless, people were short-sighted and, for example, the state compelled us to go to school. However, in the end it was the consumer who should have the final choice. He wanted to stress most strongly that the state, as such, had no interest at all. It was merely an organization through which the aims of consumers could be achieved. He hoped that it would be possible to discuss what the optimum degree of public activity was. Could we not reason this out during our discussions? If our aim was the happiness of people, there could not be any basic difference between 'socialist' and Western countries.

Chapter 23

APPROACHES TO DEVELOPMENT PLANNING

BY

HOLLIS B. CHENERY
Agency for International Development

A DEVELOPMENT programme serves a variety of purposes. It is at once a political symbol of a government's commitment to economic and social progress, a general strategy for remodelling the economy and its institutions, a basis for decisions on individual investment projects and a standard against which to measure results.

As planning has proceeded in a number of under-developed countries, it has become clear that some form of 'planning in stages' is better suited to these various needs than is a single comprehensive analysis. The basic political decisions require a general strategy or perspective while individual allocation decisions require a much more detailed and compartmentalized analysis. It has been found that both analysis and decision making can proceed better in a series of steps than by attempting a simultaneous optimizing procedure. The danger in the step-wise approach is that some decisions will become frozen at an early stage and will not be revised when a more complete analysis is available.

The present paper is concerned primarily with ways of approaching the first stage of the analysis that will reduce this danger by forcing consideration of the main alternatives. Since the theoretical relations involved are well known, I shall focus on an empirical comparison of fourteen development programmes and try to show the extent to which the strategic elements vary in practice. I shall also consider briefly the relationship between the general strategy adopted and the subsequent stages of sector planning and project evaluation.

I. FORMULATION OF A DEVELOPMENT STRATEGY

The term 'development strategy' has been borrowed from war and competitive games, but no precise definition of it is available. The concept implies a separation of more general or basic decisions from those which require only the application of agreed principles. Elements of a development strategy that are often cited are measures to mobilize savings, the extent of international trade or autarky, the balance among major sectors of production, and the nature of government interference with consumer choice.

These and other 'strategic' choices have two features in common : (a) the decision is rarely based entirely on economic factors, and (b) the outcome affects a substantial portion of the economy. In bureaucratic terms, these are the decisions that cut across departmental lines and have to be taken at cabinet level.

A more technical definition of a strategy is obtained by considering possible solutions to a detailed model of development. Although such a model might have several hundred variables, including production, exports, imports and prices for a number of commodities, each solution could probably be adequately characterized for purposes of general policy guidance by the values of five or ten variables. A strategy can be thought of as a set of values for these variables. The selection of the strategic variables is largely a matter of convenience, since a property of the system can be described in different ways.

This meaning of a development strategy may be illustrated by a specific model, which will be given in a highly simplified form to facilitate the subsequent comparison of development programmes. A model which traces the connections between the instruments of policy and the objectives which the government is trying to achieve may be called a 'policy model'. To analyse alternative development policies, the model structure must include the most significant limitations on economic growth. Many of these limits can be expressed by equations specifying the balance of supply and demand for scarce factors : capital, foreign exchange, skilled labour, or particular commodities. Other limits are of a political or psychological nature, such as the extent to which the government can increase tax collections or induce private investment by given measures. These limits are matters of judgment and cannot be incorporated in a mechanical way.

Following Tinbergen,[1] it is useful to distinguish between the variables that are of concern for development policy — social objectives and economic instruments — and the remaining ('irrelevant') variables, which are needed to describe the structure of the economy but do not directly affect the social welfare.[2] The inter-

---

[1] J. Tinbergen, *Economic Policy : Principles and Design*, Amsterdam, 1956.
[2] This distinction will vary among societies ; one country may be indifferent to whether steel is supplied from local production or imports, while another may consider it important for military purposes to produce its own supply.

relations among the policy variables are revealed most clearly in the 'reduced form' of the model, in which the irrelevant variables are eliminated.

I have elsewhere [1] suggested a procedure for using a policy model to determine alternative development strategies which allows for judgment on the more qualitative limits to development. In applying this analysis to Israel, attention was focussed on six policy variables, the first two representing the social objectives and the last four aspects of the economy subject to the government's influence or control :

(1) Gross national product, Y
(2) The rate of unemployment, u
(3) The marginal savings rate, s
(4) The level of foreign capital inflow, F
(5) The level of exports, E
(6) The growth of labour productivity, l.

In its reduced form, the twelve equations of the model are reduced to three, which correspond to three basic limitations to growth : [2]

(a) *The capital limit*

$$Y_1 = \frac{Y_o(1 + \beta f)}{1 - \beta s} \tag{1}$$

where β is the average productivity of investment and $f = \dfrac{F}{Y_1}$. This gives :

$$\frac{\Delta Y}{Y} = \beta(s + f). \tag{1a}$$

(b) *The labour limit*

$$Y_1 = \frac{N_o(1 + \gamma)(1 - u)}{\lambda_o(1 - e)} \tag{2}$$

where N_o is the initial labour force, γ is its rate of increase, and λ_o is the initial labour-output ratio.

(c) *The balance of payments limit*

$$Y_1 = \frac{(1 - \mu)}{\mu}(E_1 + F_1) \tag{3}$$

where μ is the ratio of imports to GNP.

The following comparison of two out of a number of solutions

---

[1] H. B. Chenery and M. Bruno, 'Development Alternatives in an Open Economy : The Case of Israel', *Economic Journal*, March 1962, pp. 79-103.

[2] As presented here, the model is simplified by taking a one-year time period and eliminating the breakdown of GNP into its components, which affects both capital requirements and import demand.

for the Israel economy shows the contrast between a 'low savings-high foreign aid' policy and a 'maximum savings-low aid' policy.[1] The two objectives — growth rate and unemployment — and the increase in labour productivity are held constant.

	Low Savings Policy	High Savings Policy
(1) GNP growth	7·7%	7·7%
(2) Unemployment rate	5%	5%
(3) Marginal savings rate	0·16	0·30
(4) Foreign capital inflow (as ratio to GNP)	0·08	0·04
(5) Export growth rate	13%	20%
(6) Annual increase in labour productivity	4%	4%

The result suggests that it is the required growth of exports, as much as the high savings level, that is likely to limit the possibility of carrying out the second strategy.

A final choice cannot be made among development strategies until some of their sectoral implications have been considered, since some of the structural parameters in the aggregate model will have to be modified. Some of the sectoral elements also affect the political judgment of the value of the plan. I shall therefore defer the problem of choice among strategies to the final section.

II. A COMPARISON OF DEVELOPMENT STRATEGIES

To compare the strategies actually adopted in development plans, I have selected fourteen countries having relatively comprehensive planning and published plans. The countries are shown in Table 1 ; they include two in Latin America, two in South-East Europe, three in the Near East, two in Africa, two in South Asia and three in the Far East.

Although all planning organizations experiment in a more or less formal way with alternative development strategies, the published plans usually describe only the strategy that has been selected and provide little information on the discarded alternatives. My discussion will therefore be limited to an inter-country analysis of (a) individual policy variables and parameters that can be calculated from the published results and (b) the general nature of the strategies chosen.

[1] From Chenery and Bruno, *op. cit.* Table II, solutions 1 and 4.

A. *Variation in Policy Variables*

Comparable data are available for the variables in the capital requirements and the balance of payments equations but not for the employment equation. The values of these variables in the base year of the plans, their average value over the plan period and other aspects of the plans are shown in Table 1.

For this sample of countries recent growth rates are highly correlated with present income level, to such an extent that the seven countries in the upper half all have higher growth rates for the previous four or five years than any of the countries in the lower income group, all of which grew at less than 4 per cent a year. Table 1 is therefore divided into two parts, with separate medians for each group of seven countries given for each variable.

The Capital Limit

The medians of variables in the capital-limit equation are shown in Table 2. The higher past growth rates of the high-income (H) group are due in part to higher savings rates (0·15 against 0·10), which are only partly compensated by a greater flow of foreign capital to the L group (0·06 against 0·04). In large part, the lower growth rates of the countries in the L group reflect the lower efficiency with which they have utilized new investment, their median investment productivity is only 0·24 against 0·31 for the H group.

In the plans for the two groups these differences are greatly reduced. While on the average no increase is projected in the productivity of investment in the H group, practically every country in the L group plans a large increase, with the average reaching that of the H group.

Since it starts from a poorer past performance, the L group of countries has adopted more ambitious targets than the H group. The L group typically plans to double its growth rate (from 3·1 to 6·3 per cent), while the plan median of the H group increases from 5·9 to 7·0 per cent. Much of the contrast between the planned performance of the two groups is in the expected rise in the efficiency of investment of the L group, which in large part reflects the inefficiency of their present economic organization. In the other main element, the savings rate, both groups are projecting significant increases but the gap between the groups will remain about the same. However, the median marginal savings rate of the L group (0·27) approaches that of the H group (0·325), and represents a larger increase over the past.

o

TABLE 1-A

PLAN DATA: HIGH-INCOME COUNTRIES

	Israel	Chile	Japan	Greece	Colombia	Yugoslavia	Turkey	Range	Median
				Base Year Data					
1. Population in 1960 (millions)	2	8	94	8	15	19	28	2-94	19
2. Population growth rate	4·4	2·6	1·0	0·9	2·8	1·2	2·9	0·9-4·4	2·6
3. GNP *per capita*	700	585	400	384	261	200	195	195-700	384
4. Productivity of investment β_0	0·364	0·397	0·27	0·358	0·187	0·230	NA	0·187-0·397	(0·32)
5. Foreign investment ratio (to GNP) f_0	0·143	0·018	-0·002	0·055	0·004	0·058	0·039	-0·002-0·143	0·039
6. Savings ratio (to GNP) α_0	0·110	0·118	0·302	0·148	0·198	0·313	0·124	0·11-0·313	0·148
7. Investment ratio (to GNP) I/Y	0·253	0·136	0·300	0·203	0·202	0·370	0·163	0·136-370	0·203
8. Previous growth in GNP g_0	10·6	3·95	9·9	5·9	4·0	8·4	NA	3·95-10·6	5·9
9. Export growth relative to GNP growth	1·75	1·131	1·131	2·9	-1·33	0·60	NA		1·13
10. Import ratio (to GNP) μ_0	0·30	0·128	0·094	0·186	0·144	0·180	0·102	0·094-0·30	0·144
11. Share of foreign investment ϕ_0	0·57	0·09	0	0·27	0·02	0·16	0·24	0-0·57	0·16
				Plan Data					
12. Productivity of Investment β	0·39	0·348	0·24	0·268	0·250	0·287	0·39	0·24-0·39	0·287
13. Marginal propensity to save S	0·29	0·325	0·328	0·246	0·358	0·350	0·28	0·246-0·358	0·325
14. Average foreign investment ratio	0·094	-0·002	0	0·068	0·034	0·037	0·031	-0·002-0·094	0·034
15. Average savings ratio $\bar\alpha$ f	0·151	0·156	0·31	0·166	0·200	0·354	0·147	0·147-0·354	0·166
16. Average investment ratio I/Y	0·245	0·154	0·31	0·227	0·234	0·392	0·181	0·154-0·392	0·234
17. Plan growth in GNP g	9·5	5·4	7·8	6·0	5·7	11·3	7·0	5·4-11·3	7·0
18. Relative export growth	2·00	1·78	1·00	1·46	0·75	NA	0·63	0·63-2·00	(0·123)
19. Change in import ratio μ/μ_0	0·97	0·89	1·19	1·14	1·04	NA	0·79	0·79-1·19	(0·95)
20. Average share of foreign investment $\bar\phi$	0·39	0	0	0·298	0·15	0·095	0·178	0-0·39	0·15
Plan period	62-66	62-67	58-70	62-66	60-64	62-65	62-67	..	..

396

TABLE 1-B

PLAN DATA: LOW-INCOME COUNTRIES

	Tunisia	UAR (Egypt)	Philip-pines	Nigeria	India	Korea	Pakistan	Range	Median
Base Year Data									
1. Population in 1960 (millions)	4·2	26·1	28	35	430	24	93	2·4–430	28
2. Population growth rate	2·2	2·5	3·2	1·9	2·3	2·2	2·2	1·9–3·2	2·2
3. GNP *per capita*	155	141	140	88	81	62	68	62–155	88
4. Productivity of investment β_0	(Neg.)	0·129	0·412	0·266	0·248	0·242	0·107	0·0–412	0·242
5. Foreign investment ratio (to GNP) f_0	0·146	0·071	0·010	0·058	0·025	0·164	0·061	·010–·164	0·061
6. Savings ratio (to GNP) α_0	0·044	0·104	0·130	0·099	0·143	0·037	0·067	0·037–0·143	0·099
7. Investment ratio (to GNP) I/Y	0·190	0·175	0·140	0·157	0·168	0·201	0·128	0·128–0·201	0·168
8. Previous growth in GNP g_0	–2·2	3·4	3·5	3·1	3·0	3·2	1·2	–2·2–3·5	3·1
9. Export growth relative to GNP growth	2·6	2·82	0·37	2·25	0·33	3·16	–1·8	–1·8–3·16	2·25
10. Import ratio (to GNP) μ_0	0·351	0·202	0·111	0·18	0·064	0·243	0·127	0·064–0·351	0·18
11. Shares of foreign invest-ment ϕ_0	0·77	0·29	0·07	0·37	0·15	0·82	0·48	0·07–0·82	0·37
Plan Data									
12. Productivity of investment β	0·200	0·302	0·418	0·261	0·320	0·330	0·270	0·200–0·418	0·302
13. Marginal propensity to save S	0·475	0·224	0·266	0·176	0·325	0·40	0·065	0·065–0·475	0·266
14. Average foreign investment ratio f	0·114	0·026	0·015	0·045	0·05	0·17	0·090	0·015–0·17	0·05
15. Average savings ratio α	0·190	0·193	0·147	0·108	0·161	0·095	0·067	0·067–0·193	0·147
16. Average investment ratio I/Y	0·304	0·219	0·161	0·153	0·207	0·227	0·162	0·153–0·304	0·207
17. Plan growth in GNP g	6·0	6·8	6·5	4·1	6·3	7·5	4·1	4·1–7·5	6·3
18. Relative export growth	NA	0·76	0·40	NA	·48	2·68	0·58	0·40–2·68	0·58
19. Change in import ratio μ/μ_0	NA	0·71	0·95	NA	1·48	0·82	1·40	0·71–1·48	0·88
20. Average share of foreign investment $\bar{\phi}$	0·376	0·124	0·14	0·30	0·22	0·59	0·56	0·124–0·59	0·30
Plan period	62–8	61–5	63–7	61/62–67/68	61/62 65/66	62–6	60/61 64/65	..	..

TABLE 2

MEDIANS OF VARIABLES IN THE CAPITAL LIMIT EQUATION *

Group	Marginal Savings Rate s	Average Savings Rate α	Capital Inflow Ratio f	Investment Ratio I/Y	Investment Productivity β	Growth of GNP $g\beta$	$(\alpha+f)$
Base Year Data							
High income	..	0·148	0·039	0·203	0·32	5·9	6·5
Low income	..	0·099	0·061	0·168	0·242	3·1	4·0
All countries	..	0·127	0·056	0·195	0·248	3·7	4·7
Plan Data							
High income	0·325	0·166	0·034	0·234	0·287	7·0	6·7
Low income	0·266	0·147	0·050	0·207	0·302	6·3	6·3
All countries	0·30	0·158	0·045	0·22	0·29	6·4	6·4

* Source : Table 1.

The most important difference among the strategies being followed in respect to capital formation is in the proportion that is expected to be financed from external sources. For all fourteen countries, this ratio falls from a present value of 0·26 to a planned value of 0·20, due to a rise in domestic savings rather than to a fall in the amount of external financing. The countries' reliance on external financing varies widely, and is not significantly correlated with growth rates or present income levels. Some of the determinants of this choice of strategy are discussed below.

The Balance of Payments Limit

As shown in equation (3), increases in import requirements can be met either by substituting domestic products for imports (reducing u), by increasing exports, or by increasing the inflow of foreign capital. Both in the present sample and among all countries, the import ratio shows no relation to the level of income although it varies inversely with the population of the country.[1] Among the fourteen countries, as many plans call for an increase in the import ratio as for a decrease.

The export prospects of a country are a significant determinant of its development strategy. A prospective growth of exports that is less rapid than the desired growth of GNP requires either an exceptional effort at import substitution or an increase in the amount of capital inflow. Of the six countries projecting a lower growth in exports than in GNP, India, Pakistan, Colombia and the Philippines plan to increase foreign assistance in relation to GNP while Turkey and the United Arab Republic plan substantial reductions in their import ratios and a reduction in f. The country's estimate of probable sources of foreign assistance and the initial level of capital inflow are among the factors which determine this choice.

The Employment Limit

In most of the L countries and some of the H countries (e.g. Turkey, Chile) the economy has not been growing rapidly enough to absorb the labour supply, which is not likely to limit growth in the near future. Rather, it becomes an objective of planning to hold the level of unemployment to certain limits, as in the example cited for Israel. However, a more detailed analysis of categories

[1] See H. Chenery, 'Patterns of Industrial Growth', *A.E.R.*, September 1960, p. 634, which gives the following regression equation for the import ratio: $\mu = \cdot204\,Y^{-\cdot01}N^{-\cdot28}$, where Y is *per capita* GNP (in hundreds of dollars) and N is population (in tens of millions).

399

of labour would probably show certain skills to be potential limiting factors in all cases.

B. *Types of Development Strategy*

In addition to the six variables already considered, another five or six should probably be added to any list of strategic variables. My suggestions for such a list would be :

Objectives
 (1) Growth in GNP : g
 (2) Unemployment level : u

Policy Instruments
 (3) Marginal savings rate : s
 (4) Foreign capital inflow : f
 (5) Investment productivity : β
 (6) Effective exchange rate : r
 (7) Population growth : p
 (8) Labour productivity increase : 1

Summary of Results
 (9) Manufacturing output : Xm
 (10) Agricultural output : Xa
 (11) Exports : E
 (12) Imports : M.

Although the last four variables are the results of the aggregate analysis rather than policy instruments, they form a useful link to the more detailed sectoral analysis and also include other influences (natural resources, international trading possibilities) that are not adequately reflected in an aggregate model.

Any classification of development strategies must be based largely on empirical observation rather than on theory. Of the main policy variables (nos. 1-8), there are only limited possibilities for affecting population growth and labour productivity directly in most countries (although population is an important variable in growth strategy in a few countries like Israel). As noted above, there is significant but limited variation in the productivity of investment. The range of unemployment targets among countries is also limited, since all aim at fairly full employment. We are left, then, with four variables which do vary widely among country plans and which together characterize their development strategies to a large extent. These are the growth rate (g), the average savings rate (α), the foreign capital inflow (f) and the effective exchange rate (r).

The exchange rate has not been discussed up to now, since it is not directly measurable. The effective exchange rate (or rate used

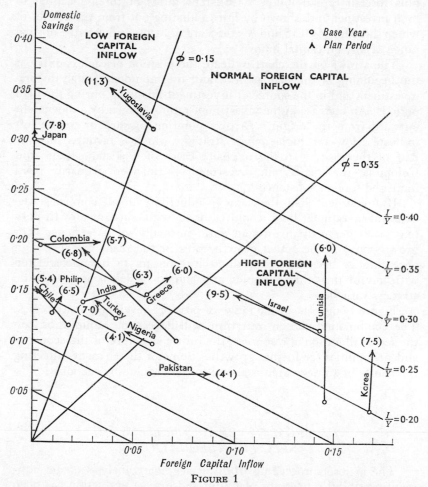

FIGURE 1

for allocation purposes) serves to adjust imports and exports to whatever value is necessary to bring the balance of payments into balance, given the rate of growth and the level of foreign capital inflow. An alternative procedure is to control imports and exports without regard for short-run comparative advantage considerations. In this case, E and M should be substituted for r as strategic variables.

The differences in development strategies stemming from the

first three variables are shown graphically in Figure 1. This chart plots the two sources of investment financing — savings and foreign capital — against each other. The parallel lines represent constant values of the investment ratio, which is the total of domestic savings plus foreign capital inflow. Constant ratios of foreign capital to total investment are shown by lines radiating out from the origin, of which those for $\phi = 0.15$ and $\phi = 0.35$ are drawn to indicate the normal range of foreign capital inflow.

The arrows on the chart indicate the position of each country at the beginning of the plan period, and the intended change in total investment and in the source of investment financing during the plan period. An increase in the investment ratio is shown by a movement outward from the origin. Arrows pointing upward or to the left indicate a low-aid, high-savings strategy, which is favoured in over half of the cases. In the opposite cases of Pakistan, India and Colombia, the increase in investment is financed primarily from increased foreign assistance.

If investment had the same productivity in all countries, the constant investment lines would coincide with constant growth lines (e.g. a 20 per cent investment ratio normally yields a 6 per cent growth rate). The actual growth rates in the plans are shown in parentheses. Investment productivity appears to be uncorrelated with any of the other variables and should be taken as a separate strategy variable.

Figure 1 suggests a wide range of possible development strategies. The combination chosen over time will have wide ramifications on the sector allocation of resources, the future structure of the economy and possibilities for further growth. Some of the elements affecting the choice of strategy are discussed in the concluding section.

III. FROM GENERAL STRATEGY TO SPECIFIC ALLOCATION

The logic of proceeding from an aggregate analysis of development possibilities to sector planning and project evaluation has been stated by several authors.[1]

Here I wish to stress two points : (1) the need to take account of all of the strategic variables in making the more detailed analysis,

---

[1] See, for example, ECAFE, Reports of the First and Second Groups of Experts on Programming Techniques, 1960 and 1961 ; Tinbergen and Bos, *Mathematical Models of Economic Growth*, 1962 ; H. Chenery, 'Development Policies and Programmes', ECLA *Bulletin*, 1958.

and (2) the need to analyse alternative strategies in sufficient detail to make the best choice among them.

Most practical work on development programming stresses quantitative balances and tends to ignore alternative sources of supply and other substitution possibilities. In its most extreme form, this approach makes sector decisions depend only on the target for national income growth, assuming fixed demand elasticities, input-output coefficients, capital-output ratios, exports and import proportions.[1] When it is followed rigidly, this procedure determines the amount of external capital as the amount needed to offset the deficit in either the savings-investment balance or the balance of payments.

The approach to sector planning from considerations of general strategy is much more flexible than the procedure just outlined. Since most under-developed countries have a considerable range of choice as to what proportion of investment is to be satisfied from foreign sources, and hence what proportion of demand is to be met from imports, this choice should also be reflected in the sector analysis. A higher value of capital inflow implies a lower effective exchange rate and higher imports. Consistency between the general strategy and the sector plan can be ensured by estimating an exchange rate from the aggregate analysis and using it to determine the volume of exports and the choice between imports and production in each sector.

An increase in external capital will also increase the overall ratio of capital to labour in the economy. This should be taken into account in the initial choice of techniques in each sector. Instead of using only income projections as a basis for sector analysis, therefore, initial estimates of the exchange rate, capital-labour ratios and the balance of payments deficit should be included.

The sector analysis also serves to refine the aggregate model and the overall strategy. The productivity of investment, imports and exports for a given exchange rate, and other aggregate magnitudes are determined more accurately from a trial sector plan than from the existing structure of the economy.[2]

IV. CHOICE AMONG DEVELOPMENT STRATEGIES

Since societies have several goals and multiple limits to their achievement, it is not desirable to choose with any finality among

---

[1] The programming technique given in UN, ECLA, *Analysis and Projections of Economic Development, I : An Introduction to the Technique of Programming*, 1955, tends in this direction, as to Soviet planning techniques.

[2] An iterative procedure for revising aggregate and sector models and relating project analysis to them is outlined in the ECAFE reports cited.

alternative strategies until their implications have been explored in considerable detail. It should be feasible to select six or eight combinations of the strategic variables as encompassing the most probable range for the final programme [1] and to develop the implications of each combination in sufficient sector detail to permit a judgment to be made on some of their secondary welfare effects.

A complete statement of a development strategy would require a tracing of the strategic variables over a considerable period of time. A longer perspective is needed to determine the desirable capital inflow in a given period, for example, since there is a limit to the amount of debt that it is advantageous for a country to undertake. The addition of the total foreign debt and the terms on which foreign assistance is supplied would help to clarify the differences in strategies shown in Figure 1.

The definition of several alternative programmes and the extension of each strategy over time helps to take account of some of the uncertainties of economic prediction. Since it is necessary to revise development programmes periodically to correct for the difference between plan and performance, it is useful to have explored a range of feasible policies and not just a single combination.

The choice among development strategies is in the final analysis a political question. The necessity to make political judgments also argues for presenting the responsible authorities with a range of possibilities, each showing costs as well as gains, rather than with a single plan.

––––––––

DISCUSSION ON THE PAPER BY PROFESSOR CHENERY

Dr. Bhagwati commented on some operational and formal problems. He thought that setting out alternatives was very helpful to planners. The meaningful specification of a utility function for planners was not possible unless they had actually seen for themselves the degree of conflict arriving from such choices. Professor Chenery's work on Israel showed that setting out alternatives was only realistic if one knew what the major constraints on growth were. The limits imposed on economic growth by organizational factors could not always be reduced, as Chenery reduced them, to problems of investment, employment or the balance of payments. Some organizational problems could be reduced to problems of these three limits. If one could not teach farmers how to grow enough food to sustain a given level of consumption, one could argue for importing the

[1] This procedure is followed in Chenery and Bruno, *op. cit.*

balance. The limiting factor was then foreign trade. However, transport could not be imported and its problems could not be dealt with in the same way.

Dr. Bhagwati thought that treating the savings ratio as an instrumental variable with a maximum value and accepting this without further analysis of the influence on savings of distribution or the sectoral composition of output might be a major obstacle to successful planning. One also needed to allow for political and ethical views on, for example, the equitable distribution of taxation. One could not do without knowing the implications of any plan for the real, post-tax distribution of income. People did not understand the role of taxation and often felt that others paid less tax than they did. Both government and public must be educated and shown that the tax burden was equitable.

Dr. Bhagwati emphasized that the static analysis Professor Chenery used in practice could be misleading in revealing the limits of a development programme. One method was to get the implications for income in the terminal year from standard assumptions about input-output matrices, exports, investments, consumption, capital-output ratios, etc. In arriving at the terminal investment of composition, and matrices, the main snag was that one got no clue to the feasibility of the growth path. Estimates of the required capital stock and its composition told one nothing, because feasibility meant working within certain parameters and constraints during the whole planning period. The alternative of collapsing all the years of a plan into a static model obscured the path by which the economy would expand. Only building up year-by-year the picture which automatically gave a definite time path could show such inter-temporal feasibility. Although Professor Chenery's model could be made dynamic this had not yet been done. One also needed to allow for yearly changes in the matrices over a given period.

Dr. Bhagwati found the idea of an import structure hard to accept. When Professor Chenery said one could have a changing level of exports and imports relatively to adjusted exchange rates, this was a substantial improvement. But could one use this idea in practice and when one was aggregating sectors? Again, how much did we need to know about aggregates in order to choose the optimum exchange rate and over what period should we define it? Should we change it from year to year or fix it for the whole period of the plan? Here again one had incidental obstacles. Year-by-year studies were best for fiscal policy, but possibly the year was not the right unit for considering exchange rates. Much of Professor Chenery's discussion of this was merely a description of blueprints and Dr. Bhagwati was doubtful about its usefulness. To depict plans in terms of a series of bottlenecks that had to be dealt with was not necessarily correct if problems of organization and so on were really the most important. Finally, what should one do if a plan ran into serious difficulties and it became clear that one would have to revise one's objectives? Could one define the 'hard core' of a plan which must not be abandoned whatever failures there were? Perhaps one should work out several alternatives, for a range of 'pessimistic' and 'optimistic' values of parameters.

Mr. Kochav said that in the list on page 400 of the paper two main objectives were a high rate of growth and low unemployment. However, the rate of growth depended on assumptions about labour requirements and one should not regard unemployment as different from the rate of growth. In some cases, a fall in unemployment depended on an inflow of capital which might be a major objective of any development plan. One might have several basic objectives on the same level. For instance, the draft Four-Year Plan for Israel was concerned with the rate of growth, an improved balance of payments and development in the South. Perhaps one should add as a fourth objective an improvement in the level of education. The stress on planning by stages was welcome, but it was needed at the branch as well as at the macro-economic level. Professor Chenery assumed that various projects were chosen on a technical basis, though this was often impossible because of an abundance of competing projects. Both technocrats and planners might put too much emphasis on the very long-run task of creating an infrastructure. Here, also, planning by stages was necessary so that one could go on to expand investment when more industrialization had been achieved. This was important where technical knowledge and skill was a major limiting factor. Over the whole period of development one would get better results than by putting too much stress on infrastructure.

Professor Bićanić (Yugoslavia) wanted the word planning used specifically. Already, participants had spoken of planning, projecting, forecasting, etc. He also felt that not enough attention had been given to the nature of aggregation. The sector, as defined by Professor Chenery, probably had a different content in each country, and mechanical comparisons might lead to wrong answers. Was it accident that Professor Chenery concentrated on income per head and not on increased capacity to produce? Similarly, the transition from stage 1 to stage 2 could not be projected in a linear function because quantitative changes occurred at an income around $200 per head. One could have faster or slower growth because of factors like changes in income distribution or in population. Similarly the capital coefficient might fall, and external economies develop. Decentralized investment could set in motion multipliers which the planners, thinking in terms of the first stage, had not anticipated.

Dr. Stanley (Ethiopia) had found the term 'planning by Stages' confusing when he read the Chenery paper. Now he knew that what was in Professor Chenery's mind was a method of analysis — by sectors rather than through aggregates. However, the term 'planning by stages' suggested so many things that one should perhaps look at other possible meanings. It could not mean carrying out plans for sectors, or individual projects, consecutively. Indeed, an earlier speaker had suggested that where there was no statistical information one could carry out only individual projects without having to make macro-economic adjustments. Such a definition of planning by stages had been unacceptable.

The planner had to take an overall view of the economy, and if he had no information he would do obvious things in fields where mistakes were not possible. However, the rest of the economy could not be allowed to decay and high priority would have to be given to collecting information about these other fields. Once statistics had been collected and institutions overhauled, one would have a second plan which was more informed and more comprehensive; a larger number of individual targets could be set. Each successive blueprint of the economy improved on previous ones in comprehensiveness, detail, scientific foundation and ability to forecast. This was the only sensible meaning of planning by stages. Dr. Stanley said he had nothing against planners going through the motions of making blueprints and rehearsing planning procedures, but he did oppose the imposition of such immature plans on living communities. He also felt that the making of blueprints was inseparable from actual development. However, while it was true that one made plans as one developed, it did not follow that one developed because one made plans. He therefore preferred to speak of planned development rather than the carrying out of plans.

Professor Kirschen said that although Professor Chenery quoted the Tinbergen definition, he did not appear to apply it on page 400. Policy instruments were generally thought of as economic variables which the government could act on directly. However, in Professor Chenery's list one found several things which were really irrelevant variables — such as labour productivity. These differed from what Professor Chenery included in his summary of results only because they came earlier in his thought and in his model. Finally, the word strategy was not altogether happy since there was no enemy. For Professor Chenery, a strategy seemed to be merely a model containing a few variables which were considered particularly important.

Mr. Heinemann (United States) wanted to call attention to some important policy problems. In recent years, economic aid had been smaller than losses to under-developed countries from worsened terms of trade. Similarly, the boom in Europe had depended on an adverse American balance of payments. It was likely that the American balance of payments problem would be dealt with as would that of the terms of trade. There were then bound to be repercussions on under-developed countries and he would expect strong pressure to increase imports from them.

Professor Wade suggested that there were two kinds of model, one the structural growth model, the other dealing with past history and predicting the future. He thought there were a number of characteristic links depending on the level of development. If the savings ratio depended on development, could not the latter be financed by domestic savings? When a country had developed, various factors could be influenced and the strategy showed that one could choose between a number of variables. The finance in an economy could come from domestic borrowing, but the selection of possible procedures was difficult mathematically since variables would change. The real problems were which variables one should choose to attack and this linked to political questions. Perhaps both models should concentrate more on looking at the extent to which internal factors could be altered.

Professor Drewnowski (Ghana) stressed the fact that analysis by stages and decision by stages were not the same thing. For analysis, the use of 'stages' was merely a question of convenience; when one was making decisions it implied the need for some kind of pattern in timing. Any choice, once made, determined the future path of the economy.

When one recognized the importance of decision stages, one could ask what these were under both capitalism and socialism. In capitalism the first stage was usually completed in the individual enterprise and mistakes were later adjusted through the market mechanism. Or perhaps one might have a strategic decision and adjust the enterprises to this by policy measures. In socialism, the strategic decision was always taken first and implemented by 'directives'. Socialism was concerned with changing economic reality. This had an important bearing on the characteristics of socialist planning in general. One must remember that the preferences of the state were always implicit in strategic decisions, and economists needed to understand the nature of those preferences.

Dr. Mars (United Kingdom) said that the addicts of programming were anxious to have matrices of coefficients. Spanish input-output tables had recently been published giving identical matrices for four years. Though the figures had not been deflated they were interesting because they gave time series for the coefficients. Some surprising changes in these coefficients were found and one could study the reasons for them. Indeed after a longer period one might be able to do some extrapolation.

Dr. Fritsch (Germany) said that his Institute had been making up for the difficulty that the study of facts was lagging behind the models. They had looked at published figures in plans and had tried to build up a standardized system of plans to define and measure strategic factors. He thought that inconsistencies within plans were a major reason for countries making unexpected requests for more foreign capital. Professor Chenery's pattern of thought was very helpful for the co-ordination of planning. It was very important to co-ordinate financial needs with the funds available from developed countries.

Professor Pajestka (Poland) agreed with planning by stages, stressing that this method had been used in many countries. Professor Chenery was concerned with a strategic draft plan, and made interesting methodological suggestions on it. Dr. Pajestka was not satisfied with this solution. The draft plan presented to decision makers should, in his opinion, be more comprehensive than was proposed. It was particularly important to indicate the various implications of the decisions about the main strategic variables since, otherwise, the policy makers could not be expected to make correct economic choices.

In Dr. Pajestka's opinion, consistency between equations was not the main worry of planners during the first planning stage. He also warned against the uncritical application of simple models consisting of 5 to 10 equations to any country and emphasized the need to select models consistent with the economic conditions and the instructions of a country.

Professor Ranis (United States) said that in preparing a plan it was customary to agree first on a given level of aggregation and then adopt particular targets and a strategy for achieving them. Unfortunately, most of the published plans Professor Chenery had looked at provided information only on the final magnitudes in the plan but not on the alternatives which the planners considered while producing it. Such information, if available, would be more helpful than the published magnitudes since it would tell one something about the flexibility and resilience of the plan in the face of (inevitable) changes in objective conditions and our knowledge of them. When one was discussing flexibility and the need for alternatives it might be useful to distinguish between those elements which were ultimately inviolate and those where there was some 'give'. For example, we knew that some plans regarded foreign aid as given but others as a residual. The points in a plan where there was such flexibility could usefully be made explicit, if not public, to assist in the inevitable adjustment process.

Professor Ranis said that investment productivity seemed to be unrelated to whether capital was domestic or imported and this was an odd result of Professor Chenery's. His own view was that the greater the proportion of foreign aid to total investment was the higher productivity would be. As for the statement that a rise in foreign aid automatically increased the capital-labour ratio, he could not see why the optimum technique would necessarily change with the size of the import surplus.

Professor Chenery said that some participants wanted more complicated models, some less complicated models and some no models at all. There was no hope in achieving a consensus of opinion and most of the questions should really have been put in the form — why did you not write a book rather than a paper?

Professor Kirschen wanted much more detailed instructions, but in fact the variables he regarded as irrelevant were sufficient. To take the analogy of a motor-car, one did not need the instruction to push the clutch to attain a given velocity because the driver could himself automatically provide the mechanism whereby he altered speed. In a general policy model, one should pick out the critical variable and set tax policy etc. on the basis of it. He thought the real need was to identify basic policy instruments.

On the relation between objectives and instruments he started from the Tinbergen definition. However, one was often concerned with an instrumental variable like unemployment, which also affected social welfare.

Professor Chenery explained that in discussing planning by stages he was not concerned purely with the distinction between decisions and analysis. He thought that initial analysis was desirable because one could then see the political variables and the need for research. The planners might do the economy no good in the first Five-Year Plan, but the second Five-Year Plan could then be improved. He agreed it was not possible to say which alternatives one should choose on the basis of an aggregate model alone and this was why he himself concentrated on a sectoral model.

When it came to deciding the direction of the economy one difficulty was that the politicians had enough trouble in handling a few variables. Decisions should be posed in terms of a few key variables. We needed to know more about the independent variables in the economy. In some cases, the number of independent variables turned out to be less than expected, and variation depended on a very small number of strategic ones. It was possible to study such variables first and to determine the details of a plan later through iteration.

At the empirical level, Dr. Bhagwati had questioned the value of comparing plans. This seemed useful if one thought one found similarities and differences. Economics was so complicated, and subject to such variation, that one was not likely to get the same solution in all cases. The discovery that one could identify a few leading categories was useful in showing a general pattern. It had been suggested that there was only one strategy — that of developing heavy industry, but if one looked at a number of plans one found considerable variation in such elements. He would certainly like to endorse what had been said about the by-products of planning studies and about the need for countries providing foreign aid to consider how this altered investment plans.

So far as models were concerned, he had always thought that these were useful either in enabling one to predict or to analyse the effects of structural change. They were probably better from the second point of view and could help under-developed countries a good deal. Economies could be assisted in adjusting to changes in the rate of growth. To complete a single plan too soon was not very important if demand caught up later, but if one was embarking upon a structural change one might have to use a plant which need never have been built for a considerable time. Dr. Chenery was not sure there was much point at present in trying to make models more dynamic. Dynamic models were more relevant to a closed economy than to a situation where there was considerable foreign aid and the input programme was flexible.

Chapter 24

DISCRETIONARY OR
FORMALIZED PLANNING

BY

PIERRE MASSÉ
Paris

1. In formalized programming a distinction is made when programme is being set up between the arbitrary and automatic parts. The arbitrary part is localized at the beginning of the process of resolution and consists of the choice of a model and the discussion of assumptions. The automatic part comprises the rest of the process, i.e. data processing with a view to calculating the unknowns.

There is no automatism in discretionary programming; it leaves complete freedom of choice at every stage of the process of resolution to overcome obstacles, make up for the lack of information or remedy anomalies when they appear. Discretionary programming may contain formalized parts but it is still discretionary so long as the transition from knowns to unknowns is not automatic.

2. Discretionary programming in which the resolution is dealt with stage by stage makes it clear when the programme is 'drifting away' from the facts and enables the appropriate corrections to be introduced at once. Its flexibility makes it appliable even when there are serious defects inherent in the material to be processed. On the other hand, it raises considerable problems for data processers and, furthermore, it is difficult to explain to people who are not initiates and makes it impossible to discuss general programme trends on equal terms.

Formalized programming cannot be partially corrected. If it gives results that are absurd, the whole process has to be undertaken again from the beginning after a search for errors which, in itself, can be a rewarding experience. On the other hand, it enables electronic machines to be used, saves time and makes it possible to investigate a larger number of variants. In addition, by concentrating the assumptions at the beginning of the process, it makes reasonable discussion easier.

3. Programming can be considered as a particular case in a process of decisions. The distinction between formalized and discretionary programming recalls that between automatic rules and

discretionary policies on which K. J. Arrow (*Statistics and Economic Policy*, Econometric Society, Cleveland, December 1956) commented in these terms. An automatic rule whose variables do not cover all the useful information available cannot be called optimal. In fact, the definition of an automatic rule soon becomes inconvenient when one is faced with a considerable mass of data. The determination of an optimal automatic rule implies the resolution of a recurrent problem of decision, which is usually impossible. We proceed by calculating an exact or approximate solution to a short decision problem. The choice of the short problem and of the computation methods are two acts of judgment which are likely to improve with time and experience. Hence there are substantial grounds for defending discretionary processes when conditions of uncertainty prevail.

The defenders of automatic rules will probably admit that any practical rule is inefficient as compared with the ideal, but they will argue that this loss is more than outweighed by the subjectivity and unpredictability of the discretionary decisions of administrators. A considerable increase in the mass of information would remove this objection ; I believe, in fact, that the role of discretionary decision would largely be diminished if our knowledge were greater, even if the policies deduced from the information cannot easily be expressed in advance by an equation.

4. Électricité de France has developed a formalized method of linear programming for its electricity production investments. It took seven years to obtain results that were completely satisfactory. The first models set up by R. Gibrat and P. Massé comprised not more than five constraints and unknowns and could therefore be solved 'by hand' ; they were of a purely academic nature. After discussing the problem with Professor G. B. Dantzig, P. Massé succeeded in setting up a programme with 60 constraints and 90 unknowns which was solved on electronic computers at DEF and the Rand Corporation simultaneously.

The difficulties encountered stemmed from the inherent logic of linear programmes for which the optimal solution can only change if one variable is substituted for another. A variable that was originally nil becomes positive but it only stops being nil to become as big as possible (at least one of the constraints into which it enters being satisfactory in the shape of strict equality). Hence the optimal solution can be locally very responsive to the modification of a single item of data.

An interesting example of this response is that of hydraulic equipment schemes, the cost of which increases as a function of the amount of equipment carried out (the decreasing efficiency of natural sites). In order to remain within the linear context, the cost growth curve was replaced by an ascending scale with five graduations. From then on, however, in accordance with the logic of linear programmes, the different categories of hydraulic equipment appear or disappear in complete graduations. Hence a slight variation in the data is sufficient to cause an appreciable change in the structure of the solution. The obvious way to remedy this instability would be to multiply the number of graduations or to turn to non-linear programming. This problem is being investigated at present.

A more curious incident occurred. We know that the electricity demand cannot be represented by a given amount of kilowatt-hours, but by a load curve, i.e. by an 'ensemble' of associated products. In the first models, this 'ensemble' was characterized by three parameters only, including the annual power and the peak winter capacity. Among the categories of equipment liable to appear in the programme, however, were gas turbines for which the capital outlay is very low, but which are expensive to operate and which are therefore suitable under good conditions for providing capacity to the exclusion of power. The solution of the first models therefore entailed using other types of equipment to supply all the mean capacity (or, in other words, all the annual power), with the gas turbines covering the entire difference between the winter peak capacity and the annual mean capacity. This result was clearly absurd since it required the gas turbines to provide an enormous capacity without producing any power.

In order to overcome this absurdity, the gas turbines were required, during a second attempt, to bear the constraint of running at least 1200 hours each year ; but the operating costs were so high that the gas turbines disappeared from the solution altogether. The obstacle was finally removed only by increasing the size of the model to permit a more subtle representation of the demand by taking account of two different typical years and by breaking each year down into five periods. In the resulting solution, the gas turbines run from 200 to 400 hours per year.

These defects are overcome by setting up a model on as large a scale as possible compatible with the resolution capacity of the computers. This increase in size gives rise to another difficulty, however, namely the risk of material errors which grow considerably with the size of the model. Roughly speaking, when this size is multiplied by k, the number of coefficients and therefore the risks of error are multiplied by $k2$ and the time required to produce the solution (hence the cost of using the computer) by $k3$.

This is why Électricité de France multiplied its precautions. The calculations are performed twice, if possible by different methods ; checks are made to ensure that the process is coherent ; the cards fed into the machine are triple perforated. And yet one error eluded every check : this was the inversion of the sign for an inequality. The mistake was only discovered afterwards through the absurdity of the result.

This illustrates one advantage of linear programming which offsets the drawbacks described above : owing to the very fact that the solution varies in every respect or not at all, there is a minimum risk of accepting erroneous results. Generally speaking, if the solution is not the right one, it is absurd.

Électricité de France has now succeeded in setting up a satisfactory model covering three successive plans with 250 constraints and slightly more unknowns. In spite of this marked progress, it is not possible to introduce each project with its possible alternatives into the programmes. The features of the programmes consist of categories of power stations as opposed to individual stations, the categories being defined by representing the facts diagrammatically, since the latter are particularly responsible in the sphere of hydraulic equipment.

The framework plotted by the overall programming therefore has to be supplemented by marginal studies defining the value of each project or each variant.

5. The problem of planning an economy is infinitely more complex than the programming of even the largest sector. The programming of Électricité de France covers five products, whereas the French plans — even in their initial outline — cover 28 highly aggregated production sectors with a hundred or so sub-branches.

One much more important basic difference is that EDF programming stems from a single decision centre, whereas French planning brings a large number of decision centres into play. However, the state is a privileged decision centre and the concerted development objective of the plan directs the activity of firms and the behaviour of individuals. In addition, regular statistical factors play a part in many cases. In that way we know roughly the surplus saving and the surplus consumption of different kinds caused by a surplus in the overall income. Similarly, we roughly know the rate of expansion of the different branches as a function of the growth rate of the economy. Hence the freedom to launch an undertaking, to work, to save and to consume is not incompatible with having a development sketch drawn up by the planner.

It should be added that this initial sketch is subsequently supplemented and rendered more explicit with the aid of representatives of the very people who will have to take the actual decisions within the framework of the plan. This second stage in drawing up the plan is the task, in particular, of the modernization commissions (one per branch), plus a few co-ordinating commissions comprising civil servants, heads of firms and trade unionists.

It should also be added that, apart from the differences mentioned above, there is a quite remarkable similarity between EDF programming and the planning of the economy.

Both of them proceed by groups and not by units, EDF by categories of operations as opposed to individual operations, the French plan by relatively aggregated branches instead of by firms or products.

The similarity can be taken even further. EDF supplements its programming by more detailed calculations performed marginally to the comprehensive programme. Similarly, the French plan is fined down by marginal adjustments which are made whenever possible (particularly in the power and transport sectors). In the latter case, we can even interpret the role of the Market as being an incessant adjustment function marginal to a previously prepared Plan.

French planning as applied hitherto has been essentially *discretionary*. The philosophy of its methods has been described on numerous occasions and in any case does not come within the scope of this paper. We shall simply recall that as far as the Fourth Plan is concerned, it starts from a level for the final demand which corresponds to the assumption chosen for the growth of the gross domestic product and of the structure of consumption desired for that level. Complementary assumptions on foreign trade and on the investments required to carry the expansion beyond the last year of the plan enable the level of activity to be determined for each one of the 28 branches forming the national economy. Hence a table (in volume) is obtained showing the trade balanced by the aggregated outputs of these branches. This is followed by the study of the balance in value to give prices and incomes and to relate them to consumption and saving. Lastly, three discretionary growth variants have been drawn up for the Fourth Plan with rates of 3 per cent, $4\frac{1}{2}$ per cent, and 6 per cent respectively for the gross domestic product.

A certain amount of work has been done on formalization, such as the NATAF variable price model,[1] but the whole of the procedure has largely remained discretionary.

---

[1] 'Le Modèle à moyen terme à prix variables, SEEF' (*Les Études de comptabilité nationale*, No. 3, 1962, Imprimerie Nationale, Paris). Co-author, M. Thionet.

This situation, which has the advantage of being flexible, nevertheless has several drawbacks. In particular, the investigation of growth rate variants has given rise to some misunderstanding. *In the first instance*, the counterpart to more rapid growth was an increased share of investment in the national product, i.e. a correlative reduction in the share of consumption. These were clear and calculated advantages and drawbacks. But a *second* counterpart, which was less perceptible to non-specialists, lay in the decrease in the balance of payments surplus, i.e. in the acceptance of a greater risk. According to the discretionary line of thinking of the experts, there was even a *third*, and perhaps not sufficiently explicit, counterpart which was an increased effort of technical innovation, industrial dynamism and disciplined income. In fact, these last two counterparts have not been clearly discerned or felt, so that the preference of the Investment and Planning section of the Economic and Social Council naturally went to the 6 per cent variant and the choice of the Commissariat Général au Plan and then of the government had to lag behind slightly. It could be added that if the surplus growth rate were considered — wrongly — as the consequence of the surplus initial investment alone, we should arrive at an unrealistic figure for the interest rate implicit in the Fourth Plan. These misunderstandings confirm the disadvantages of the 'subjectivity' and of 'discretionary decisions' and the need for a complete and accurate explanation of the calculation assumptions.

6. In approving the Fourth Plan, the French Parliament voted in favour of the agreement of the government, a provision instituting, a preliminary debate on the general trends of the plan before the Parliamentary Assemblies. More exactly, the government will be required to put a bill involving the approval of a report on these general trends before the Parliament in good time. If the debate is to be clear and the vote free from ambiguity, the report will obviously have to put forward several variants, including that proposed by the government. The presentation of these variants increase the interest of formalization. As a result of this formalization, all the assumptions have to be rendered explicit and localized at the origin of the process, thereby reducing the risks of misunderstanding to a minimum and facilitating reasonable discussion on an equal footing. In addition, time and money will be saved by using machines for all work of a repetitive nature.

This trend towards formalization only affects the first stage in setting up the plan, i.e. that of the sketches. The second stage, that of 'concertation' is discretionary by nature since it consists of dialogues, conflicts and arbitrations. This was the case, in particular, of the estimate aim for a surplus balance of payments for the Fourth Plan, the point on which the modernization Commissions and the foreign trade experts could not agree. In his recent book *Le IVᵉ Plan français*, M. François Perroux has clearly described the decision taken which was in the nature of a compromise. He stresses that 'it has not been calculated with a view to an optimation' and qualifies it as 'a rather complex result of : (a) inquiries sent to exporters, (b) assessments made by Ministries responsible for foreign trade, (c) projections (in the most hazardous of all fields) by government departments'. What must be added to this analysis is that the process followed in this second stage of setting-up the plan is in conformity with the philosophy of concertation since there is no weighting automatic mechanism of the different opinions with a view to revealing an optimum.

7. Before speaking of the methods contemplated for drawing up the initial sketches of future plans, it should be recalled that there are two different levels of optimization, namely :

— optimization at the technical level which is preliminary and subordinate and can be handed over to the planning experts ;
—optimization at the political level which comes second in time, but is intrinsically dominant and is bound up with the political factors in the country.

The fact that the main optimization comes second in time should not be surprising. Political choice would lose its meaning if it were not to be exercised between technically optimized variants.

The existence of two levels of optimization causes a distinction to be made between two sets of variables :

— the set X of 'political' variables which condition the demand (and which would appear in the collective demand function if this could be formulated). Work, the different types of consumption and social investment, emigration from rural areas, professional or regional migrations, etc., are political variables.
— the set Y of 'technical' variables, which are the levels of activity of the different branches, the volumes of imports and exports, the greater or lesser degree of capitalism in the production process for each branch, etc.

In the initial aim, the criterion of technical optimization would have consisted of minimizing the initial investment for a given set of values for political variables. This is the way Chenery and Kretschmer operated in their investigations on the Mezzogiorno. After inspection, it appeared preferable to follow a suggestion of

R. Mercier and maximize the final consumption C^2. In the following description X will therefore designate more precisely the set of political variables except for C^2. The maximization of C^2 is in point of fact an incorrect expression since C^2 is of the nature of a vector. We shall say $C^2 = C^1 \alpha \Delta C$, C^1 being the consumption in the last year before the plan, C an increase in consumption of given structure and α a parameter to be maximized.

Technical optimization then consists of maximizing C^2 (i.e. α in fact) with X being given. This occurs under a certain number of constraints, the chief two of which we shall mention.

One consists of fixing the productive investment of the last year of the plan so as to guarantee future expansion beyond the plan. The other consists of fixing the surplus desired for the balance of payments (or alternatively the desired probability of a credit balance) which characterizes the 'safety' of the solution obtained.

If $\hat{C}^2$ is the result of the technical optimization under constraint, political optimization will consist of having a certain number of X_i given and of choosing between the different $(X_i \hat{C}_i^2)$ supplied by technical optimization.

This choice is bound up with political considerations. It is the planner's responsibility, however, to clarify it, in particular by supplying factors permitting an assessment of the comparative utilities or non-utilities of the different X_i. For instance, the choice between food, journeys, cars, the telephone, television, housing, schools, hospitals, and so on can be usefully clarified by comparisons with other countries.

8. The progress made towards the formalization of sketches calls for some caution if it is thought desirable to remain within the limits of effectiveness. In particular, it does not appear possible in a first attempt to rely entirely on technical optimization as described above in order to build up a formalized central sketch which can be considered as wholly valid. It was therefore decided to build up a *central discretionary sketch* Σ for a reasonable 'ensemble' X of values for political variables by improving on the methods followed during the preparation of the previous plans, while still remaining on the same general lines.

On the other hand, an attempt will be made to construct a *number of formalized variants* V_i, corresponding to different 'ensembles' X_i, very near to X. It will not be possible, however, to make a valid comparison of Σ and V_i since the transition from Σ to V_i entails a change of data (the replacement of X by X_i/X), and also a change of method (the replacement of a discretionary process by a formalized process). A valid comparison is only possible from a *formalized central sketch E*. However, as we have said above, a formalized central sketch stemming from technical optimization cannot be considered as wholly valid. The true value criterion of E will be that of being 'reasonably close' to Σ. The constraints required for this purpose will be introduced into the technical optimization leading to E.

That is to say if $(X, \hat{C}^2)$ is the 'ensemble' of political variables corresponding to E and $(X_i, C^2{}_i)$ the 'ensemble corresponding to V_i, the neighbouring 'ensembles $(X_i C^2)$, $(X_i C^2{}_i)$, accompanied by the relevant comments, will be submitted to the choice of the political assemblies. We have stressed the words near and neighbouring twice in the text. We believe that we can rely on formalization for small-amplitude variation whereas, at least in the first attempt, we would be much more circumspect in contemplating large-amplitude variations.

The content of the 'ensembles' X and X_i are now being investigated. Several political variables have been quoted above, others may be contemplated. It will also be necessary to ask whether the variations in the components of V_i can be considered as additives in the event of successive variations in each of the components of X_i.

9. We have so far considered the V_i variants corresponding to the *deliberate* choice of 'ensembles' of political variables X_i controlled by the collectivity. But there are also Z_i 'ensembles' of exogenous variables which elude the control of the planning collectivity, either because they are controlled by external centres of decision like the other industrialized countries of the West, the Eastern European countries or the Neutral block, or because they correspond to 'choices of Nature' in a universe governed by the laws of probability or by an uncertainty to which a probability cannot be allotted. If account is taken of the Z_j, the W_{ij} variants corresponding to the 'ensembles' (X_i, Z_j, C_{ij}), will have to be compared. This raises the problem of a criterion for choice in the unknown.

10. The foregoing considerations form a framework, the contents of which have yet to be specified. The choice of technical variables, political variables and exogenous variables is in itself a complex problem. In a first stage, the most meaningful variables will have to be accepted in each case. At the same time models in physical quantities and values will have to be constructed, beginning with very simple diagrams. Under these circumstances, the Fifth Plan can be no more than a first step towards the formalization of sketches.

DISCUSSION OF THE PAPER BY M. MASSÉ

Sir Robert Shone (United Kingdom) outlined the British approach to planning. Its feasibility and value was being tested by a first project covering the years 1961–66. The aim was to raise the rate of growth from about 2¾ per cent to 4 per cent, and to raise the rate of productivity increase from about 2 per cent to something over 3 per cent. In Section 2 of the Congress, Mr. Maddison had argued that European countries with a productivity growth rate below 3 per cent should raise that rate to at least 3 per cent. The present figure was lower in both the U.S.A. and U.K.

The problem was being tackled in the U.K. in a way broadly similar to that outlined by M. Massé and both the discretionary and formalized approaches were being adopted. A provisional model was being checked by discussions with a number of industries and by work on more general problems. The model would be reconsidered in the light of this. Work was also proceeding with Professor Stone on a formal model of the economy. Formalization could use the speed of computers and enforced rigorous thinking, but it might not have developed to a stage at which it could help substantially in this first project.

In the U.K. a major concern was with changes that would give faster growth. Raising productivity and improving management was not a merely technical issue ; it involved public and political questions. Yet, in M. Massé's paper, the degree of capitalization was taken as a technical factor. The level of investment, which was certainly one factor affecting productivity, led on to questions of taxation, the treatment of investment income, equity and so on. It was difficult to regard policies on these matters as solely technical. Similarly, the development of training and apprenticeship was needed. This again involved agreement and action on public problems. The British approach, therefore, associated government, management and unions closely with work on planning and with the responsibilities involved in achieving the objective.

Professor Perroux (France) held that even a partly-deterministic programme was out of line with both the reality and atmosphere of contemporary science, which was non-determinist in the scientific sense. Science attempted to introduce probability coefficients into its equations, or to reformulate them in stochastic systems. There was a big difference between such efforts and practical planning or programming.

Professor Perroux stressed the need for reconciling the kind of investment models used by Électricité de France with a discretionary, global plan. M. Massé had raised the whole issue of how to co-ordinate specific projects, whose secondary and tertiary costs and revenues one could not overlook, within the national plan. Professor Perroux did not accept that the activities of Électricité de France constituted sectoral planning as M. Massé implied.

Record of Discussion

Professor Perroux argued that it was important to take account of leading industries or sectors. Statistics clearly showed that there were some 'growth' industries which expanded more rapidly than industry as a whole. There were also the expansionary effects of absolutely new industries, like atomic energy. Whatever kind of growth model one used, it must allow for such effects.

Professor Perroux also stressed the need to reconcile projections showing equilibrium between the sectors of the economy at some future date with partial, interpretative models. This was a difficult combination to achieve, and the French Plan had been unable to allow for it from the beginning. The most acute problems arose over relations between industry and agriculture and between production and distribution.

The French Modernization Commissions had a double role. They gave firms the opportunity to make known their investment intentions and thereby enabled them to avoid duplicating investment; they also offered opportunities for reaching agreements, and this meant that there was the permanent danger of oligopolistic collusion.

Professor Mossé (France) said there was a deep-seated preoccupation with planning in France. The object of economics should be to study decision-taking. So far, decisions in France had been taken either by the Commisariat du Plan or by the Modernization Commissions. He felt that these had patronal links with the industries concerned, and would like to put the point rather more strongly than Professor Perroux had. There was a kind of oligopolistic collusion between the technocrats and the oligopolists. He thought it most regrettable that there was no really democratic decision-making process.

Professor Mossé felt that techniques of planning were good, but was more doubtful about objectives. French planners proceeded by forecasting through extrapolation rather than by deliberate planning. Since the forecasts were reasonable, they would prove correct, but this did not mean that planning had any influence. There was also a distinction to be made between growth and development. Growth was a purely arithmetic process; development was the result of changes in structure. The French planners had left aside the fundamental question of the distribution of the national income, and he felt there had not been sufficient harmonization of the plans of nationalized and private industry in France. Plans could be realized on paper, but this did not show how far the results achieved had merely reflected the deliberate choices of oligopolists.

Professor Mossé felt that by regional planning one should not mean merely working out the local effects of global decisions. One should look at each region, making horizontal plans, and see how it could be developed harmoniously. To eliminate conflict between multi-regional and multi-sectoral planning new methods should be devised. Techniques of planning were not everything. We needed to know how far the underlying wants of consumers were being satisfied.

Dr. Loutfy (Egypt) said no one denied the vital need for reliable and detailed statistics if one was to plan. The French planning organizations worked clandestinely and France's economic organizations were not sufficiently informed. Industrialists did not know which sectors had too much or too little investment.

To throw some light on the economy and obtain co-ordinated planning it was necessary to introduce standardized methods of calculating and, more important, publish statistical and accounting data. He believed that the introduction of such systems was essential for planning, if one was to avoid maladjustments between sectors and frame a plan which met all the needs of a modern economy.

Dr. Krelle (Germany) said that some people in Germany were understandably critical of planning after the experiences of the 1930s and '40s. He thought that the French example was a reasonable one in that it preserved the price mechanism and allowed consumers and some investors to make their own decisions.

The French Plan was in one respect a kind of forecast of private consumption and investment ; in another, it was a guide for the economic policy of the government. He thought that this type of planning combined the advantage of a free-market economy with the necessity for long-range projections and he was in favour of it.

As to the methods used, he had some comments. Maximizing final consumption as a device for determining the planned figures, seemed to him to be more of propaganda value in showing the benevolence of the planners than to reflect the real forces of the market or of government action. If anything was to be maximized at all, it was the preference function of the politicians, given the most probable reactions of private firms and consumers.

To offer only three alternative rates of growth over-simplified the problem. Wider policy alternatives should be presented, including such things as alternative tax rates and the expenditure programmes of the government. Formal and discretionary elements should be connected in order to bring in the judgment of experts, especially in the first stages of preparing the plan. Expert judgments should be used as a supplement to state the appropriate behavioural functions in the different sectors of the economy. In later stages the more formal procedures of econometric model-building and social accounting would predominate, so that the policy makers could be shown the effects of changes in policy parameters as a basis for decision. The Dantzig decomposition principle might be used to combine different sub-plans for regions or branches into a general, optimal plan. Thus, freedom of choice in consumption and private investment, on the one hand, and democratic procedures in making policy decisions, on the other, could be combined with the advantages of a rational long-range government economic policy.

Professor Dorfman (United States) said that a major difficulty was fitting planning into the parliamentary procedure. The importance of having an objective function that reflected government preferences had been emphasized. The only way to establish this was to consult parliament; the mathematicians could not extrude such a function. Since the beginning of the IEA Congress, stress had been laid on the need to fragment the planning process and use iterative procedures, thereby achieving optimal plans. But the iterative process was supposed to take place wholly within the walls of a planning agency with no consultation of the legislators until a plan with one or two variants had been produced. There was then not enough time or scope for detailed reiteration. In the U.S.A. a procedure to bridge this gap seemed to be developing through the activities of the Joint Economic Committee of Congress. Legislative leaders worked closely with the administration, enabling the latter to send out trial balloons in order to define objectives. This might make it possible to define the preference function by bringing in parliamentary influences at an early stage.

Mr. Kochav (Israel) suggested that when several alternative rates of growth were offered to the Cabinet and the legislature, both would tend to choose the highest one. But they would not give sufficient attention to the policy measures required to achieve it.

Mr. Skolka (Czechoslovakia) supported the view that discussion gave the best results. In Czechoslovakia discussion had been based on pioneer linear-programming studies, particularly of transportation in food and chemicals. The first study was not particularly successful through lack of data.

Discretionary planning forced the use of new tools in two ways. First, there was parametric programming, of which he had no experience yet. Second, simple methods could give good sub-optimal results and a variety of solutions. The latter had been developed in Czechoslovak transport.

Dr. Cukor (Hungary) said that, to M. Massé, Hungarian planning would be discretionary. Interest in the application of mathematics was increasing, however, and this formalized planning started from linear models similar to those mentioned by Mr. Skolka. One example was a study of cotton weaving. In this textile study, there had been no difference between the discretionary and formalized mathematics; the mathematical model had been considered as purely supplementary.

It was then thought that it would be useful to set up models for the whole economy, proceeding from information on investment to an optimal solution for the whole economy. In constructing a global model it had been found best to deal with particular branches in a special way by special processes and thereby improve the basic information about the whole economy. He therefore wondered what were the links between the work done in Électricité de France and the overall French Plan. The results of all computations depended upon the accuracy with which one could measure future needs. He was not certain which methods could be used, but it was clear that simple extrapolation was not very accurate.

Professor Chenery (United States) said that the French 'central sketch' represented a combination of political possibilities and several of these possibilities made up what he described as a development strategy. The problem was to find an optimal combination of policies. No one suggested that no models should be used and the question was therefore how to combine a formal model with some political variants. There was an evolutionary process and he agreed that one would have to begin in a discretionary way and develop progressively more formality.

Professor Bourrières (France) thought that the difficulty of formalized planning in under-developed areas stemmed largely from its linear character. This was probably not important in developed areas ; there was sufficiently little variability for the method to work. In under-developed areas the rate of development was rapid, the economy was far from equilibrium and linear models were therefore not very successful. As Professor Perroux had said, we needed to link the elements of any economy. We should look on it as made up of a number of connected vessels containing liquid. In a developed economy there were large vessels with wide pipes connecting them, so that the level of liquid in all parts of the economy changed simultaneously. The under-developed countries had both large and small vessels but many of the pipes connecting them were either narrow or blocked. It was therefore very hard to know how to operate on the economy. Should one move labour from agriculture to improve industry and raise standards of living ? Or should one develop agriculture as a base for industry ? A linear solution was not likely to be possible. One had to creep forward by trial and error, although even here linear models might be useful in some sectors, say, where the expansion of cotton production could lead to a big growth in consumption and a high yield on capital. Linear models could be used to study important sectors or to show the orders of magnitude of the effects of changes in other sectors.

M. Maillet (Luxembourg) suggested that the desire to present several variants of a plan to policy makers and possibly to the public would cause difficulties if the parameters given by past experience were likely to change. For example, with very different rates of growth, one would get much more, or much less, automation, more or less redistribution of income, etc. To the extent that the balance of payments was a limiting factor, he wondered whether it was possible to plan for a country entering an organization like the EEC which was bound to affect trade patterns.

Mr. Gern (Switzerland) said that the structure of production had important social and cultural consequences, particularly in new countries where social structures were disrupted. The fact that the level of income was the least bad measure of the standard of living did not excuse the planners from looking beyond the effects of their actions on things to their effects on people. Moreover, these factors should be included among the objectives of the plan in the form of constraints or optima.

M. Massé outlined the drawing-up of the Fourth French Plan in Figure 1.

The first line represented the initial stage of the planning procedure.

Record of Discussion

The government considered the initial sketch of the plan and sent it to the 25 Modernization Commissions. The results of their work went on to the Economic Council which adopted a final draft plan, and sent it to Parliament. In the Fourth Plan, for the first time, the Economic Council was brought in at the initial stage. Its opinions were broadly followed. In the Fifth Plan, it was intended to bring Parliament in to discuss the outlines of the plan immediately after the Economic Council had done so. Only then would the Modernization Commissions set to work.

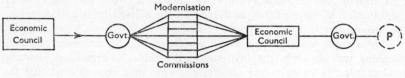

FIGURE 1

Since the orientation of a development plan must be essentially political, political discussion in Parliament should take place as soon as possible. The early political discussion should consider approximately ten variants. This would meet one of the suggestions made by Professor Perroux in his book on the Fourth Plan, where he suggested that the basic alternatives should be put to all. An attempt would be made to formalize the variants, while the central sketch would retain its usual discretionary character.

Formalization was not a mystique and one should never formalize for its own sake, only when its advantages outweighed its drawbacks. Sir Robert Shone had mentioned the work of Professor Stone, who had developed a very interesting model for formalizing a growth programme. This would be important in the U.K. where the first stage of planning certainly required an effort at formalization.

M. Massé explained the way in which variants were used, in the table below.

	h	$\frac{I}{Y}$	ΔA	θ (or $\hat{C}^2$)
0	40	20%	$-100{,}000$	5%
1	$+2$	0	0	$+0{\cdot}35\%$
2	0	$+2\%$	0	$+0{\cdot}40\%$
3	0	0	$-20{,}000$	$+0{\cdot}25\%$
	$+0$	20%	$-190{,}000$	6%

Row 0 represented the central sketch, though the figures were hypothetical, h stood for hours; $\frac{I}{Y}$ stood for the investment ratio; ΔA meant the change in agricultural population, which was a major problem in French economic evolution; θ represented the rate of growth.

425

Rows 1, 2 and 3 showed changes compared with row 0. Row 1 represented the first variant of the central sketch. It showed that if the working week rose to 42 hours this would increase the rate of growth by, say, 0·35 per cent. The second variant showed the effect on growth of a 2 per cent rise in the investment ratio. The third variant showed the effect of a bigger reduction in the agricultural labour force. Other possible variants could allow, for instance, for a different fiscal policy. Indeed, one could have more than one possible change in any one row. The government and parliament would be asked, in effect, to choose which combination of variants they preferred, in the sense that it would be best for the country.

An example of the way in which variants could be combined in actual planning was shown in the final row in the table. Formalized planning tended towards an economic optimum. This final row showed that the optimum was a 40-hour week, a 20 per cent investment ratio and a fall of 190,000 in the agricultural labour force. Since the initial sketch was not formalized, the constraint of a fall of only 100,000 in the agricultural labour force had been introduced arbitrarily. One then had, moving away from the optimum, a constraint on the formalized model, and might get, not the optimum 6 per cent rate of growth, but a rate of 5·1 per cent. Similarly, an investment ratio of 19·8 per cent introduced as a constraint might reduce the rate of growth to 5 per cent.

There was the problem of using a terminal year. It was true that this meant an arbitrary cut in a continuous process, as Professor Arrow had pointed out. For this reason, Électricité de France had used three successive plans. One was a comparison with the discretionary programme of the past; the second set out present decisions; and the third allowed for possible future modifications. This third plan showed what would be done today, but allowed for the fact that the arbitrary cut in the process made at the terminal year introduced difficulties. As for establishing links between matrices, Professor Clopper Almon at Harvard had developed a method of doing this, using differential equations which could be integrated over time. The model could not be used in France as it stood, but might be adapted.

Planning in France had begun in the form of studies of key-sectors analogous to those mentioned by Professor Perroux in the discussion. It had moved from these few basic activities to an overall study of balanced growth, partly as a result of criticisms of partial planning. More detailed work was now needed to show which sectors led others. An economy evolved over time, and one might look on this evolution as a sequence of disequilibria. Moreover, the world changed rapidly and no plan could be expected to remain entirely valid for four years. One needed instruments which would enable basic objectives to be maintained. The third plan had been adjusted for its final two years and the same might be done for the fourth. The U.S.S.R. now had a 'moving' seven-year plan and France might well come to this.

Record of Discussion

M. Massé thought the formation of the EEC might lead either to a collapse of French planning or to a common EEC development policy, if not a plan, say on fuel or automobiles. M. Massé felt it was certainly necessary to improve statistical and accounting data to solve problems as they occurred. Psychological resistance to change was also important. Although it was difficult to look more than four years ahead, the future needed to be considered and efforts had been made in France to look really far ahead.

Chapter 25

BEHAVIOURAL AND TECHNICAL CHANGE IN ECONOMIC MODELS [1]

BY

RICHARD STONE AND ALAN BROWN
Cambridge University

I. INTRODUCTION

TECHNIQUES of sector planning is a large subject on which it would be difficult to get beyond generalities in a short paper. Our work on this subject is at the model-building stage and we have recently described its general lines in [1].[2] Here we shall select one aspect to write about : the problem of freeing economic models from their dependence on parameters appropriate to the past. We all know that tastes and techniques change, that new commodities and processes are introduced, but too often we continue to view the future through the spectacles of the past as if none of these things ever happened. These problems become all the more insistent in disaggregated, sectoral models. What, then, are we to do about them ?

II. THE PROBLEM

Any economic model contains a number of parameters which must be estimated before the model can be applied. The usual practice is to begin by looking at the past and to estimate parameters as constants in regression equations. In some cases the procedure is even simpler : input-output coefficients are usually obtained as ratios of inputs to outputs in a single input-output table.

Again, as a general rule, relationships to be statistically and computationally manageable are expressed initially in a simple form. Thus inputs are taken as constant proportions of the corresponding output, demands are taken as linear or log-linear functions of income and prices. With proportional relationships, elasticities are always unity ; with linear relationships, elasticities tend to unity ; with log-linear relationships, elasticities are constant.

[1] The work on consumers' expenditure referred to in this paper is part of a project jointly undertaken by the authors and D. A. Rowe of the National Institute of Economic and Social Research, London ; that on inter-industry relations is part of the Growth Project of the Department of Applied Economics, Cambridge University, and owes much to the work of our colleagues.

[2] For figures in square brackets see Section *VIII*, List of works cited, pp. 438-9.

Generally speaking we do not believe in these simplifications. As a means of describing past experience, they may be adequate ; but some doubt always arises as to whether they will be reliable if continued into the future. These doubts frequently find expression in the introduction of residual time-trends into econometric relationships. In such cases time is regarded as a catch-all for slowly changing influences which have not been introduced explicitly. In any field of economics it is easy to see that such factors exist, but it would be helpful if they could be made to influence the relationship in a more subtle way than simply raising or lowering the whole function systematically as time goes on.

These problems are particularly important if we are concerned with models of economic development and growth. In this case we are interested in the value of parameters in the more or less distant future. In many cases these will not be well approximated by values derived from the past.

In our work on a growth model for Britain we are trying to handle these difficulties in two ways. First, we try to derive from past experience information about the way in which parameters are changing. This depends on a suitable mathematical formulation of the relationships we are studying. Second, we plan to submit the outcome of these changing relationships to economists and technicians in industry who may be able to comment on their realism. Although it would be convenient to us to short-circuit the first stage and adopt from the outset estimates made by outside specialists, we cannot do this because of the difficulties of human communication. The particular parameters which enter into a specific economic model are not as readily comprehended in industrial circles that their estimation can be left to outside specialists. But once they are estimated and their implications worked out, many specialists can be found who will comment on the results and contribute to making better estimates. In this way we can start to bring outside expert knowledge to bear on economic models.

In this paper we shall concern ourselves with the first stage : the formulation of relationships with changing parameters. We shall illustrate our methods by two examples : demand functions and input-output coefficients.

III. DEMAND FUNCTIONS WITH CHANGING PARAMETERS

Our problem here is to analyse consumers' demand into a number of groups in a consistent manner. For this purpose we propose to express each quantity demanded as a particular linear function of total expenditure and each of the prices of the system. The resulting linear expenditure equations have been described as [1, 5, 6]. In their static form they can be formulated as follows :

$$\hat{p}e = b\mu + (I - bi')\hat{c}p$$
$$= \hat{p}c + b(\mu - p'c). \tag{1}$$

In (1), p is a vector of prices, $\hat{p}$ is a diagonal matrix of prices and e is a vector of quantities bought : $\hat{p}e$ is therefore a vector of expenditures. The symbol denotes total expenditure and b is a vector of parameters whose sum is unity. The symbols I and i denote respectively the unit matrix and the unit (column) vector so that i', the transpose of i, denotes the unit (row) vector. Finally, c is a matrix of constants and $\hat{c}$ is a diagonal matrix with these constants in the diagonal.

The second row of (1) enables the behaviour of this demand system to be described in a simple way. If they operated in accordance with it, consumers would buy certain fixed quantities of each commodity, the elements of c, at the current prices of the period, p. The total cost of these committed quantities is $p'c$. Consumers would then allocate their supernumerary income, $\mu - p'c$, over the different commodities in proportion to the elements of b.

Many readers may agree with us in accepting this system as a reasonable first approximation. It is additive, has no money illusion and has a symmetric substitution matrix. For a complete system of n commodities, only $2n - 1$ independent parameters have to be estimated. To be balanced against these advantages there are limitations. The system relates to groups of substitutes, it cannot accommodate complementary or inferior groups ; its Engel curves are linear ; its Marshallian demand curves are hyperbolae and so never elastic.

But a more severe limitation, perhaps, if we are interested in the development of consumption over time is the constancy of the parameters, b and c. It can hardly be imagined, for example, that committed expenditure for transport was unaffected by the advent and development of the motor-car or that the proportion of supernumerary income devoted to food has not fallen as the country has got richer. How shall we change the form of (1) to allow for these possibilities ?

Reflection will show that we cannot add residual trend terms on to (1) without destroying its theoretical properties. We can, however, make the vectors b and c functions of any exogenous variables we choose. For example, we can make them linear functions of time, and this is the method we shall adopt in the following section. In this case we define b at time θ, b_θ say, as

$$b_\theta = b^* + b^{**}\theta \qquad (2)$$

and we define the corresponding c_θ as

$$c_\theta = c^* + c^{**}\theta. \qquad (3)$$

In (2) we must have $i'b^* = 1$ and $i'b^{**} = 0$ so that $i'b_\theta = 1$ for all values of θ. Fortunately these requirements are met by least-squares estimates as a consequence of the adding-up theorem.

IV. A NUMERICAL EXAMPLE

In order to illustrate this method we have divided private consumption per head in Britain into eight classes and used data based on [4, 8, 9, 11] for the years 1900 to 1960 with the omission of 1914–19 and 1940–47. The method of calculation is an iterative one in which we assume starting values for b^* and b^{**}, calculate c^* and c^{**}, use these estimates to revise the initial b^* and b^{**} and continue in this way until the whole calculation converges, that is, until the sum of squares of the residuals changes by less than 1 part in 10,000 from one cycle of calculations to the next. The values are given in Table 1 below. Ten complete cycles were needed for this degree of convergence.

TABLE 1

PARAMETERS FOR EIGHT CONSUMPTION GROUPS, 1900–60

	b^*	b^{**}	c^*	c^{**}
1. Food	0·1997	− 0·0039	23·58	0·332
2. Clothing	0·0927	0·0021	7·95	0·043
3. Household	0·1621	0·0021	19·88	0·154
4. Communications	0·0145	− 0·0004	0·34	0·026
5. Transport	0·1853	0·0016	3·93	0·165
6. Drink and tobacco	0·1537	− 0·0019	8·43	0·058
7. Entertainments	0·0102	− 0·0008	2·76	0·075
8. Other	0·1819	0·0012	8·03	0·064
Total	1·0001	0·0000	74·90	0·917

A comparison of the ** values with the * values in Table 1 shows that the elements of b and c are subject to very considerable change over time. The implications of these changes for demand analysis are extremely interesting but this is not the place to go into such details. For the present purpose we need to know how far the proposed system of equations is capable of representing the changing pattern of consumption. Some indication is given in Table 2 below which compares the calculated consumption per head in 1900 and 1960 with the observed consumption per head in those years. In this table all the entries are expressed at 1938 prices and the calculated expenditures are divided between committed expenditures and expenditures out of supernumerary income.

TABLE 2

CONSUMERS' EXPENDITURE PER HEAD AT CONSTANT PRICE

(£ 1938)

		Committed Expenditure	Expenditure from Sup. Inc.	Calculated Total	Observed Total
1. Food	1900	13·81	8·09	21·90	21·32
	1960	33·74	1·11	34·85	34·73
2. Clothing	1900	6·66	1·05	7·71	8·29
	1960	9·27	2·24	11·51	11·53
3. Household	1900	15·37	2·98	18·35	18·16
	1960	24·59	3·71	28·30	27·66
4. Communica-	1900	−0·42	0·80	0·38	0·24
tions	1960	1·12	0·04	1·16	1·16
5. Transport	1900	−0·94	2·45	1·51	2·28
	1960	8·99	4·00	12·99	13·58
6. Drink and	1900	6·74	10·50	17·24	16·66
tobacco	1960	10·19	1·02	11·21	11·47
7. Entertain-	1900	0·56	0·66	1·22	1·27
ments	1960	5·04	−0·23	4·81	4·78
8. Other	1900	6·15	4·46	10·61	10·07
	1960	9·98	3·31	13·29	13·12
Total	1900	47·93	30·99	78·92	78·29
	1960	102·92	15·20	118·12	118·03

The first column in this table contains the elements of c in 1900 and in 1960. Thus committed expenditure per head on food at 1938 prices is estimated at £13·81 in 1900 and £33·74 in 1960. But total real food expenditure per head did not rise as fast as this because the amount spent out of supernumerary income was much reduced : from £8·09 in 1900 to £1·11 in 1960. We can see from the bottom of the table that at 1938 prices supernumerary income per head is estimated at £30·99 in 1900 and £15·20 in 1960. In the case of food this reduction was accentuated since in 1900 the proportion of supernumerary income devoted to food is estimated at 32 per cent as against 8 per cent in 1960.

If we add these two components of expenditure together we obtain the total calculated real expenditure per head which, in the case of food, works out at £21·90 in 1900 and £34·85 in 1960. These values are fairly close to the observed values shown in the last column of the table. The same is true of most of the other comparisons.

On the positive test of Table 2 we may conclude that the proposed model gives a good first approximation to consumers' behaviour and we may go on to consider ways of improving it in detail. But we should remember that if there had been no change in the pattern of consumption we could probably have done about as well with a much simpler model. However, the pattern of consumption did change as is shown in Table 3 below.

TABLE 3

PATTERNS OF CONSUMERS' EXPENDITURE

(Per mille)

		Current Prices		Constant 1938 Prices	
		Calculated	Observed	Calculated	Observed
1. Food	1900	335	327	279	272
	1960	310	309	295	294
2. Clothing	1900	88	94	98	106
	1960	101	100	98	98
3. Household	1900	240	237	234	232
	1960	214	210	239	234
4. Communica-	1900	5	3	5	3
tions	1960	8	8	9	10
5. Transport	1900	33	50	19	29
	1960	94	99	110	115
6. Drink and	1900	136	132	220	213
tobacco	1960	129	132	95	97
7. Entertain-	1900	24	25	15	16
ment	1960	35	35	41	40
8. Other	1900	138	132	136	129
	1960	108	107	113	111
Total	1900	1000	1000	1008	1000
	1960	1000	1000	1001	1000

On the improvement of the basic model, there are four lines on which we are working at present.

First, to estimate the parameters we use the method of least squares in a two-stage iterative programme. The sum of squares which we minimize is the unweighted sum of the residuals in all equations in all time periods. If this were the right thing to do the method would be efficient; but it is probably not the right thing to do, partly because the expenditure groups are of very unequal size and partly because some of these change considerably over time. We could probably gain plausibility for our simple method by choosing the groups more evenly. Failing this, we are driven to generalized least-squares with a non-scalar covariance matrix.

Second, we should have some difficulty with the present method if we wanted to analyse simultaneously not eight or a dozen expenditure groups but forty or fifty. Fortunately we can get round this problem because the linear expenditure system is decomposable. This means that we can analyse a number of main groups, as above, and then analyse independently the components of each group using only the total expenditure on the group and the prices of the components. A complete, consistent system can be built up from this information.

Third, although the model we have described makes allowance for changes in tastes and new commodities, it does not allow for adaptations of behaviour that take time, as in the purchase of durables. We already have a programme for a dynamic linear expenditure system with constant coefficients and it should not be very difficult to elaborate this to allow for changing coefficients. The problem here is likely to be insufficiency of data.

Finally, the most serious problem in projecting the coefficients arises from the very magnitude of their changes. If a component of b has a downward trend the time will come when it will become negative. Such a negative value has no economic meaning in the linear expenditure system: all elements of b must lie between 0 and 1. This suggests the need for some restriction on the elements of b^{**} or some change in the form of the time trends.

V. INPUT-OUTPUT WITH CHANGING PARAMETERS

Just as we find that the parameters of consumption functions change, so we may be sure that the same is true of input-output coefficients. If we had as much information on inter-industry relationships as we have on consumers' behaviour we could tackle this problem by methods similar to those we have just outlined. But, as a rule, the information available is much less, being in fact restricted to a single input-output table. All that we can hope to measure year after year are the marginal totals of the input-output table. The column vector of marginal output totals is the difference between the gross outputs of industries and the final demands made upon them. The row vector of intermediate inputs is the difference between the same gross outputs and the primary inputs into the different industries. If this kind of information is available then, as we have shown elsewhere [7] we can use it to bring an old input-output table up to date.

In order to do this we made the simplifying assumption that changes in input-output coefficients are attributable to three causes : first, changes in prices ; second, the substitution of one product for another ; and third, changes in the degree of fabrication applied by any one industry to its material inputs. On the further assumptions that the second factor operates uniformly along the rows of the table and that the third factor operates uniformly along the columns of the table, we can formulate the problem as follows. Let A_o be a known, initial matrix of input-output coefficients and let A be the unknown matrix for period 1 which we desire to estimate. Let p be a price vector whose elements are the ratios of prices in period 1 to prices in period 0 and let r and s be vectors of unknown coefficients. Then, on the assumptions made,

$$A = \hat{r}\hat{p}A_o\hat{p}^{-1}\hat{s}$$
$$= \hat{r}A^*\hat{s} \tag{4}$$

say, where the circumflexes denote diagonal matrices formed from the vectors they surmount and $\hat{p}^{-1}$ is a diagonal matrix of price reciprocals.

If we have an intermediate output vector, u say, an intermediate input vector, v say, and a vector of gross outputs, q say, for period 1, then

$$Aq = u \tag{5}$$

and

$$qA'i = v \tag{6}$$

where A' denotes the transpose of A and i denotes the unit vector.

We can make an initial estimate, u_o say, of u by permultiplying q by A^*. Thus

$$A^*q = u_o. \tag{7}$$

In general $u_o \neq u$ but we can force an equality by an appropriate multiplication of the rows of A^*. Thus

$$(\hat{u}\hat{u}_o^{-1}A^*)q = u. \tag{8}$$

If we regard the expression in brackets as an estimate of A it can be seen that it satisfies the row conditions but not the column conditions. These can be satisfied by substituting for A from (8) into (6) followed by an appropriate multiplication of the columns of A^*. Thus

$$\acute{q}A^{*\prime}\hat{u}\hat{u}_o^{-1}i = v_o \tag{9}$$

and

$$\acute{q}(\hat{v}\hat{v}_o^{-1}A^{*\prime}\hat{u}\hat{u}_o^{-1})i = v. \tag{10}$$

If we regard the term in brackets as a revised estimate of A we can see that it now satisfies the column conditions, but not in general the row conditions. We can, however, repeat the cycle of operations until we obtain convergence with both row and column conditions satisfied. Thus after $(n+1)$ iterations we shall obtain

$$(\hat{u}^{n+1}\,\hat{u}_o^{-1}...\hat{u}_n^{-1}\,A^*\hat{v}^{n+1}\,\hat{v}_o^{-1}...\hat{v}_n^{-1})q = u_{n+1}. \tag{11}$$

This process is certainly convergent for any A^* with non-negative elements, and so, for sufficiently large n, the term in brackets in (11) may be taken as an estimate of A.

By these means we can form an estimate of A from A_o which agrees with known marginal totals of intermediate output and input. The problem of projecting A into the future is thus reduced to projecting price relatives and the coefficient vectors r and s. If we made a number of calculations at successive intervals we could find out how far the elements of r and s changed in a regular way. If we are unable to do this we can only base trends on the values observed over the period 0 to 1.

VI. ANOTHER NUMERICAL EXAMPLE

In our work on British economic growth we have taken as A_o a coefficient matrix for 1954 based on the official Yellow Book [10]. From this we have calculated a matrix of intermediate product flows for 1959, set out in [7]. A more detailed matrix for 1960 obtained by a modification of this method will shortly be given in [2]. But so far we do not possess a second matrix sufficiently comparable with the one given in the Yellow Book to provide a test of the method.

We have fortunately been able to work out a test in collaboration with two Belgian colleagues working on similar problems. The detailed results of this experiment have been set out by Paelinck and Waelbroeck in [3]. Briefly, they have worked out for Belgium input-output matrices with 21 industries for 1953 and 1959. They provided us with the 1953 matrix and the connecting price vector and we calculated a 1959 matrix by the method described above. The elements of this calculated matrix were within 1 per cent of the direct estimates with some ten exceptions. A further analysis showed that most of these exceptional results could quite easily have been foreseen. A typical example is as follows:

Over Belgian industry as a whole there was a tendency to replace coal as a fuel. The element of r for coal mining was therefore less than one, as one would expect. But one of the industries was coke ovens in which coal entered not as a fuel but as a raw material, and here the coal input per unit of output naturally did not fall as it did in other industries. In an effort to accommodate this fact, a certain amount of strain was set up in the adjustment process. Thus distortions were introduced in other parts of the table and even so the input of coal into coke ovens was badly estimated. However, this is a fact which is known up to date from fuel and power statistics. It can therefore be supplied from outside and A_o can be adjusted after the input of coal into coke ovens has been removed both from the inter-industrial matrix and from the output of coal and of coke. Thus this source of strain disappears and the outside estimates can be added back after the adjustment process to give a complete table.

In the end we decided to treat six cells of the table in this way, partly because the cause of the trouble was fairly obvious and so could have been foreseen and partly because up to date direct estimates were readily available. The results of the experiment are summarized in Table 4 below.

TABLE 4

ALTERNATIVE DISTRIBUTIONS OF ERROR IN THE ESTIMATION OF
INPUT-OUTPUT COEFFICIENTS

(Calculated *less* observed)

Range of Error ‰	Naïve Model	Model 1	Model 2
≥ 10	10	6	0
7-9	2	4	0
4-6	5	10	7
1-3	36	61	63
0	132	117	129
−1-3	58	55	58
−4-6	14	9	8
−7-9	6	5	4
≤ 10	7	3	1
Σ	270	270	270

The original matrix contained $21^2 = 441$ elements, but of these 171 were zero and so the table relates to the remaining 270 elements. The naïve model consists in assuming that the 1953 coefficient matrix applied to 1959. While in many cases this is true, there are 17 cases in which the error is greater than 1 per cent. Model 1 consists in a straightforward application of the iterative adjustment method described above. In this case the number of elements in error by more than 1 per cent is reduced to 9. Model 2 consists in setting 6 elements equal to their 1959 values and applying the algebraic method to the remainder. In this case there is only one element with an error of more than 1 per cent (its value is $-1\cdot4$ per cent) and, compared with the naïve model, 250 rather 226 elements lie within a range of ± 3 per mille.

We may conclude that this method, involving a small measure of direct knowledge and a mathematical adjustment programme, provides a means of bringing input-output tables up to date with the kind of information that is generally available and of projecting them into the future. The choice of trend forms for r and s is of course made easier if a number of comparable, past tables are available. In any case the projections can be regarded simply as providing agenda for discussions with economists and technicians in industry about their probable future input requirements, discussions which would all too easily evaporate into generalities and misunderstanding without some definite figures to comment on.

VII. CONCLUSIONS

We have tried to open up the question of estimating changing parameters in economic models, a question which seems to us of particular importance for models relating to future growth and development. Common observation tells us that parameters change but it does not tell us which changes are important or what to do about it. The problem is often ignored in practice, partly because traditional economic thought is largely static (tastes are assumed constant in conventional demand theory) and partly because economic information is limited (input-output coefficients are usually estimated from a single table several years out of date). The proper response to these difficulties is not to throw away traditional theory and statistics but to develop them to a more acceptable degree of realism.

VIII. A LIST OF WORKS CITED

1. Cambridge, Department of Applied Economics, *A Computable Model of Economic Growth*, No. 1 in *A Programme for Growth*. Chapman and Hall, London, 1962.

Record of Discussion

2. Cambridge, Department of Applied Economics, *A Social Accounting Matrix for* 1960, No. 2 in *A Programme for Growth*. Chapman and Hall, London, 1962.
3. Paelinck, J., and J. Waelbroeck, 'Étude empirique sur l'évolution de coefficients input-output', *Économie appliquée*, Tome XVI, No. 1, 1963, pp. 81-111.
4. Prest, A. R., assisted by A. A. Adams, *Consumers' Expenditure in the United Kingdom*, 1900–1919. Cambridge University Press, 1954.
5. Stone, Richard, 'Linear expenditure systems and demand analysis : an application to the pattern of British demand', *The Economic Journal*, Vol. LXIV, No. 255, 1954, pp. 511-27.
6. Stone, Richard, *Input-output and National Accounts*, O.E.E.C. Paris, 1961.
7. Stone, Richard, and J. A. C. Brown, 'A long-term growth model for the British economy', in *Europe's Future in Figures*. North-Holland Publishing Co., Amsterdam, 1962.
8. Stone, Richard, and Others, *The Measurement of Consumers' Expenditure and Behaviour in the United Kingdom, 1920–1938*, Vol. I. Cambridge University Press, 1954.
9. Stone, Richard, and D. A. Rowe, *The Measurement of Consumers' Expenditure and Behaviour in the United Kingdom, 1920–1938*, Vol. II. Cambridge University Press, forthcoming.
10. U.K. Board of Trade and Central Statistical Office, *Input-Output Tables for the United Kingdom*, 1954. Studies in Official Statistics, No. 8, H.M.S.O., London, 1961.
11. U.K. Central Statistical Office, *National Income and Expenditure*, H.M.S.O., London, annually.

DISCUSSION OF THE PAPER BY PROFESSOR STONE AND MR. BROWN

Professor Kirschen (Belgium) said that the paper dealt very neatly with two problems confronting the forecaster or model builder. On the problem of forecasting changes in consumption patterns, he wondered first on what basis total household consumption had been divided into the eight mutually-exclusive categories of Tables 1 to 3. Second, the available information covered forty-seven years and was used to estimate four parameters only, 2 b's and 2 c's. Could one replace the first three equations by non-linear functions giving a better description of the facts, but still displaying consistency ? Or should one sacrifice some consistency to accommodate the extremely variable growth patterns of the components of consumption ? Finally, was the first row of equation (1) really necessary, since the explanation ran entirely in terms of the second row ?

Turning to the projection of input-output coefficients, Professor Kirschen mentioned some research done in the University of Brussels in an attempt to project, five to ten years ahead, the fifty most important coefficients in a matrix containing about 800 non-zero figures. Unlike Mr. Brown, they had enlisted the help of industry from the very beginning and found that industrialists were usually able to reply to the questions asked. Sometimes industry was asked directly for the required coefficient such as the input of coal in electricity production. At other times, industry preferred to forecast both terms of the fraction, especially when a switch was forecast in the pattern of inputs, but the use of one input was unavoidable. For example, the gas industry had to use some supplies which no other industry could, and to find other inputs for the rest of its output. The industrial forecasts were not always accepted, but the information was still useful. He concluded that the method of adjustment suggested in the paper should be used only where the necessary information could not be obtained directly for the very many small flows of the matrix.

Mr. Skolka (Czechoslovakia) said that the method of estimating changes in input-output coefficients was simple and astute and the experiment on Belgian data showed that it worked well. However, he wanted to point to some problems. First, the method was based on the simplified assumption that changes in the coefficients were caused by three things, namely changes in prices, the substitution of one product for another and changes in the degree of work done by an industry on its inputs of material. While the first two assumptions were realistic, the third could lead to inaccuracy in calculation. Second, the way in which others had used this method showed that it could be useful in arriving at coefficients for the period between the drawing up of two inter-industrial balances or for the short-run extrapolation of coefficients. For both of these one needed data on marginal output and on intermediate output. The paper did not explain clearly, however, how the elements of the r and s vectors should be estimated or whether the authors had attempted such estimates.

There was a tendency to look upon input-output coefficients deterministically, but it would be better to try to deal with them statistically. However, an input-output coefficient was an average with a certain variation. It was probable that small variations were more typical for important coefficients with high values and that bigger variations occurred with less important coefficients with small ones. This meant that one could evaluate differently the accuracy of estimates obtained by using the Belgian data according to the variability of individual coefficients. For some, an accuracy of about 1 per cent would be sufficient; others would require much greater reliability.

The Stone-Brown method was linked with the possibility of arriving at an inter-industrial balance in the estimate of statistics and planning in individual countries. Most Western countries prepared input-output tables only at considerable intervals, and did so from censuses of manufacturing and current statistics. In this case, the method might be suitable for interpolating and extrapolating the coefficients.

Record of Discussion

In the Soviet Union, Poland and Hungary, inter-industrial balances were already completed. A balance would be prepared for Czechoslovakia for 1962. In the Soviet Union and Czechoslovakia, data on building and industry came from special statistical investigations and the influence of secondary production on the coefficients was excluded. In the Soviet Union and Poland, detailed input-output balances of important commodities had been drafted in physical terms. Besides balances from past data, planning balances based on accepted data had been begun. Simultaneously, Czechoslovakia, the Soviet Union, Poland and Hungary, were carrying out tests with the input-output method for regions, sectors, groups of firms and individual firms. Some economists thought it would be useful to create a system of such tables, starting with the enterprise and extending to the whole economy. However, this would be difficult and time consuming. It would also require systematic statistics, similar or identical in content to input-output coefficients, especially those in physical units. In such conditions, the problem of estimating was fairly easily solved, but the problem of aggregation was very difficult.

Professor Lombardini (Italy) reported that he had made a similar study to that of Messrs. Stone and Brown, calculating the technical coefficients for 1955 and 1959 in an Italian region. He had found great stability in these coefficients.

Professor Chenery (United States) had been wondering whether one could apply the Stone-Brown method to other countries, especially under-developed ones. The model took advantage of the ability of the computer to systemize the work of others and it was certainly true that with computers one could consider alternatives. However, this was primarily a forecasting and not a planning model, since there was no systematic procedure for optimizing. Though in the U.K. there was not much need for experiment with patterns of imports and exports, in under-developed countries these could vary greatly. Professor Tinbergen had said that the accelerator was more useful in the long run. This appeared to be true in the sense that one found that if there were a fixed capital-output ratio in the U.S.A. one would require twice as much investment as one actually had. However, in the long run, one might be able to use a flexible accelerator allowing for excess capacity.

Professor Chenery said a study of Japan had been made for the past of what was being done here for the future. Input-output tables for 1914–35 and for 1954 showed that much progress in Japan was due to technical development. The application of the Stone-Brown model might give one even more insight into Japan's economy. The model would also be useful in any comparisons of inputs and outputs.

Professor Cukor (Hungary) said that the paper began from a statistical basis for input-output calculations. Should this be extended universally? To use input-output tables for planning one would need several of them. In Hungary, there was now a 50-sector table for 1957 and one with about 100 sectors for 1959. The difficulty lay in comparing the two tables.

Since it was difficult to produce comparable tables for all dates, part of the reason for using the Stone-Brown method was lost, although it remained interesting. The discussion of the substitutability and the degree of transformation between factors seemed rather simplified. Changes in technique could be very different in different industries. Developments like the substitution of coal and oil did not happen everywhere. There had been much in .he chemical industry, but less in electricity, where coal could be economically used.

The results from using the model on Belgian data were impressive, but he wondered what results one would get from bigger changes and a bigger matrix. As Mr Skolka had said, it was not only a question of the size of the change, but of its importance as well. One could get the main coefficients quite readily from past data without using input-output tables. He suggested that as many as possible of the coefficients should be acquired directly and the remainder via the Stone-Brown method.

Professor Dorfman (United States) thought that everyone would have to follow the new trend of trying to forecast what could not be forecast. Economics was not a tidy subject. For example, under-developed areas could not be content with existing input-output coefficients. They desired not to forecast trends but to make changes. The planners' problem was to decide which input-output coefficients he wanted, remembering the difficulty of changing them. Linear models and linear programming were inadequate when technical coefficients were subject to change. We should therefore campaign against linear programming in this kind of work, and advocate more general methods.

For example, in Sector I, we might know input and capital per man. Capital per man was in effect an input-output coefficient, but to some extent under the control of the planners. One also had certain demand relationships between various goods. Since the situation in all the remaining sectors of the economy was similar, the problem of the planner was how best to apply the limited capital available from domestic savings and foreign aid. He had to allocate it among sectors. As a first approximation, one could guess marginal productivity in the final plan and allocate to each sector the capital that would give this marginal productivity in each industry. One was then in the pleasant linear-programming situation of having all the coefficients, and could work out a provisional programme. From the dual, one could get new estimates of marginal productivity. If these were not the same as in the first guess, one could make a second approximation and re-compute the new state of capital, labour and other coefficients. One could then go on to the third approximation. Even if this procedure did not converge, one could make changes until the dual gave the same results as the data fed in. One could introduce as much data as one had and deal with highly non-linear problems as a succession of linear ones.

Mr. Brown replied to the discussion. The answer to Professor Kirschen was that the eight categories into which household consumption had been divided were chosen experimentally. He agreed with Professor Kirschen that getting 32 parameters from forty-seven years' data appeared to represent rather low efficiency, but attempts would be made to improve the usefulness of the model, for example, by considering the dependence of the parameters on time. Consistency conditions had been found important and one of these was that the models should add up. The problem had been eased by separating current expenditure from expenditure on durable goods, the equations for the latter being more complicated. He agreed that it would be better to use direct data and this might well be best in an 'under-developed' country like the U.K., where one had to wait a long time for the results of infrequent censuses.

Mr. Brown agreed that his results were not exclusive, but one could estimate only a limited number of parameters and it was a question of choosing the best method. It had seemed that the row-column multiplication was most useful, though often changes were much more subtle, as column 2 of Table 4 showed. He and his colleagues had therefore calculated the (r)'s and (s)'s but could not put them into the tables. Much could be learned when, as in Belgium, one had comparable matrices for different periods. It was true that the distribution of consumer demand depended on income distribution and on prices. Both of these emerged at the end. One could feed back the demand functions until one got the same results as those fed in.

In the U.K. model they had tried two variants. First, they had put in exports and allowed the rest of the results to follow. Second, they had allowed imports to depend on past trends and found the necessary level of exports. There had been no attempt to reach an optimum solution since there was not enough data to produce a realistic one. The intention was to study sensitivity and the problem had been taken to the point of finding which were the quantitatively-important factors.

Professor Cukor had asked questions about the effect of using a bigger and bigger model but Mr. Brown did not know the answers. Indeed, he thought it would be interesting if one *could* know them. He was attracted by Professor Dorfman's suggestion and agreed that in under-developed areas the main problem was how to change the coefficients.

Chapter 26

OPTIMUM ORGANIZATION OF A NATIONAL ECONOMY: BRANCH AND TERRITORIAL PLANNING

BY

G. SOROKIN

The U.S.S.R. Academy of Sciences

PUBLIC ownership on the means of production predetermines the unity of a national economy, and makes imperative its co-ordinated and planned development. The plan for the development of a national economy sets the all-important ratios of public production : between accumulation and consumption, between manufacture of the means of production and consumption articles, between production and circulation, industry and agriculture, between production and labour resources, etc. This is the national economy development aspect of planning.

The development plan of the Soviet Union, while reflecting the unity of the entire socialist economy, reflects also its division into branches of national economy and economic areas, and the established all-state and local administration of national economy. In this connection a single development plan of the U.S.S.R. is elaborated in respect to branches, economic areas, Union Republics, Oblasts, Areas and Autonomous Republics. Such a composition of the plan is a result of the objective process of the division of labour (by branches and territories), and it also specifies the organization responsible for the fulfilment of the plan by assigning tasks to Union Republics, Oblasts and other administrative units.

The organic combination of total development and of branch and territorial planning allows for a comprehensive approach to be made to the economic tasks, leads to the drawing up of optimum plan. The data on the rate of growth of national economy including the growth of national income and consumption constitute the criteria of successful planning. The data on the rate of growth of the Soviet economy are widely known, so we shall quote only a few figures which show how the Seven-Year Plan is being fulfilled.

The totals of the economic construction of three years of the Seven-Year Plan attest to great success of the planned socialist

444

economy. The gross industrial output of the U.S.S.R. in 1959–61 increased by 33 per cent instead of 27 per cent, as estimated by the control figures of the Seven-Year Plan. The gross agricultural output in the same period increased by 59 per cent, though such rates of growth still did not satisfy the speedily growing requirements. National income, retail turnover of goods, labour productivity in industry are growing in accordance with the level of average annual targets of the Seven-Year Plan or higher.

In 1961 the rate of growth of industrial production in the U.S.S.R. was 9·2 per cent, and in the United States — 1 per cent. The amount of steel smelted in the Soviet Union increased by 8 per cent, and in the United States — decreased by 1·7 per cent. The output of electric power in the U.S.S.R. was raised by 12 per cent, and in the United States — by 4 per cent. The extraction of oil in the Soviet Union increased by 12 per cent, and in the United States —by 2·5 per cent, etc.

Thus the volume of production reached in the U.S.S.R. with regard to that of the United States was : in steel, 78 per cent ; cement, 94 per cent ; cotton textiles, 59 per cent ; woollen textiles, 131 per cent ; leather footwear, 73 per cent ; sugar (made of local raw material), 164 per cent. On the whole the industrial output in the U.S.S.R. in 1961 amounted to more than 60 per cent of the American output.

The planning experts of the Soviet Union are tirelessly seeking new effective methods of synthetic, branch and territorial planning, as well as planning in industrial enterprises and collective farms.

The organization of the Soviet planning is in general outlined in the long list of books; therefore this paper deals with the changes which have occurred in recent years in organization and methods of planning as a whole, as well as in drawing up branch and territorial plans which are parts of the single plan of the national economy development.

The development of the planning techniques, the increasing role of the three above-mentioned aspects of planning (all-state, branch and territorial) are predetermined by the changes in economic and political life.

The Soviet Union has set a grandiose plan for developing its national economy up to 1980. The volume of industrial output is to be increased not less than sixfold, and agriculture — approximately by 3·5 times as compared to 1960. The complete technical re-equipment of the entire national economy will be effected. It is planned to achieve the higher level of consumption than in any of the capitalist countries. In order to keep the planned rates of growth it is necessary to maintain a strictly proportion-wise development of national economy, harmonious correlation of its branches, to carry out the speediest overcoming of the relative lag of agriculture. In other words the implementation of the general twenty-year plan raises the responsibility of planning bodies in balancing the economy, in a more comprehensive estimation of all demands of national economy which is developing as a single whole. Alongside this the progress of technology extraordinarily quickly increases the number of production branches ; division of labour leads to the emergence of new branches. Swift development of technology changes the purpose of industrial branches and revolutionizes the production structure. The mutual co-ordination of the development of branches, active influence on the production structure, technical re-equipment of branches — all this provides for the all-round branch planning, while the increase in the number of branches and the growth of the scope of production increases the volume and significance of the branch plans.

The interbranch division of labour is supplemented by the territorial division of labour. The single national development plan synthesizes and relies on plans for all-round development of large economic areas. The rationalization of ties between areas is an important pre-condition of optimum fulfilment of the single development plan. The drastic increase of the role of Eastern areas is a characteristic feature of the planned division of labour in the Soviet Union. The development of the Eastern areas, with the priority on geological survey, construction of roads, enterprises and houses, supply of labour — all this naturally raises the role of territorial planning.

Demands for the most optimum organization of planning have lately been increasing because of the fact that the U.S.S.R. national economy is developing as a part of the world socialist economy. The rapid growth of the international socialist division of labour is increasingly influencing the planning of the U.S.S.R. national economy in all its aspects. Both the general rates of economic development and the development of individual branches, and the territorial planning are co-ordinated with the plans of other socialist countries.

The changes in the organization of state management has also greatly influenced the planning. The increase of the Union Republic's role in managing economy, the elimination of branch ministries and the setting-up of economic councils, the establishment of territorial-industrial boards, both in Oblasts and Republics, have radically changed and strengthened the territorial planning. In planning by Republics and Oblasts the territorial plans coincide with the administrative borders, which has not been the case before when the all-state plan was divided by enlarged economic areas which included many administrative units. Therefore territorial plans were not in the past given to any administrative body. Now the territorial planning became more efficient; the Oblast and Republic bodies' plans contain strictly defined tasks and they can effectively organize work for fulfilling industrial plans.

The strengthening of the role of Republics and Oblasts in planning was carried out on the basis of developing the principles of democratic centralism; alongside the transfer of many planning functions to the Republics and Oblasts, further consolidation of the centralized planning was carried out, a more correct co-ordination of all-state and territorial plans was achieved.

Life raises the demands to the organization and techniques of planning in all directions : for ensuring unity and proportionate trends in the entire national economy, for consolidating branch and territorial planning. The combination of such planning leads to the drawing up of the optimum plan. The science and practices of the Soviet planning in recent years have made certain achievements ; they became enriched by new methodological and methodical devices to which attention might be drawn.

For the achievement of unity of the single development plan and the necessary proportionalism, the methodology of drawing up the balance of national economy, of synthetic and natural balances has been improved. Proposals for the scheme of the balance of national economy have been elaborated. There are recommendations on the application (with the characteristics of distributive relations) of the so-called rated prices which are closer to the value by all commodity groups. This, apparently, will permit the clarification of a more realistic correlation between accumulation and consumption, as well as between subdivisions of public production. Alongside the national economy balances there are widely used in the U.S.S.R. the estimations of public product and national income by the Union Republics. The interbranch balance was drawn up in 1959 and 1960 for more than 80 branches of national economy and 150 commodities. Thus the interbranch relations were reflected and full input for the manufacture of this or that kind of goods was determined.

The interbranch balance reflects more than four thousand production relations, out of which five hundred are of decisive importance which cover 95 per cent of all material input in national economy. The determination of full material and labour input per unit of goods permits to more exactly take note of interrelations in

447

the development of manufacture of various products. The aggregate requirements in labour, raw and other materials for the manufacture of finished goods.

In the estimation of full labour input by production branches the following distribution of workers by branches has been obtained : production of consumer goods, about 50 million people ; production of the means of production, 30 million people ; unproductive sphere, about 17 million people. These figures in particular attest to an insufficient labour productivity in agriculture.

As to the full input of raw and other material, it came out that these expenditures were considerably higher than direct ones. Thus the complete input in rolling ferrous metals per item are higher, 1·2-3·1 times, than the direct expenditures ; input in coal extraction, 1·1-5·5 times (depending on the quality), etc. The coefficients of the complete national economy inputs can be made use of in all instances when it is necessary to follow the whole value link emerging in the obtaining of the finished goods. In particular, they might be found useful in the solution of such problems as the formation of prices, efficiency of capital investments, determination of export-import programme.

The methodology of drawing up natural balances is also progressing. In connection with the ensurance of technological progress the working out of the balances of equipment is being perfected. Especially interesting are the balances of the means of integrated mechanization and automation. The comparative analysis of balances for mutually replaceable products (oil, coal and other fuels, metals and plastics, wood and plastics, wood, metal and concrete products) is coming into wide use on which basis the manufacture of the most suitable materials is organized or expanded. The methodology of drawing up the man-power balances depending on the demands of highly mechanized and automated production and with due account of raising the general educational level and qualification of workers is being perfected. The man-power balances by micro-areas are assuming much importance because they permit to more exactly earmark the man-power resources and facilitate better substantiation of the plans for their use.

Considerable progress has been lately noted in the development of branch planning. The work of selecting optimum types of enterprises, designing the most perfect technological systems and technically advanced equipment, modernizing the existing enterprises is carried out on a large scale. All this proves that attention has been focussed on the planning of the newest, most advanced technology. The planning of technology requires a specific approach to the solution of the problems. In this connection demands are raised on the quality of the branch planning and the planning of enterprises. Only the planning of a branch as a whole enables us to determine a correct proportion between a branch and the national economy, to co-ordinate the volume of production of this or the other product with the requirements of the population and the state. Attention must be given to the estimates of the long-term requirements in many kinds of industrial and agricultural products, in particular, possible scope of the consumption of foodstuffs, clothing and footwear on the basis of scientifically substantiated quotas. The final selection of the development plans for this or that branch is increasingly connected with the expediency of expanding a particular production, with the efficacy of capital investment into various branches. Certain work has been carried out for selecting criteria of efficacy of capital investments and new equipment, and their application to individual branches.

The territorial planning of the U.S.S.R. has as its basis 15 Union Republics, 17 large economic areas and more than 100 administrative areas (Oblasts). Administrative areas mainly are parts of the Union Republics, and in some cases geographically coincide with their boundaries. Each of the Transcaucasian, Baltic and Central Asian Republics forms its own economic area. The Russian Federation is subdivided into 10 areas, the Ukrainian Republic — into 3 areas ; the Kazakh Republic forms the Kazakh economic area. The Byelorussian and Moldavian Republics whose borders coincide with those of economic administrative area are not included in the number of economic areas.

The established set-up made it possible to render the territorial planning more active. The Republics and the Oblasts, alongside the elaboration of plans for their own territories, take an active part in drawing up an all-state plan. In large economic areas Councils were organized for co-ordination and planning. They are called upon to study and consider the most important problems of integrated development of national economy in the territories of large economic areas. Proposals for the most efficient utilization of production funds, natural and man-power resources with due account of the local and state interests must be worked out. As a result of making the territorial planning more active great importance was gained by the regional balances of production and consumption, by plans of integrated development of areas, comparative estimations of the expediency of developing enterprises in this or that area. The task of getting closer the economic and cultural levels of individual territories is being solved in which connection a system of indicators was worked out which characterized the degree of development of different areas.

The non-interruption or continuous principle is a new feature in the organization of the national development, branch and territorial planning. It means, for example, that the work on a prospective plan is being done without interruption, and it is supplemented annually by new targets in order to have always a prospective plan for 5-7 years.

Thus the Seven-Year Plan is calculated for 1959–66. With non-interrupted planning, in drawing up an annual plan for 1959 it was necessary to determine targets for 1960–66, and in preparing a plan for 1960 — the targets for 1961–67, i.e. to have a seven-year plan in full volume, with the compensation of already fulfilled time-limits. Uninterrupted work over a prospective plan gives a clear perspective of economic development, allows to carry out capital construction discreetly, with due account taken of all factors. Had there not been uninterrupted planning, it would have come out by 1964, 1965, i.e. by the end of time-limits set by the 21st Congress of the CPSU for the fulfilment of the Seven-Year Plan, that national economy did not have specifically elaborated prospects, which would have introduced the elements of fortuitousness into the construction plans. The principles of uninterrupted planning do not in any case concern the directive nature of the duly adopted prospective plans, for the fulfilling of which the state bodies are responsible before the public. The task consists of introducing the uninterrupted planning into economic councils and enterprises.

The mathematical methods and the newest computing techniques are being employed on a large scale.

The planning calculations are often of mass character and are very complex. They can and must be rationalized with the help of mathematics. Computing centres have been set up in the U.S.S.R. State Economic Council and some other planning bodies. The mathematical methods and the modern computing techniques are used in calculating interbranch balance of production and distribution of production, different methods of material and technical supply, in determining comparative efficacy of capital construction, plans for setting up enterprises, optimum schemes of mass transportation, complete labour input for the manufacture of individual kinds of products, etc.

The computing centre of the U.S.S.R. State Economic Council is in particular working on the drawing up of interbranch balances, is elaborating the diagram of the distribution of workers and employees by the level of wages for 1965, 1970, 1975 and 1980 with due account of the necessary funds for regulating the remuneration for work done in various production branches, is studying the popular consumption and is making estimates of optimum sets of foodstuffs, the requirements of the population in foodstuffs and durable use articles by stages of the general prospective plan, and is making studies of optimum distribution of cement and combine harvesters production.

For the specification of estimates, programmes based on special economic and mathematic methods should be worked out. For the extensive application of mathematical methods and computing machines it will be necessary to work out scientifically based norms of consumption of the means of production and consumption articles, as well as other norms, necessary for the planning and project estimates, and to change the existing planning and registering documents in order to obtain material for adequate processing in the computing machines. The correct selection of original methodological positions determined by political economy, theory of planning and other economic sciences is a condition for successful application of mathematical methods in planning.

These are the basic aspects in the modern organization of national economy, branch and territorial planning in the Soviet Union.

DISCUSSION OF THE PAPER BY PROFESSOR SOROKIN

M. Bénard (France) said that in recent years some economists who were interested in formulating decision models for national economies were becoming more cautious. Professor Tinbergen called for a programme in several stages instead of a system of equations and inequalities. Professor Chenery wanted to replace rigid optimization by largely-discretionary development strategies. Formalized planning was thus losing ground to discretionary planning.

However, economists from a variety of countries with considerable experience of planning, including the U.S.S.R., seemed to be moving from purely discretionary planning to formalized planning. Both M. Massé and Professor Sorokin appeared to support this. Was this the result of a purely theoretical debate ; or were there practical reasons for it ? M. Bénard thought the latter was true.

Highly-formalized national planning made sense only on two conditions. It required that there should be no major alterations in the social structure, income distribution, consumption and spending habits, and so on. For all these would disrupt relationships within the economy.

M. Bénard argued that technical change or alterations in the proportions of the productive system were much more easily foreseen and measured. Formalized planning also required statistical data that was accurate enough to allow realistic estimates of the parameters and variables in the models used.

M. Bénard thought it obvious that these conditions held neither in under-developed countries nor in countries undergoing political or social revolution. Planning in the U.S.S.R. before 1939, and in under-developed countries today, was therefore discretionary. If there were formal models, these were only partial.

In an industrialized country, with long experience of long- or medium-term planning, a growing number of problems and choices had to be faced while, at the same time, the mass of data available become more and more unmanageable. Successive approximation became more and more difficult, and the danger of confusion compelled the use of more rapid and rigorous methods. At the same time, the planners in these countries saw the limits of formalized planning more clearly. If decision-models had to cover the whole economy, it was not clear that they could deal with the problems of branches and regions as well as with micro-economic problems. The decentralization of decisions became necessary, but the decentralized authorities had to possess not merely power but the ability to make their local decisions without contradicting central ones.

We all knew how Oskar Lange had shown that the establishment of a rational price system, even if it only took account of 'shadow prices', was indispensable. It alone would allow correct output and investment decisions to be made by branches, regions and firms. The formalization of national plans compelled some decentralization of decisions, but this, in its turn, presupposed some formalization. These dialectical links between the formalization and the decentralization of planning did not exhaust the question. One knew that the translation of macro-economic decisions into micro-economic ones could, in theory, be carried out centrally in physical terms. The solution to the 'dual' of the problem allowed one to establish a rational price system and, always in theory, permitted considerable decentralization.

In practice no centralized system of physical planning could provide a rational price system that allowed decentralization. Again, the existence of a rational price system did not ensure the respect of local decision-takers for overall central decisions, especially when the decisions were taken in the private sector. However, it seemed that these remarks could usefully lead to the questions everyone wanted to put to Professor Sorokin.

Mr. Markowich said Professor Sorokin referred to an optimal plan. Did this mean a mathematical optimum in the sense of one arrived at by an input-output table or simulation techniques?

Professor Leonard (United States) noted that the paper referred to eighty branches. He wondered whether there were more and if the further ones were also included in Russian planning. When the paper spoke of the division of labour, did this take account of the appearance of new branches, because new techniques were being developed ? 'Rated' prices were mentioned on page 447 ; how did these differ from market prices ? The 'Unproductive' sphere was mentioned. What activities did this include ? Was defence in it ? And what about capital goods ?

M. Bénard (France) wondered whether the Gosplan usually produced alternative plans between which it had to choose. For example, in Russia a choice had to be made between the rate of growth of income and a desirable price structure. Could the best combination of the two be chosen ? In shaping these alternatives were there formal macro-economic models based on production functions with either complementary or substitutable factors ?

Professor Sorokin mentioned continuous planning where each year one added a year on to the end of the plan and eliminated one from the beginning. At the end of any Seven-Year Plan did one then have a complete plan for the following seven years which had been built up a year at a time ? Such a second seven-year period must be planned in a way that was compatible with longer-term planning, which in the Soviet Union now extended to 1980. How were the two reconciled ?

M. Bénard wondered if input-output matrices were used in the U.S.S.R. to determine the output of branches then and, if so, how final consumption and investment was arrived at for any year and then allocated between branches. Or was production determined for basic industries like oil and chemicals and was global output built up from this ?

It was obviously difficult to forecast technical change over a long period and it was known that big changes occurred. How did Soviet planning deal with future changes in the structure of production within industries and regions ? Also, since the production techniques used in ten years' time would depend, not only on knowledge, but also on decisions taken during those ten years, could one itemize the input-output tables to take account of developments over time ? Professor Sorokin had mentioned work on optimization of consumption of food stuffs. Some details were known, but there was also mention of the planning of household goods, including clothing. Any such analysis must also take account, not only of what production the state thought possible or desirable, but also what consumers wanted. How were these two reconciled ?

On prices, we knew that a technical solution to the planning of production could be arrived at, but one first had to know the distribution of surpluses between branches. These could be allotted in proportion to output, investment or hours worked. According to the method chosen the funds allocated to each branch, and therefore its investment decisions, would be affected differently.

Professor Mossé said that, only recently, French planning had been concerned with the objectives of each branch of the economy. In the second stage, there had been a geographical projection of what was to be done in each region for each branch. Now French planners were more interested in regional planning, starting from the production figures for each local area and integrating them to get the output for the region.

Professor Bourrières said that the Russian annual rate of growth appeared to be under 9 per cent, which on reasonable assumptions about the capital-output ratio implied an enormous investment effort, with an investment quota approaching 35 per cent of GNP. How was the necessary diversion of resources from consumption achieved? So far as decentralization was concerned, it had formerly been said that the Central Office gave orders about production targets to regions and even firms. There appeared to have been some softening of this procedure recently and he wanted to be told about this. He had visited Russian firms and had heard managers say that their own plans were usually accepted quickly and without changes. Did this mean that the Gosplan allocated firms' production targets on the basis that whatever a firm offered to do was the most that it could do and that any production in excess of the output offered by existing firms could only come from the building of new ones?

Professor Marczewski said that Russia was planning to increase agricultural output over twenty years at an average of 10 per cent per annum, with a more rapid rate of increase in the near future and a slower one later on. Agricultural output had been growing by about 5 per cent per annum. There had recently been some stagnation, especially in livestock production and the elimination of personal holdings was being suggested. He wondered how the 10 per cent rate was arrived at. Making full allowance for the considerable increase in investment in agriculture that was planned, he wondered what technical and organizational improvements allowed the Soviet planners to allow for such extraordinary rates of growth.

Professor Marczewski noted that while there had been a tendency, since 1957, to allow firms to reinvest their profits on their own initiative, a reversal of the process was occurring. The reason seemed to be that investment had risen beyond the levels foreseen by the planners and therefore conflicted with central decisions. Was there now a trend towards limiting such decentralization of investment decisions? What was the machinery for co-ordinating central and local investment planning?

We knew that, until recently, the Mutual Economic Assistance Council had played only a minor role and that co-ordination of Eastern countries' plans consisted mainly in organizing bilateral relations between each People's Democracy and the Soviet Union. However, since 1960 an effort seemed to have been made to establish real multilateral co-operation.

Theoretically, such co-operation aimed at an optimum in terms of the national product. The aim would be to maximize production in each member country or in one member country, or to maximize the joint product of all member countries. The solutions implied were clearly not the same. Again, if the aim was to maximize the collective product, income transfers to those countries making the biggest sacrifices might be made. Was it the practice to co-ordinate both production and distribution in this kind of way?

Record of Discussion

M. Lisle said that since incomes in the U.S.S.R. could double in ten years because income was rising at 6 or 7 per cent per annum, he wondered how the planners predicted the division of income between consumption and savings and also between consumer goods. He could see how one could set up nutritional standards, for food as a whole, but how did one predict the demand for meat rather than dairy products, or fruit rather than vegetables ? Finally, while it might be possible to have set nutritional standards for food, he found it difficult to see how one could have such standards for durable consumer goods. What ideas did the Russians have ?

Professor Leonard noted that Russian output quite often exceeded the forecast target. Did the big increases in industrial and agricultural output predicted for 1980 represent cautious estimates, or were they intended to allow for fortuitous or unpredictable increases ?

Professor Cukor (Hungary) said that Hungary, being a small and poor country, found international trade important. International trade was very difficult to plan and Hungary had made a number of market studies, beginning with mathematical models for a few branches.

He could see that continuous planning made it necessary to distinguish plans according to length. To produce an engineer would require six years formal training and perhaps five years experience to make him really valuable. One had to allow such a period to elapse.

Mr. Kade (West Germany) found a lack of concrete information in the paper. This was unfortunate, since Soviet economic theorists were now abandoning much of their dogmatism and engaging in such things as inter-industry analysis. Valuable work was being done in the Laboratory for Mathematical and Statistical Techniques in Planning, in Siberia. There had been remarkable changes in Soviet planning since 1957 and participants had hoped to hear more from Professor Sorokin about planning methods.

How was the plan conceived at the different levels ? Was there a formal model of linear or non-linear programming, or was there a simpler iterative method ? Similarly, were the rates of growth of income and consumption important or could one not arrive at these with the input-output method ? Above all, what exactly was being done in the field of inter-industry analysis ? We were told that there was to be an input-output table for 1962. How detailed would it be and would it be in real and/or value terms ? What were the technical coefficients ? What were their norms or estimates ? Were the prices current ones ?

Investment criteria in the U.S.S.R. must not merely solve allocation problems, but allow for decentralization. In the past, much of the work here seemed to have represented either variants of the Western marginal efficiency criteria or purely dogmatic statements. What progress was being made towards working out applicable criteria in the U.S.S.R. ?

Chapter 27

FRONTIERS AND INTERRELATIONS
OF REGIONAL PLANNING

BY

JACQUES R. BOUDEVILLE
Lyons University

FROM the standpoint of the economist, the region has three facets.

The region can first be characterized by its degree of uniformity ; it is more or less HOMOGENEOUS.

Secondly, the region can be investigated as a function of the extent to which it is integrated or less POLARIZED.

Lastly, the region can be examined from the standpoint of the aim pursued ; it is a programmed or PLANNED region.

It is the last of these notions that essentially concerns us today. The problem is one of determining the frontiers of the region as effectively as possible in order to achieve the aims in view. This administrative layout then emerges as the instrument of a long-term economic policy.

This approach gives rise to a basic question and two essential features.

Should the region and its programme be conceived for the region alone as a function of the nation ? The answer depends on two typical features.

The region is a very open space with little coherence. It is accessible to the movements of all goods for which there is a national market — (66 per cent).[1] It is coherent and interrelated only for goods for which the market is essentially regional (33 per cent), such as building, foodstuffs, road transport, telecommunications, water, gas, electricity, trade, services and local government. It contrasts with the nation, the greater part of whose trade takes place within its frontiers. Small Free-Trade countries like Switzerland and Belgium, whose size and population can be compared with those of the Rhône Alps or North Italy, are typical from this point of view. About 50 per cent instead of 33 per cent of their trade is within the frontier.

In point of fact, very little is known of the trade within the region. Generally speaking, three types of information are available :

[1] See below, p. 461.

456

(1) Rail traffic, assessed in tons according to a scale of rates adjusted to the operational requirements of this mode of transport ;

(2) The intensity of road traffic on the national highways classified by the type of vehicle ;

(3) The intensity of river traffic assessed in tons according to a scale of rates which differs from that used for the railways and for general statistical purposes.

All the above can only give a guide or rather — because of the road traffic — an approximation of the regional polarized space, as well as perhaps some data for cross-checking thanks to the matrix of rail transport for movements of goods supplying a national market. Trade within the region and between regions has therefore to be determined indirectly.

It emerges from these considerations that the *frontiers of the programmed region* can be conceived in two ways.

Firstly, they may tend to enclose a territory with the highest possible interdependence and coherence. Hence the polarized region would appear best suited to the creation of regional plans.

Secondly, the frontiers of the regions may be conceived according to the trade that links them, so that one can take the most useful action as regards this trade since it is preponderant (66 per cent).

In short, the question is one of knowing which to plan, i.e. interregional trade or trade within the region. Before replying to this question, the idea of programme, prospect and economic decision has to be clarified.

In investigating the types of analysis that can be used to set up effective programmes, stress should be laid on the difference separating the terms forecast and prospect. Let us take as our aim an economic variable, i.e. income or employment or the equilibrium of the balance of payments.

At the end of a given period in the future, the variable selected as the end in view has two values : the *forecast* value and the *desired* or *required* value. They are quite separate. The role of the political instrument is to foster this difference between forecasts and prospects. The role of the model of decision is to present only the relationships between political instruments and objectives.

In achieving a given aim, political instruments have an effectiveness and a productivity which varies. Like all productivities, it is the reciprocal of the cost.

Within the geographical framework this cost may be reduced to a minimum and the effectiveness boosted to a maximum considering the economic interrelations retraced by the model, i.e. by the whole of the *decision relationships*.

All in all, the problems raised by the space context of the development of the territory are regulated by a key idea.

Because the intensity of the regional interrelations dictates the economic frontiers, the programme for the largest possible unit must be imposed on the spaces composing it.

We shall therefore examine this idea and the layout of the frontiers for the planned region in order to determine the content and hierarchy of the programmes.

I. THE NOTION AND LAYOUT OF FRONTIERS

Professor Leontief recently put forward, at the Collège de France,[1] a model of analysis for interregional trade based on the notion of gravitation. This leads at the present time to the most up-to-date operational notion of the region defined by its *external trade*.

On the other hand, in emphasizing that the polarized space is a field of force [2] whose growth is a function of its leading industries,[3] Professor Perroux defines the region by its internal cohesion and its polarization, i.e. by its *internal trade*.

The two notions — one of them more abstract, the other more realistic, as can be seen merely from looking at a map of the industrial regions [4] — both have the great merit of being based on a fundamental feature in the working of our economies, namely the asymmetrical interrelation.

This dominant feature is spontaneously adapted to the notion of the model. It is quite the opposite with the notion of homogeneity which describes the point of departure or of arrival, but which does not tend towards the conception of a pattern of action and development. It does not seem that the point of view of homogeneity alone enables the frontiers of the programmed regions to be drawn. What of the notions of internal and external trade ?

(A) The examples of Lyons and Italy enable us to *discard the homogeneous frontier*.

The average *per capita* income and its complementary factors are a synthetic index of the development or under-development they

[1] In March 1962.
[2] *Économie appliquée*, No. 2, 1950.
[3] 'Points de développement et foyers de progrès dans l'économie du XXe siècle', PUF, 1961.
[4] Cf. the map of M. Le Filatre published by the INSEE.

enable to retrace. They are nevertheless an obstacle that has to be overcome.

In France, the frontier of homogeneity clearly cuts right through the Massif Central and the Rhône-Alps area. It separates the Puy-de-Dôme, Loire, Rhône, Isère and Savoie from its peripheral fringe, i.e. the Cantal, Haute-Loire, Ardèche, Hautes-Alpes. On the other hand, it does not cut between Auvergne and Rhône.

On the other hand, the frontier of social and economic polarization as seen from a simple road map emphasizes the sociological and commercial attachment of the Ardèche, the Drôme and the Hautes-Alpes to the triangle of development formed by Grenoble, Lyons and Saint-Étienne. It marks the attachment of the Haute-Loire and the Cantal to Clermont-Ferrand.

The same phenomenon is found in Italy where, however, the example of the Mezzogiorno might suggest the opposite. The ISTAT has divided Italy into three regions, North, Centre-West and South not only because of the level of development as measured by the average *per capita* income, but also because of the diversity of the growth rates bound up with different polarizations and attractions.

In the centre, Latium is polarized by Rome and is split in half by the homogeneous frontier. In addition, the Marches and Umbria are much nearer the South than Emilia-Romagna.

It is remarkable, in fact, that the most dynamic space is not in the traditional North polarized by the Turin, Genoa, Milan triangle after the manner of the Rhône-Alps region, but rather the Centre-West.

Hence, even Italy, where the size of the regions would be favourable, is not broken down in accordance with a criterion of homogeneity. Another notion must be used.[1]

(B) An *abstract frontier* can be defined by the external trade of the region.

We shall consider in turn, the basis, layout and criticism of this frontier.

A large number of national regions and all the urban regions are more than 66 per cent open. Trade with the outside is, in fact, the motive element of the space under consideration. From every point of view, it has a preponderant importance. It is this rather than internal trade which should be at the origin of the definition of the region. The region is based on the machinery of inter-regional trade. It is knowledge of this trade that will form the principle set forth.

[1] Homogeneity is satisfactory for an economic programme only in so far as it coincides with the polarization, cf. below.

A model of this trade pattern based on the principle of information or gravitation is given by Leontief.[1] A regional couple AB, say Eastern France and Brittany, with its trade currents is thus considered. But these currents are not independent of the competition from the other regions CDEFGH and of the layout of their frontiers. This layout will be all the more satisfactory the better the AB currents are predicted by the model.

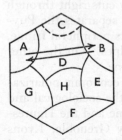

By coupling regions CF and ED, etc., the layout of the frontiers A and B as well as of the frontiers of the regions foreign to the pair of spaces considered can be improved in turn. Gradually, an optimum layout is reached.

We feel that this method is dangerous for two reasons:

(1) It places complete confidence in the theoretical model, the validity of which has not yet been proved and may confuse the issue ;[2]

(2) Since external trade is markedly more unstable than internal trade, the frontiers defined in this manner will be essentially mobile, which is a nullifying obstacle to a four-year programme.

The frontiers could only be stabilized at the cost of extreme division, which gives rise to the elementary cell of the firm and the household.

Fortunately, there is a third conception of the frontier.

(C) A concrete frontier defines *the polarized region*.

The polarized region is defined as a heterogeneous space, the different parts of which are complementary to each other and conduct among themselves, and especially with the dominating poles, more trade than with the neighbouring region.

---

[1] Its fundamental equation is :

$$Xigh = \frac{Xigo \; Xioh}{Xioo} (Cig + Kih) \; digh \; \Sigma \; igh$$

where

$Xigh$ = export of the commodity i from region g to region h
$Xigo$ = total production of commodity i in region g
$Xioh$ = total consumption of commodity i in region h
$Xioo$ = total production or consumption of i
Cig = influence parameter of the other producing regions
Kih = influence parameter of the other consumer regions
$digh$ = reciprocal of the distance gh
igh = 1 or 0.

[2] We feel that it is essential for the experiment to be made in France, but on the frontiers of the polarized region.

The region is therefore an aggregate of contiguous elementary units whose internal index of attachment is stronger than the index of attachment with the neighbouring space of the same order. Such a continuous ensemble has a maximum intensity of internal trade and hence maximum sociological cohesion. It is achieved by trial and error. It is not unique but is a function of the scale, i.e. of the number of regions — 100, 20 or 10 fixed *a priori*. At the limit — and contrarily to the earlier notion of the frontier leading to the firm and the household — it ends in the regional autarky of the nation.

In practice, as the trade is not well known, the polarized region is defined firstly by the poles, the hierarchy of which forms the background, and secondly by the road and telecommunication links which connect them on a regional economic scale.

Merely by superimposing the INSEE map plotted by M. Le Filatre on the map showing the intensity of the growth in road traffic, the layout of the contours of 20 and 10 large French regions can easily be distinguished by eye.

The regional metropolis is defined by its tertiary composition and by the diversity of its industrial functions. In practice the two indices are often related, hence the possibility of making a hierarchical classification.

(D) *The adaptation of the polarized region to the programmed region* is bound up with both its size and the availability of technicians, trades union executives and local administrators.

The minimum economic *size* is on the scale of the small European nations such as Denmark, Switzerland, Belgium and Holland. The above table gives the area, the population, the overall and *per capita* incomes of these countries and that of the 6 main regions out of the 21 regions for the French programme, as well as the figures corresponding to North-West Italy.

It seems that a region of 30,000-40,000 square kilometres containing 4-5 million inhabitants and with a regional income of about 4 million dollars at 1958 prices can lay claim to an integrated regional life, if not to a national life. This corresponds closely to 10 large French regions. It is only at this scale that social accounting and regional programmes are forcibly required. Only the Rhône-Alps region and the North Region approach these dimensions. They are therefore in our opinion the two test programme regions.

Similarly the union of Lorraine and Alsace, together with part of Franche-Comté, would form a typical European region.

In addition, Brittany and Aquitaine should be added as an *under-developed* programme region.

As a comparison, it is interesting to *measure the degree of internal*

TABLE 1

SMALL COUNTRIES AND PROGRAMMED REGIONS (1957)

	Area in Sq. Km.	Population	Density	Income $ Million	Per capita Income	External Trade* on GNP	External Trade* on Total Output
Switzerland	41	5,429	131	7,699	1510	36%†	20%†
Denmark	43	4,547	106	4,889	1086	54%†	36%†
Belgium	30·5	9,154	300	10,161	1130		68%‡
Netherlands	32·5	11,480	354	10,868	1087		
Rhône Alps	44	3,631	86	4,299	1194		
Lorraine	23 ⎫	1,971 ⎫	91	2,438 ⎫	1219		
Alsace	8 ⎬ 31	1,211 ⎬ 3,182	154	1,366 ⎬ 3,804	1139		
Brittany	28	2,341	83	1,892	779		
Aquitaine	42	2,191	54	2,033	924		
North	12	3,393	287	4,477	1317		
Italy (North-West)	58	12,600	217				

* Average (imports-exports).
† According to Delahaut et Kirschen, *Cahiers économiques de Bruxelles*, No. 1, pp. 119-20, No. 10, p. 165, calculated from a national matrix in twenty branches.
‡ Calculated from a regional matrix in sixteen branches.

coherence, we dare not say autarky, of very open countries like Belgium and the Netherlands.

By comparing the average of imports to the gross national product, abnormally high proportions are obtained. In point of fact, the national product only accounts for terminal products and hence a fraction of the total national output. The totality of the external transactions is compared with a fraction of the internal transactions.

An input-output table of order 20 would provide a better comparison. In 1933 Belgium worked to the extent of a fifth of its total output in goods and services to satisfy the rest of the world. In return it received about one-fifth of the total consumption that it required for its functioning. However, this ratio — one of the highest in the world — is exceeded by the Netherlands, where it amounted to 36 per cent. In France the average ratio of imports and exports to the gross national product is about 15 per cent and the average share of imports and exports in total output (table of order 12) is about 10 per cent.

For the Rhône-Alps area, a calculation of the degree of 'opening' can be made from a regionalized 16-branch inter-industrial table.

Local activities include branch 04 Electricity, Gas and sundry, branches 13 to 19 Building, Transport, Trade, Services, totalling NF 7175 million.

Two-thirds of the coal output, i.e. NF 178 million and about half of the agricultural and food industries, i.e. 1106 million have to be added. Out of a total of 24,000 million, these 8459 million accounts for about 31 per cent. By adding the textile and chemical materials stemming from the above activities, the figure becomes 32 per cent.

In 1953 the exports from the European countries of the OEEC to the rest of the world amounted to 23,000 million dollars and the total sales (final and intermediate) to 504,000 million, i.e. about 4·5 per cent.[1] Does this mean that the nation is to Europe as the region is to the nation ? But this question poses in turn the question of the content and hierarchy of the programmes.

II. THE CONTENT AND HIERARCHY OF THE PROGRAMMES

Confronted with the three aspects of the region, i.e. the homogeneous region, the polarized region and the planned region, it is

[1] E. S. Kirschen, *La Structure de l'économie européenne en 1953*, OEEC, 1958.

customary to set up three types of regional programmes relating to rural regions, urban regions and river basins.

In any event, this is not a question of economic planning based on the notion of interrelations and integrated programmes. This is only technical planning containing a number of sociological ancillaries. Apart from the cases in Italy and Brazil, economic planning proper, in the field of action, remains localized on a national level.

Now as Professor François Perroux has said, the priorities in a development plan cannot be solved by the narrow procedure of specific projects. They have to be integrated in the framework of the overall forecast, i.e. urban, regional or national.

By bearing in mind the need for a distinction of scale and the absolute necessity of integrating direct and indirect effects into coherent and connected plans, we can consider in turn :

(A) The regionalization of national programmes.
(B) Polarized programmes based on an urban hierarchy.
(C) Interregional river basin development programmes.
(D) Interregional programmes between supra-national economic communities.

We only outline the first two points here, since the others have already been gone into elsewhere.[1]

(A) *The regionalization of national programmes*

(1) A distinction has to be made between the national market and growth and the regional markets and growth. Hence the regions are brought into contact through the nation as a whole.

(2) Two difficulties arise :

— in the markets, the intermediate demand is as large as the final demand ;
— as regards the supply, the costs of a given industry do not have the same structure in every region.

(3) Although it is a very slow process to build up a regional matrix, it is fortunately easy to regionalize a national matrix by aggregation if the latter is sufficiently detailed. Furthermore, it is of interest to break it down into three relatively independent and hierarchical blocks, namely :

(a) the agricultural complex ;
(b) the industries and services depending on the final demand ;

[1] Cf. *Les Espaces économiques*, Collection 'Que sais-je ?', PUF, 1961. *Les Programmes économiques*, Collection 'Que sais-je ?', PUF, 1962.

(c) the basic industries depending on the intermediate demand whose centre of decision is national and the weight very considerable, compared with the industries of the other two groups.

(B) *Polarized programmes based on an urban hierarchy*

Industry is urbanized in order to derive full benefit from a saving on expenses external to the firm. But sufficient diversity is necessary for an urban centre to become a pole of development. The mere effect of income analysed by conventional accounting methods is powerless in a community that is too open.

The problem consists of bringing the urban turnover, at constant prices, up to a maximum — allowing for the constraints of space and labour — as a function of the technical matrix and the salary cost of the town. This is the problem of the industrial zones. This point has been dealt with in earlier studies of the Association de Science Régionale de Langue Française, particularly in the Regional Operational models, *Cahiers de l'ISEA*, series L, No. 9.

Within the framework of the regional programme, if the metropolis is to fulfil its role as co-ordinator, it must receive the most comprehensive range of newly-installed industries allowing for the above constraints. The satellite towns will develop through more far-reaching specialization as a function of the particular advantages they have to offer.

Errors of method have to be avoided. Care must be taken not to use the system of the urban-based economic multiplier to account for diversified urban growth. In its general shape $E = (1 - k)^{-1} n$,[1] the urban multiplier is only a fairly rough aggregate tending to make a saving on the study of economic interrelations. In its pseudo-matricial form, it is a preposterous mathematical exercise. It is the purchasing factors that are stable, not the sales factors. They can only both be so in the case of homothetic growth.

In conclusion, Regional Economy is a science of decision. It presupposes the determination of aims, the use of means and the choice of the most effective instruments to achieve those aims.

From this point of view, two dangers are apparent in a concerted economy. Firstly, the pattern of the regional programmes is as much professional as administrative. The same problems of demarcation and hierarchy face trade-union organization and local authorities.

[1] E = total employment ; n = national employment ; k = percentage represented in total employment by local employment.

Secondly, the problem of bringing to light the interrelations of the economic trends and the coherence of the means and aims requires the presence of a regional command familiar with the new techniques which, although simple no doubt, are of sufficiently recent date in their first decade to be misunderstood or unknown. At the outset, it will be essential to remain confined to a minimum while setting store for the future.

Admittedly, excellent regional schemes have been carried out without the aid of modern techniques. The Roman aqueducts and Gothic cathedrals did not wait for Strength of Materials calculations to be architectural feats.

Similarly, we can admire the work of the pioneers of our time. Nevertheless, the role of the economist is to produce general rules superseding the old empirical approach and piecemeal work, which is always expensive.

Three principles are essential. In constructing a regional policy, the polarized region is the best instrument of economic analysis. Secondly, the region should not be considered in itself regardless of the nation as a whole. Lastly, if a policy of expansion is to be successful, it is more important to throw light on the resources available than to list the deficiencies.

———

DISCUSSION OF THE PAPER BY PROFESSOR BOUDEVILLE

Professor Lombardini (Italy) suggested that a region should be defined according to the purposes of one's analysis. One might be assessing the perspectives of economic development there. Or one might be dealing with the implications of hypothetical changes in some exogenous variables and parameters for the structure and dynamics of the region. Analysis might also help planners to co-ordinate their interventions in a particular area.

For the first purpose, a region should be defined in terms of links between productive sectors. In a rapidly-developing region this was easy. Many activities would be connected with the region's rapidly-growing industries, especially if this growth was concentrated in a few big firms, which had a large number of relatively small firms as suppliers or sub-contractors. Changes in the rate of growth in a region depended mainly on technical and economic development in these leading industries and on the actual or potential facilities which the region could offer after government intervention.

The aim would be to create poles of development, each pole being characterized by the concentration of some basic activities. If a country was dominated by a number of separate poles of this kind, there should be no difficulty in determining the boundaries of each region, especially if there were no strong links between the poles of development. If a region was so defined the coefficients of an econometric model for it could be built up. Research on the Turin region had shown that the technical coefficients in its matrix were quite stable. The commercial coefficients — the percentages of input bought from firms within the region and the percentages of output exported — were less stable. Problems arising from the instability of the coefficients could be dealt with more effectively if the regional analysis was carried out simultaneously with an analysis of the whole country. By comparing regional input-output tables with the national one, light could be thrown on the different degrees of technical and economic development in various regions and the relationships between them. Regional analysis enabled one to make reasonable guesses about possible changes in some of the parameters of the national model; labour productivity was the accelerator. Similarly, analyses of the whole economy helped one to foresee possible changes in some of the regional coefficients.

Professor Baudin (France) said that in France the word region meant an area smaller than the nation and the paper regarded the nation as the maximum area for a region. However, in the IEA the word '*régional*' was always used to translate the English word 'regional', although this did not mean the same thing. The IEA had held 'regional' conferences for Africa and was considering one for the Mediterranean countries. The word 'region' suggested common interests, but how could one use such a concept for the whole Mediterranean area or for Europe ? The Mediterranean area was certainly not homogenous. If it had a pole, the pole was formerly Rome. As for planning it was hard to see how this could be done today on a regional basis if countries like Egypt and Israel were both included in the Mediterranean region.

In Latin America one saw inter-dependence and co-operation only between states of similar economic strength and at similar stages in development. Thus Colombia, Ecuador and Venezuela had formed an international group, but Argentina and Brazil were not members. They were at a different level of development.

M. de Maud'huy (France) was struck by Professor Tinbergen's feeling, shared by many people, that regional planning was intended to raise the level of economic development in under-developed countries. His own experience suggested that while planning was difficult in under-developed areas suffering from unemployment, urban planning, for example, was difficult and complex in developed regions with full employment. In his own region, income was high, but there were relatively few schoolchildren and engineers had to be imported. They were emptying the under-developed parts of France. Regional planning had to be general and this applied to both developed and under-developed countries. In the latter, the aim should be to give equilibrium and balance to the economy. The regional planners would have to accept overall objectives set for them at the national level. There were some difficulties, therefore, in reconciling regional needs with national aims. If one were going to co-ordinate plans at the national level it would be necessary to have a flexible notion of the region and he was afraid of too much centralization. In France, the regions had probably benefited from the existence of a group of men who could interrelate decisions, since they already knew the essence of the problem. However, it would be necessary to move beyond this, especially in European planning.

Dr. Mulder (Italy) said that Professor Boudeville was trying to define the geographical frontiers of a region within which one could plan, and made the distinction between homogeneous and polarized regions. The first were characterized by such things as a low income per head. The latter were determined by the degree of economic integration — the intensity of trade. How far were these regions homogeneous sociologically ? Were they characterized by a common conception of life, a sense of belonging, a common folklore, etc. ? Experience indicated that local planning, say, in a village, was useless unless sociological factors were considered. Was not the same true of a regional development programme ? He saw no *a priori* reason why the polarized region should coincide with the region as a sociological unit.

Professor Bourrières (France) congratulated Professor Boudeville on having had the courage to give a figure for the size, population and income of what could be called a region. He had suggested 30,000 to 40,000 square kilometres, 4 to 5 million people and an income of 4 million dollars. These figures were only sensible in a European framework and it was hard to decide whether area, population or income was the most important criterion. Professor Bourrières was particularly interested in the relevance of these criteria in under-developed areas, where the existence of deserts, forests and areas with very high population meant there was no coherence between the three criteria.

His own solution for Africa would be to suggest that a region should have between 4 and 5 million people, unless population density was high. This would mean that many new African countries represented only part of a region, while Nigeria had several regions.

With India or China one would not have 100 regions in each country, because income was very low. One might well have to regard an area with 40 million people as a region. He approved of M. Boudeville's approach, because it meant that when a country did develop, one changed one's concepts. This was not merely a theory, but suggested practical measures.

Professor Isard (United States) emphasized those points where he thought time would bring a change in analysis. As a regional scientist, he thought of a system of regions in terms of interdependent economic, social and political factors. One also had a hierarchy of regions, with the world itself as the highest-order region. Professor Tinbergen had focussed attention on the nation, or political region. Professor Boudeville had broken this down into metropolitan or polarized regions and we could disaggregate still further to the sub-metropolitan, the water-shed or even the neighbourhood region. He thought it was correct for Professor Boudeville to approach the polarized region in the way he had done since it raised a set of critical problems which could be attacked with the available techniques. However, other approaches were also relevant and would become even more relevant as time went on.

We must bring in non-economic factors and it was in this way that he felt the Tinbergen model would be improved in ten years' time. As Professors Boudeville and Lombardini had said, a national model or plan was often looked at as relating to a set of linked regions. However, while it was necessary to integrate the regions at the national level, the region itself should be looked upon as an integrate unit. He felt the need to introduce into economic analysis some tools from other fields, such as statistical decision theory. Planners had to look at political, as well as economic, feasibility. Simulation techniques could enable one to confront the decision makers with all possible alternatives, discover which they thought satisfactory and so bring political feasibility criteria into a model. National and regional plans could then be more satisfactorily reconciled.

Professor Mossé (France) wondered why Professor Boudeville was concerned with frontiers between regions, when these were being broken down between nations. It was important not to regard the region as a unit with rigid frontiers. While actual planning meant that one was concerned with a particular area, it was also important to consider links between regions.

Professor Mossé looked with some displeasure on the tendency towards centralization in France. Regional planners should not concern themselves merely with the geographical projection of some national objective. They must take account of local needs and demands and he felt that these could be given much greater weight than in the past.

Professor Boudeville explained that the fundamental difficulty of defining regions in terms that would apply to both under-developed and developed countries was that the region was not the same at all stages of economic development. In under-developed countries the pricing system was inefficient and prices charged often had no economic rationale. Analysis must therefore be based more on income than on anything else. A polarized region must have common statistical data and commercial links. He felt that mobility and sociological, or even spiritual, factors could be allowed for. In Europe, regions were often determined by the location of key industries and the role of industrialists in the region was important. They also needed technicians to conceive and carry out a plan. There were few such planners, but it was essential to reconcile regional and national objectives. At present, France's regional planners were a group of men moving from region to region. He thought it important that towns should not only know how much they sold outside their boundaries,

but where their products went.   One could then define regional, national
and international goods.   There had been a very interesting study of the
coal trade for 89 French regions, and such analysis could study the evolution of technical coefficients and commercial relations.   They would lead
to regional models for some kinds of goods.

Professor Boudeville did not think one should follow Plato in defining
regions, although there seemed to have been a classical division between
internal and external causality in his paper.   He felt one should go farther
and consider the use of various poles, as Professor Isard had done.   The
polarized region was the optimum for applying linear operators to stable
relationships.   He agreed that there was no complete homogeneity within
the Mediterranean Basin, but thought one could oppose this region to
that of the 'Men of the Sea'.   There was certainly no doubt that the
Mediterranean Basin was largely made up of under-developed areas.

Chapter 28

REGIONAL PLANNING
AND URBAN DEVELOPMENT

BY

E. A. LISLE

University of Paris

THE preparation of the fourth French plan (1962–65) was the occasion for an important effort to programme the residential and collective equipment of large cities over the next fifteen years. Urbanization of the population is one of the dominant characteristics of our time.[1] It is legitimate therefore to approach the problem of regional planning through the programming of urban equipment.

To plan, fifteen or twenty years hence, requirements in housing, elementary and secondary schools, advanced education facilities, hospitals, technical, social and cultural equipment, involves making a long-range forecast of the city's economy. Given present capital equipment, its capacity and degree of obsolescence, given also standards of occupancy to be maintained or attained, future requirements will depend first on a replacement and renewal policy with regard to existing constructions, secondly on a forecast of population growth analysed by age and sex and located by districts.

The population forecast is itself the result of two trends : natural growth and net immigration, the latter being far more important than the former. Immigration is caused by two factors : economic attraction due to new employment opportunities and attraction exercised by the city itself for certain types of population who come as permanent or long-term residents (students, the sick, the retired, etc.). In the case of new employment opportunities, two subgroups should be distinguished : opportunities induced by population growth (construction, retailing, transportation and public utilities, education and local administration, etc.); autonomous employment opportunities, in sectors which do not cater for residents but whose activity is outwardly turned. A fifteen- or twenty-year forecast of the economic growth of the city is therefore, through its incidence on employment, the centre-piece of a programme of residential and collective capital equipment even though new employment opportunities are not the sole cause of immigration.

In practice, nevertheless, the programming of urban capital

[1] Jean Gottman, *Megalopolis*, 20th Century Fund, New York, 1961.

471

equipment only fans out into problems of regional economic development in units of a certain size : towns of 300,000 to 500,000 population,[1] conurbations of 1,000,000 or more [2] or when a town of 50,000 to 100,000 is set — for the purpose of studying its investment requirements — within the *urban network* [3] of the five or six neighbouring towns of similar size.

A forecast of economic growth is thus the basis of any programme of residential and collective equipment. The implementation or non-implementation of the programme will in turn help or hinder the economic growth anticipated in the region.

This paper will analyse the economic magnitudes which must be forecast regionally in order to draft a capital equipment programme. The forecasting methods will then be described and the significance of the results assessed.

I. REGIONAL ECONOMIC MAGNITUDES REQUIRED FOR PROGRAMMING URBAN INVESTMENTS

The drafting of a long-range programme of residential and collective capital equipment does not require setting up regional economic accounts, which at best are too often but a servile imitation of national accounts. It is unnecessary, for instance, to draw up regional balance sheets by commodity groups for they are not relevant to the problem at hand besides being of little economic significance and most difficult to establish. Two sets of variables are, however, fundamental : demographic data ; incomes.

To estimate and project these magnitudes requires statistical data on concepts borrowed from population censuses and national accounts. They are summarized in the following table.

Demography

In a Western country like France a population growth rate of 1 per cent per annum may be deemed high without, however, being of much importance compared to a productivity growth rate of 4 or 5 per cent per annum. For a city, on the other hand, population growth rates of 2 or 3 per cent per annum are common and are at the root of capital equipment requirements, location problems and

---

[1] Such as Toulouse, Nice, Bordeaux, Nantes.
[2] Such as the District of Paris, the Lille–Roubaix–Tourcoing conurbation, the Lyons region, Marseilles and its outer belt (Aubagne, Gardanne, Aix, Salon, Étang de Berre).
[3] Such as the Nîmes–Montpellier–Sète–Béziers–Narbonne network.

traffic difficulties — more generally of all problems of land use, that specifically rare factor — which face us in towns today.

Population censuses are the best source of demographic data. They are unfortunately infrequent and slow to exploit, with the result that the picture they give is quickly out of date in rapidly-growing towns. They have to be brought up to date through

VARIABLES NEEDED TO PROGRAMME URBAN CAPITAL EQUIPMENT

Economic Agents	Demography	Incomes
Firms	Number of establish-ments (by sector) Employment (by sector) — overall — by district — commutation	Operating account — by sector and legal status (e.g. companies, self-employed)
Households	Number and size of houses — by district Number and age-sex structure of households — overall — by district	Appropriation account Distribution of incomes
Local authorities	Employment	Appropriation and capital accounts

sample surveys of population or employment, social insurance registrations, house construction statistics, the registrar of births and deaths, the electoral roll, etc.[1]

Incomes

Three categories of income are relevant to a programme of capital equipment :

income of resident households which on the one hand determines the level of the effective demand for housing, thus governing the volume and the structure of the largest item in a city's capital formation ; on the other hand the purchasing power of households is a basis for the rates and taxes levied by local authorities ; value added by firms in the region : this is both a source of households' income and of local authorities' revenue ;

[1] In some countries a declaration of residence is compulsory at each change of address. Migratory movements can thus be traced with some accuracy.

local authorities' revenue whose volume finally determines the borrowing or the self-financing capacity of the city for its capital equipment programme.[1]

Except for local authorities' revenue, these different forms of income are difficult to estimate. In the case of firms, a consolidated operating account may be drawn up, showing value added estimated as the sum of its parts : wages and salaries, employers' insurance contributions, indirect taxes, gross trading profit. In France, data exist on a departmental basis for the first three items. The fourth one must be estimated from the other three by means of national coefficients.

In the case of households, sample surveys are strictly the only means whereby an appropriation account can be drawn up and income distributions plotted. In France sample surveys are available covering the nine regions defined by EEC. It would be unwise to extrapolate the results of these surveys to narrower regions. When surveys are lacking it is necessary to estimate the income of households by means of the operating account of firms (wages and salaries paid out, unincorporated business profits) and the appropriation account of local authorities and social insurance services (wages and salaries, pensions, insurance benefits). The approximation to households' overall income thus arrived at may be checked by the local income tax returns of private persons.[2]

II. FORECASTING THE ECONOMIC MAGNITUDES

Although it is unnecessary to set up a complete set of regional accounts, it is vital for the projection that the accounts drawn up be strictly comparable (as regards definitions, schedules and methods) to the corresponding national accounts which are the framework of the national economic development plan. For, as a first approximation, a projection of the regional economic variables will be attempted homothetically with respect to the comparable national magnitudes.

[1] State subsidies to local authorities vary considerably (in France) according to the type of capital equipment. Taking the capital equipment programme as a whole, however, they are a complementary source of funds : the main financial resources are those which the local authorities must raise out of, or borrow on the strength of, their own revenue.

[2] A pilot attempt was made to draw up these accounts in the Bouches-du-Rhône department in the South of France. For the whole department 27 sectoral consolidated operating accounts were drawn up covering all firms (later a similar set of accounts were drawn up covering all firms in the District of Paris). For the whole department and for the towns of Marseilles and Aix separately, the appropriation accounts of households were drawn up ; for Aix, the appropriation and capital accounts of the government sector were drawn up.

The results thus obtained will then be corrected in order to take account of local development projects.

The Homothetic Projection

To each sector in the region under survey, represented by its level of employment and its value added, are attributed the rates of growth of output and productivity anticipated for the same sector on the national level over the period of the development plan. Projections of employment and value added by sector are deduced which will act as a working hypothesis in the second stage of the forecast.

The Revised Projection

Two sets of corrections are brought to bear on this working hypothesis.

First, the employment trend provides a basis upon which to build a population forecast. This in turn generates a feed back projection of new employment opportunities induced by overall population. The value added projection on the other hand provides a first approximation of households' income which, via the propensity to consume function, feeds back a revision of the output forecast for the retail and personal service sectors of the region. Thus after a few iterations — not yet formalized, by a model — the original projection of employment, population and incomes is revised.

Simultaneously this forecast is submitted to sectoral working parties (made up of representatives of the local and central government and of local trade associations and leading firms) comparable, on the regional level, to the national committees for modernization and investment which work out, in France, the details of the national economic development plan.

The sectoral working parties criticize and revise in each sector the forecasts of employment and output on the basis of development plans under way and projects in hand. The incidence of these revisions is then estimated in terms of income.

The forecasts of employment and population [1] thus obtained are the basis of the urban capital equipment programme defined in terms of the population's material requirements subject to standards of occupancy and a given renewal policy to be achieved by a certain date. The estimated cost of this programme must then be set

---

[1] The population forecast is arbitrarily corrected, where necessary, to take account of residential immigration not linked to economic growth.

against the financial possibilities of the city. These are deduced from a projection of running costs (analysed by broad categories, whose trends are statistically estimated from time series) and a forecast of public revenue based on the probable trend of assessable matter (value added, households' income) and assumptions concerning the rates of local taxes.

The comparison between the city's capital outlay requirements and its financial possibilities determines an order of investment priorities, in other words leads to a set of political decisions, for the socially or technically optimum programme (within a given horizon) is generally subjected to financial restraints.

III. CONCLUSIONS

The foregoing remarks amount to a progress report summarizing three years' experience in a French department : aims, problems, methods. The aim was to programme the urban capital equipment of one or more cities in a region.

The problems were mostly of a statistical nature : knowledge of the demography and economy of a region are at present inadequate (in France) to attain the objective aimed at.

The method consisted in drawing up and projecting a few tables of population statistics and economic accounts comparable to the corresponding national accounts but not integrated in a full set of regional accounts.

Besides the immediate usefulness of the analysis of population, employment and incomes for the long-range programming of urban capital equipment, two further contributions to regional economic analysis should be mentioned.

The first one concerns the economic dependence of the region with respect to the rest of the world. In the process of estimating the components of value added, one has to distinguish the establishments whose indirect taxes are paid by a head office situated outside the region under survey ('fiscal emigration'). The level of employment or the value added of these establishments set against the comparable magnitudes of the whole sector provides an indicator of dependence of the sector with respect to decision-making units outside the region. What is true of each sector is true of the whole economy and provides an indicator of the dependence (or of autonomy) of the region as a whole with respect to the rest of the country (world). In the case of particularly dynamic regions 'fiscal immigration' may well take place thus indicating the degree of influence or attraction of the region on the rest of the world.

A second result of the foregoing analysis is to help define the 'critical mass' beyond which a region has a likelihood of seeing its economic growth develop spontaneously, below which it requires external stimuli to maintain its level of activity-distinguishing, in the terminology of the fourth French plan, regions where government economic policy need only follow up development and regions where it must set the pace. The size (and density) of population, its social and professional structure and incomes, are a first set of factors defining this 'critical mass'. The degree of dependence reflected in fiscal migrations are another. The volume (in terms of employment and value added) and especially the nature of tertiary activities is a third. This sector is one of those most expected to expand in coming years, servicing the resident population (retailing, personal services, etc.), the population residing in the city's sphere of attraction (university facilities, hospitals, entertainment, etc.), as well as the manufacturing industries of the town and its region (head offices, commercial, financial and research departments, insurance, banking, commodity and securities markets, etc.).

The economy of a region is centred on that of the large city which constitutes its metropolis : at one and the same time, mass-consumption market, source and training centre for labour, location of the administrative, social and more generally collective capital equipment servicing households and firms.

A forecast of the demographic and economic development of a region is a necessary basis for a long-range programme of urban investments. But the latter in turn, because of the weight of the metropolis in the regional economy, because too of the structurating qualities of urban capital equipment, emerges as a natural starting point for regional planning.

DISCUSSION OF THE PAPER BY M. LISLE

Professor Lajugie concentrated on two points of method. First, M. Lisle had said that the establishment of long-run programmes for urban areas did not require comprehensive regional accounts. If this meant that we could not afford to wait until regional accounts were developed he would agree, since we must use what data we had. However, this was very much a second-best method and we ought to be aiming to build up regional, and even urban, accounts for each agglomeration. Without them no coherent plan was possible. He was also surprised that M. Lisle did not press for a regional balance for each product. He agreed that this was hard to calculate, but it did have an economic meaning. Data for each product and each sector were indispensable to our knowledge of the various circuits of trade and production, which in a sense defined an agglomeration. He did not think such statistics would be artificial and while he agreed that, at first, we should have to break down the national accounts to get regional figures, he hoped that, as soon as possible, true regional accounts would be produced at the regional level. Experiments in France showed that this could be done.

In the second part of his paper, M. Lisle proposed the homothetic method for regional forecasting — the application of the national co-efficient to regional data about basic variables. This was very dangerous. The aim of regional policy was to reduce disparities between regions and using this method was likely to perpetuate them. Although one could make adjustments, the method was a bad one. For example, France was aiming to increase its tertiary sector. If one raised the amount of tertiary activity in every region to the national average, one would get too much tertiary activity in areas like Aquitaine, where there was no industrial base. It would be much better to aim at achieving the ideal rate of growth for each individual region.

Mr. Kochav said that M. Lisle had described the framework of the information needed for regional planning. This might be very suitable for regions which would develop in an organic way, but in a new city or region development was not an organic process. It represented an organized effort to build up a region or city rapidly under the pressure of immigration, resettlement and political decisions. It was often assumed that by building houses and providing basic services one could attract the necessary industry, but if this did not happen there would be unemployment of a kind that might not exist in existing cities with 'traditional' employment. A comprehensive plan for any new area was therefore necessary. The difficulties of a new city were well known. Costs of transport, energy and water might be higher and part of the population attracted to the improved houses or other facilities might be unskilled.

All these problems could be overcome, but only through subsidies from the central government. Unfortunately a comprehensive plan required vast amounts of detailed information, not least on costs, and such information was essential in assessing the kind of industry which could safely be set up in a new area. Great stress would have to be laid on functional training and education which would be lacking in a new area.

M. Maillet (Luxembourg) saw some contradiction between M. Lisle's insistence that one should plan housing etc. on at least a ten-year basis and his belief that one could use forecasting techniques. These could only look ahead five years at the very most and became very unrealistic if one pushed them farther ahead.

Professor Boudeville (France) said that a study had been carried out in Lyons, projecting employment rather than links between the industries.

Unfortunately all industrial expansion seemed to take place in new industrial zones rather far from the existing urban areas. One needed to know the degree of complementarity between industries, for this would inevitably be changed brutally when other industries moved in. For, example, the introduction of the petro-chemical industry would mean that highly-capitalistic processes replaced labour. This made it difficult to provide employment, and realistic plans for growth had to take account of the effects of investments in new industries.

M. *Lisle* agreed fully with Mr. Kochav's insistence on the need for training. The fact that he had not said more about it in his paper did not mean that he underestimated its importance. Some departments of France were likely to find development hampered by a lack of educational facilities.

He agreed with M. Maillet that there was some contradiction between the distance one had to look ahead in planning the building of hospitals schools and public utilities and the possibilities of accurate forecasting. However, one might hope that the increased dynamism of a region which came about when new industry was introduced would allow sufficient new industry to be attracted.

What Professor Lajugie had said was quite fundamental. M. Lisle reported there was some controversy in France at present over the feasibility of working out regional activities and he wanted to qualify what he had said in his paper. In some fields it had been important to work out economic models. For example, in the U.K., after 1939, it had proved necessary to produce national income accounts in order to show the dangers of inflation in Keynesian terms. In France, a similar global model had been disaggregated and the resulting system of accounts used as a framework for the whole economy. There was, however, no regional model for development and this was why he had said that only the national system of accounts could be applied to regions. The ultimate aim must be a policy for regional development, though at present this could not be based on any complete model. One method was to develop transport, technology, housing, hospitals, etc., which could be done by the local political authorities. A model would give one a programme for the collective equipment for a region, but the state would then have to play some part.

On the homothetic method, M. Lisle stressed that one should not work out one's policy on the basis of the national figure, but correct the national figure for each region in agreement with the local political authorities. He stressed that the co-ordination of regional policy could take place only on a national basis.

SECTION 4
THE STABILIZATION OF PRIMARY PRODUCING ECONOMIES

Chairman : W. A. LEWIS
Vice-Chairman : M. BYÉ
Rapporteur : HELEN THOMPSON

Chapter 29

ECONOMIC DEVELOPMENT
AND WORLD TRADE

BY

W. ARTHUR LEWIS
University of the West Indies

DURING the nineteenth century economic development overflowed from Europe and North America into Asia and Africa and Latin America by means of international trade. There were the usual substantial benefits. The trader brings new ideas : new tastes, which stimulate effort, and new techniques, which stimulate innovation. Additional income was generated, and though much was taken as profit, much remained behind not merely to add to local consumption, but also to finance ports, railways, electric power, water and other public utilities, and also indirectly through taxation to pay for schools, hospitals, a framework of law and public administration, and other public services. Some local industries were destroyed by imports, and others, such as human porterage, gave way to new techniques, but the net effect was undoubtedly a great increase in the capacity to produce real income.

The process, though beneficial, generated immense resentment in Asia and Africa and Latin America. This resentment is in sum the resentment which any one of us feels against being dependent on somebody else. The momentum of growth was in Europe and North America. The development of the outlying continents happened only by way of reaction to what happened in Europe or North America. The outlying continents were in this sense peripheral, and nobody likes to be peripheral. It takes a good deal of sophistication to be able to say 'I don't mind his using me for his own purposes so long as he pays me well', and even in neutral contexts this has an immoral flavour. The outlying continents built up increasing resentment of the fact that their economic development depended on the pace set in Europe and North America.

Specific resentments included the following :

(1) Foreign trade was dominated by foreigners, buying the materials their economies needed, and pushing the sales of what their economies produced. Much production for export was also

483

dominated by foreigners, especially in plantations or mines, though some crops were grown by peasants. Foreigners also assumed control of the government, and in most cases used this control to advance their own country's economic interest. But the principal cause of the domination by foreigners was that they were the principal source of investment capital, of technical know-how and of marketing contacts.

(2) The foreigners were interested primarily in imports and exports, and did little to stimulate production for the home market. The incomes they paid out locally were to some extent spent on local goods, whose output was thereby stimulated. But whereas much thought and money were given to eliminating obstacles which stood in the way of developing production for export, similar thought and money were not devoted to eliminating obstacles in the way of production for the home market.

(3) The relative share of foreigners in the proceeds was considered unduly high. Foreigners reserved to themselves the best paid jobs, and took in profits sums which seemed large when compared with what they paid in wages or taxes or purchases of local products and services. The terms of trade also caused concern. The terms of trade must move unfavourably to tropical producers so long as they offer to the outside world an unlimited supply of labour available at a wage determined by low productivity subsistence production, since increased productivity in tropical export industries must, in competitive conditions, result in lower prices rather than in higher wages.

(4) Because the economy was dependent, it fluctuated in accordance with cyclical fluctuations transmitted from Europe and North America, rather than in accordance with self-generated movements.

These four characteristics are not all equally essential to the concept of economic dependence. The essence of the independent economy is that it has a momentum of its own, in the sense that the annual rate of investment, and the flow of innovation, are not mainly determined by external causes. These are relative terms. All developed economies have some degree of dependence because they trade. To speak of independent and dependent economies may trap the unwary, but it is quite valid to speak of more dependent and less dependent economies, with say the U.S.A. towards one end of the scale, and Jamaica towards the other end. Britain lies somewhere in between, and is obviously less dependent today than it was thirty years ago.

Having a momentum of one's own is not incompatible with any

one of the characteristics which caused resentment. A country's development may be directed primarily at its own home market, and yet it may be dominated by foreigners and dependent on foreign investment. Conversely, it may be dependent in the sense that its fluctuations derive largely from foreign trade, and yet it may be a mature economy, exporting capital and capitalists. Again, adverse terms of trade are not a necessary result of dependence on foreign trade ; for even if labour for export industries be infinitely elastic in supply, land and minerals are not, so a country can do well out of the rents of scarce types of land or climate or location, or out of mineral royalties. If the emphasis is on momentum, then foreigners, foreign investment and terms of trade are not necessarily symptoms of dependence.

The share of foreign trade in the national economy is more relevant to determining dependence but even this is not decisive. For first we must note that some export trades resist external influences better than others. Some are less subject to fluctuations — in general, the demand for consumer goods fluctuates less than the demand for capital goods. Also some traders are more aggressive : they keep on selling when the rest have stopped, so that in a sense one can think of the Japanese economy during the 1930s as being for this reason less dependent on external influences than other economies with equal proportionate ratios of foreign trade. More important than these differences is the capacity of a country to adapt itself swiftly to adverse external influences. Thus the British economy in the nineteenth century had a remarkable momentum of its own, despite the high ratio of foreign trade, because, as foreign investment diminished, home investment was stepped up. In fact its twenty years' secular (or Kuznets) cycle is actually the reverse of the American in timing. Economic dependence usually springs from dependence on foreign trade, but countries with equal trading ratios are not equally dependent.

Since neo-classical economics does not use the concept of momentum it does not allow for the distinction between greater and less dependence, and the subject is not treated in the traditional texts on international trade. The classical economists were much concerned with such matters, but when they invented the Law of Comparative Costs, and bequeathed its simple arithmetic to become the foundation of the neo-classical theory of international trade, statics supplanted dynamics. This kind of analysis was therefore driven underground into Marxist and nationalist writings. However, there is nothing Marxist in studying momentum ; or in sharing anti-colonialist resentments. Independence, inter-dependence and dependence are found as much in the socialist as in the non-socialist world.

Inside the anti-colonialist world, the resentment of dependence ranges over the degrees of sophistication. At the lowest level it is directed against all the superficial phenomena of the current situation : against foreigners, international investment, the export of profits, exports, imports and neglect of the home market. Whereas at refined levels it is seen that all these hated phenomena have contributed to economic development, and that if they were merely swept away, a dependent country would relapse into even greater poverty. Thus it is recognized that while it is better to have an independent growing economy than a dependent growing economy, it is also better to have a dependent growing economy than an independent stagnant economy.

Men do learn from experience. Most of the men to whom national independence has brought political power, have at some time preached the cruder forms of anti-colonialist economics. But within a few years (often a few months) of attaining power they have usually begun to see that economic dependence is better than stagnation. From talk of driving out foreign investment, many Ministers have switched to spending much of their time in wooing foreign investors, offering guarantees and inducements superior to those offered to their own nationals. Equally, the promotion and safeguarding of export interests has become a major political concern of the new nationalist leaders, even where the export industry is dominated by foreigners.

This change of attitude can be justified by recognizing that one can reduce economic dependence without having to reduce exports. Becoming independent means developing one's own momentum by acquiring a propensity to invest which is not much affected by external events. This means developing a considerable propensity to invest for the home market. If investment for export markets were already very large, an increase in investment for the home market might necessitate a reduction in investment for exports, but in the less developed economies, where the rate of investment is usually low, what is more to the point is an increase in the total level of investment. In most of the less developed countries the problem is not to cut investment for exports, but simply to develop side by side a considerable investment for the home market.

How to increase investment for the home market is outside the terms of reference of this paper ; other sessions of this conference will handle this problem. Foreign trade is not irrelevant : it facilitates investment for the home market creating demand, public utilities, education, savings and so on. Sooner or later its influence and example must stimulate domestic production. However, economic policy no longer waits for what might be a natural evolution, over a long period of time, and modern planners now concentrate on giving to production for the home market most of the thought which used formerly to be given exclusively to eliminating obstacles to exporting.

This can easily be overdone, as they are learning rapidly. Developing home production is not a simple substitute for developing export production. On the contrary : in most cases you cannot produce more for home consumption unless you also produce more for export.

The marginal propensity to use goods of the kind which are being imported always exceeds zero. Hence any development which raises real income, must increase the demand for goods of a kind hitherto imported. If the economy imports its raw materials and its capital goods, the marginal propensity to import will be particularly large. The difficulty also exists on the side of exports, since the marginal propensity to use goods of the kind hitherto exported also exceeds zero, and in some cases, as in Latin America and India since the war, development may eat up exports.

Hence any increase in production for the home market must put a strain on the balance of payments unless it is adequately import substituting. The planner neglects foreign trade at his peril. If each time investment increases, and production begins to rise, the economy is faced with rising imports of food, raw materials and capital goods, or with increased home consumption of exportable goods, not matched by import substitution or by extra exports, the resulting balance of payments deficit not merely threatens the currency's stability ; but also deprives the home market of purchasing power, deflates demand and profits, and so brings the expansion to an end. The economy simply cannot get off the ground. How familiar we now are with this process in economies as different as say Britain, and India and Chile. It is now almost a rule of thumb that, in the absence of foreign borrowing, the possible rate of economic growth is limited by the rate at which you can increase net foreign receipts, whether by exporting more, or by substituting for imports. If one neglects foreign trade in one's planning, either the plan fails, or one is driven to ever-tightening restrictions on imports.

We thus see that it is not an accident that in the past economic development has usually started because of an increase of exports. Attempts to start developments for the home market may have been frequent, but they will have been aborted by the balance of payments difficulties which then deflated the home market. Development based on exports puts money into the home market, and so stimulates production for the home market ; but development based on home production takes money out of the market, to purchase imports, and is therefore self-deflating. We can also see why the nineteenth century was relatively free of balance of payments problems when compared with the twentieth century, although it was a century of such tremendous development. Development based on exports resolves balance of payments crises, while development based on production for the home market creates balance of payment crises.

This is just one aspect of the theory of balanced growth, at which it is now fashionable to sneer. Most of what is written is irrelevant, since it uses the development of export industries as proof that unbalanced growth is possible. In so far as the doctrine is concerned with the pattern of demand, the fact that it is the possibility to export which releases an economy from the restraints of unbalanced growth has always been integral to the theory.[1] The proposition that it is necessary to balance the patterns of demand and supply is concerned only with the limitations of the kind of development which is directed to supplying the home market. The theory says : 'If you increase A, you will have to cut back unless you also increase B'. It does not say : 'If you wish to increase A, you must first increase B', or 'you must increase B simultaneously'. Hence it cannot be disproved by showing that growth always takes place on one front at a time, or in some other unbalanced way. Like Toynbee's tautology, the theory is that if challenge is not met by response, it will result in failure. If you increase the production of A in circumstances where B is complementary to A, you will face a challenge, in the shape of a shortage of B. If you respond to this challenge, you will move to greater heights ; if you do not, you will fail. The anti-balanced growth writers stress that challenge is good, and that the opportunity for response which it offers is the heart of the process of growth ; while the balanced growth theorists, faced with planners who have been getting into serious trouble by neglecting the necessity for response, have been emphasizing that challenge without response leads to failure. One can argue about which of these emphases is more useful at any particular time ; to argue about which is more correct, as so much of the literature does, seems rather childish.

Whatever the theorists may have been writing about balanced growth, a decade of balance of payments crises has served to re-

---

[1] The point is made explicitly in my *The Theory of Economic Growth*, pages 277-80, published in 1955.

habilitate exports in the eyes of the anti-colonialists. They no longer ask whether it is wise to try to expand exports ; their question is rather what is the prospect for exports in a rapidly developing world.

The answer seems to be that the prospect is as good as ever. The quantum of world trade increased in the thirty-five years before the First World War at an average rate of 3·4 per cent per annum.[1] From 1950 to 1960 the average rate was 6·2 per cent per annum.[2]

Both manufactures and primary products are growing faster, in relation to world production, than was the case before 1913. We can take world manufacturing production as a rough index to the growth of world demand. From 1881 to 1913 the ratio of the average annual percentage increase in trade in primary products to the average annual percentage increase of world production of manufactures was 0·81. The ratio had risen, between 1950 and 1960 to 1·04. The base had also risen, since the annual rate of growth of manufacturing which was 4·0 per cent before 1913, averaged 5·2 per cent after 1950.

This increase in world trade, relatively to world production, is not as remarkable as it may seem at first sight, since it follows a period when world trade was well below its 'normal' level in comparison with production. During the Great Depression of the 1930s, world trade in primary products fell about 12 per cent below its normal level in relation to production (by the test of these average ratios) and by 1950 the quantum of world trade in primary products was 17 per cent below the calculated level.[3] It is not therefore strange that trade should now grow relatively faster than before ; indeed at current rates of growth, the quantum of trade in primary products will not attain 'normal' until 1966, after which it would again be 'normal' for the rate of growth of trade to fall below the rate of growth of production.

We have, of course, no knowledge of what is 'normal'. The structure of world trade changes continuously, and we have no reason to expect pre-World-War-I ratios to be still valid post-World-War-II. Yet, one must observe that this kind of remark was made all the time between 1880 and 1930, a period of fifty years, and yet the basic ratios did not change during that period. In any case all we are saying is that it is not strange that the Great Depression era, in

[1] Calculated from League of Nations, *Industrialization and Foreign Trade*, p. 157.

[2] The figures used in this paper from United Nations sources exclude the production and trade of the U.S.S.R.

[3] See my article 'World Production, Prices and Trade, 1870–1960, *The Manchester School of Economic and Social Studies*, May 1952. The figures for 1950 have been revised.

which international trade lost ground, relatively to production, has now been succeeded by a period in which international trade is regaining ground, relatively to production, and that we must not assume that this is more than a temporary phase.

At the same time, this analysis interprets the facts differently from the authors of *Trends in International Trade*.[1] These authors found that world trade in primary products in the middle 1950s was rather low, by comparison with 1928. They assumed that this must be due to long-term structural factors, and adduced the usual explanations (low income elasticity of demand for food, decline in the growth rate of European and North American populations, more economical use of raw materials, substitution of synthetic materials, etc.). Our ratios show that the phenomenon can be explained without resort to such explanations, which have, in any case been at work for many decades. The major decline in trade occurred within the first five years of the early thirties ; and the decade of the fifties has been a period not of decline but of an extraordinarily high growth rate of international trade in primary products. In my Manchester School article of 1952 I fell into the trap, when speculating about what might happen in the 1950s, of forgetting that the fall of trade in the 1930s might be matched by a rise of trade relatively to production in the 1950s. Most other authors writing on this subject fall into the same trap, and comparing the 1950s with the 1920s, deduce either that there has been a permanent change to a lower absolute level, or that there has been a permanent change to a higher rate of growth. We shall not be entitled to start speculating about permanent changes until the short-fall of the 1930s has been completely eliminated.

If the trade in primary products is growing at an abnormal rate, the trade in manufactures is growing even more spectacularly. From the 1870s until 1950 the share of manufactures in world trade, by value, remained more or less constant, through boom and slump. Divergencies between the growth in quantum of manufactures and of primary products were always completely associated with equal proportionate movements in relative prices. However, since 1951 the share of manufactures by value has steadily increased and by 1960 it was 11 points above the average [2] (54·0 as against 42·8), a difference much bigger than at any previous time (previous differ-

[1] Published by GATT, October 1958.

[2] Measurement is complicated by the fact that the classification of manufactures has changed. On the old basis used by the League of Nations statisticians, manufactures averaged 36·9 per cent from 1881 to 1938, and was 40·1 in 1938. On the new basis used by the United Nations statisticians, manufactures were 46·5 per cent in 1938. I have therefore translated the 1881/1938 average to 42·8 on the new basis.

490

ences have seldom exceeded 2 points). This change is most encouraging to those under-developed countries which, because of scarcity of arable land relatively to population, have to base their development on increasing imports of agricultural products matched by increasing exports of manufactures. To a country like India, now sorely beset by balance payments difficulties and ever-increasing numbers, it is heartening to know that world trade in manufactures is buoyant, so that, while doing her utmost to expand agricultural output, India can hope to find markets for the manufactures which she must export in rapidly increasing quantities if she is to solve her problems.

However, in discussing manufactures, as in discussing primary products, it is too early to speculate on permanent changes. World trade in manufactures lost ground relatively to production during the 1930s, so a rapid revival in the 1950s is not an occasion for making deductions about long-term trends. World trade in manufactures may be divided into four parts ; a part which exchanges against primary products, a second part which exchanges against other manufactures, a third part exchanging against invisibles, and a fourth part representing foreign investment. We can explain the relative constancy of the share of manufactures in world trade by saying that the part which exchanges against primary products has in the past moved in the same proportions as the other three parts. There is, however, no law causing this to happen. During the 1930s the exchange of manufactures against manufactures fell just as much as the exchange of manufactures against primary products. In the course of the 1950s, however, the exchange of manufactures against manufactures has revived even faster than the exchange of manufactures against primary products, and so the share of manufactures in world trade has risen. We cannot guess how much of this change will prove permanent. It is quite feasible that when the exchange of manufactures against manufactures reaches what used to be its 'normal' level, in relation to production, its rate of growth will decline. Since this will happen before the trade in primary products reaches its 'normal' level, it is then even possible that the share of manufactures in world trade may decline again, and stabilize at around 43 per cent. In the middle 1960s we shall be able to speculate more confidently about such matters, with the aid of additional hindsight.

Developing countries are interested not only in the prospects of the rate of growth of international trade, but also in what is happening to the terms of trade. Here the post-war experience has been favourable to primary producers. Dividing by the index number of the price of manufactures, the price of food entering world trade, taken as 100 in 1913, was at 94 in 1929, at 84 in 1937 and at 107 in 1960. For primary products as a whole, the terms of trade in 1960, based in 1913, were at 98, and their average level for the decade of the 1950s exceeded that of any decade in the preceding 100 years.

This situation was not stable, because it was not based on increased consumption. It was due, in the first place, to a temporary deficiency of supplies, resulting from the war. Between 1938 and 1948 world manufacturing production increased by 46 per cent, whereas production of raw materials increased only by 20 per cent, and production of food only by 6 per cent. These deficiencies were eliminated in the 1950s. It is true that during the 1950s, manufacturing grew 30 per cent faster than before the First World War (5·2 per cent per annum as against 3·9), but the rate of growth of world food production (2·9 per cent per annum) was nearly 50 per cent up, and the rate of growth of raw materials (3·7) was also considerably higher than before 1913. This catching up of supplies would itself have caused the favourable terms of early post-war years to give way to lower prices. In addition, the Korean War, heavy stockpiling and other war scares, kept primary product prices well above normal levels in the early 1950s, so that, as conditions returned to normal, some decline was inevitable. The terms of trade for primary products declined 15 per cent between 1954 and 1960, and are continuing to fall.

In my Manchester School article of 1952 I showed that one could get an excellent fit for the terms of trade by using world manufacturing as an index of demand, and matching it, in the case of food, with world food production, and in the case of raw materials with a series which assumes a constant annual increase in productive capacity. The same formulae yield a good post-war fit, but only if one leaves out the years before 1952 or 1953. In the earlier post-war years (and especially in 1950/52) prices are so much affected by war scares that the index of manufacturing, though it presumably remains a good index of consumption, cannot serve as an index of demand.

In the inter-war period the formula for the price of food (H) was

$$\log H = a + 0·58 \quad \log M - 1·49 \quad \log F. \quad (R = 0·95)$$

where H is the index of the terms of trade for food (base = 10·0), M the index of world production of manufactures, and F the index of world production of food. From this formula one can calculate that, if food production were increasing by 2 per cent per year, it would take an annual increase of manufacturing of 3·5 per cent to keep relative prices constant.

When applied to the period 1952 to 1960 the results are [1]

$$\log H = a + 0 \cdot 26 \quad \log M - 1 \cdot 54 \quad \log F. \quad (R = 0 \cdot 99).$$

The elasticity of demand is the reciprocal of the coefficient of F. Since this comes to $0 \cdot 67$ in the inter-war period, and $0 \cdot 65$ in the period 1952/60, we know that we are on the right track. We note, however, the sharp fall in the coefficient of M. Since food production was increasing by $2 \cdot 7$ per cent per annum between 1952 and 1960, the coefficient of M tells us that world production of manufactures would have had to be increasing by 17 per cent per annum to keep the price steady. In other words, the price in the early 1950s was much higher than could be supported by the underlying conditions of consumption and supply. Once the stock-piling and war scares had subsided, the price would have to fall substantially to reach normal levels.

The position with respect to raw materials was the same. The formula for this, for the period 1881/1913 was

$$\log \mathcal{J} = a + 0 \cdot 86 \quad \log M - 0 \cdot 0131 N. \quad (R = 0 \cdot 85).$$

For the period 1921/38

$$\log \mathcal{J} = a + 0 \cdot 86 \quad \log M - 0 \cdot 0142 N. \quad (R = 0 \cdot 97).$$

And for the period 1953/60

$$\log \mathcal{J} = a + 0 \cdot 84 \quad \log M - 0 \cdot 0243 N. \quad (R = 0 \cdot 99).$$

where $\mathcal{J}$ is the index of the terms of trade for raw materials, and N the number of years from any given date.

We observe that the coefficient of M remains unchanged over the two world wars and eighty years.[2] The coefficient of N (which is logarithmic) tells us by how much the price would fall in any year if manufacturing stayed constant. The answer was virtually the same in the first two periods ($3 \cdot 1$ and $3 \cdot 3$ per cent); but in the 1950s the answer had risen to $5 \cdot 5$ per cent, indicating that prices could remain constant only if manufacturing increased by $6 \cdot 9$ per cent per annum. As in the case of food, prices were too high in the

[1] These results are for five-year moving averages in the inter-war period, and for three-year moving averages in the post-war period. The post-war regression coefficient is misleadingly high, because the number of terms is small. The quality of the fit has to be observed by inspection.

[2] This incidentally throws doubt on the proposition that there has been a sharp structural decline in the demand for raw materials in manufacturing. The processes of economy and substitution are not new. The demand for raw materials increases less than the demand for manufactures, but there is no evidence of a change in the proportionate rates of increase. If I had to bet, I would guess that the pre-war coefficients for N, F and M will all hold when prices are no longer influenced by war scares.

early 1950s, and were bound to drop as the hot and cold wars began to come to an end.

Whether prices are yet normal we cannot say, but in any case there is another reason why the immediate outlook for primary producers is bad.

According to one small school of economists, production is subject to a cycle of about eighteen to twenty years, which is sometimes called the Kuznets cycle, after the great pioneer in this field. When the Kuznets cycle is in its upswing, Kitchin recessions are minor, create little unemployment, and can be dismissed by such euphemisms as 'a rolling readjustment'. But when the Kuznets cycle reaches its downturn, Kitchin's become violent, unemployment is persistent, and Kitchin booms peter out before full capacity is reached. Believers in the Kuznets cycle prophesied that the 1950s would have only minor crises, but that around the year 1960 the major industrial countries would enter a period when unemployment was naggingly persistent, and the rate of growth of production below average. Having written in these terms in 1955, I do not find the present situation in the U.S.A., or Britain, difficult to interpret, and worldwide stock exchange crashes come as no surprise.[1] We shall not have a great depression, like those of the seventies or the nineties or the thirties, because we understand these things much better than did our forefathers, but it will be at least another five years before we resume the carefree progress of a Kuznets upswing.

This has special relevance to primary producers, since the terms of trade for primary products are so sensitive to business depressions. The immediate forecast is not good, but I make no claim to be a prophet. A scientist confines himself to extrapolating trends. 'If the future turns out to be like the past, it will such and such.' But whether the future will be like the past is any man's guess, and the use of statistical methods to frame one's guess does not add to its authority.

It is now time to bring this discussion to a point. The simplest way to do this is to sum up the propositions which I have sought to establish.

(1) The terms of trade have been abnormally favourable primary products since the Second World War. The current decline was inevitable, and will continue until there is a Kuznets upswing of production in North America and Western Europe.

(2) There is no reason to believe that world trade is losing ground. Trade normally grows less rapidly than manufacturing

---

[1] W. A. Lewis and P. J. O'Leary, 'Secular Swings in Production and Trade', *The Manchester School*, May 1955.

industries. The proportionate ratio declined sharply in the 1930s and 1940s, and rose sharply in the 1950s. Neither the currently low ratio of trade to production, compared with the 1920s, nor the currently high rate of growth of trade relatively to production, should be assumed permanent ; the facts are compatible with treating the 1950s as a transition period during which the ratios of the 1920s are being re-established.

(3) Reducing economic dependence involves increasing production for home consumption relatively to exports ; but an economy cannot develop unless it either exports more or produces substitutes for imports. Where possibilities for import substitution and foreign deficits are limited, the possible rate of economic growth is a direct function of the rate at which exports can be expanded.

APPENDIX

	Production		Trade		Prices		
	Manu-factures	Food	Manu-factures Ratio	Primary Products Quantum	Manu-factures	Food	Raw Materials
1913	100	100	37·0	100	100	100	100
1938	155	133	40·1	119	72	58	51
1938	50	80	46·5	90	50	31	35
1948	73	85	44·0	77	103	99	104
1949	74	83	43·3	86	98	92	97
1950	84	89	43·7	90	86	91	92
1951	91	92	45·9	94	102	102	132
1952	93	96	47·7	95	104	101	107
1953	100	100	48·4	100	100	100	100
1954	102	100	48·2	105	98	100	100
1955	112	103	49·0	113	99	96	102
1956	117	106	50·2	122	103	97	102
1957	121	107	52·0	129	106	98	105
1958	118	113	52·7	120	106	94	97
1959	131	117	53·0	139	106	89	97
1960	140	119	54·0	152	109	88	98

Source : United Nations, *Statistical Year Book*, and Lewis and O'Leary, *op. cit.*

DISCUSSION OF THE PAPER BY PROFESSOR LEWIS

Dr. Bhagwati, opening the discussion, thought that Professor Lewis in his paper had made too much of the generalization that the growth of a country was limited by its export receipts. Professor Lewis' description of expansion leading to balance of payments pressure followed by a decline of domestic activity was too standardized and did not fit important individual cases. Growth and the balance of payments could interact in many ways. Exports could be the agent of expansion, as was believed to have been the case in nineteenth-century Britain. In a modern planned economy foreign trade was more likely to be looked on as an alternative process of production, a technological possibility for development. In this context, although many under-developed countries might feel that exports were a bottleneck in the process of increasing the rate of investment and/or growth, this was not necessarily so. In some cases, including India, the limiting factor in raising the rate of investment was the low level of marginal saving. However, given their capacity or willingness to save, developing countries could legitimately be concerned with the gains from trade and the future prospects of exports and imports in their relation to each other. This was an extremely complicated and difficult task for a planning authority.

Professor Chenery said that there were two separate factors limiting growth — a low rate of savings, and the difficulty of expanding exports, and that the question of which factor was stronger had to be considered in each case. He agreed with Professor Lewis that in under-developed countries there was often a bias against exports. Planners tended to over-emphasize import substitution, and neglected the dynamic possibilities of exports. *Professor Walker* agreed with Professor Lewis that, anyhow for small countries, growth depended on exports. A recent study showed that for 25 small countries since 1950 imports had increased at a substantially higher rate than national product, and there was no sign of import ratios falling with growth. *Professor Lewis* maintained that exports were a brake on growth not only for small countries but also for such large ones as India.

Professor Lewis thought that it would be useful to discuss the merits of stabilization of export prices. If the link between export prices and domestic prices could be broken, e.g. by marketing boards, or counter-cyclical taxation, or monetary policy, stabilization might not be necessary. Primary producer countries, who could not rely on the willingness of richer countries to co-operate in commodity agreements, might be well advised to follow this policy. *Dr. Aubrey*, however, felt that, in so far as exports influenced domestic income, investment and growth, measures such as 'smoothing' would be valuable in neutralizing those effects of instability which hindered development. *Mr. Onitiri* said that the problem of stabilization had to be studied in its relation to economic development, which was the primary aim of under-developed countries. Stabilization confined to a smoothing operation round a long-term trend was not worth while : an attempt must be made to improve supply elasticities in under-developed countries. The opportunity for structural adjustments offered by the high export earnings of the early fifties had been lost ; some substitute must be found.

Record of Discussion

There was some discussion of the level at which prices should be stabilized. *Professor Lewis* observed that some under-developed countries wanted prices stabilized at above market level, which was really a requirement for aid from more developed countries. *Dr. Adler* pointed out that terms of trade might be too favourable for primary producers : there was a real danger that high prices for raw materials would encourage the use of substitutes.

There was criticism from *Dr. Bhagwati* and *Professor Walker* of what were taken to be Professor Lewis's optimistic predictions of a more favourable future for the trade of primary producing countries, derived from a supposedly 'normal' base-year situation. *Mr. Stanovnik* also contested Professor Lewis's assumption that the development of trade since the war was normal. The figures used were calculated by the UN, leaving out the Eastern European trading area, in which the ratios of industrial production to trade differed from that of other parts of the world.

Mr. Stanovnik, Professor Servoise, Mr. Kapferer and *Professor Chenery* all believed that manufactures would have to have a place in the future exports of under-developed countries. There was a feeling that the pattern of trade must alter ; *Professor Servoise* and *Mr. Stanovnik* predicted that there would be less opportunities for trade between the under-developed and industrialized countries and that trade between the under-developed countries themselves would have to grow. In this connection *Professor Servoise* and *Mr. Kapferer* stressed the value of regional integration in providing a larger market.

Dr. Bhagwati took issue with Professor Lewis's adoption of the 'aggregated' approach, in which all under-developed countries were taken together and deductions as to their future exports and terms of trade made on the basis of averages. Dr. Bhagwati argued that the future course of the terms of trade of the developing countries and its significance for their trade and investment policies could be studied usefully only in the context of a detailed analysis of all the factors affecting supply and demand in foreign trade for individual countries. *Professor Walker* also felt that looking at the aggregate world picture had been responsible for Professor Lewis's apparently optimistic assumptions as to the future of world trade. The prospects for some regions, such as Africa, and some individual countries, were more gloomy.

Chapter 30

COMMODITY TERMS OF TRADE OF PRIMARY PRODUCING COUNTRIES

BY

M. L. DANTWALA
Bombay University

I. INTRODUCTORY

THE significance of the movement of the (commodity) terms of trade to the primary producing countries arises from two distinct phenomena : (1) the short-term fluctuations in the terms of trade and their destabilizing effect on the economies of the primary producing countries ; and (2) the possibility of a secular trend which may have certain implications for their economic policies. The prevalence of short-term fluctuations in the terms of trade of primary products is an accepted fact and remedies have been suggested for their elimination, though the effectiveness with which each one of these would operate is subject to some doubt.

In this paper, we are concerned only with the secular trends in terms of trade. The past experience in this regard and the analysis concerned with it have been briefly examined within the permissible limits of space. It is obvious that a variety of complex factors influence the movement of the terms of trade over time. We have tried to examine some of these and taken a view of the likely trends in future. There are factors which would strengthen the terms of trade of the primary producing countries as well as those which would tend to weaken them. The direction of the resultant is too difficult to predict ; but one thing appears clear. The constellation of circumstances which resulted in exceptionally favourable terms of trade for the primary producing countries between 1938 and 1953 is not likely to recur in the near future. With the return to the prewar relationship between the export and import prices, the sluggishness in the growth of their trade will be more fully reflected in their balance of trade and payments position and weaken their import capacity. 'The share of what non-industrial areas as a whole were able to finance from current export earnings fell during the period 1953–57 from approximately 90 to 60 per cent.' [1] Coming as it

[1] GATT, *International Trade*, 1959.

498

does, at a time when their aspirations and (if one may say so) their impatience for economic development are mounting, the situation will pose a formidable challenge to economic statesmanship. It is said that 'A step-up in development by 2 per cent will need a rise of more than 10 per cent in imports of capital goods'.[1]

II. FACTORS INFLUENCING THE TERMS OF TRADE

The terms of trade of primary producing countries evidently depend upon the relative intensity and elasticity of demand for their exports and imports. For an appraisal of these characteristics, it is necessary to review the trends in international trade in regard to some of its characteristics. A close study of these reveals the following features which are germane to the discussion of terms of trade.

(1) World trade in primary products is not expanding proportionately with the growth in the manufacturing output. The index of manufacturing production with 1928 as the base was 246 in 1955–1957 while the index of exports of primary commodities was no more than 132 ; the index of exports of manufactures stood at 203. The contrast becomes less sharp with 1948 as the base. Manufacturing production increased by 58 per cent and the export of primary commodities by 44 per cent as against an increase of 95 per cent in the export of manufactures. A variety of factors account for the sluggishness in trade in primary commodities. Apart from the income-elasticity effect, the sluggishness may be due to (i) domestic supplies replacing imports, (ii) raw material saving technology and shifts in composition of manufactures production, (iii) growth of synthetic substitutes and better utilization of scraps and (iv) supply deficiencies.

(2) The share of the primary producing countries in the total trade as well as the trade in the primary products has been more or less stagnant since 1938 and declining since 1948. In other words, the industrial areas are becoming increasingly self-sufficient. As Nurkse put it : 'They are becoming each other's best customers'. In 1960 almost 50 per cent of the import requirements of the industrial areas for primary products are supplied by the industrial areas themselves. To what extent the slowing down of demand and the shift in the source of supply are due to autonomous demand factors in industrial areas and to inelasticities of physical supply and high prices of primary producing suppliers is a matter which needs careful investigation.

[1] *Ibid.* p. 50.

(3) Import demand of the primary producing countries, on the other hand, has been growing and appears to be price inelastic. This imbalance between the export earnings and import requirements has been clearly reflected in the growing balance of trade and payment deficits of the non-industrial areas and their shrinking foreign exchange resources.

III. ATTEMPTS TO MEASURE TERMS OF TRADE

In spite of the well-known difficulties of concepts and measurement in dealing with the subject of terms of trade, attempts have been made to measure the terms of trade of (1) primary products and (2) export-import terms of merchandise trade of individual countries. As for the former, the broad facts are fairly well known. Primary product prices display a clear tendency to fall more steeply than prices of manufactures in depressions and rise more rapidly during booms. Thus, during the inter-war period (1913–38), the terms of trade were adverse to primary products. After the outbreak of the Second World War, the position was reversed, and right up to the end of the Korean War boom (1953), the trade terms were distinctly favourable to the primary products. The estimates of the change in terms of trade vary with the choice of commodities included in the index. Accordingly, the estimates of change between 1928 and 1955–57 in the terms of trade between primary commodities and manufactures range from an improvement of 25 to 33 per cent. Since 1953, however, the trend has been once again reversed. Between 1953 and 1959, export prices of all primary products declined by 5·5 per cent, while those of manufactures rose by 7 per cent. The terms of trade value of 'agricultural products' declined by 20 per cent.[1] The peculiarity of this period is that unlike earlier cycles both the volume and the unit price indices have turned in favour of manufactures.

Yates has an interesting observation to make on this phenomenon. He observes : 'In 1896–1900 a 6 per cent rise in price ratio (for manufactures) went with a 20 per cent fall in quantum ratio. In the inter-war period, a 20 per cent improvement in the terms of trade was associated with a 13 per cent opposite movement in the quantum relative. By 1953 the position is further transformed : a price relative rise of 4 per cent accompanies a rise in the quantum relative of 23 per cent and for other years in the 1950s the position is similar. Taking the three periods, 1896–1900, 1928–38 and the 1950s, a rise

---

[1] FAO, *The State of Food and Agriculture*, 1961, p. 31.

in the relative unit values of manufactures has progressively less and less adverse effect on the export volume of manufactures.' [1]

As in the case of the trends in the movement of primary commodities in world trade, the aggregation of all primary commodities in a single group hides divergent movements in the terms of trade (real unit values) of the sub-groups and even in individual commodities within such groups.

Taking the entire period from 1927–29 and 1955–57, the 'real' unit values for most of the primary commodities — except rubber which declined by 31 per cent, jute (–7 per cent), cotton (–6 per cent), wheat (–15 per cent) and butter (–34 per cent)—improved in varying measures ranging from more than 60 per cent for copper and lead, 40 per cent for coffee and cocoa, 33 per cent for petroleum, 31 per cent for tobacco and 14 per cent for tea. Since 1946–48, however, a large number of commodities experienced a deterioration in their real unit values : the entire food group (–24 to –32 per cent), jute (–34 per cent), lead and zinc (–17 and –3 per cent) and butter and sugar (–7 and –2 per cent). Even petroleum lost 2 per cent. The only commodities to gain were copper (+71 per cent), bauxite and aluminium (+49 per cent), rubber (+47 per cent) coffee (+104 per cent), tea (+21 per cent).[2]

Obviously, both the demand and supply conditions have influenced the divergent trends in the movement of real prices of primary commodities. Taking the entire period from 1927–29 to 1955–57, there are commodities like minerals for which the buoyant world demand could not be matched in spite of impressive increase in production. Consequently, their terms of trade improved. In the case of aluminium, however, the increase in production more than adequately met the rise in demand, resulting in deterioration in its 'real' unit price. On the other hand, in the case of cereals, supply could not be adjusted to the relatively stagnant demand, resulting in the deterioration of their real prices. For the beverage group as a whole, though production increased more rapidly than world demand, its real prices also improved, presumably because of the rising domestic demand.

Terms of Trade of Primary Producing Countries

It is well known that the pattern of movement in terms of trade of primary producing countries does not run parallel to that observed

---

[1] P. Lamartine Yates, *Forty Years of Foreign Trade*.
[2] United Nations, *World Economic Survey*, 1958, Table 7. Real Unit Values refer to import values deflated by world manufacturing unit value.

for the primary produce *vis-à-vis* manufactures. The difference arises because some of the primary producing countries are themselves not insignificant importers of primary produce — 20 to 25 per cent of their total imports consist of primary produce — and some of the so-called semi-industrialized countries are slowly expanding their exports of manufactures. Thus, whereas the terms of exchange of all primary exports against manufactured goods improved by about one-third between 1928 and 1955–57, the primary exporting countries experienced only a negligible improvement of 4 per cent in the terms of trade of their exports against their total imports.[1]

Between 1928 and 1937–38, the unit value of exports from non-industrial countries declined from 100 to 69, while that of their imports came down only to 80, thus resulting in the deterioration of the terms of trade of the former. During the war and thereafter till 1955, the respective unit values of exports and imports of non-industrial countries rose to 197 and 184 (1928 = 100) revealing a considerable improvement in their terms of trade since 1937–38.[2] Since 1954 the trend is once again reversed. The terms of trade of the primary exporting countries in 1959 were about 14 per cent below the 1950 level.[3]

The table below based on the classification adopted in the United Nations publications, viz. developed and under-developed areas, summarizes the trends in the movement of terms of trade for these respective areas and some of the individual countries.

TERMS OF TRADE
(Index 1953 = 100)

	1938	1948	1951	1957	1960
Developed areas	107	101	94	98	105
Under-developed areas	75	90	112	98	96
North America	123	108	91	100	106
Western Europe	107	101	93	99	105
Africa	68	92	116	99	97
Latin America	63	90	106	94	85
Middle East	89	97	114	108	106
Australia, New Zealand, Union of South Africa	80	91	116	88	76
Asia	84	91	118	97	110

[1] *UN Economic Survey of Asia and the Far East*, 1959.
[2] GATT, *Trends in International Trade*, p. 26.
[3] *UN World Economic Survey*, 1959.

IV. FORECASTS OF FUTURE TRENDS

The discussions concerning terms of trade have revolved round a statistical examination of the behaviour of the terms of trade, interpretation of the same with a view to ascertaining the distribution of 'gains of trade' between broad groups of trading countries, analysis of the impact of divergent pattern and rates of economic development upon the terms of trade, statistical and analytical predictions concerning future behaviour of terms of trade, and the impact of the above upon trade relations and economic development policies of newly industrializing countries. Professor Raul Prebisch's thesis concerning the historical decline in terms of trade of primary producing countries *vis-à-vis* manufacturing countries and the extrapolation of the historical trends as a probable pattern of behaviour in the future has been supported as well as refuted by many writers. Prebisch maintained that the gains of productivity in developed countries would tend to be taken over in the form of real wages and not transferred to importing countries in the form of lower prices. Productivity improvements in under-developed countries, on the other hand, would be largely reflected in the form of a fall in prices, thus transferring most of the gains to the importers in the developed countries. The existence of population pressure and the phenomenon of unlimited supply of labour would tend to keep wages at a low level in the primary producing countries. An additional factor tending to the detriment of the primary exporting countries is the low income elasticity of demand in the developed countries for primary exports. To this, Professor Singer has added an additional factor. Technological changes in the developed countries, whether autonomous or induced, tend to cheapen the cost of substitutes of primary products and at the same time enable the discovery of newer substitutes. Professor Prebisch's thesis is contested on the ground that (i) the empirical evidence was derived from a narrow base of British experience, (ii) no allowance was made for improvement in the quality of manufactures and appearance of new products, and (iii) it ignored the great decline in inward (to Britain) freight rates.

In direct opposition to the Prebisch thesis, Professor Colin Clark, in his *Economics of 1960* (written in 1940–41) predicted that the terms of trade would have moved in favour of agriculture by a factor of as much as 1·9 by 1960 in comparison with the base period of 1925–34. A decade later, he stated that he would like to adhere to his earlier conclusion and added that something like these terms of trade will persist till 1970.[1]   Professor W. A. Lewis made a major contribution to this subject in his essay on *World Production, Prices and Trade, 1870–1960*).[2]   In a separate section of this essay he made a calculation of the likely movement of production, prices and trade in primary products and manufactures and came to the conclusion that the terms of trade of primary products would improve by 22 to 39 per cent above 1924–35, respectively, on 'lower' and 'higher' assumptions.   The estimates of Professor Clark and Professor Lewis, however, are not strictly comparable among other things because of the difference in coverage.   Professor Clark had taken account of the effects of the further industrialization of the Soviet countries, while Professor Lewis had not.   Looking at these estimates two years after the end of the fifties, it is clear that Professor Lewis' estimates are closer to what has actually happened.   Even so, the divergence is not insignificant.

It is not the purpose of this paper to examine why and where estimates went wrong.   Still it would be useful to state the main assumptions of the two distinguished economists and check them with what appears to have actually happened.   The main factors in Professor Clark's estimates were :   (1) enormous transfers of capital from developed to under-developed regions ;   (2) rapid growth of population particularly in the under-developed regions and its impact on domestic consumption and exportable surplus ;   (3) the relatively slow increase in agricultural productivity ;   (4) a somewhat high estimate of income-elasticity of demand ;   and (5) a price-elasticity of demand in the neighbourhood of -0.5.   With his pessimism regarding supply and optimism regarding demand, he estimated that 'for each one per cent per annum that the supply falls short of demand, we must allow a two per cent per annum rate of change in the terms of trade'.

The major 'high' and 'low' assumptions in Professor Lewis' estimate were :   (1) a rate of growth in world manufacturing production (3.9 to 5 per cent per annum) ;   (2) rate of growth of food production (1.3 to 2 per cent per annum) ;   (3) an incremental relationship between manufacturing production and volume of trade in primary products (0.87) ;   and (4) a movement in the prices of raw material (derived from the experience of 1921–38).

Looking retrospectively, it would appear that the higher of the two assumptions of Professor Lewis in regard to manufacturing and food production was nearer the mark.   Trade in primary products as

[1] 'Problems of Long-Term International Balance', UNESCO, *Social Science Bulletin*, Spring, 1951.
[2] *The Manchester School of Economics and Social Studies*, Volume XX.

well as manufactures also expanded during the fifties more rapidly than estimated by Professor Lewis. As for the prices of food and raw materials, the deterioration was much larger than anticipated with the result that as against his estimate of the movement in terms of trade of primary products ranging from 97 to 110, the actual decline was 24 per cent from 1950 and 15 per cent from 1953.

The table below reproduces Professor Lewis' estimates and gives alongside some of the recent broadly comparable data. The categories and assumption of the two sets of statistics are not identical and their juxtaposition was a matter of mere convenience.

| | 1960* (1950=100) | | | |
	Lower Assumption	Higher Assumption	1960† (1950=100)	1960† (1953=100)
Manufacturing production	147	163	167	140
Primary production	—	—	136	120
Food production	114	122	135	119
Prices of raw materials	100	110	—	—
Agricultural raw materials	—	—	69	88
Minerals	—	—	87	92
Prices of food	92	110	76	81
Trade in primary products	135	143	—	—
Trade in manufactures	131	157	203	156
Terms of trade	97	110	76	85

Sources :
  * *The Manchester School of Economic and Social Studies*, Vol. XX.
  † United Nations, *Statistical Year Book*.

The deterioration in the terms of trade of primary commodities during the 1950s and particularly since 1954 is not disputed. The point is whether what took place after 1951 was a return towards the normal relationship distorted by the war-time disorganization in the supply of many primary products and further aggravated by the stock-piling rush induced by the Korean War, or an emergence of an entirely new trend symptomatic of the years to come ? The answer to this question depends upon many complex factors. However, an attempt is made to assess some of these in what follows.

V. APPRAISAL OF FACTORS AFFECTING FUTURE TRENDS

(1) Factors Affecting Demand for Primary Products from Industrial Countries

The relevant factors here are growth of population, rate of growth, the technological quotient of raw material input in finished product and income and price elasticities of demand. While the rate of growth of population and economic activity have been such as to stimulate demand for primary products, the declining proportion of raw material input in manufacturing production, either because of technological factors, growth of synthetics or shifts in the composition of manufacturing production, has an opposite effect. The income-elasticity naturally varies with the type of primary product concerned. It is well known that food items have a fairly low income elasticity. As for the agricultural raw materials and minerals, the demand for them grows (though at a slower rate) with the growth in economic activity. If the latter grows fast enough, there is no reason for the total demand to lag behind even the growing available supplies.

It is difficult to say anything very definite about the price elasticities. Here, both the uncertainties in regard to supply as well as the price factor have relevance inasmuch as they affect the search for synthetics. Where there are competing suppliers, the price factor for the country concerned would result in a shift in the source of supply rather than affect the total demand. Given a particular rate of growth of manufacturing activity, the demand for their raw material content becomes fairly well determined and the price factor is not likely to significantly affect production decisions. In view of this, it may be said that the demand for the raw material is fairly price inelastic in the short run.

(2) *Supply from Non-Industrial Countries*

On the supply side, the 'fifties were a very peculiar decade. Some of the primary producing countries have not yet recovered from the disruption in their production due to war when confronted with the sudden upsurge in demand culminating in the Korean War boom. With limited supplies, prices soared high giving them exceptionally favourable terms of trade. Since then, production has been picking up and it is our expectation that, thanks to the build-up of the infrastructure, during the 'sixties production will expand more rapidly. We think that the improvement in technology will postpone the emergence of diminishing returns for quite some time. The availability of this increased production for exports is, however, likely to be curtailed by the rising domestic demand from the rapidly growing population and rising incomes consequent upon large investment expenditure. There is even evidence that some of the primary producing countries are becoming net importers in regard to certain groups of primary products. The faster the rate of growth, the larger will be the domestic demand. This would obviously not affect all commodities uniformly. For quite a few, the domestic demand is not significant. It should, however, be noted that the growing domestic use of primary production may have an import-saving and even export-promoting effect in regard to some categories of manufactures. On the whole, economic development in many of these countries is likely to be anti-export biassed, more so if there is excessive emphasis on capital goods production and too little on raw material and consumption goods production.

As to the likely price trends, though as we stated earlier both production and productivity are likely to grow, this may not be reflected into lower prices because of the inflationary pressures and the compulsion to permit gains of productivity to factors in the shape of higher rewards than in lower prices.

(3) *Import Demand of Non-Industrial Countries*

In contrast to the demand of the industrial countries for the primary products of the non-industrialized countries, the demand of the latter for imports of capital goods, maintenance materials and even for food is likely to be high, inflexible and indifferent towards prices in view of their commitment to the programme of rapid economic development.[1] The only limiting factor will perhaps be their import capacity determined by their export earnings, capital transfers under free and open market and foreign aid. If the idea gains ground that the lion's share of import capacity should be allocated to imports of capital goods, the import capacity will be further impaired through a fall in export earnings. Yet, there is likely to be a great temptation to follow a policy of brinkmanship.

(4) *Supply from Industrial Countries*

The rapidly rising manufacturing capacity of the industrial countries is fully capable of physically meeting this rise in import demand. There are hardly any supply inelasticities to be feared here. Yet it is difficult to say whether the growing production and productivity in the industrial areas will be reflected in lower prices of exports of manufactures. Here again, the claims of higher rewards to domestic workers may have precedence till they begin to produce adverse effects on the export market and in turn on domestic economic activity. Another factor to reckon with would be the possibility of

---

[1] The near disappearance of oilseeds exports from India and sugar exports from Indonesia illustrate the point. In India, national income increased by 22 per cent between 1953 and 1957, while quantum of imports grew by 59 per cent.

competition from the Centrally Planned Economies and its impact on the offer terms of the industrial areas.

IV. CONCLUSIONS

A synoptic judgment on a question which involves so many diverse factors is difficult to arrive at. Some thirteen years ago, Professor Robertson felt that 'strong and persistent forces were making it progressively more difficult for the manufacturing populations of Western Europe to earn from overseas the requisite fodder alike for their own fastidious stomachs and for their insatiable machines', and adds, 'we ought to have perhaps foreseen the emergence of the revolutionary notion that some day one thousand million Asiatics would take it into their heads to expect to have enough to eat'.[1] Within just over a decade, how dramatically has the situation changed ! Leaving aside the Asiatics for the present, the Overseas, particularly North America and Oceania, are knocking at the frontiers of the European Economic Community for the privilege of looking after the fastidiousness of European stomachs ; and gifting away not inconsiderable quantities for the hungry stomachs of the Asiatics also ! As for insatiable machines, their appetite for 'fodder' is becoming somewhat dyspeptic. The one thousand million Asiatics, or rather their governments, have developed — perversely it may seem to the West — more appetite for machines than for food, machines which they are finding 'progressively more difficult' to obtain not because the developed nations do not have enough, but because their 'fastidious stomachs and insatiable machines' do not want enough 'fodder' from the under-developed areas with which the machines could be bartered. It should, however, be admitted that the appetite of Asian stomachs and machines is growing.

Anyway, in the early 'sixties, whether the supply terms of primary commodities are high or low, their exports do not offer any bright prospects to the non-industrial areas as a source for augmenting export earnings. This does not mean that the source should, therefore, be neglected. On the contrary, there is no escape from making the best of the difficult bargain. Even if they accept the strategy of 'Balanced Growth', a start cannot be made without substantial imports of capital goods and maintenance material, which will have to be paid through export earnings ! The primary producing countries must do their very best to improve the productive efficiency of their export products (whether the demand for them is expanding

[1] *Lloyds Bank Review*, July 1949, quoted by Colin Clark, *op. cit.*

or receding). Alfred Marshall spoke of 'the splendid markets which the Old World offered to the products of the New'. He had obviously in view what were known as Regions of Recent Settlement (RRS). If such splendidness still exists, the non-industrial areas would like to share it.

The industrial countries would sooner or later realize that *Commonness* cannot be confined to the narrow continental boundaries. Probably a second look at their resource allocation would reveal areas in which shifts in favour of imports might be to the mutual advantage of themselves and the exporting primary producing countries. The scope for this may be considerable as was shown in a recent publication in which it was estimated that 1 per cent reduction in the production of primary commodities in North America and Western Europe relative to consumption would augment net imports by over 9 per cent, though it would appear that the 'higher income' primary producers would be the more substantial beneficiaries from such larger imports. Yet, in view of the disturbing imbalance which has developed in international trade between the developed and the under-developed areas, the possibilities of a purposeful and selective shift in the agricultural protection policies needs to be fully explored.

With all respects to Nurkse, the nineteenth-century international trade did not act as an Engine of Growth for the bulk of the under-developed areas. Even when it did provide a stimulus to domestic production, it created dual economies with a built-in stagnation in the rest of the economy. The fault may not be on one side alone. However, a point of seminal importance is to ask : what role international trade will play in the latter half of the twentieth century in the economic development of the non-industrialized areas ? Professor Nurkse, till his last days, argued fervently to demonstrate the loss of the propelling and growth-transmitting power of the engine of international trade during the twentieth century. Valiant attempts have been made to combat this pessimism. Whatever may be the final verdict of the distinguished experts in the field, at least one thing appears clear : unless wise economic statesmanship prevails in the field of international economic relationship, we may find the domestic Dual Economies of the nineteenth century progressively being transformed into a Dual International World.

(The discussion of this paper is recorded after Chapter 31.)

Chapter 31

THE TERMS OF TRADE

BY

H. M. A. ONITIRI
University College of Ibadan

M y terms of reference call for 'a review of what is known historically of long-term movements in the terms of trade plus a discussion of factors relevant to speculations about future trends'. This is a large and controversial subject, and the literature is quite extensive. In this brief survey, I cannot hope to explore the subject fully in all its aspects. What I propose to do is to draw attention to the main issues, particularly as they bear on the problems of economic development. Before turning to this task, however, a few remarks about the uses and limitations of the terms of trade in the sphere of development may provide a useful background to the discussion. Since controversy has raged as much on the accuracy of the statistical estimates of the terms of trade as on the economic and welfare interpretations to be placed upon them, one does not need to be apologetic about treading again a time-worn path. I propose, then, to divide the discussion into three parts. The first part will consider the usefulness of various measures of the terms of trade in the analysis of development problems ; the second will examine the historical movement ; and the third will discuss the future prospects.

I. SIGNIFICANCE OF CHANGES IN THE TERMS OF TRADE FOR ECONOMIC DEVELOPMENT

There is a two-way relationship between the terms of trade and economic development. Firstly, changes in the terms of trade influence the pace of development and the pattern which it takes ; and secondly, the pace and pattern of development have important repercussions on the terms of trade. Specifically, the focus of interest may be one or more of the following aspects of the relationship :

(i) changes in the balance of payments ;
(ii) changes in the national income ;
(iii) changes in the financial resources for economic development ;

510

(iv) the international distribution of the gains from trade, particularly as between manufacturing countries and primary producers ;

(v) the distribution of the gains from international investment between investing and borrowing countries ; and

(vi) the efficient allocation of productive resources.

The first three aspects are closely related, and so are the fourth and fifth. All six feature prominently in the literature of the post-war years, although different authors have usually emphasized particular aspects. Various United Nations reports which have been devoted wholly or partly to the terms of trade have been concerned mainly with the first three aspects ; [1] R. Prebisch [2] and H. W. Singer,[3] whose contributions are now usually referred to as the 'Prebisch-Singer thesis', are concerned largely with the fourth and fifth, and so is G. Myrdal.[4] Several authors dealing particularly with measures for short-term price stabilization, have usually emphasized the importance of the sixth. The theoretical expositions by H. G. Johnson [5] are particularly useful for the analysis of the fourth and fifth. The study by C. P. Kindleberger [6] elucidates the problem in all its aspects. While the various studies dealing with prospective movement of the terms of trade do not usually specify a particular point of interest, concern with the fourth aspect seems implicit in many of the writings.[7]

The Terms of Trade and the Trade Balance

Both the net and the gross barter terms of trade are widely used in the analysis of changes in the balance of trade. However, in this

[1] The most important of these reports are : *Relative Prices of Exports and Imports of Under-Developed Countries* (1949, II. B, 3) ; 'Relative Prices of Primary Products and Manufactures in International Trade' (E/2455, 1953) ; 'Repercussions of Changes in the Terms of Trade on the Economies of Countries in the Process of Development' (E/2456, 1953) ; *Measures for International Economic Stability* (1951, II. A, 2) ; *Measures for the Economic Development of Under-Developed Countries* (1951, II. B, 2) ; *International Compensation for Fluctuations in Commodity Trade* (E/CN. 13/40).

[2] *The Economic Development of Latin America and its Principal Problems* (UN E/CN. 12/89/Rev. 1, 27th April 1950).

[3] 'The Distribution of Gains between Investing and Borrowing Countries', *Papers and Proceedings of the American Economic Association*, May 1950.

[4] *Economic Theory and Under-Developed Regions*, London, 1957 ; *An International Economy*, London, 1956.

[5] *International Trade and Economic Growth*, London, 1958 ; *Money, Trade and Economic Growth*, London, 1962.

[6] *The Terms of Trade — A European Case Study*, New York, 1956.

[7] See especially Colin Clark, *The Economics of 1960*, London, 1944 ; W. A. Lewis, 'World Production, Prices and Trade, 1870–1960', *Manchester School of Economics and Social Studies*, Vol. XX, 1952 ; and M. K. Atallah, *The Long-Term Movement of the Terms of Trade between Agricultural and Industrial Products*, Netherlands Economic Institute, Rotterdam, 1958.

context, the two measures suffer from the limitation that they are ratios, whereas in the analysis of changes in the balance of trade we are usually interested in absolute changes. A change in the net or gross barter terms of trade can be unambiguously related to a change in the ratio of the values of exports and imports and not to the absolute change in their difference. Thus, if Ve, Vi are value indices ; Pe, Pi the indices of average values ; Qe, Qi the quantum indices ; where the subscripts e and i refer to exports and imports,

$$\frac{Ve}{Vi} = \frac{PeQe}{PiQi} = T \times G,$$

where T represents the net barter terms of trade (index of average value of exports divided by index of average value of imports) ; and G, the gross barter terms of trade (index of quantum of exports divided by index of quantum of imports). It follows from this relationship that an increase in T (G remaining constant), or an increase in G (T remaining constant) will necessarily increase the ratio $\frac{Ve}{Vi}$. However, except in the trivial case where trade is balanced in the base year, this relationship does not unambiguously indicate the effect on the trade balance (measured as the absolute difference between the values of imports and exports) of the movements of prices and quantities in external trade. It is, therefore, of little practical application in the real world where the trade of individual countries is hardly ever balanced. Firstly, in such circumstances, an increase in the ratio $\frac{Ve}{Vi}$ does not necessarily indicate an improvement in the trade balance in money terms ; it may well be associated with a condition of deterioration or no change ; and similarly, a decrease in the ratio $\frac{Ve}{Vi}$ may be associated with an improvement or no change in the trade balance in money terms. Secondly, holding T (or G) constant would not necessarily eliminate the influence of price (or quantity) movements on the trade balance in money terms. In short, provided that trade is unbalanced in the base year, the trade balance in money terms may change one way or the other as a result of equal percentage changes in prices and quantities, even though the three ratios $\frac{Ve}{Vi}$, T and G remain unchanged. This limitation of T and G for the analysis of absolute changes in the trade balance is now well recognized in the literature.[1] Yet instances can still be

---

[1] See, for example, United Nations, *op. cit.*, *Relative Prices* etc., p. 123, and C. P. Kindleberger, *op. cit.*, p. 279 *et seq.*

found where the effect of price movements on the trade balance is incorrectly regarded as reflecting the effect of movement in the terms of trade ; [1] or where the effect of the terms of trade is incorrectly regarded as reflecting the effect of price movements.[2]

C. P. Kindleberger, who explicitly recognizes this limitation of T and G, still believes that the analysis of $\dfrac{Ve}{Vi}$ in terms of G and T 'gives us a less ambiguous insight into the relationship among volume, prices and the trade balance. They eliminate the price-level effect by expressing the trade balance not as the difference between the value of exports and imports but as the quotient of the value of exports divided by that of imports. . . .' [3] This argument, however, is far from convincing, and for precisely the reasons adduced in its support. It is not doubted that the relationship between T and G on the one hand, and $\dfrac{Ve}{Vi}$ on the other, is a unique algebraic relationship. But what more ? What is the analytical value of the trade balance expressed as the quotient of the value of exports divided by that of imports ? This is probably a debatable point, but the present writer would venture to suggest that this measure has very little application to practical problems. Not only does the analysis of the trade balance in terms of T, G and $\dfrac{Ve}{Vi}$ eliminate the price-level effect, it also eliminates the effect of changes in volume level of external trade ; and because these two factors are eliminated, the analysis does not furnish a complete explanation of the relationship among volume, prices and the trade balance, measured as the difference between the values of imports and exports (which is what we are usually interested in), nor does it furnish a complete explanation of the relative influences of prices and quantities on the trade balance (which is another point that Kindleberger was interested in).[4] Either we must dispense entirely with the notion of the terms of trade in the analysis of changes in the balance of trade and speak merely of the effects of movements in prices and quantities ; or we must conduct the analysis in terms of T and G and the price and volume levels of external trade. In view of the

[1] See, for example, R. G. D. Allen and J. E. Ely (Eds.), *International Trade Statistics,* chapter 10, pp. 210-11.

[2] This error may be present in several studies which attempt to measure the effect of changes in the terms of trade on the national income. For example, the statement by R. C. Geary that the 'trading gain' should be nil when import and export price indices are equal cannot be regarded as generally valid unless it is assumed that trade is balanced in the base year. See Phyllis Deane (Ed.), *Income and Wealth,* Series IX (Studies in Social and Financial Accounting), pp. 3-8.

[3] *Op. cit.* p. 284.   [4] *Ibid.* pp. 284-6 and Table 12-2.

importance which the terms of trade has now assumed and also because a change in the price level of external trade by itself may be very important, the latter course is probably the better alternative. While there are statistical difficulties in defining the price level of external trade, these difficulties are in the nature of the problem and do not constitute a valid reason for abandoning this kind of analysis altogether.[1]

The Terms of Trade and the National Income

The limitation of the analysis of the trade balance in ratio form shows up even more clearly if our interest shifts from the trade balance to the national income. While, other things remaining unchanged, an increase (or decrease) in the trade balance in money terms, amounts to an increase (or decrease) in the national income in money terms, no such symmetry exists between the trade balance in ratio form and the national income. A change in the price level of external trade will influence the national income in money terms independently of a change in the net barter terms of trade in just the same way as it influences the trade balance in money terms. And in circumstances where the price level and the net barter terms of trade have opposite effects on the trade balance in money terms, they would likewise have opposite effects on the national income in money terms. It is therefore possible that, even if other elements in the national income remain unchanged in real or money terms, an increase in T may be associated with a decrease in the national income in money terms, and conversely a decrease in T associated with an increase in the national income in money terms. This is why it may be considerably misleading to consider the effect of the terms of trade without taking into account the effect of changes in the price level of external trade.

More intractable difficulties arise when we are interested in the national income in real, rather than in money, terms. This aspect of the problem has been extensively discussed particularly in the context of national accounting.[2] Admitting that in certain circumstances movements of international prices do influence the national income in money terms independently of movements in the real

---

[1] Kindleberger defines the price level of external trade as the simple average of the import and export price indices ; it is, however, also possible to define it as the weighted average of the import and export price indices, the weights being the respective values of imports and exports in the base year (in case of base-weighted prices indices). In either case, the definition makes sense only where import and export prices move in the same direction. Perhaps this is an argument for confining this kind of analysis to this special case. Cf. C. P. Kindleberger, *op. cit.* p. 282.   [2] See especially Phyllis Deane (Ed.), *op. cit.*

values of imports and exports, the problem is to find an appropriate price index with which to deflate the trade balance in money terms in order to ascertain the real gain or loss resulting from the movement of international prices. Reviewing various opinions on this problem, R. C. Geary [1] distinguished between two classes of what he described as 'surplus-deflators', namely (i) price deflators which depend in some linear way on import and export price indices; and (ii) price deflators which do not. He himself expressed preference for the deflators of class (i) particularly because they satisfy one condition to which he attaches much importance, namely that the trading gain should be nil when export and import price indices are equal. The implication of this conclusion is that only a change in the net barter terms of trade should give rise to real gain or loss; it completely ignores the possibility that a change in the price level of external trade without a change in the nct barter terms of trade (i.e. equal percentage increases or decreases in import and export prices) may, in some circumstances, give rise to real gain or loss. For example, if a country has a trade surplus in the base year, equal percentage increases in import and export prices which result from general world inflation will, in the current year, increase the trade surplus in money terms; and if the surplus is used in the same period to extinguish external liabilities the money value of which has not been affected by the general inflation, there would obviously have been a real gain. A price deflator of class (i) would be irrelevant in this particular case, while the index of the price of external liabilities would seem to be more appropriate. Once it is admitted that surplus deflators other than those which depend linearly on import and export price indices, may sometimes be relevant, it becomes necessary to take account not only of the terms-of-trade effect but also of the price-level effect, in assessing the real gain or loss from the movement of international prices.

This problem touches upon another one which was indicated in the United Nations report, *Relative Prices* etc.[2] Studies of the terms of trade are usually based on simultaneous price relations and take no account of time-lags between the sale of exports and the expenditure of the proceeds on imports, or between the purchase of imports and the subsequent sale of exports to pay for them. While a considerable part of foreign trade is, in fact, simultaneous in nature, there are periods when such time lags may be very important. (For example, during the Second World War when many countries were using a large part of their export proceeds to build up their foreign assets rather than to purchase imports; and in the current

[1] Phyllis Deane (Ed.), *op. cit.* p. 8. [2] P. 124.

period, when many countries are buying imports with the proceeds of foreign loans which would have to be repaid with the proceeds of future exports.) In such circumstances, figures of the terms of trade based on simultaneous price relations would have to be interpreted with great caution and with due reference to other factors.

The Terms of Trade and the Provision of Financial Resources for Economic Development

The income terms of trade undoubtedly represent a great improvement over the net barter terms of trade as an indication of the availability of financial resources for economic development. However, it is itself subject to the limitation that it takes no account of changes in the price level of external trade. As we have seen, such changes may influence the trade balance in money terms and, therefore, the financial resources available for economic development. It may also be noted here that failure of the income terms of trade to take account of the price level of external trade limits its usefulness as an index of the gains from trade. This limitation applies whether it is the income terms of trade itself which is regarded as the index of total gain from trade [1] or whether it is the income terms of trade less the volume index of exports which is so regarded.[2] In either case, a change in the price level of external trade may influence the gains from trade independently of a change in the net barter terms or in the volume of exports.

The Terms of Trade and the Distribution of the Gains from Trade

Recent theoretical expositions by J. Bhagwati [3] and H. G. Johnson [4] provide a useful frame of reference for a discussion of this problem. In particular, these expositions clearly illustrate the now generally accepted proposition that an adverse movement of the net barter terms of trade, resulting from an expansion of the volume of trade, does not necessarily indicate a welfare loss, and may well be associated with a welfare gain. On a statistical level, it is now generally agreed that, in spite of the statistical difficulties involved

[1] As J. Viner does in *Studies in the Theory of International Trade*, p. 563.
[2] As C. P. Kindleberger does in his own study (*op. cit.* p. 288). The author mentions that he took this concept of the gains from trade from the United Nations Report, 'Repercussions of Change in the Terms of Trade, etc.', *op. cit.* p. 18, note 8.
[3] 'Immiserizing Growth; A Geometric Note', *Review of Economic Studies*, XXV (3), No. 68, June 1958; 'International Trade and Economic Expansion', *The American Economic Review*, XLVIII, No. 5, December 1958.
[4] *Op. cit.*

in measuring productivity, the single factoral terms of trade considerably improves on the net barter terms of trade as an indication of the gains from trade. However, several statistical problems remain. The first group of problems relates to making allowance for the changing quality of traded goods and the appearance of new goods on the import list. And the second group concerns the calculation of a single terms of trade series for manufacturing and primary producing countries in conditions where (1) different countries adopt different methods of valuing imports and exports, and (2) the terms of trade may improve simultaneously for both parties owing to improvements in transportation, etc.

Another kind of problem which is particularly relevant to the Prebisch-Singer thesis is that the terms of trade which relate to the trade of a particular country may be quite different from the terms of trade of the nationals of that country. In cases where foreign enterprises play an important role in the national economy, it may be useful to make a distinction between the terms of trade of the country as a geographical entity (which may be referred to as the 'domestic' or 'territorial' terms of trade) and the terms of trade of the nationals of the country (which may be called the 'national' terms of trade). It is not unlikely that changes in the two terms of trade may diverge widely. Indeed, the worsening of the position of primary producers emphasized by Prebisch and Singer may have revealed itself more in the movement of the 'national' terms of trade than in that of the 'territorial' terms of trade. The difficulties of measuring the 'national' terms of trade would, of course, be immense ; and the distinction would, no doubt, evoke criticism. But I still venture to put forward the idea for what it is worth.[1]

The Terms of Trade and the Allocation of Productive Resources

One of the most important topics of current discussion among economists is the relevance of comparative cost theory to contemporary problems of economic development. The topic has proved very controversial and I do not want to dwell on it in this paper. One is impressed, however, by the considerable stress laid in the literature (especially in discussions of measures for short-term price stabilization) on the need to preserve the long-term trend of international prices, so that these prices may properly perform their

[1] This idea is, in fact, not a novel one. For example, H. Myint makes a similar but slightly different distinction between the 'external' and 'internal' terms of trade. See H. Myint, 'The Gains from International Trade and the Backward Countries', *The Review of Economic Studies*, Vol. XXII (2), No. 58, 1954–55, pp. 132–3.

function of directing resources along the most efficient channels. At the same time, the opinion is frequently expressed that diversification of national economies through economic development is the ultimate solution to the problem of short-term instability. While economic development for stability may simultaneously increase the national income, it is possible that too much preoccupation with stability may, at least in the short run, slow down the increase in the national income. The crucial problem is to explore the possibilities where both kinds of development overlap, and where they do not, to strike a proper balance between them. What requires to be emphasized is that the need to develop for stability constitutes a structural argument for departing somewhat from the paths of development indicated by the guiding light of international prices. Furthermore, the difficulty of forecasting the future course of prices is itself another argument for increasing the flexibility of national economies through economic development.

The foregoing analysis is intended to indicate some of the difficulties involved in using measures of the terms of trade for the analysis of practical problems. These difficulties have led some economists to doubt the usefulness of further research on this subject.[1] However, misused as the concept of the terms of trade has been, especially in official reports, it remains a useful tool of economic analysis. The studies which have been made of past movement of the terms of trade have generated much argument, but they have shed considerable light on the course of economic history. It is to these studies that we must now turn.

II. HISTORICAL MOVEMENTS OF THE TERMS OF TRADE

Several studies by the United Nations and by professional economists bear on this aspect of the problem.[2] Probably the most important, and certainly the most quoted and criticized, is the United Nations study, *Relative Prices of Exports and Imports of Underdeveloped Countries*. The conclusion reached by this study is summarized in the following paragraph : [3]

Such general statistical data as are available indicate that from the latter part of the nineteenth century to the eve of the Second World War, a period of well over half a century, there was a

[1] See, for example, H. Staehle, 'Some Notes on the Terms of Trade', *International Social Science Bulletin*, Spring 1951, p. 417. (Quoted by C. P. Kindleberger, *op. cit.* p. 1, footnote 2.)

[2] A summary of the results of the most important of these studies is given in M. K. Atallah, *op. cit.* pp. 5-11. [3] P. 7.

secular downward trend in the prices of primary goods relative to the prices of manufactured goods. On an average a given quantity of primary exports would pay, at the end of this period for only 60 per cent of the quantity of manufactured goods which it could buy at the beginning of the period.

A later study of the same organization, *Commodity Trade and Economic Development*, questioned the validity of this finding, particularly on the ground that it fails to take account of the improvement in the quality of traded goods. However, this study itself observed that :

> The facts which are beyond doubt are that the secular movements in the terms of trade are substantial ; and that the movement was in favour of manufacturing countries from the nineteen-twenties to the nineteen-thirties, and has been unfavourable, at least to some manufacturing countries, in recent years.[1]

The series calculated by W. A. Lewis [2] shows an unfavourable trend for primary produce from about 1883 down to the eve of the Second World War. The series of A. H. Imlah on the British terms of trade from 1796 to 1913 shows a clear unfavourable trend against British exports until about 1874, since when it showed a slightly favourable trend up to 1913.[3] That compiled by Colin Clark [4] for the period 1800 to 1940 revealed broadly the same trend as Imlah's up to 1900 and a favourable trend for exports up to the eve of the Second World War. From his extensive study of Europe's terms of trade, C. P. Kindleberger [5] concluded that 'no series is completely representative of the world terms of trade between primary products and manufacturers' and that, on the face of the evidence, 'it may be fair to conclude that there is no long-run tendency for the terms of trade to move against primary products in favour of manufacturers'. 'On the contrary,' he maintained, 'if allowance is made for the unprovable but generally accepted fact that the improvement in the quality of manufactures over the past eighty years has been greater than that of primary products, the terms of trade may have turned against manufactures and in favour of raw materials per unit of equal quality, however that may be defined.' Theodore Morgan has recorded a similar opinion. Examining data for six countries — U.S.A., India, Japan, New Zealand, the Union of South Africa and Brazil—he found no general worsening of the price position of primary

[1] P. 12.   [2] *Op. cit.*
[4] *Economic Elements in the Pax Britannica*, pp. 94-8.
[3] *The Conditions of Economic Progress*, London, 1951.
[5] *Op. cit.* p. 263.

producers.[1]   Finally, the GATT Report, *Trends in International Trade*, records the opinion that : 'The terms of trade in the post-war period were more favourable to non-industrial countries than in 1938, but recently turned against them while still on a level not far from the 1928 position'.[2]

The general picture which emerges from the large volume of evidence accumulated in these studies, reveals five more or less clearly defined phases, corresponding roughly to the following periods : (i) 1800–1880, (ii) 1880–1913, (iii) 1914–38, (iv) 1939–52 and (v) 1952–60.   The first and fourth phases displayed generally favourable movements for primary produce, while the remaining three displayed generally favourable movements for manufactures.   In so far as the various studies overlap, there is a wide measure of agreement among them as to the course of the terms of trade in the five phases distinguished.   The main source of disagreement is about the trend over a period covering three or more of these phases.   While some of the studies indicate that the trend has been unmistakably against primary produce, others (notably C. P. Kindleberger and Theodore Morgan) [3] deny that any such trend is noticeable.   There is also a wider correspondence of views as to the major influences at work in each phase than there is about the importance to be attached to the long-term underlying forces of demand and supply influencing the trend over the whole period.   With regard to the movement of the terms of trade in each phase, the most important influences usually emphasized are summarized in Table 1.   Concerning the long-term trend, the statistical difficulties of calculating a world series and of adjusting for changes in the quality of traded goods as well as changes in the composition of trade, will continue for a long time to bedevil the discussion of this problem.   But even if it is supposed that the statisticians (after allowing for quality changes etc.) agree that an unfavourable trend against primary produce is, in fact, noticeable, the interpretation of this trend in terms of an inherent tendency (implicit in the nature of the demand and supply functions) for the terms of trade to move against primary produce may still be hard to justify.   While it cannot be denied that long-term underlying forces of demand and supply — such as the operation of Engels' law, the tendency for raw material input per unit of manufactures to decline, the normal growth of population, the spread of industrialization to new areas and the progress of technical knowledge — have been at work all through the period, it can be argued that

[1] 'The Long-Run Terms of Trade between Agriculture and Manufacturing', *Economic Development and Cultural Change*, Vol. VIII, No. 1, October 1959.
[2] P. 6, para. 24.   [3] *Op. cit.*

the influences of these factors may have been largely overshadowed by the major disturbances to world trade which occurred during this period. Such major events as the two world wars and the economic depression of the nineteen-thirties have certainly had some effects on the long-term demand and supply functions, quite apart from their temporary influences. While the whole period has been long enough for the long-term trend of the terms of trade to reveal itself, it is quite possible that these major disturbances may have greatly distorted the picture. If the past offers any guidance at all as to the influence of long-term factors on the terms of trade, it is the period before the First World War which seems to offer such guidance. Although this period was dominated by the Industrial Revolution and actually witnessed some revolutionary developments, events were on the whole less revolutionary than in the subsequent period. And, in spite of the fact that statistics for the period before the First World War are far less reliable than those for the subsequent period, the various studies reveal a far greater measure of agreement for the former period than for the latter. However, much has happened to the international economy since the First World War and the experience of the period before that war is now of interest largely because it illustrates, as compared with recent history, contrasting patterns of trade and development.[1] The indeterminacy of the long-term trend of the terms of trade between manufactures and primary produce is strongly emphasized by P. T. Ellsworth,[2] and more recently by G. Haberler.[3] In criticism of the Prebisch-Singer thesis, these authors stress the statistical problems of estimation as well as the difficulties of attaching a welfare significance to a particular movement of the terms of trade.

While the position taken by Prebisch and Singer is not easy to support solely on the face of the statistical evidence (because of the major disturbances to the international economy during the period involved), certain factors need to be taken into account before a full assessment of the situation can be made. The first factor — already mentioned — is the possibility that the 'domestic' terms of trade may be quite different from the 'national' terms of trade, and that the latter, more than the former, may have reflected the effect of the monopolistic arrangements to which Prebisch and Singer refer. The second factor is that the level of the terms of trade for primary

[1] This comparison forms the main theme of the lecture by Ragnar Nurkse, *Patterns of Trade and Development*, Oxford, 1961.

[2] 'The Terms of Trade between Primary Producing and Industrial Countries', *Inter-American Economic Affairs*, Summer 1956.

[3] *International Trade and Economic Development*, National Bank of Egypt, Cairo, 1959.

produce generally, as opposed to their movement, may have been influenced at various times and in various ways by the nature of the political relations between the producing and the consuming countries. For example, the traditional pattern of trade of colonial territories has usually been weighted in favour of their metropolitan countries and this has had the effect of giving them sometimes better and sometimes worse terms of trade than they would have got by the free play of demand and supply for their products in the world market. There seems to be general agreement that the bulk-purchase scheme, undertaken by the British government during and immediately following the Second World War, and the discriminatory restrictions of the Sterling Area during the same period, have, on the whole, had the effect of lowering the terms of trade of some British Colonies below what they would have been in the absence of these arrangements.[1] Contrary examples are the maintenance of a sheltered market in Britain for West Indian sugar, and by France for the products of her former overseas territories. For these reasons, in interpreting the historical movement of the terms of trade with reference to the international distribution of the gains from trade, it is important to bear in mind that the terms of trade are only one, and not necessarily the most important, factor in the situation.

III. FUTURE PROSPECTS

Attempting to predict the future course of the terms of trade is, as someone has said, like trying to write history in advance. However, a few such attempts have, in fact, been made. Three of these — those by Colin Clark,[2] W. A. Lewis [3] and M. K. Atallah [4]— are particularly significant, both for the results achieved and for the light which they throw on the factors relevant to such speculations. The results obtained by Colin Clark and W. A. Lewis, as regards the level of the terms of trade around the year 1960, have already

---

[1] On the effect of bulk-purchase arrangements, see Charlotte Leubuscher, *Bulk Buying from the Colonies*, especially Part III. On the effect of Sterling Area restrictions, see A. C. L. Day, *The Future of Sterling*, chapter 7. C. P. Kindle-berger emphasized the difficulties of making a total assessment of bulk-purchase agreements, but concluded : 'it is likely that Britain's bargaining power, together with the loyal support of her Dominions, made it possible for her to continue bulk-buying only during the period of seller's markets when it was to her advantage' (*op. cit.* p. 80). One of the difficulties involved in making a total assessment of bulk-purchase can be illustrated with reference to West African cocoa during the war. The purchase of the whole of the West African crop was guaranteed by the British government, even though, in the early years of the war, a large quantity of cocoa had to be destroyed owing to lack of shipping space. (Cf. C. Leubuscher, *op. cit.* p. 21.)　　　　　　　　　　[2] *The Economics of 1960.*
[3] *Op. cit.*　　　　　　　　　　　　　　　　　　　　　　[4] *Op. cit.*

been examined against the actual level towards the close of this period. Dr. Enrique Lerdau [1] has found that, on the supply side, both results seriously underestimated the post-war growth in the supply of primary commodities ; while, on the demand side, Lewis' assumptions proved to be more realistic. Both authors, therefore, overestimated the favourable movement for primary produce, although Lewis' estimate was much closer to the actual event than Clark's.

M. K. Atallah's approach to the problem is the most elaborate of the three. He worked with three mathematical models corresponding to various basic assumptions about the supply and demand functions ; and under each model, he examined several special cases corresponding to different assumptions as to certain key variables. The assumptions underlying each model and the calculations of the terms of trade for one decade after 1952-54, based upon them, are reproduced in Tables 2 and 3, and the accompanying notes. The author himself believes that it is Model III which describes 'in a more explicit way the interplay of the factors which influence the terms of trade' [2] and among the result of these models, he expresses preference for those shown in columns 8 to 11 of Table 3, which indicate that (with 1952–54 = 100) the terms of trade of industrial for agricultural produce will lie between 67 and 89, the actual level depending on the values chosen for the capital-output ratios in industry and agriculture, the elasticities of output with respect to capital in both sectors, the elasticity of industrial output with respect to labour and the rate of saving in the industrial sector.

How well do these estimates stand against the present level of the terms of trade ? The latest figures (1953 = 100) given in the United Nations *Monthly Bulletin of Statistics* indicate the export price indices for food and non-food agricultural products to be, respectively, 85 and 92 in the third quarter of 1961. These indices combine to give a weighted index for all agricultural products of 88. The export price index for industrial products in the same period is 110, so that the terms of trade of industrial for agricultural products is 80. Now, considering the difficulties involved in obtaining the calculated results, this figure is remarkably close to some of those shown in columns 8 to 11, and particularly to those in columns 10 and 11 of Table 3. This rough correspondence does not, of course, indicate conclusively that the real world has behaved more or less like the model during this period. Quite apart from the major

---

[1] 'Stabilization and the Terms of Trade', *Kyklos*, Vol. XII, 1959, Fasc. 3, pp. 362-74. [2] *Op. cit.* p. 74.

simplifying assumptions underlying the model and explicitly recognized by the author as limiting the results,[1] the predicted increases
in production have been quite different from the actual increases.
The production indices for agricultural and industrial products given
in the same United Nations source are, respectively, 115 and 145.
These figures diverge rather widely from the predicted increases on
which Dr. Atallah's calculations are based. For the figures in
columns 8 to 11 of Table 3, the predicted increases in production
range from 22 to 31 per cent for agricultural products, and 25 to 30
per cent for industrial products. On the basis of the actual increases
in production, we should expect a far less deterioration in the terms
of trade for agricultural products than has actually taken place. In
a complicated model such as this, the source of error is not easy to
detect. One possible explanation is the increasing tendency in
world trade for more and more manufactured goods to be exchanged
for each other rather than for primary commodities ; but it could
also be that the values chosen for some of the variables do not
correctly represent the actual values. Furthermore, it is not unlikely
that the actual levels of agricultural and industrial productions in
the period (1952–54) were quite different from the initial values
assumed. In spite of these comments, I think that it would be
readily agreed that Dr. Atallah's models represent an advance in
our thinking on this subject, and I would agree with H. W. Singer
that 'to test such forecasts in the light of actual experience is
essentially an unkind, even though necessary undertaking'.[2] The
disadvantage common to all models — and which is in the nature
of the problem — is that the results obtained are not likely to be
sufficiently precise to provide a useful basis for economic policy.

Descending from mathematical models to basic facts, it is now
fairly well established that there are factors on the demand side
making for a relative weakness of primary commodity prices. No
one seriously doubts that Engels' law still operates, or that technological and structural changes in the industrial countries are likely
to cause the demand for primary inputs to lag behind the increase in
the general level of activity. The imponderables are on the supply
side. In particular, the effect on supply of the progressive industrialization of primary producing countries is a factor that cannot
readily be assessed. While much would depend on the progress of

[1] The major assumptions are :

    (i) the high level of aggregation of products,
    (ii) the division of countries into industrial and agricultural producers and
    (iii) the uniformity of expenditure patterns in both countries.

[2] 'Epilogue' on the symposium on 'Stabilization and Development of Primary
Producing Countries', in *Kyklos*, Vol. XII, 1959, Fasc. 3, p. 398.

economic development in these countries and on the pattern which it takes, the speed of progress in this direction will itself depend on the future course of the terms of trade. Indeed, it is already feared that, in the absence of a massive increase in foreign aid, the process of development in the primary producing countries may be considerably slowed down if the terms of trade remain at their present level. Dissatisfaction with the existing trend of the terms of trade lies behind much of the concern with the problem of short-term instability, and explains the frequent references to the concept of 'fair' or 'appropriate' prices in recent discussions of international commodity problems.

This latter point leads one to pose the question : What functions do we expect international prices to perform in future, as regards the relations between industrial and primary producing countries ? While economists have, subject to certain reservations, sought to uphold the role of prices in the allocation of productive resources, there is a large body of opinion, especially among the primary producers themselves, which believes that international prices must be sufficiently favourable to sustain the development of the less developed countries. This question is bound up with several other controversial issues — such as the best form of granting foreign aid

TABLE 1

MAJOR EVENTS INFLUENCING THE TERMS OF TRADE
BETWEEN MANUFACTURES AND PRIMARY PRODUCE

Period	
1800–1880	Expansion of manufacturing production, and lowering of manufacturing costs, associated with the spread of the 'industrial revolution'.
1880–1913	Increase in the supply of primary produce associated with the opening up of new lands, migration, capital investment and the cheapening of transportation.
1918–1938	Expansion of primary production during the war years ; and the economic depression of the nineteen-thirties.
1939–1952	Destruction of sources of supply of primary produce during the war ; increase in demand for primary produce during the Korean War.
1952–1960	Aftermath of the Korean War ; development of synthetic substitutes for primary produce.

—which are strictly outside the scope of this paper. However, for many reasons (some of which economists themselves have supported) the role of international prices in allocating resources does not particularly appeal to countries whose economies are essentially unbalanced. This seems to be the crux of the problem. Furthermore, uncertainties about the future course of international prices partly explain the emphasis usually given in development programmes to the diversification of the national output. It has been repeatedly stressed in the literature that economic development is the ultimate solution to the problem of short-term instability of the terms of trade ; it can also be said that it provides the answer to the long-term problem.

TABLE 2

THE TERMS OF TRADE OF INDUSTRIAL FOR AGRICULTURAL PRODUCTS ONE DECADE AFTER 1952–54, AS CALCULATED BY M. K. ATALLAH (MODELS I AND II)

	Model I			Model II
η_2	-0.9			-0.5
η_1	1.0	0.72	0.48	0.50
$\beta_2 = 0.70$ $\alpha_1 = 0.01$	1.19	1.09	1.02	1.03
$\beta_2 = 0.70$ $\alpha_1 = 0.03$	0.94	0.89	0.84	0.64
$\beta_2 = 0.30$ $\alpha_1 = 0.01$	1.28	1.15	1.06	1.10

Source : M. K. Atallah, *The Terms of Trade between Agricultural and Industrial Products*, Table XIX, p. 70.

Notes: η_2=price elasticity of demand for agricultural products,
η_1=income elasticity of demand for agricultural products,
α_1=annual rate of technical progress in the agricultural sector,
β_2=labour exponent in the industrial sector (i.e. elasticity of industrial output with respect to labour).

Assumptions underlying Table 2

(1) Agricultural production increases by a constant annual rate.
(2) The industrial production function includes two factors of production : labour and capital ; the function is linear and homogeneous.

TABLE 3

THE TERMS OF TRADE OF INDUSTRIAL FOR AGRICULTURAL PRODUCTS ONE DECADE AFTER 1952–54, AS CALCULATED BY M. K. ATALLAH (MODEL III)

(1)	$\alpha_2 = 1$				$\alpha_2 = 0.5$		$\alpha_2 = 0.25$		$\alpha_2 = 0.15$	
	(2) $\frac{c_1}{p_1}=3$; $\frac{c_2}{p_2}=3$	(3) $\frac{c_1}{p_1}=3$; $\frac{c_2}{p_2}=5$	(4) $\frac{c_1}{p_1}=2$; $\frac{c_2}{p_2}=4$	(5) $\frac{c_1}{p_1}=1.5$; $\frac{c_2}{p_2}=4.3$	(6) $\frac{c_1}{p_1}=1$; $\frac{c_2}{p_2}=4$	(7) $\frac{c_1}{p_1}=1$; $\frac{c_2}{p_2}=3$	(8) $\frac{c_1}{p_1}=0.5$; $\frac{c_2}{p_2}=3$	(9) $\frac{c_1}{p_1}=0.5$; $\frac{c_2}{p_2}=4$	(10) $\frac{c_1}{p_1}=0.5$; $\frac{c_2}{p_2}=3$	(11) $\frac{c_1}{p_1}=0.5$; $\frac{c_2}{p_2}=4$
$\beta_2 = 0.70$ $\sigma_2 = 0.11$	0.73	0.71	0.59	0.53	0.61	0.65	0.71	0.67	0.82	0.79
$\beta_2 = 0.30$ $\sigma_2 = 0.11$	0.79	0.73	0.64	0.56	0.68	0.72	0.76	0.72	0.89	0.85
$\beta_2 = 0.70$ $\sigma_2 = 0.20$	0.77	0.73	0.63	0.55	0.66	0.69	0.74	0.71	0.86	0.84

Source : M. K. Atallah, *The Terms of Trade between Agricultural and Industrial Products.*

Notes: β_2 = labour exponent in the industrial sector (i.e. elasticity of industrial output with respect to labour),
σ_2 = rate of saving in the industrial sector,
α_2 = capital exponent in the agricultural sector,
c_1 = capital stock in the agricultural sector,
c_2 = capital stock in the industrial sector,
p_1 = volume of agricultural production,
p_2 = volume of industrial production.

(3) Industrial population increases at a constant proportional rate of growth.

(4) The volume of savings in each sector is a constant proportion of income in that sector, but total savings in both sectors are invested in the industrial sector.

Assumptions underlying Table 3

(1) Agricultural production requires fixed proportions of capital and labour ; labour is assumed to be abundant, so the only effective limit on production is capital ; technical progress results in a fixed annual rate of increase of production.

(2) The industrial production function includes two factors of production : labour and capital ; the function is linear and homogeneous.

(3) Industrial population increases at a constant proportional rate of growth.

(4) The volume of savings in each sector is a constant proportion of income in that sector ; and investment in each sector depends on the savings of that sector.

(5) The ratio of the agricultural products demanded to the industrial products demanded depends on the total money income of both sectors and the prices of their products.

(6) The demand function for agricultural products implies a price elasticity of -0.5 and an income elasticity of 0.5.

DISCUSSION OF THE PAPERS BY PROFESSOR DANTWALA AND MR. ONITIRI

In discussion there was substantial agreement that terms of trade had been adverse to primary producers for some time. *Mr. Economides* made the point that manufacturers were often in a position themselves to fix prices, whereas competing primary producers had to accept them. Higher prices for food and raw materials were therefore reflected very quickly in prices of manufactures and the benefit to their producers was only temporary. The benefits from lower prices of food and raw materials were shared between trade-unionized workers and industrialists and were not passed on in prices of manufactures.

The true terms of trade between primary producers and industrial producers, as indicated by ratios of *per capita* income generated in agriculture to those generated in the whole economy of industrial countries, were very adverse to primary producers. The prospects for primary producing countries were for a continuation of the adverse terms of trade.

Record of Discussion

Professor Tyagunenko and *M. de Jouvenel* were among those who felt that the position of primary producers *vis-à-vis* industrialized countries was weak and likely to remain so. *Professor Tyagunenko* believed that the position would get worse as the ratio of consumption of raw materials to industrial output in the more developed countries declined.

Professors Reubens and *Tyagunenko* believed that diversification of the economy and in particular industrialization were the appropriate remedies for under-developed countries suffering from adverse terms of trade. Professor Tyagunenko advocated industrialization on a broad base, including heavy industry and the manufacture of producer goods, although this programme might have to be modified for the smaller countries.

In the context of diversification *Dr. Johnston* stressed that developing countries needed also to expand agricultural exports, which could often be done without diverting substantial resources from the industrial sector. It was a question of determining relative priorities. *Dr. Bhagwati* also wanted the cost of diversification in terms of real income to be weighed.

Part of the discussion was addressed to the methodology of determining terms of trade and the validity of some of the cruder forms of index. *Professor Lengellé* and *Professor Dupriez* were among those who commented on the methodological problems of constructing meaningful indices. *Professors Walker*, *Wade* and *Gannagé* were concerned with the problem of aggregation. *Professor Walker* felt that generalizations about terms of trade, which were themselves an amalgam of individual movements of prices and groupings of countries, were not of much help to individual countries. However, these aggregates could be broken down into their component parts to give guidance on specific policy issues. *Professor Gannagé* thought that global terms of trade had little meaning where favourable terms affected one sector only of a country, such as foreign oil companies. Would it be possible to develop sectoral terms of trade, taking account of the structure of the economy?

There was some discussion about the possibility of predicting the future course of terms of trade, and its usefulness in policy making. *Dr. Zellner* argued that the use of econometric models could provide better guidance on the effect of terms of trade on balance of payments than could unscientific guesses about the future. *Professor Wade* was also in favour of using econometric techniques. *Mr. Onitiri* said that he was not against model building. With all their limitations indices of terms of trade had to be used. The outlook for terms of trade should not affect the allocation of resources between production and export, but between different types of domestic production, in fact the rate of development.

Chapter 32

LONG CYCLES OF ECONOMIC GROWTH: DOES THE KONDRATIEFF CYCLE STILL SURVIVE TODAY? *

BY

LÉON H. DUPRIEZ
Centre de Recherches Économiques, Louvain

IT was my intention, at first, to present here a brief survey of historical and theoretical work on the long cycles [1] which we call Kondratieff. This would have included an analysis of the problem indicated in the title ; but on reflection, I preferred to limit myself to that problem alone, for various reasons.

We are rapidly accumulating material on long-term economic trends prior to the industrial revolution and we are beginning to see an explanation for them ; but it does still seem too early to attempt a true synthesis, such as I have tried to present for the economic movements of the industrial revolution itself — first in my *Mouvements économiques généraux* [2] where I included supporting statistical series, and later, in more theoretical form, in *Philosophie des conjonctures économiques.* [3]

Furthermore, the study of the Kondratieff itself has been somewhat overshadowed since the war by other concepts of economic evolution. In recent years, the only author who has shared my approach of looking for the Kondratieff in general long-term movements has been Gaston Imbert. [4] So there is not much work which I could have summarized had I wished to do so.

Yet, if we want to see the course of history in perspective and also to determine the theoretical validity of the Kondratieff at present,

* Translation from the French by Elizabeth Henderson.
[1] In English the word 'cycle' has traditionally been associated not only with the short cycle but also with the longer Kondratieff cycle. The author, writing in French, had deliberately avoided the word cycle (in French he had used the word 'movement'). Unfortunately no convenient English term is available to convey the meaning of these longer swings.
[2] L. H. Dupriez, *Mouvements économiques généraux*, Institut de Recherches Économiques et Sociales and Nauwelaerts, Louvain, first edition 1947, second edition 1951.
[3] L. H. Dupriez, *Philosophie des conjonctures économiques*, Institut de Recherches Économiques et Sociales and Nauwelaerts, Louvain, 1959.
[4] G. Imbert, *Des Mouvements de longue durée Kondratieff*, Aix-en-Provence, 1956.

we have to try and find out whether, since 1945, the economy still moves in a phase of such a cycle or whether modern economic policy has introduced other forms of movement.

This is the problem to which I shall try to give an answer, or at least the elements of an answer. The problem appears all the more interesting just because economic thinking nowadays proceeds along rather different conceptual lines.

I. THE PROBLEM

After 1919 it soon became evident that the economy was entering a long downswing. The Harvard Economic Service recognized it as early as 1923 behind the price stability of a cyclical upswing. From 1930 onwards, the phenomenon assumed such dimensions as not to be overlooked, although its 'spontaneous' duration remains an unresolved enigma. Imbert dates the end of the movement with 1935, others consider this assumption as tenuous and prefer to regard the long downswing as continuing until the political break of 1939.

Be that as it may, there can be no doubt at all that the end of the war in 1945 constituted the point of departure for a new evolutionary pattern, the general lines of which have remained consistent until our own days. In any discussion of Phelps Brown's characteristics of these movements, we must first define their climacterics, which can legitimately be expected to provide an initial broad indication of the present phase of the economy. We shall then have to analyse what typical movements of the past can be retraced in more recent times and to define their bearing on the climacterics of the last seventeen years.

The known recurring features of the Kondratieff have been studied in the framework of the industrial revolution and of those countries which were its pioneers. There remains the question, therefore, what, if any, conclusions can be drawn with respect to non-industrialized countries and to the periods of their insertion into the industrial economy.

II. TRACING THE PHASE OF THE KONDRATIEFF

The first thing the statistical analysis we propose to conduct here will have to do, therefore, is to identify those developments of the past seventeen years which can be interpreted as a continuation of the long cycles as well as those which, on the contrary, deviate from the traditional pattern. There is certainly no reason to suppose *a priori* that past models will fully repeat themselves in the structural evolution of our economy. We shall have to arrive at some judgment of principle both on the relative importance of movements of the traditional type and on their theoretical significance.

The principal element of the economic climate remains the general movement of the price level, or more precisely, of the price structure in relation to factor costs. The price trend conditions a great variety of economic decisions, which are consciously or unconsciously subject to its influence. This is true no less of decisions bearing on quantitative developments as of those involving qualitative and structural changes in the production process.

Since these are long-term influences, they are bound to have a visible impact on the rate of expansion of economic activity and on the rate of increase of productivity. We are justified, therefore, in trying to define the climacterics of the Kondratieff in terms not only of price trends, but also of production and productivity trends.

In my *Mouvements économiques généraux* I argued that the movements of the Kondratieff had a profound influence on the shape of secular expansion ; it will be recalled that this argument was based on the statistical analysis of prices, production, factor returns, transport, trade and other 'real' aspects of the economy. I found, however, that these movements were not motive forces of the economy, but rather themselves conditioned by monetary relationships of various kinds ; nevertheless, they remained the fundamental means of transmission through which the Kondratieff made its impact on the economy.

Quite apart from climacterics, therefore, we have to trace the development of the determinant monetary relationships. As a starting point for the analysis below, I would briefly recall a few basic points such as I formulated them in the above-mentioned book.

(1) The theory of secular development is complete and coherent without any reference to monetary factors, but the latter have to be introduced into the discussion of periods which, while not secular, are longer than those covered by the Juglar. In the Kondratieff, in particular, monetary developments appear to be dominant.

(2) There exists no mechanism by which the money supply is automatically adjusted to the demand for money at constant price levels (or, conversely, which ensures stability of the average ratio between the value of the money unit and its purchasing power) ; some movements must, therefore, be expected *a priori*.

(3) The problem cannot be reduced, as Cassel did, to one of price movements under the influence of metallic money supply ; this is

too simple a view and one, moreover, which fits only some definite historical circumstances.

(4) The really decisive monetary developments have to be looked for at the level of monetary, and especially fiduciary, circulation and of credit.

(5) Credit variations deprive monetary movements of their autonomy as motive forces of the economy, in so far as the demand for credit itself depends on the climate of the economy.

Monetary developments are the most difficult to assess, given that they no longer obey their own natural laws but, increasingly, respond to more and more open intervention ; the economic climate is today fashioned also by new policy measures. A case in point is repressed inflation.

III. TURNING POINTS

Let us assume, as a working hypothesis, that all these above-named principles lead us to recognize in the conditions of the economy since 1945 the determinants of a Kondratieff upswing. Apart from fluctuating intensity (as in the nineteenth century, too) the relevant influences were at work throughout the period, and this is as far as historical judgment can go — barring, of course, the expectation of a turning point in the more or less immediate future, which would confirm that we are indeed faced with an alternating phase and not with the projection of any more durable expansionary movement. It is quite obvious that no such turning point has occurred during the last few years, as regards either the prevailing tendencies or the climate.

But this brings us up at once against a very delicate point of theory. If we interpret developments in historical terms, we may rightly say that we can still recognize a Kondratieff phase and there-fore argue that the theoretical construction of alternating phases persists, though in changing form. If this is so, we should clearly stick to the traditional way of thinking. But then, there is the more utopian context of the 'new economics', in which economic move-ments are regarded as susceptible of guidance through action on certain key factors. In this context it would, no doubt, still be admitted that recent developments have, under many aspects, much in common with the long upward waves, but it would also be argued that this type of development is beneficial because of the stimulus it provides and that it tends to be perpetuated by modern economic policy. In this view the long upward wave would then be merely the transition to a new type of evolution.

Which of the two views is true ? It is now seventeen years since the war has ended, and we must scan the immediate future for some indications, especially for any sign that reasons for a turning point may, or are likely to, make their appearance. If we can find such reasons, the Kondratieff keeps its historical features. If we cannot, we may have to adopt another view.

The problems of the future to be examined in this context include, in particular, the attrition of policies of repressed inflation, the fact that full employment of the factors of production disrupts exponential growth trends and makes it impossible to extrapolate them secularly, the growing abundance of capital, tools and supplies in relation to needs, and, last but not least, the waxing strain on international liquidity. Overlaying all this, we have, as F. Simiand says, the changing prospect of successive generations acting differently in response to the conditions created by their elders.

IV. PRICES, PRODUCTION AND PRODUCTIVITY

Let us first have a look at general price trends, since these are, traditionally, regarded as indicators of the direction of Kondratieff movements.

Over the entire period 1946–61, the cost-of-living index has displayed greater average annual rises than during the long upswing of 1887–1913 (see Chart 1) ; the actual range of increase is between 1·8 per cent in Belgium and 4 per cent in Great Britain. These figures compare with 1·06 per cent in Great Britain, 1·26 in Germany and 1·82 in the United States during the earlier period. But the strong upward thrust spent itself in 1951 ; since then the annual average rise of the cost-of-living has been only 1·2 per cent in the United States, 1·23 in Belgium, 1·53 in Germany and 2·77 per cent in Italy. In any event, the width of the movement remains of the same order of magnitude as in the past.

Wholesale price indices are more difficult to interpret, because of the sudden shock of additional demand in 1951, when markets were still short of supply ; the developments since 1953 convey a better picture of current trends (see Chart 2). Here we encounter certain divergences which will need some explanation. In the United States, industrial wholesale prices rose at an annual average rate of 2·79 per cent between 1947 and 1961, as compared with 1·54 per cent before 1913. Public opinion has seized upon this phenomenon and labels it inflation, even though it is not so much in excess of the British wholesale industrial price rise of 2·05 per cent annually between 1897 and 1913. Since 1951 the relevant U.S. prices have been rising only by an average 1·21 per cent a year. Inflationary fears are certainly shared by nations which have a period of repressed inflation behind them, but quite legitimately not by others. In Italy and Belgium, for example, the wholesale price indices for industrial products were no higher in 1961 than they had been in 1953.

In their turn, agricultural wholesale prices generally had a falling tendency — through alternating ups and downs until 1953, and then slow and steady, as evidenced by the American and Belgian indices. In Italy, on the other hand, wholesale agricultural prices have been rising at an annual average rate of 0·85 per cent. By contrast, we see a generally rising trend for the period 1897–1913, ranging from 1·35 per cent in Great Britain to 2·78 per cent in the United States.

Looking at individual prices (as shown in two examples in Chart 3) it will be seen that these overall moderate movements mask profound structural changes due to a variety of causes. European coal prices, for instance, have been rising under the impact of decreasing returns, while American ones fell as a result of better techniques. Iron and steel prices have been falling in a more and more competitive marginal international market, while rising in the basic domestic markets under the pressure of growing costs. The falling trend of international wheat prices is due to an enormous expansion of acreage and to an improvement in farming techniques. Stationary or falling textile prices due to technical progress and market saturation, contrast with rising building construction prices, due to opposite reasons. Many other examples could be cited.

While some individual prices, therefore, have a falling trend, other and more important ones are rising, especially hourly labour costs. This is a case where modern developments cut right across earlier known Kondratieffs ; their divergence from wholesale prices implies a much more rapid pace of technical progress. Between 1945 and 1961, increases in wage costs ranged from 4·58 per cent on an average in the United States to 7·13 per cent in Germany ; by comparison, we have a range of 0·94 per cent in Great Britain to 2·57 per cent in the United States in the period ending in 1913, and of 0·6 per cent in the United States to 2·19 per cent in Germany prior to 1872. The divergence is profound, and testifies to a strong increase in the marginal productivity of labour.

Generally speaking, then, the price system as a whole definitely displays a long-term upward movement. Individual prices are largely immune against reductions due to technical progress and growing supply, in so far as adjustments as between labour costs and product prices come about mainly by wage increases. Equilibrium imposes no undue strain on inventories. Repressed inflation weakens and disappears thanks to upward adjustments of the internal price system. We are in the presence of what neo-Wicksellian theory regards as an inflationary price-wage spiral.

Let us now take a look at the impact of these facts on production and productivity, which are traditionally regarded as conditioned by the economic climate.

We can be brief on this subject, because there is nothing much we can say on the consequences of the Kondratieff. We need merely establish the overall direction of the impact.

The volume of industrial output has been expanding strongly and systematically since 1946 (see Chart 3). The following comments may be made :

(1) Although least strong in the United States, where expansion started on high levels after reconversion of the greatly increased wartime capacities, the annual average rate of growth of the volume of industrial output was still 3·6 per cent ; this is much the same rate as during the years 1898–1914, when, however, it was higher than in other countries. The United States thus finds itself at the other end of the range at present.

(2) The very high rate of expansion in the European Economic Community (8·28 per cent) reflects reconstruction and structural change in industry, as well as the concentration of industrial populations. Europe has caught up with the United States, but this rate of expansion cannot be sustained in the secular period (it would imply multiplication by 2819 in a hundred years !) and the present state of full employment constitutes an immediate obstacle to any extrapolation of this rate of growth.

(3) For the rest, all the growth tendencies taken as a whole cannot be extrapolated either for any length of time ; expansion will have to proceed at a more moderate pace wherever full employment of the factor labour is approaching.

(4) Developments are all the more subject to short-term cyclical fluctuations as elements of re-expansion are slackening.

Previous long upswings generally implied a slow increase in physical productivity and heavy reliance on the growing employment of labour. This has not been so since 1946. Automation, the proliferation of specific tools, the improvement in the specific qualities of raw materials, etc., uninterruptedly raised physical productivity. This fits better into Schumpeter's theory, where the upswing is linked to the application of dominant techniques, than do the earlier upswings with their more extensive and less intensive efforts.

Current rates of increase in physical productivity, on the contrary, imply rapid intensification sustained by so much effort that we are probably right in placing the movement into the secular rather than the merely long period (Chart 3). We have no means of making comparisons with the past in terms of overall manufacturing industry ; but what we know of individual industries suggests that the rate of increase has been fast everywhere since 1946, even in Great Britain. Here again Europe stands out with rapid productivity increases underlying its growth. We are not far from the relations prevailing in 1936–38, which suggests that countries will, in the near future, develop in a more uniform fashion and at a more moderate pace.

Wage costs rose throughout the period nearly as much as hourly physical productivity, but have not quite caught up with it (Chart 1) ; the slight remaining difference is explicable in terms of stronger capital intensity and the growing importance of white-collar workers. However, in comparison with 1936–38, wages recently rose somewhat more than productivity, which testifies to a strengthening of the position of labour. The process of economic imputation has worked correctly and uninterruptedly.

As regards interest rates, the period began in the United States and the countries of repressed inflation with cheap-money policies, since low interest rates are stimulants in the context of full-employment policies. But the latter had to give way to counter-cyclical policies and now bond yields are high. In some countries of Europe high yields have dropped to more normal levels. Markets are now much more uniform than they used to be.

It is hardly surprising that bond yields should be rather high after seventeen years of prosperity ; but the real reason is the size of government demand for capital funds. The capitalization rate of shares is now so low that many future prospects will have to be reconsidered in the light of the production forecasts mentioned above. The capital market's capacity to meet the claims of business companies does not appear to have been impaired by the latter's large-scale and prolonged recourse to the market.

V. MONETARY DEVELOPMENTS

As I did in my *Mouvements économiques généraux*, I shall try, here too, to analyse the monetary aspects of the recent long wave by starting with metallic money — on which Kondratieff and Cassel originally placed unduly heavy emphasis — and then go on to note circulation, credit and the conditions of monetary policy, according to Simiand. I shall try to assess the tendencies and prospects of new problems in the light of the decisive part always played by monetary developments in long cycles.

Starting from relatively low levels (27·5 per cent below 1936–38), gold production has grown by 3·1 per cent on the average over the whole period under consideration. This is not much in comparison with overall industrial production. Until 1953, the pace was very slow indeed, under the influence of highly unfavourable prices — or unfavourable, at any rate, in terms of rising factor costs. New production methods then redressed the situation, and gold production has been rising since 1953 at the rate of 4 per cent for the whole world, and 7·67 per cent for South Africa, whose share in world production has become more and more dominant. But this more favourable tendency coincided with the period of least rising prices.

If the possible impact of gold production on price systems is to be properly assessed, new production has to be considered in relation to monetary gold stocks. The proportion of new production at present seems quite insufficient. In 1936–38 the proportion exceeded 4 per cent, having climbed from 2 per cent since 1920. In 1946, we find 2·26 per cent and by 1961 still no more than 2·95 per cent. Gold production was seriously deficient over the whole period, even though the most recent figure seems to tally with the norm established in 1930 by the League of Nations. But now the underdeveloped countries are increasingly adopting monetary forms of economy, not to speak of the rapid growth of industrial societies.

Furthermore, non-monetary uses of gold and hoarding have absorbed large quantities of gold since the war, whereas in the inter-war period gold had been almost wholly concentrated in currency reserves. Over the period under consideration, non-monetary uses and hoarding swallowed up 60 per cent of new production. The political crises of 1951 and 1956 and the lack of confidence in money in 1960 led to large-scale hoarding. Central banks are rightly reluctant to cut themselves off from the market and to let the price of gold soar on the black market — which indeed would finally discredit monetary gold and would openly confer a nominalist character on the gold exchange standard.

As a result of all these influences liquidity reserves have been rising only slowly. For the ten countries under consideration [1] the rate of increase as a whole was only 1·27 per cent a year over the period 1946–61. This falls seriously short of the liquidity requirements of the international monetary system. For the whole world

[1] United States, Great Britain, Germany, Canada, France, Italy, Japan, Belgium, Luxemburg and Sweden. These countries were chosen because their currencies are at present most widely convertible.

the rate of increase was 1·43 per cent. The shortage is all the more serious as reserves are now more scattered than they used to be and as the country which provides additional reserve currency has been losing gold at the rate of 1·5 per cent a year.

The very fact that the world's foreign exchange reserves (especially in dollars) grew in thirteen years from 13·8 to 23·3 billion dollars testifies with all the necessary clarity to the need to overcome the shortage of gold backing. If the system today appears incapable of expanding any further or is even threatened by contraction, this may become a reason to suggest that a turning point in the Kondratieff is imminent.

While the gold base has serious implications on long-term problems, the relations of the monetary and the price system have to be assessed in terms of monetary circulation. Let us examine the aggregates for our ten selected countries, since we cannot establish larger aggregates with adequate accuracy.

Total means of payments increased at the conservative rate of 3·04 per year, which was slower than industrial production and probably also slower than national income, though less so. However, there were no doubt some surpluses of means of payment at the beginning of the period. Certainly the movement as such is not inflationary. It seems to have responded well enough to the normal functioning of the institutions (or to needs, as Tooke would have said), the system being left to adapt itself without interference from policy decisions regarding the money stock.

Even so, the money stock increased more than the gold stock (which rose by only 1·27 per cent annually), so that the fiduciary issue (backed by domestic credit) increased by 5·59 and monetary circulation backed by foreign exchange by 8·57 per cent annually.

These developments are in line with the pattern of previous long upswings (cf. *Mouvements économiques généraux*, vol. II, p. 170); both in 1848–72 and in 1897–1913 reserves declined and fiduciary circulation expanded vigorously. However, in the present financial structure, where rediscounts by concentrated banking systems are low, the main burden of credit creation falls on foreign exchange.

The low proportion of rediscount in the total volume of money supply deprives my earlier historical interpretation of some of its validity with respect to the importance of the fiduciary issue : but the underlying economic phenomenon, namely, the economy's proportionately more heavy recourse to the banking system in the long upswing, is still in evidence, even though its final effect is obscured by the strength of the deposit banks. Credit extended to private business has risen by 10·12 per cent a year on the average, with a marked acceleration of the pace since 1953. This is well in excess of the rate of economic expansion, even if corrected for intervening price rises, and therefore clearly commits the commercial banking system.

However, the effects of the latter's commitments on the credit system varied over the period. Until 1957 private credit extended by central banks kept rising, while in any case never exceeding about 5 per cent of commercial credit ; later it fluctuated cyclically, but stopped rising. By contrast, since 1955 sight deposits at central banks increased from 15 to 30 per cent of the fiduciary issue. It follows that bank liquidity has been increasing.

Finally, desired — or better, real — cash balances shed some light on the differential effects of money supply on prices. The United States and Great Britain entered the period with their war inflation unhampered by monetary reform or credit restrictions. However slowly their circulation increased, it could not prevent prices from rising, because people dipped into their cash reserves. Germany started from the bottom up and had no problem of price inflation, in spite of strong monetary expansion. Thanks to devaluation, France had a somewhat similar pattern of real cash balances.

In concluding this analysis, it might be worth pointing out that there has been no revolutionary change in monetary institutions since 1946 ; they simply developed along the line of greater liberalism — and one which ultimately is more liberal in substance than in form. In other words, money as an institution gradually improved its working. This too, is typical of long periods of prosperity (see *Mouvements économiques généraux*, p. 193). Of all the developments we described, this is probably the one least susceptible of extrapolation.

Because of the complexity of observed monetary movements, we need some overall judgment to assess the manner of their effect on the relationship between monetary and real factors.

Although the gold base of the world monetary system makes its own impact felt imperatively, it no longer directly rules the monetary system's quantitative developments. The separation was gradual before 1914, and after 1920 we had a sharp break. From then on the respective rates of expansion diverged openly — not without creating internal structural problems for our monetary system.

Even though technical progress in South Africa eliminated the danger that gold production might be held back by rising costs at constant prices, according to the Kondratieff model, not nearly enough new gold reached the currency reserves. The share of monetary gold dwindled because it had to compete with speculative and commercial buying in the same market.

At the other end of the scale, bank credit expanded vigorously, implying growing banking commitments as in all long periods of upswing ; business 'needs' come to the fore. The money supply for direct use (bank notes and current accounts) increased less than circulation, but this may be explained by the abundance of means of payment in many countries at the beginning of the period. The development of the money supply does not seem to play a very active part in the Kondratieff, but responds readily to the divergent influences of cash holdings and credit.

The divergences between means of payments and domestic credit caused no difficulties to the banking system ; the relative diminution of rediscounts and the accumulation of deposits at central banks testify to the growing strength of national banking systems. By contrast, the divergences between money supply for direct use and the gold backing did lead to an increase in foreign exchange reserves in a unilateral and too exclusive form, which weakened the position of the reserve currencies predominantly used for this purpose. It is at this point that the Kondratieff movement requires structural reform of the world monetary system.

Finally, it must not be overlooked that the climate of government policy has generally been inflationary. Governments were always ready to step in with monetary measures to make good every slightest economic deficiency. Political pressure in this direction has found powerful support in the 'new economics' with its accent on the maintenance of money flows. However, the impact of policies of this kind on the long movement weakened in the course of time, in so far as the international monetary order left less and less room from freedom of action at the national level.

VI. LONG CYCLES IN UNDER-DEVELOPED COUNTRIES

Before concluding our investigation, let us take a look at the incidence of the long cycle outside the industrial world, that is, under-developed countries with scarcely diversified economies, often producers of the world's major raw materials. Unfortunately, we have no clear framework for current analysis in the absence of historical synthesis — for which, in any event, we do not possess the necessary material. All we can do, therefore, is to draw on what fragmentary indications we have.

First of all we must warn the reader against a naïve form of interpretation. The long downward movement from 1920 to 1939 was characterized since 1925, and even more so since 1930, by so heavy a fall in raw material and food prices that the terms of trade of the areas at the fringe of the world market deteriorated catastrophically. Direct loss of purchasing power was heavy, but heavier still were the disorganizing effects on the economy and public finance.

This might suggest that the central phenomenon of the long cycle in under-developed countries is the development of the terms of trade and the resulting income variations expressed in the current balance of trade. The long cycle would then appear as a direct consequence of relations with the industrial world. But such an interpretation would be somewhat hazardous for any period other than 1920–29, when many fringe countries already had a fairly developed monetary economy which was highly sensitive to a restricted number of export activities.

Furthermore, we should not allow our minds to be obfuscated by the terms of trade for goods : given technical progress, only the exchange ratio expressed in factors of production, or more specifically in wages, is really meaningful, and it may upset all our superficial conclusions.

For instance, up to 1872 the primary producing countries' terms of trade improved considerably against Great Britain, owing to British technical progress ; in terms of wages, it should have been the other way round. Between 1872 and 1896 the terms of trade moved in the other direction ; but agricultural prices collapsed in 1877, just when American crops expanded so much — and the victim was European, not American, agriculture. Finally, in the inter-war period, the drop in the price of palm oil corresponded to the shift of exports to plantation countries, which again proves the relevance of the exchange ratio in terms of factors. All in all, no valid conclusions can ever be drawn without a careful study of the respective developments of nominal and real wages.

In its turn, monetary history is full of warning examples. The breakdown of bimetallism in 1876 inaugurated a period of declining prices, just as the devaluation of sterling and the dollar did later ; but, by sticking to the silver standard, India (together with the rest of Asia) escaped the monetary impact of the Kondratieff on prices and production.

At the present time, when practically all economies are monetary and highly interdependent, it is more natural to ask how the primary producing countries are drawn into the long cycle through their participation in its processes than to argue in terms of commercial impact. It is in this sense that we must look at the terms of trade, which alone lend themselves to graphical representation (Chart 7).

The development of the terms of trade was entirely dominated by the transition of the economy from scarcity to abundance of agricultural produce. By political accident, the scarcity reached its peak in 1951, when it further improved the producing countries' already unusually favourable terms of trade. While returning to more normal levels, the terms of trade then remained good until some time between 1954 and 1957, according to the commodity and the country concerned. Since then, supply has been large and elastic, and prices have dropped. Once more we have escaped Ricardo's dire forecasts of the exhaustion of cultivable land.

However, recent developments have nothing in common with the 'great thaw' of 1930. Current prices certainly do put some producers under severe pressure, but allow others, who are better placed or better equipped, to expand production to the detriment of their neighbours. Here again we should examine the exchange ratio in terms of wages and there is every reason to suppose that we should then not find deterioration in all cases, but improvement in some.

There is no prospect of any quick and immediate disappearance of food and raw material surpluses — partly because, in the aggregate, these commodities occupy an undue place in development plans, and partly because the producers' income is protected so that they need not adjust their output to market conditions. No political solution to the conflict between progress and current security is in sight which might be expected to raise market prices.

This must be regarded as a datum of the problem for the next few years. We must, furthermore, expect the course of economic events to be influenced by the world's new political features. The disappearance of the colonial system will weaken the link between exports and local development to the benefit of more integrated structures. But it is too early to evaluate the other consequences of the new political pattern both for separate economies and the world economy as a whole. Linear extrapolation of the past would certainly not seem to be in order.

COST OF LIVING AND WAGES

Index 1936-38 in national currency

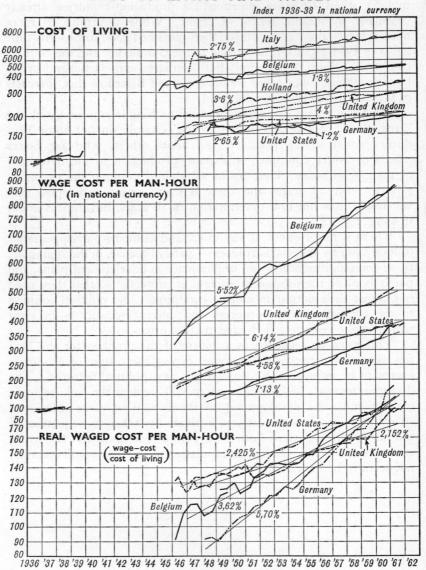

CHART 1

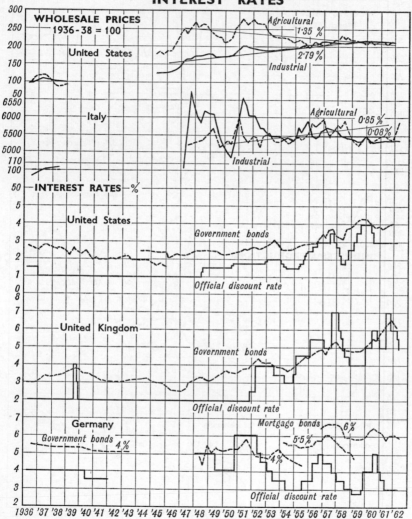

WHOLESALE PRICES AND INTEREST RATES

CHART 2

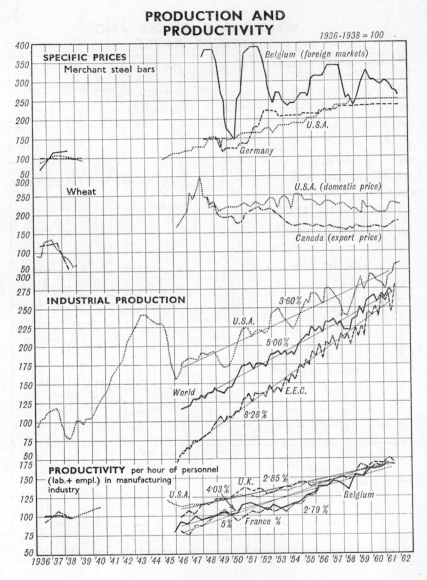

PRODUCTION AND PRODUCTIVITY

1936-1938 = 100

SPECIFIC PRICES
Merchant steel bars

Belgium (foreign markets)

U.S.A.

Germany

Wheat

U.S.A. (domestic price)

Canada (export price)

INDUSTRIAL PRODUCTION

3·60%

U.S.A.

5·06%

World

E.E.C.

8·28%

PRODUCTIVITY per hour of personnel
(lab.+ empl.) in manufacturing
industry

U.K. 2·85%

U.S.A. 4·03%

Belgium

2·79%

5% France %

1936 '37 '38 '39 '40 '41 '42 '43 '44 '45 '46 '47 '48 '49 '50 '51 '52 '53 '54 '55 '56 '57 '58 '59 '60 '61 '62

CHART 3

546

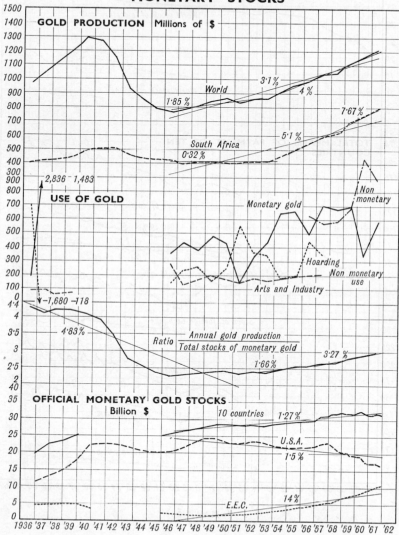

CHART 4

MEANS OF PAYMENT

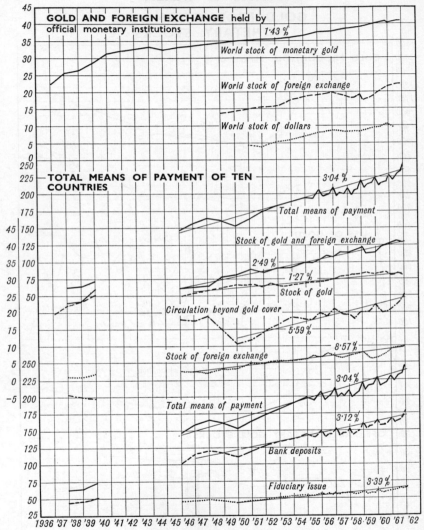

CHART 5

CREDIT AND DESIRED
CASH BALANCES

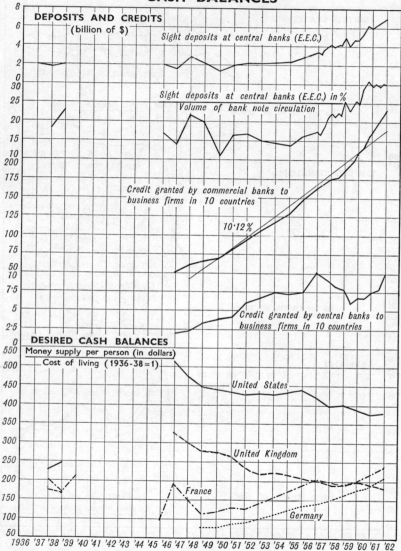

DEPOSITS AND CREDITS
(billion of $)

Sight deposits at central banks (E.E.C.)

Sight deposits at central banks (E.E.C.) in %
Volume of bank note circulation

Credit granted by commercial banks to
business firms in 10 countries

10·12%

Credit granted by central banks to
business firms in 10 countries

DESIRED CASH BALANCES
Money supply per person (in dollars)
Cost of living (1936-38 = 1)

United States

United Kingdom

France

Germany

1936 '37 '38 '39 '40 '41 '42 '43 '44 '45 '46 '47 '48 '49 '50 '51 '52 '53 '54 '55 '56 '57 '58 '59 '60 '61 '62

CHART 6

549

TERMS OF TRADE

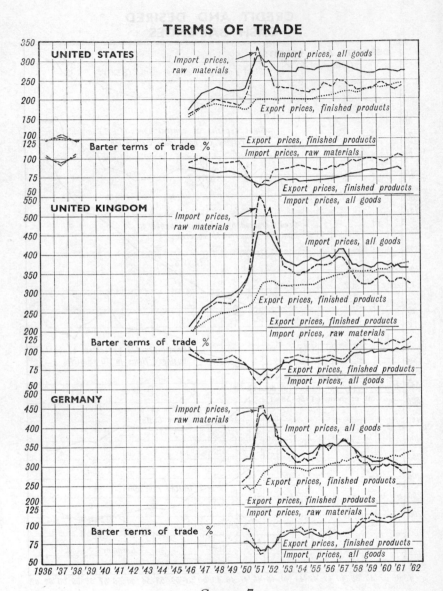

CHART 7

Record of Discussion

DISCUSSION OF THE PAPER BY PROFESSOR DUPRIEZ

THE discussion in this session was concerned mainly with the reality of the concept of the Kondratieff cycle itself, and with the validity of trying to use it in relation to recent periods.

Professor Patinkin doubted whether the idea of the Kondratieff cycle was well established. Most of the basic data in Kondratieff's original paper (of 1926) were monetary series not related to physical product. Detailed studies of cycles in the United States showed no evidence of the existence of long cycles. Even if the existence of long cycles were established there were other possible types, such as the 'Kuznets cycle' of 20-25 years.

Professor Khérian made the point that it was impossible to base on statistical data any judgment about the existence of long-term cycles in under-developed countries. The former French Indo-China, for instance, had had only one qualified statistician for the whole region. The four successor states were handicapped by the short time during which their statistical organizations had functioned, and could so far provide only approximate data.

Madame Delivanis was in agreement with *Professor Dupriez*, who maintained that there was good authority for the existence of the Kondratieff cycle. She was not convinced by the evidence of the studies of cycles in the United States cited by Professor Patinkin. As for the monetary bias of the original paper Professor Dupriez explained that in his exposition he had dealt particularly with monetary movements because he felt them to be a most significant element in long-term cycles.

On the question of applying the concept of the Kondratieff cycle to recent years, *Professor Patinkin* thought that the seventeen years from 1945 (the period discussed by Professor Dupriez) should be compared with immediately preceding years (although war years perhaps should not be included) and not with a period of upswing at the end of the nineteenth century. He was also not happy about starting the period under scrutiny in 1945, with its heritage of suppressed inflation. He wondered how one could decide on the basis of 17-years' evidence whether an upswing was part of a 25-years' or a 50-years' cycle.

Professor Weiller felt that the present-day preoccupations of developing countries with the elasticity of demand for exports of certain typical products and with import substitution were quite different from those which had formed the background of the original studies of the 'Kondratieff cycle'. Further, the agricultural protectionism which had been practised in the past in countries now developed could have no relevance to the problems of present-day under-developed countries depending primarily on agricultural exports.

Madame Delivanis believed that we were now approaching a Kondratieff downturn, although this might have less intensity than in the past.

Problems in Economic Development

The United States and Western European economies had had more stability since 1945, partly on account of government intervention. Less developed countries too might show smaller fluctuations in so far as their own disturbances were a reflection of those of more developed countries.

Chapter 33

INTERNATIONAL COMMODITY
ARRANGEMENTS

BY

DR. GERDA BLAU
Director, Commodities Division,
Food and Agriculture Organization of the United Nations *

1. THE main purpose of this paper is to consider the scope and limitations of international commodity arrangements as instruments for promoting economic stability and growth, particularly from the point of view of the less developed countries. In the closing years of the war and in the immediate post-war years very high hopes were entertained of the creation of a widespread network of individual commodity agreements as part of a new international economic order. The paucity of concrete results achieved so far stands in striking contrast to this. There have been a large number of resolutions by the United Nations and Specialized Agencies and other inter-governmental organs urging the negotiation of commodity agreements ; there has also been a great deal of preparatory work and discussion concerning individual commodities. Yet, in the seventeen years since the end of the war, international agreements have been concluded for only five commodities — wheat, sugar, coffee, tin and olive oil. Of these, the only two presently functioning as agreements which qualify as producer-consumer agreements and contain some operative provisions designed to influence world trade, are those for wheat and tin.[1] The total value of world trade in the

* The views expressed in this paper are the personal views of the author and do not commit the organization to which she belongs.

[1] The International Sugar Agreement continues formally in force until the end of 1963, but its operative provisions have ceased to function as from the beginning of 1962 owing to the failure of governments to reach agreement on the re-formulation of quotas. For coffee, there has been a succession of one-year producers' agreements by which the governments concerned agreed to limit exports. A new coffee quota agreement on more comprehensive lines, including the participation of importing countries and intended to run for a period of three years, is at the stage of negotiation. The olive oil agreement, although negotiated in accordance with the rules of the Havana Charter, provides only for a series of co-ordinated national measures without attempting to influence international trade (which in the case of olive oil merely accounts for about 5 per cent of world production and consumption). Good progress has been made in recent months with preparatory work on an international agreement for cocoa.

553

five commodities for which agreements have been concluded in one form or another, accounts for about 10 per cent of world trade in primary products. The proportion of trade actually covered by agreement provisions is considerably less.

2. In recent years, there has been a growing sense of disappointment, particularly on the part of the primary producing countries, with the limited results attained so far. Increasing attention has been paid to other techniques which could serve either as a substitute for, or as a complement to, the working of international commodity agreements. At the same time, efforts continue to be made by governments to overcome the obstacles that have hitherto frustrated the conclusion of more effective commodity agreements on standard lines and also to explore the possibilities of new types of agreements of a more comprehensive kind.

Objectives of Commodity Agreements

3. International commodity agreements can, in principle, be devised to serve one of five objectives or a combination of them :

(i) They can attempt to raise, or uphold, export earnings by means of arrangements among producers, restricting production or exports or both — the pre-war commodity agreements concluded in the 1930s were mainly of this type (and their experiences have illustrated some of the difficulties of effective operation of such arrangements in the forms then applied).

(ii) They can attempt to promote economic stability, both in the producing and in the consuming countries, by preventing undue fluctuations of prices and quantities traded but without interfering with long-term trends.

(iii) They can endeavour to mitigate the problems and hardships of such long-term adjustments as may be required in cases of persistent disequilibrium between production and consumption, particularly under conditions of inelastic supply and demand.

(iv) They can try to counteract the shrinkage of markets which may result from protectionist measures or preferential arrangements in importing countries.

(v) They can be used as instruments for inter-governmental commodity programming by governments on more comprehensive lines, taking account of trade on both commercial and concessional terms, of national policies relating to production, prices and stocks, and of the close links between problems of commodity trade, aid and development programmes.

4. One of the main difficulties in the actual negotiation of international commodity agreements has been that the participating

554

governments have not always been fully conscious of which of these five objectives they were mainly aiming at ; nor were they fully conscious of the extent to which any one of these objectives, or a combination of them, could be successfully attained by one or the other of the standard types of agreement techniques. The primary exporting countries have been naturally interested not just in the stability of prices but in securing reasonable returns in terms of the manufactured goods which they are buying — in much the same manner in which the primary producers of the developed countries are mainly interested in obtaining some degree of parity of purchasing power in relation to the rest of the economy. The importing countries, on the other hand, have been mainly interested in securing more stable conditions of trade and have been prepared to consider any measures influencing the levels of exporters' returns, over an average of years, only in so far as such measures formed part of a process of orderly adjustment of production to the changing conditions of the world markets. Hence the emphasis in chapter VI of the Havana Charter (which was intended, and still serves, as a code of guiding principles governing international commodity negotiations) that no interested government should be excluded from negotiations, and further that 'participating countries which are mainly interested in imports of the commodity concerned shall, in decisions on substantive matters, have together a number of votes equal to that of those mainly interested in obtaining export markets for the commodity'. The provisions of chapter VI of the Havana Charter imply that the two main objectives of international commodity agreements are to prevent or moderate pronounced fluctuations in prices but without interfering with long-term trends, and to provide a framework for facilitating adjustments between production and consumption, having regard in both cases to the desirability of securing long-term equilibrium between the forces of supply and demand. In other words, the main objectives are those stated under (ii) and (iii) above.

Balance of Bargaining Power

5. The provisions of the Havana Charter which prescribe that producers and consumers should have equal weight in shaping the provisions of an international agreement are obviously important and commendable from the point of view of international ethics. At the same time, they have undoubtedly made the negotiation of individual commodity agreements more difficult than during the inter-war period of largely unilateral approaches by producers or by

their governments. For these provisions of the Charter imply that an agreement is negotiable only as regards matters on which there is an identity of interest of both parties, or on points on which a 'bargaining balance' can be reached — i.e. where the advantages of adhering to the agreement are assumed to balance its disadvantages, from the point of view of each participant.

6. Indeed, it is only in regard to the moderation or elimination of price fluctuations that there is a clear identity of interests between the exporting and the importing countries — though even here the interests of the exporting countries (which in typical cases derive the great bulk of their foreign income from the sale of one or a few primary commodities) are very much greater than those of the importers whose economies are not greatly affected by changes in the price of any one of these commodities.

7. The postulate of non-interference with long-term trends implies that prices resulting from an agreement should not differ, on the average over a number of years, from what they would have been in the absence of an agreement. Since the future is unknown, this 'neutral price' can be definitely ascertained only *ex post* whereas the technical solution of the problem presupposes that it is known *ex ante*. In the absence of such pre-knowledge any commodity agreement of this kind necessarily partakes the character of a speculative deal — a deal which can be justified as a form of insurance against the risk of undue losses resulting from large and unexpected price variations. The fact that the conclusion of price-stabilizing commodity agreements has proved so difficult in practice appears to indicate that neither exporters nor importers were really prepared to pay a substantial premium for this kind of insurance. Moreover, for a number of commodities it is difficult, or impossible, to speak of a representative world price. And as to the interests of exporters, their *main* concern, of course, has been with prospects for their total export proceeds (depending on volume as well as price) — and with the average level of export proceeds over a number of years, measured in terms of import purchasing power, not merely with short-term fluctuations in money terms.

8. Added to this is the fact that in recent years (since 1954) the primary exporting countries have been faced with a slow deterioration in their terms of trade resulting from an unfavourable trend of commodity prices in relation to the prices of manufactures. The impact of cyclical changes has become relatively less important. Yet, for a solution of the trend problem the types of commodity agreements which have been the subject of international discussion and negotiation in the 1950s are not, in themselves, a sufficient instru-

ment. Nor do these agreement-techniques take sufficient account of the need for improved co-ordination of national policies in developed countries.

Three Standard Types of Agreements

9. Three types of agreements have been negotiated and their subsequent history illustrates the same fundamental difficulties.

10. The first of these is the *multilateral contract agreement*. The main feature of such an agreement is that it contains an obligation on importers or exporters to buy or sell certain guaranteed quantities. These guarantees have to be implemented at a stipulated maximum price, or stipulated minimum price, whenever the free-market price reaches or exceeds these limits. To be reasonably effective such a multilateral contract agreement should cover a high proportion (say two-thirds) of the total trade of the participants and the spread of prices between the floor and the ceiling should not be too wide. It would then protect the real national income of both the importing and the exporting participants from the major ill consequences of fluctuations in the world price, whilst preserving the free-market price as a mechanism of adjustment for securing a balance between world production and consumption.

11. The only case of a multilateral contract agreement is the International Wheat Agreement. The original Agreement of 1949 provided for guaranteed quantities which covered about two-thirds of world trade ; the maximum price was $1·80 per bushel and the minimum price was stipulated to fall progressively from $1·50 in the first year covered by the agreement to $1·20 in the fourth and final year. During the four-year period world prices were running continuously above the stipulated maximum ; importing participants availed themselves of their right to buy the agreed quantities at the stipulated maximum price, so that no less than 95 per cent of the guarantees were effective. As it turned out, therefore, the 1949 Agreement operated entirely in the interests of the importers. When the Agreement came up for re-negotiation in 1953, the major exporters were successful in securing a rise in the stipulated maximum price to $2·05, and of the stipulated minimum price to $1·55, throughout the subsequent three-year period. This was achieved at the expense of the withdrawal of the United Kingdom, whose representatives expected — correctly as it turned out — a decline in world prices. During the period covered by the second Agreement, some other importers also withdrew. As a result, the proportion of world trade covered under the second Agreement dropped to 25 per

cent as against 60 per cent in the case of the first. When the Agreement was re-negotiated for the third time in 1959, the idea of guaranteed quantities was abandoned and was replaced by a simple undertaking of member-importing countries to purchase a minimum percentage of their commercial requirements from member-exporting countries, as long as prices move within a stipulated range, but without any obligation to buy guaranteed quantities at the minimum price. The exporters retain the obligation to sell at the maximum price, if called upon to do so by importing countries, an amount equal to the annual average of importers' purchases over the previous four years (minus transactions already made within the Agreement year).[1] This new type of Agreement has made it possible to bring in the great bulk of commercial world trade, but only at the expense of eliminating some of the former operative provisions concerning rights and obligations, particularly those relating to purchases of specified guaranteed quantities at the minimum price. In any case, during the period covered by the four Agreements the significance of the world price of wheat as a mechanism of adjustment has been progressively undermined, partly because it has more and more been set by the two largest exporters and partly because, faced with growing surplus supplies, the exporters have been disposing of an increasing proportion of their supplies under special arrangements on concessional terms.[2]

12. The second type of agreement, of which particularly high hopes were entertained in the early post-war years, consists of the institution of an *international buffer stock*, which stabilizes prices by an obligation to buy whenever the world price falls below a certain minimum and to sell when the price rises above a certain maximum (and possibly combined perhaps with a discretionary right to buy or sell between these limits). The well-known problem of a buffer-stock scheme of the provision of adequate finance to enable the authority to carry out its functions is closely related to the difficulty of successfully forecasting the future relationship between supply and demand, and securing international agreement on a range of prices which is consistent with the prospective movement of the long-term world price which secures a balance of supply and demand. Unless the trend of this long-term world price is stable or rising, a buffer stock is not likely to be successful in ironing out the fluctuations from the trend for more than a limited period of time. The

---

[1] The latest Agreement, which started operating in 1962, is similar in character to the 1959 Agreement. The minimum and maximum prices have been raised to $1·62 i/2 and $2·02 i/2 per bushel. The U.S.S.R. is a member of the current Wheat Agreement.

[2] This point will be further considered in paragraphs 20 and 21 below.

reason is that with a falling trend the necessary downward adjustment of the operating range of prices cannot be secured with sufficient promptitude, even if the experts were successful in distinguishing between what is a fluctuation and what is a trend. With a rising trend the same difficulty arises, but since this does not impair the finances of the buffer-stock authority (on the contrary, it tends to strengthen them), it does not prevent it from resuming operations subsequently once agreement has been secured on the revision of the operating range of prices.

13. The only buffer-stock scheme covered by international agreement is the International Tin Agreement, which, however, provides for contingent export control as well as for a buffer stock. As it has turned out, this is one of the few commodities for which in recent years the relationship between world consumption and production has been favourable to producers. Nevertheless, the scheme ran into heavy waters less than two years after its inception in 1956, when the tin price fell heavily and the manager of the buffer stock used up all his cash resources (including some supplementary resources) in the purchase of tin without succeeding in stabilizing the price. Subsequently, the world price was held up by the export controls provided in the Agreement. Over the first full year of control, the overall reduction of exports by participating countries was no less than 41 per cent and over the second full year it was 36 per cent. Despite this, and on account of considerable supplies from the Soviet Union, the price collapsed temporarily in the last quarter of 1958 but recovered rapidly in the subsequent year, aided by an arrangement with the U.S.S.R. about exports.

14. The third type of agreement is an *export-restriction agreement*, which makes provision for the limitation of exports in so far as this is necessary in order to secure some degree of stability of prices. The Havana Charter laid down specific conditions with which the operation of such an agreement should comply, designed mainly to protect the interests of consumers and to prevent the imposition of too rigid a pattern of production. The effectiveness of an export-restriction agreement depends to a very large degree on the comprehensiveness of the agreement, i.e. on the extent to which it brings under control all important sources of export, actual and potential; on the extent to which substitutes are available; and on the importance of international trade of the commodity in relation to world production and consumption. Moreover, to be effective, an export restriction scheme logically requires the regulation of output by *individual producers* and not only of exports by the countries as a whole. Failure to secure world-wide participation in a quota arrangement on the

part of exporting countries is less serious in so far as importing countries are brought in as participants and undertake to discriminate (in one way or another) against non-participating exporters. At the same time, the very features likely to strengthen the effectiveness of a quota restriction agreement as an instrument for raising, or upholding, export earnings in the short run — such as comprehensiveness of membership, stringent quota provisions and strict adherence on the part of both exporters and importers — also are those likely to endanger the long-term prospects for the industry as a whole, by impeding change, sheltering high-cost producers and generating centrifugal forces which may eventually lead to the collapse of the whole arrangement. Great care must be taken, therefore, to set quotas realistically, to allow for sufficient flexibilty, and to encourage such structural adjustment and co-ordination of production and price policies as may be required to promote efficiency and progressive diversification in the primary exporting countries as well as the strengthening of markets in importing countries.

15. Apart from the International Tin Agreement, to which reference has already been made in connection with its buffer-stock features, the only post-war instance of an operating agreement of this kind is the International Sugar Agreement.[1] The Agreement, in the form negotiated in 1953, relied on a system of export-quotas for the so-called 'free-market' sector which accounts for less than one-half of world sugar trade and provides the balance of requirements not covered by special trading arrangements. It differed from the export-quota agreements concluded before the war in that it contained automatic provisions for an increase in the quotas whenever the world price exceeded a certain maximum for 30 consecutive days, and for a decrease in the quotas when it similarly fell below a certain minimum ; and in that it imposed an obligation on importing countries to procure a certain part of their supplies from participating exporters. The exporting countries agreed to regulate their production so as to avoid the accumulation of stocks in excess of 20 per cent of their annual output. The initial export quotas fixed each year in the light of estimated requirements were adjusted thereafter on the basis of price movements with the object of maintaining the price within the range of 3·25 to 4·35 cents. Prices remained fairly stable, near the minimum of the range, until 1956 when a short European crop and comparatively low levels of reserves coincided with the strong stimulation of demand caused by the Suez crisis.

---

[1] The new draft agreements for coffee and cocoa are also based on export quotas (for traditional markets), supplemented in the case of the draft coffee agreement by some provisions for the regulation of output.

With prices running well above the maximum of 4·00 cents, all quotas and limitations became automatically inoperative until late 1957 when prices again moved within the range. In the following year, the original provisions were amended to allow for automatic and discretionary quota adjustments at various points within the initial price range. In more recent years, the efficacy of the Agreement has been impaired by the drastic changes in the pattern of trade following the cessation of arrangements between the United States and Cuba. Since January 1962 all operative provisions have been suspended owing to the inability of participating governments to agree on the distribution of quotas.

16. What the record of operations of these three types of agreements has shown is that it is extremely difficult to deal with the problem of price stability in isolation and to conclude agreements which succeed in stabilizing prices but without interfering with what the trend of prices would have been in the absence of such agreements.[1] The problems of trend and fluctuations, whilst they do logically call for different kinds of remedies, cannot, in fact, easily be separated and treated apart from each other outside the world of economic textbooks. The agreements operated in post-war years have succeeded in serving some limited objectives, but they have not proved capable of dealing with the two main sets of commodity problems which call for action : the need for some assurances, particularly to low-income exporting countries, of fairly stable and remunerative average levels of export proceeds for a number of years ahead, say for the five-year periods normally covered by national development plans ; and the need for improved international co-ordination of *national* policies of the developed countries.

Different Categories of Commodities

17. Before we can further consider the implications of post-war experience, it is necessary to look at the problem in more concrete terms, in the light of the main features of the actual patterns of

---

[1] It would, of course, be an exaggeration to say that the difficulty of securing agreement over prices or quotas was the sole, or even the main, factor responsible for the failure to reach agreement in the case of a number of commodities where a great deal of preparatory work was done to consider possible forms of regulation, and where there was a clear desire on behalf of both exporting and importing countries to reach an agreement of some kind — as, for example, in the cases of cotton, rubber, cocoa and rice. There are serious technical difficulties connected with grading, standardization, storage qualities, and limitations imposed on the effectiveness of controls due to competition from synthetic materials or other close substitutes. Account must also be taken of the structure of the market which, in the case of rice, for instance, is characterized by a network of bilateral trading arrangements that could not easily be dispensed with. All these factors add to the difficulties of formulating obligations capable of clear interpretation.

world commodity trade. One of the reasons for the comparative lack of success so far has been that in many of the inter-governmental discussions of commodity questions the problem has been approached in a generalized way without sufficient regard to the basic differences between different groups of commodities. Indeed it is one of the merits of more recent inter-governmental consultations, particularly those connected with the Common Market, that they have drawn attention to (though they have far from solved) the different kinds of problems which need to be considered for different categories of products.

Commodity Exports of the Developed Countries

18. It is not always realized that no less than one-half of the total value of world commercial exports of primary products [1] both originates in and is absorbed by the developed countries of North America, Western Europe, Oceania and Japan. The bulk of such trade consists of temperate-zone agricultural products, mainly foodstuffs. The pattern of trade in this group of commodities is very largely influenced by the domestic agricultural stabilization and support policies of virtually all the importing countries and of the United States (which, of course, is the largest exporter), with the funds required for the support of agriculture being drawn from the non-agricultural sectors of the countries concerned. This is a very important difference from the situation prevailing in under-developed countries where virtually all incomes are low and where agriculture accounts for the dominant part of the national income. In such countries there are no resources available for the price support of agricultural export commodities. Indeed, the export-producing sectors of these economies are often called upon to provide economic assistance for measures to raise productivity in the even poorer agricultural subsistence sectors and for purposes of development and diversification generally.

19. The existence of an extended network of domestic agricultural policies has got important consequences. It must be recognized that a network of such measures provides an effective barrier against any sudden large-scale contraction of agricultural incomes such as occurred in the Great Depression of the early 1930s. At the same time, the existence of independent national policies of price and output regulation has created a situation in which the patterns of production for some of the most important commodities (such as wheat) have been completely divorced from

---

[1] Excluding petroleum and the exports of the centrally planned economies.

world supply and demand relationships, involving large and growing excess stocks in some of the exporting countries. These policies have led to the introduction of export subsidies, or of two-price systems on behalf of the exporters, and of varying forms of import regulation on behalf of the importers.

20. The emergence of structural surpluses — a consequence of very remarkable technological progress and not only of the national policies — has resulted in new forms of trade flows, on concessional terms, from the developed mainly to the under-developed countries.[1] It has not been found possible up till now to bring such concessional trade within the operative provisions of the International Wheat Agreement (which is the sole international agreement in operation for a predominantly temperate-zone staple commodity). However, a beginning has been made in evolving a new code of international ethics through the acceptance, by most of the governments concerned, of a flexible set of principles [2] which encourages constructive uses of surplus supplies, mainly in low-income food-deficit countries, and at the same time provides some safeguards for the interests of commercial exporters. It has also been found possible to secure the acceptance by a large number of governments of a set of principles concerning national price stabilization and support policies [3] which reflects the highest common denominator of international understanding obtainable so far among governments with differing and partly conflicting policies. These attempts to arrive at sets of agreed principles, which are formally accepted by governments but which do not imply any contractual obligations and which carry no sanctions, are, nevertheless, of importance, particularly in view of the fact that governments have been generally reluctant up till now to accept contractual obligations that interfere with their sovereign rights in shaping domestic policies.

21. Thus, whilst the domestic agricultural policies of the developed countries have lessened their incentive, as compared with the early 1930s, to insure against violent price changes by means of international agreements, their incentive to secure access to markets has been increased as a result, and the promotion of the latter objective requires commodity agreements of a different character. The current discussions on the Common Agricultural Policy in

[1] So far mainly from North America to the food-deficit regions of Asia and also to a number of Latin American and African countries.
[2] *FAO Principles of Surplus Disposal and Guiding Lines* : FAO document C 551/22, Appendix A, Rome, July 1955. The main feature of these principles has also been incorporated, since 1959, in the consultative provisions of the International Wheat Agreement.
[3] *National Agricultural Price Stabilization and Support Policies : Guiding Principles Recommended by FAO* : FAO, Rome, 1961.

Brussels in relation to the Commonwealth and other trading partners, though still in a very preliminary stage, show an increased willingness to work for international agreements of a much more comprehensive type for temperate-zone foodstuffs. Such agreements would comprise trade both on commercial and on concessional terms and also some guarantees of access to the European consuming markets, as well as policies concerning prices, production, and stocks in the participating countries.

Commodity Problems of Under-developed Countries

22. With regard to the other half of world commodity trade, which originates from the under-developed countries, the nature of the problems is quite different. This trade consists primarily of tropical agricultural products (though it also includes some temperate-zone agricultural exports from semi-developed countries of Latin America) and to a lesser extent of minerals. About three-quarters of this trade is absorbed by the developed countries, mainly North America and Western Europe, which thus absorb about 85 per cent of the world imports on commercial terms of all primary products.[1] In the case of these tropical export products and minerals, in contrast to temperate-zone foodstuffs the problem of the narrowing of markets due to protectionist measures by the importing countries exists only in a few cases (notably sugar),[2] though analogous problems arise on account of preferential arrangements which may now become more important owing to the European Common Market. On the other hand, the markets for exports of raw materials from the under-developed countries (with some exceptions, such as petroleum) are affected by other causes : the growing use of synthetic materials of various kinds, the reduction of the amount of raw materials required per unit of finished product, and a shift in the pattern of industrial production which has caused a decline in the relative importance of industries heavily dependent on imported materials. Added to this

[1] The only commodity which is mainly traded *among* under-developed countries is rice. This accounts for a large part of their share of world imports of primary products (although not more than 4 per cent of world rice production enters into international trade). Mention should also be made of the as yet quantitatively unimportant, but expanding flow of trade from the under-developed countries to the U.S.S.R. and other centrally planned economies, which might become a potentially important balancing factor in the world trade for primary products. (China exercises a rather special role as an unpredictable, but occasionally important, exporter or importer of a range of primary products.)

[2] For this reason the primary exporting countries have relatively little to gain from the usual kind of multilateral negotiating for the reciprocal reduction of tariffs and quantitative restrictions. Indeed, they may tend to lose since their own exports are not predominantly hampered by trade restrictions whilst the concessions made in return may handicap them in developing new industries.

there is growing evidence of a structural over-production for a large number of tropical products, due to an increase of yields resulting from the important technological improvements of recent years, as well as the large increase in plantings (due to the high prices of the early 1950s) which are only now coming into production. Moreover, the very spread of 'development consciousness' of the under-developed countries has meant that increases in production have been encouraged, even of commodities whose world prospects have been known to be unfavourable, so long as they have offered a promise of increased export earnings of the particular country concerned. Available projections of the main tropical products for the period up to 1970 [1] indicate a growing excess of world production over world consumption, even on the most optimistic assumptions concerning the growth of demand in the high-income countries. There is scope for some increases in the relatively less prosperous areas, where the income elasticities of demand are still relatively high, and in countries where consumption is now held down by high internal revenue duties,[2] but, by and large, unless present trends are rapidly reversed, it is unlikely that the growth of consumption can keep pace with the projected increases in production.

23. The only long-term remedy is the economic development of the under-developed countries themselves. This would allow a diversification of their domestic production. They would then become less dependent on a few basic commodities for their export earnings and less dependent also on imports to cover their essential needs. On the other hand, the prospects of their economic development are greatly dependent on their ability to maintain and increase their foreign receipts, both through trade and aid. The developed countries of the world are beginning to recognize the fact that the 'commodity problem' of the under-developed countries is not something separate from their development problem, but that the two are intricately involved with each other. This should open the way to a new approach to international commodity arrangements — not from the narrow viewpoint of improving the functioning of particular markets, but as part of a comprehensive programme of economic assistance to the under-developed areas. The provisions of the Treaty of Rome provide evidence of a certain awareness of this, in that the various aspects of economic aid to under-developed regions — stable prices and markets, financial assistance, long-term planning

[1] *Agricultural Commodities — Projections for 1970* ; Special Supplement to the FAO Commodity Review 1962 ; FAO, Rome, 1962.
[2] The European Economic Commission has recommended to the members of the Common Market — the main group of countries which impose heavy revenue duties on these products — to abolish them within the next few years.

of production structures — are considered together. Unfortunately, they single out a narrow group of countries — the overseas associated members of the Common Market — for such comprehensive treatment. Nonetheless, if their envisaged programmes do materialize, the need to extend the same treatment to the other under-developed areas of Asia, Africa and Latin America will become the more obvious.

24. If one may hazard a guess as to the directions in which the thinking of the advanced countries anxious to assist the development of the poor areas of the world is likely to develop in the future, it will be in the direction of a joint comprehensive programme. Such a programme would provide not only aid but also multilateral long-term purchase contracts for their exports. This alone would give them a sufficiently firm basis for the elaboration of development programmes geared to a definite knowledge of the external conditions with which they will be individually confronted.

25. It is obvious that it will take years, in the best of circumstances, before the governments of both the developed and the under-developed countries are prepared to face up to the need for such comprehensive long-term planning on an international scale, and before they are ready to accept its obligations. It will take further years before such a joint comprehensive programme, related to both trade and aid, can be worked out. In the meantime, the position of the under-developed countries is deteriorating and their needs are pressing. The export proceeds from the sale of primary commodities (excluding petroleum) has shown very little rise from the (pre-Korean) year of 1950 to 1957, and has been falling since that time. Their future prospects in the light of current production and consumption trends are unfavourable and their financial reserves are already under considerable strain. The question is what can be done *now* to alleviate the situation until such time as more comprehensive measures can be put into force.

26. There is, of course, a great deal which the under-developed countries could do on their own to improve their position — as, for example, through increased efforts to raise productivity levels in their subsistence sectors, aided by land reform ; the elimination of waste both in their public expenditures and in their personal consumption ; fiscal reforms and the introduction of improved marketing techniques, such as Marketing Boards, which could serve as a means of syphoning off revenue from the exporters as well as the purpose of stabilizing producers' prices. Further consideration of these problems would, however, go beyond the scope of this paper, which is primarily concerned with international policies.

Compensatory Financing

27. The pressing need of under-developed countries is for more resources, particularly of foreign exchange, to sustain their development programmes. The flow of economic aid has increased fairly rapidly in recent years but it must be remembered that it still constitutes only a small fraction of the total foreign receipts of the under-developed countries, and the rise in aid has failed to compensate for the deterioration of their terms of trade in recent years. The first objective must be seen in a reversal of the adverse *trend* of export earnings, aided where necessary by policies of structural adjustment in both exporting and importing countries. In addition, however, the under-developed countries also urgently require assistance for replenishing their liquid reserves and for moderating the impact of fluctuations in their current export receipts. This second objective could be assisted by more liberal lending policies of the International Monetary Fund and it could be supported further by the adoption of proposals contained in the recent United Nations Experts' Report on compensatory financing.[1]

28. The experts put forward a scheme for the creation of a central fund, called the Development Insurance Fund, into which all member countries would pay contributions and against which members would make financial claims which would be paid automatically in stated circumstances. Such claims would be based on the decline of export proceeds in a particular year as against the average of the three preceding years, and would cover a proportion, say 50 per cent, of the shortfall thus defined in excess of a minimum shortfall of say 5 per cent for which no compensation is payable. Two alternative types were envisaged and the experts thought that there would be some merit in adopting a scheme which made use of a combination of both. Under the first type of scheme, the compensatory payments are in the nature of a cash settlement, which does not have to be repaid in the future. Under the second type of scheme, the payments take on the character of a contingent loan, which needs to be repaid if the export proceeds of the subsequent five years are high enough to allow it (i.e. out of the excess of export receipts over the three-year base period) but not otherwise. As regards the contributions the experts recommend that countries should contribute a percentage of their national income (possibly

---

[1] *International Compensation for Fluctuations in Commodity Trade*, United Nations, New York, 1961. The Committee of Experts consisted of I. H. Abdel-Rahmah, Antonio Carrillo Flores, Sir John G. Crawford (Chairman), Albert G. Hart, S. Posthuma and M. L. Qureshi.

graduated in relation to *per caput* incomes), whilst low-income primary producing countries should contribute a fixed percentage of their export receipts. The experts estimate that the annual gross claims on the basis of a 50 per cent compensation and a 5 per cent minimum reduction would have amounted to $383 million per year on the average for the years 1953–59 for the under-developed countries, whereas the claims of the high-income countries would have averaged $85 million on the same basis. The necessary contributions, on the other hand, assessed on all countries' export proceeds at a standard rate, would have amounted to $326 million annually on the high-income countries and $142 million from the high-income to the low-income countries ; thus involving an annual net transfer of $241 million from the high-income countries to the low-income countries on the assumption that all benefits took the form of cash settlements. The merit of this scheme is that it gives a certain insurance against hardship ; the beneficiaries in return for their contributions — in much the same way as that in which citizens of the modern state receive benefits in exchange for contributions in cases of sickness, unemployment, etc. And just as in the case of compensatory social insurance schemes, where part of the cost is borne by the state out of general taxation, the contributions are not levied on a full actuarial basis. The adoption of such a scheme would give partial protection to under-developed countries against the effects of both cyclical fluctuations and also (though to a much lesser extent) against an unfavourable trend of commodity prices, not only in relation to any particular commodity but to commodities in general. In this way it would secure some of the same objectives, as far as the stabilization of foreign income is concerned, as a network of commodity agreements. On the other hand, it should be emphasized that the experts' proposals, even if adopted in full, are little better than the standard types of commodity agreements adopted so far as protection against unfavourable price trends ; and, as we have repeatedly stated, it is unfavourable price trends rather than fluctuations which are likely progressively to constitute the dominant problem for under-developed countries in the coming decade.[1]

[1] Following the publication of the UN Experts' Report in 1961, the Organization of American States published a proposal for the establishment of an international fund for the stabilization of export receipts. This was evidently influenced by the ideas of the United Nations Experts. Like the UN Report, the OAS proposal assumes that compensatory finance should be available to cover a proportion (two-thirds up to a maximum of 20 per cent of previous exports) of any shortfall of actual export proceeds, below their average in the previous three years. Like the UN Report, the OAS proposal also envisages that the high-income countries make a larger contribution to the fund than the low-income countries. The OAS scheme departs, however, from the recommendations of the UN Experts

The Role of Commodity Agreements

29. The adoption of such a compensatory finance scheme would not, of course, obviate the need for individual commodity agreements. As the UN experts themselves emphasize, compensatory finance is complementary to commodity agreements and not an alternative to them. But we must be clear as to the objectives which individual commodity agreements should serve. In particular, it must be recognized that commodity agreements cannot be successful in stabilizing prices and in securing reasonable terms of trade unless they also succeed in bringing world production and consumption into balance. This naturally cannot be a matter of international agreements alone but requires a close co-ordination between international and national policies. The main objective of commodity agreements should, therefore, be looked upon as an orderly method through which patterns of production and trade can best be adjusted to the requirements of world demand over a longer period. From this point of view, quota arrangements or the multilateral contract provide some of the elements required, provided that, unlike the existing agreements, they provide for the co-ordination of national policies of all countries concerned and for the joint programming and adjustments, as required, of production patterns in both exporting and importing countries and of measures influencing consumption, internal price levels and related commercial and fiscal policies, not only for measures relating directly to the regulation of exports and imports.

The Role of Consultations

30. Such co-ordination, while it could be assisted, on certain conditions, by export-restriction and multilateral contract agreements, calls in addition for a commodity-by-commodity approach of a broader kind. It is relevant here to mention that in the postwar period, in addition to commodity *agreements* which contain

in three respects. In the first place, compensatory finance will only be available to low-income countries and not to all countries, as under the UN scheme — the arrangements would thus no longer retain the character of a universal insurance scheme. In the second place, it envisages that the fund be financed by a single once-for-all payment, of which $600 million would be contributed by the low-income countries and $1·2 billion by the high-income countries. In the third place — and this is the most important difference — the compensation payments envisaged under the OAS proposals are in the nature of loans which have to be repaid in a maximum of five years irrespective of the levels of export proceeds of the borrowing countries. The UN experts, on the other hand, recommend that the compensatory payments should either be outright cash settlements, or else contingent loans, which only required to be repaid if the recipients' export earnings rose sufficiently within a specific period.

binding obligations between the contracting parties, international commodity *consultations* have proved of very real benefit in the actual solution of commodity problems, even when they did not eventuate in any formalized agreement. At one time commodity study groups were regarded as no more than an essential preliminary in arriving at international agreements, the tasks of which were accomplished once negotiations for a definite agreement had been opened. Experience with the Wheat Agreement and the Sugar Agreement has shown, however, that the continuing organs which were set up in connection with these agreements — the International Wheat Council and the International Sugar Council — by constituting a forum for consultation and for comprehensive annual review of the situation and prospects of the world market, and of the plans and programmes of individual countries, have provided very valuable services to participating governments, quite apart from their operational functions. In addition, the study groups which have been set up for a wide range of commodities — grains, rice, cocoa, coffee, cotton, wool, rubber, coconut, citrus fruit, non-ferrous metals — have already provided a widespread network of consultative machinery, which has undoubtedly assisted the co-ordination of national policies through the intense and mutual study of common problems. There can be no doubt that with increasing emphasis on the importance of commodity export earnings for the viability of under-developed countries, consultations, quite apart from more formal and mechanized arrangements, will have a major role to fill.

Need for a Concerted Attack

31. The conclusions to be drawn from our analysis are not of the spectacular kind. There is no single panacea, no magic waving of the wand which would enable us to solve the world commodity problem in all its complexity. Indeed, an attack on any single front can reach only a limited objective. But it has perhaps been shown in this paper that there are a number of ways in which a genuine effort is likely to produce some useful results. What is needed is a concerted attack on a number of fronts — long-term lending and aid as part of a comprehensive development programme ; compensatory finance ; international agreements for the regulation of production, for co-ordinated planning in the creation of a new capacity and for the provision of guarantees of access to markets ; long-term purchase agreements, conditional and unconditional ; continuing consultations between governments, both commodity-by-commodity and in close link with wider discussions on trade, aid and development planning,

including also confrontations of plans of individual countries — all
of which should be pursued simultaneously and with vigour.

DISCUSSION OF THE PAPER BY DR. GERDA BLAU

Professor Wallich, opening the discussion, took up the question of the
desirability of stabilization. The advantage of not interfering with
fluctuations was that it usually resulted in more gains to the producer
and increased output. In previous discussions the general view had been
that stabilization should consist of smoothing out fluctuations, but not
interfering with the trend. His own view, however, as suggested above,
was that stabilization did alter the trend. Pure stabilization could be
tackled from within a country through marketing boards, etc., but not
much had been done in this direction. It appeared that what producers
really wanted was an improvement in their terms of trade.

There was general agreement, as in earlier discussions, on the weakness
of the bargaining position of primary producing countries, on account of
the probable future over-supply of many commodities. *Professor Wallich*
held this view, as did *Mr. Joy* and *Mr. Bevin*, who agreed with the remark
made in a previous session that manufacturers tended to set prices, while
primary producers had to accept them. In this respect his own country,
New Zealand, was just as vulnerable as Ghana. *Mr. Joy* pointed out
that developed countries had been too successful in short-term stabilization policies, subsidizing agriculture from the proceeds of industry and
aggravating the long-term problem of over-supply. Developed countries
would in the long run have to stop primary production in competition
with under-developed countries.

As a consequence of the weakness of primary producers it was accepted
by many of those present that industrialized countries would have to find
some way of helping the under-developed primary producers. This led
to a debate on the relative merits of commodity agreements and compensatory schemes of the types described by Dr. Blau in her paper as
having been formulated in the recent United Nations Experts' Report
and proposed by the Organization of American States respectively. The
consensus of the meeting appeared to be against commodity schemes,
mainly because of their inappropriateness in conditions of over-supply.

Professor Wallich was in favour of compensatory arrangements for this
reason, and because higher prices for producers tended to be dissipated
in consumption. *Mr. Economides* made the point that the compensatory
scheme suggested by the UN should be based on the movements in terms
of trade or primary producers, and not simply on their export prices. A

point in favour of compensatory payments made by *Dr. Aubrey* was that they did not demand, as commodity agreements did, predictions as to future prices. An element of flexibility was given to the UN scheme by payments being either in the form of a loan or grant. Both forms provided needed foreign exchange, but grants in addition provided a stimulus to incomes. *Mr. Desai* felt that if the need was to help the whole economy rather than merely producers within it, compensation payments were superior to commodity agreements.

Professor Wallich and *Mr. Liesner* thought that the arrangements suggested among EEC countries for variable levies on imports of foreign produce might become the germ of an idea for channelling funds internationally to primary producers.

There was some feeling that neither commodity agreements nor compensation payments were desirable and that diversification and development should be the paramount consideration in aiding primary producer countries. *Professor Weiller* expressed this view, maintaining that in many of the tropical African countries, where commercialization of the subsistence sector and the spread of a money economy were not making progress, there was a conflict between the desire to stabilize prices for primary producers and the need for further diversification. *Professor Johnston* also thought that aid in development was a better way to help than trying to offset the decline in prices of primary products through price assistance funds. He felt that though there was a good case for restricting production of commodities where output was running well ahead of demand, restrictions should be concentrated on countries that had already achieved some diversification and were able to transfer resources. Exceptions should be made for certain very under-developed countries (e.g. in tropical Africa) where there was scope for expanding exports based on existing subsistence food production. The opportunity cost of this expansion was low and the benefit great in generating increased incomes among the rural population and spreading a money economy as well as in the immediate acquisition of foreign exchange. Even with falling prices it would benefit these countries to produce and export more.

Professor Lengellé and *Dr. Zellner* were pessimistic about international trade planning and commodity agreements. Professor Lengellé thought that one of the reasons for failure was the wide variety in the organization and cost structures of suppliers of primary products. Dr. Zellner pointed out that even within countries agricultural planning usually failed and the difficulties of worldwide planning were much greater. Therefore development aid should not be linked with commodity schemes. It would be best to let market forces work freely and then use aid to facilitate adjustments.

Dr. Aubrey doubted whether Dr. Blau's point that increased trade with the centrally planned economies would be a stabilizing influence was always valid, and *Mr. Ulin* pointed out that sales of minerals from these countries had sometimes depressed prices. Dr. Blau agreed that countries with centrally planned economies would only be a stabilizing factor if they absorbed more tropical products.

In conclusion *Dr. Blau* saw hope in the linking of trade with aid to help countries in adjustment and diversification. Compensatory schemes were modest in extent and should be part of, not replacing, aid. She felt that in all these spheres there was need of continuing and closer contact between inter-governmental planning and academic thought.

Chapter 34

MARKETING BOARDS

BY

D. WALKER
University of Exeter

IT is proposed to use a good deal of the space that is available to discuss some stabilization aspects of the operation of Marketing Boards in Uganda. An attempt will be made, however, to draw some general conclusions from these experiences and also to touch on some of the other aspects of the working of such Boards.

I. BACKGROUND : THE UGANDA ECONOMY

The country is poor. Even when subsistence output is included gross domestic product *per capita* is only about £23 and money product £16. The economy is dependent on agriculture and related forms of economic activity. This is so both with respect to the domestic product and even more so with respect to exports. The agricultural sector narrowly defined constitutes some 58 per cent of domestic product and 47 per cent of cash product. As regards exports, with the exception of about £2·5 m. of copper ore, almost all, in a total of about £40 m., are agricultural. Foreign trade is most important, exports constituting some 40 per cent of money product and imports 25 per cent. Coffee and cotton completely dominate the export scene, amounting to about 80 per cent of total export earnings; though a growing contribution is being made by tea and copper. The employee sector is small and most people earn their living as peasant farmers. Only about a quarter of a million people earn wages or salaries.

The ordinary African peasant farmer is responsible for most of the agricultural cash production and, therefore, for most of the exports. All the cotton and most of the coffee is produced in this way.

African agriculture is still to a considerable extent subsistence farming. About three-fifths of the area under cultivation is used to produce food for the farm family's own consumption. In terms of

574

money value, however, the value of output produced for the market exceeds the imputed value of subsistence production. The bulk of the output produced for the market is exported, but there is a growing volume of food sales to the towns. The farm unit is small, and production for the market is in very many cases regarded as subsidiary to the production of food.

During the post-war years attempts have been made to develop and encourage other forms of economic activity besides peasant agriculture. Large sums of money, for example, were invested in the development of hydro-electric power in the expectation that the provision of such power would remove the most important factor preventing industrialization. On the whole, results have been disappointing and the manufacturing sector is still very small, constituting about 6 per cent of domestic product. There have also been developments in plantation agriculture, particularly in tea and sugar, but such activities still only amount to about 10 per cent of the output of the money agricultural sector.

We noted above the importance of exports as a generator of money incomes. It follows that change in the volume of exports and — which is of special importance in the present context of stabilization — in the prices obtained for the main export commodities have very considerable primary and secondary effects on the level of money incomes and expenditures. To a very substantial extent stabilization policy in Uganda has to be concerned with erecting a barrier between export earnings and the distribution of such earnings to the factors of production that combined to produce them. Given the likelihood of considerable fluctuations in export earnings it is necessary — if it is desired to avoid fluctuations in the level of domestic output — to establish some mechanism which will limit or prevent such fluctuations being reflected in the level of domestic expenditures. Such a policy involves withholding of part of export earnings in some stabilization or other reserve in a period when there is a cyclical increase in prices or action — say by way of an increase in taxation — to reduce the incomes of other sections of the community and the accumulation in a reserve fund of the additional revenue. Corresponding changes in the reverse direction would be required in the case of a fall in export earnings. It will be noted that we are here taking a broad view of stabilization ; considering the economy as a whole rather than the incomes of particular sectors or groups in the economy.

There is little doubt that in recent years external price movements have been the most important factor making for fluctuations, and it is believed this is likely to continue. This is not to deny that there can be other important influences. There can be crop failures and the failure to gather or sell a crop. Investment expenditure is often dependent on overseas finance and the decisions of overseas firms and governments and can be affected by non-economic considerations. There can develop a recession due to credit restrictions by the banks and the operation of the inventory cycle. There can be political difficulties which affect local calculations of risks and expected profits.

One last introductory point. Uganda's currency is provided by the East African Currency Board. The East African shilling is issued by the Board against payment of sterling, and is redeemable at all times. Under this arrangement any increase in currency in circulation formerly required a corresponding increase in the sterling assets of the Board. Since 1955 this is not entirely the case as the Board is now empowered to invest part of its assets in local East African securities. Even with this change there is little scope for a stabilization policy which utilizes deficit financing, either with the help of a Central Bank or directly through the printing of notes, as part of its machinery. In these conditions budget deficits can only be incurred if the government in good times has accumulated a reserve fund — or if it can borrow overseas (or obtain grants) to meet the deficit. Similarly, additional subsidies to farmers can only be made if reserves have been accumulated. Though I have made this point following a statement on the institutional set-up I must not be taken as implying that institutional changes — the establishment of a Central Bank, etc. — would permit much greater flexibility. There is little scope for deficits financed by credit creation as a counter cyclical device in an economy such as Uganda which is so dependent on foreign trade and foreign capital flows, and this is of crucial importance when considering stabilization policies.

II. BACKGROUND : MARKETING BOARDS

During the war years coffee and cotton were purchased in bulk by the British and other allied governments and the Uganda government established marketing arrangements to organize the purchase of these crops from the growers and their eventual export. As the export price became a negotiated price, determined as a result of bargaining between governments, it was not surprising that the Uganda government found it desirable to establish each year a fixed price at which the crops would be purchased from the growers. In the beginning the price to the grower was closely related to the expected export price, but as the Uganda government's bargaining position improved (and after the war as the free world price began to rise) local producer prices fell behind the level that the export price would justify and by 1948 about £10 m. had accumulated in a reserve fund.

It is not proposed to discuss the war-time and immediate post-war period as in all respects it was exceptional and the arrangements that were organized were entered into so as to meet the war-time problems as they arose and were not the consequence of any particular theory or carefully thought-out plan. All that may usefully be said is that the accumulation of funds was the product of three rather different considerations. Prices to producers were kept low to some extent because the government wished to avoid inflation ; this was a real possibility because of the difficulty in war-time conditions of obtaining a higher level of imports. Secondly, there was the fear that higher prices for cotton and coffee would discourage the growing of food crops. A third reason was that export prices increased faster than expected thus producing an increase in the reserves greater than the level planned or expected.

In 1948 the marketing arrangements were reorganized. Marketing Boards — the Lint Marketing Board and the Coffee Industry Board — and corresponding Price Assistance Funds were established for cotton and coffee respectively. Out of the accumulated war-time profits referred to above £3·9 m. was allocated to the Cotton Fund and £0·5 m. to the Coffee Fund ; the remainder of the £10 m. was earmarked for various development projects. Tables 1, 2 and 3 reveal the general effect of the policies followed by the Boards since they were established. Up to about 1954 the Marketing Boards were accumulating funds, whereas since that date they have not ; and in the case of coffee there has been a very considerable rundown in the fund.

[Tables 1, 2 and 3 follow]

TABLE 1
THE COTTON SECTOR, 1950–61

Year	Payments to Growers		Export Taxes		Marketing Board Surplus		Ex-Farm Income £ m.
	£ m.	% of Ex-Farm Income	£ m.	% of Ex-Farm Income	£ m.	% of Ex-Farm Income	
1950	7·6	52	2·9	20	4·1	28	14·6
1951	10·7	40	5·9	22	10·4	38	27·0
1952	12·3	46	6·0	22	8·4	32	26·7
1953	10·7	76	2·9	21	0·4	3	14·0
1954	13·3	72	3·5	19	1·5	8	18·4
1955	11·9	75	3·1	20	0·8	5	15·8
1956	13·0	78	3·4	20	0·4	2	16·7
1957	13·5	80	3·4	20	0·1	— *	16·9
1958	13·2	104	2·3	18	− 2·8	− 22	12·7
1959	12·1	104	2·0	17	− 2·5	− 21	11·6
1960	10·9	77	2·3	16	1·0	7	14·2
1961	12·9	91	2·3	16	− 1·0	− 7	14·2

* Less than 1 per cent.

Source : *Uganda Statistical Abstracts.*

TABLE 2
THE COFFEE SECTOR, 1950–61

Year	Payments to Growers		Export Taxes		Marketing Board Surplus		Ex-Farm Income £ m.
	£ m.	% of Ex-Farm Income	£ m.	% of Ex-Farm Income	£ m.	% of Ex-Farm Income	
1950	1·7	27	1·2	19	3·3	53	6·2
1951	3·0	31	1·9	19	4·9	50	9·8
1952	3·8	43	1·7	19	3·3	38	8·8
1953	5·1	67	1·3	17	1·2	16	7·6
1954	8·5	79	1·8	17	0·4	4	10·7
1955	16·6	114	2·9	20	− 4·8	− 33	14·7
1956	9·7	86	1·9	17	− 0·3	− 3	11·3
1957	11·0	73	3·8	25	− 0·2	1	15·0
1958	11·8	77	2·8	18	− 0·7	5	15·3
1959	14·1	93	2·2	15	− 1·2	− 8	15·2
1960	14·0	132	1·0	9	− 4·3	− 41	10·6
1961	10·6	118	0·3	3	− 1·9	− 21	9·0

Source : As in Table 1.

TABLE 3

THE STATE OF THE PRICE ASSISTANCE FUNDS

Date	Cotton		Coffee	
	Amount at Date £ m.	Change between Dates £ m.	Amount at Date £ m.	Change between Dates £ m.
31.12.48	3·5		0·5	
31.12.49	5·6	2·1	1·1	0·6
31.12.50	8·6	3·0	4·5	3·4
31.12.51	21·4	12·8	9·1	4·6
31.12.52	22·4	1·0	12·7	3·6
31.12.53	20·3	− 2·1	14·8	2·1
30. 6.54	21·8	1·5	15·2	0·4
30. 6.55	18·8	− 3·0	11·9	− 3·3
31.10.56	19·4	0·6	10·3	− 1·6
31.10.57	20·4	1·0	10·7	0·4
31.10.58	13·1	− 7·3	12·0	1·3
31.10.59	11·3	− 1·8	11·6	− 0·4
31.10.60				
31.12.61	11·7	0·4 *	5·0	− 6·6*

* Change between 31.10.59 and 31.12.61.

Notes on Table 3

1. Sources : *Statistical Abstracts and Sessional Paper*, No. 2 of 1962.

2. Between 1952 and 1955 £18·2 m. was transferred from the cotton Price Assistance Fund to the African Development Fund. These transfers are *not* shown as withdrawals in the Table.

3. In 1957–58 £5 m. was borrowed from the Cotton Fund to finance government capital expenditure. It is not thought that this money can really be regarded as available for price assistance purposes and it has been shown as a withdrawal from the fund in 1957–58.

4. The following points were made in Sessional Paper No. 2 of 1962 with respect to the claims on the two funds :

(a) Cotton. About £3·5 m. is required for crop financing each year. About £1·25 m. is tied up in unmarketable local securities. About £1·75 m. is committed for price assistance purposes with respect to the 1961–62 crop.

(b) Coffee. About £4·25 m. is required for crop financing. With the announced price for the 1961–62 season, about £2·25 m. will be required for price assistance purposes.

5. It would seem, therefore, that about £5 m. is available in the case of cotton for *future* price support purpose and little for coffee.

Notes on Table 3 (continued)

6. It will be noted that there is no exact comparability between the statistics in Tables 1 and 2 relating to the Marketing Boards and those in Table 3. There are two main reasons for this. The figures in Table 3 are inclusive of the interest on the funds whereas those in Tables 1 and 2 are not. And, second, the figures in most cases relate to slightly different time periods.

7. The following three points may be added here with respect to Tables 1 and 2 :

(a) The figures above and below the line, i.e. those relating to 1950–53 on the one hand and 1954–61 on the other, are not completely comparable.

(b) The following figures represent the combined cotton and coffee position for 1948 to 1949 :

	Payment to Growers	Export Taxes	Marketing Board Surplus	Ex-Farm Income
1948	3·7	1·5	1·8	7·0
1949	8·3	3·0	4·9	16·2

(c) Ex-farm income represents the income the producers could have received if there had been no export taxes and if the Marketing Board had pursued a 'neutral' policy, i.e. all transport, marketing and processing costs have been deducted.

In considering the broad statistical picture it is important to appreciate that there have been a number of changes in the overall policies followed by the Boards. Three phases may be distinguished.

First : the changes of 1948 did not make any real difference as regards policy. As is clear from the tables, prices to the growers continued to be well below that justified by the export price. To a very substantial extent this occurred almost accidentally ; for export prices continued to increase, and in setting the producer price the Boards tended to pay attention to the current price. There was, however, an element of deliberate intent. The government believed in the period 1948 to 1953 that export prices were at artificially high levels and that a very sharp break in prices was just around the corner ; some experts even feared that prices similar to that of the late 1930s might return. Believing this it seemed right on a number of grounds not to allow the high export prices to be too much reflected in the domestic economy ; in particular it was felt that domestic costs and prices would be pushed up out of line with the true long-run position and that the accumulation of funds would enable the economy to adjust itself more smoothly when the expected fall in export prices occurred. However, little of this was explicitly stated.

The tables also show that considerable sums were raised in export taxation (these taxes were imposed on a sliding scale basis) during the period. Expenditure lagged behind income and thus the activities of the government itself as well as the activities of the Marketing Boards imposed a restraining influence on the level of domestic incomes and expenditures.

Two important policy changes were made in 1952–53. It was decided (and publicised) that in fixing the prices announced to the grower at the beginning of each season the basis should be the best estimate possible of the world price — subject to the payment of export tax. The policy of deliberately accumulating surpluses was abandoned. The policy adopted was in essence one of an intra-seasonal price guarantee and the object of the Price Assistance Funds was to enable this guarantee to be made and thus cover any unexpected changes in the world price occurring within a season. Given this policy it seemed that the accumulated funds of the Boards were excessive. It was decided that a Cotton Fund of £20 m. was sufficient and that any excess should be made available to the government to finance development projects of special importance to the African community. Eventually about £18 m. was transferred in this way. In 1957–58 the Cotton Fund was further depleted when £5 m. was lent from it to the government to help finance the capital expenditure programme.

Since the announcements of 1953 there has been no clear-cut, unequivocal statement of policy as regards the price policy of the Boards and the use of the funds but in recent years the decisions of the Boards and speeches of Ministers indicate that the 1953 policy is not being followed. There has been, for example, a departure from the policy of intra-seasonal price guarantees in the case of coffee. In January 1959 the coffee price was reduced from 80 cents to 65 cents three months after it had been fixed and it is now policy that up to three such changes can be made during a season. As regards cotton, deliberate payments were made from the fund in 1958 and 1959 to maintain incomes as world prices fell (and because poor crops were expected), and there have been a number of references in ministerial speeches and government statements to the ability of the Price Assistance Funds to cushion the growers and the economy against falls in export prices and earnings ; and these references have envisaged something very much more than intra-seasonal price stabilization. No general policy statement has, however, been made.

III. STABILIZATION : STATISTICS

Stabilization activities in Uganda since 1948 have to be considered in the light of the economic pressures on the country. Of crucial importance have been the changes in export prices and sales. Some of the main movements are set out in Table 4. What is particularly striking is :

(a) The rapid increase in the value of exports from 1948 to 1952 and — after a severe dip in 1953 — the relative stability for the next ten years.

(b) The rapid rise to 1951, fall to 1953 and then relative stability in the cotton export price. Also striking is the stability of the cotton export volume during the whole period.

(c) The great and continuous increase in the volume of coffee sales throughout the period and the rapid rise in the export price to 1954 followed by a great fall. It is interesting to contrast the coffee position in 1951 and 1961. Export sales proceeds were roughly similar but between the two periods the volume index went up from 138 to 328 (1950 = 100) and the price index declined from 119 to 51 (1950 = 100).

We noted above the importance of export earnings in the economy. The rapid increase in these earnings in the early part of the period had, therefore, a marked effect, and ex-farm incomes and the Domestic Product increased rapidly. In these years, however, government action had a considerable disinflationary impact ; both the Marketing Boards and the government itself accumulating substantial surpluses (export tax receipts contributed very substantially to the budget surpluses) ; thus erecting a barrier between the flow of export earnings and their transmission to producers. In this way the effects of the export boom on the level of domestic expenditures, output and prices was much reduced. In more recent years these accumulated funds have been used to finance government deficits, and to enable cotton and coffee growers to receive incomes in excess of that justified on market considerations. These disbursements have been an important element in maintaining the level of domestic incomes in the face of declining export prices. It should be noted, however, that the increase in the volume of coffee exports has been of equal importance.

Table 5 shows the magnitude of the stabilization measures. The swing of about £27 m. between 1951 and 1961 represents a very considerable fiscal contribution to stabilization. In 1951, 25 per cent of money domestic income was withheld in the form of reserve funds and was thus not available for spending ; in 1961 it is probable

TABLE 4

FOREIGN TRADE: SOME VOLUME AND PRICE INDICES

	1948	1949	1950	1951	1952	1953	1954	1955	1956	1957	1958	1959	1960	1961
Value of exports,* £ m.	13·9	23·5	28·9	47·4	47·7	33·6	41·1	42·3	41·5	46·9	46·4	43·2	42·5	
Value of imports, £ m.	9·0	12·5	15·4	22·1	24·3	25·7	25·2	34·0	28·1	27·0	27·0	25·5	26·0	
Exports														
Volume index	(70)	98	100	110	113	103	116	136	135	147	151	160		
Price index	(63)	83	100	150	146	114	122	108	105	105	100	97		
Cotton exports														
Value, £ m.		17·3	16·7	28·7	29·9	16·8	20·9	16·4	19·3	17·5	18·1	15·4	14·9	16·7
Volume index		112	100	99	109	96	113	88	108	97	112	107	95	99
Price index		108	100	173	165	105	111	111	107	108	97	86	93	101
Coffee exports														
Value, £ m.		2·9	8·3	13·6	12·3	11·5	13·5	20·1	15·7	21·6	20·8	18·7	17·0	14·0
Volume index		113	100	138	122	111	110	235	194	262	245	277	367	328
Price index		35	100	110	122	125	147	103	98	99	102	82	54	51

* Domestic exports and re-exports.

Source: *Uganda Statistical Abstracts.*

TABLE 5

THE IMPACT OF THE STABILIZATION MEASURES

	1950	1951	1952	1953	1954	1955	1956	1957	1958	1959	1960	1961
A Excess of government revenue over expenditure	2·7	3·5	0·5	−3·1	−2·3	−3·8	−2·7	−4·9	−3·0	−3·0	−4·4	−5·4
B Marketing Boards with holdings	7·4	15·3	11·7	1·6	1·9	−4·0	0·1	0·3	−2·1	−3·7	−3·3	−2·9
Stabilization Contribution Amount	10·1	18·8	12·2	−1·5	−0·4	−7·8	−2·6	−4·6	−5·1	−6·7	−7·7	−8·3
D As % of Money Domestic Income	19	25	15	−2·1	−1	−8	−3	−5	−6	−7	N.A.	N.A.
E As % of Gross Domestic Product					*	−5	−2	−3	−3	−4	−5	−5
F As % of Gross Money Domestic Product					*	−7	−2	−4	−5	−6	N.A.	N.A.

* Less than 1 per cent.

Sources: *Statistical Abstracts. The Geographical Income of Uganda, 1950–56. The Gross Domestic Product of Uganda, 1954–59.* The need for column D on the one hand and columns E and F on the other arises because a consistent series exists on the basis described in Source (2), see Table 6, for the period 1950–59. Another series on a rather different basis (described in Source (3)) exists for the period 1954–61. There is no official series on a comparable basis for the whole period.

584

that about 8 per cent of money domestic income was injected into the economy thus enabling a higher level of output and income to be achieved than would have been possible if such injections could not have taken place ; as would have been the position if reserve funds had not been accumulated in the years of high prices.

It seems fairly clear that in general terms these fiscal measures have had a stabilizing influence on the economy in the sense that without them there would have been bigger fluctuations in the levels of domestic prices, employment and incomes. If the Marketing Boards and the government had not accumulated surpluses in the early part of the period there is little doubt that there would have been quite severe inflationary pressures and money incomes and prices would have increased rapidly as increasing expenditures met fairly inelastic (in the short run) supplies of both domestically produced goods and imports. Of perhaps greater long-term economic significance would have been the effects of the reaction as the boom collapsed. In the absence of reserves accumulated in the early 'fifties domestic expenditures in the late 'fifties and early 'sixties by the government and by cotton and coffee growers would have been considerably below the level achieved. They would, therefore, have been far below the level that would have obtained if there had been no withholding policy in the early 'fifties. It is believed that the secondary effects of this on investment, public confidence and economic and social development generally would have been serious. (It is appreciated that this judgment is based on a number of assumptions, e.g. that a great boom in the early 'fifties would not have had a tremendous *permanent* effect on the level of economic activity, etc.)

At the general aggregative level, then, I would judge the stabilization policy to have been reasonably successful. It seems doubtful if it is desirable or possible to try in detail to prove that there has been *stabilization* in a technical sense. This might be attempted along the lines suggested in Table 6, but deficiencies in the basic data as well as the influence of factors only loosely (if at all) connected with the fiscal measures — e.g. the great increase in coffee output — would make such an attempt a hazardous operation.

IV. STABILIZATION : OTHER ASPECTS

In discussing the operations of Marketing Boards, economists in recent years have often been critical on the following two points. They have suggested, first, that the Boards have not followed

TABLE 6

STABILIZATION EFFICIENCY

	1948 to 1949	1949 to 1950	1950 to 1951	1951 to 1952	1952 to 1953	1953 to 1954	1954 to 1955	1955 to 1956	1956 to 1957	1957 to 1958	1958 to 1959	1959 to 1960	1960 to 1961	1961 to 1962	Average Change Amount £ m.	As % of Average Income
A Change in Money Domestic Income, £ m.	24·1	5·8	-11·5	10·2	7·4	-1·0	5·3	-2·9	0·3						7·6	9
B Change in Money Private Income, £ m.	11·6	9·2	4·4	8·5	12·6	-4·3	3·2	1·1	2·5						6·4	9
C Change in Gross Domestic Product, £ m.							11·5	1·4	5·1	0·1	2·3	1·9	0·1		3·2	2
D Change in Private Domestic Product, £ m.							16·7	-2·0	3·0	4·3	5·0	0·4	2·5		4·8	3
Cotton and Coffee																
E Change in ex-farm incomes	16·0		-1·3	-13·9	1·4		-2·5	3·9	-3·9	-1·2	-2·0	-1·6			5·2	20
F Change in growers' incomes	4·4		2·4	-0·3	6·7		-5·8	1·8	0·5	1·2	-1·4	-1·3			2·8	15

(1) Sources: As in Table 5.

(2) Lines C and D are needed as well as lines A and B as continuous series do not exist for the whole period with respect to either Domestic Income or Gross Domestic Product.

(3) In connection with the Cotton and Coffee sector, changes between 1949 and 1950 and between 1953 and 1954 and 1954 have not been computed as this would have involved comparisons between statistics which are not really comparable.

(4) The main difference between Money Domestic Income (A) and Money Private Income (B) is that the former includes the proceeds of Export Taxes and the withholdings of the Marketing Boards whereas the latter does not—though it does, of course, include the injections from the Marketing Boards. To a substantial extent the differences between the two sets of figures is a result of the stabilization activities of the government and Marketing Boards.

(5) The same points can be made with respect to the differences between C and D. (See pp. 37-8 of The Gross Domestic Product of Uganda, 1954-59.)

consistent, carefully considered, publicly announced policies and, second, that they have been used as revenue collecting organizations, thus disguising as a price assistance contribution what turns out to be — in effect — a tax.

Both these criticisms can be made with respect to the Uganda Boards. As regards the first, we noted that up to 1953 there was no clearly stated policy ; and that very soon after policy was stated departures from it took place. At the present time it would be difficult to state clearly existing policy — and it has not been stated. It seems in practice to be a mixture — the content of which changes from time to time — of the following :

(a) Intra-seasonal price guarantees linked to the expected world price. In the case of coffee, however, changes can and have been made during the season.

(b) A willingness to use the Price Assistance Funds to offer a price above that justified by the export price in certain conditions, e.g.

(i) If a very poor crop is expected.
(ii) If the expected world price is very low.

Clearly the time is approaching when shortage of funds will not permit the Board to engage in income support policies, but so long as funds are available it seems to be policy to interfere from time to time in this way.

As regards the second charge we have already noted how in 1948, 1953–55 and 1957–58 considerable sums were diverted from Price Assistance Funds to the exchequer to finance government expenditure.

On the whole, I am not impressed by criticism of the above kind.

Concerning the second charge I would agree that it would have been preferable if the funds eventually utilized by the government had been collected through export taxes rather than through the Marketing Board organization, but I do not consider that any great issue of principle is involved. The government had to pass legislation to obtain the use of the funds : just as legislation would have had to be passed to collect money in taxation.

As regards the first criticism I believe it to be somewhat naïve. Given the circumstances of the late 1950s, for example, when low export prices were in prospect and there was a very considerable reserve in the Price Assistance Funds — more than an amount required for intra-seasonal price guarantees — it seems not unreasonable for the funds to be used to provide an element of income support.

U

Both of the criticisms seem to arise from a desire to have the Marketing Boards operating either entirely independently of the government or acting under legislation which, though perhaps circumscribing their freedom of action, also reduces the opportunity for government interference. I suspect that either of these possibilities is outside the range of practical politics — and probably rightly so. If the Marketing Boards are concerned with a country's main export crops they are concerned with a large and vital sector of the economy and it is unrealistic to imagine that the governments will not wish to influence the prices that producers should get for their produce and have an important say in determining the use of any funds which the Marketing Boards may have at their disposal. It seems to me that it is necessary to accept that the government must be involved in all the Marketing Board's crucial decisions and that it is right that in connection with these decisions the wishes of the government should prevail — particularly in those spheres where the decisions have very widespread repercussions.

I accept the necessity for governmental overlordship and the critical comments below relate, therefore, more to the government than the Marketing Boards.

One of the effects of the policy described above of first accumulating funds in government and Price Assistance reserves and then disbursing them (in part by increasing the rewards of producers but mainly to finance public expenditures) has been to develop a large public sector — one perhaps too large to be easily supported by the ordinary revenue of the state at existing levels of export prices.

Between 1950 and 1953 total government expenditure doubled, increasing from £8 m. or 11 per cent of domestic incomes to £17·5 m. or about 18 per cent of domestic incomes. During the post-war period as a whole total expenditure went up more than five-fold and in 1961–62 it was running at around 30 per cent of Gross Money Income.

There are, of course, particularly in a poor country such as Uganda, always many desirable and needed projects awaiting finance, and as funds accumulated in reserves the pressures built up for a considerable increase in government expenditure. The additional spending increased substantially the size of the public sector — particularly as a good part of it was devoted to capital schemes which in the result had very substantial (and permanent) recurrent implications. By the late 1950s the country had acquired a range of public services somewhat out of line with its economic strength at existing levels of export prices. Though rates of taxation have been increased a number of times during the last five years there was a deficit on current account of some £1·5 m. on a current budget of £19·6 m. in 1961–62 and one of £3·7 m. on a capital programme of £5·5 m.

Since 1950 some £85 m. have been spent by the government from funds derived directly from the cotton and coffee growers. Due to the rise in world prices and the operation of export taxes and the Marketing Boards very large funds were mobilized. It is not easy to form a judgment as to the value of this whole operation from a development point of view, but the following points are relevant for such a purpose :

(a) On the whole the expenditure of the government has not had a very great effect on output ; it has not yet been very productive. In the early years there was a great attempt to develop the infrastructure through investment in power and communications and a good deal of public money also went into building up cement and textile industries and assisting in the establishment of copper mining and refining. In the middle years the emphasis was on the development of education and medical services. Only now, under pressures of revenue shortage, is emphasis really being devoted to methods of increasing agricultural output and incomes fairly quickly. On the other hand Uganda has now got a good infrastructure and has a much better supply of educated personnel than many other emerging African countries.

(b) It is difficult to be certain of the extent to which economic development was held back by the withholding policy and — even more difficult — to assess how the strength of the economy today would have looked if a different policy had been followed. The following points may be considered :

(i) We have noted the great increase in the output of coffee. Even with the heavy taxation, coffee was a very profitable crop for the African grower in the early and middle 1950s and it seems doubtful if output would have expanded much more if prices had been higher. Even with present prices and price expectations the Uganda government is not finding it easy to limit the expansion in production, as it feels it should as part of its obligations under the World Coffee Agreement.

(ii) With cotton it is another story. Throughout our period the price offered to the growers has been low ; both absolutely in relation to the input of effort, etc., required and, relatively, as compared to the effort required to produce a similar income from coffee. Areas in which both coffee and cotton could be grown shifted to coffee and in areas where only cotton could be grown there was no great enthusiasm for its production. In part, of course, the low effort/price for cotton is a reflection of world prices and agronomic considerations : it is also true, however, that the withholding policy hit cotton producers more than coffee producers. This has been particularly important in recent years when due to the world coffee situation a considerable increase in the output of cotton is required. I believe myself that cotton production could have been increased quite substantially by a judicious use of higher prices and an intensive effort to get improved methods of cultivation and spraying introduced.

(iii) Perhaps the most serious criticism of the whole Marketing Board and withholding policy was the encouragement it gave to the belief that a country such as Uganda could isolate itself in an economic sense from the rest of the world. Having been told in the early 1950s that producer prices must be held below the level justified by export prices, producers in the late 1950s and early 1960s were not satisfied when told that world prices only permitted a particular, low, producer price. Not surprisingly there is pressure for subsidies and it is easy to get into the somewhat ludicrous position of recent years of using large sums of money to subsidize the incomes of coffee growers and thus encouraging production at a time when the government is trying to restrict output.

On the government side the policy followed was a reflection in part of their way of seeing economic development as an organized and orderly process. The idea that development implies private entrepreneurs — some of them getting rich and most of them going bankrupt — starting small industries and transport organizations and being forceful, awkward nuisances, was foreign to the tidy-minded colonial administration. Such views inhibited the acceptance of a policy of allowing much higher incomes to accrue to the producers in the hope that this would not only stimulate agricultural development but would spill over and stimulate growth in other sectors — particularly into small-scale industrial and commercial enterprises of the 'back yard' type.

It will be clear from what has been written that it is not easy to consider the stabilization aspects of policy separately from other matters. The accumulation of funds imposed a heavy burden on cotton and coffee producers and this raises questions both of equity and of the effects on output. Similarly, the disbursement of funds in the late 'fifties raises issues beyond those of stabilization — questions as to the effect on the overall public finance position and as to whether the funds were spent wisely. As already stated it is considered that in the broad the *stabilization* impact of the government's actions have been significant and beneficial. It is also believed that it was right to take advantage of the steep rise in primary product prices to increase the effective tax rate on coffee and cotton producers and use the resources thus made available for general development purposes. On the other hand it is considered that the withholding policy was carried too far in the early 'fifties — particularly in the case of cotton — and also that a better use could have been made of the resources which were obtained. Three final points on stabilization :

(1) The actions of the Uganda authorities since the end of the war both through the Marketing Boards and through more orthodox public finance measures does seem to indicate that a small primary producing country can through its own internal policies greatly limit the disturbing impact of export fluctuations on its domestic economy.

(2) When considering the stabilization problem it is important to distinguish between measures and policies aimed in the first instance at stabilizing the export sector — presumably with the eventual objective of stabilizing the economy as a whole — and measures and policies which attempt *directly* to stabilize the whole economy. In practice both variants withhold income from producers in the export sector in periods of boom. In slump conditions, however, producers in the export sector receive support from the accumulated reserves under the first approach whereas under the second the reserves are likely to be used to finance a government deficit and thus permit a higher level of government expenditure than would otherwise be possible. In Uganda both policies were followed. What is of great importance in the present context is that the role of Marketing Boards as a stabilization device is *mainly* important with respect to a policy directed at the export sector. If the object of policy is general stabilization — which in my view is what it should be — then it is believed that taxation devices — particularly sliding-scale export taxes — and budget deficits and surpluses are more straightforward and useful devices and weapons from a stabilization aspect than making use of the Marketing Board machinery.

(3) In the paper I have not touched on many of the practical difficulties associated with operating a stabilization policy. These are well known, and I will just mention four which seem to be of great importance :

(a) The great difficulty of price forecasting and therefore of distinguishing between a secular and cyclical trend.

(b) The difficulty of estimating the rate of change of prices and therefore of estimating the reserve fund needed for operating an intra-seasonal price stabilization scheme.

(c) The difficulty when operating a policy of general stabilization of varying the level of government expenditure as a counter-cyclical device.

(d) The difficulty of introducing any form of stabilization system at a time when the price level is tending downwards.

V. MARKETING ARRANGEMENTS

It would take us too far from the main subject of this paper to consider in any detail the whole marketing structure in Uganda for cotton and coffee but it is necessary to make clear the place of the Marketing Boards.

In the case of cotton the Board announces each year before planting begins a price which is the *minimum* that will be paid at the time of harvesting. Since 1953 this has been based on a fairly conservative view of the expected export price which will be realized by the crop. Later in the season — before harvesting — a final price is announced which has often been substantially above the 'planting price'. This new price takes into account (in an upward direction only) new information concerning the expected export price and — in very recent years — the expected yield of the crop and general (income) stabilization considerations. The 'harvesting price' cannot affect the acreage put to cotton, but it can affect the proportion of output that is picked and — perhaps — the acreage planted in the following season. We should really refer to announced *prices* for different prices are announced for the two main types of cotton grown : growers also receive premiums for sorting their cotton into two classes, 'good' cotton and 'stained' cotton and in turn substantially higher prices are paid (and announced) for the 'good' than for the 'stained' cotton.

In part arising out of the administrative requirements for offering fixed (selling) prices to producers the 'processing' (ginning) sector of the industry is remunerated by the Board on a fixed margin basis, its size being determined on a cost-plus formula which is reviewed from time to time. After processing, the Lint and Seed come into the hands of the Board and are eventually sold by auction. The Board arranges for the transport, insurance, etc., of the crop to the export port. The Board has a monopoly position and no cotton may be exported without passing through its hands.

I should like to make four points rather dogmatically with respect to these arrangements :

(1) In the case of an annual crop like cotton I believe that the

grower welcomes the announcement of a guaranteed minimum price before beginning planting. I believe that given the many risks and uncertainties which beset a small mainly subsistence peasant farmer in Africa that a guaranteed price has a considerable incentive effect. There are ways of achieving this which do not involve having a Marketing Board but I doubt if they are so effective.

(2) I believe the cost-plus system of rewarding the ginners has given this side of the industry too big a share of the export earnings. There is a case either for a review of the basis of calculating the formula or else for finding a way to introduce real competition into the industry whilst maintaining the system of guaranteeing effective minimum prices to the growers. If freedom were given to the ginners to compete and if realistic minimum prices for the growers were not enforced there is the danger of collusion amongst the processors leading to the growers' price being forced down.

(3) The administrative costs of the Board have been low and have been more than offset by the reductions in transport and insurance costs that the Board has been able to secure because of the scale of its operations. By performing the 'uncertainty bearing' function which is a heavy charge on private enterprise traders in the absence of a Marketing Board the potential proceeds of the producers have been increased. The Board's work in seeking new markets, in improving quality and in representing the industry at the many international gatherings which are necessary in these days of 'controlled trade' is also important.

(4) The Board is appointed by the government. Members of the Board and its staff are not civil servants and the Board has considerable freedom in its day-to-day operations. Prices to be offered to growers and other major decisions have to be approved by the government.

The coffee position is less straightforward and it will have to be considered even less adequately than was cotton.

Till comparatively recently almost all the coffee produced by Africans was exported through the Board and the general marketing arrangements were as follows.

The Coffee Board originally announced its buying price at the start of the season but this policy of a single announced price has now been abandoned and prices may be changed up to three times a season. (The change took place after the great fall during the 1955 season when the Price Assistance Fund was reduced by £4·5 m.) As coffee is a tree crop there is not the same case for a seasonal guarantee as there is in the case of cotton. Changing the price in mid-season can, however, have a bad effect on quality as peasants tend to strip trees of unripe berries if they anticipate a fall in price. The price is set for *Kiboko* — the local name for the sun-dried coffee cherry which is the form in which most of the coffee is sold by the peasant farmers. As with cotton, the curers received a fixed margin and in due course the Board auctioned the coffee for export.

This whole structure is now very much under review. For two main reasons. The first reason arises out of the fact that at the *Kiboko* stage quality cannot be distinguished and the remuneration of growers has depended on the weight presented. In turn the processors receive a fixed margin per unit (of weight) processed. Only at the final stage when the Marketing Board sells the coffee for export does quality affect the price. With these arrangements emphasis is on quantity rather than quality with the effect that the quality has been poor and has, indeed, tended to become poorer — which is particularly serious in the present state of the coffee market. To get a real improvement a number of changes are required :

(i) The grower must be persuaded (and equipped) to 'rough hull' his coffee so that quality can be assessed at the primary buying stage.

(ii) The grower must be offered a substantial premium for quality.

(iii) The processor's remuneration formula must be weighted so as to encourage him to 'reject' poor coffee.

It is not easy to see how (ii) can be combined with a guaranteed price of the existing type. A possible way of trying to meet the difficulties is one involving a loosening of the whole structure. If the growers are equipped to 'rough hull' and if the Board *buys* from the processors and offers big differentials for quality then these differentials would tend to be passed back to the growers which would in turn have an encouraging effect on quality. What would have to be watched in these circumstances is the possibility of the price to the grower being depressed by collusion of the processors in a weak market. To limit the possibility of this the Board could announce not only the price at which it will purchase but what it thinks this *should* mean as a producer price.

The second reason why the structure is under review is that during the last few years a considerable proportion of African produced coffee (at the present time about 30 per cent) has been marketed outside the Marketing Board machinery. Associations of growers may purchase and process coffee produced by their members and sell it in the open market whereas curing works and hulleries must sell to the Board. The Board no longer has a monopoly and this leads to a number of complications. In order that the growers who form Associations might continue to enjoy the protection of the

Price Assistance Funds they are allowed to sell to the Board at the controlled price if they wish. If the controlled price is above the export price they do, otherwise they do not. A good deal of 'illegal' movements to Associations take place if the export price is above the controlled price. The fact that Price Assistance Funds exist and that Associations are allowed to sell to the Board does in effect give them both the opportunities which flow from dealing in the free market and the security of the Marketing Board system.

When, as at the moment, the Uganda Board is trying to follow the African Coffee Agreement and refusing to sell below the agreed floor price the Associations can and do sell. In these special circumstances the Board probably needs powers to have some control over total exports. This might also enable it to control effectively the pattern of exports and ensure that Uganda gets a maximum return for the agreed volume of permitted exports.

VI. CONCLUDING NOTES

Though I have been concerned in the paper with Uganda's Marketing Boards it is believed that the discussion has a good deal of relevance with respect to Boards of a similar type, i.e. Boards dealing with export crops produced mainly by peasant farmers. There are, of course, Marketing Boards — notably those in Kenya and the Rhodesias — which are mainly concerned with crops produced mainly for domestic consumption : I have not touched on the problems of such Boards.

In discussing the Boards most attention was directed at their stabilization activities. In the previous section, however, I did discuss — though very briefly and inadequately — the role of the Boards as *marketing* organizations. In my view it is important to distinguish between the two roles. For it is quite possible to be in favour of the *government* pursuing a policy of overall stabilization and yet being utterly opposed to introducing a Board between producers on the one hand and processors and exporters on the other and thus impede the operation of free market forces.

My final point relates to the danger of fighting old battles — which I am conscious of having done ! The large surpluses that accumulated in Price Assistance and other funds ten to fifteen years ago were the result in large part of a quite exceptional period. These surpluses have now almost gone. The trend of world export prices looks like being downward for the next five to ten years and it seems doubtful if Marketing Boards or governments in the near future will be able either to tax very severely the grower or subsidize him from accumulated funds. The great and heroic days of Marketing Boards seem to be over. Yet in my view they still have a useful role to play, in two respects. In the first place in the performing of the commercial functions already discussed ; in 'protecting' the grower and in generally assisting the interests of the industry through research, sales promotion, and improving the efficiency of the marketing arrangements. And in the second place through a policy of price guarantees — especially with annual crops. This should be on at least a seasonal basis but if the reserves would permit it a price policy based on one of the moving average systems would be even more desirable. It is thought that any ambitious scheme of income stabilization should be firmly in the hands of the government for such schemes involve the economy as a whole and general questions of fiscal equity and development strategy ; and even though the Marketing Board's machinery may be used it should be seen to be government rather than Marketing Board policy.

DISCUSSION OF THE PAPER BY PROFESSOR WALKER

Professor Walker in introducing his paper emphasized that it was almost entirely concerned with those Marketing Boards which dealt with commodities produced for export by small-scale peasant farmers, such as the Cotton and Coffee Marketing Boards of Uganda.

Professor Walker stated that if the governments of primary producing countries wished to stabilize their economies it was necessary for them to break the link between export earnings and the level of spending in the domestic economy. For in such economies movements in the level of expenditures generating domestic income tended to be determined by what was happening in the export sector. Autonomous movements in domestic investment or consumption expenditures tended to be of little importance from a stabilization point of view ; fluctuations in the aggregates arose on the whole from fluctuations in export earnings. Not only was it important to separate the export sector from the rest of the economy but it was also important — in the absence of external assistance — to accumulate some of the proceeds arising in a period of high export earnings in the form of foreign exchange reserves so as to enable an appropriate level of imports to be financed in a period when export earnings were lower but when, due to stabilization measures, the level of domestic income was maintained.

Stabilization policies could be considered either as directed at the export sector alone, or at the whole economy. In both cases there was need for the export sector to be taxed in boom periods and a fund accumulated. With the first approach, however, the fund was used in a slump to subsidize the producers of the export crops, whereas in the second it was used by the government to finance general development expenditure. For stabilizing the export sector Marketing Boards were the obvious instrument ; for stabilizing the economy as a whole, however, they were by no means so necessary. Professor Walker believed that on the whole it was desirable to think of stabilization in the context of the economy as a whole and that such a responsibility fell clearly upon the government and should be carried out through general fiscal and monetary measures, e.g. through budget surpluses and deficits, sliding scale export taxes, counter-cyclical expenditure policies and changes in the reserve ratios of banks, etc.

On the assumption of the government accepting general responsibility for stabilization the case for Marketing Boards tended to rest not on stabilization arguments but on 'marketing' arguments such as the incentive effect of seasonal price guarantees, the protection of producers from uncertainty and from the possible collusion of processors, the ability to secure new markets and to take action to improve quality and standards, and the general economies of large-scale operation in the marketing of crops for export.

Professor Johnston, opening the discussion, said that Professor Walker had documented a most interesting case of a government having been able to hasten development by the use of funds accumulated in a period of high export earnings through the mechanism of Marketing Boards. He believed, however, that in future, countries like Uganda should pay more attention to more orthodox methods (such as land or income taxes) of taxing the agricultural sector.

Professor Walker and *Mr. Modi* also spoke in favour of taxation policies as the best instrument for the government in attempting to stabilize the economy. Mr. Modi pointed out that marginal producers of coffee, cotton and sisal, who had to pay income tax as well as export taxes, were forced out of business. *Professor Weiller* suggested that Marketing Boards might still be appropriate for countries with a taxation system not yet developed enough to be an instrument for budgetary anti-cyclical policies.

There was a difference of opinion as to whether profits derived from the operation of Marketing Boards should be used for general development or for the benefit of producers themselves. *Madame Delivanis* and *Professor Servoise* believed that in developing countries, where fiscal resources were small, governments were justified in taxing the export sector in the interests of general development. *Mr. Onitiri* and *Mr. Suliman* felt that the export sector should not be expected to bear the brunt of development costs. Mr. Onitiri described how in some newly independent countries governments had taken over Marketing Boards and their accumulated reserves for general development purposes in an unwise manner. Surpluses derived from marketing should be spent directly on the crop-producing areas, and the co-operation of the producers themselves should be enlisted. *Mr. Bevin* described the working of the Dairy Board, the Meat Board and the Wool Board in New Zealand. These boards functioned with government collaboration, but in different ways, to protect the producer. They had all been able to build up reserve funds in the period of high export prices, but as prices fell, the reserves had declined, and it was felt that with the prospect of further price falls, the marketing boards were likely to run into difficulties. *Professor Dantwala* also observed that the success of Marketing Boards depended on successive rises and falls in export prices. Uganda had been fortunate in starting the experiment when prices were rising and it was possible to accumulate a reserve fund.

Many participants stressed the importance of the technological functions of Marketing Boards as distinct from the stabilization functions. *Professor Johnston* thought that the arguments in favour of Marketing Boards were strongest in the case of export crops where the boards might hope to control quality. The most important thing was to increase output and productivity by agricultural research and educational programmes. *Professor Reubens* also stressed the importance of research and education on the growth and storage of crops, soil treatment, etc., particularly where producers were small, ill-educated and bound by tradition.

There was much support for the idea of co-operative societies. *Professor Johnston* thought that a network of co-operatives was more flexible and economical than a Marketing Board, and could help with distributing supplies to farmers and with agricultural credit, as well as with marketing. *Mr. Modi* shared this view, and *Mr. Onitiri* spoke of Marketing Boards as forming the apex of a network of producer co-operatives. *Professor Dantwala* agreed that at first sight marketing co-operatives seemed to be the right solution, but added that great difficulties had been encountered with them in India, where farmers appeared to prefer to sell to traders.

Mr. de Widt and *Mr. Karp* had misgivings about certain types of stabilization schemes which they felt perhaps underestimated the individual producers capacity for self-help.

Chapter 35

THE INTERNATIONAL TIN SCHEME

BY

H. HEYMANN
London

IN his letter, earlier this year, inviting me to prepare this paper, the President of the International Economic Association, after referring to the more general subjects covered by Gerda Blau and David Walker, wrote : 'Professor Arthur Lewis is anxious that there should also be a paper on one of the more interesting actual commodity schemes and has suggested the tin scheme.' With the stress of Section 4 of this Congress on economic growth and the instability of primary producing economies as a rule connected with their output of specific industrial raw materials or basic foodstuffs outpacing the growth in demand, this choice might, at first sight, appear surprising. After all, tin is the only major primary commodity, current production of which is unable to meet demand, although consumption in the free world is still limping behind the level it had reached as long ago as the end of the 'twenties.

In spite of this apparent contradiction, however, tin has been the only suitable choice. Disregarding the outcome of the recent United Nations conference on coffee, which had not yet begun when this paper was completed, and the unrepresentative agreement on olive oil, there are in existence only two inter-governmental schemes besides tin, namely those on sugar and wheat. The International Sugar Agreement, which is an export regulation scheme, and the International Wheat Agreement, representing a multilateral contract between its member exporting and importing countries, though providing comprehensive platforms for collaboration in the International Wheat and Sugar Councils, respectively, have so far been frustrated by the conflict of national policies — over which they have no direct influence — with international needs. The regulation of sugar exports into the free world market, indeed, is at present in abeyance for want of agreement on the basic export tonnages for 1962 and 1963.

The tin scheme, like that for sugar, is basically an export regulation scheme which, by setting strict limits to stocks in member producing countries, also exercises control over their output. But, as I will show later in greater detail, the tin scheme, in addition to the regulation of exports, and of stocks in producing countries, also provides — alone among all global commodity schemes, past or present — for fully integrated buffer stock operations. Indeed, so far as its armoury of regulatory weapons is concerned, the tin scheme is the most powerful inter-governmental commodity scheme economic history has so far known.

My task in this paper is to give an account of this scheme — its frame, its application and its results — and to draw the lessons from the experience gained. But in order to remove the risk of confusion, I must first draw attention to an important aspect of the current tin situation which is bound to overshadow the international tin market for years to come.

Under two acts, passed by Congress in 1939 and 1946, respectively, the United States government accumulated a strategic stockpile of tin which, on the evidence of recently declassified information, amounted at the end of 1961 to 349,000 long tons, the equivalent of world production, exclusive of the Soviet Union, for two full years. Not less than 164,500 tons out of this huge total have been declared surplus and legislation freeing 50,000 tons for disposal has been passed in June. Although the U.S. government, including President Kennedy personally, have given assurances to tin-producing countries that their markets will be protected against disruption and that they, as well as the International Tin Council, the governing body of the tin scheme, will be consulted before actual disposals begin, the uncertainty created resulted in a slump of the cash price for tin from this year's 'high' so far of £974 per long ton on 19th March, to a new 'low' for thirteen months of £845 on 19th June.

By the time this paper was completed the promised consultations had not yet begun and with prices still fluctuating violently from day to day, the position remained very much in flux. I will bring it up to date in the introduction to this paper at the Congress. Meanwhile, although stockpile disposals are bound to gain influence on the tin scheme in future, they must not be allowed to mask, or be used for, serious shortcomings in the results of the tin scheme in the past. The desperate efforts of the Tin Council since the spring of 1961 to secure supplies of tin from the United States government, have proved beyond dispute that, after five years of collaboration under the post-war tin scheme, supplies from non-commercial stocks have become necessary to meet demand and prevent prices from running away. This is the relevant point. The problems now created by the threat of over-abundant stockpile disposals are quite a different matter, which must not be allowed to obscure the judgment in regard to the merits or demerits of the tin scheme.

Now let us come to the subject proper, starting with an outline of the evolution and the basis of post-war collaboration on tin. In October 1946 an international tin conference, convened by the United Kingdom government, arrived at the conclusion that, ultimately, a tin surplus was likely to arise and that, accordingly, continuous inter-governmental review of the tin position was required. For this purpose the conference recommended the establishment of an International Tin Study Group, comprising the principal producing and consuming countries. The first meeting of that group was held in Brussels in April 1947 and the group established its headquarters in The Hague in January 1948. Already at its third meeting, in October 1948, a Drafting Committee for a tin regulation scheme was appointed and at its fifth meeting, in March 1950, when international allocation of tin had only just ended, the Study Group passed a resolution by majority vote, requesting the Secretary General of the United Nations to convene a negotiating conference. That conference, indeed, began at Geneva on 25th October but, as in the meantime the outbreak of the Korean war had forced up tin prices to quite fantastic levels, the conference decided on 21st November 1950 to adjourn. Its second session began exactly three years later and, by 9th December 1953, it had completed the text of the first post-war agreement on tin. It did not come into operation until 1st July 1956 and expired at the end of June 1961. Meanwhile, its successor, the second post-war agreement, had been drawn up by a United Nations conference in New York in May and June 1960 and, as the two agreements differ only in some practical details, but not in their basic conception, they can conveniently be summarized together.

Both post-war agreements on tin are of five years' duration and consist of twenty-two articles plus three annexes in the first and six in the second agreement. Their main objectives are largely identical. They are in short : to prevent excessive fluctuations in the price of tin, to achieve a reasonable degree of price stability on a basis which will secure long-term equilibrium between supply and demand, and to ensure adequate supplies of tin at prices which the first agreement defined as 'reasonable' and the second describes as 'fair to consumers and providing a reasonable return to producers'. Among the additional, and more general, objectives, article I of the second agreement contains a novel one, namely 'to keep under review the long-term need for the development of new deposits of tin'.

The tin scheme, as already mentioned, is governed by an International Tin Council, which is led by an independent chairman and on which the member governments are represented as either producing or consuming countries. In contrast to the international agreements on wheat and sugar, the tin scheme does not place tangible operative obligations on consuming countries, although in case of need such obligations could, of course, be voluntarily agreed on an *ad hoc* basis. The nearest approach to this was experienced in August 1958, when the U.K. and the Netherlands subjected imports of tin from the Soviet Union to controls, which remained effective until early 1959.

The agreement aims at stabilizing market prices within a predetermined range, which can at any time at either end, or both ends (floor and ceiling), be changed by simple distributed majority, that means by separate simple majorities of the producing and consuming member countries. The Council has two weapons to stabilize market prices within the agreement price range, namely, first the regulation of exports from the producing countries — and, through the control of stocks, under article XII of both agreements, also of production — and secondly, buffer stock operations in the open tin market.

The Council considers at least once in each calendar quarter the statistical position and prospects of the metal, and in the light of its findings it can declare quarterly 'control periods' with a total for permissible exports. This total is being divided among member producing countries in proportion to their 'percentages', which are being revised periodically in the light of changing conditions. Neither of the two post-war agreements on tin place general limits on reductions in permissible exports, as the international sugar agreement does. The Tin Council, however, is not allowed to declare a control period unless it finds that at least 10,000 long tons of tin metal are likely to be held in the buffer stock by the beginning of that period, although under certain conditions this figure can be reduced to 5000 tons. Limitations of exports in each control period depend on a positive Council decision for that period and, as these decisions require a simple distributed majority, consuming countries are able, if their majority is determined to do so, to prevent the imposition, or maintenance, of export restrictions.

The operation of the buffer stock is, within the framework of Council instructions, the responsibility of the Buffer Stock Manager. He is required to sell tin at the agreement maximum price (provided that he has physical tin at his disposal) and to buy tin at the floor price of the agreement (provided that he has the necessary cash). Between the floor and the ceiling the agreement price range has been subdivided into three 'sectors'. In the 'lower sector' the buffer stock may enter the market as a buyer if its Manager considers it necessary to prevent prices falling too steeply, while in the 'upper sector' it may sell tin to prevent the market price advancing too fast. In the 'middle sector', however, the pool must remain inactive, unless the Tin Council decides otherwise ; under the first agreement such a decision required a simple distributed majority, but under the second, separate two-thirds' majorities of the producing and consuming countries have become necessary.

Only producing member countries are required to make contributions to the buffer stock. The first post-war agreement provided for a buffer stock of 25,000 tons of tin metal, a figure which has been reduced to 20,000 tons in the second agreement. Both agreements contain provisions for voluntary contributions to the buffer stock but the second agreement, in addition, also allows the Tin Council to borrow funds for the purposes of the buffer stock. In case of need, therefore, the stock under the second agreement could, in spite of its smaller initial size, be expanded far beyond its forerunner under the first agreement. The second agreement includes one other provision which the first did not contain. Under it, the Tin Council may authorize the Buffer Stock Manager to buy from, or sell to or for the account of, a governmental non-commercial stock. In concluding this summary it should be mentioned that both agreements contain identical provisions for action in the event of a tin shortage, which include the collection of estimates of supplies and requirements and the making of recommendations to ensure maximum development of production and equitable distribution of available supplies.

These are the main provisions of the tin scheme. In regard to both, their comprehensiveness and the extent of their applicability, they have never been equalled, or even approached, by any other inter-governmental commodity scheme. Now I will give an outline of their use in practice and of the results achieved. But, in order to give you a clear and balanced picture I will have to switch back more than three decades, because the seed for, and the spirit of, co-operation under the post-war tin scheme were not created in the Palais des Nations in Geneva or at United Nations Headquarters in New York, where the two agreements were negotiated in 1953 and 1960, respectively. Their origin is rather to be found in a letter to the Editor, which appeared in *The Times* (London) on 6th June 1929. It is this letter which set the ball rolling, and its contents, in spite of all the basic principles of Chapter VI of the I.T.O. Charter and the ending of the Colonial era in all tin-producing countries after the Second World War, having remained the underlying philosophy of collaboration under the tin scheme ever since.

In its nature that letter, which was signed by 12 leaders of British tin-mining interests in Malaya, Nigeria, Siam and Burma, represented an appeal for the formation of a Tin Producers' Association, able to represent and protect the industry. It pointed out that the tin-mining industry had reached a 'crucial turning point', with the world's need for tin constantly growing — by as much as 25,000 long tons, i.e. about 17 per cent, in the two preceding years — and no fresh sources of any consequence discovered for many years. In spite of the rising demand, so the letter continued its argument, the market price for tin had over the past five years fallen by £85 to around £200 a ton, enough to reduce the revenue of producers by £10,000,000 in a full year. The writers claimed that a large proportion of world consumption of tin was being satisfied from production, of which the costs are either near, or actually higher than, the prevailing market price, and they concluded their argument by stating that 'within reasonable limits the question of price is of no great consequence to consumers on account of the infinitesimal amount of tin employed in the principal products'. Any scheme, the letter suggested, which would provide 'reasonable stability both of price and supply' would, accordingly, be welcomed.

Well, the letter achieved its object. The proposed Tin Producers' Association was formed in the summer of 1929 and at its first general meeting in December 1929, Sir Philip Cunliffe-Lister (now Lord Swinton), the first chairman of the Association — who later, as Colonial Secretary, played a great part in the evolution of pre-war British colonial commodity policies — was already able to inform members that producing interests in the Netherlands East Indies and in Bolivia had agreed to participate in a scheme to secure an equilibrium between supply and demand of tin.

In explanation of some references in the letter to the Editor of *The Times* in June 1929 and of some features in collaboration under the pre- and post-war tin schemes to which it paved the way, I should here interject a few remarks about the structure of tin production and tin consumption. The world's tin is being derived from a range of deposits found in three North-South furrows of the earth's crust. The richest extends from Siberia through South East Asia to Australia ; it supplies two-thirds of the world's tin and includes its foremost producing countries, namely Malaya and Indonesia. The second furrow extends from Cornwall and the Iberian Peninsula via Nigeria and the Congo to South Africa, while the third is being represented by the mountain range along the western parts of North and South America, although it provides an important source of tin only in Bolivia. The last two furrows account very roughly for one-sixth each of world production. Geological conditions differ greatly from area to area and mining operations range from dredging and washing away alluvial deposits in the valleys and river-beds in South-East Asia to deep-rock mining high up in the Bolivian Andes. Geological conditions and mining methods alone would have resulted in very wide differences in production costs. But structural influences, namely the relative lack of capital concentration and the resulting splitting-up of the industry into an extremely large number of very unequal units, have increased these differences to truly remarkable proportions. Any policy, therefore, which tries to serve the interests of the whole tin-mining industry by a common price, is bound to raise problems, and to have consequences, the nature of which will be obvious to every economist.

Tin as a constituent of bronze has been one of the earliest metals used by men, and some of its properties make it indispensable today in many uses. Thus, tin has the lowest melting-point of all major metals, it is extremely malleable and ductile, shows unusual resistance to corrosion and fatigue and it is non-toxic. As a direct result, the packing of food (mainly in tinplate), solder and a number of other alloys, headed by bronze-bearing metals and other anti-friction metals, have become its main uses. Being employed mainly for coatings and in alloyed form, the amount of tin used per unit of end product is, indeed, relatively small. But to deduct from this that, within reasonable limits, the question of price is of no great importance to consumers is driving the point too far. Some uses of tin, like tinfoil, collapsible tubes and the tin content in most alloys have been greatly reduced over the past thirty years for simple considerations of cost.

But the main limiting factor in tin consumption over the same period has not been the price as such, but the actions enforced under the tin scheme before and after the war to raise the price to, and to sustain it at, a predetermined level. In practice this meant frequent shortages of supplies, and as on top of this tin was acutely short during the Second World War and the early post-war years, tin-consuming industries had to put up with rather difficult supply conditions over such a long period that the way was paved for exceedingly far-reaching tin-saving devices. In particular the progressive change-over from the mechanical hot-dip method to the electrolytic deposition method of coating in the manufacture of tinplate, has reduced the average amount of tin used per unit of tinplate to such an extent that world consumption of tin for tinplate (which still accounts for 40 to 45 per cent of total tin consumption) has hardly increased since 1929 although, meanwhile, world production of tinplate has been trebled. In spite of the fact that during the same period quite a number of new uses for tin have been developed — tin is being served by one of the best collective development organizations in existence, namely the Tin Research Institute — world consumption of tin, exclusive of the Soviet Union, has not yet fully recovered to the level of over 180,000 long tons, it had reached by 1929, the year the drive for a tin scheme was begun. Between 1951 and 1960 that figure averaged only 150,600 tons per annum, although it rose from 149,000 tons in 1958 to 162,000 tons in 1959 and 180,000 tons in 1960, before reacting to 176,000 in 1961.

As I had pointed out before this diversion into the structure of tin production and tin consumption, the preparations for a voluntary cut in the tin output had reached an advanced stage by the end of 1929, and voluntary restrictions were initiated in February 1930. It became, however, soon obvious that the split-up of the tin-mining industry in too many units of different size and efficiency hampered progress and by the end of the autumn of 1930 the Council of the Tin Producers' Association had agreed to a Dutch proposal that the governments of producing countries should be asked to administer and enforce the scheme. By March 1931 indeed an inter-govern-mental scheme between the main producing countries entered into force ; it turned out to be the first of a series of four consecutive agreements which kept co-operation alive until the end of 1946.

The regulation of the tin market under these agreements between producing countries very much followed the 'philosophy' which the sponsors of the Tin Producers' Association had developed in their letter to *The Times* in 1929. Prices became the main preoccupation and in order to lift market prices to the level aimed at — around £230 a long ton — and keep them there, production had to be sharply curtailed over extended periods. Undoubtedly price stability over the period as a whole during which the pre-war scheme was in operation was enhanced, even though the range between the highest and lowest prices in 1937 — from £180¾ to £311½ — was the widest for any year since 1920. But the price paid for this achievement was a heavy one. A lot of bad feeling was caused among consumers, especially in the United States, while the serious and continuous under-employment of resources not only caused social hardship in producing countries but also sapped the enterprise of producers, among whom restrictionism virtually became a frame of mind.

Under-development in the 'thirties and over-exploitation of mines during the war — in South-East Asia in 1940 and 1941, and in the rest of the world, headed by Bolivia, from 1942 to 1945 — had already greatly reduced the potential output of tin mines in the free world when peace was restored. By the time the first post-war scheme came into operation in 1956 this decline had made a great deal more progress because internal unrest in South-East Asia, and especially in Malaya and Indonesia, had prevented adequate development work during almost the whole of the first post-war decade, while in Bolivia the nationalization of the greater part of the industry in 1952 resulted in dislocations which have not been overcome to the present day. Clearly, the threat of a potential shortage of tin has always been in the background since the end of the Second World War and it has been due only to the relatively low rate of consumption that it was not forced right into the open at a much earlier date than it eventually has been.

Still, the approach towards the tin problems under the post-war scheme remained much the same as in the 'thirties. Under the pre-war agreements all the operative provisions of the 1953 scheme — export restrictions, limitations of stocks in producing countries and integrated buffer stock operations — had already been developed and the only real change, which the compliance of the post-war agreements with the United Nations principles brought about, namely equal representation of producing and consuming countries, remained a weak spot. While the six producing member countries of both post-war agreements accounted from the start in 1956 for more than nine-tenths of the tin output in the free world, the fourteen consuming countries participating in the 1953 agreement covered barely two-fifths of free world consumption. Through the adherence of Japan to the 1960 agreement, this share has now been brought up to around 45 per cent. But the United States and Western Germany, whose combined consumption of tin in 1961 was in excess of the total for all the fifteen present consuming member countries of the scheme put together, remained outsiders to the present day. Consequently, the representation of consuming interests on the Tin Council *vis-à-vis* the strong and united front of producing countries remained too weak, with the result that prices — their absolute level and their stability — became once again the only preoccupation of the International Tin Council in applying the provisions of the tin agreements of 1953 and 1960.

When the first post-war agreement became operative in mid-1956, the cash price of tin was fluctuating around £735 a long ton, which happened to be in the neutral 'middle-sector' of the agreement price range, determined by the 1953 United Nations conference at from £640 to £880. Soon after the implementation of the scheme the political Suez crisis had emerged and, in the closing quarter of 1956, cash tin rose for the first time since 1953 above the new maximum price of the agreement of £880. The buffer stock was unable to intervene because it had not yet any tin at its disposal.

As soon as the Suez crisis subsided Bolivia pressed for a higher agreement price range and in March 1957, the Tin Council, indeed, decided to raise the minimum price from £640 to £730, while leaving the maximum price unchanged at £880. This meant that the sub-divisions of the agreement price range for buffer stock operations were automatically adjusted to £730-£780 as 'lower sector', £780-£830 as 'middle sector', and £830-£880 as 'upper sector'. Whatever the economic merits of Bolivia's claim for a higher agreement price might have been, the timing of the Council decision of March 1957 could not have been worse. In the spring of that year world market prices for commodities generally were on the decline after their advance during the political Suez crisis, and the United States economy had entered a recessionary phase, resulting in quite a sharp reduction in its tin consumption. Experience gained under the pre-war tin scheme had strongly confirmed that swimming against the tide of commodity prices in general can be extremely costly. But, quite obviously, the Buffer Stock Manager showed no inclination in the spring of 1957 to act in accordance with that lesson. The poor timing of the Council's price decision as such had raised enough doubts, but the tactical errors committed by the buffer stock immediately following that decision virtually invited trouble.

Although at that time the market price for tin was only slightly below £780 a ton, the highest level at which support operations were allowed within the revised agreement price range, the buffer stock entered the market from the beginning of April 1957 onwards with such vigour as a buyer that, within three months, it had accumulated a reserve of over 3900 tons of metallic tin. As consumers were forced into reserve by this intensive pool activity the Buffer Stock Manager allowed market prices from July 1957 onwards to fall gradually until, by 9th October, they reached for the first time the new agreement minimum of £730, which the buffer stock was compelled to defend.

At this point the buffer stock committed another tactical error with disastrous psychological consequences. Instead of supporting simultaneously all international key prices for tin, and spot as well as forward prices, the pool limited its support operations to the cash price on the London Metal Exchange. Producers, consumers and dealers alike drew the conclusion from this practice that the pool might not be able financially to maintain its support of the agreement minimum price for long and began to dispose of every ton of tin metal they could spare through the buffer stock supported cash contract of the London Metal Exchange. With an avalanche of tin sales from every possible quarter developing, the market was thrown into a serious crisis of confidence.

Of course, the buffer stock was not provided with the means of coping with such an unnatural situation and, although member producing countries, early in 1958, agreed to place a voluntary 'special fund', over and above their full regular contributions, at the disposal of the Buffer Stock Manager, the Tin Council had to resort to export restrictions in an effort to regain control of the market.

The first 'control period' began on 15th December 1957 and limited exports from the producing countries to a figure equivalent to $71\frac{1}{2}$ per cent average quarterly exports in the base-year ended September 1957. In the second and third calendar quarters of 1958 this equivalent was cut to 60 per cent and in the last quarter of 1958 and the first quarter of 1959 it was further reduced to 52 per cent. But, with consumers forced into reserve for want of confidence, and with tin from unorthodox quarters, including the Soviet Union, still being thrown on the market in sizeable quantities, the Tin Council experienced a serious defeat. On 18th September 1958 the Buffer Stock Manager, owing to the exhaustion of funds at his disposal, had to withdraw from the market. As a direct consequence, the London cash price for tin, which since the previous October had been pegged by the pool at the agreement 'floor' of £730, slumped on that day by as much as £90 to £640. By a strange coincidence this decline equalled the amount by which the minimum price of the agreement had been raised in March 1957.

Fortunately, in spite of this calamity, member countries of the agreement continued to co-operate with each other and, with exports from the producing countries compulsorily restricted to not much more than half their normal rate and with consumer and trade stocks reduced well below a safe minimum, the artificially created tightness of supplies began to gain the upper hand in the autumn of 1958. By the beginning of October the market price had recovered to the agreement minimum of £730 and before the end of the same month it was self-supporting around £750. Indeed, during the winter of 1958–59 the market would have turned firmer still, but for a regular trickle of sales by the Buffer Stock Manager. By the end of February 1959 the entire stock of more than 5000 tons, acquired in the previous spring and summer with the 'special fund', had been sold and, although in the closing week of the same month the market price advanced into the 'middle sector' of the agreement price range (£780 to £830), the Tin Council remained excessively cautious.

It is true the relaxation of export restrictions was commenced in the second quarter of 1959, when permissible exports were raised from 52 to 60 per cent of the quarterly average in the base-year, and further gradual increases followed in each of the next four control periods. But, although the Buffer Stock Manager, having been authorized by the Council to operate in the 'middle sector' of the agreement price range, reduced his tin reserve in the course of 1959 from 23,325 to 10,050 long tons — and let me remind you that the buffer stock must hold 10,000 tons of tin to allow the Council to declare a control period — export restrictions were not lifted until the beginning of October 1960. The Tin Council did not even allow exports to be raised in order to replenish the heavily depleted stocks in the buffer pool; its reserve remained at 10,000 odd tons from the end of December 1959 to the end of March 1961. Meanwhile, as I have already mentioned in reviewing the structural changes of tin uses, world consumption of the metal began to rise quite strongly since early 1959, having overtaken the restricted world mines output already since the beginning of 1958.

When, at long last, export restrictions under the tin scheme were lifted in the autumn of 1960, it soon became obvious that three decades of a decline in the world's developed tin resources, followed by nearly three years of compulsory restrictions under the post-war scheme, had reduced the productive capacity and flexibility of the tin-mining industry to such an extent that it was no longer able to make ready use of its regained freedom.

With shipments from the producing countries failing to reflect any material increase and with demand still expanding in the early months of 1961, the market position began to reflect dramatic features. By 7th April 1961 the London cash price for tin surpassed for the first time since 1956 the critical point of £830 and, in doing so, penetrated into the 'upper sector' of the agreement price range. Small sales by the buffer stock slowed down the advance in April and early May. But, with the excessively depleted buffer stock obviously in a tight corner, speculators entered the market and forced up the price. The level of £880, the maximum price of the agreement, which the Buffer Stock Manager was required to defend, was reached by 7th June. After a stand of no more than 10 market days, the buffer stock had to concede defeat; in the afternoon trading session of the London Metal Exchange on 20th June 1961 the Chairman of the Tin Council announced that the buffer stock had exhausted the stocks of tin at its disposal and had, accordingly, withdrawn as a seller of cash tin on the market. Already on the following day the market price rose above £900 and, after touching £939 on 23rd June, it closed the month of June 1961, and with it the lifetime of the first post-war tin agreement, at £910 per long ton.

The exhaustion of the reserve of physical tin in the buffer stock on 20th June 1961 virtually marked the end of regulating the international tin market through the post-war scheme — at least so for the time being. But, before summing up and drawing conclusions, I want to give you a brief outline of developments in the tin market and of collaboration under the tin scheme since the middle of 1961.

Ever since the withdrawal of the buffer stock in June 1961, the state of the tin market has been determined by two factors over which the Tin Council had no control, namely the deficiency of supplies and the uncertainty emanating from the U.S. stockpile disposal policy. By 1st September 1961, the day before the U.S. General Services Administration asked Congress to free 50,000 long tons of tin from the national stockpile for disposal, the London cash price had advanced to £993½ a ton, its highest level since the closing stages of the Korean boom in 1952. The prospect of legislative action in the United States had a sobering influence on the international tin market throughout last autumn and winter, but a serious break in market prices, to which I have already drawn your attention, did not occur until the spring of this year, when Congressional hearing on the proposed legislation for stockpile releases threw the tin market into yet another crisis of confidence. At the time this paper was completed the position remained so much in flux that I will have to bring it up to date at the Congress in Vienna.

Meanwhile, owing to the dislocation of the international tin market, the majority of the operative provisions of the second post-war agreement on tin had, at least temporarily, become irrelevant by the time that agreement entered provisionally into force on 1st July 1961. At its first meeting under the new agreement immediately after that date the International Tin Council took two tangible steps. In the first place it informed the U.S. Administration of its desire to enter into consultation regarding releases of tin from the American stockpile. This move was in May 1962 followed up with increased urgency in a message sent by the Heads of Delegations on the Tin Council to the U.S. Secretary of State. In reply to that message consultations have been promised but, by the time this memorandum was completed, they had not yet taken place.

The second step taken by the Council early in July 1961 concerned the accumulation of the buffer stock under the second agreement. Inevitably, the Council noted that, owing to the prevailing shortage of tin, it would not be appropriate to require that any part of the new buffer stock should be contributed in the form of physical tin. The entire pool contribution was, accordingly, called up in cash.

At the same Council meeting, however, the most pressing point on the agenda, namely the application of article XIII, providing for action in the event of a tin shortage, got stuck because the producing member countries insisted that the attainment of the objectives of the agreement required an immediate increase in the agreement price range. On this matter, however, a compromise could not be reached at the time and the first Council meeting had to be adjourned. On its resumption in October 1961, the producing member countries submitted a joint proposal to raise the floor price of the agreement from £730 to £800 and the ceiling price from £880 to £1000 a ton. With seven-eighths (exactly 879 out of 1000) of the votes of consuming countries cast against it, the proposal failed to secure the required 'simple distributed majority'.

But the matter was not left to rest. In January 1962, when the future of the agreement after 30th June 1962 was at stake because of non-compliance with the minimum ratification provisions, it was taken up once again. On this occasion a compromise was reached. It raised the floor price by £60 to £790 and the ceiling price by £85 to £965. Within this new price range the 'lower sector' will be £790 to £850, the 'middle sector' £850 to £910 and the 'upper sector' £910 to £965. Only after this decision on agreement prices did Bolivia complete its ratification formalities and, in doing so, enabled the second post-war agreement to enter into force definitely on 21st February 1962.

This, then, is the account of the tin scheme and its application. As the most comprehensive and strongest inter-governmental commodity scheme ever applied in practice, it certainly deserves a great deal of attention. But I do not think that the experience provided will be of much encouragement in assessing the power of commodity schemes in stabilizing commodity markets or primary producing economies. It has certainly shown that a powerful armoury of regulatory weapons does not represent an adequate substitute for economically balanced objectives and the results of the tin scheme, both before and after the war, have been fashioned decisively by the fact that its real sponsors, and its governing body, were too much inclined to mistake restrictionism for conservation and rigidity for stabilization.

This negative conclusion cannot, in my opinion, be materially altered by the fact that the post-war tin scheme, as already its forerunner before the war, made unquestionably quite a strong impression on tin prices. It is true, the average cash price for tin on the London Metal Exchange for the years 1956 to 1961, at £791·3 per long ton, was lower than the 1950 to 1955 average of £829·6. But this comparison can give a wrong impression because the period from the beginning of the last decade until the initiation of the tin scheme half-way through it included the phase of the Korean boom when, mainly as a result of intensive United States stockpiling, tin prices recorded their highest level in history so far. Almost certainly tin prices during four, if not five, of the past six years would have been lower but for the regulation of the market by the scheme. And, while the range between the highest and lowest prices was as wide as £125 in 1958 and £214 in 1961, export restrictions and buffer stock operations limited it to £74 in 1957, to £54½ in 1959 and to £43 in 1960 respectively.

In spite of the fact, therefore, that the buffer stock ran out of money in September 1958 and out of tin metal in June 1961 — thus causing very sharp fluctuations in these two years — the impact of the tin scheme on tin prices, if viewed in isolation, has been quite encouraging. In spite of a number of strong dissenters among tin-mining industry leaders, the majority of tin-mining companies are indeed not dissatisfied with the results and, even some independent economists have, on the evidence of the tin price performance over the past six years, expressed favourable opinions about its achievements.

But, what I have tried to bring out in this paper, is the fact that the results of the tin scheme cannot be assessed on the performance of tin prices in isolation. The attainment of the price objectives by every available means has been so much the guiding light of the International Tin Council that it virtually lost sight of every other factor, including supplies. Its attempt in 1957–58 to enforce the revised agreement minimum price not only resulted in the exhaustion of the buffer stock's cash resources but also forced the Council to resort to sharp restrictions of exports, and of production. And, in the process, the entire tin industry was thrown into a crisis of confidence.

This experience made such a powerful impression on the Tin Council that it overshadowed its actions during almost the whole remaining lifetime of the scheme. Not only were export restrictions maintained for a full two years after the buffer stock crisis in September 1958, but also the pool holdings of tin metal were reduced to the permitted minimum without any effort being made to replenish them. This excessively restrictive enforcement of the price objectives of the scheme ran so much counter to the structural conditions of the tin producing and consuming industries that it transformed a surplus, which since 1959 has been only imaginary, into a genuine and frustrating shortage. As a direct result, the hopes entertained in 1956, that the introduction of the tin scheme, by increasing confidence among producers in their future, would bring about a long overdue effort to tackle development arrears were sadly disappointed. Instead of facilitating the strengthening of the production base for the future, the impact of the scheme laid idle a great part of the existing capacity over extended periods with all the resulting economic and social consequences to producing countries. Moreover, the shortage of tin caused by excessive restrictionism hit the market at the very time when world consumption, due mainly to the economic growth on the European mainland and in Japan, was approaching for the first time since 1937 the level it had shown in 1929. Consumption during the past twelve months seems to indicate that the shortage of supplies and the rise in prices have at least for the time being, interrupted that trend.

But, although the Tin Council has lost control of the tin market since the spring of last year, collaboration under the scheme has never been more urgent than now. Unless the confidence of tin producers and consumers in their future can be strengthened the outlook for the industry will be bleak indeed. On the production side there is no more time to be lost in overtaking the arrears of development, accumulated over a period of more than three decades if a serious and continuous shrinkage of supplies is to be prevented. Tin consumption requires adequate supplies at economic prices if the encouraging trend of recent years is not to be reversed. The pending disposals from the U.S. stockpile could perform the constructive purpose of both gaining time for the long overdue strengthening of the tin production base and keeping consumers adequately supplied so long as newly produced supplies remain deficient. But to ensure this without seriously disturbing the stability of the market, and undermining confidence, a close co-ordination of stockpile disposals with new production will be indispensable.

In this direction the tin scheme will face a new and important task which will bring the Tin Council into direct contact with the main critic among Western governments of its past policies. In the interest of the future balance of the tin industry it is to be hoped that this contact will be constructive. It could give the tin scheme the more flexible and more expansive approach which it has so far been lacking to the detriment of the best interests of its own member countries.

Record of Discussion

DISCUSSION OF THE PAPER BY MR. HEYMANN

Mr. Heymann, in a written introduction which was read to the meeting, said that the details of the U.S. authorities' plan for releases from their tin stockpiles were not yet available. Meanwhile the International Tin Council was supporting the price of tin at an increased price through purchases for the buffer stock. While this might be reasonable as a short-term counter to the possible effects of U.S. disposals it could be a de-stabilizing influence in the longer run. It was most desirable that there should be co-ordination of policy between the U.S. authorities and the International Tin Council, and also less preoccupation on the part of the latter with short-term price support, and more concern for the long-term balance of supply and demand. He believed that commodity schemes could be useful, if properly administered, to level out short-term fluctuations but were not suited to deal with difficulties caused by structural changes in production or markets.

Dr. Aubrey, opening the discussion, gave the latest information on the proposed U.S. sales of tin from the strategic reserve. These proposals were modest, the 160 tons a week to be sold representing only 5 per cent of average weekly world production, and being about equal to the current gap between demand and supply.

Dr. Aubrey felt that any attempt to 'manage' a commodity by open-market operations inserted a new element of speculation into the situation, and might even widen the swings it was supposed to contain. It might also, if profits from the operations went to producers, arouse the suspicions of other parties. He believed that, although Mr. Heymann was right in pointing out the defects of administration of the tin scheme, it did not necessarily follow that commodity schemes were inherently bad. If they could be fitted into a more general context, embracing the development of primary producing countries, their restrictive tendencies might be offset.

There was a discussion as to whether 'management' of the market in a commodity really fulfilled the same function as speculation and whether the effect was likely to be stabilizing or not. *Mr. van der Laan* felt that 'management', where discretionary powers were in the hands of a pro-ducers' ring, would not produce significant expectations about the future because it would be known that the manager would always act in one way, i.e. in the interest of the producers. *Dr. Zellner* could not see what function the manager of a commodity scheme could perform in his open market operations that could not be as well performed by speculators. Although there was some support for the view that 'management' would have a stabilizing effect on the market, *Professor Weiller* questioned whether in fact speculation tended to limit fluctuations as it was supposed to do. *Professor Lewis* took the same view, pointing out that speculators worked on a rising or falling market and left when movement ceased. They had no interest in a stable market.

Problems in Economic Development

Some doubt was expressed about the desirability of the manager of a buffer stock making a profit out of his operations, but it seemed to be felt that this profit might usefully be appropriated for development.

The point made by Mr. Heymann in his paper that the operation of the tin scheme had tended to reduce output was questioned by *Professor Lewis* and *Dr. Zellner*. Professor Lewis believed that the shortage of supply of tin was due to special factors such as revolutions in South-East Asia and Bolivia. Mr. Zellner felt that it was in the very nature of the tin scheme — a cartel-like arrangement — to weaken the structure of production. *Dr. Aubrey* thought that Mr. Heymann had not meant to accuse the Buffer Stock Manager of causing shortages, but of aggravating them at a critical juncture by keeping controls on too long. *Mrs. Yossundara* said that the Buffer Stock Manager could not always be blamed for the failure of supply to expand when required. National governments, favouring small producers, might impose more severe restrictions on large producers. When restrictions were lifted the large producers were unable to expand production quickly.

Professor Lewis felt that the main lesson to be learned from the tin scheme was that the buffer stock was too small. It should be large enough to cope with small fluctuation-changes of 5-10 per cent in production or consumption. Larger fluctuations — such as those caused by the Suez crisis — were unsuitable for buffer stock operations, and in such conditions the manager should hold off from the market. *Dr. Aubrey* was not certain if buffer stocks were appropriate for any commodities apart from tin, and *Mr. Kane* pointed out that the difficulties experienced in agreement on tin, which was in limited supply, showed how much more difficult it would be to work out an agreement for commodities such as coffee or wheat where supplies fluctuated and were increasing.

INDEX

Entries in the Index in Black Type under the Names of Participants in the Conference indicate their Papers or Discussions of their Papers. Entries in Italics indicate Contributions by Participants to the Discussions

Index

Index

Index

625

Problems in Economic Development

THE END

PRINTED BY R. & R. CLARK, LTD., EDINBURGH